# AMERICAN
# FOREIGN POLICY

# AMERICAN FOREIGN POLICY
## FDR To Reagan

## James E. Dougherty
St. Joseph's University

## Robert L. Pfaltzgraff, Jr.
Fletcher School of Law and Diplomacy,
Tufts University

*1817*

**HARPER & ROW, PUBLISHERS, New York**
Cambridge,  Philadelphia,  San Francisco,
London,  Mexico City,  São Paulo,  Singapore,  Sydney

*Sponsoring Editor*: Marianne Russell
*Project Coordination and Cover Design*: Caliber Design Planning, Inc.
*Compositor*: Typographic Alternatives, Inc.
*Printer and Binder*: R. R. Donnelley & Sons Company


**American Foreign Policy: FDR to Reagan**
Copyright © 1986 by Harper & Row, Publishers, Inc.

**Library of Congress Cataloging in Publication Data**

Dougherty, James E.
  American foreign policy.

  Bibliography: p.
  Includes index.
  1. United States—Foreign relations—20th century.
  2. Presidents—United States—History—20th century.
  3. United States—Foreign relations administration.
  I. Pfaltzgraff, Robert L.  II. Title.
E774.D66 1986    327.73    85–21963
ISBN 0-06-041696-3

        87  88  9  8  7  6  5  4  3

# Contents

## Chapter 3   Truman and the Postwar American Shaping of the Global System    46

## Chapter 4   The Eisenhower Administration: A "New Look" in Foreign Policy    93

**Chapter 5**    The Foreign Policy of John F. Kennedy: Years
of Idealism    142

**Chapter 6**    The Foreign Policy of Lyndon Johnson: From
Tragedy to Disillusionment    193

**Chapter 7**    The Nixon/Ford Administration and a New
Structure for World Peace    240

## Chapter 8    The Carter Administration: World-order Politics Beyond Containment    284

## Chapter 9    The Reagan Foreign Policy: A Quest for Restored Purpose and Strength    340

# Preface

This is a textbook on United States foreign policy since the Second World War. Recognizing that a large number of university and college students take no more than one course in the field of foreign policy, we have included an introductory chapter setting forth main traditional themes of American diplomacy. Although we do not consider this an adequate substitute for a regular course encompassing the earlier period, we nevertheless deem it essential that the reader be able to place the past half century in a broader historic context for an understanding of certain continuing or recurring factors.

We have chosen to base the organization of this text on presidential administrations from Franklin Roosevelt to Ronald Reagan rather than purely on geographical regions or functional themes. We have done this not only for the obvious reason that in the American constitutional system presidents are placed at the center of foreign policymaking. Although the external or the internal environment in which defense and foreign policies are formulated necessarily lies beyond presidential control, the president formulates the political and philosophical approaches that infuse the administration's foreign policy and shape the national mood. A president sets the priorities and focuses the nation's attention through speeches, press conferences, briefings, leaks, and a variety of other communications; pressures, cajoles, and persuades Congress to support specific policies; selects the departmental and agency heads, ambassadors, principal military officers, advisers, and other administrative personnel who assist in the evolution and execution of policy; and manages at least in part the flow of the news while making the most important decisions on sensitive security matters, especially in time of crisis.

In addition to overseeing U.S.–Soviet affairs, every president has had to devote a great deal of attention to transatlantic relations. Most have faced critical challenges in the Middle East and in the Asian-Pacific area, as well as in the Western Hemisphere. Such continuing functional issues as deterrence and defense doctrines, arms control, foreign economic policy (including international development and assistance, and trade, tariff, and monetary policies), and participation in international organizations have borne the imprint of each administration that has had to deal with them. This is not to suggest the absence of important elements of continuity in American foreign policy — a theme that is highlighted in the various chapters of this volume. Instead of trying, therefore, to fit the foreign policy of each president into a rigid matrix, we have sought to deal more or less proportionately with problems and issues, regional and functional concerns, and specific programs, crises, and decisions as they arose. We have attempted to place events within the international and domestic settings that confronted the presidents and those who advised them or carried out their policies. It is not surprising, then, that such topics as national security in the nuclear age, the Atlantic Alliance, U.S.–Soviet or Sino–American relations, arms control negotiations, conflicts in the Middle East or East and Southeast Asia, the economics of the Marshall Plan, the Alliance for Progress, and the European Common Market, and crises such as Berlin and Cuba receive extensive coverage because of their salience on the national-security agenda of decision makers within the respective administrations in which such events occurred.

Dr. Dougherty has benefited much from overseas lecture tours, sponsored by the Department of State/U.S. Information Agency, which have brought him into contact with embassy personnel, university scholars, and research centers in Britain, Belgium, Denmark, Norway, Sweden, The Netherlands, the Federal Republic of Germany, Japan, Korea, and Indonesia, and from intensive exchanges with colleagues in a variety of organizational contexts: the International Institute for Strategic Studies (London); the International Studies Association; the International Arms Control Symposia held in Ann Arbor and Philadelphia; a dozen Strategy for Peace Conferences at Arden House and Airlie House; lectures and discussions at the National War College, the Air University, the Inter-American Defense College, and the Foreign Service Institute of the Department of State. Among the many who have helped to shape his perspectives Dr. Dougherty would single out the following friends and colleagues at Saint Joseph's University: Professors Lawrence J. Bell, David Burton, Elwyn F. Chase, Frank Gerrity, and Anthony J. Joes.

Dr. Pfaltzgraff has received a variety of beneficial insights into American foreign policy from many colleagues in discussions held under the auspices of the Institute for Foreign Policy Analysis and the International Security Studies Program of the Fletcher School of Law and Diplomacy at Tufts University. Its many colloquia and annual conferences have provided an opportunity for the examination of numerous policy issues set in broader theoretical and strategic context. Together, the Institute for Foreign Policy Analysis and the International Security Studies Program of the Fletcher School have furnished a variety of occasions for an examination of issues drawing connections between conflict theory and strategy. Dr. Pfaltzgraff is also indebted to the Fletcher School of Law and Diplomacy for the numerous opportunities that it has provided, both inside and outside the classroom, for the testing of theoretical approaches to international relations by reference to the real world of policy and diplomacy. He wishes to convey thanks to Deans Emeritus Edmund A. Gullion and Theodore L. Eliot, Jr., as well as to John P. Roche, Interim Dean, and Uri Ra'anan, Chairman of the International Security Studies program.

The authors also express thanks for intellectual encouragement and insights from Dr. Jacquelyn K. Davis, Executive Vice-President of the Institute for Foreign Policy Analysis, and to Dr. Charles M. Perry of the Institute's senior staff. Research assistance was provided by Mark Eddington, Chung Min Lee, Robert Lister, and Tamah Swenson. For administrative support, thanks are extended to Robert C. Herber, and for secretarial help to Mary D'Amore, Marjorie Duggan, and Annette Yauney of the Institute for Foreign Policy Analysis, all of whom assisted in the preparation of the manuscript for publication.

James E. Dougherty
Robert L. Pfaltzgraff, Jr.

# chapter 1

# Main Themes and Tensions in the American Foreign-Policy Tradition, 1776–1933

After two centuries of political experimentation, we, the people who are organized as the United States of America, find it difficult to reach agreement concerning the role we wish to play and the direction we want our country to take in world affairs. Compared to the older European nations, ours is still a young country. It is also much more heterogeneous, the result of the in-gathering of a great variety of ethnic and linguistic groups, religions and philosophical convictions, and ways of life. Throughout our history, our foreign policy has oscillated erratically between activism and passivity, between vigorous internationalism and complacent isolationism, between aggressive imperialistic impulses and guilt-ridden self-abnegation, between intolerant arrogance at some times and matchless magnanimity at others. It is small wonder that other peoples find us difficult to understand.

Our political leaders and foreign-policy makers, subject to the unpredictable fluctuations of popular moods and opinions, have for the most part sought to pursue the national interest by formulating a pragmatically realistic policy that runs somewhere between the extremes dictated by ideology or emotion. Yet presidents, who with their secretaries of state and other advisers are responsible for charting the nation's course within the international community, have always had to recognize the limits that necessity frequently imposes on political choice. No government can accomplish all that its citizens want it to accomplish at any given time. The consequences either of taking action or of doing nothing in a particular situation must always be carefully weighed. Potential gains must be evaluated in the light of costs and risks involved.

The president, as principal agent for formulating foreign policy, is often at loggerheads with Congress and is either urged on or restrained by advisers. Both the executive and the legislative branches of the government, which in our constitutional system have complementary parts to play, constantly feel conflicting pressures from the voting public, political parties, organized interests, the mass media, churches, and competing units of the bureaucracy, as well as from actors outside the American political system—foreign governments, international organizations and alliances (such as the United Nations, the North Atlantic Treaty Organization, the European Economic Community, and the Organization of Petroleum Exporting Countries), multinational corporations, and nongovernmental entities (such as political parties, religious bodies, peace movements, and even terrorist groups). In a turbulent international environment, it is no simple task to fashion a coherent and consistent foreign policy.

From the time of Washington's first administration onward, the American people have often been divided over what constitutes an effective foreign policy. It was not extraordinarily difficult for our early presidents to forge and carry out a realistic policy based on their conception of the national interest, even though irate mobs might burn them in effigy. Since the latter part of the nineteenth century, however, the conduct of American diplomacy has become a more complex affair, burdened with more ideological and emotional baggage, and our political leaders have felt increasingly tempted to engage in moralizing rhetoric or to expound abstract principles of political philosophy which have not always been well suited to concrete international reality. There can be no question that religious-philosophical ideas and values should—and do—play an important part in guiding the lives of all peoples. But a healthy, fruitful idealism must remain in contact with empirical reality. When our visions diverge too widely from the world as it is rather than as we would wish it to be, they can become counterproductive. The history of American foreign policy since the World War II has been a history of a national effort, sometimes successful and sometimes not, to strike a tolerable balance between realism and idealism, between commitments and capabilities, and between politics as a utopian dream of re-creating the world in our own romantic self-image and politics as the art of knowing what it is really possible for us to do. Before we delve into the intricate problems of U.S. foreign policy in the period since World War II, however, it will be instructive to review the main themes and tensions of the American foreign policy tradition before that time.

## FOREIGN POLICY IN THE YOUNG REPUBLIC

The 13 American colonies, from the very beginning of their struggle for independence, recognized the international balance-of-power system's realities, one of which was their own need for foreign assistance. Without French help, the American Revolution might not have succeeded. The Continental Congress dispatched Silas Deane, Arthur Lee, Benjamin Franklin, and John Adams in a quest for aid from England's principal rival, and the wily Franklin played deftly upon French misgivings about an Anglo-American reconciliation to win an alliance that Louis XVI had not previously been eager to enter.

The American colonists had shown not only that a war of rebellion could be successfully waged against royal rule, but also that such a war—far from being the crime it had always been considered to be in European history—could be morally justified and that its leaders could be portrayed before the world as "standard bearers whose banners . . . and devices proclaimed a new philosophy of man."* The United States was the first "ideological" state in history—not only in the sense of being publicly and morally committed to the quest for democratic equality and individual liberty for its citizens, but also in the sense of making this commitment a foundation of its policy within the international system.

In its origins the United States of America reflected a mixture of realist and idealist thought. The new nation was able to enter the European balance-of-power system and take advantage of it for the purpose of achieving its own independence, at the same time that it professed to be separating itself from that system and striking a new note in history. It was able to do this by appealing both to the national interest of the French government and to the romantic rationalism of those intellectual disciples of Rousseau who looked upon Americans as "children of nature."

The brilliant diplomacy of the Revolution, however, was in danger of being wasted as a result of the weakness of the government under the Articles of Confederation. In addition to compelling domestic political and economic incentives for strengthening and unifying the government of the young nation, the desire on the part of conservatives to buttress the international bargaining position of the United States was another powerful motive for developing a centralized government under a federal constitution. When the new basic instrument was forged, it was a product of many compromises among political philosophies, states, sections and socioeconomic interests. Powers for conducting foreign affairs normally reserved in the older European nation-states to the executive—powers to appoint diplomatic envoys, to make treaties, to declare war, to raise and support the armed forces, and to control foreign commerce—were here divided between the president and the Senate or the whole Congress. By thus dividing powers between the two branches, the Constitution seemed almost to invite an historic struggle over the privilege of directing American foreign policy.

The fledgling republic immediately adopted a pragmatic approach to foreign policy. Its leaders were unwilling to allow popular emotional prejudices to affect adversely the national interest of the militarily weak country. The nation found its sympathies divided when Britain and France were at war during the Napoleonic period. The Federalists, led by Washington, John Adams, and Alexander Hamilton, along with most of New England and industrial, shipping, and financial concerns sided with Britain, as did conservatives who favored monarchical institutions and religious tradition. The Republicans, led by Jefferson and Paine, along with agricultural interests and the intellectuals who

*L. C. B. Seaman, *From Vienna to Versailles* (New York: Harper & Row, 1963), pp. 32–33.

admired the liberal principles of the French Revolution, were decidedly pro-French. Against those who contended that the United States owed a debt of gratitude to France, Hamilton argued the case for diplomatic realism and a policy of neutrality. We should indeed be grateful to France, wrote Hamilton, but a government must base its policies on self-interest. France had acted not altruistically but pragmatically to advance its own interests, and had already received its reward in the weakening of the British Empire. A United States just trying to get on its feet could not substantially help France, but it could greatly hurt itself. Hamilton's Anglophile realism prevailed over Jefferson's Francophile idealism. Those two mainstreams of thought, variously modified, have endured throughout American history.

Washington, in his Farewell Address, stressed the need for prudent statesmanship. He urged Americans to observe good faith and justice toward all nations, and warned of "permanent, inveterate antipathies against particular nations and passionate attachment for others." His most famous statement was this one:

> Europe has a set of primary interests which to us have none or a very remote relation. Hence she must be engaged in frequent controversies, the causes of which are essentially foreign to our concerns. Hence, therefore, it must be unwise in us to implicate ourselves by artificial ties in the ordinary vicissitudes of her politics or the ordinary combinations and collisions of her friendships or enmities.

Most historians agree that Washington did not intend by this that the United States should turn toward isolationism, although his words would often be quoted by isolationists for that purpose. (Incidentally, he did not warn against "entangling alliances"; that phrase was Jefferson's.)

A president may sometimes feel compelled to take an action that is inconsistent with his ideals. Jefferson, an anti-imperialist at heart, achieved the greatest imperial acquisition in American history, doubling the nation's size not by force of arms but by purchase of the Louisiana Territory after setting aside his own "strict constructionist scruples" regarding the Constitution. He showed his antimilitarism by demobilizing one-third of the army and putting most of the navy in mothballs, but later had to order punitive action against the pirates of Tripoli. Although he disdained the balance-of-power theory, he quietly hoped that it would work to the advantage of the United States—that is, that Napoleon would break British dominance at sea, while Britain and its allies would prevent Bonaparte from achieving hegemony on the European continent. Both Jefferson and his successor, James Madison, sought to preserve American neutrality in the Napoleonic Wars by applying restrictive economic measures. Their policies of embargo, however, were not at all successful. These policies were hard to enforce, and it was often difficult to determine whether their depressing effects at home were more damaging than those felt by foreign nations. Western and Southern agricultural interests, convinced that their economic woes were due to British trade policy (the infamous "orders-in-Council"), gave rise to a party of warhawks. These resentments, combined with anger over the high-handed British practice of impressing seamen from American ships on the high seas, led to the rather confusing War of 1812, fought for causes and motives, some of them contradictory, on which American historians have never been able to reach a consensus.

## THE MONROE DOCTRINE AND CONTINENTAL EXPANSION

Europe's wars had deeply divided the American people. The Congress of Vienna, which restored peace, enabled them to turn their attention inward and westward, away from Europe's balance-of-power politics. The Monroe Doctrine of 1823 symbolized the new mood of an America ready to become preoccupied with its own "manifest destiny." Since 1810, most of Spain's colonies in the New World had managed to gain their independence and declare themselves republics. (Portugal's Brazil had become an independent empire.) The United States during Madison's presidency had been sympathetic to the cause of the rebels, but avoided actively assisting them. Now President James Monroe's chief concern was that other European powers might intervene to help Ferdinand VII, the absolutist Bourbon recently restored to the Spanish throne, to reestablish Spain's control over the former American colonies. If that happened, Britain stood to lose trade diverted in the previous decade from Spanish to English ports. The British were not keen about republican governments, but to preserve their commerce they showed a willingness to cooperate with the United States to discourage any reversal of the Latin American situation. The astute Secretary of State John Quincy Adams persuaded President Monroe that it would be more dignified for the United States to assert its principles unilaterally, not only against Spanish aspirations but also against Russia (then expanding its influence along the Pacific coast of North America), rather than "come in as a cock-boat in the wake of the British man-of-war."

Monroe decided to act alone in declaring the end of European colonization in the entire Western Hemisphere. In his annual message to Congress of December 2, 1823, he reiterated Adams' principle that

> the American continents . . . are henceforth not to be considered as subjects for future colonization by any European powers . . . We owe it, therefore, to candor and to the amicable relations existing between the United States and those powers that we should consider any attempt on their part to extend their system to any portion of this hemisphere as dangerous to our peace and safety.

European kings found it an arrogant affront to the Old World for an upstart republic to redefine unilaterally the international law of colonization, especially when that republic lacked the power to enforce its proclamation. But the Americans knew that if put to the test they could count on the support of Britain and its navy. The Monroe Doctrine had no real legal effect, but it put the Europeans on notice that the young federal republic would henceforth regard hemispheric security as an essential—indeed, the primary—element of its national interest.

Much of American history in the nineteenth century pertained to the southward and westward expansion of the national frontiers, beginning with the acquisition of Florida by cession from Spain, in return for which the United States renounced its claims to Texas and the Southwest, which were then part of Spanish Mexico. Mexico, however, soon gained independence from Spain and proceeded to centralize its control over Texas. The freedom-loving Texans, finding Mexico's domination intolerably oppressive, won their independence in 1836 and entered the Union nine years later. Although the United States had acted with propriety in regard to Texas, annexation led to war and troubled U.S.–Mexican relations for a long time. Any designs that the United States had had on Canada had long since dissolved with the Rush-Bagot Agreement of 1817, which laid the foundation for the demilitarization of the boundary between the two countries. President James K. Polk warned Europe not to try playing balance-of-power politics on this side of the Atlantic by thwarting the territorial growth of the United States, pointedly applied the Monroe Doctrine to the Pacific Northwest, and arranged for the cession of New Mexico and California to the United States. The 1853 Gadsden Purchase of what is now part of Arizona and New Mexico, plus the 1867 purchase of Alaska from Russia, rounded out the expansion of the United States on the North American continent.

The building of the continental United States was an imperialistic enterprise, as the making of every great nation-state is. Along the way, there were occupations and settlements both legal and illegal, border incursions and infiltrations, followed sometimes by the fomenting and support of rebellions. The native American Indians, looked upon as opponents of civilization, were generally treated shabbily and driven from their hunting grounds and sacred places. There were numerous instances of military commanders and diplomatic envoys exceeding their instructions in dealing with the Indians. Such quasi-official acts are what imperial expansion is made of, but for the most part the crudest and harshest activities were carried on by private individuals or groups without the authorization of the United States government. On the whole, American continental expansion was far less violent and more benign than that of the other comparable imperial powers. Beyond the original 13 states, nearly the whole empire on the North American continent was acquired without war but rather through purchase, negotiation, or uncoerced annexation, and with the voluntary consent of the overwhelming majority of the people concerned. Moreover, as Dexter Perkins has pointed out, "the process of growth had not led to the acquisition of territory containing important unassimilable elements," and each area was brought into the Union on a footing of complete equality with the older states.

The Civil War was a critical period. Secretary of State William Seward feared that European states, jealous of American growth, might try to apply the balance-of-power mechanism known as "divide and rule" to weaken the emerging rival. Britain favored the separation of the Confederacy from the Union, quickly recognized the belligerency status of the South under international law, and proclaimed its own neutrality. The South relied on "King Cotton diplomacy" to win British support, believing that Britain would need Southern cotton for its textile mills, but Egyptian and Indian cotton at low prices undermined that hope. Moreover, President Abraham Lincoln's Emancipation Proclamation of 1863 greatly improved the moral position of the Union in the eyes of the English people, whose abolitionist sentiments were stronger than their attraction to the genteel ways of the Southern aristocracy. France under Emperor Napoleon III was also tempted to take advantage of the Civil War to intervene in Mexico and place the Austrian Habsburg Prince Maximilian on its newly created monarchical throne, but once the war was over the U.S. government had at its disposal a large military force with combat experience. France's challenge to the Monroe Doctrine quickly collapsed, and the hapless Maximilian was abandoned to face a firing squad.

Following the Civil War, Americans were so preoccupied with binding up the nation's wounds, settling the Western lands, building the transcontinental railroad, and promoting commerce that few of them could get very excited over foreign policy. It was perhaps a characteristic of the American isolationist tradition that secretaries of state were not expected to bring any diplomatic experience to their post, and from the Civil War onward none did before John Hay at the close of the century. During the British–Venezuelan boundary dispute, President Grover Cleveland's secretary of state, Richard Olney, insinuated that the United States could force the arbitration of any dispute arising between a European power and a Western Hemisphere state, thereby provoking a distinguished British diplomat, Lord Salisbury, to lecture Olney on the correct meaning of the Monroe Doctrine. In the end, Britain arrived at an amicable settlement with Venezuela because of its embroilment with the Boers of South Africa, who had the backing of Kaiser Wilhelm. Although Cleveland was by no means an imperialist, his strong stand on Venezuela may unwittingly have aroused imperialistic passions in American hearts.

## THE GREAT DEBATE OVER IMPERIALISM

Many Americans had harbored imperial or expansionist aspirations in the latter half of the nineteenth century, but those impulses had been restrained. They were not so much a matter of a desire for territorial aggrandizement as for support of peoples struggling for political liberty and human rights. John C. Calhoun had earlier warned his fellow citizens against thinking that it was the mission of the United States to spread civil and religious liberty around the globe. Our liberty could best be preserved, he said, by adopting a course of moderation and justice toward all nations, thereby serving as a model of how liberty-loving peoples conduct themselves. Conflict in Cuba produced terrorist atrocities and a ruthless Spanish counterinsurgency strategy. Newspapers owned by William Randolph Hearst and Joseph Pulitzer ignited the emotions of imperialists and humanitarians alike. After the U.S. battleship *Maine* was blown up in Havana harbor (an event for which blame could never be fixed), the "yellow press" and the jingoes made war inevitable. The "splendid little war," as John Hay, then U.S.

ambassador to the Court of St. James's, called it, lasted only three months. Spain's forces suffered decisive defeats in Cuba, Puerto Rico, and the Philippines. Puerto Rico was ceded to the United States, along with Guam, and Spanish sovereignty over Cuba was declared at an end. On the eve of the war, Congress had unanimously subscribed to the position that the United States disclaimed any intention to exercise sovereignty, jurisdiction, or control over Cuba and was determined, following pacification, to leave the government of the island to its people. On the subject of the Philippines, not a word had been said. Indeed, little thought had been given beforehand to an issue that would spark a great debate as one century gave way to another. There was some expectation that a U.S. victory would lead to an independent Philippine republic. But business interests, the U.S. Navy, and American Protestant churches had other ideas for the islands, as did those political leaders who advocated an imperialist policy.

It is in dealing with end-of-century imperialism that the economic interpreters of American history come into their own. Prior to the 1890s, American business, preoccupied with satisfying the demands of an ever-expanding domestic market, had been relatively apathetic about export trade—more so than during the early part of the century. But the three decades after the Civil War witnessed a remarkable growth of industry and railways, a quadrupling of the gross national product, and a quintupling of the manufacturing index. The surplus of production over consumption (which was presumed to be a cause of the recent depression) created an unprecedented situation which led to a conscious search for foreign markets, though not necessarily for colonial territories.

Modern historians who have been influenced by Marxist thought and by the Hobson-Lenin explanation of imperialism as the highest stage of capitalism have not been able to apply to the United States of the 1890s the under-consumption–oversaving hypothesis concerning the quest for foreign areas in which to invest surplus capital, for the simple reason that the United States was a net importer of capital up to 1914. They have insisted, therefore, that the search was for foreign markets for goods, especially in Latin America and the Far East.

It is incorrect, however, to place too much emphasis on the economic explanation of U.S. foreign policy even in the "grand epoch" of American imperialism at the end of the century. During the 1890s U.S. exports averaged only about 7 percent of the gross national product, and more than 80 percent of those exports went to Canada and Europe, while only 13 or 14 percent went to Asia and Latin America, the regions of imperial acquisition.

Business and industry generally, preferring a stable, predictable international environment for trade, were opposed to the war. However, once hostilities broke out and the Philippine Islands became a possible prize of war, the business community quickly and mistakenly perceived them as a potential boon—a market in their own right and a commercial gateway to the Asian mainland at a time when all the European powers were carving out spheres of economic interest in China. The U.S. Navy, strongly influenced by the writings of Captain Alfred Thayer Mahan, coveted the Philippines for their strategic value as a Pacific outpost. The transition from sails to steam created a need for coaling stations. Many argued that if the United States did not take the islands, someone else—probably Germany or Japan—would. President William McKinley, in one of the most famous statements of rationale in American diplomatic history, narrated how—after praying for divine guidance—he decided to annex the Philippines because the United States could not give them back to Spain, nor allow them to be turned over to our commercial rivals in the Orient, nor leave the Filipinos to their own devices (for they were unfit for self-rule). So, he said, there was nothing left to do except to take all the islands and educate, uplift, civilize, and Christianize their inhabitants (this last despite the fact that Spanish missionaries centuries earlier had made the Filipinos the only predominantly Christian people in Asia).

Since the president's decision required the Senate's consent, there followed a great debate between anti-imperialists and imperialists. The former group consisted of liberal politicians from both major parties, university intellectuals, journalists, literary figures, and industrial and labor leaders. The anti-imperialists were appalled at the prospect of bringing a distant, ethnically and culturally alien people under the American flag without its consent, and also fighting to suppress a guerrilla insurgency it had earlier supported—that of Aguinaldo.

These opponents of annexation called it unconstitutional, opposed to liberal principles, and no less reprehensible than the behavior of the colonial oppressor, Spain. Such an imperial policy, in their eyes, was bound to corrupt our own republican institutions, embroil the United States with the European colonial powers in the Far East, and lead to increased defense spending that would burden all the people while benefiting only a small segment of the business community. The anti-imperialists had intelligence and eloquence, but they lacked leadership and organization and were too few in number to buck the tide of expansionist sentiment then sweeping over the country.

The imperialist movement, led by Senator Albert J. Beveridge, Senator Henry Cabot Lodge, and Theodore Roosevelt, then assistant secretary of the navy—all disciples of Mahan—believed that one of the hallmarks of national power is ability to conduct foreign commerce; that commerce requires a merchant marine backed up by an effective navy; that the great maritime empires of history had all achieved their position largely because they possessed powerful navies and overseas colonies to provide a network of bases; and that the United States in the 1890s was woefully deficient in the basic requirement of naval power. If the United States was to achieve national greatness and make its full contribution to that basic common interest of civilization, the upholding of law and justice in international society, then the American people must abandon their isolation, begin to look outward, and take whatever steps were necessary to lay the foundations of naval power.

The imperialists were for the most part Social Darwinians who believed that Charles Darwin's new hypotheses regarding biological evolution, natural selection, and "survival of the fittest" were fraught with implications for an understanding of competition and conflict in social relations and world politics. They were convinced that Anglo-Saxon people, having demonstrated their superior fitness by the high degree to which they had developed democratic institutions, scientific-industrial arts, human freedom, and civil rights, now had the natural mission of suppressing barbarism everywhere and elevating the level of civilization of the whole world.

Subsequently, President Theodore Roosevelt justified his decision to recognize an independent Panama freshly broken off from Colombia on the grounds that the Panama Canal project must be pushed forward because it was designed for the benefit of world civilization and was being obstructed by the blackmailing avarice of the wretched regime in Bogotá. In truth, the imperialists were not primarily interested in seeking a mere economic advantage for the United States. Their real concern was for power, prestige, Anglo-Saxon supremacy, and the ennobling work of civilizing the world.

The war with Spain had brought the United States out of its isolation and preoccupation with internal developments. Within a very few years, the country seemed to abandon its anticolonial tradition in a fit of imperialistic frenzy. The factors that enabled the Manifest Destiny tradition to overwhelm the anticolonial tradition were multiple: political, economic, religious, and strategic. The American people wanted power, prestige, commerce, a navy, foreign bases, equality with the European imperial powers, and a sense of global, civilizing mission. The nation's most influential publicist in this century, Walter Lippmann, writing during World War II, declared that the acquisition of the Philippines had been a grave mistake, for it involved a commitment far exceeding U.S. military power, and for Lippmann there could be no rational foreign policy except where commitments were kept in proportion with power.*

The debate at the turn of the century showed that a portion of the American people were no less prone to imperialistic urges than portions of the people in other relatively powerful countries. It also demonstrated that the United States was the first imperial power in history to feel uncomfortable, even guilty, about its role and to experience the impact of large-scale public criticism over the political immorality of taking control of other peoples by right of conquest. Half a century later, the ingrained anticolonial tradition in American thought would triumphantly reassert itself.

## THE OPEN DOOR POLICY

Having established its predominance in the Caribbean and gained a strategic foothold in the Far East, the United States had to start acting the role of a great power just when the European imperialist states were beginning to transfer the balance-of-power playing field to the unfamiliar terrain of Asia, where no one was quite sure of the rules and where Russia and Japan enjoyed certain natural advantages that they did not have elsewhere.

When China's crumbling Manchu Dynasty found itself the object of a scramble on the part of the Western nations for spheres of economic interest and political control, the United States sought to ensure for its own industries a fair

---

*Walter Lippmann, *U.S. Foreign Policy: Shield of the Republic* (Boston: Little, Brown, 1943), pp. 7, 26.

share of the Chinese market—that "limitless market" of which Western capitalists had dreamed in vain for nearly a hundred years, which then accounted for perhaps only 3 percent of the country's foreign trade. This led to the policy known as the "Open Door," implying guaranteed equal commercial opportunity for all nations. Britain, controller of the bulk of China's foreign trade and long opposed to the compartmentalization to which China was being subjected by Germany, Russia, Japan, and France, supported the "Open Door" idea as proposed by John Hay—at least initially.

Secretary of State Hay was eager to nurture the budding Anglo–American friendship, but he had to battle lingering isolationism. Most Americans still wanted the good feeling of power and prestige that goes with a strong navy and imperialist adventures, but they did not wish to abandon their isolationism, much less assume the full range of responsibilities entailed by their new position as a world power. Hay did not seek to abolish the spheres of interest, but merely to obtain pledges of commercial impartiality. Eventually even Britain, hedging its bets, was willing only to give guarantees contingent on the grant of similar guarantees by other powers, most of which responded with evasive or ambiguous replies.

After the outbreak in China of a fit of nationalist frenzy known in the West as the "Boxer Rebellion," involving the murder of Christian missionaries and attacks on foreign legations in Peking, the United States contributed 2500 men to an international expeditionary rescue force of 20,000 soldiers. Hay circulated a note to the powers reiterating the principle of equal trade and declaring it to be U.S. policy to uphold respect for China's political independence as well as its territorial and administrative integrity, but making it clear that the United States was not prepared to take any military action to enforce the Open Door policy. Not comprehending the forces at work in the Far East, the American people tended to attribute the outcome of such power struggles to their own virtue. Believing almost as firmly in the principles of the Open Door as in those of the Monroe Doctrine, they seemed to think that their foreign-policy tradition could be maintained merely by reasserting the old moralistic ideals which their new overseas commitments contravened.

Theodore Roosevelt continued to support the Open Door policy with diplomatic means, but without committing the United States to such active involvement in Asian politics that the application of force might become necessary. In the Russo–Japanese War of 1904–1905, Roosevelt, who understood the balance of power better than his moralistic pronouncements might indicate, preferred an outcome that would permit Russia to retain a position in the Far East as a counterweight to the growth of Japanese power. Acting as conciliator, he brought the two belligerents together at Portsmouth, New Hampshire, and a peace treaty was signed on September 5, 1905. Although the terms of the settlement were favorable to Japan, the Japanese people were not happy with the Portsmouth Treaty. Roosevelt was made the scapegoat for an unpopular yet necessary peace. From that time onward, the U.S.-Japanese relationship began to deteriorate in spite of all that the president did to try to effect a realistic, friendly adjustment to the emergence of Japan as a formidable new power in the Far East. The two nations reached some fragile understandings over the Philippines, Korea, Manchuria, their respective territorial possessions in the Pacific, and the independence and integrity of China and the principle of the Open Door within that empire, but the Japanese were deeply offended by evidence of racial prejudice and discrimination against their people in California. Despite Roosevelt's effort to work out a "gentlemen's agreement" on immigration, the cloud of mutual Japanese–American distrust could not be entirely dispelled.

Roosevelt's immediate successors lacked his feeling for the Asian situation. President William Howard Taft and his secretary of state, Philander C. Knox, were both corporation lawyers. They relied heavily on the efficacy of legalistic approaches to and financial instruments of foreign policy. Both believed that government and business should cooperate to their mutual benefit, working together to promote American markets and investments abroad while at the same time accomplishing the nation's foreign-policy objectives. "Substituting dollars for bullets"—Taft's own phrase—was the essence of what came to be known as "dollar diplomacy." Taft and Knox made some unrealistic proposals for the financing and administration of Asian railways, with support only from Germany. Apparently neither one understood the balance of power in Europe or in Asia, much less the evolving connection between the two. Russia and Japan were strongly opposed to the U.S. plan. Britain was allied with Japan and had already come to terms with Russia over Persia in 1907. Russia and France had formed their alliance against that of Germany and Austria. Neither Britain nor France was about to offend its partner to the east to please Taft and Knox. Prior to Taft's presidency, many Chinese had looked on the United States as their country's only disinterested friend among the great powers. Now, for the sake of promoting international business interests, the United States looked as though it were willing to join the predators. Washington's policy had the unintended effect of exacerbating the situation, arousing nationalist resentment in China against foreign economic exploitation and helping to bring on the Sun Yat-sen Revolution of 1912, which overturned the Manchu Dynasty.

Within two weeks of assuming the presidency, Woodrow Wilson repudiated his predecessor's dollar diplomacy. The United States returned to its role as China's disinterested friend and guardian of the Open Door by becoming the first power to grant recognition of the Chinese republicans as the *de jure* and not merely the *de facto* government of China. When World War I broke out and Japan attacked the Germans in the Shantung Peninsula, China's feeling of dependence on the United States increased markedly.

## THE UNITED STATES AND LATIN AMERICA AT THE TURN OF THE CENTURY

There had not been a great deal of political interaction between the United States and Latin America in the nineteenth century. For the most part, Latin American governments regarded the Monroe Doctrine as being in their own interests as much as in those of the United States. "Yanqui imperialism" did not make its appearance as a term of opprobrium in intrahemispheric relations until the turn of the century.

The interests of the United States in the Caribbean were more salient to the American public than those in Asia—specifically, the construction of an interoceanic canal, which became a prime objective of U.S. policy. Securing the approaches to such a canal was a major consideration in fixing the status of Cuba after the war with Spain. European observers fully expected American expansionists to annex the island outright, but liberal anti-imperialists would not have stood for that. The Platt Amendment of 1901 made Cuba for all practical purposes a protectorate of the United States.

For half a century, the United States and Britain had agreed to cooperate in the building of a canal, which neither nation was to control exclusively or to fortify. In 1901 Britain, eager to develop ties with the United States, made a concession in the Hay-Pauncefote Treaty, agreeing that the United States could control and fortify the proposed canal after all. Every student of American diplomatic history knows about the controversy over the siting and building of the canal. The Panamanians, with the connivance of interested parties in the United States and with the assurance of support from an officially "noninvolved" U.S. government, carried out a musical-comedy revolution that separated Panama from Colombia. Theodore Roosevelt immediately recognized Panama as an independent state, with which he finally concluded a favorable canal treaty in a presidential election year. There is no point in trying to throw a mantle of political-legal niceties over Roosevelt's Panama Canal policy, since he himself never did. He defended his actions by appealing to collective civilization's mandate to construct a new highway for that civilization. History has faulted him not for presiding over a great engineering accomplishment, but rather for the political way things were done. With a little patience, they might have been done better, without sowing seeds of bitter fruit.

In the early years of the century, North–South hemispheric relations were marked by several instances of rather high-handed U.S. action. To preclude European intervention, which might otherwise be justifiably undertaken in response to chronic wrongdoing and financial irresponsibility on the part of Caribbean governments, Theodore Roosevelt asserted the right of the United States to exercise an "international police power." Under this Roosevelt Corollary to the Monroe Doctrine, he and his two successors—William Howard Taft and Woodrow Wilson—carried out several political-military interventions into the Dominican, Haitian, Nicaraguan, and Mexican republics, taking over the collection of customs, protecting foreign investments, chasing bandits, punishing insults to the United States and terrorist attacks on U.S. citizens, imposing martial law, and withholding recognition from governments unable to meet the constitutional test of free elections. These actions, undertaken for a mixture of motives—economic and strategic self-interest, humanitarianism, and the moral idealism of a nation convinced that it alone possessed the vision and power needed to bring order out of chaos in a benighted region—were condemned by liberal anti-imperialists in this country and by nationalists throughout Latin America.

## U.S. ENTRY INTO WORLD WAR I

The American people, insulated by geography from the threats of aggressive neighbors, had long tended to be more idealistic than Europeans about international politics. Utopian theories, it is true, were largely a product of European Renaissance and Enlightenment philosophers who propounded blueprints for world organizations that would guarantee permanent peace, but American politicians seemed to take those utopian visions much more seriously than did their European counterparts. On both sides of the Atlantic, among large segments of both the intellectual elite and the general public, faith had grown steadily in the ability of governments to avert war through the devices of international law, arbitration, and the diplomacy of reasonable compromise. Hopes ran high that the vehicles of burgeoning international transport, trade, and communication—the railway train, the steamship, and the telegraph—would usher in an era of friendship and interdependence among industrial nations that would make modern warfare, fought with large armies and the destructive military technology becoming available, economically unprofitable and politically inconceivable to the ruling elements of civilized nations.

Neither diplomats, nor lawyers, nor arbitrators, nor disarmament conferences were able to avert the tragedy of the First World War. To most of the causes of that war, the geographically aloof Americans could scarcely relate. After all, they had always been suspicious of alliances. While believing in a big navy for the protection of their maritime commerce and for the defense of their shores, they abhorred arms races, standing armies, and compulsory service. They had always looked favorably on arbitration as a method of resolving disputes. Initially, there was a widespread feeling, somewhat isolationist in inspiration, that a war in Europe did not touch our vital national interests and that accordingly neutrality was the best course to pursue. President Wilson urged the American people to be impartial in thought and action. It was the nation's duty to remain at peace, he said, so that it might exert the mediating force of moral principle. Being neutral, however, was not easy. For several years U.S. relations with Britain had been getting better while those with Germany had been deteriorating.

From the very beginning, the war had an impact on the United States and its economy. Wilson decided that a policy of neutrality was not incompatible with the sale of American goods to the belligerents. U.S. trade with Europe, which had been increasing, dropped off sharply after the outbreak of war. Within a few months, however, exports to Britain and France rose rapidly, while sales to Germany declined to a trickle for the simple reason that Britain controlled the seas and was able to enforce a blockade of the Central Powers. The Germans argued that, although not strictly speaking a violation of international law, the lopsided pattern of U.S. trade in effect belied the proclaimed U.S. policy of neutrality. The United States attempted to assert neutral rights on the basis of concepts adequate for the nineteenth century but not for the twentieth, since they did not take into account such crucial technological developments as mines and submarines. This effort was bound to end in failure. Early in 1917, the Germans announced a policy of unrestricted warfare against all ships in enemy waters. Berlin apparently assumed that even though this policy would bring the United States into the war on the side of the Allies, Germany could defeat Britain and France before America's vast resources could be mobilized, transported, and put into play on the far side of the Atlantic.

Wilson had long sought to mediate the conflict, but this disinterested leader of high moral principles was pained to suffer the usual fate of the mediator—to be suspected by each side of playing the adversary's game. Whereas Wilson spoke of "peace without victory," both the Allies and the Central Powers were willing to negotiate a settlement only on the most favorable terms following military victory. His threat to lead the United States into war on the Allied side failed to deter the German government from embarking on unrestricted submarine warfare. Horrified to see the country drifting inevitably toward war, Wilson nevertheless insisted that U.S. merchant ships be armed. Early in April 1917, when Wilson with great reluctance yet with soaring eloquence asked for a declaration of war, Congress voted it overwhelmingly and gave Wilson his saddest triumph.

Historians have passionately debated the question: Why did the United States enter the war when it did and on the side of the Allies? Explanations deriving from Marxist economic determinism have abounded, beginning with the superficial and discredited "devil theory" that U.S. entry was engineered by "merchants of death," munitions makers and bankers who stood to profit from going to war. It has also been argued that the volume of U.S.-Allied trade and investment between 1915 and 1917 gave the United States an ever-increasing stake in an Allied victory. In every country there are groups that gain from war, but no one has ever demonstrated satisfactorily that economic interests predominated in the mind of the idealistic professor-turned-president who despised economic interests as a basis for a statesman's choice.

Beyond economic interests, several other motives have been suggested: (1) to punish Germany for invading Belgium and sinking passenger liners; (2) to ensure victory for the democracies and make the world safe for democracy; (3) to vindicate neutral rights and uphold the principle of freedom of the seas; (4) to bring the war to an end and help shape the peace as the only power selfless enough to pursue a steadfast course of righteousness toward the creation of a better world order; (5) to protect the national interest by preserving or restoring the European balance of power against the hegemonic aims of an autocratic, militaristic Germany. In sum, it is safe to say that the decision to enter flowed from a combination of political and economic self-interest and the altruistic conviction that the American people were doing the right thing.

Although Wilson favored the cause of the Allies, he did not wish to be linked to their war aims or to be informed about the secret wartime treaties and agreements that the Allies had entered into among themselves. In his Fourteen

Points he enunciated his own noble aims in a "war for freedom and justice and self-government amongst all the nations of the world . . ."*

In the give-and-take of peace negotiations at Versailles, however, Wilson felt compelled to make many pragmatic compromises inconsistent with the exalted principles enunciated in the Fourteen Points. Faced with problems involving the boundaries of the successor states of the Austro-Hungarian Empire, the disarmament of Germany, the rights of national minorities throughout Eastern and Central Europe, the disposition of the Rhineland and the Saar, the redistribution of Germany's former colonies, mandates for the nascent states of the Arab world, and national antagonisms in territorial disputes from Western Europe to the Far East, the president justified all his compromises on the grounds that they enhanced the prospects for his League of Nations—thus making the connection between the peace treaties and the League's Covenant acceptable to the far-from-idealistic politicians of Europe. The only goal that in his mind could not be compromised was that of setting the League in motion as a permanent process of adjusting international differences nonviolently. All the imperfections in the peace treaties could be corrected later. He was quite rigid in demanding his own way, and frequently displayed a lack of prudence as well as a self-righteous arbitrariness.

At the end of the war, American moral fervor was running high. An overwhelming majority of the American people and five out of every six Senators favored a U.S. role in the League of Nations for the sake of peace. As time went on, and the Senate Foreign Relations Committee, chaired by Henry Cabot Lodge, kept asking questions and adding reservations, the idealism subsided. Many thought that the Versailles settlement merely perpetuated the old order and froze the territorial status quo. Some of the nation's leading literary figures were giving expression to a mood of bitter disillusionment with war, and this trend reinforced the natural tendency of the American people to turn inward, toward isolationism and noninvolvement and away from any foreign commitments that might lead to future wars. Senator William E. Borah of Idaho, a leading isolationist, sincerely argued that this country could best serve the causes of peace and freedom by tending its own garden as a model to the world. Wilson suffered a serious stroke, which removed the leading advocate of the League from the active scene, yet he hoped that the 1920 presidential election could be turned into a referendum for ratification of his Covenant, not Lodge's. By that time, however, the American people had lost interest in the Wilsonian vision of a peaceful world organized around the concept of collective security. The Covenant was never ratified. The United States later made a separate peace treaty with Germany.

*Among his points were the following: open covenants, openly arrived at; freedom of the seas alike in peace and in war; equality of trade conditions among all nations; reduction of national armaments; a readjustment of all colonial claims, with equal weight for the interests of populations and governments; the evacuation of all occupied territory; self-determination for the peoples under Austro-Hungarian and Turkish rule; the formation of a general association of nations that would guarantee political independence and territorial integrity to all states. (The full text of the Fourteen Points can be found in Ray Stannard Baker and William E. Dodd, eds., *Public Papers of Woodrow Wilson: War and Peace,* 2 vols. [New York: Harper and Brothers, 1927], Vol. I, pp. 159–161.)

## ISOLATIONISM BETWEEN THE WORLD WARS

Tired of Wilson's summons to noble endeavors, the American electorate responded overwhelmingly to Warren G. Harding's call for a return to "normalcy." Although Harding in his campaign for the presidency had voiced a vague commitment to an "association of nations," he interpreted the results of the 1920 election as a mandate against the League of Nations and for withdrawal from international involvement. For several months the U.S. Department of State refused to acknowledge any communications from the League's headquarters in Geneva. Later, however, the United States began to cooperate actively with League bodies working in such specific nonpolitical, functional fields as the control of white-slave (prostitution) and drug traffic, as well as in disarmament discussions.

The Senate maintained a cool reserve toward any proposal that might conceivably be interpreted as tending toward the limitation of its sovereign independence by subordinating it to international decision making. American diplomats, steeped in a legalistic tradition of conducting foreign policy, favored strengthening international law by having the United States play an exemplary membership role in the World Court (the Permanent Court of International Justice), but the Senate at first demurred and years later granted approval with reservations that the World Court could not accept. Subsequent efforts by Presidents Herbert Hoover and Franklin Delano Roosevelt to bring the United States into the international judicial body proved futile. Throughout the 1920s the United States, while assiduously avoiding commitments that would impinge on its freedom of action, continued to favor initiatives designed to promote peace. These included arbitration agreements, "cooling-off" treaties, and, most important, naval disarmament. The United States and Britain, anxious to avert a costly competition in naval armaments for which there was little enthusiasm on either side, persuaded Japan, France, and Italy to take part in the Washington Conference of 1921–1922, which led to a ten-year moratorium on new capital-shipbuilding programs, the scrapping of 66 ships from the three leading navies with a total tonnage of nearly 2 million, and the acceptance of future naval ratios based on existing naval strength—a ratio of 5:5:3:1.75:1.75 for the battleships and aircraft carriers of the United States, Britain, Japan, France, and Italy, respectively. The Five-Power Naval Treaty, which was to run until December 31, 1936, served to attenuate naval-armaments rivalry at the level of capital ships and shifted competition to cruisers, destroyers, and lesser classes of ships not limited. The Washington naval treaty was only temporary in its results. It saved Britain and the United States a good deal of shipbuilding costs, but was later criticized for having lulled the United States into a false sense of security in the Pacific.

The United States relied heavily on good-faith agreements in the interwar period to promote international peace. These included: (1) the Four-Power Treaty of 1921, whereby Britain, Japan, France, and the United States professed respect for one another's insular possessions in the Pacific; (2) the Nine-Power

Treaty (the Four plus Belgium, China, Italy, the Netherlands, and Portugal) of 1922, proclaiming respect for the sovereignty, independence, and territorial integrity of China—a multilateral pledge that did not help China at all in the 1930s; and (3) the Kellogg-Briand Pact of 1928, by which more than 60 nations sanctimoniously renounced war as "an instrument of national policy," many with sweeping reservations safeguarding their national interests. The ineffectiveness of this "promissory note" approach to international stability and peace was amply demonstrated by the apparent paralysis of states in face of the Japanese attacks on Manchuria in 1931 and on China in 1937; Italian premier Benito Mussolini's assault against Ethiopia in 1935; Italian Fascist, German Nazi, and Soviet Communist military intervention in the Spanish Civil War of 1936-1939; Nazi Germany's remilitarization of the Rhineland in 1936, in violation of the Versailles and Locarno Treaties:   and Adolf Hitler's takeover of Austria and Czechoslovakia in 1938.

Foster Rhea Dulles has concluded that the most significant aspect of American foreign policy during this critical period of incipient international instability was an "unhappy alliance between idealism and irresponsibility."* The American people were becoming preoccupied with domestic economic issues. Ever ready to strike the proper moral pose, they espoused high-sounding principles and legalistic formulas, perhaps because a vestige of that distinctively American utopianism to which Wilson had earlier appealed made it impossible for them to admit publicly that what happened on the other side of the world was no concern of theirs. But they were reluctant to make any sacrifice of economic interest, much less of life, to undergird the rhetoric of peace and righteous indignation.

To make matters worse, U.S.-European relations during the 1920s were seriously disturbed by a complex of economic issues involving war debts, war reparations, patterns of capital-investment flow, and tariff policies. European governments had borrowed $10 billion from the United States. When the British proposed a mutual cancellation of war debts, Congress and the State Department balked, since this measure would have placed the heaviest financial burden on the net creditor nation—the United States. The Europeans, having borne the severest human and physical losses in the war and aware that the United States had benefited from wartime trade, believed that the Americans ought to contribute to the common war effort by writing off the indebtedness that resulted from the tragedy. But there was no precedent for cancelling contractual debts out of political considerations, and no institutional mechanism or process for absorbing such huge losses.

From the beginning, Europeans linked reparations to debt payments. The British declared their policy to be to demand no reparations beyond those necessary to pay creditors, thus shifting onto the United States the onus for demanding reparations from Germany. The United States insisted that reparations were a purely European affair (since Americans sought none) and that the

*Foster Rhea Dulles, *America's Rise to World Power, 1898-1954* (New York: Harper & Row, 1963), p. 166.

two issues be kept separate, but to no avail. Throughout the middle and later 1920s, American investment capital flowed to Germany and sparked an industrial revival that enabled Germany to make its reparation payments, and this enabled the Allies to meet their debt-service schedule. But the wartime transition in the United States world position from net capital-importer to a creditor nation was not accompanied by commensurate changes in foreign trade patterns and policies. The strong American economy continued to produce an export surplus, while Congress revised tariff barriers in the Fordney-McCumber Act of 1922 and the Hawley-Smoot Act of 1930. The debtor nations of Europe could not sell enough in the American market to earn the dollars needed to meet their obligations and were forced to ship large amounts of gold, thereby destabilizing their own credit structures. As the Great Depression deepened and world trade contracted from 1930 onward, President Hoover sought to ease the mounting pressure on European economies, especially that of Germany, by calling for a one-year moratorium in 1932 on debt and reparations payments. This plea was applauded as a statesmanlike move, but it was not sufficient to reverse the downward cycle. After the moratorium, debt payments were never fully resumed except by Finland. In the end, the United States had no choice but to sustain the loss. This aggravated the Depression and reinforced isolationist and neutralist sentiment within the American body politic throughout the 1930s.

# chapter 2

# The Foreign Policy of Franklin D. Roosevelt:
## From Isolation to Wartime Diplomacy

Franklin Delano Roosevelt's inauguration as president in January 1933 brought no revival of Wilsonian ideals in foreign policy. During his election campaign, Roosevelt, having taken the pulse of an isolationist electorate, opposed entry into the League of Nations. When he pronounced the oath of office, the deepest economic crisis in American history was plunging all the industrial nations into frantic national particularism. He would soon feel compelled to adopt policies that appeared to sabotage the London Economic Conference of 1933, which was convened to devise ways of lifting the world out of the Great Depression by providing for currency stabilization through some mode of international convertibility now that governments were going off the gold standard. Without such a solution, world trade would continue to plummet. Roosevelt, like other national leaders, feared that policies designed to manipulate currency for purposes of promoting international trade (still not of prime importance in the U.S. economic picture) would interfere with his programs for domestic recovery.

## RELATIONS WITH LATIN AMERICA AND THE FAR EAST
## IN ROOSEVELT'S FIRST TERM

The only reference to foreign affairs made by Roosevelt in his first inaugural address was to the "Good Neighbor" policy, actually begun by Hoover. U.S.-Latin American relations underwent steady and substantial improvement during the Roosevelt presidency, thanks largely to the diplomatic efforts of Secretary of State Cordell Hull and his assistant, Sumner Welles, to put the Hoover–FDR Good Neighbor policy into practice. At the December 1933

Pan-American Conference in Montevideo, the United States concurred in the resolution that "no State has a right to intervene in the internal or external affairs of another." The United States withdrew its military forces from Nicaragua in 1933 and from Haiti in 1934, following a reciprocal trade agreement to provide financial stability for the island republic. In 1934 negotiations with Cuba led to the abrogation of the Platt Amendment and its companion treaty of 1903, which had long rankled the Cubans. Steps were taken between 1933 and 1939 to end the U.S. protectorate over Panama and to provide for joint defense of the canal. Roosevelt travelled to the Buenos Aires Inter-American Conference of December 1936 for the purpose of multilateralizing the responsibility for the enforcement of the Monroe Doctrine to protect hemispheric security against a foreign threat.

While liquidating its interventionist image in Latin America, the United States also altered its imperialistic posture in the Far East. Congress in 1934 passed the Tydings-McDuffie Act, which provided for the complete independence of the Philippines after an orderly 10-year transition period. (Despite the four years of wartime chaos, including Japanese occupation, the United States fulfilled its commitment on July 4, 1946, less than a year after the war in the Pacific came to an end.)

## U.S.–SOVIET RELATIONS IN ROOSEVELT'S FIRST TERM

The first serious diplomatic problem Roosevelt confronted was that of which policy to adopt toward the vast continental power on the opposite side of the earth. Following the withdrawal of its troops from Russia in 1920, the United States had shunned official relations with the Soviet government for 13 years. The Republican administrations adhered to the nonrecognition policy of Woodrow Wilson. Apart from the members of the American Communist party, a minority of leftist intellectuals, and a very few conservatives—like Senator Borah, who usually marched against the majority—most Americans wanted to have nothing to do with the Bolshevik regime, which they considered godless, ruthless, anticapitalist, and filled with ill-will toward the American system. Herbert Hoover organized a substantial relief program in Russia for humanitarian reasons. American business firms obtained lucrative commercial contracts under Lenin's New Economic Policy (1921–1925) of inviting capitalist help after the chaos of the "war communism" period, and also under Stalin's First Five-Year Plan (1928–1933). They found it extremely difficult to deal with the state trading monopoly, but were willing to tolerate frustrations for the sake of export profits, especially as the Great Depression deepened.

Soon after his inauguration, President Roosevelt sought to open discussions with the USSR to normalize relations. Attracted to personal diplomacy, FDR bypassed his secretary of state and called on the services of William C. Bullitt, who had been a member of the U.S. delegation at Versailles and had visited Russia in 1919, where he had had talks with Lenin. By this time the "Red scare" of the early 1920s had subsided, but Moscow's longtime refusal to pay compensation for property confiscated from U.S. corporations and to honor debts of the Tsarist regime still constituted a stumbling block to renewed diplomatic relations. In 1933, however, both countries were interested in turning over a new leaf, partly perhaps out of a common apprehension of Japan, which seemed bent on an expansionist policy in Asia.

Roosevelt and Soviet Foreign Minister Maxim Litvinov negotiated the terms of recognition, under which the USSR agreed to abstain from propaganda in the United States, allow religious freedom to American citizens in the Soviet Union, negotiate an agreement guaranteeing a fair trial to Americans accused of crime in Russia, and reopen the question of financial claims. Recognition took effect on November 16, 1933, and Bullitt became the first ambassador to the Soviet Union. There was not much improvement in Soviet attitudes or behavior, much less in Soviet–U.S. trade, despite the high hopes of American capitalists. Stalin's brutal purge of the Communist party and his even more horrible campaign to liquidate the *kulaks* came to light in the mid-1930s. After two years, a disillusioned Bullitt resigned his ambassadorial post.

## U.S. NEUTRALITY AND THE OUTBREAK OF WAR

As the world crisis deepened and dictatorships opposed to the international status quo grew stronger, the American body politic sought through congressional action to guarantee U.S. noninvolvement in the affairs of foreign countries. A growing belief that it had been a mistake for the United States to go to war in 1917—at great cost to itself and with no thanks from the Allies after the war—produced a series of neutrality laws between 1935 and 1937.

Neutrality legislation at first prohibited the sale or export of arms to any belligerent and their transport in American vessels, and authorized the president to forbid U.S. citizens to travel on belligerent ships except at their own risk. Subsequent enactments forbade loans to belligerents and all travel by Americans on ships of belligerents, even at their own risk, but authorized the president to list nonmilitary goods that belligerents might purchase and transport in their own ships—the "cash and carry" provision.

The Neutrality Act of May 1937 called on the president to invoke the foregoing provisions whenever he "found" a state of war existing abroad. When Japan attacked China in July of that year, the Roosevelt administration, sympathetic toward China and fearful that the strict application of neutrality law would be to the disadvantage of victims of aggression, refrained from invoking the law on the grounds that it did not "find" a war, and permitted the export of arms to the hapless Chinese government of Chiang Kai-shek. In October 1937, when Roosevelt called for a "quarantine" of aggression, the reaction of public and press was far from favorable. In January 1938 Congress narrowly defeated the proposed Ludlow Amendment to the Constitution, under which a declaration of war would not be valid until it had been approved in a national popular referendum.

British Prime Minister Neville Chamberlain and Foreign Secretary Lord Halifax pursued throughout 1938 what they themselves frankly called a policy of appeasement toward Mussolini and Hitler. They were prepared to abandon nonrecognition of Italy's Ethiopian conquest and to placate Hitler at the expense

**CHRONOLOGY OF EVENTS MOVING THE UNITED STATES FROM NEUTRALITY TO WAR, 1939–1941**

| | 1939 |
|---|---|
| August 23 | Nazi–Soviet (Ribbentrop–Molotov, or Hitler–Stalin) Non-Aggression Pact paves way for start of World War II by dividing the territory of Poland while assigning Finland, Estonia, Latvia, and Bessarabia to the USSR and Lithuania to Germany. |
| September 1 | Germany invades Poland. |
| September 3 | Britain declares war on Germany; France reluctantly acknowledges a state of war; Italy declares intention to remain neutral. |
| October | American foreign ministers meeting in Panama issue a declaration establishing a neutrality zone of from 300 to 1000 miles around the Western Hemisphere (except for Canada, which has entered the war) and warning non-American belligerents against the commission of hostile acts, but without enforcement provisions. |
| September–October | Nazi-Soviet Pact is revised; Germany receives more of Polish territory and assigns Lithuania to the USSR. Polish territory is incorporated into Germany and the Soviet Union. In Paris a Polish government-in-exile is established (later to move to London). Soviet Union occupies Baltic states of Estonia, Latvia, and Lithuania. |
| November 4 | President Roosevelt signs Neutrality Act of 1939, prohibiting American ships from carrying passengers or cargoes to belligerent nations, prohibiting American passengers from traveling on belligerent ships, prohibiting belligerents from selling securities in the United States, and requiring military and nonmilitary exports to warring countries to change ownership before leaving American ports. |
| November 30 | Soviet Union attacks Finland and meets stiff resistance. |
| December 14 | League of Nations expels Soviet Union for aggression against Finland. |

| | 1940 |
|---|---|
| March 12 | After a bitter "Winter War," Stalin's Red Army crushes the valiant resistance of the Mannerheim Line and forces Finland to surrender and cede the Karelian Peninsula. |
| April 9 | Germany attacks Denmark and Norway. The Danes order an immediate cessation of hostilities. The Norwegians resist bravely, but briefly and in vain. King Haakon flees with his government to England. An Anglo–French expeditionary force lands in Norway but meets with disaster. |
| May 10–27 | German forces suddenly attack Belgium, the Netherlands, and Luxembourg. The Dutch government, anxious to preserve neutrality, awaits "complete certainty of German aggression" before requesting Anglo–French aid, but it is too late. Winston Churchill replaces the discredited Neville Chamberlain as British prime minister. Dutch Queen Wilhelmina escapes to England with her government. Four days after the attack, the Dutch military orders a cease-fire. Belgian resistance, with help from British and French forces, lasts 18 days but crumbles after Allied units are caught in German pincer. British evacuate 338,000 Allied troops in "miracle of Dunkirk." |
| June 5–22 | Germany carries out *blitzkrieg* against France and is joined five days later by Italy, in what Roosevelt calls Mussolini's "stab in the back." French defenses quickly crumble. After outflanking the Maginot Line, German troops occupy Paris June 14. Third Republic votes itself out of existence, to be replaced by Marshal Henri Pétain's Vichy regime. De Gaulle announces from London that he will lead the forces of Free France. |

| | **1940** |
|---|---|
| June 30 | Foreign ministers of the American Hemisphere issue the Declaration of Havana, embodying the principle that territory held in this hemisphere by a non-American power (meaning Denmark, the Netherlands, or France) could not be transferred to another non-American power (meaning Germany). |
| August | "Battle of Britain" begins with German Luftwaffe bombing attacks designed to knock out the Royal Air Force and pave the way for Germany's planned cross-Channel invasion. |
| August 31 | Roosevelt, with congressional approval, inducts first units of the national guard into the federal service. |
| September 2 | Roosevelt, bypassing Congress, enters an executive agreement with the British government, trading 50 overage World War I destroyers to Britain and receiving in exchange 99-year rent-free leases for base sites in Bermuda, the Bahamas, Jamaica, St. Lucia, Trinidad, Antigua, and British Guiana. |
| September 16 | Burke-Wadsworth Selective Service Act becomes law, instituting first peacetime conscription in U.S. history. |
| September 27 | Germany, Italy, and Japan sign Tripartite Pact in Japan and announce it to the world as a defensive alliance to keep the United States out of the world conflict. |
| October 27 | Mussolini's army invades Greece. |
| October 30 | Speaking in Boston just days before his election to a third term, Roosevelt tells American mothers: "I have said this before, but I shall say it again and again and again: Your boys are not going to be sent into any foreign wars." |
| December 29 | Roosevelt, in a radio "fireside chat," says that the United States must become "the great arsenal of democracy." |

| | **1941** |
|---|---|
| January 6 | Roosevelt in his annual message to Congress calls for Lend-Lease Act to provide military aid to any country whose defense the United States considered vital to its own security, thereby clearly committing the United States to the cause of British victory. |
| March 11 | Lend-Lease Act becomes law. |
| April 9 | Roosevelt signs agreement with Danish minister in Washington bringing Greenland within "sphere of cooperative hemispheric defense." |
| April 13 | Soviet Union and Japan conclude Neutrality Pact. |
| June 22 | Hitler invades the Soviet Union. |
| July 7 | United States and Iceland conclude agreement similar to that regarding Greenland. |
| July 26 | After Japan speeds up military moves through Southeast Asia, Roosevelt freezes Japan's assets in the United States and begins to cut oil shipments. |
| August 10 | Roosevelt and Churchill meet at sea and issue Atlantic Charter. |
| September | German U-boat fires torpedoed at U.S. destroyer *Greer.* Roosevelt issues order to shoot on sight. Proposal that President Roosevelt and Japanese Premier Prince Konoye meet collapses over terms. United States and Britain sign agreement in Moscow promising to provide military assistance to the Soviet Union. |
| October | U.S. destroyer *Kearny* torpedoed off Iceland in a battle with German submarines. Destroyer *Reuben James* torpedoed and sunk off Iceland. Roosevelt declares that "the shooting war has started." |

of Czechoslovakia. Roosevelt seemed resigned to accept the European democracies' appeasement policy for lack of any realistic alternative.

In July 1939 the isolationists in the Senate and the House scored their last triumph by emaciating the administration's proposals to permit arms shipments on a cash-and-carry basis. Only after war broke out on September 1, 1939, with Germany's invasion of Poland, did popular sympathy for the victims of aggression and the cause of democracy mount high enough for Roosevelt to overcome the opposition of the isolationists. Even then, in order to get the neutrality laws revised, Roosevelt had to justify his efforts on the grounds not of aiding Britain and France, but of strengthening American's ability to preserve its neutrality.

The American people were not isolationist in the sense of wanting to turn their backs on the outside world with moral indifference. American novels and short stories, movies and plays, newspaper editorials and books, and radio commentaries of the time often reflected a keen awareness of how much hinged on the outcome of the struggle between the totalitarian and democratic systems. Yet Americans hoped desperately that President Roosevelt could chart a wise course, preserve freedom of choice, steer clear of war, and somehow make everything turn out right in the end. As early as 1938, Roosevelt began to speed up U.S. defense programs for building ships and aircrafts. His administration agreed in January 1939 to sell bombers to France. Six months later, the president gave Tokyo the required notice for terminating a commercial treaty that had allowed Japan to purchase certain war-related materials, including scrap iron, from the United States. Yet subsequently, for almost the first two years of the war, he sought to divide Germany from Japan, or at least to avoid doing anything that would push Tokyo into committing its forces actively in the war against the interests of the American, British, and Dutch democracies in Southeast Asia.

When the European war started in 1939, more than three-quarters of the American people expected Britain and France to win, and this opinion scarcely changed during the seven-month period of inaction on the Western front, variously called "the phony war," *sitzkrieg,* and *la drôle de guerre.* Ironically, the only fighting in Europe was in Finland, victim of Soviet aggression, for whose people the Americans felt much sympathy because of their fidelity to war-debt obligations. In January 1940 Roosevelt called for the production of 50,000 planes a year. By this time, the cash-and-carry program was beginning to help Britain and France, but in contrast to World War I there was no question of granting credits or using American ships. The fact that Stalin was in league with Hitler as a result of the Nazi–Soviet Non-Aggression Pact meant that the two leading totalitarian states were lined up against the democracies, and this made U.S. aid less controversial than it might otherwise have been.

The democratic nations were jolted out of their complacency in April when Denmark and Norway fell, again in May when the invasion of Belgium and Holland demonstrated that policies of neutrality offered no security whatever, and most of all in June when Germany's panzer divisions overran crumbling French defenses along the Maginot Line. (See "Chronology of Events Moving the United States from Neutrality to War, 1939–1941," pp. 23–24.) Following the

French collapse, only 30 percent of the American people still expected an Allied victory. But in Britain Neville Chamberlain had been replaced by the redoubtable Winston Churchill one day after the invasion of the Low Countries. One of Churchill's first steps to rally the nation was to form a wartime coalition cabinet of Conservatives and Labourites. Roosevelt in June 1940 similarly appointed to his cabinet two Republicans—Henry L. Stimson as secretary of war and Frank Knox as secretary of the navy.

Upon becoming prime minister, Churchill immediately and urgently requested FDR to render aid. The stamina displayed by the British during the Battle of Britain in August and September aroused hope for the democratic cause. Actually, both the British and the Germans in the late 1930s had overestimated the power of German bombers to wreak rapid devastation. Germany's failure to bring Britain to its knees necessitated the cancellation of Operation SEA LION, Hitler's plan to invade England, which the German navy had no chance of carrying out unless the *Luftwaffe* first gained complete command of the skies.*

## TOWARD AN ANGLO–AMERICAN ALLIANCE

The "destroyers-for-bases" deal, under which the president authorized the transfer of fifty overage U.S. destroyers to Britain in return for 99-year rent-free leases of British territory in the Western Hemisphere for the construction of bases, indicated that the two English-speaking democracies were moving toward a de facto alliance. The initial response to the Anglo–American exchange was favorable. Even the Republican presidential candidate, Wendell L. Willkie, supported it for at least a few days, but a few weeks later he was branding it "the most dictatorial and arbitrary act" of any president in American history. Willkie's increasingly strident charges that the reelection of Roosevelt would almost certainly mean war forced the president to alter his thematic emphasis and to campaign more actively. Worried about reports concerning the shifting mood of the electorate, FDR trimmed the sails of his political strategy and came out fighting for peace during the last two weeks before election day, declaring that his military-preparedness efforts were designed for the sole purpose of ensuring that the nation could remain out of the war into which Willkie accused him of leading the country. On November 5 Roosevelt polled 27.2 million votes to Willkie's 22.3 million. The debate over foreign policy probably had not decisively affected the outcome of the election; the great majority voted either their gratitude for New Deal policies or their protest against them and against Roosevelt's flouting of the tradition whereby no president served more than two terms.

The third term opened with Roosevelt proposing a Lend-Lease Act for massive military aid to Britain, thereby provoking a titanic debate in Congress. Isolationists bitterly opposed to lend-lease argued that it would lead ineluctably to the convoying of ships carrying arms to Britain. Germany would have no choice

---

*See Chester Wilmot, *The Struggle for Europe* (New York: Harper, 1952), Chapter 1; Gordon A. Craig, *Germany, 1866–1945* (New York: Oxford University Press, 1978), pp. 723–724; and George H. Quester, "Strategic Bombing in the 1930's and 1940's," in his *Deterrence Before Hiroshima* (New York: Wiley, 1966), pp. 82–122.

but to interdict the flow of supplies from the "arsenal of democracy" to its forward bastion in Britain, and thus the United States would eventually be drawn into the war in spite of all Roosevelt's solemn pledges to the contrary. Lend-lease, declared its critics, was incompatible with neutrality. By the spring of 1941 the American people were feeling less neutral; the government's policy was much less so. Roosevelt, denying any intention of instituting convoys, began cautiously to authorize "neutrality patrols" in order to safeguard the ships transporting arms. The undeclared shooting war in the North Atlantic was about to begin. The formal initiation of hostilities, however, came as a result of developments on the opposite side of the world, where relations between Washington and Tokyo had been deteriorating since the expiration of the naval limitation treaties in 1936.

## PEARL HARBOR: THE UNITED STATES IS DRAWN INTO THE WAR

When Japanese armies attacked China in July 1937, the government in Tokyo was not thinking about an eventual war with the United States. The bombing and strafing of the U.S. gunboat *Panay* on the Yangtze River in December brought an immediate apology and a promise to pay compensation. Neither the army nor the navy of Japan had any interest in provoking conflict with the United States. Indeed, for some time the two services were not agreed on assessing foreign threats and opportunities, the army fixing its eyes on the Soviet Union as a menace to Japan's position in Manchuria while the navy favored expansion southward through French Indochina toward Thailand, British Malaya, and the Dutch East Indies, sources of rubber, tin, and other strategic raw materials—above all oil, the lifeblood of navies. While expanding its navy, seizing offshore islands, and blockading Western commercial interests in China, Japan continued to refrain from provoking an isolationist America into war. Roosevelt, however, in 1938 and 1939 tightened economic policy toward Japan—limiting financial credit and the export of airplanes and aircraft parts, high-octane aviation fuel, scrap metal, and machine tools.

As war came to Europe, Japan's leaders perceived potential gain in merging the Far Eastern and European conflicts by taking advantage of Germany's victories to penetrate the European colonial territories in Asia. Upon the collapse of France in June 1940, Japan sent forces into French Indochina and demanded that Britain close the Burma Road over which military supplies were reaching China. September 1940 witnessed the signing in Berlin of the Tripartite Pact, linking the three principal aggressors in Asia and Europe. Japan recognized the leadership of the Axis powers in establishing a new order in their region, while the Axis recognized Japan's new order in East Asia. The signatories also promised to assist one another if any one should be attacked by a power not yet a party to either the European or Asian conflict. Thus the Tripartite Pact was not a genuine mutual defense alliance, but rather a political instrument aimed at keeping the United States neutral by threatening it with war in the Atlantic and the Pacific simultaneously. If successful, the pact would discourage Roosevelt from over-committing the United States to Britain and would enable Hitler to win his war in the west; it would also enhance Japan's freedom to pursue its southward course of expansion toward self-sufficiency. The pact has been termed a blunder for Japanese diplomacy, for it was concluded after Germany's ability to win the Battle of Britain had already been cast into grave doubt.*

Roosevelt's global strategic outlook had long dictated that aid to Britain must hold the highest priority. Aware that the danger of war in the Atlantic was on the rise from the late summer of 1940 onward, and that the U.S. Navy was not prepared for serious trouble in two oceans, the president sought to avoid pushing Japan over the precipice into war. To show strong disapproval of the aggression against China, Roosevelt and Hull felt obliged to apply economic pressure and to keep alive the threat of greater punishment if Japan persisted in its course. Just as some elements in Tokyo kept hoping in vain that the United States would acquiesce in Japan's effort to establish a "co-prosperity sphere" in Asia, so Roosevelt and Hull apparently hoped that moderate elements in Tokyo would regain control from the militarists, place distance between themselves and the Axis, and pull Japanese troops back from foreign occupied territory.

The problem confronting the Roosevelt administration was to determine what measures would deter Japan from opting for war yet would not actually provoke Japan into war. Once the Japanese speeded up their march through Southeast Asia in July 1941, it became extremely difficult to formulate effective economic sanctions that did not have serious and immediate military implications. The Japanese government exhibited a peculiar talent for provoking responses from Washington that were bound to look like unfriendly acts. The Japanese perhaps underestimated the American determination to defend British and Dutch interests in the region.

In an effort to halt the Japanese, Roosevelt froze all Japanese assets in the United States on July 26, 1941, thereby enabling him to cut off the flow of oil to Japan, as his secretaries of war and navy had been urging. Admiral Harold Stark, chief of naval operations, was strongly opposed to the oil embargo because he was convinced that this would tilt the scales toward war in the Pacific; he deemed the navy unprepared for war, even though he thought that every day's delay of entry into the Atlantic war jeopardized Britain's survival. Apparently he still thought of the wars in Europe and Asia as separable. No one could be certain whether the Japanese navy, which had previously been opposed to reckless adventures but for which oil was of critical importance, would insist that Tokyo come to terms with the United States or would advocate war in order to ensure a supply of oil.

From July to November, there were signs that both sides were still looking for a *modus vivendi,* but their fundamental objectives, requirements, and demands were incompatible. The authors consider Bruce M. Russett's basic hypothesis unconvincing that war was avoidable and unnecessary; that the Japanese attack was a direct result of the embargo and "merely climaxed a long

---

*Frank W. Ikle, "Japan's Policies Toward Germany," in James W. Morley, ed., *Japan's Foreign Policy, 1868–1941: A Research Guide* (New York: Columbia University Press, 1974), p. 327; and Paul W. Schroeder, *The Axis Alliance and Japanese–American Relations, 1941* (Ithaca, N. Y.: Cornell University Press, 1958), pp. 29–47.

series of mutually antagonistic acts."* In fact, it was not possible for the Roosevelt administration to avoid putting any pressure on Japan and to pursue instead an appeasement policy of rewarding the Japanese militarists for a decade of mounting aggression.

As early as January 1941, U.S. Ambassador Joseph C. Grew had warned the Department of State concerning a rumored Japanese plan to carry out a surprise attack against the American naval base at Pearl Harbor, Hawaii. This, combined with other circumstantial evidence, has given rise to recurring suspicions that President Roosevelt was somehow responsible for the disaster at Pearl Harbor, either by permitting it to happen while leaving the fleet exposed to what he knew was an impending attack or even by maneuvering the Japanese into attacking so that he could bring a unified America into the European war through the back door.** Actually, although American naval strategists had long included an attack on Pearl Harbor among their standard war games, no credence was given the rumor reported by Ambassador Grew. On November 27, 1941, the War Department sent the following message to Lt. General Walter C. Short, army commander in Hawaii:

> Negotiations with Japan appear to be terminated to all practical purposes . . . Japanese future action unpredictable but hostile action possible at any moment. If hostilities cannot, repeat cannot be avoided the United States desires that Japan commit the first overt act. This policy should not, repeat not, be construed as restricting you to a course of action that might jeopardize your defense. Prior to hostile Japanese action you are directed to undertake such reconnaissance and other measures as you deem necessary but these measures should be carried out so as not, repeat not to alarm civilian population or disclose intent. Report measures taken.

General Short, concluding that the avoidance of war or of giving any pretext for war was the paramount consideration, riveted his attention on the precautionary commands not to provoke the Japanese or to alarm the local civilian population and focused on the danger of internal sabotage rather than external attack.

Political and military leaders in Washington called for readiness, yet downgraded the danger—which, as the Japanese bombing of Pearl Harbor on December 7 proved, was all too real. Incompetence, shortsightedness, nonchalance, and lethargy could be found at all levels from the president on down—as they always can be found in retrospect. Gordon W. Prange's well-documented study contains the judicious conclusion that there are no scapegoats, no villains in the drama, no American president acting as puppeteer to Japanese decision makers.† The fundamental disbelief that it could happen was at the root of the

---

*Bruce M. Russett, *No Clear and Present Danger: A Skeptical View of the U. S. Entry into World War II* (New York: Harper & Row, 1972), p. 20.

**See, for example, Charles Callan Tansill, *The Back Door to War* (Chicago: Henry Regnery, 1952).

†Gordon W. Prange, Introduction to *At Dawn We Slept: The Untold Story of Pearl Harbor* (New York: Penguin Books, 1982), pp. xi–xii.

tragedy. Pearl Harbor may have been the miracle Roosevelt hoped for to shock the American people out of their isolationist illusion—which it certainly did—but Japan, not he, was the maker of that miracle.

## WARTIME DIPLOMACY

Just as Tsarist Russia's participation in World War I had until March 1917 tarnished the cause of the Allied democracies, so the Anglo–American partnership against Hitler was compromised and complicated by its link to Soviet imperialist designs and the totalitarian dictatorship of Josef Stalin throughout World War II. Stalin was shrewd enough to realize that the Russian people would not make heroic sacrifices for the Bolshevik idea. Consequently, he not only permitted but encouraged the revival of traditional religious, historical, and cultural themes to stimulate nationalist fervor. In the United States, conscious efforts were made to deemphasize Soviet communism and to exalt "Mother Russia" as well as the enduring friendship between the two countries. In the spring of 1943, Stalin made the ostentatious but almost meaningless gesture of dissolving the Communist International (Comintern), whereupon the U.S. Communist party dissolved itself for the duration of the war. Nevertheless, many in the West shared Churchill's deep distrust of the power to the east, which Hitler's invasion had made a *de facto* ally. The Grand Coalition was always an uneasy alliance, although Stalin got along much better with Roosevelt than with Churchill.

While the war was on, there was more to unite the interests of the Western democracies with those of the U.S.S.R. than to divide them. From June 1941 onward, Roosevelt and Churchill were agreed that aid to the Soviet Union was imperative, and a formal agreement on military-equipment assistance was signed in Moscow on October 1, 1941, while the German armies were driving toward the Soviet capital. Stalin wrote of his sincere gratitude in accepting Roosevelt's offer of a billion-dollar loan without interest charges. By mid-1942 Britain and the United States had shipped to the Soviet Union, at heavy cost in ships sunk, some 2.8 million tons of equipment, including 4400 tanks and 3100 planes.

World War II stimulated the most intensive diplomatic intercourse among powerful heads of government and their envoys (Hull, Eden, Molotov, Harriman, Hopkins, and Beaverbrook) ever seen within the international system—conferences and face-to-face meetings, letters, notes, cables, and phone conversations. Roosevelt and Churchill conferred with each other on seven different occasions in addition to their two meetings with Stalin at Teheran and Yalta and their meeting with Chiang Kai-shek in Cairo (from which Stalin and Molotov stayed away because the Soviet leader did not wish to reach any conference agreements with the Chinese government). Churchill also met twice with Stalin in Moscow. Finally President Harry S. Truman (who succeeded Roosevelt on April 12, 1945) and Stalin met with Churchill and later with Clement Attlee (who became prime minister in 1945) at Potsdam. Space permits only the most important issues treated in these conferences and other communications to be summarized in this section.

Stalin was quite pleased with the determination of Roosevelt and Churchill to assign strategic priority to defeating Germany before Japan (toward which the USSR was neutral). On January 1, 1942, while Churchill was in Washington, he, Roosevelt, Molotov, and Chinese Foreign Minister T. V. Soong, along with the representatives of other nations, signed the United Nations Declaration, pledging each country to "employ its full resources, military or economic," against the Axis powers and to make no "separate armistice or peace with the enemies." Members also subscribed to the "common program of purposes and principles" of the Atlantic Charter, but these were not spelled out in the declaration, because the Soviet Union would not abjure all territorial changes that were not in accord with the freely expressed wishes of the people concerned. Nor would it promise to respect the right of all peoples to choose their form of government and to restore self-government to those from whom it had been forcibly removed. The fact that the Soviet Union would give only qualified approval to the principles of the Atlantic Charter was an indicator of a deep political-ideological fissure in the coalition. It was papered over then, but would reopen in the closing stages of the war.

**The Issue of the Second Front**

The most divisive strategic issue within the wartime coalition pertained to the opening of a second front, which Stalin naturally demanded as early as possible to relieve the German pressure on the Soviet Union. Roosevelt and Churchill were in disagreement on this. Churchill, who had watched Stalin sitting out the war as a treaty partner of Hitler all through the Battle of Britain, thought that the Western allies were sending plenty of their own much-needed war matériel to the USSR. He favored an indirect, peripheral, nibbling strategy over an invasion into the heart of German strength. Roosevelt and Stimson wanted a frontal cross-Channel assault as early as possible, and in May 1942 the president promised Stalin that the formation of a second front could be expected before the end of the year. The British, who regarded themselves as superior strategists to the Americans, tentatively accepted the U.S. proposal but became doubtful and then opposed until Germany had been weakened and there had been an adequate buildup of Allied forces in the British Isles. Churchill strongly preferred a landing in North Africa in the fall of 1942. Roosevelt eventually accepted the idea for the sake of Anglo–American solidarity, but left it to Churchill to travel to Moscow in order to let a disappointed Stalin know of plans for a landing in North Africa instead of a second front in France.

The Anglo–American invasion of North Africa in November 1942 complicated the relationship between the English-speaking allies and the French. Almost all of North Africa was under the control of the militarily feeble Vichy regime, with which the United States had maintained diplomatic relations, much to the chagrin of American liberals and General Charles de Gaulle. De Gaulle received support from Churchill and recognition from Stalin as leader of the Free French. Roosevelt, however, suspecting that the self-appointed leader was not as representative of the French people as he made himself out to be, neither liked nor supported him.* American diplomacy struck many liberals at the time as somewhat shady,** but it was amply justified insofar as it produced a substantial political-strategic gain at an extremely low cost in lives.

The triumphant operation in North Africa was soon followed by a Roosevelt–Churchill conference in Casablanca in January 1943, just two weeks before the German surrender at Stalingrad and four months before the collapse of Axis forces in North Africa. Stalin was invited but declined, pleading the responsibities of military command just as a counteroffensive was becoming possible. Churchill and his military staff once again proved more suasive than the U.S. high command, which was still impatient to launch a cross-Channel thrust into *Festung Europa.* It was decided that the next move would be into Sicily. Stalin, who had denied that the North African invasion had relieved any German military pressure on his forces, would again be upset. Realizing this, and perhaps hoping to remove from Stalin the temptation of entering into separate peace talks with the Germans, Roosevelt used the occasion of the Casablanca Conference to announce the war-aim policy of "unconditional surrender by Germany, Italy, and Japan." This announcement struck a note of confidence as Allied forces were preparing to mount the initiative on several fronts in 1943. But it was criticized in many quarters as calculated to stiffen enemy resistance, weaken the resolve of Germans who might otherwise have moved to overthrow Hitler, and prolong the war.

From Sicily, Allied forces in the west moved on to the Italian mainland on September 3, nine days after a badly shaken Mussolini had been dismissed by King Victor Emmanuel III, placed under arrest, and succeeded by Marshal Pietro Badoglio as head of a new parliamentary government.† In October, the Badoglio government was allowed to achieve the status of a co-belligerent—but not an ally—of the Western powers. Stalin was resentful over the separate Anglo–American armistice negotiations with Italy as inconsistent with the United Nations Declaration of January 1, 1942, but since there were no Soviet forces anywhere in the Mediterranean region, his complaint carried little weight. Besides, the Germans dug in and remained determined to make the Allies' peninsular campaign as costly as possible—which they did. Thus it was not possible to speak of a real peace settlement.

---

*Roosevelt and Hull were irritated and embarrassed when de Gaulle ordered his forces to seize the tiny Vichy-held islands of Saint-Pierre and Miquelon south of Newfoundland, despite the establishment of a hemispheric neutrality zone under the Panama Declaration of 1939.

**A related aspect of diplomacy which came in for criticism pertained to Roosevelt's friendly correspondence with General Francisco Franco, the pro-Axis dictator of Spain. Since the expeditionary forces came ashore in Algeria and Morocco, on each flank of the Spanish Protectorate, the Allies deemed it important to neutralize the 150,000 Spanish troops in the region and to discourage a Spanish move against Gibraltar. Roosevelt reassured Franco that the United States would "take no action of any sort which would in any way violate Spanish territory," that the two countries were "friends in the best sense of the word," and that he believed the Spanish government wished to remain outside the war. (Arthur P. Whitaker, *Spain and Defense of the West* [New York: Praeger, 1962], pp. 11–14.)

† A week later Mussolini was rescued by a Nazi pilot and became a puppet ruler for the Nazis in an artificial "social republic" in northern Italy.

It has often been mistakenly assumed that Churchill was alone among Western leaders in understanding the postwar geopolitical implications of wartime military operations and that if his advice about a second front in the Balkans had been followed, the Soviet Union might well never have been able to make the gains in Eastern Europe that it made in the closing stages of the war. Actually, the president in 1943 recognized the need for American forces to reach Berlin as soon as the Russians did, in case Germany should suddenly collapse. Although he wanted a second front on the Continent, he did not want it at the cost of heavy U.S. casualties, for that could jeopardize not only the nation's ability to bear the brunt of the war in the Pacific but also its willingness to shoulder postwar international responsibilities. Therefore he did not feel as strongly as his military chiefs about opening the second front as early as possible. He and his staff finally agreed that the cross-Channel invasion must come by May 1944.

### The Teheran Conference

Once the timing had been set for the Operation OVERLORD invasion of occupied France across the English Channel, the way was clear for the first meeting of the Big Three leaders—Roosevelt. Churchill, and Stalin—at Teheran, Iran (then Persia), on November 27–December 1, 1943. En route to the Persian capital, the first two met with the Nationalist Chinese (Kuomintang) leader Chiang Kai-shek at Cairo. Stalin, because of his posture of neutrality vis-à-vis Japan, did not wish to take part in discussions in which the Pacific war and its aftermath were the principal subject. The Cairo Three promised to prosecute the war against Japan to the latter's unconditional surrender and to restore to China all territories taken by Japan, such as Manchuria, Formosa, and the Pescadores. During the Teheran talks, Stalin gave no indication that he wished to aid Mao Zedong, the Chinese Communist leader, against Chiang, and he explicitly endorsed the intention concerning the return of Chinese territories.

Stalin understood where the real power resided in the Anglo–American alliance. Churchill and his people had more experience in international diplomacy, but the British Empire was in a long-term structural decline, although the wily old anti-Bolshevik Churchill was expected to do whatever he could to revitalize British imperialism and obstruct the expansion of Soviet influence at war's end. In contrast, Stalin regarded Roosevelt and the Americans with a healthy respect, for the mantle of leadership in the world of prodigious capitalist production had long since passed from Britain to them. Stalin perceived that he could exert greater influence over Roosevelt—a shrewd domestic politician whose comprehension of international affairs would undoubtedly have been more sophisticated had he possessed Churchill's wider experience. Stalin went out of his way to ingratiate himself with Roosevelt, to avoid offending him in face-to-face meetings, to appeal to his anticolonial sentiments against Churchill's imperialist inclinations, and to defer to his views as arbitrator when differences arose between Churchill and himself, knowing that Roosevelt would often bend over backward to appear objectively neutral rather than a member of an Anglo–American capitalist cabal against Stalin. Roosevelt found Stalin amiable and charming as a person and impressive as a political leader. He was pleased to hear Stalin's assurance that the Soviet Union would enter the war against Japan as soon as Germany was defeated.

## The Normandy Landing and de Gaulle

On June 6, 1944, two days after Allied armies entered Rome, an American-British armada, the mightiest ever gathered, carried out Operation OVERLORD on the beaches of Normandy. General Dwight David Eisenhower proved himself eminently successful as a soldier-diplomat in his role as supreme commander of the Allies' massive expeditionary force.

De Gaulle was not informed of the timing of the invasion until the evening before. Roosevelt and Hull had abandoned their reservations about the leader of the French Committee of National Liberation only when it became clear that he was widely regarded as the leader of Free France and that he alone could effectively appeal to all elements of the French resistance to unite their efforts in support of the Allied invasion. Even then, Roosevelt was slow to recognize de Gaulle's committee as the de facto provisional government of France. De Gaulle and French forces were allowed to lead the liberation march into Paris on August 25. De Gaulle immediately demanded that the Big Three become the Big Four to make decisions about the future of Germany. He traveled to Moscow in December to negotiate a Franco–Soviet mutual assistance pact aimed at Germany, thereby reviving a 50-year-old alliance. As the Big Three prepared for their final meeting at Yalta early in 1945, de Gaulle asserted that he should participate. Churchill agreed, Stalin was noncommittal, and Roosevelt's firm opposition prevailed.

## The Allies and a Defeated Germany

The terms of unconditional surrender posed no great problems. It had been decided that Germany should be completely disarmed and compelled to pay reparations for war damage inflicted on the Allies, but no agreement was reached on exact amounts. Germany was to be divided into three nearly equal occupation zones, with Berlin as a separate zone of joint occupation subdivided into distinct sectors of responsibility. The Soviet Union was to occupy the eastern zone, while the British and Americans were to divide western Germany between them—the Soviet leader did not care how. (Later, he agreed that there could also be a French zone so long as it was carved out of the western sector.) Under the original Roosevelt plan, Berlin would have been the intersecting point of the three zones, thus giving each power assured access, but in the end the Soviet zone boundary ran more than 100 miles west of Berlin, and little attention was paid to the question of access rights. That oversight would make Berlin a source of international friction for many years.

The British and the Americans disagreed over zonal divisions. The British, whose forces were already deployed in the north, wanted the northwest zone, where they would be close to the Low Countries (which they knew well), would be able to oversee German naval disarmament, would enjoy shorter supply lines and could carry out their occupation with the least economic expense. Roosevelt, however, wanted American forces, which were deployed to the south, to exchange the southwest for the northwest sector, where they would have easier access to German and Dutch ports for redeployment to the Pacific. Moreover, he did not wish to make U.S. forces dependent on lines of communication through France, perhaps because of his strained relationship with de Gaulle or perhaps because he expected political conflict and instability in that country. He finally gave in to the British on the condition that there be U.S. control of and assured access to the ports of Bremen and Bremerhaven.

At their second Quebec conference in September 1944, Roosevelt and Churchill initialed an agreement embodying a proposal put forth by U.S. Secretary of the Treasury Henry Morgenthau, Jr., that the Germans' industrial warmaking potential in the Ruhr and Saar areas be dismantled by the Allies whose industries had been destroyed. Under the Morgenthau Plan, Germany was to be converted into "a country primarily agricultural and pastoral in its character." The proposal was subjected to considerable ridicule by seasoned diplomats and the press. Both Roosevelt and Churchill pulled away from that drastic proposal within a month after the former admitted that he was staggered by its implications and had no idea how he could have initialed it, for although he favored controls, the Morgenthau Plan went far beyond his intention.

### The Dumbarton Oaks and Yalta Conferences

Churchill and Stalin had shown less interest than the American president in pressing for the postwar establishment of an international organization to maintain peace and security. But at a seven-week conference on the Dumbarton Oaks estate in Washington, D.C., from late August to early October 1944, representatives of the Big Four (with the British and Americans meeting separately with the Russians and Chinese) produced agreement on the basic structure of the General Assembly and Security Council of the new United Nations. The General Assembly would embody the principle of the equality of member states, and the Security Council was founded on a recognition that peacekeeping would depend on the unanimity of the four Great Powers, whose special responsibility would involve the veto privilege. This was not a Soviet proposal; Roosevelt, remembering the fate of Wilson's League Covenant at the hands of the Senate, insisted on the right of veto, but Roosevelt and Churchill favored some limitation on its use in Security Council voting so that it would not extend to procedural matters, nor to Security Council consideration of a dispute to which one of the Great Powers was a party. On the question of representation in the General Assembly, the Soviet Union demanded 16 seats—one for each of the socialist republics in the Union. Roosevelt rejected the demand, and at one point even countered with the puckish suggestion that the United States should then have to be given one vote for each of the 48 states. Recognizing the fact that the British Commonwealth would have six members in the General Assembly, and acknowledging Stalin's concern that the Soviet Union could be isolated and outvoted by the West, the United States and Britain agreed at Yalta to support a compromise whereby the USSR would receive two additional seats for the Ukrainian and Byelorussian republics, and the Soviet Union acceded to the Western plan to limit the use of the veto in the Security Council.

Not long after his electoral victory over Thomas E. Dewey in 1944, a tired Roosevelt set off for the Crimea to meet Stalin and Churchill for the last time. Ever since the summer of 1944, Stalin had become noticeably more difficult to deal with as his armies moved beyond Soviet frontiers into Finland (which would be neutralized but not occupied), Romania, Bulgaria, Hungary, and Poland. In October 1944, Churchill and Stalin in Moscow discussed what amounted to spheres of influence in postwar Eastern Europe. Roosevelt, not wishing to be associated with such a concept, did not bestow his formal blessing on it, but neither did he interpose objections to it.

Roosevelt was primarily interested in securing a specific Soviet commitment on participation in the war against Japan. Stalin undoubtedly intended to enter the Pacific war before it was over so that he could help shape the peace settlement in the Far East, but he played hard to get in an effort to build up the price that the Allies would pay for his aid, and he was not ready to fix a date for entry. Roosevelt, sponsor of Chiang's China for membership in the Big Four, also sought Soviet cooperation in resolving differences between Chiang's Kuomintang and Mao Zedong's Communists. Although Stalin was extremely critical of Chiang, he conceded that Chiang was the only national leader at the time who might have a chance of uniting China. Apparently he did not expect Mao's Communists to prevail over Chiang.

### The Polish Question

No issue of wartime diplomacy placed a heavier strain on the Grand Coalition than that of Poland, which came to symbolize the inability of the Western democracies and the Soviet Union to bridge the political differences that divided them so deeply. The two major sets of related questions pertained to frontiers and to the form of government that Poland was to have. The Allies managed to agree on frontiers, however bitter the final solution may have been to Polish nationalists, but they could not agree on the form of government because the Western democracies, if they remained faithful to their own basic values, could never give their approval to the political system that the Soviet Union, thanks to the Red Army, was in a position to impose on Poland.

As a direct consequence of the Nazi–Soviet Nonaggression Pact of August 1939, Stalin one month later had occupied and annexed eastern Poland—about two-fifths of its total area—thereby incorporating into the USSR about 5 million Poles and an equivalent Byelorussian and Ukrainian population, the latter in provinces that once belonged to the Tsars but had been lost by a weakened Russia in 1921. The London-based Polish government-in-exile refused to recognize the Soviet annexation of Polish territory in the east. Then in 1943 at Teheran, Churchill used three matchsticks to illustrate to Stalin how Poland could be moved westward, as it were: the Soviet Union would retain its zone in the east and

Poland would receive territorial compensation in the west, up to the Oder and Neisse rivers, at the expense of Germany. Stalin, a hard bargainer, said that he would be willing to pull back from the Molotov-Ribbentrop Line to the old 1920 Curzon Line, provided that the USSR could annex the northern part of East Prussia, including the port city of Konigsberg. Churchill, expressing sympathy for Soviet security needs, concurred in these changes, but insisted that there must be a strong Poland, able to play an independent part in the European security system. Roosevelt was in tacit agreement on the need for boundary revision, but with his eye on 6 or 7 million voters of Polish extraction in the United States, he told Stalin that he could not participate in any decision on the subject either at Teheran or during the following year prior to the 1944 election.

Churchill sought to persuade the London Poles to accept the Teheran understanding and make the best of it, but Premier Stanislaw Mikolajczyk and the other political and military leaders of the government-in-exile were adamant in their rejection, contending that Britain, which had originally gone to war in 1939 to save Poland from Nazi aggression, was now abetting Soviet partition. Churchill warned that Britain and the United States would never wreck the wartime alliance by employing military force against Soviet claims, based as they were on harsh but immutable political-military realities. Mikolajczyk appealed to Roosevelt, but to no avail, because the president—even apart from electoral considerations—did not wish to become involved in any decision making that would entail guarantees concerning postwar Eastern Europe.

Washington and London gradually shifted their concern from the issue of frontiers to that of Poland's postwar government. For more than two years, Stalin had been conducting a prolonged campaign to discredit the London Poles and to establish the presumption that the pro-Communist Union of Polish Patriots (later to evolve into the Lublin Committee) would become the government of the country after it had been "liberated" by the Red Army. Soviet–Polish relations were poisoned by the discovery in April 1943 of the mass graves of several thousand Polish army officers in the Katyn Forest, part of the Polish territory occupied by the Soviet Union from 1939 to 1941, and by Stalin's betrayal of the Polish underground army of General Tadeusz Bor-Komorowski, which carried out a valiant uprising from August to October 1944.

As the Red Army approached the capital, a Polish-language radio station in Moscow appealed to the people of Warsaw to rise up and harrass the German occupation forces in their retreat, but once General Bor had given the signal for the insurrection to begin, the radio in Moscow lapsed into silence, Soviet planes over Warsaw and Soviet artillery ceased all activity, and the Red Army's ground offensive came to a halt. Stalin remained deaf to appeals from Churchill and Roosevelt to help Bor's beleaguered Home Army of 40,000 partisans, and he refused to allow British and American planes to land on Soviet territory if they aided what he branded as an irresponsible, reckless, and criminal adventure in Warsaw. In effect, Stalin saw to it that the military arm that would have supported a free representative government in Poland after the war was liquidated, not by the Red Army but by four German divisions in Warsaw. The uprising was crushed in eight weeks. At Yalta it was a foregone conclusion that the Moscow-rigged

Lublin Committee would constitute the postwar government of Poland, despite assurances that "free and unfettered elections" would be held soon.

## The Decision to Build the Atomic Bomb

There was tragic irony in the fact that Hitler's rise to power in Germany coincided with an intensification of scientific research and rapid discovery in atomic physics. The exodus of German, Hungarian, and other scientists such as Albert Einstein, Max Born, Leo Szilard, and Edward Teller—several of them refugees from Hitler's racist policies—brought to the United States a group of first-class theoretical minds deeply disturbed at the prospect that the Nazis might be the first to develop "the ultimate weapon." Nils Bohr, a Dane, encouraged them.

In 1939, four weeks before war broke out, Einstein signed a letter informing Roosevelt that in the immediate future, "it may become possible to set up nuclear chain reactions" conceivably (but not certainly) leading to the construction of "extremely powerful bombs of a new type." The president indicated that he wanted action, and four months later the Army and Navy, with some skepticism, allocated $6000 to purchase the uranium and graphite needed for an experiment to determine whether a chain reaction could be achieved. Further research convinced top government scientists that the United States should pursue the matter seriously. Organization of the Manhattan Project was entrusted to Major General Leslie P. Groves. The first successful operation of an atomic reactor and demonstration of a chain reaction took place in a makeshift laboratory beneath the football stadium of the University of Chicago on December 2, 1942. When American forces took Strasbourg in November 1944, it was learned that German atomic efforts were not even as advanced as those of the United States had been three years earlier. Some scientists connected with the Manhattan Project began to have second thoughts about proceeding with the construction of an atomic bomb. It was too late, however, to shift the most costly scientific enterprise in history into reverse. Robert Oppenheimer, scientific head of the project, convinced his colleagues that they had an intellectual obligation to complete the work and validate the theory. Many physicists became concerned about the uses to which the weapon might be put and began to discuss possible methods of establishing international controls over atomic energy in the postwar period. Szilard and Bohr were particularly concerned lest the development of atomic weapons in the United States arouse Soviet fears and lead to a new form of power struggle in the future. Bohr advocated collaboration with the Soviet Union to ward off suspicion and competition. Roosevelt agreed with Churchill, however, that the secrets of the new bomb should not be shared with Stalin.

## Roosevelt's China Policy

In the Asia-Pacific theater, Japan had quickly conquered the Philippines, Malaya, Burma, and the Dutch East Indies, while compelling American, British, Dutch, and Australian forces to retreat ignominiously. The U.S. Navy began to mount an initiative as early as June 1942, when it defeated the Japanese fleet at

Midway. That was a turning point in the war, after which the Japanese lost the Solomon Islands, New Guinea, and nearby archipelagoes, at the same time being bypassed and isolated in other islands that they held. Moreover, American submarines began to exact a heavy toll on Japanese ships, and these losses seriously depressed the economy. Thoughtful politicians in Tokyo began by 1943 to doubt that Japan could win and to speak of a compromise peace, but the military would not tolerate such defeatist suggestions, especially in view of the Roosevelt-Churchill policy of unconditional surrender. As late as 1944, Japan was able to carry out a large-scale offensive in southwest China. Despite a major Japanese setback along the Indo-Burmese frontier, U.S. planners expected a long bloody struggle.

Roosevelt saw Soviet participation and Chinese political military unification as conditions for the final campaign against Japan. As early as 1942, he proposed that Chiang place his Nationalist Kuomintang forces under the command of the American general Joseph W. ("Vinegar Joe") Stilwell, but the generalissimo procrastinated. In June 1944, the president dispatched Vice-President Henry Wallace on a fact-finding mission to Chungking, the Nationalist capital. Roosevelt was anxious to avert civil war between the Nationalists and the Communists,* and to bring about better Sino–Soviet relations, Wallace, noting that the best Kuomintang troops were deployed against the Communists to the north, concluded that Chiang was more preoccupied with the struggle against Mao for internal control of China than with the war against the external aggressor. Mao was no less concerned with Chiang, but he was shrewder in that he cultivated popular support for his "liberation army" by conducting limited operations against Japanese forces. When Wallace pressed for a united Chinese military effort against Japan, Chiang warned that Washington was being deceived by the Soviet propaganda line that Mao's followers were not real Communists, only agrarian reformers—an interpretation that gained wide currency in American intellectual circles in the early postwar years. At Chiang's urging, Wallace recommended that FDR send a top-level personal representative to Chungking.

Roosevelt appointed as his personal representative (later ambassador) General Patrick J. Hurley, a personal friend and former secretary of war in the Hoover administration. Hurley was a charming, flamboyant, and often erratic character who had little knowledge of China. Convinced that the Nationalists were stronger—a correct assumption, from the military standpoint—he believed that Chiang alone could unify the country. U.S. foreign service officers in China, however, saw Chiang's government as corrupt, inefficient, too closely aligned with a small group of bourgeois moneylenders and landlords, and thus alienated from the masses. In the eyes of these "China hands," the Communists were politically stronger because they were closer to the peasants and were associated with popular reforms.

In September 1944, after receiving from General Stilwell a report on the deteriorating situation in Burma and China, and fearing that China might soon

---

*The Communists were the left wing of Sun Yat-sen's original revolutionary party, the Kuomintang; they broke off after Sun's death in 1925.

be knocked out of the war, Roosevelt sent an urgent appeal to Chiang through Stilwell: if China was to be saved and not completely overrun by the Japanese, Kuomintang forces must be placed under Stilwell's command. By that time the general and the generalissimo despised each other,* and Chiang suspected Stilwell of drafting the ultimatum. Refusing to be dictated to by Roosevelt, he demanded that Stilwell be recalled and General Albert C. Wedemeyer be appointed in his stead. Hurley traveled to Yenan and hammered out a complex agreement with Mao for the unification of all Chinese military forces under a national coalition government. Hurley, excessively optimistic on the possibility of compromise, underestimated the profound ideological differences between the Nationalists and the Communists. Chiang rejected the idea of a coalition because he assumed that Communists could never take part in a coalition except as a tactical prelude to a complete takeover of power.

**The Final Stages of the War**

The Yalta conference had left many important issues unresolved, or only apparently resolved. Stalin did not agree at all with Roosevelt and Churchill on the meaning of "free elections" in Poland or elsewhere in Central and Eastern Europe. As the Red Army rolled westward into countries that Stalin regarded as naturally disposed to decline the honor of forming his security zone, it become obvious that he was determined to arrange the postwar shape of things in that zone according to Soviet security interests, regardless of how the Western democratic leaders might interpret the wartime agreements. What Stalin wanted was a new and more effective *cordon sanitaire* of his own making, a protective belt facing westward. Churchill was more skeptical than Roosevelt concerning Stalin's intentions, but even Roosevelt—by now exhausted and ailing—began to realize after Yalta that the West faced some hard bargaining with an intransigent ally over both European and Far Eastern questions. Nevertheless, he continued to hope that the wartime allies would manage somehow to extend their collaboration indefinitely into the postwar period, perhaps because he seemed to take it for granted that American public opinion would not support U.S. military occupation of Europe for more than a year or two. Thus Roosevelt bent over backward at times to meet Stalin's demands, making concessions to speed up Soviet entry into the war against Japan and to win Soviet support for a stable Europe.

As the war drew to a close, the USSR's old ideological animosity toward capitalist states, which had been subdued from 1941 to 1945, began to reappear. In March 1945, Soviet Foreign Minister Vyacheslav M. Molotov sent notes to Washington and London protesting against Anglo–American talks with German officers in Berne, Switzerland, on the possibility of a surrender of German forces in northern Italy. A few days later, Molotov insinuated that the Western Allies were trying to conclude a separate peace with Germany. Stalin informed the

*Chiang was probably aware that Stilwell usually referred to him as "the Peanut."

president that Molotov would not be able to attend the United Nations Conference in San Francisco, scheduled to open a month later. Roosevelt complained to Stalin that he was "frankly puzzled" by the discouraging lack of progress in carrying out the Yalta decisions, especially on Poland. Stalin kept up his criticism of the Berne negotiations, which in his view were enabling Anglo–American troops to advance rapidly into the heart of Germany without meeting any resistance. It was quite understandable, of course, that Germany's armed forces should fight furiously against the advancing Red Army in the east while hoping that British and American forces would occupy most of the country, and perhaps arrive in Berlin before the Russians. No negotiations were necessary for that.

U.S.–Soviet relations, then, were disintegrating when Franklin Delano Roosevelt died less than three months after being inaugurated for his fourth term as president. The sudden death of this leading personality at such a critical moment compounded the ambiguities that were already inherent in the international diplomatic situation because Roosevelt had preferred to postpone settlement of the most difficult political issues until after military victory had been secured. The suave, aristocratic, eloquent New Yorker was succeeded by a plain-speaking man from Missouri, shrewd in domestic politics but inexperienced in foreign affairs and largely in the dark about his predecessor's wartime diplomatic dealings.

## FOREIGN-POLICY DECISION MAKING UNDER ROOSEVELT

When Roosevelt took office in 1933, the traditional assumptions concerning the formation and conduct of American foreign policy remained intact and unquestioned. The U.S. Constitution established a mechanism whereby public policy was based on a combination of the popular consensus about the general direction in which the country ought to move and elite expertise concerning the formulation of specific policies and tactical decisions to implement them. In a democracy, the people elect the executive and the legislature, which share responsibility in varying degrees for weighing the desirability, costs, and consequences of alternative courses of action or inaction in the international arena. The general public, however, while influencing the choice as to the ultimate destination on which the ship of state has embarked, can neither chart nor navigate its precise course.

Because of natural advantages which inhere in the executive—unity of decision and command, superior sources of information, secrecy, and the ability to take action quickly when necessary, especially in a crisis—all political systems vest the plenary power to take foreign-policy initiatives in that branch. The Supreme Court, in the case of *United States* v. *Curtiss-Wright Export Corporation* (1936) referred to the "very delicate, plenary and exclusive power of the President as the sole organ of the Federal Government in the field of international relations." Justice Sutherland, speaking for the Court, said that "congressional legislation which is to be made effective through negotiation and inquiry (abroad) . . . must often accord to the President a degree of discretion and freedom from statutory restriction which would not be admissible were domestic affairs alone involved." The Court itself throughout its history had abstained completely from passing judgment on the constitutionality of any action of a president in the realm of foreign affairs.

Roosevelt chose as his secretary of state a Tennesseean, Cordell Hull, a man trained in the law who had served 22 years in Congress. Hull had no diplomatic experience, but he was an expert in fiscal matters, especially tariffs. Roosevelt selected him not out of personal friendship, nor for his high moral principles, but probably because Hull was a power in the Democratic party who had helped FDR get the nomination in Chicago, who enjoyed a fine reputation with Congress and who would be able to make it appear that the new administration sincerely favored reviving international trade through tariff reduction (even though Roosevelt was no less an advocate of national economic protectionism than other government leaders at the time). Hull believed that high tariffs were a major contributor to international instability and tensions in the 1930s. He is perhaps best remembered for his ardent advocacy of the Reciprocal Trade Agreements Act of 1934. A Jeffersonian democrat at home and a Wilsonian idealist abroad, Hull had a deep aversion to power politics and the concepts of balance of power and spheres of influence, and an equally strong attachment to international law, organization, and morality. In his substantive outlook, he was not less utopian than the Virginian who went to Princeton, Trenton, and the White House, but he faulted Wilson for having neglected his relations with Congress and for turning foreign policy into a subject of partisan conflict. Hull carefully avoided those tragic mistakes.

From 1933 until 1937, Roosevelt was compelled to devote most of his attention to combating the effects of the depression. These were the years of Hull's maximum influence in the making of foreign policy. Hull was a hard, steady, plodding worker who strove for reciprocal tariff cuts and other international economic adjustments based on the perception of enlightened self-interest by governments. He also did much to build the inter-American system by lending credibility to the central tenet of Roosevelt's Good Neighbor policy—nonintervention in the affairs of the Latin American republics—even while persuading them to close ranks for the sake of hemispheric security. Along the way, he exhibited a capacity for giving vent to his moral indignation and lecturing other diplomats for their governments' unconscionable breaches of international decency—as he did the unwitting Japanese envoys within hours after Pearl Harbor. Esteemed by Congress and public alike, he was virtually immune to press criticism, and he served longer than any other secretary of state in American history—nearly 12 years—before retiring for reasons of age and health after the November 1944 election. He was a Wilsonian to the end, striving to lay the foundations for a hopeful new international order of peace in the United Nations.

Roosevelt and Hull respected each other, but they were never close and friendly, always rather formal, and they did not always see eye to eye. Hull wanted more ambassadorial posts to go to professional diplomats rather than to donors to party coffers. The president gave the secretary a free hand to administer and reorganize the business of the State Department, which FDR, like some of his successors, deemed stodgy and sluggish. The conservative Tennesseean, however, was not a reformer or a daring innovator. He presided over the last decade of a traditional department before it moved to Foggy Bottom.

From 1937 onward, as the international situation grew worse, Roosevelt's interest in foreign affairs quickened. With the approach of the war, the White House became more and more the center for decision making for the great foreign policy issues, while Hull continued to manage the flow of routine diplomatic business. He deeply resented the fact that his undersecretary, Sumner Welles, who was much more Roosevelt's type, had direct access to the president and often recommended initiatives that Hull considered sufficiently impulsive to warn against, sometimes successfully. Hull's utility lay in his critical mind, which may have seemed excessively cautious when it came to citing reasons for taking no action at a particular time but which occasionally saved the president from hasty or imprudent steps.

Foreign policy was much simpler in the 1930s. There was no foreign aid and very little instantaneous news from abroad prior to Pearl Harbor. There was no National Security Council, no integrated Department of Defense, no Central Intelligence Agency, no Joint Chiefs of Staff. A War Council began meeting with the president during 1941, but Hull was a member only up to the formal declaration of hostilities, after which military decision making dominated, with little systematic analysis of political implications. Roosevelt became increasingly dissatisfied with the professional diplomats, especially those like Loy Henderson, Joseph Grew, and Hull himself who were abidingly suspicious of Stalin's regime. Anxious to speed Lend-Lease aid first to Britain and later to the USSR, he established direct contacts with Churchill and relied on Harry Hopkins and W. Averell Harriman as his personal envoys to Stalin.

The war brought a proliferation of new organizations: the Office of War Information, the War Protection Board, the War Food Administration, the Office of Lend-Lease Administration, the Economic Warfare Board, the War Shipping Administration, the Office of War Mobilization, the Office of Strategic Services, and several others. Between 1940 and 1945, the number of personnel in the State Department nearly quadrupled. There was a pressing demand for reorganization. The task was carried out during 1944 by Undersecretary of State Edward R. Stettinius, a skilled administrator from the world of business—General Motors and U.S. Steel. Stettinius refashioned and rationalized the geographical and functional divisions of the department, putting similar tasks in the same offices and drawing more efficient lines of reporting to relieve top officials of routine decisions and give them more time for policy analysis and long-range planning.

Stettinius, acting under the exigencies of war, moved the department from traditional to modern procedures. By the time Hull stepped down, Stettinius was a natural choice to succeed him, in view of the fact that Roosevelt was then making the most important decisions through summit diplomacy—not only Big Three meetings but regular communications—and he needed a technician who could channel position papers and policy options to him and relay his own decisions back to State for implementation. Stettinius was a man of useful talents, but creative thinking in foreign policy was not among them. He carried on Hull's dedicated work on behalf of the United Nations, clarifying for Stalin and Churchill at Yalta the arrangements for voting in the Security Council and doggedly winning the argument on that subject at San Francisco against an obstreperous Molotov.* Finally, of Stettinius it must be said that he had an eye for competent personnel. His undersecretary was Joseph C. Grew; Dean Acheson was in charge of international economic policy; other assistant secretaries included William L. Clayton and Archibald MacLeish, the latter responsible for the new Division of Cultural Affairs.

Roosevelt was neither the first nor the last president who sought to shape at least some crucially important foreign policies independently of the State Department. The president's constitutional entitlement to play the most direct possible role in foreign affairs could not be questioned. The president must always have the best policy advice available, and the professional diplomatic establishment usually is, or should be, the logical source for such advice. Even when the most creative advice is available outside the State Department, it is still essential that the professional foreign service be kept fully up to date on current developments. No president has ever made more sweeping foreign policy decisions, while keeping the State Department in such a state of doubt or darkness, than did Franklin Delano Roosevelt.

Roosevelt in wartime had a peerless ability to make far-reaching political decisions, often in the name of military necessity, without being subjected to constant critical review by Congress, much less overruled by that body. His adversaries fumed when he concluded the destroyers-for-bases deal with Britain, but they were unable to lay a glove on him because his uncanny sense of timing saved him at any particular juncture from going beyond what public opinion was ready to support. As the international danger of blatant aggression by antidemocratic regimes loomed larger, his influence with a predominantly Democratic Congress increased to the point where he was able to overcome a powerful isolationism and replace neutrality legislation with the Lend-Lease Act.

Once war was formally declared, he became, in the words of Clinton Rossiter, a virtual constitutional dictator. A charismatic leader and noteworthy strategist, an eloquent master of radio communication arts and a commander-in-chief who seemed to know exactly what had to be done, and who did it with a flair never before seen in Washington, he inspired such public confidence that Congress and the press scarcely dared to challenge him, lest they be accused of jeopardizing the national war effort. The nation's newspaper publishers supported what was in the eyes of most Americans a just war for human liberty and decency against totalitarianism. Most of the working press stood in awe of FDR as the nation's number one newsmaker and accorded him a deference unique among modern inhabitants of the White House. One cannot imagine another leader persuading Congress to authorize $2 billion for a secret weapon whose

---

*Although Hull dealt with Churchill and Stalin at Moscow in October 1943, he never accompanied FDR to the summit meetings at Casablanca, Cairo, or Teheran.

nature could not be divulged—the largest sum ever spent for a single project up to that point in history. Roosevelt was the last president to enjoy such a prerogative. World War II was a watershed in the history of American foreign policy, as his successor would learn. Even though it converted the United States from an isolationist recluse to the leading internationalist actor on the global stage, the war also brought profound changes in the linkage between domestic politics and foreign policy.

# chapter 3

# Truman and the Postwar American Shaping of the Global System

During the last full month of the war in Europe, a dramatic transition in American leadership took place, from Franklin Delano Roosevelt to Harry S. Truman. FDR had selected Truman in 1944 as a replacement for a vice-president who had already become politically controversial, Henry A. Wallace. Truman was neither a friend of Soviet communism nor a Red-baiter. When the Nazis attacked the Soviet Union in June 1941, he had indicated that he would not mind seeing the two totalitarian powers exhaust each other in a war of attrition, but after Pearl Harbor he looked pragmatically upon the USSR as an ally deserving of American aid. Within a short time, he would have to take the measure of Stalin and allow Stalin to take his measure in the tests of will over Poland, Germany, and other major issues. But the first decision he was called on to make, an hour or so after being sworn into office, was whether the San Francisco Conference on the United Nations should proceed on schedule to put in final form the charter for Roosevelt's modified version of Wilson's idealistic plans for an international peacekeeping organization.

Foreign observers of U.S. foreign policy have often wondered about the American penchant for international organization. The United States, of course, unlike the countries of Europe from which it sprang, has no immediate neighbors who have throughout history been seen as threats to security. In this century, therefore, when technology has made the world seem smaller, the leaders and representatives of the American people have tended to perceive foreign wars and other conflicts as disruptive of international peace and order, and thus as potential though remote threats to a predictable international environment. Long before being locked in actual struggle with foreign powers, they have interpreted as dangerous to their own well-being and safety aggressive, expansionist behavior by more distant nations, driven by ideologically hostile blueprints of what the global system ought to be. Americans, shaped by their own frontier experience, developed a preference for meeting challenges abroad, and for parrying security threats before they reached their own shores. In the nineteenth century, that tendency produced the Monroe Doctrine. In the twentieth, there was a hope that it could be done by organizing for collective action with similarly motivated peaceful states to preserve or restore world order. That explained the Americans' initial flirtation with the League Covenant, which they quickly repudiated. They then pursued the less demanding policy of preaching moral sermons to the world in the period between the wars. After World War II, they returned to the idea of universal collective security with much more gusto, but hedged their bets by providing in the United Nations Charter for a more limited regional form of collective defense.

Even while war was still being waged, leading figures in both major parties, as well as an overwhelming majority of the American public, had agreed that the United States could not be allowed to repeat its earlier mistake of lapsing back into a complacent isolationism once the conflict was over. The Republican presidential candidates of 1940 and 1944, Wendell Willkie and Thomas E. Dewey, were joined by such one-time stalwart isolationists as Senators Robert A. Taft of Ohio and Arthur H. Vandenberg of Michigan in calling for responsible U.S. participation and leadership in an international organization for the maintenance of peace. The foreign secretaries of the Big Four met at Moscow in October 1943 and announced the plan to form the United Nations. When Secretary of State Cordell Hull returned from that conference, he gave voice to his own lingering Wilsonian idealism by proclaiming that "there would no longer be need for spheres of influence, for alliances, for balance of power." The new organization, however, would be born under more favorable auspices than the defunct League of Nations. Resolutions introduced into the House of Representatives by J. William Fulbright of Arkansas and into the Senate by Tom Connally of Texas affirmed the need for a new world organization. Only a few diehard isolationists resisted the popular tide of what would come to be known as internationalism.

Truman did not hesitate for a moment in deciding that the San Francisco Conference should be held as planned. Stalin changed his mind and agreed that Molotov would go to San Francisco and would also stop off to meet Truman in Washington. The new president was determined to state his position clearly and firmly on the necessity of keeping agreements. Truman was receiving advice from officials in the Department of State and military officers who were less inclined than Roosevelt had been to make concessions to Moscow merely to demonstrate good will and obtain Stalin's cooperation. At the same time, Truman inherited his predecessor's policy of enlisting Soviet participation in the war against Japan and in launching the United Nations on a viable basis. In his view, without Russia there would not be a world organization. Nevertheless, when Molotov called on Truman in Washington, the president, using sharp tones, told the foreign minister that Poland was a symbolic test of whether their two countries could work together on the basis of the Yalta understandings, and reminded him that no president could get Congress to approve appropriations for postwar economic collaboration unless there was wide public support for them. He emphasized that the Yalta agreements could not be a one-way street. "I have never been talked to like that in my life," said Molotov. "Carry out your agreements," Truman retorted, "and you won't get talked to like that."

By mid-April 1945, Anglo-American forces were preparing to link up with Soviet forces in Central Europe. A question arose as to whether the western allies should push eastward as far as possible or should crush German resistance along a less rapidly moving front while waiting for the Soviet army to move into the occupation zones approved by Roosevelt and Churchill at Quebec in September 1944. Churchill was now anxious for the Western allies to gain control of as much German territory as possible for purposes of postwar bargaining. He was particularly interested in seeing British and American forces capture Berlin, and Foreign Secretary Anthony Eden expressed the hope that American troops would liberate Prague. Churchill argued that the occupation zones had been drawn hastily at a time in 1942—before Quebec, indeed before the Allied expeditionary forces made the Channel crossing on D-Day, and long before the battle for Germany had begun—when no one could foresee the advances that would actually be realized by April 1945. The prime minister did not want an early automatic fallback by Western allied armies to lines coinciding with the occupation zones. But General Dwight D. Eisenhower and General George C. Marshall, then chief of staff, insisted that Berlin was not a militarily important objective and that soundly conceived military operations should not be set aside for political considerations—which in any case would prove to be ephemeral, because the Western allies could be expected eventually to withdraw their forces to the agreed occupation boundaries. Truman essentially concurred with their judgment that American troops should not be exposed to greater danger than was necessary. He deemed it desirable to control Berlin, Prague, and Vienna, but the Russians were in a stronger position to take them and bear the cost. Besides, he did not want to give them an excuse for breaking agreements.

## THE DECISION TO USE THE ATOMIC BOMB

Truman knew nothing of the Manhattan Project until after he became president, when he was briefed by Secretary of War Stimson. Since the atomic bomb was not successfully tested until July 16, 1945, at Alamogordo, New Mexico—more than two months after the end of the war in Europe—the question of its use against Germany never arose. But there had long been an assumption at the highest levels that the weapon would be used if it should become available before the war was over. Several scientists who had strongly supported the bomb project as a deterrent to the use of a potential German weapon were opposed to employing the bomb against Japan, which had never been assumed to be trying to produce an atomic weapon. Acting on the advice of James F. Byrnes (the senator from South Carolina who was Truman's choice to succeed Edward R. Stettinius as secretary of state after the San Francisco Conference), the new president appointed an ad hoc committee to advise him on atomic matters, chaired by Secretary Henry L. Stimson.

One of the options urged by some scientists in the late spring of 1945 was a demonstration use of the bomb. The suggestion was considered briefly by the policymakers but rejected as impractical for several reasons: problems of communication between adversaries, the possibility that Japanese military observers of a demonstration might just argue endlessly about its significance, the fear that the bomb might turn out to be a dud and the fear that American prisoners of war in Japan might be concentrated in the target area if the time and place of the explosion were known in advance. With Navy Undersecretary Ralph Bard as the only dissenter, the committee recommended a military use without warning. Truman, Byrnes, and Stimson were determined to use the full power of the United States with maximum shock effect to bring about the unconditional surrender of Japan as early as possible in order to eliminate the necessity for an amphibious invasion of the home islands.

Since the atomic bombing of Hiroshima and Nagasaki has aroused so much moral and political controversy, it must be set in context. Truman, a new president, had inherited an unknown weapon at the end of a long, bloody war. By the 1930s, the bombing of urban-industrial centers had come to be taken for granted by the West in the cases of Ethiopia, Spain, and China as an inevitable wartime result of military technology. World War II began with the bombing of Polish cities and Rotterdam by the Germans, which were soon followed by aerial attacks on Berlin and London. Prior to the dropping of atomic bombs on Hiroshima and Nagasaki, even greater numbers of civilians had died in saturation and fire-bombings of Leipzig, Dresden, Tokyo, Osaka, and Nagoya.

U.S. policymakers expected Japanese forces to wage a furious, protracted last-ditch struggle to defend every square mile of the home islands. General Douglas MacArthur and Chief of Staff George C. Marshall estimated that the final assault on Japan could cost from a half million to a million American casualties and a much larger number of Japanese lives. Given the situation, perhaps the only factor that might have led the United States to abstain would have been the known possession of a comparable capability by Japan to strike a retaliatory blow at, say, San Francisco and Los Angeles. Japan, however, possessed no deterrent. The case can be made that the atomic bombing of the two Japanese cities, although it clearly violated the traditional moral and civilizational principle of "discrimination," which prohibited the direct killing of innocent noncombatants, was marginally justifiable under the principle of "proportionality," on the grounds that it quickly ended the war and prevented a much greater total amount of death and destruction.

## THE POTSDAM CONFERENCE AND ITS AFTERMATH

The last of the allied wartime conferences was held at Potsdam, a suburb of Berlin, during the last two weeks of July 1945. The *dramatis personae* were changing. Roosevelt was replaced by Truman, a plain-talking, straightforward man, sufficiently aware of his lack of experience to keep his mind open to advisers and

State Department position papers, yet also quite decisive (sometimes hastily so), determined to carry through with a course of action once embarked on it, and stubborn enough to be almost unbudgeable once he had made up his mind. This was to be his first and only meeting with the diplomatically more experienced, ruthless, and crafty Stalin, with whom he got along well personally despite the fact that they were constantly at loggerheads over the issues. Churchill was accompanied in the first phase of the conference by his deputy prime minister, Clement Attlee, the mild-mannered leader of the Labour party. Before the conference was over, Churchill and Attlee returned to London for Britain's first parliamentary election in ten years, as a result of which Labour defeated the Conservatives and Attlee became the prime minister. Of the original Big Three, Stalin alone remained.

Naturally, the conference was dominated by questions pertaining to the shape of postwar Europe (especially Poland and Germany) and the final stages of the war in the Pacific against Japan. Truman wished to demonstrate continuity with the lines of Roosevelt's policies, insofar as those lines could be discerned. During the last few months of his predecessor's life, Truman had no way of knowing how rapidly suspicion between the United States and the Soviet Union had been increasing. FDR himself was quoted as saying: "Averell is right; we can't do business with Stalin. He has broken every one of the promises he made at Yalta."* Truman, although determined to be firm with the Soviet leader, was also anxious to work out compromises conducive to a stable postwar peace and a viable United Nations capable of preserving that peace.

All the Allies represented at Potsdam (de Gaulle was not a participant) were in agreement that Germany, though divided into four occupation zones, should be treated as a single economic unit according to centralized policies jointly formulated and approved by the Four-Power Control Council. It was probably unrealistic from the start to expect much consensus within the council beyond the general goals of demilitarization, de-Nazification, and democratization for the defeated enemy. When it came to implementing the policies of disarming military units, rooting out Nazis from political positions, and allowing the formation of democratic political parties, mutual recriminations were hurled. The only area in which genuine cooperation was achieved was in the establishment of the Nuremberg War Crimes Tribunal, which by October 1946 had found 19 leading Nazi figures guilty and sentenced 12 of them to be executed.** Within six months of the Potsdam Conference, it was clear that centralized policies for treating the whole of Germany as a single economic unit were out of the question.

---

*Quoted in W. Averell Harriman, "Russia and the Cold War," in Robert D. Marcus and David Burner, eds., *America Since 1945* (New York: St. Martin's Press, 1972), p. 5n.

**The Nuremberg trials came in for much subsequent criticism on purely legal grounds, since they were conducted by the victors without impartial judges from neutral countries or consultants on German legal procedures; they went beyond the traditional principle that only states and not individuals are subject to international law; and they seemed to violate the prohibition against *ex post facto* justice by prosecuting as crimes actions that had not previously been clearly defined as crimes under international law. Quincy Wright, "The Law of the Nuremberg Trial," *American Journal of International Law* 41 (1947), 38–72; and Robert K. Woetzel, *The Nuremberg Trials in International Law* (New York: Praeger, 1950).

## Potsdam and European Questions

U.S. and British officials at Potsdam agreed that a vengeful peace should not be imposed, for that approach in 1919 had helped to pave the way for Hitler in 1933. With Western Europe in economic shambles and millions of refugees being displaced westward, American and British policymakers were convinced that Germany, far from being dismembered and punitively repressed, had to be rehabilitated industrially if prolonged economic chaos in Europe was to be averted. The British recalled that reparations had played a part in bringing on the interwar depression, and U.S. policymakers remembered that, by being linked to war debts, the burden of reparations had been passed on to American taxpayers. Truman, Churchill, and Attlee backed away from precise dollar reparation figures, thinking that division of the country had rendered meaningless any figures for total reparations and formulas for interzonal transfers of capital from dismantled factories, current factory output, and food. There was wrangling over the imposition of an undemocratic government on Poland and over Poland's western border, which the West identified with the Eastern Neisse and the East with the Western Neisse. The Soviet Union had assigned a 40,000-square-mile zone in East Germany to Poland for administration. The United States and Britain protested at the Soviet decision to give Poland a "zone of occupation" and de facto control of German territory up to the Oder and Western Neisse rivers without consulting the Western allies, who wanted the settlement of boundaries to await the peace conference. Stalin contended that it was a zone of administration, not occupation, and that the formal revision of boundaries could be made at the peace conference.

Truman and Stalin clashed over favorable surrender terms for Italy, which the United States wanted because Italy had been the first enemy state to quit the war. The Soviet Union also objected to the refusal of the United States to recognize the governments of Hungary, Bulgaria, and Romania until after free elections had been held in those countries. The United States rejected the Soviet demand that the Montreux Convention of 1936, which had given Turkey control of navigation through the Bosporus and Dardanelles straits and the right to close them in time of war or threat to Turkey's security, be replaced by a system of joint Soviet–Turkish control.

In the end, Byrnes worked out a complex but not very durable compromise on reparations, the Polish territorial issue, and the East European satellites. Potsdam, like Yalta, produced what Feis has called "porous agreements . . . loosely stitched fabrications rather than sturdily woven compromises," which made it easy for each side to think that it was observing them while accusing the other of flagrant violations. Given the profound differences between the Soviet Union and the Western allies—political, economic, social, ideological, and strategic—nothing better was to be expected from the meeting of the two new world powers along the storm front that now ran through Europe. The best the leaders of the wartime allies could do under the circumstances was to pass all the insoluble problems along to the foreign ministers who were to convene a few months later, while hoping vaguely that either they or the nascent United Nations might be able to create a climate more favorable to settlements.

**Potsdam and Japan**

The situation with regard to Japan was quite different, largely because of the way the war ended. We referred earlier to Roosevelt's efforts to enlist Soviet participation in the final stages of the war in the Pacific and Stalin's efforts to raise the price of Soviet entry, especially in the form of territorial, political, and commercial concessions in the Far East. Roosevelt and Churchill granted those concessions at Yalta, in return for Stalin's assurance that the Soviet Union would enter the war against Japan within two or three months after the final victory had been won in Europe. Once Truman, Byrnes, and Stimson received word of the successful A-bomb test at Alamogordo the day before the Potsdam Conference began, they quickly lost interest in paying any price for a Soviet declaration of war against Japan.

Prior to Potsdam, Stimson, at the urging of the ad hoc committee on atomic-energy matters mentioned earlier, had advised Truman that he ought to consider informing Stalin about the bomb in order to avoid unnecessarily arousing his mistrust when it was used. Faced with Soviet demands at Potsdam, however, Truman, Byrnes, and Stimson agreed that Stalin would be told only enough to head off subsequent charges of deception. A full week after the test, therefore, Truman, without actually mentioning the nature of the weapon, casually informed Stalin about a "very powerful explosive" which would be used against Japan and which the Americans thought "will end the war." Stalin, equally laconic, showed no surprise but merely said that he was glad to hear about the weapon and hoped that good use of it would be made against Japan. Either Stalin did not fully comprehend the significance of the news, or else he was feigning indifference, not wishing to appear impressed or to let Truman think that the bomb represented an important new factor in diplomacy.

Following the Japanese defeat on Okinawa, the Tokyo government, at the wish of Emperor Hirohito, put out peace feelers through Moscow. Japan and the Soviet Union were not at war, having signed a five-year neutrality pact in April 1941. The Japanese wanted Stalin to act as an intermediary to find a way of bringing the war to an end on terms less harsh and dishonorable than unconditional surrender. They did not know that Stalin had already promised to go to war against Japan. The Soviet leader did not inform Washington of this overture, but the U.S. Navy had broken the cable code in which diplomatic messages were transmitted between Tokyo and Moscow. When Truman raised the question with Stalin at Potsdam, the latter merely intimated that it would not have been the act of a loyal ally to seek better terms for Japan than the English and Americans had set. Stalin, in all probability, had already determined that important Soviet interests in the Far East could be served at low cost by entering the war against an exhausted enemy at the right time. General John R. Deane referred to what he called a "strange race" in the summer of 1945, Japan trying to get out of the war and the Soviet Union trying to get into the war before it ended.* Neither the Russians nor the Americans, of course, knew how close Japan was to collapse; that

---

*John R. Deane, *The Strange Alliance* (New York: Viking, 1947), chap. 15 and 16.

has remained a matter of spirited debate to this day. American political and military leaders, as we have noted earlier, expected a bitter, costly invasion.

President Truman was probably also motivated to use the atomic bomb against Japan in order to terminate the war before the Soviet Union entered it, thereby denying Stalin a strong voice in the Far Eastern settlement. It cannot be denied that after his exposure to Soviet intransigence at Potsdam, Truman was determined that the Japanese occupation not follow the German pattern of divided zones of responsibility. The Soviet Union, hoping to gain joint control over Japan and to acquire additional territorial and other advantages in East Asia, declared war on August 8, 1945, two days after the crew of the *Enola Gay* dropped the first atomic bomb on Hiroshima, and before Stalin had obtained the concessions he had been seeking on China. The Russians replaced the Japanese for a time as occupiers of Manchuria and North Korea, but they did not win the joint control of Japan that they had demanded.

## FROM WARTIME ALLIANCE TO COLD WAR

For more than two decades, a debate has raged on American university campuses between "orthodox" and "revisionist" historians over the origins of the cold war. The authors have written elsewhere that, according to the older, "orthodox" interpretation that prevailed until the early 1960s,

> the Soviet Union was impelled in its foreign policy by two mutually reinforcing tendencies toward expansion—a Communist ideology avowedly bent on the destruction of the Western capitalist system, imposed upon a much older Russian tradition of universal messianism and a Tsarist policy of constantly probing for areas into which influence might be extended. During the interwar period, the Soviet Union had not disguised its hostility to the Western capitalist-democratic states; during the war, it had been a somewhat difficult ally—scarcely grateful in the eyes of the West for aid received . . . [albeit] delayed, as in the case of Stalin's call for a second front. The policy elites responsible for formulating U.S. policy during and after the war—the so-called Establishment—were never entirely comfortable at being allied with Josef Stalin, and they were not eager to extend what had been a wartime necessity into the postwar period, once it became apparent that the Stalinist system, which had pushed a Russian military power to unprecedented westward frontiers in Central Europe, was replacing wartime collaboration with a revived intransigence.*

Most of the orthodox historians were of the opinion that the U.S.–Soviet cold war was the inevitable result of the sudden confrontation in the Central European power vacuum of two diametrically opposed political-economic systems, each imbued with its own powerful ideological view of how human society should be organized on the international level. The orthodox chroniclers—virtually all political scientists and historians before the 1960s—were

*James E. Dougherty and Robert L. Pfaltzgraff, Jr., *Contending Theories of International Relations: A Comprehensive Survey* (New York: Harper & Row, 1981), p. 240.

inclined to assume that if blame had to be assigned for the onset of the cold war, the greater portion had to be levied against the Stalinist regime, which had seized control of Eastern Europe with strong-armed tactics supported by the presence of the Red Army; had engaged in intemperate denunciations of Western proposals for the postwar occupation of Germany, European recovery, and political cooperation in the United Nations; and, by lowering what Churchill called an "iron curtain" from the Baltic to the Adriatic, had manifested a degree of hostile isolationism unknown in the history of modern industrial states.

In contrast, the revisionists argued that the cold war between the Soviet Union and the United States could have been avoided if only the latter had pursued different policies. Revisionist critics included William Appleman Williams, D. F. Fleming, Gar Alperowitz, Barton J. Bernstein, Gabriel Kolko, David Horowitz, and Henry Magdoff. The revisionists were far from agreeing among themselves regarding the origin of the cold war. Fleming, a Wilsonian idealist at heart, along with Bernstein, faulted the personalities of Truman and his advisers for reversing Roosevelt's policy of trying to understand and get along with the Russians. Other revisionists, including Williams, Kolko, Horowitz, and Magdoff, were not at all content to explain the deteriorating relationship in terms of a change of presidents. They sought a more fundamental, structural cause dating back to the American imperialist surge at the turn of the century, hypothesizing that U.S. industrial capitalism could solve its internal contradictions only by globalizing its influence and eventually building, under the aegis of the so-called military-industrial complex, a huge arsenal of armaments and a worldwide network of military bases, alliances, and aid agreements to achieve its goals. Alperowitz and Kolko differed in their explanations of the U.S. decision to employ atomic weapons against Japan, the former stressing the diplomatic purpose of influencing Soviet behavior in Eastern Europe (which, if that really was the purpose, failed completely) and the latter emphasizing the military considerations discussed previously. Generally speaking, the revisionists blamed the United States, but not the Soviet Union, for employing all available levers of foreign policy in pursuit of its own national interests during the immediate postwar period.

Many of the revisionists rationalized Soviet behavior on the grounds that the Soviet Union had been deeply concerned about its security ever since the Allied intervention of 1918. As Cecil V. Crabb has noted, every nation is entitled to security, and one nation's fixation with security imperatives may arouse a sense of insecurity among other nations. The revisionists peremptorily condemned the discontinuance of wartime aid to the USSR after the war was over. They were much more muted when it came to criticizing Soviet policies of political repression in Poland, East Germany, Czechoslovakia, Hungary, Romania, and Bulgaria during the postwar decade. Revisionism, Crabb explained, was intellectually fashionable because it was novel and stimulating, as well as challenging to the older, official explanation favored by the power structure.

The authors of this text are inclined to trace the cold war to the fact that the two principal victorious powers had vastly different historical, cultural, political, and economic backgrounds, and occupied geopolitical space on opposite sides of the globe, so that their postwar relationship was bound to produce a dialectical clash once the common enemy had collapsed. Each side had a sense of universal mission, along with the energy, resources and *élan vital* to carry it out. Each was committed to the pursuit of objectives consistent with its own values and at least partially incompatible with those of the other. That is the recipe for irreducible and protracted conflict, which under the circumstances then prevailing could hardly have been averted if a president had not died, or if this rather than that aid policy had been applied at a particular "critical" juncture.

### The 1946 Crisis in Iran

Most historians of the cold war, whether orthodox or revisionist, have tended to focus on U.S.–Soviet wrangling over Germany and Eastern Europe, the deterioration of economic relations, and the role of the atomic bomb, while paying somewhat less attention to power struggles in the Near and Middle East. Prior to 1941, Americans had scarcely been aware of any "national interests" in that region of the world which has since achieved the status of a strategically pivotal area. By war's end, U.S. elites had no doubt that those interests were growing, even though their precise nature was still unclear.

The British, in contrast, had long felt particularly sensitive to developments in the Eastern Mediterranean and Southwestern Asia. In the nineteenth century, they assumed a special responsibility to support the Ottoman Empire against the probing pressure of Tsarist Russia, ever in search of warm-water ports. After initially opposing the construction of the Suez Canal as a French threat to the line of "imperial communications" to India, Britain later became the canal's principal protector. Emerging from World War II in a politically, militarily, and, above all, economically weakened position, the British realized that they would have to start educating their unseasoned American cousins on the importance of the straits, the Nile valley, the Persian Gulf, and the Horn of Africa. The task would not be easy, thought the British, because the Americans manifested a peculiar political naiveté, derived from a sentimental anticolonialism that had been deeply rooted in the national ethos ever since 1776.

Shortly after the Nazi invasion of Russia in 1941, the Soviet Union and Britain, almost duplicating an Anglo–Russian move in 1907, demarcated spheres of influence in Iran (Persia) and jointly moved military forces into that country in August 1941. Soviet troops took over a northern zone and British troops a southern zone, following the destruction of the Iranian navy and the abdication of the Shah. They did this to protect against a possible German effort to gain control of Iran's oil while mounting an attack against the Baku oil fields. When U.S. lend-lease aid began, American forces established a Persian Gulf Command, with military service (but not combat) missions and civilian technicians, to facilitate the transport of 5 million tons of wartime supplies to the Soviet Union. At the Teheran Conference, the Big Three pledged themselves to maintain the independence, sovereignty, and territorial integrity of Iran, as guaranteed by the

Tripartite (Soviet–British–Iranian) Treaty of January 1942. To minimize any appearance of occupation, the Allies had promised in that treaty to remove all foreign forces from Iranian territory within six months after the war with Germany and its associates came to an end.

Within their zone Soviet forces disseminated communist propaganda, stirred up Kurdish nationalist sentiments against the Iranians, and supported the communist Tudeh ("Masses") party in open warfare against the central Teheran government. When Teheran sent army reinforcements northward in November 1945, they were halted by Soviet troops. A month later, the Tudeh (now renamed the Democratic party) proclaimed the "autonomous republic" of Azerbaijan. Secretary Byrnes, in Moscow just before Christmas 1945, expressed to Stalin his disbelief that 1500 poorly equipped Iranian troops posed a serious threat to 30,000 well-trained and fully outfitted Soviet soldiers. The deadline set by the London Conference of Foreign Ministers for the complete evacuation of foreign forces from Iran was March 2, 1946. All American and British forces had departed prior to that date. The Soviet Union, after showing signs of leaving, apparently ordered its units to settle down in northern Iran.

On January 19, 1946, at the very first session of the United Nations Security Council, the Teheran government, with U.S. backing, formally charged the Soviet Union with interfering in Iran's internal affairs, thereby violating the UN Charter and other treaty obligations. The Soviet Union, which was then relatively isolated in the United Nations (which it regarded as a pliable instrument of U.S. foreign policy), piously denied all charges and took the offensive by accusing British troops in Greece and Dutch troops in Indonesia of posing threats to peace and security. The Security Council could do little except urge the Soviet Union and Iran to negotiate a solution.

By early March 1946, just when Winston Churchill was delivering his "iron curtain" address at Fulton, Missouri and warning that relying solely on the United Nations would be tantamount to appeasement, the situation looked quite ominous. Soviet military deployments in Iran were reported to be increasing. British and American newspapers were speculating on the possibility of war. There followed a confusing period of efforts to raise the issue of Iran in the Security Council again, ambiguous progress·of negotiations between Moscow and Iranian Premier Qavam to establish a proposed Soviet-controlled joint oil company (later aborted), and the ultimatum to Stalin from an exasperated Truman, who later claimed to have threatened that unless Soviet troops withdrew completely, U.S. forces would be sent back into Iran.

Iran and the Soviet Union exchanged notes of agreement on August 4, promising Soviet military withdrawal by May in return for the validation of a treaty authorizing the formation of a joint Soviet–Iranian oil company, subject to the approval of the Iranian Majlis (parliament). It was agreed that the Azerbaijan problem would be worked out legally and peacefully between the Iranian government and the people of Azerbaijan, with a spirit of benevolence toward the latter. The Soviet Union never did obtain its oil concession because the Majlis rejected the accord, but Moscow did not bother to protest. Its own behavior had served as a spark to Iranian nationalist feeling. This in turn led to growing criticism of Britain's oil operations in the southern part of the country, and helped pave the way for Prime Minister Mossadeq's nationalization of the Anglo–Iranian Oil Company in 1951. The 1946 Iranian crisis also aroused the suspicion of American policymakers concerning long-range Soviet aims in the vicinity of the Persian Gulf. The fact that the United States chose to handle the crisis, at least publicly, through the United Nations Security Council enhanced the prestige of that fledgling body, while simultaneously confirming the Soviet conviction that the new international organization was a tool of Anglo–American diplomacy.

## Containment and the Truman Doctrine

According to Churchill, Stalin had agreed that Britain could exercise "90 percent influence" in postwar Greece. Yet when the British landed in Greece and the Germans withdrew in late 1944, Greek Communists attempted to seize power in Athens and engaged the British in bitter warfare for several weeks. The British finally prevailed, but the end of the war found Greece physically battered and economically impoverished. In August 1946 the Communists, with external support from Yugoslavia, Bulgaria, and Albania, renewed their bid for power by launching guerrilla war in the north. The crisis for both Greece and Turkey was coming to a head at about the same time.

To understand the rationale underlying the Truman Doctrine, one must consider the interpretation of the Soviet threat that was slowly taking shape in the minds of American policymakers during the year following Churchill's "iron curtain" speech. Truman, recognizing that the country was in a demobilization mood, did not immediately give that speech his formal endorsement. Throughout 1946, however, leading officials in Washington began to think along lines articulated most clearly by George F. Kennan as what came to be called the "strategy of containment." In February 1946 Kennan, a career diplomat and expert on Soviet affairs who was soon to become the first director of the new Policy Planning Staff in the Department of State, sent an 8000-word telegram from Moscow to Washington containing his views on the nature, aims, and behavior of the Soviet system. Comparing Kennan's message to Sir Eyre Crowe's famous 1907 memorandum on Britain's relations with France and Germany, John Lewis Gaddis has noted that seldom in the history of diplomacy does one individual set forth, within a single document, ideas powerful enough to redirect a nation's foreign policy.*

Kennan's famous telegram was adapted to article form and published in *Foreign Affairs* in July 1947, and his analysis was elaborated in other writings and in lectures at the war colleges. He rejected the utopian Wilsonian assumption that governments should ignore power realities and pursue only international harmony, characterizing it as an inadequate foundation for the conduct of American diplomacy. Since armed conflict cannot be finally eliminated from international

---

*John Lewis Gaddis, *Strategies of Containment: A Critical Appraisal of Postwar American National Security Policy* (New York: Oxford University Press, 1982), p. 19.

affairs, thought Kennan, war is not always evil nor peace always good if legitimate national interests are jeopardized. National security, he held, depends not on a United Nations that deals in illusion but rather on a stable equilibrium among the various hostile interests and forces in the world.

Kennan, not surprisingly, deemed it naive of U.S. policymakers to assume that it would be easy to establish normal relations with the Soviet Union by winning either Stalin's trust through open-handedness or his respect through fair bargaining. Soviet foreign policy, in Kennan's view, depended on internal Soviet structural factors rather than on what the United States did or did not do. The Soviet leadership (i.e., Stalin) knew no other way to govern than by cruel, repressive dictatorship and therefore needed to project a hostile international environment in order to survive and justify its heavy-handed methods. The United States could do nothing, however magnanimous, to dispel Soviet suspicions, which were deeply rooted in an ideology that postulated an implacable enmity between socialism and capitalism and the inevitable overthrow of the latter by the former (which meant, in effect, the triumph of the Soviet Union over the West). Stalin and those around him were insecure fanatics and self-righteous doctrinaires who were incapable of compromising with rivals at home or abroad.

Because it postulated an innate antagonism between socialism and capitalism, said Kennan, the Soviet Union could not perceive a community of aims between itself and other powers, and when it signed documents that seemed to indicate the contrary, that was only a tactical maneuver in dealing with the enemy. Moscow's conduct of foreign policy was marked by secretiveness, lack of frankness, duplicity, deep suspicion, and basic unfriendliness of purpose. This would continue until the internal nature of Soviet power changed. Convinced that the Russians would be difficult to deal with for a long time, he warned against Americans who will always see signs that "the Russians have changed."

The policy of the United States, Kennan concluded, should be one of long-term, patient, but firm containment of Russian expansionist tendencies. Given the wartime destruction and the postwar exhaustion of Soviet society, its problems of backwardness in many sectors inhibiting needed economic development, and the internal stresses of a Communist party uncertain of its ability to maintain control through future leadership transitions, Kennan questioned the immutability of the Soviet power system. He suggested that by persevering in a policy of containment of the spread of communism, the United States could increase the strains within the Soviet system and compel it to face the alternatives of breaking up or mellowing.

It was in Western Europe that the need for containment was perceived as most urgent. The weather in Western Europe—meteorological, economic, and political—during the winter of 1946–1947 was worse than it had ever been during the war. Snow disrupted road and rail transport, and deep cold brought traffic on frozen rivers and canals to a halt. Britain was especially hard-hit by local food shortages, electric power cuts, the immovability of coal, factory closings, and rapidly rising unemployment. Not only in Britain, however, but on the Continent, too, the economic and political future of Europe was viewed with despondency, despite the conclusion of peace treaties with Italy, Romania, Bulgaria, Hungary, and Finland. Politically well-informed Western Europeans were uneasy when they eyed the colossus to the east and contemplated their own vulnerability to the kind of external pressure being applied against Greece and the internal pressure of Communist parties in Italy and France bent on exploiting chaos.

Despite Secretary of State Byrnes's emphasis on "patience and firmness," Henry Agard Wallace, former secretary of agriculture and vice-president under Roosevelt and now Truman's secretary of commerce, addressing a Democratic political rally in New York's Madison Square Garden in September 1946, parted company with the administration, expressing the fear that American anti-communism and the toughening U.S. stance toward the Soviet position in Eastern Europe would lead to a third world war. Byrnes and the State Department were furious over what appeared to be an announcement by the secretary of commerce of a fundamental change of direction in U.S. foreign policy toward a softening of attitude vis-à-vis the Soviet Union. After Byrnes threatened to resign, Truman fired Wallace, who eventually became a presidential candidate for the left-wing Progressive party in 1948.

Such was the background against which the British ambassador in Washington, Lord Inverchapel, delivered to the U.S. government on February 21, 1947, word that for economic reasons His Majesty's government would find it impossible to grant further financial assistance to Greece and Turkey after March 31, 1947. Although the Truman administration had known for months that the British faced increasing financial difficulties in meeting its commitments in the eastern Mediterranean, it was nevertheless surprised by the announcement of an impending deadline. Since no funds were readily available for Greece and Turkey, they would have to be voted by Congress, which knew nothing of the emergency and which was dominated by a Republican majority in a budget-slashing mood.

Meanwhile, Secretary of State Byrnes had been succeeded by General George C. Marshall in January 1947. Few Americans in the postwar era have been held in such high esteem as Marshall. On the same day the president submitted his nomination as secretary of state, the Senate gave its unanimous consent. Dean Acheson agreed to stay on as undersecretary for what would prove to be six fateful months.

On Greece and Turkey, Truman decided to call the majority and minority leaders of Congress to the White House and spell out the urgency of the problem to them. After briefings by Marshall and Acheson, the once-isolationist Senator Arthur Vandenberg of Michigan said that if the president would convey that same message to Congress, he and most of his colleagues would support him. The rest was largely a formality. The president appeared before a joint session of Congress on March 12, 1947, and requested $400 million in assistance for Greece and Turkey to curtail Soviet expansionism. There was a sense in the country that history was turning a corner. After two months of probing debate, the Greek-Turkish Aid Act passed the House by a vote of 287 to 107 and the Senate by 67 to 23. The Truman Doctrine marked official recognition of the fact that the cold war had begun, and that the United States would henceforth pursue a strategy of containment, beginning in Europe.

## Communist Coup in Czechoslovakia

Western liberal elites had always looked with favor and admiration on the constitutional democratic experiment in Czechoslovakia during the interwar period. Among all the new successor states created at the end of World War I, Czechoslovakia was the only one to preserve its democratic features until the outbreak of World War II. Many in the West experienced guilt when their leaders went to Munich to seek "peace in our time" at the expense of the young republic. The Soviet Union, which was not invited to Munich, vowed that it would defend Czech freedom even if no other power did, but it did nothing to resist the tide. There can be no doubt, however, that Moscow was friendlier toward the Czech government than toward others in Eastern Europe, which it regarded as reactionary.

During the war, Czech units fought with all the Big Three allies against the Germans, and took part with the Red Army in the liberation of Prague. U.S. forces entered Czech territory on April 13, 1945, and Churchill urged Truman to direct Eisenhower to take Prague and as much of Czechoslovakia as possible. Truman referred Churchill's suggestion to Eisenhower, who replied that he would not attempt any move that he deemed militarily unwise. Because he regarded the Czech republic as an historic friend and wartime ally, Stalin did not employ his usual heavy-handed tactics in that country, but withdrew the Red Army and allowed the democratic state to reorganize itself with Communists in the government.

For more than two years after the war, the governing coalition headed by President Eduard Benes and Foreign Minister Jan Masaryk, with Communist Klement Gottwald as prime minister and eight other Communists in the cabinet, sought to maintain a balanced policy of friendship with East and West. For a while, the country offered an example of how a freely elected government in Eastern Europe need not pose a threat to Soviet security. Early in 1947, Russian and local Communists had completely eliminated the leadership of non-Communist parties from the governments of Hungary, Romania, and Bulgaria. When Czechoslovakia, regarding itself as part of a wider Europe, showed interest in the Marshall Plan (discussed below), it incurred Moscow's displeasure. In February 1948 Communist-controlled police units in Prague, advised by Soviet Deputy Foreign Minister Valerian Zorin and backed by the threatening presence of the Red Army on the nation's borders, carried out a coup by terror, arresting all potential opponents and accusing them of conspiring with the United States to execute a reactionary, capitalistic counterrevolution. To spare his country a bloodbath, Benes, now in poor health, turned over the reins of power to Gottwald. Two weeks later, the fractured body of Jan Masaryk was found on the cement courtyard of the Foreign Office. The official explanation was suicide. Western democratic opinion was profoundly shocked. The Communist takeover probably did more than any other single event to pave the way for the Atlantic alliance a year later. The coup in Czechoslovakia provided the initial stimulus for the Vandenberg Resolution, which opened the way for U.S. participation in NATO.

## The Berlin Blockade

The diplomatic negotiations toward an Atlantic alliance were sustained by the Soviet threat to the West embodied in the Berlin blockade. In June 1945, when the Allied armies withdrew to their respective zones of occupation, Western access rights to Berlin were taken for granted. There were arguments over which routes could be used and how many trains per day could pass from the Western zones to Berlin, but there was no question as to the right of the Western occupying powers to send troops and supplies to their garrisons in Berlin. In the fall of 1945, the Four-Power Control Council agreed on train passage from the Western zones and on free and unhindered use of three air corridors by the Western occupiers but no clear, written agreement on road and rail access had ever been reached.

By the spring of 1948, tension over Germany between the West and the Soviet Union was at breaking point. As a result of mounting disputes over the dismantling of manufacturing and power plants by the Soviet Union for war reparations, permissible levels of industry, the inability or refusal of the Soviet authorities in the eastern zone to ship food westward, and occupation policies in general, the British and American zones, with the French sometimes following reluctantly, were moving toward closer cooperation among themselves. Each side blamed the other for causing the breakdown of the quadripartite administration of a unified Germany, when actually the cause was the existence of two incompatible models of what the government of Germany should be. In view of Molotov's vituperative attacks at the London Conference in late 1947, George Marshall, with the backing of Ernest Bevin and Georges Bidault, declared that any all-German government established to function under the existing circumstances of basic disagreements within the Control Council would be powerless, and he moved that the conference stand adjourned.

The failure to reach a diplomatic solution in London led quickly to Western initiatives toward the formation of a mutual defense alliance, the creation of a West German government, and the participation of West Germany in the Marshall Plan. Soviet sources began suggesting that the division of Germany would lead to a change in the status of Berlin. In April 1948 the Russians began to interfere randomly but increasingly with ground traffic to and from Berlin, prompting American and British authorities to rely more heavily on air passage. The Soviet member announced that the four-power *Kommandatura* in Berlin was being dissolved because, in violation of the Potsdam agreements, the Western zones were being combined economically and a new currency introduced. The Allied Control Council never met again.

General Lucius Clay, military governor in the U.S. occupation zone, fearing that the ultimate purpose of the tightening noose was to force the Western powers out of Berlin, urged Washington to approve an unmistakably firm response, backed by force if necessary. Clay was sure that if the United States demonstrated sufficient resolve, the Soviet Union would back away from a confrontation. Secretary Marshall and U.S. military chiefs, however, deemed it unwise to base national policy on such a bluff. They pointed out that the United States, lacking forces in Europe to match those of the Soviet Union, would face a humiliating retreat if the bluff should be called. Clay was authorized to reassert U.S. occupation rights but not to allow the guards on the trains to attempt to force their way through if stopped, which they were on April 1. Neither side was ready to initiate the use of force.

In June, Soviet officers "temporarily" halted all rail and road traffic from the West into Berlin for "technical reasons," which were soon transformed into a denial of the Western powers' rights in Berlin. Some of Truman's advisers wondered whether holding Berlin was worth the potential risk. Clay had warned that if Berlin fell, West Germany would be next and the entire U.S. position in Europe would be threatened. In his view, the future of democracy required the United States to stand fast. Truman never doubted it, and countenanced no discussion on that point, only on how to uphold U.S. rights. The Soviet Union was in a position physically to obstruct ground traffic, leaving to the United States the option of initiating force under disadvantageous conditions. Since the United States had clearer title to the use of air corridors, which would shift the onus of introducing force to the Soviet Union, the Truman administration chose the air route.

The U.S. Air Force was not at first enthusiastic about the idea of airlifting supplies not only to the military garrison but also to the 2 million people of West Berlin, fearing that such a massive logistical operation would drain off Air Force strength from other areas and expose a large number of aircraft to danger. Planes were called into service from all points. By October, nearly 5000 tons of supplies were being flown into Tempelhof airfield every day. In April 1949, on one day 1398 Allied planes, landing every 61.8 seconds, carried a record 12,941 tons. Over less than 11 months, 2.3 million tons of supplies were ferried into the city in the greatest single exercise in airborne logistics in history. So high did popular morale in West Berlin become that Stalin, seeing that the blockade had become counterproductive, quietly lifted it in May 1949.

## THE MARSHALL PLAN FOR EUROPEAN ECONOMIC RECOVERY

The spring of 1947 found the economies of Western Europe languishing in a state of near-paralysis and the bulk of the population chronically depressed. Signs of wartime devastation were still to be seen everywhere—in the destruction of physical plant, housing, and transport systems and in the eyes and bodies of people who had lived through seven years of wartime and postwar strain, fear, malnutrition, and tragedy. Each of these countries was experiencing grave shortages of one sort or another—food, coal, fertilizer, livestock and grain feed, raw materials, and machinery or parts essential for putting factories back into production. To make matters worse, the pool of the unemployed and hungry had been swollen by the return of demobilized troops to the civilian economies and even more so by the influx of millions of refugees from Eastern Europe.

Europe had massive needs for imports, but no way to pay for them. Foreign-exchange holdings had been liquidated during the war and could not be replaced without a revival of international trade, which was virtually nonexistent.

The United States had already poured about $9 billion worth of aid in a variety of forms, including a $3.75 billion loan to Britain in 1946, directly and bilaterally to the recipient countries. Although these efforts mitigated dire emergencies as they arose, they were of little avail when it came to spurring genuine rehabilitation, because they were not part of any coherent plan.

The principal architects of European economic recovery were George F. Kennan, Dean Acheson, Undersecretary of State for Economic Affairs William L. Clayton, career diplomat Charles ("Chip") Bohlen, and, of course, George C. Marshall, whose name Truman wanted attached to the famous plan which the soldier-statesman unveiled in a 1500-word message at the Harvard University commencement on June 5, 1947. Marshall, convinced that Europe was disintegrating and that the patient was "sinking while the doctors deliberate," demanded immediate U.S. action, had ordered Kennan to form a policy planning staff in the State Department and to give top priority to the European problem. Kennan was convinced that the political and psychological self-confidence of Western Europe must be strengthened with economic aid. It would be important, however, for the United States to treat the European region as a whole, instead of giving piecemeal aid to this country and that. Only by inducing the Europeans to work out an integrated approach among themselves and to present a comprehensive statement of their needs would it be possible for the United States to provide effective assistance.

In his Harvard address, Marshall said that the program was to be a joint U.S.-European one, but the responsibility for coordinated planning was to rest with the European recipients. Kennan had urged that the offer be open to the Soviet Union and its Eastern European satellites, for their participation would soften Soviet hostility to the West and help to keep open the economic ties between Eastern and Western Europe, whereas their refusal would place the blame for dividing Europe squarely on Moscow.

Many policymakers in Washington were opposed to the offer of aid to the Soviet Union. They thought that, after the arguments advanced to support the Truman Doctrine, Congress would never approve the expenditure of the taxpayers' money to strengthen the Soviet economy. Others thought that if the Soviet Union decided to participate, it would do so only for the purpose of sabotaging the program, perhaps by withdrawing at a critical juncture. The Truman administration did not expect the Soviet Union to participate in what it was bound to regard as a plot to strengthen American-based international capitalism, but it wished to avoid the appearance of deepening the division of the world and so the door was left open to the east.

Western Europe's response was enthusiastic. Ernest Bevin, foreign secretary in Britain's Labour government, who had been alerted in advance by Acheson, immediately got in touch with his French counterpart, Georges Bidault, to arrange an early meeting in Paris, to which Molotov was also invited. Molotov, too, seemed favorably disposed to Marshall's aid offer at first, although he insisted that the Soviet Union would want to submit its own separate list of needed goods instead of coordinating its planning with the Western economies. After receiving further instructions from Stalin, however, Molotov abruptly changed his attitude to one of intransigent opposition. *Pravda* accused the United States of trying to gain control of the European economies and interfering in the internal affairs of European states in order to forestall an impending capitalist depression. The Soviet government, no doubt fearful of Western influence in its Eastern European satellites, declined on behalf of Poland, Romania, and Yugoslavia and warned Czechoslovakia (half a year before the Communist takeover) not to participate. The Czechs withdrew most reluctantly, and the international thermometer kept dropping toward the cold war point.

Regardless of the Kremlin's reasons for opposing the Marshall Plan, its reaction turned out to be a serious blunder. Moscow's implacable hostility toward a generous and far-sighted policy on the part of the United States—even though it was also motivated by the enlightened self-interest of a producer in need of prosperous foreign markets—helped to unify the Western Europeans in coordinating their recovery plans.* The Organization for European Economic Cooperation (OEEC) was formed among 19 countries by April 1948, and at the same time the European Recovery Program (ERP) was launched with funding by the U.S. Congress. The original requests totaled $30 billion. Congress, which cannot legally appropriate funds beyond the budget year, spoke of morally committing itself to about $6 billion per year for four years. Europe's requests were later scaled down to $17 billion. By the time the four-year program ended in 1952, Congress had authorized only $12.5 billion in aid grants, but that amount proved sufficient to stimulate productivity and regional integration.

The year 1950 saw the creation of the European Payments Union (EPU)—a clearinghouse for intra-European payments (i.e., the multilateral cancellation of surpluses and deficits) that increased the efficiency of aid funds and the liquidity of the members. The dollar gap was closed; trade was liberalized; during the first decade of the OEEC, Western Europe achieved full currency convertibility, doubled its foreign exchange reserves, and achieved an average annual GNP growth rate of almost 5 percent per year. The Marshall Plan was the most successful foreign economic aid program in history because the Western Europeans had the political leadership, administrative skills, and technological know-how to make it work. Most important, it signaled the awareness of the governing elites in the United States and Western Europe that their countries would henceforth be economically interdependent. Thus it laid the foundation for the subsequent intertwining of their political-military security in the North Atlantic Alliance.

## PALESTINE AND MIDDLE EASTERN POLICY

From the earliest days of his presidency, Harry Truman had to grapple with the thorny issues of Palestine and the Zionist demand for the creation of an independent state of Israel. Zionism was a Jewish nationalist movement founded in

---

*The French and Italian Communist parties, at Moscow's urging, greeted the "Martial Plan" with vitriolic propaganda and worked to subvert the aid programs with strikes, violent demonstrations, and sabotage.

Europe at the end of the 19th century by Theodor Herzl in reaction against the anti-Semitic tendencies latent in European nationalisms. Prior to World War I, Zionists united around the proposition that Jews, long scattered throughout the world as a result of the Diaspora, or scattering, of biblical times, must create a political and territorial base of their own. During World War I, British Foreign Secretary Lord Balfour issued a declaration to the effect that His Majesty's government favored the establishment of a "national home" for the Jewish people in Palestine. This was done to win Zionist support for Britain's cause in the war against Germany. As soon as word of the Balfour Declaration reached the Arabs, whom the British were supporting in a revolt against the Ottoman Turks, the Arabs accused London of betraying them, and the conflict over Palestine began in earnest.

After the war, the League of Nations designated Britain as the mandatory power for Palestine. Throughout the two interwar decades, the London government increasingly found itself in the middle between Zionists and Arabs. The British gradually acceded to Zionist pressure for higher quotas of Jewish immigrants into Palestine, especially during the era of Hitler's persecution. Each time London permitted immigration, it solemnly assured the Arab inhabitants of Palestine that their rights would not be jeopardized. The Arabs, however, became more and more disenchanted with Britain, and even bitterly hostile, except when London, to win Arab support against Germany and Italy, made concessions to the Arabs, which would then draw anathemas from the Zionists. But it cannot be denied that the overall change in the internal balance of power during the British Mandate was in favor of the Zionists.

President Truman has often been accused of having played domestic electoral politics with the question of Palestine. In fairness to him, it should be pointed out that during the 1944 campaign both the Republican and the Democratic party platforms had called for unrestricted immigration into Palestine. Governor Thomas E. Dewey of New York and Senator Robert A. Taft of Ohio were just as ready as Truman to use the issue in order to win Jewish votes, but once the question was drawn into the vortex of electoral politics, the president was in a much better position than anyone else to do something about it. Truman was personally very sympathetic to the Jews and their anguish in the wake of the Holocaust, although at times he became irritated by Zionist pressure tactics. He did not hesitate to approve a proposal for 100,000 immigrants to Palestine and to forward it to Prime Minister Attlee in September 1945. From 1945 to 1948, principal State Department figures—Stettinius, Acheson, Lovett, Henderson, Kennan, and Marshall—warned Truman against making commitments to the Zionists that would jeopardize vital U.S. interests in the Middle East, especially the friendship of Arab governments and assured access to oil.

The British, upset by the president's position, were opposed to further large-scale Jewish immigration because they assumed—correctly—that it would exacerbate the mounting tensions in Palestine and would intensify Zionist demands for the creation of Israel. Already Haganah, the illegal Jewish army, and two terrorist groups—Irgun Zvai Leumi and the Stern Gang—were stepping up activity against both Arabs and British in Palestine. When Truman agreed to

London's proposal that the whole problem be studied by an Anglo–American committee of inquiry, the Zionists accused him of reneging on his commitment. In April 1946 that committee recommended immigration of 100,000 but rejected the idea of a separate Jewish state and called for retention of the British mandate. The British, shot at by both sides, quickly became frustrated and disillusioned over their role. A second Anglo–American team formulated a plan for a federated Palestine, consisting of autonomous Jewish and Arab provinces plus separate status for Jerusalem and the Negev, all under central British administration. This compromise further dismayed the Zionists, who were convinced that only in an independent state could Jews find security.

In October 1946, with congressional elections impending, Truman endorsed the Jewish Agency's proposal for a "viable state" in an adequate area of Palestine as a result of partition. The king of Saudi Arabia accused the United States of breaking its promises to the Arabs. The British, who kept pointing out that the Balfour Declaration favored "a national home for the Jews in Palestine," not a separate Zionist state, were furious and felt betrayed. Foreign Minister Ernest Bevin, speaking in the House of Commons, charged Truman with playing electoral politics with an issue that required delicate international diplomacy.

The British, exhausted by World War II, made clear their view that partition could be imposed only by force and their intention that British troops would not be used for this purpose. Truman, on the advice of the Joint Chiefs of Staff, had more than once expressed a comparable determination with regard to U.S. troops. Britain turned the question over to the UN General Assembly, which in the spring of 1947 appointed a Special Committee on Palestine (SCOP) to study the matter and report back by the fall. A majority of the 11-member committee recommended separate Jewish and Arab states and the assignment of the Negev to Israel. On November 29, 1947, the General Assembly voted in favor of partition by a vote of 33 to 13, with Britain, China, Yugoslavia, Ethiopia, and six Latin American states abstaining. The Arab states, other Islamic members (Afghanistan, Iran, Pakistan, and Turkey) and Greece, India, and Cuba voted against partition. The United States, the Soviet Union, France, and most European and Latin American members voted in favor of partition The Soviet Union had earlier favored a single binational state, but finally voted for separate states, probably to reduce the British imperial presence in the Middle East and in the expectation that partition would radicalize the Arab world.

The resolution was, of course, only advisory, not legally binding, since the General Assembly is not an international legislature. The Palestinian Arabs, asserting historic rights to the entire area of the Mandate, refused to accept the resolution and to establish a truncated state for themselves. Britain rejected all responsibility for enforcing the resolution and announced that it would turn Palestine over to the United Nations six months later, on May 14, 1948.

The pace of military conflict picked up immediately. On December 5 the United States embargoed the sale of arms to the Middle East. Kennan's Policy Planning Staff in the State Department prepared a memorandum lamenting that the United States was supporting the extreme objectives of political Zionism to the detriment of its own security interests. The memorandum predicted that

Moslem animosity would jeopardize existing oil and pipeline concessions, trade, and air-base rights, would open the Middle East to Soviet political and military penetration, and would arouse worldwide anti-Jewish and anti-Western sentiment for trying to meet Jewish needs and quiet the West's conscience at the expense of the Palestinian Arabs. It concluded that partition could not be implemented and recommended a shift to the creation of a UN trusteeship.

After appearing to approve the State Department's retrenchment from partition to trusteeship, Truman was prevailed upon to see the Zionist leader Chaim Weizmann, whom he admired, in a private meeting of which the bureaucracy was not notified. Truman assured Weizmann that the United States still backed partition. The very next day, Warren Austin, head of the U.S. delegation to the United Nations, with the backing of a State Department that was under the impression the President had approved the notion of a trusteeship, at least for the time being, made a formal address appealing for a trust status. Once again, the Zionists exploded. Truman, writing in his diary that he had never been made to feel so much like a liar and a double-crosser, noted that there were people in the State Department who were trying to cut his throat.

Israel proclaimed its independence effective the moment the British Mandate ended—at 6:00 P.M. on May 14, 1948. Truman, suspecting that the Soviet Union might try to preempt the United States by granting diplomatic recognition first, immediately announced U.S. recognition while the issue of trusteeship was still being debated, much to the consternation and indignation of many national delegations to the United Nations. One day later, Egypt, Syria, Jordan, Lebanon, and Iraq declared war on the new state, hoping to regain control of "enemy-occupied" Palestine. Although the Arabs had known for a long time what was coming, they had failed to make preparations, and when the crisis broke they were unable to unite on a strategy. Humiliated in defeat, they were forced to make separate truces on ignominious terms without formally recognizing either Israel or an end to the state of war. The result was the displacement of nearly a million Palestinian refugees to neighboring Egypt and Jordan, the stimulation of a virulent spirit of Arab nationalism which fed on anti-Western and anti-Zionist imperialism, the festering of revolutionary discontent against the corrupt Arab regimes widely blamed for the defeat, and the emergence of the Arab–Israeli conflict, the source of regional instability that persists to this day.

## UNITED STATES POSTWAR POLICY IN ASIA

Despite the increasingly intensive interest of the United States in Japan and China since the latter half of the nineteenth century, American elites—both political and military, with a few notable exceptions—were less familiar with the Asian than with the European scene. They were not well prepared to understand or to cope with China's problem of transition to a postwar world.

Chiang's government signed a Treaty of Friendship with the Soviet Union in August 1945 and accepted the Far Eastern provisions of the Yalta agreements in order to gain Stalin's formal recognition of China's sovereignty over Manchuria, to limit Soviet expansionism in the region, and to restrain Russian aid to

Mao's forces. On the surface, Chiang's position as national leader seemed assured. His was acknowledged as the legitimate government by all the victorious anti-Axis powers. His prestige was at least temporarily enhanced by the restoration of all Chinese territories seized by Japanese forces. Even Stalin apparently expected Chiang's rule to last. But Chiang was not able to prevent the Communists in the north from accepting the surrender of Japanese divisions, with their arms, despite the fact that the United States helped to transport a half million Nationalist troops to the interior and the north. Meanwhile, the Soviet Union allowed the Chinese Communists to acquire Japanese arms in Manchuria, which, along with the American arms seized from the Kuomintang, enabled Mao's forces to take over Manchuria. Moreover, eight years of international and civil war had caused widespread disruption of agriculture and trade, destruction of the nation's feeble production and transport systems, and rampant inflation. Mao, vastly superior to Chiang not only as a military strategist but also as a political propagandist, managed to pin on the Kuomintang the blame for virtually all the economic chaos that plagued China at the war's end.

President Truman was deeply chagrined in November 1945 to learn from a ticker-tape news story that Hurley had resigned as ambassador and had released to the press a letter to Truman justifying his action and accusing the State Department of subverting his efforts. Hurley, like many other Americans, adhered to a conspiracy theory of contemporary history. Unable to comprehend the profundity of wartime social upheavals and the power of revolutionary forces operating in China for a third of a century, he blamed events in that country on obtuseness if not treachery in the State Department. Truman prevailed upon General Marshall, a year before he was to become secretary of state, to assume the post vacated by Hurley. Marshall was more balanced and prudent, but no more successful than Hurley in solving an increasingly insoluble problem: reconciling the rival parties in a civil war. At one point Marshall appeared to have worked out an agreement for the establishment of a coalition and the unification of all military forces once the Nationalists had cut their divisions by half. When Marshall was called back to Washington for a consultation, desperate power-driven extremists on both sides shaped the course of events, and the chances for a genuine *modus vivendi*, which had never been good, dissolved altogether.

Marshall had been assigned a hopeless and a thankless task. Chiang could not fight the Communists and reform China from within all at the same time, assuming that he was interested in reform in the first place. From 1946 onward, his sole hope lay in U.S. military intervention, but by the time he was willing to assign a real directing role to an American general, in conjunction with significant U.S. military aid, it was too late. What was long lamented as the "loss" of China to communism could have been prevented only by dispatching sizable American forces, and at no time following the termination of the Pacific war was that ever politically feasible. Chiang was doomed when the United States inevitably assigned top priority in the immediate postwar period to the containment of Soviet communism in Europe rather than Chinese communism in Asia.

Ever since the first American imperialist surge into the Pacific at the end of the nineteenth century, Republicans had shown more interest in Asia than

Democrats had. There was, consequently, a significant "Asia First" constituency in the United States, especially along the West Coast, which thought that Democrats bred in Eastern cities and universities were disposed to ignore U.S. interests in Asia in their preoccupation with Europe. Moreover, a strong pro-Nationalist China lobby was active in Washington, headed by Chiang's ambassador, V.K. Wellington Koo, and buttressed by occasional visits from Chiang's charming wife. Truman and Marshall eventually became disenchanted with Chiang, concluding that U.S. aid to the Nationalists was becoming futile, serving more to enrich the bank accounts of Chiang's associates than to defeat the superior strategy of Mao. Once that disillusionment set in, the China lobby, Senator Joseph McCarthy of Wisconsin, and other vehement critics of Truman, Marshall, and the State Department began to exploit a rising tide of anti-communism throughout the country. The closing months of 1948 witnessed the massive offensive of Mao's forces that would bring final victory to the Chinese Communists in the following year. By the beginning of 1949, all of Manchuria was under the control of the Communists, who then proceeded to extend their sway throughout northern China. Everywhere the discredited Nationalists were in retreat. In September Mao Zedong announced the establishment of the People's Republic of China, with its capital at Peking. Nanking, Canton, and the Nationalist capital at Chungking were taken in October. Two months later, Chiang Kai-shek, the Kuomintang cabinet, and the remnants of the Nationalist armed forces—about half a million men and their families—withdrew to the island of Formosa (the Portuguese name for Taiwan), a hundred miles from the mainland. Chiang was never to leave the island from which, for the next quarter of a century, the Nationalists asserted their futile claim to be the only legitimate government of the Chinese people. "Who lost China?" became a rallying cry of Truman administration foes.

The problem, as many policymakers in the Roosevelt-Truman administration defined it, was to come to terms with the new forces in Asian nationalism, which combined with Japan's subsequent militarism, aggression, and occupation to tumble most of the European colonial empires in the East—British, French, and Dutch—during the war or soon afterward. Roosevelt, naively believing that the United States and the Soviet Union shared an anticolonial tradition, was not at all enthusiastic about helping Britain to restore its prewar colonial rule. The American military chiefs did not want the British to play a significant role in the closing stages of the Pacific war. Roosevelt seemed more anxious to persuade the Soviet Union to enter the war against Japan than to give the British, French, and Dutch any major parts to play in the liberation of Southeast Asia. He was willing to see the Netherlands East Indies revert to temporary Dutch administration because Queen Wilhelmina had promised eventual self-government, but he still wanted those islands to be liberated mainly by U.S. forces in order to make sure that her pledge was honored. The British were allowed to liberate Sumatra because of its proximity to Singapore, then capital of Malaya. In August 1945, just before the end of the war, the Japanese occupying authority proclaimed the independent Republic of Indonesia. The Indonesians quickly took a liking to independence (*merdeka*), and when the Dutch returned a few months later, they ran into stiff national resistance under the leadership of President Achmed Sukarno. The Dutch attempted to suppress the nationalist movement and to establish a sort of commonwealth relationship, but the effort was unsuccessful and led to civil war. A UN team arranged a truce aboard the U.S.S. *Renville* in early 1948, and thus it can be said that the United States, with a benevolent eye, facilitated the formal transfer of sovereignty to Indonesia that took place in November 1949.

The United States tried to cleanse its own anticolonial conscience of its "sinful imperialist venture" in the Philippines at the turn of the century by carrying out the promise embodied in the Tydings-McDuffie Act of 1934. In spite of more than four years of war, occupation, and postwar economic dislocation, the Philippines were granted independence on July 4, 1946—right on schedule. Because of the war, however, the Filipinos had not been adequately prepared for democratic self-rule. During the early years of indepedence, much of the $1.5 billion in economic aid given by the United States was diverted to wasteful or corrupt uses, while many downtrodden Filipinos were attracted to the band of communist insurgents known as the Hukbalahaps.

Despite its own disappointing experience in regard to the Philippines, the United States looked with favor on the achievement of independence by India and Pakistan in 1947 and by Burma in 1948.* The British, not at all happy over the anticolonial attitudes and policies of the Americans (who themselves had been the first to leave the British Empire), suspected Washington of working to reduce and, if possible, replace the presence and influence of Britain in Southeast Asia, the Indian Ocean–Persian Gulf area, and the Nile valley.

The United States scored its most remarkable postwar success in Japan. The sudden surrender of that country, coupled with U.S. insistence that any Russian forces entering the home islands must be placed under the control of the Supreme Commander, Allied Powers (SCAP)—that is, General Douglas MacArthur—precluded effective Soviet participation in the occupation.** Japan escaped the fate of becoming a divided country like Germany, and this made the task of postwar democratic reform much easier. The United States took over Japan's former mandated islands in the Pacific, as well as the Bonins and the Ryukyus, including Okinawa. The United States also assumed jurisdiction over Japan's former Pacific mandates—the Marshall, Caroline, and Marianas islands, which were confirmed in 1947 as U.S. trusteeships by the United Nations.

MacArthur ruled the defeated nation as a virtually absolute yet benevolent and surprisingly popular dictator. Under his aegis a new constitution replaced that of the Meiji Restoration of 1868. The emperor was retained as a symbol but was deprived of political authority in favor of a British-style parliament-cabinet system. The military establishment was dissolved; in Article 9 of the new constitution the use of war as a means of settling international disputes was

---

*India and Pakistan became republics within the British Commonwealth; Burma became a republic outside it.

**The Soviet Union declared war on Japan on August 9, 1945, only five days before the emperor announced the surrender. Soviet forces occupied the southern half of Sakhalin, along with Habomai, Shikotan, and other northern islands.

renounced forever; the big business combines *(zaibatsu)* were partially broken up; land reform brought limits to the size of farm holdings; political parties were allowed to organize; the press was given freedom; women received the franchise for the first time; labor unions were encouraged and granted the right to strike.

Within four years, the man William Manchester called the "American Caesar"* had presided over the conversion of Japan from an aggressive totalitarian regime into a peaceful democratic state that would soon astound the world with its economic miracle. The Soviet Union complained frequently about American unilateralism in the postwar shaping of Asia's principal industrial power, but it was in no position to do much about it. The transformation of Japan proceeded at such a rapid pace that the State Department's Office of Northeast Asian Affairs questioned how long a people as proud as the Japanese would tolerate foreign occupation, however benign. A Japanese settlement was under consideration and negotiations began even before the writing of a peace treaty was given new urgency by the outbreak of the Korean War (discussed below). The Pentagon argued that negotiating a peace treaty was premature, and its arguments to this affect became more insistent after the North Korean aggression. U.S. diplomatic officials, however, were apprehensive that if the growing Japanese desire for independence was frustrated too long, resentment would mount against the occupying power and the gains made for democracy in Japan after 1945 would be dissipated.

Work on a Japanese peace treaty got under way in May 1950, with principal responsibility entrusted, in the interest of bipartisanship, to John Foster Dulles, who would have been Thomas E. Dewey's secretary of state had the 1948 election turned out differently. Dulles, an accomplished negotiator, presented a completed treaty to a conference convened in San Francisco in September 1951. The Soviet Union and its Eastern-bloc satellites attended the conference, but Acheson's rules of procedure thwarted their efforts to subvert the final draft of the treaty, which was based principally on Anglo–American cooperation.

## THE NORTH ATLANTIC TREATY

However important the Marshall Plan may have been for resuscitation of the Western European economies, it provided no guarantee of security against the possibility of military attack by the colossus to the east. Western Europe was growing stronger in the economic dimension but weaker in the military. Although the United States enjoyed a monopoly of nuclear weapons, the Europeans, next door to the world's greatest land power, felt a growing sense of insecurity when they thought of the imbalance in conventional forces. By mid-1947, the United States had demobilized from 12 million to 1.5 million under arms. Many feared that Stalin would expand his imperial sway into any power vacuum he could safely fill.

Probably the Soviet Union, exhausted by a war that had brought it 20 million casualties and widespread destruction, was not at all prepared to attack

*William Manchester, *American Caesar: Douglas MacArthur, 1880–1964* (Boston: Little, Brown, 1978).

westward. In politics, however, perceptions are often more important than realities when it comes to assessing threats. The Soviet Union was on the political, psychological, and military offensive in the last two years of the war and the years immediately following. It can scarcely be doubted that the American atomic monopoly failed to inhibit Stalin's readiness to press as far as possible in Poland, Iran, Greece, Turkey, divided Berlin, and throughout Eastern Europe. Stalin himself ridiculed the significance of atomic weapons in international politics, while exalting the classical principles of strategy, of which he was a master. In view of the fact that the Communist party leaders in France and Italy, Maurice Thorez and Palmiro Togliatti, were declaring to their countries' respective parliaments that when the Soviet Red Army arrived at the national borders the people would greet it as an army of liberation, the nervousness of the Western Europeans was hardly surprising.

The Prague coup of February 1948 not only speeded up congressional authorization for Marshall Plan credits but also spurred Britain, France, and the Low Countries to sign the Brussels Treaty in March 1948, creating a regional collective defense organization. On that same day Truman asked the Congress to restore the military draft. The initial impetus for this group, which would later be expanded into the Western European Union (WEU), came from Ernest Bevin, Georges Bidault, Paul Henri Spaak of Belgium, and N.F. van Kleffens of the Netherlands. For more than two years after the war, most European governments had been reluctant to abandon hope in the idea of universal collective security embodied in the United Nations and to form a regional collective defense organization such as was permitted by Article 51 of the UN Charter. (This was exemplified in the Organization of American States, or OAS, established by the United States and 21 Latin American republics under the 1947 Rio Pact.) On June 11, 1948, the Senate by a vote of 64 to 6 passed a resolution calling for "association of the United States, by constitutional process, with such regional and other collective arrangements as are based on continuous and effective self-help and mutual aid, and as effect its national security." This resolution, named for Senator Vandenberg, marked a revolution in U.S. foreign policy. It acknowledged that henceforth the security of the United States would be entwined with that of Europe and paved the way for the formation of the North Atlantic Alliance in the spring of 1949.

The architects of the North Atlantic coalition were thinking at first in political rather than military terms. They certainly did not regard a Soviet invasion as imminent, but they anticipated that the prolongation of the military imbalance would create such serious psychological and political problems as to jeopardize the stability and economic well-being of Western Europe's democracies. Europe was badly in need of an injection of self-confidence. A purely Western European defensive alliance would not suffice, for at that time West Germany could not be included because of political opposition among the members of the WEU—France, the Low Countries, and Britain. What was required was nothing less than a formal American guarantee of European security.

Initially, the alliance was to be formed by the joining of the United States and Canada with the Western European Union states. Almost immediately Norway, worried about the close ties between the Soviet Union and Finland, wanted to be included in an Atlantic alliance. So did Italy, which, under Alcide de Gasperi, saw itself as part of the continental economy rather than as a Mediterranean country. President Truman was not at first ready to accept Italy's membership because this would extend the treaty's scope to the Mediterranean and because Italy's earlier alliance record was poor. France, however, insisted on Italy's inclusion. It was thought that Denmark should be brought in because of the significant position of Greenland in the North Atlantic, and so should Iceland for a similar reason. Dean Acheson favored membership for Portugal, despite the fact that it was a nondemocratic corporate state under the authoritarian rule of Antonio de Oliveira Salazar, largely because of the strategic importance of its mid-Atlantic Azores, where the United States later built an airbase at Lajes.* That made 12 Atlantic allies.

In Article 2 of the ensuing North Atlantic Treaty, the signatories promised to contribute toward peaceful and friendly international relations by strengthening their free institutions, promoting conditions of stability and well-being, and eliminating economic conflict. This meant that the North Atlantic Alliance would go beyond the old-fashioned purely military alliance and would assume positive goals of political and economic cooperation. Article 3 specified that the parties, "separately and jointly, by means of continuous and effective self-help and mutual aid, will maintain and develop their individual and collective capacity to resist armed attack."** Article 5 contained the critical clause that might one day activate the treaty:

> The Parties agree that an armed attack against one or more of them in Europe or North America shall be considered an attack against them all and consequently they agree that, if such an armed attack occurs, each of them, in exercise of the right of individual or collective self-defense recognized by Article 51 of the Charter of the United Nations, will assist the Party or Parties so attacked by taking forthwith, individually and in concert with the other Parties, such action as it deems necessary, including the use of armed force, to restore and maintain the security of the North Atlantic area.

## NATO and the Constitutional Question

During ratification hearings, several senators expressed concern that Article 5 might commit the United States automatically to war and that the Senate's constitutional function would be bypassed. This was essentially the same fear for its prerogative that the Senate had manifested over the collective security provisions of the League of Nations Covenant. Acheson trod a razor's edge, stressing that in a future crisis the allies could expect the United States to do what

---

*Britain was favorably disposed because Portugal was its oldest extant treaty partner, a relationship dating back to 1386.

**The North Atlantic Treaty Organization (NATO) was the integrated military command structure established to carry out coordinated defense plans under the treaty.

it deemed necessary to fulfill its obligations, but it would take action in accordance with its own constitutional processes. A Gallup opinion poll in May 1949 showed 67 percent of the American people in favor of the treaty and only 12 percent opposed. The Senate consented to ratification on July 21, 1949, by a vote of 82–13. Within a week after signing the instrument of ratification, Truman submitted a military assistance bill to Congress requesting $1.16 billion in military aid for Europe. On August 24, 1949, the North Atlantic Treaty brought into effect America's first peacetime alliance commitments since 1800, when the old alliance with France was dissolved.

Having intervened twice in European wars *after* they had begun, the United States now sought to deter another war by making its intentions known before aggression occurred. How was deterrence to be achieved? Would it be necessary for the United States to send a substantial contingent of troops for permanent deployment in Europe? When Senator Bourke Hickenlooper of Iowa put that question, Acheson's answer (which, he later admitted, was stupid) was a "clear and absolute 'no.' " The general assumption was that deterrence could rest on U.S. strategic bombers carrying atomic bombs. At that time the United States possessed a monopoly of those weapons, but that came to an end in late 1949, when the Soviet Union carried out its first successful test of a similar bomb. Nevertheless, the long lead enjoyed by the United States obviated worries about the ability of the United States to deter a total, nuclear third world war. The outbreak of the Korean War in June 1950, however, made Europeans acutely aware of the possibility of limited conventional war.

By early 1951, the administration considered it necessary to send troops to Europe, and this brought another round in the constitutional debate. Congress was naturally sensitive to a transatlantic deployment of six or so divisions whose presence might mean that the United States would someday be confronted with a situation in which the legislative branch would have no choice but to declare war. President Truman, for his part, was anxious to preserve the prerogatives of the president as commander-in-chief of the armed forces. When asked at a press conference whether congressional approval was needed to send American troops to Europe in addition to the two divisions already there, his answer was an unequivocal "no," at which point Senator Taft accused him of usurping the Senate's war power. Truman reasserted the authority of the president to send troops abroad in fulfillment of U.S. treaty obligations, making it clear that he would consult Congress but not ask its permission to do so, for that would negate the administration's duty to execute a plan for European defense as already required by the North Atlantic Treaty, previously approved by the Senate and now part of the law of the land. Truman won the argument, largely because even the Senate's strict constructionists did not wish to obstruct his administration's efforts to shore up the defenses of Western Europe.

### The Issue of West German Rearmament

When General Eisenhower was named the first Supreme Allied Commander, Europe (SACEUR), in December 1950, he found that Soviet ready divisions outnumbered those of the Western allies by almost 10 to 1. The Europeans were not interested in a strategy of fallback in the face of a massive onslaught, followed by a process of liberation, after the pattern of World War II. The French, the Dutch, and the Belgians in particular insisted on a "Forward Strategy" of defense as far to the east as possible—that is, at the Elbe River. The logical corollary of this proposition was that West Germany would have to be rearmed; certainly the countries formerly occupied by the Germans would not defend them against attack if the Germans did not fight for their own territory. The corollary was a discomfiting one, because many of Germany's neighbors, when they thought of defending themselves in the future, had Germany as well as the Soviet Union in mind. The North Atlantic Council, meeting in New York in September 1950, took up the question of a political and military role in the alliance for the newly established Federal Republic of Germany, but more than four years elapsed before the occupation regime ended and a quasi-sovereign West Germany under Konrad Adenauer's chancellorship was finally admitted to NATO. The French proposal for a European Defense Community as a check on West German rearmament is part of the European integration movement's history.

## INTEGRATION OF WESTERN EUROPE

In 1948 Churchill had called for the creation of a "United States of Europe." The Council of Europe and the various organizations set up to pursue Marshall Plan objectives provided 15 governments with considerable practice in taking a larger regional view of their economic, social, and other functional problems. In May 1950 French Foreign Minister Robert Schuman, sensing that West Germany would eventually become part of the Atlantic defense structure and wishing to bring Germany's war-making industrial capacity under international supervision, put forth a bold plan (conceived by Jean Monnet, a dedicated supranationalist) for a European Coal and Steel Community (ECSC). The plan envisioned a common market and high authority for that basic productive sector, built on Franco–German cooperation and open to participation by other European governments. Italy and the Benelux states (Belgium, the Netherlands, and Luxembourg) joined, while Britain—for a variety of political and economic reasons, including wariness of international decision-making organizations and concern for its own competitive position and social welfare programs—remained outside.* Truman and Acheson welcomed the Schuman overture as "an act of constructive statesmanship ... in the great French tradition" and lent their support to the economic integration of Western Europe, with "the Six" as the core of the arrangement.

The favorable reception accorded to the Schuman Plan led France to try to resolve the problem of German rearmament by extending the concept of supranational integration to the military level. The government of René Pleven drafted a proposal for a European Defense Community (EDC) and presented it to the National Assembly in October 1950. Under the plan, the armies of the Six

---

*British Foreign Secretary Ernest Bevin charged that Schuman and Acheson had "cooked up" the plan and kept him in the dark until after it had been publicly announced. Acheson conceded later that the affair had been badly handled, and that the failure to consult London in advance probably exacerbated its negative reaction.

on the Continent (but not France's overseas forces) were to be merged into one common army. For operational efficiency, national-language units would be retained up to the divisional level, while corps and higher commands, as well as supply and other auxiliary services, would be internationally integrated. Thus there would be German soldiers, but no German army and no German general staff. In the end there would be no EDC either, despite strong support for the plan from the United States, for the French who conceived this radically imaginative scheme in 1950 scuttled it in 1954, thereby necessitating other arrangements for West Germany's admission to NATO. (These arrangements will be treated in Chapter 4.)

The North Atlantic Council, meeting at Lisbon in February 1952 (just seven weeks before Eisenhower resigned as SACEUR to run for the presidency), approved extremely ambitious goals for arming the Alliance. By 1954, there were to be 40 combat-ready divisions (exclusive of those needed for Greece and Turkey), 56 reserve divisions, and 1,000 aircraft. Seasoned officials throughout Western capitals were skeptical. Churchill was already telling Parliament that greater reliance would have to be placed on nuclear weapons so that defense expenditures could be cut.* Before the end of 1952, Paris informed NATO that it would not be able to increase its military contribution to Alliance forces on NATO's Central Front because of France's costly military involvement in guerrilla warfare in Indochina. The U.S. Congress was unwilling to grant additional military aid before the Europeans strengthened their own conventional defense efforts. Adenauer knew that his government lacked sovereign independence, yet always insisted that the Federal Republic of Germany must be treated as an equal partner as it became more fully integrated into Western Europe.

The Soviet Union, which had sought to block the establishment of a separate West German government in 1949, made a final, all-out effort in early 1952 to head off the Federal Republic's economic and military incorporation into the West. On March 10 Soviet Foreign Minister Andrei Vishinsky sent a note to the Three Western occupying powers calling for a unified Germany, the withdrawal of all foreign troops and bases from German soil within a year, the banning of organizations "inimical to democracy," equal civil and political rights for all German citizens (including former military officers and Nazis), and a prohibition against Germany joining a military alliance against any power whose armed forces had fought Germany in the war. The boundaries agreed on at Potsdam would be made permanent, and Germany's armed forces would be strictly limited.

All three Western foreign ministers—Dean Acheson, Anthony Eden, and Robert Schuman—regarded the Soviet initiative as a "golden apple of discord," tossed westward to disunite the allies and to negate the progress that they had painstakingly made in the past 16 months toward building a defense structure. At

---

*In October 1952, Britain became the third power to achieve atomic-weapons capability by conducting an explosion in the Monte Bello Islands off Australia. The Soviet Union had successfully tested in 1949.

the same time, they recognized that Vishinsky's proposal was superficially attractive to many: to Germans who desired reunification; to the French, Dutch, Belgians, Danes, Norwegians, and others who feared West German rearmament; and to all who wished to put an end to the cold war by placating the Soviet Union. Acheson coordinated the Western replies, with the cordial concurrence of Adenauer, who was deeply committed to an Atlantic-oriented policy for the Federal Republic. The allies replied to Moscow that the formation of an all-German government must precede the convening of a conference to draft and sign a peace treaty, and that free all-German elections, as well as the free conditions necessary for such elections, would be prerequisites to the setting up of a single government. They reminded Moscow that a UN commission had been appointed to check on the conditions for free elections, and that West Germany and West Berlin had made arrangements to facilitate such an investigation. Would East Germany and East Berlin do the same? That question was enough to prevent the Vishinsky proposal from going any further. It became increasingly clear from 1952 onward that the Adenauer government would shun the appeals of the rival Socialist party for reunification through neutrality and demilitarization and would base the security and prosperity of the Federal Republic on closer ties with the Atlantic–Western European nations.

## U.S. Policy Toward Spain

Truman and Acheson were roundly criticized by conservatives in Congress and elsewhere for their policy toward Spain. At the San Francisco Conference, the Big Three had voted to bar from United Nations membership any regime installed with the help of Axis military forces. In December 1946 the UN General Assembly urged members to recall their ambassadors from Madrid. The U.S. post had been vacant since December 1945, and the mission was headed by a *chargé d'affaires*. Truman and Acheson would have nothing to do with Spain while Franco remained in power. A majority in Congress, however, led by conservative Senator Pat McCarran of Nevada, wanted to extend economic aid to Spain at a time when every other country in Western Europe was benefiting from the Marshall Plan. The Defense Department—the Navy at first and later the Air Force—looked forward to having military bases in a country of considerable strategic value at the western end of the Mediterranean. Acheson was concerned lest a U.S.–Spanish military agreement, even outside NATO, would offend Britain, France, and other allies and would arouse suspicions of a U.S. intention to defend Europe from behind the Pyrenees. Although Truman vetoed Spain's inclusion in the Marshall Plan, Congress voted a separate $100 million loan authorization in 1950. The president irritated the friends of Spain by refusing to consider the loan mandatory and withholding the funds until U.S. interests dictated their disbursement. After the UN ban on ambassadors was lifted, Truman was still emotionally opposed to appointing one, not only because of the issue of fascism but also because he was convinced that Catholic Spain was violating the religious liberty of Protestants. Acheson at State and Marshall at Defense gradually came around to accept the position of the "Spanish lobby"—Acheson because he deemed the use of an ambassadorial ban to achieve internal political changes unwise and doomed to failure, Marshall for military reasons. Truman was reluctantly worn down, an ambassador was named, and the way was paved for an economic-military agreement to be signed in 1953 by the Eisenhower administration.

## THE KOREAN WAR

None of the leading figures in the Truman administration doubted by the end of the 1940s that the cold war was moving into high gear. There was a growing desire in Washington to spell out the containment doctrine more clearly in operational terms. After Kennan resigned as director of the policy planning staff at the end of 1949, the task of drafting a more precise policy statement was assumed by a small group of State and Defense officials headed by Paul H. Nitze. The resulting document in early 1950 was National Security Council Paper No. 68, known as NSC-68, which was somewhat more alarmist than Kennan had been in defining the Soviet threat, and more urgent in its prescriptions. Kennan would have agreed that Soviet goals in the Stalinist period were "wholly irreconcilable" with those of democratic societies, but whereas Kennan wished to prevent the USSR from gaining control of industrial power centers, he did not insist upon defending every point around the Soviet perimeter. The authors of NSC-68, concerned about the adverse political and psychological consequences of any successful communist aggression, believed that in a bipolar world any Soviet expansion would mark a defeat for free institutions everywhere. They therefore called for higher taxes and cuts in nondefense expenditures to finance a major U.S. military buildup commensurate with the responsibility of the nation as leader of a seriously threatened free world. Given the prevailing budgetary mood of the public and Congress, such recommendations would have run into very heavy opposition had it not been for the outbreak of the Korean War.

Korea was to be Truman's tragedy. No one could have suspected such a thing at the end of World War II. Throughout its history, Korea had often been treated as a pawn by stronger Asian powers, as either a coveted prize or a buffer for China, Russia, and Japan. Japan, ascendant after its victories over China and Russia at the turn of the century, annexed Korea in 1910. In the Cairo Declaration, the United States, Britain, and China agreed that in due course Korea should become independent. At Yalta, an informal agreement was made that the Big Four (including the Soviet Union) would administer an interim trusteeship. When Stalin asked whether foreign troops would be stationed in Korea, Roosevelt said no and the Soviet dictator concurred. Upon the sudden collapse of Japan, the United State and the Soviet Union landed troops in Korea in early September 1945 to accept the surrender of Japanese forces south and north of the 38th parallel, which had been chosen arbitrarily by MacArthur as a temporary dividing line.

Because the surrender of Japan came unexpectedly early, MacArthur was not prepared to occupy Korea with properly trained forces, much less military leaders sensitive to the politics and culture of the area. For a while, Koreans in both sections of the country, hungry for the fruits of liberation, came to feel that they had merely traded one form of occupation for two new ones hardly less arrogant. Confronted with economic and political turmoil, the U.S. military was inclined to restore civil order by depending on some of the rightist elites who had collaborated with the Japanese conquerors. Syngman Rhee, a Korean patriot who had exiled himself to the United States in 1910 and obtained advanced degrees at Harvard and Princeton, returned to his homeland as the leader of a conservative national independence movement.

It soon became clear that neither power would allow Korea to be united under the auspices of the other. Nevertheless, Washington, not at all eager to assume the full burden of responsibility in South Korea while becoming increasingly preoccupied with the Soviet threat to Western Europe, began to look for a graceful way of phasing out the U.S. presence in Korea. All the same, the Truman administration did not want to see the entire Korean peninsula pass to Communist control, for it was thought that this would have a devastating impact on relations with Japan. The administration, therefore, turned to the United Nations for a solution. The General Assembly, with Moscow dissenting, called for a nationwide Korean assembly to be elected in 1948, after which a national government would be formed, followed by the withdrawal of Soviet and U.S. troops. A UN commission, barred from entering North Korea, conducted elections in the southern part of the country on May 10, 1948. Syngman Rhee was elected president of the Republic of Korea, the capital of which was Seoul. A few weeks later, a new Communist government was proclaimed for North Korea, its capital at Pyongyang and its chief Kim Il-sung.

The United States was determined to withdraw its occupation forces from Korea before the end of 1948, while continuing to furnish economic aid to Rhee's government. In December 1948, at U.S. urging, the UN General Assembly declared the Republic of Korea (that is, of South Korea) to be the legitimate government of the whole country. The Rhee government, which had already shown tendencies toward authoritarianism, interpreted this declaration to mean that it was entitled to extend its control over the North by force. The United States wanted Rhee's army strong enough to defend South Korea, but not to attack across the 38th parallel. General MacArthur, commander-in-chief for the Far East, advised Washington that the Republic of Korea's prospects of defending itself against a full-scale invasion by a more heavily armed North Korea was poor.

Prior to the scheduled withdrawal of U.S. troops at the end of June 1949, a National Security Council study addressed the contingency of a North Korean invasion. Rejecting the option of a unilateral U.S. military intervention, the NSC staff recommended an appeal to the UN Security Council, with the possibility that the United States might take part in a UN-sanctioned international police action if an invasion did take place. The NSC recognized that an all-Communist Korea would enhance the USSR's political and strategic position vis-à-vis China and Japan and would adversely affect U.S. interests throughout the Far East. On January 12, 1950, Acheson delivered a speech on U.S. China policy to the National Press Club in Washington. The speech, an apologia against the "loss of China" charge, was designed to demonstrate how a militarily superior Chiang had been overthrown by the politically more powerful forces of revolutionary nationalism, which Mao knew how to exploit. The secretary of state, reiterating a statement made by MacArthur during an interview in Tokyo less than a year before, defined the defense perimeter of the United States as stretching from the Aleutians to Japan to the Ryukyus to the Philippines. Korea was not "specifically excluded" from that defense perimeter, as it would subsequently often be put, but it certainly was not included in the area that the United States would defend unilaterally as essential to its own security. Acheson said that if an attack on the Republic of Korea should occur, reliance would have to be placed on local resistance and on the commitments of the civilized world under the Charter of the United Nations to help defeat aggression.

For that speech, Truman and Acheson would later be pilloried, not only by extremist partisans of Senator McCarthy but even by more responsible Republicans, including presidential candidate Dwight D. Eisenhower, for having virtually "invited" Communist aggression against the Republic of Korea. Seldom did any commentator make the point during those years of recrimination that the United States was totally unprepared, in view of its overall military posture, from 1946 onward to offer a credible deterrent guarantee to South Korea. Neither the incumbent Democrats nor the opposition Republicans had championed greater defense preparedness during that period.

The feared attack came on June 25, 1950. Truman, who had paid a weekend visit to his Missouri home, flew back to Washington while the UN Security Council was meeting. The Soviet representative, Jacob Malik, had walked out of the Security Council in January 1950 to protest the refusal to seat Communist China in place of the Nationalist government. Everyone wondered whether he would end the boycott that day and veto any U.S.-inspired action, but he did not appear. Since the prevalent assumption was that North Korea would not have dared to launch the attack without Stalin's authorization, some speculated that the USSR might have approved the attack to spoil the Japanese peace-treaty negotiations that were then getting under way. The possibility cannot be discounted that Stalin did not expect an early reaction from Washington and that Moscow could not react quickly enough to instruct Malik to return to the UN.

Truman and his principal advisers quickly agreed that the United States had to make a timely and decisive response or else watch the United Nations, not to mention its own prestige in the Far East, suffer a rapid collapse. MacArthur was placed in charge, for two reasons: (1) it was axiomatic that the United States must contain communism, and the doctrine of containment was not limited to Europe and (2) U.S. officials did not expect any rapid countermove by the Soviet Union. By the end of the first week of the war, MacArthur had recommended that American ground units up to two divisions be sent from Japan to stem the tide. U.S. civilian officials and military leaders were not keen about committing large numbers of troops to a vulnerable peninsula on the edge of the Asian mainland—a peninsula whose strategic value was not rated high in the age of total war. The commitment was made, however, because the attack in Korea was perceived as an attack on the United Nations, on the postwar global balance of power, and on

**CHRONOLOGY: FIRST WEEK OF THE KOREAN WAR**

| | |
|---|---|
| June 25, 1950 | North Korean invasion force, spearheaded by seven divisions (90,000 men), supported by tanks and aircraft, breaks through five South Korean divisions spread along the border. |
| | Accusing North Korea of breach of peace, UN Security Council votes 9–0 (Yugoslavia abstaining), calling for cessation of hostilities and North Korean withdrawal, and appealing to UN members to render every assistance in executing the resolution. |
| | President Truman meets at Blair House with Dean Acheson, Defense Secretary Louis Johnson, Chairman Omar Bradley and other members of the Joint Chiefs of Staff, Secretaries of the Army, Navy, and Air Force, and four State Department principals. |
| | General MacArthur is authorized to speed shipments of military equipment to South Korean forces and to employ his forces in pursuance of UN resolution. U.S. Air Force ordered to protect Kimpo Airport near Seoul. Seventh Fleet directed to proceed north from Philippines and to prevent any attack from China on Formosa and vice versa. |
| June 26, 1950 | U.S. Air Force and Navy ordered to give all-out support to Korean forces, confining their effort to south of the 38th parallel. |
| June 27, 1950 | U.S. sends note to USSR requesting effort to restrain North Koreans. North Koreans capture Seoul. |
| June 28, 1950 | Senate votes unanimously to authorize president to invoke selective-service laws and call up reserves. MacArthur flies to Korea for personal reconnaissance. |
| June 29, 1950 | MacArthur recommends commitment of American divisions to prevent a rout. After consulting with National Security Council and JCS, Truman approves use of U.S. combat troops in Pusan area to protect supply operations and evacuation of American citizens. Truman considers offer of 33,000 Nationalist Chinese troops by Chiang Kai-shek, but postpones decision on advice of Acheson, who fears that their move into Korea might provoke Chinese Communist intervention. Moscow, in reply to U.S. note, blames South Koreans for having originated attack. |

the reliability of the U.S. pledge to defend its allies—not so much the Koreans as the Japanese and Western Europeans.

Within two weeks of the outbreak of war, British Foreign Minister Bevin and Indian Prime Minister Jawaharlal Nehru were urging Washington to make concessions to the Communists, especially about Formosa and the Beijing government's admission to the United Nations, in return for a cease-fire in Korea. Acheson, with Truman's approval, made it clear that the United States was willing to discuss a peaceful resolution of those issues on their merits, but not under the duress of blackmail then being employed, since that would merely whet the Communists' appetites for further aggression elsewhere. Since the United States possessed a Security Council mandate for counteraction in Korea, it was by no means ready to allow the Soviet Union to shift the debate from unmistakable

Communist aggression in Korea to other questions that, under the terms of the United Nations Charter, would be politically much murkier and less relevant to the organization's function of dealing with breaches of the peace. Acheson's basic principle was that one never negotiates under the threat of force unless no other choice is available.

By August 1950, the UN army—consisting principally of U.S. and Korean forces, with smaller units contributed by more than a dozen other countries (nearly all U.S. allies)—held only a small perimeter around the southeastern port city of Pusan. In September, however, MacArthur seized the initiative and carried out a brilliant flanking maneuver with an amphibious landing at Inchon on the west coast near Seoul. Within two weeks, MacArthur's forces had regained control of the country up to the 38th parallel. What was their new UN mandate to be? Since Soviet UN representative Malik had returned to the Security Council that body was paralyzed into inaction. To circumvent the veto, Acheson offered a "uniting for peace" plan to increase the effective role of the General Assembly when the Security Council was unable to act.*

Several policymakers in the Truman administration were in favor of crossing the 38th parallel to remove the danger of a future attack on South Korea and to create conditions of stability that would permit realization of the UN's 1947 goal—a unified, independent, and democratic government of Korea.** At the end of September, Acheson, Marshall (who had succeeded Louis Johnson as secretary of defense), and the Joint Chiefs of Staff recommended and Truman approved a plan that authorized MacArthur to cross the parallel and destroy the North Korean armed forces—provided that Soviet or Chinese armed forces did not intervene. On October 7 the General Assembly repeated its call for a united, free Korea by a vote of 47 to 5. The American public wanted a permanent solution to the Korean problem, not an ambiguous compromise that would leave the situation where it had been on June 24. To the administration, punishing the Soviet Union for supporting aggression against the United Nations by rolling back communism's borders in Asia appeared increasingly attractive, for it would hearten Japan and might prompt a policy reorientation in Beijing. This was to be undertaken, however, only if it involved no risk of general war.

Mao Zedong and Zhou Enlai, both in public speeches and in diplomatic communications through India's officially neutral but privately pro-Chinese Ambassador K. M. Panikkar and Prime Minister Nehru, warned that the People's Republic of China would not tolerate the approach of U.S. forces toward its border. Most American policymakers were inclined to discount the probability of Chinese intervention as a bluff, because such a move would contravene China's interest in being seated at the United Nations. Truman was urged by his White House aides to arrange a Wake Island meeting with MacArthur. They thought it

---

*The British foreign officer warned that a majority of the General Assembly might not be friendly in the future, but Britain joined in sponsoring the plan.

**George F. Kennan and Paul H. Nitze, then director of the Policy Planning Staff, were opposed to going north of the 38th parallel because of the increased danger of conflict with Soviet or Chinese Communist forces.

would be a dramatic touch just three weeks before congressional elections, and they noted that Roosevelt, with an eye on the 1944 presidential election, had met MacArthur in Honolulu in July of that year. Truman was not at first eager to engage in a political stunt, but he finally decided to talk to the one he called "God's right-hand man" to find out whether he thought China would enter the Korean War. MacArthur did not think so. Neither did the U.S. Central Intelligence Agency nor most policymakers in Washington, even though they were less certain than MacArthur that organized resistance through Korea would be ended by Thanksgiving and U.S. forces back in Japan by Christmas.

In late October 1950 the Chinese began to move into Korea as "volunteers," for Peking, which was by no means in a strategically strong position, had no way of knowing what the U.S. reaction might be. Within a few weeks, MacArthur's UN forces were under assault from more than 200,000 Chinese troops, backed by two reserve armies in Manchuria. When ordered by the Joint Chiefs of Staff to postpone the bombing of bridges across the Yalu River, over which Chinese forces were pouring into North Korea, MacArthur persuaded Truman to authorize the bombing. But when MacArthur requested permission to engage in hot pursuit across the Yalu of Manchuria-based MIG-15s that were attacking UN forces, permission was denied because of the objections of allies who had forces in Korea, especially Britain, which had established diplomatic ties with Beijing. Instead of reaching the Yalu, MacArthur's "end-the-war" offensive confronted a massive Chinese counteroffensive, and the UN forces were pushed back. By November 28 the UN offensive collapsed and MacArthur said, "We face in entirely new war." Disaster had struck.

From that time on, the Korean War became a protracted struggle of attrition. At a press conference on November 30, President Truman hinted that the United States was actively considering the use of the atomic bomb in Korea, and that the military commander in the field might have the power of decision, even though the Atomic Energy Act of 1946 provided that only the president could order the use of atomic weapons. His remarks sent shock waves around the world. Prime Minister Attlee, reflecting a widespread British fear that the Korean conflict was distracting the United States from the Soviet threat to Europe and pushing the world toward the abyss of general war over what the British regarded as less-than-vital interests in Asia, flew to Washington to urge Truman to keep the Korean War localized.

MacArthur was vociferously opposed to limiting the war and to accepting the handicaps that were being imposed on his operations—no major reinforcements, no bombing beyond the Yalu of bases in Manchuria or targets in China, no unleashing of Chiang's forces to fight in Korea (partly for fear of alienating India), no naval blockade of Chinese coastal ports (because this would hurt allied trade and jeopardize the position of Hong Kong), and no threat—not even an implied one—of employing atomic weapons (so as not to arouse Asian anti-American sentiment, divide the Western alliance, and lose the mantle of UN support for U.S. policy). MacArthur displayed the pique of a military commander who believed that he was being required, for political reasons with which he disagreed, to fight with one hand tied behind his back.

When MacArthur went public in his criticism of U.S. strategic policy, especially in a letter to the Republican leader of the House of Representatives, Joseph W. Martin, and in what appeared to be his own ultimatum to Communist China, not cleared with Washington and the United Nations, Truman had no choice but to regard this as a direct challenge to his authority as president and to the traditional U.S. principle of civilian supremacy over the military. For his open defiance, MacArthur was relieved of all his commands on April 10, 1951, and replaced by General Matthew B. Ridgway. MacArthur—the hero of Bataan, Leyte, and Inchon, the Supreme Allied Commander in the Pacific, the "proconsul to Japan," and the commander of the United Forces in Korea—returned to a tumultuous welcome by the American people and Congress (he had never come back home after the war) while the president dug in to weather the ensuing storm of abuse from his critics.

At the beginning of the Korean War, Truman's decisiveness had been quite popular with the public, Congress and both political parties (except for a few extremists), the European allies, and the United Nations. Even Henry Wallace applauded his policy. Early in the war, with U.S. and UN forces bravely holding the Pusan perimeter, support still ran high. It rose even higher after Inchon, when it seemed that all Korea might be liberated. Four months after the outbreak of hostilities, China entered the war, cautiously at first but more boldly as the signals from Washington made it clear that the United States was determined not to become involved in a wider war with the Soviet Union or China. Many subsequent commentators have pointed to the fear of a nuclear war. In retrospect, it seems unlikely that anything the United States might have done in 1950–1952 could have goaded the Soviet Union into an all-out war with a United States vastly superior in atomic capabilities. At the time, however, responsible decision makers had to proceed with caution. They knew that the United States could not simply accede to the wishes of the European allies, for as the leading global power it had obligations in the Far East not shared by the Europeans. At the same time, they realized that the Communist threat was greater in Europe, where U.S. interests were primary. As a rejoinder to MacArthur's famous aphorism—"There is no substitute for victory"—the administration could quote General Omar Bradley—"the wrong war at the wrong place at the wrong time."

In June 1951, as the fortunes of war were running modestly in favor of the UN forces, the Soviet Union proposed truce talks. This overture precluded a UN tactical offensive (which was more feasible militarily than politically). In contrast to 1918, when the Allies had insisted on continuing their offensive operations until the armistice was actually signed, this time the United States accepted the Communists' demand for a virtual cessation of hostilities prior to the opening of truce negotiations. This proved to be a major blunder, for it relieved all offensive pressure on the Communist forces at a critical point in the conflict. It also enabled the Communists to employ a variety of delaying tactics to prolong the truce negotiations for a frustrating year, punctuated by ten months of grueling but stalemated warfare. The bargaining power of the Chinese Communists and the North Koreans increased in inverse proporton to the declining willingness of the United Nations to resume military operations. With each passing month, the

UN police action in Korea became more contemptuously known as "Mr. Truman's war," for which the president and his secretary of State were held more accountable than the North Koreans, the Chinese Communists, or the Soviet Union.

In the final analysis, the Korean War produced an impact far beyond the peninsula where it was waged. By graphically demonstrating the willingness of Soviet and Chinese Communists to support or employ military aggression against the ideals of the United Nations and U.S. strategic interests, it stimulated the American public to tolerate an increase in defense spending to 15 percent of gross national product, a level several times higher than was deemed possible before June 1950. The American defense buildup ultimately redounded to the military advantage of NATO. The gauntlet hurled down in Korea also speeded up the process by which the European allies accepted the necessity of West German rearmament. The war undoubtedly hastened the drafting of a peace treaty for Japan, as well as a U.S.–Japanese mutual security agreement.

At home, because the American people were utterly unaccustomed to an ambiguous war in which political considerations took precedence over military ones, the Korean conflict produced a profound division within the American polity. It contributed to the wave of right-wing anti-intellectual hysteria known as McCarthyism, which began as a witch hunt against a State Department alleged to be "thoroughly infested" with Communists responsible for plotting the loss of China and, indirectly, the hostilities in Korea. The bitterness of that period not only hurt the Democrats in the 1950 and 1952 elections but also made it impossible for the administration to consider following the British lead by recognizing Peking, particularly after the General Assembly condemned the People's Republic of China as an aggressor against the United Nations. Finally, the Korean War gave rise, not immediately but in the latter 1950s, to a great strategic debate about the implications for U.S. defense policy of limited war in the nuclear age.

## EFFORTS TOWARD INTERNATIONAL CONTROL
## OF ATOMIC ENERGY

For more than a year before Hiroshima and Nagasaki, scientists associated with the Manhattan Project, aware not only of the atom's danger as a destructive force but also of its great potential for peaceful benefits, discussed the problem of controlling the new form of energy. In late 1945 Secretary of State Byrnes appointed then-Undersecretary Dean Acheson to chair a committee that would draft a plan to be presented in the United Nations.* The result of the committee's deliberations was the Acheson-Lilienthal Report of March 1946, which formed the basis of the Baruch Plan, the first postwar proposal for nuclear disarmament, named for Bernard Baruch, an eminent advisor who became the first U.S. representative on the UN Atomic Energy Commission. The plan's basic as-

---

*The group included, among others, Vannevar Bush, James B. Conant, Leslie R. Groves, John J. McCloy, J. Robert Oppenheimer, and David E, Lilienthal—names that carried significant weight.

sumption was that the monopoly of nuclear technology then possessed by the United States would not last much beyond five years. The plan called for the creation of an International Atomic Development Authority within the framework of the United Nations. The IADA would conduct all "intrinsically dangerous activities" in the nuclear weapons field; would own and control all sources of critical materials and related installations; would carry on continuous research in nuclear weapons and all phases of atomic energy, so that no state could ever surpass it in technical knowledge; would license all national and private nuclear activities (such as peaceful atomic projects); would approve the structure, design, and capacity of all atomic installations and reserve the right of inspection in any nation at any time without advance warning. IADA was to be politically responsible to the Security Council and General Assembly of the United Nations, without being subject to any nation's veto power—the latter condition having been Baruch's major contribution. It was to exercise exclusive control over all stockpiles of atomic weapons, which were to be distributed in such a way that a preponderant amount would never be available within the borders of a single nation. New projects for atomic development would also be located according to the same principle. If any country seized the installations within its borders, this move would trigger the inspection system, and the facilities of IADA would be placed at the disposal of the UN in sufficient time to enforce the renegade's compliance with international obligations under the threat of superior force.

There was reason to wonder whether the Senate would approve the IADA if a treaty should be negotiated. It never came to that, however, because of the USSR's persistent objections.

Some observers at the time wondered why the Soviet Union did not take advantage of the opportunity to internationalize the American nuclear monopoly. In retrospect, it is not difficult to see that acceptance of the Baruch Plan was not in the Soviet Union's perceived national interest, for it would have thwarted Moscow's own high-priority objective of duplicating the U.S. achievement. It would have led to an infringement of Soviet national sovereignty by an international body and would have subjected the socialist economic planning process to outside capitalist interference, if not control. Finally, since the United States was the only country that had ever made an atomic bomb, the Soviet leadership perceived a real danger that American scientists and engineers would merely perpetuate the U.S. technological monopoly under the guise of an international authority. The USSR was determined to get its own A-bomb, which it was entitled to do under the rules of the nation-state system. Notwithstanding Baruch's ominous warning—"We are here to make a choice between the quick and the dead . . . We must elect world peace or world destruction"—the goverment of no major power was yet ready to exchange the rules with which they were familiar for a new set of standards for governing a radically transformed and disarmed world.

Throughout the late 1940s, U.S. military planners gradually drifted toward greater reliance on the American atomic monopoly to counterbalance Soviet conventional superiority. After the Soviet Union conducted its first atomic explosion in 1949, the U.S. Congress—previously anxious to keep the defense budget as low as possible—showed itself willing to increase military appropriations for aid to the NATO allies and for more atomic weapons. The Joint Congressional Committee on Atomic Energy, headed by Senator Brian McMahon of Connecticut, favored a broader array of nuclear weapons and strategic bombardment (by B-36s) as the foundation of U.S. foreign policy and military deterrence in an ideologically divided world. There was increasing talk of a super-bomb, a hydrogen weapon based on the theoretical possibility of thermonuclear fusion rather than atomic fission, with an energy release 100 to 1000 times greater and a destructive power (measured in area damage) 20 to 100 times greater than that of the Hiroshima bomb. There was some concern that the Soviet Union might proceed quickly toward the production of such a weapon.

Key policy advisers to the president advocated an H-bomb project as the U.S. rejoinder to the Soviet atomic blast (which had stirred an unprecedented sense of vulnerability in the American public). The scientific community was divided. Ernest O. Lawrence, Edward Teller, and Karl T. Compton supported the project; J. Robert Oppenheimer, James Conant, Enrico Fermi, and I. I. Rabi—all of whom had favored building and using the A-bomb—were opposed on moral grounds to what they regarded as a potential instrument of genocide. The failure to make progress on the Baruch Plan for international control, combined with the danger that the Soviet Union might build the H-bomb first, leaving the United States with no deterrent, plus the fact that news of the H-bomb possibility had leaked out to create both congressional and public pressure, led Truman early in 1950 to make the building of the hydrogen bomb a matter of urgency.

Truman was president during the first seven and a half years of the nuclear era. During that time, no headway was made on international arms control, perhaps largely because of the wide disparity in the atomic capabilities of the United States and the Soviet Union. The latter, rejecting year after year Western plans for controls, safeguards, and inspection, mounted a worldwide propaganda campaign to "ban the bomb" by mutual public declaration. Although the campaign was intensified after the outbreak of the Korean War and its effect was supplemented by the Stockholm Peace Appeal and unfounded communist charges that U.S. forces were waging "germ warfare" against North Korea and China, the Western powers steadfastly ignored Soviet demands for modes of disarmament that amounted to mere promises to denounce and abolish weapons without any means of verifying compliance. Moscow's psychological warfare efforts, however, cannot be called unsuccessful, for they managed to persuade millions of people around the world that the United States wanted nuclear war while the Soviet Union was a great champion of peace, and that American (but not Soviet) nuclear strategies and weapons were evil and a threat to the whole world.

## FOREIGN-POLICY DECISION MAKING IN THE TRUMAN YEARS

Each president, it seems, faces a unique set of problems that emerge continuously from the changing domestic and international scenes. When Truman entered the presidency, the United States was preparing to ride a tidal wave of postwar internationalism. Many Americans were impatient for foreign intervention, especially in Eastern Europe and China, to make sure that historical forces developed in conformity with American principles and wishes. The two critical years 1947 and 1948 found Truman confronted with a Republican-dominated Congress, segments of which (from both parties) were quick to blame him for failing to take a firmer stand in one part of the world or another, even through they refused to countenance the military programs of force that a firmer stand would have required.

Truman assumed office with no experience in foreign affairs. He had met FDR only twice outside of cabinet meetings, and he had never met Stettinius, whom he inherited as secretary of state. Unlike his Democratic predecessors, Wilson and FDR, Truman did not have a Colonel House or a Harry Hopkins.* Whereas the earlier Democratic presidents in this century had had problems with their secretaries of state in wartime, either disagreeing with them or lacking confidence in their advice on the most critical issues of foreign policy, Truman believed in reaching foreign-policy decisions through proper organizational channels. Moreover, for the most part he trusted the good judgment of the three secretaries of state he appointed: James F. Byrnes (at least for a while) as a politician, George Marshall as a man, and Dean Acheson as a diplomat.

### Truman's Secretaries of State

The end of the San Francisco Conference, at which Stettinius climaxed his brief (seven-month) career as secretary by steering the United Nations Charter through to signature, provided an opportunity for Truman to fill the post with his own appointee. Byrnes had broad experience—30 years in Congress (both houses), 16 months on the Supreme Court, and two and a half years in charge of the Office of Economic Stabilization, where he became known as the "assistant president." He accompanied Roosevelt to Yalta and thus met Stalin before Truman did. When Truman named him secretary, the Senate gave unanimous approval to a long-time club member without hearing or debate, although a few senators thought that he was too much inclined to the art of political compromise to deal firmly with the likes of Stalin, as if the dictator were only a Republican curmudgeon.

Byrnes believed that the members of the Grand Alliance had paid such a heavy price in their unified effort to defeat Nazi Germany that their inevitable postwar differences could be resolved without serious difficulty. At Potsdam, he found the Russians willing to compromise, after hard bargaining, on procedural matters (such as the establishment of the Council of Foreign Ministers) but unbudging on substantive issues related to Germany and Eastern Europe. Byrnes's public protest in October 1945 against the dangers of rapid U.S. postwar demobilization was not enough, in the eyes of conservative critics, to offset his

---

*He did, however; continue Roosevelt's practice of employing Averell Harriman for occasional special missions—for example, in the Anglo-Iranian oil dispute of 1951, not because of any personal relationship as close as that between FDR and Hopkins, but because of Harriman's experience and prestige in dealing with Moscow (not to mention his prestigious position in the Democratic party).

willingness to recognize the new governments of Hungary, Romania, and Bulgaria. Even Sumner Welles criticized Byrnes for departing from Roosevelt's Yalta principles. Byrnes acquired a reputation as being too soft on the Russians for what he considered his own realistic acceptance of postwar facts that the West was unwilling to bear the price to change. In a trying period of polarizing attitudes, the president himself probably began to wonder whether Byrnes, because of his reputation, may have been making too many important foreign-policy decisions without adequate discussion or White House approval. Byrnes spent 350 of his 562 days as secretary on trips away from Washington. By January 1947, the man who stood for the preservation of U.S.-Soviet unity through compromise had outlived his political time.

For nearly a year, Truman had in mind George C. Marshall, then on his special mission to China, as a successor to Byrnes. The president had the highest admiration for the eminent wartime chief of staff, whom he called "the greatest living American." No professional military officer had ever before been named secretary of state. Marshall, however, was more than a military man. He had attended every wartime conference at which Roosevelt was present and had also been at Potsdam with Truman. As a military figure who had never engaged in politics—indeed, had never even voted—he could serve as a unique symbol of bipartisanship in foreign policy. The Senate Committee on Foreign Relations took 20 minutes to recommend confirmation and on the same day the Senate gave unanimous consent, the last time a secretary was endorsed without being subjected to careful scrutiny. Despite Marshall's outstanding reputation, Truman received some criticism for blurring the distinction between the civilian and the military in the conduct of foreign affairs.

Marshall, like Truman, appreciated careful staff preparation as the basis of efficient decision making. He had little patience with endless hand-wringing and self-paralyzing discussions of policy alternatives, but he was willing to probe deeply whatever factors were involved in the most critical decisions. Preoccupied with preparations for the Moscow Foreign Ministers' Conference in March 1947, Marshall largely delegated to his undersecretary, Acheson, the task of working out the details of the Truman Doctrine of aid to Greece and Turkey. Tension between the requirement that the secretary become involved in international negotiations and the requirement that foreign policy and the department be administered from Washington is inevitable, but Truman, Marshall, and Acheson handled the problem rather well. Marshall, keenly aware of the need for a centralized long-range perspective in foreign policy, created the Policy Planning Staff within the Department and put George F. Kennan in charge. The team of Truman, Marshall, Acheson, Kennan, and Clayton, as noted earlier, produced the Marshall Plan, as well as U.S. participation in NATO and the idea of technical assistance for the "underdeveloped" countries (as they were then called)*—probably the most creative trio of initiatives in the history of any nation's diplomacy up to that time.

---

*This last program was known as "Point Four" because of its place in Truman's January 1949 inaugural address.

Marshall and Truman deeply respected each other, but they clashed seriously at times—never more than over the question of U.S. policy toward Palestine and the independent state of Israel. Marshall was the spokesman for the State Department, professing to embody the long-range national interest of the United States against the president's White House advisers. Some of the latter advocated a humanitarian course on behalf of the survivors of the holocaust, while others were thinking of Jewish votes in the 1948 election. The divergent outlooks gave rise to embarrassing breakdowns in communication between Washington and the U.S. Mission to the United Nations. When Truman overruled the State Department, Marshall showed himself to be a loyal soldier and obeyed.

Dean Acheson became secretary of state at the start of Truman's second administration, after an illness forced Marshall's resignation. By this time the Senate Foreign Relations Committee was in a mood to ask probing questions about Acheson's attitude toward the Soviet Union. The anti-Wilsonian Acheson, who believed in pursuing national security through the balance of power rather than through pious appeals to moral principles, and whose credentials as a principal architect of the Truman Doctrine were impeccable, had little difficulty in winning Senate confirmation by a wide margin. However, his troubles mounted over the next four years. The postwar debate over what Roosevelt had "conceded" to the Soviet Union at Yalta had begun to cover the executive with a cloud of suspicion. The cloud was darkened by misgivings over U.S. policy toward China. Marshall himself, during his last months in office, had come under congressional fire for playing down the report of General Albert C. Wedemeyer (Stilwell's successor), which advocated an extension of the Truman Doctrine to Asia for the purpose of propping up Chiang's Nationalists.

In an effort to preserve bipartisan support on foreign policy, Truman assigned important posts to Republicans John T. McCloy, Paul Hoffman, and Robert Lovett. Acheson who thought that the secretary of state should not spend a lot of time away from Washington at conferences abroad, prevailed on the president to entrust the task of drafting the Japanese peace treaty to John Foster Dulles, an experienced negotiator on good terms with the Dewey and Taft wings of the Republican party. Truman's acquiescence thereby advanced Dulles's chances of becoming the next Republican secretary of state.

### Reorganization of the Structure

During Truman's tenure, major changes occurred in the organizational structure of the executive branch for the conduct of foreign and defense policy. To begin with, the executive office itself, which consisted of only about a dozen advisers and staff assistants in April 1945, underwent rapid expansion to include several new agencies: the National Security Council, the Council of Economic Advisers, the Office of Defense Mobilization, and the others. A number of older departments and agencies assumed additional functions related to foreign affairs, requiring new coordinating committees. Membership in the United Nations, the North Atlantic Treaty Organization, and the Organization of American States (or

OAS), established by the 1947 Pact of Rio, required organizational mechanism within the U.S. executive branch. The State Department was reorganized in 1944, 1945, and 1949, and the Foreign Service was modernized in 1946. The president, who became a sort of chief of staff of a sprawling labyrinth, received a special assistant for international responsibilities in 1950, an office that would become quite powerful in later administrations.

The National Security Act of 1947 created a new Department of Defense to integrate the work of the three service departments—Army (formerly the War Department), Navy, and Air Force (formerly the Army Air Corps). The three branches of the military were not united in a single service, but retained their separate identities at the subcabinet level. The Joint Chiefs of Staff, in existence since 1942, was regularized in 1947 to serve as the principal source of military advice to the president and the executive departments and agencies.* The act established the National Security Council to assess and appraise the objectives, commitments, and risks of American foreign policy in the light of the nation's actual and potential military power, and to advise the president on the integration of domestic, foreign, and military policies relating to national security. Finally, the 1947 legislation brought the U.S. government's various information-gathering efforts; overt and covert, together in the Central Intelligence Agency.

The membership of the National Security Council has changed frequently over the course of time, along with the needs of decision making. Under Truman it usually consisted of the secretaries of state and defense, the Joint Chiefs of Staff. the director of central intelligence, the director of the Office of Defense Mobilization, the director of the Foreign Overseas Administration, and the three service secretaries until they were dropped in the 1949 reorganization, when the vice-president was added. The council normally met once a week and was chaired by the president. It gave advice that he was, of course, free to accept or reject. It coordinated the work of the departments, especially State and Defense, where national-security issues were at stake. The council had a career staff, a planning board, and an executive secretary. These prepared agendas and policy papers through interdepartmental discussion (or negotiation) prior to consideration by the full council. The NSC contributed to most foreign-policy decisions, including those related to the Berlin Blockade, the Atlantic Alliance, the military assistance program, and the Korean War. However, its role was limited by several factors: (1) the unwieldiness of its meetings when members were accompanied by staff assistants; (2) the cumbersomeness of its procedures in drafting policy papers; and (3) the personality and jurisdictional clash between Dean Acheson and Louis Johnson (until the latter was replaced by Marshall in 1950). When a crisis arose and key decisions had to be taken quickly, as on the day after the North Korean invasion of the South, Truman preferred to call together the principal advisers he wanted, most of whom were NSC members, without invoking the time-consuming formalities that had to precede a council meeting. Acheson certainly liked it that way, too, for it preserved the flexibility that he was convinced the

*In 1952 Congress gave the commandant of marines an equal voice with the other three chiefs on questions affecting the Corps.

policymaking process required. It also prevented the insertion of a bureaucratic wall between the president and the secretary of state, and it reduced the likelihood of recommendations based on bland, ambiguous compromises—"agreement by exhaustion" among rival fiefdoms—rather than the clear-cut responses to critical challenges that both he and the president were good at formulating.

Truman has been ranked as a "near-great" president, primarily for his foreign-policy decisions. Although his popularity rating dipped on occasion to a lower point than that of any postwar president—even Nixon's after Watergate—his reputation has grown. By selecting Byrnes and Marshall, he minimized friction with Congress, but as time went on his administration had to bear blame for the "loss" of China and the frustrating agony of Korea—war of a type to which the American people were not accustomed. He had to contend with three lobbies—the Zionists, the Chinese, and the Spanish—in controversies over thorny political questions that could be settled not by appeals to international law but only by executive decision. Throughout his second term, he and Acheson felt compelled to keep the war in Asia limited so that priority could be given to building the alliance with Western Europe. The efforts to globalize containment on opposite sides of the world had to be kept in proportion.* Some of their problems arose from imponderable and inescapable human elements. Acheson, for example, undoubtedly provoked resentment for the fastidiousness of his dress, his aristocratic air of superiority, the quickness of his mind, and the occasional sharpness of his tongue. Together he and Truman, the "average man" turned president, made quite a paradoxical pair of decision makers, who did much to shape the postwar world.

---

*George F. Kennan later subjected his own containment theory to reinterpretation, insisting that he had not intended as much emphasis on military means as the Truman Doctrine embodied. During the Vietnam War, he also contended that containment was meant mainly for Europe, and in any event had become meaningless in Asia after China went communist in 1949. But when the Korean War started in 1950, the U.S. response through the United Nations was looked upon generally as an application of the containment theory, and Kennan did not then demur at such an interpretation.

# chapter 4

# The Eisenhower Administration:
A "New Look" in Foreign Policy

In November 1952, 20 years had elapsed since the Republican party had won a presidential election. Two Democratic presidents, Roosevelt and Truman, had led the United States through periods of transformation, from the Great Depression to victory in World War II to the emergence of the United States as a superpower. The accomplishments of the Truman administration following World War II had been remarkable: the formation of a bipartisan foreign policy based on a national consensus that a return to isolation was incompatible with American interests; the initiation of the Truman Doctrine in support of Greece and Turkey; the development of the Marshall Plan to help ensure the economic recovery of devastated Western Europe; the sowing of the seeds of democracy in West Germany and the creation of the Federal Republic of Germany; the founding of the Atlantic Alliance; and the signing of a peace treaty with Japan and the rebirth of that nation under representative government. These, however, were eclipsed by the Korean War, which contributed to the belief, held by a large number of Americans, that it was time for a change of leaders.

Although it produced an eloquent candidate in Adlai Stevenson in 1952, the Democratic party, after two decades in power, was perceived as a party of views and programs whose time had passed. Although the United States, in the Truman administration, had entered an era of economic growth and prosperity that in the decades to follow was to lift larger numbers of Americans to unprecedented affluence, the early 1950s were marked by deep political divisions. The stature that Truman has acquired as his administration has receded into history could not readily be foreseen in the turbulence of the partisan battles of the waning years of his presidency.

At the zenith of its power, the United States seemed to many Americans unable or unwilling to master the forces that were shaping the world in the second half of the twentieth century. Containment of communism was perceived as a static and reactive approach to foreign policy. Instead, opponents of the Truman administration contended, the United States should pursue a more activist policy designed not simply to halt communist expansion, but to reverse its momentum and even to liberate peoples in Eastern Europe who had fallen under Soviet rule. The frustration of having vast power but being unable to use it creatively and effectively to forestall perceived threats to national security contributed to the Truman administration's decline in popularity and helped to shape the policy issues that dominated the presidential campaign of 1952.

## THE END OF THE KOREAN WAR

The most important issue was the Korean conflict. Unlike Vietnam nearly a generation later, Korea had not produced mass demonstrations and bitter differences of opinion at home. By 1952, however, Korea symbolized the limitations, whether self-imposed or dictated by objective circumstances, of American power. In contrast to the decisive victories won by American forces in World War II, the United States had found itself, less than a decade later, in a military stalemate that could not be altered unless the conflict were expanded both in geographic scope and in level of military commitment. In the closing days of the presidential campaign of 1952, the Republican candidate, Dwight D. Eisenhower, had announced that, if elected, he would go to Korea in order to find an honorable solution to the war.

Although the Truman administration was criticized for the stalemate in Korea, negotiations for an armistice had been underway since July 1951. In the autumn of 1952, the talks had bogged down on the issue of repatriation of prisoners of war, many of whom in the hands of United Nations forces did not want to be returned to North Korean or Chinese Communist authorities. Fearing that such persons would face, as Truman put it, "slaughter or slavery" if repatriated, the United States rejected the idea of any compromise and instead intensified military operations as a means of inducing the enemy to reach a settlement at the conference table. Whatever the actual significance of Eisenhower's "I will go to Korea" announcement in enhancing the prospects for an armistice, its immediate effect was undoubtedly to contribute to his landslide victory on November 4, 1952. Although Eisenhower, as president-elect did travel to Korea in December 1952, the Korean War dragged on for several months into his presidency and ended with the signing of an armistice in Panmunjon on July 27, 1953. The line separating the two Koreas did not differ substantially from the 38th parallel, across which North Korean forces had attacked South Korea in June 1950. In August 1953 the United States signed a security treaty with the Republic of Korea—as it was to do with a large number of other states during the Eisenhower administration. These treaties extended American defense commitments from the Truman administration's focus on Europe and Japan to a security perimeter that extended from Northeast Asia to the Middle East. By the time it ended, the Korean War had taken the lives of 32,629 Americans; 103,284 more had been wounded in battle.

Meanwhile, Stalin had died on March 4, 1953. His death, in the Eisenhower administration's view, marked the beginning of a period of transition in the Soviet leadership until Nikita Khrushchev's emergence at the top of the Soviet Union's political hierarchy in the mid-1950s. Within several weeks of the Stalin's death, the Chinese altered course and accepted a plan for voluntary repatriation of prisoners of war held by the United Nations Command. However, the truce negotiations once again became deadlocked in May 1953. The Eisenhower administration, in a message from Secretary of State John Foster Dulles to Prime Minister Jawaharlal Nehru of India, to be forwarded to Chinese authorities, indicated that it might use atomic weapons if the conflict could not otherwise be ended on acceptable terms. The transfer of nuclear warheads to Okinawa as a signal of intent, together with prospect that other measures might be taken—the bombing of bases in China and the blockade of the Chinese coast—may have enhanced the prospect for a truce.

## DULLES'S THREE THEMES: CONTAINMENT, LIBERATION, AND RETALIATION

If Korea was symptomatic of the frustrations in American foreign policy of the early 1950s, no less disturbing was the issue of the extension of Soviet power into Eastern Europe and the circumstances that had produced the imposition of communist rule. The Republican party platform of 1952 had denounced the Yalta agreements and called for a dynamic American strategy based on liberation rather than what seemed to be simply the reactive policy of containment pursued by the Truman administration. The idea of liberation of captive Eastern European peoples had been embraced in the presidential campaign of 1952 and had appealed especially to members of ethnic groups. However, Eisenhower limited his support for the idea to peaceful means, thereby skillfully appealing to its advocates within his own party without embracing a strategy that would probably have called for greater resources than the administration was prepared to commit. To many Republican critics, the Yalta agreement, by condemning Poland to communist rule, had symbolized the impotence of the United States against Soviet domination, as well as a failure to support democratic forces.

In May 1952, before he became secretary of state, Dulles had prepared an essay whose twin themes were retaliation and liberation. He proposed that the United States adopt a military strategy based principally on American superiority in air power and nuclear weapons. Communist aggression would be met not by means similar to those used against us and our allies, but by those military capabilities in which the U.S. was superior at geographic points where an adversary would be most vulnerable. Thus Soviet superiority in numbers of conventional forces would be countered by the technological advantages possessed by the United States. This became the basis for the changes adopted by the

Eisenhower administration, which in the years following the Korean armistice reduced conventional forces and thus defense spending by increasing the reliance of the United States on nuclear weapons. The Eisenhower administration's deemphasis of conventional warfare made possible a reduction in the size of the Army from twenty divisions at the end of the Korean War to fourteen by 1957. The Navy, however, was reduced only slightly, while the Air Force was to be increased from 115 to 137 wings. There were to be reductions in U.S. forces stationed overseas, together with greater reliance on the ground forces of allies and the development of a mobile reserve based in the United States. The "new look" strategy was to be a nuclear one.

The administration decided in October 1953 to deploy battlefield nuclear weapons in Europe. By the early 1950s the United States had developed low-kiloton nuclear weapons that made atomic deterrence a feasible concept for the NATO Central Front. In December 1954 the NATO Ministerial Council reached agreement on the stationing of tactical nuclear weapons in Europe, and between 1954 and 1957 the Atlantic Alliance evolved a military policy for the use of such weapons in the event of a Soviet attack against Western Europe. The emphasis on nuclear weapons as both deterrent and defensive shield was peculiarly suited to a period when the United States faced little danger of retaliation from the Soviet Union—a condition that lasted for years after the Soviets launched their first Sputnik in the autumn of 1957, thus demonstrating a hypothetical capability of launching nuclear warheads that might strike targets in the United States. Nuclear strategy was seen by the Eisenhower administration as an alternative to the attrition of conventional warfare of the type that had sapped U.S. energies in Korea. It accorded with the notion that the United States should be prepared to use military power only if its vital interests were threatened, but that once having decided to do so, American policymakers should be able to escalate to whatever level was necessary in order to prevail. Such was the conceptual basis for a national-security policy whose central element was the certainty of deterrence in order to minimize the likelihood of miscalculation on the part of an adversary.

The liberation theme, as developed by Dulles, stood in sharp contrast to the concept of retaliation. While retaliation embraced the notion that the United States would use whatever weapons, including nuclear ones, that it deemed necessary to defend its vital interests in response to a military attack, liberation represented an effort to take the offensive against the Soviet Union, but strictly by means other than the use of force. Eisenhower and Dulles recognized, even before the election, that a liberation policy based on military force would involve the likelihood of war with the Soviet Union, the prevention of which was a cardinal objective of the Eisenhower administration. But it was equally apparent that the Soviet Union was most vulnerable in Eastern Europe, a fact that became apparent first in the riots that erupted in East Germany in June 1953 and then in the unrest in Poland and the uprising that brought in Soviet troops to restore communist rule to Hungary in the fall of 1956.

The dilemma confronting the Eisenhower administration was apparent. The United States could use such instruments as Radio Free Europe to encourage the forces opposed to Soviet rule, but those elements would inevitably be crushed by the Soviet Union. The use of peaceful means of persuasion by the United States would not succeed in countries where Soviet interests were of such importance as to warrant the use of overwhelming military force. We did not possess the conventional capabilities to counter such power, nor would the escalatory threat inherent in the concept of retaliation have been applicable in these circumstances. Hence the liberation concept, in retrospect, can be seen both as a response to the domestic political context of the times and as the expression of a perceived need to move from a strictly defensive, reactive policy to one of active pressure against an adversary's vulnerabilities.

## THE U.S. RESPONSE TO THE INDOCHINA WAR
## AND TO THE FRENCH WITHDRAWAL FROM SOUTHEAST ASIA

A strategy of rapid military escalation as the basis for deterrence, or avoidance, of conflict as a result of enemy miscalculation seemed most applicable to Western Europe, where the commitment contained in the Atlantic Alliance and the perception of U.S. vital interest was strongest. However, the first test of the Eisenhower strategy took place in Southeast Asia in 1954. The insurgent Viet Minh forces led by Ho Chi Minh mounted their final offensive at Dien Bien Phu in North Vietnam against the forces defending what remained of France's overseas possessions in the region. France had never fully reasserted its rule over Indochina after the end of World War II and the Japanese wartime occupation of most of Southeast Asia. Just before the end of his presidency, Truman had approved an increase of $30.5 million in defense funds for Indochina in response to a resolution adopted by the NATO Council in December 1952 identifying Alliance interests with those of France in Indochina. By the time Truman left office, the United States was underwriting as much as one-half of France's costs in Indochina; this was to rise to three-quarters by 1954, when France was finally defeated. While assisting France, the United States repeatedly had called for independence for Vietnam, Laos, and Cambodia. Thus American policy, from the Truman to the Eisenhower administrations, continued to support French policy, while seeking—ineffectively, as it turned out—to influence Paris toward a negotiated settlement providing for independence. The end of the Korean War had permitted China to increase its support for the Viet Minh forces fighting against France. In the early months of 1954, the French position had been weakened to the point of collapse as Viet Minh units launched an attack against French forces along that segment of the border with China and Laos which General Henri Navarre, France's commander in Indochina, had chosen to defend. France appealed for direct American military intervention.

### Eisenhower Rejects Military Intervention

To judge from the increased share of the war effort borne by the United States in 1954, the Eisenhower administration attached even greater importance to Indochina than had its predecessor. In fact, both Eisenhower and Dulles had proclaimed the strategic importance of Indochina's raw materials and geographic location. The loss of Indochina, it was thought, would open other countries in Southeast Asia to communist attack.

However, Eisenhower believed that France, in refusing to agree to grant independence if military victory was achieved, had made the pacification of Indochina impossible. Therefore, Eisenhower reasoned, the likelihood of success was not sufficient to justify a direct U.S. commitment in the form of air or ground forces. A military victory could be won only with the support of the population of Indochina and military forces contributed by other allies.

Thus the United States was not prepared to intervene militarily not only because of likely local opposition, but also because psychologically it would be important, as in the Korean War, for any such military action to be taken as part of a broader international coalition. The principal European power capable of intervening was Britain, but Churchill's government was firmly opposed to any such action. Nor were Australia and New Zealand willing to commit forces to Indochina in support of France. Last but not least, the Eisenhower administration, with the Korean War scarcely over, was not willing to risk military involvement in another costly Asian conflict. Eisenhower remembered the criticism that Truman had received for failing to obtain congressional authorization for military action. American military intervention in the form of air and ground forces, which Eisenhower was determined to avoid, would have required in his estimation a declaration of war by the U.S. Congress. Nevertheless, the United States vowed that it would intervene directly if China committed its own forces to the war in Indochina. Contingency plans for such U.S. intervention included the use of atomic weapons against military targets in China. Here again, however, any U.S. decision to commit military forces to the war in Indochina in the event of direct Chinese involvement would probably have depended on the willingness of other Southeast Asian states and Britain to join in such action.

## The Geneva Conference of 1954

After the French defeat at Dien Bien Phu, Pierre Mendès-France become premier in June 1954, pledging to secure a peaceful settlement by July 20. In late April, less than two weeks before the fall of Dien Bien Phu, a conference had been convened in Geneva in which the United States reluctantly participated with Britain, France, China, and the Soviet Union. The meeting had been organized as a result of a Soviet proposal, which France had viewed as a means of negotiating a settlement that would minimize its mounting losses. The rapid deterioration of France's military position in the spring and early summer, together with Mendès-France's determination to extricate his country from the Indochina War, lent increasing urgency to the Geneva Conference. On July 21, 1954, an agreement was reached in Geneva providing for the division of Vietnam at the 17th parallel. Ho Chi Minh's forces occupied the territory north of that line, while a noncommunist government was established in South Vietnam, with the United States as its chief external supporter. Although not a signatory of the Geneva accords, the United States pledged not to oppose them. The settlement at Geneva provided for nationwide elections to be held by 1956. The United States saw the creation of South Vietnam as an opportunity to strengthen a noncommunist barrier to expansion from the north. The United States supported Ngo Dinh Diem as the successor to the discredited Emperor Bao Dai, with whom France had sought to work in the preceding period as an alternative to Viet Minh rule. Although North Vietnam was lost, the Eisenhower administration hoped to add South Vietnam to a security perimeter being fashioned by the United States along the Asian periphery. American policy was to focus on military aid to build up indigenous forces (which France had conspicuously failed to do), while extending economic assistance and encouraging the Diem regime to broaden its base of support by increased democratization.

Although Vietnam, together with the states of Laos and Cambodia created from Indochina, was prohibited by the Geneva accords from joining a military alliance, this did not prevent the United States from forming a collective defense organization consisting of other states in the region. In keeping with its emphasis on associating the United States with other countries committed to the defense of weak states, the Eisenhower administration in 1954 designed the Southeast Asia Treaty Organization (SEATO) as a central element of U.S. policy, with Britain, France, Thailand, the Philippines, Australia, and New Zealand joining the United States as members.

The differences between the Atlantic Alliance and SEATO were readily apparent. Unlike NATO, the new organization failed to attract as members some of the most important states of the region: Indonesia, Burma, and Malaysia. Its provisions for collective action lacked the strength and automatic nature of those in the North Atlantic Treaty. SEATO never evolved the elaborate integrated command structure of NATO, nor did it provide the basis for an allied military strategy or large-scale commitments of forces by member states. Although Vietnam, Laos, and Cambodia were not directly associated with SEATO, a protocol was written into the treaty extending its protection to include Indochina. The limited effectiveness of SEATO can be seen in the fact that, having played at most a peripheral role in the Vietnam War, it was formally dissolved on June 30, 1977, two years after the fall of South Vietnam.

## THE QUEMOY-MATSU CRISES

Only weeks after the signing of the Geneva accords, tensions rose once again in East Asia. The government of mainland China announced that it intended to extend its control to the island of Taiwan (then called Formosa). On September 3, 1954, Communist Chinese forces began shelling Nationalist Chinese fortifications on Quemoy and Matsu, islands close to the mainland, but then, as now, occupied by Nationalist forces from Taiwan. Quemoy and Little Quemoy are located directly opposite the port of Amoy. Matsu stands athwart the harbor of Foochow. They had been used by the Nationalists as bases for commando raids into communist-controlled territory. Because of their location, only nine miles from the mainland and 100 miles across the Formosa Strait from Taiwan, they were psychologically important to Chiang Kai-shek as potential bridgeheads in any plan to restore his position in China. For the same reasons, the People's Republic of China saw the Nationalist presence on the islands as unacceptable. In any military strike against Taiwan itself, the occupation of the offshore islands would be a necessary preliminary step.

In December 1954 the United States concluded a bilateral defense treaty committing itself to the defense of Taiwan and the nearby Pescadores Islands without explicitly agreeing to defend the offshore islands. In an exchange of letters between Dulles and the Chinese Nationalist ambassador to the United States in early December, the administration sought to protect Taiwan from possible attack and at the same time ensure that Chiang did not use the offshore islands to mount an offensive against the mainland without the consent of the United States. So long as the administration held firm in its resolve not to abandon Quemoy and Matsu, while at the same time extending a formal security guarantee to Taiwan itself, it would be possible both to satisfy the domestic U.S. supporters of Chiang Kai-shek, many of whom were members of the Republican party, and to defuse what seemed to be a potentially dangerous situation in East Asia. Having just been faced with the extension of Communist rule above the 17th parallel in Vietnam, the United States was not prepared to accept the defeat of the Nationalist government on Taiwan.

The escalation of military action from the mainland against the Tachen Islands, located about 200 miles northwest of Taiwan, in January 1955 led the United States to make naval units available to assist in the Nationalist evacuation, while at the same time strengthening Chiang's forces on Quemoy and Matsu. In March 1955, the Eisenhower administration sent the signal that, in the event of a direct Chinese military assault on the offshore islands, the United States might be forced to respond, possibly with atomic weapons, against military targets on the Chinese mainland. Whatever the causal link, these warnings were followed, in April 1955, by a conciliatory statement from China's Foreign Minister Zhou Enlai during a meeting of Third World States in Bandung, Indonesia. This led, in turn, to a positive American response and the opening of discussions in Geneva between U.S. and Chinese diplomats on the issue of the offshore islands.

Such talks were begun in Geneva and transferred to Warsaw in 1958. In themselves, they had no discernible effect on the dispute over the offshore islands, but the United States and China continued to meet at the ambassadorial level through the next decade until, in the early 1970s, the two countries moved toward full normalization of relations. In late August 1958 the Chinese Communists resumed the shelling of Quemoy, announcing once again that they would seek to liberate Taiwan. This action followed a military buildup by Chiang Kai-shek's forces on the offshore islands to 100,000 troops, nearly one-third of the entire Nationalist Army. These carried out commando raids from Quemoy against mainland targets. The Eisenhower administration was not prepared to give Chiang Kai-shek the freedom of action to commit his own forces and, by inference, those of the United States to war with the People's Republic of China. Nor was Eisenhower willing to permit Mainland China to defeat the Nationalist forces on Taiwan or to force the abandonment of the offshore islands. Again, Eisenhower resorted to ambiguous statements of American intent that left open the possibility of various forms of escalation

U.S. military action in fact consisted only of the Seventh Fleet's escorting Nationalist shipping to the three-mile territorial limit just off Mainland China for the resupply of Chiang's forces on Quemoy. In October 1958 the Chinese Communists announced that they would bombard Quemoy only on alternate days. Thus the crisis cooled, with the Eisenhower administration having once again acted effectively to prevent seizure of the offshore islands. While referring to the United States during the crisis as a "paper tiger," the mainland government failed to elicit from the Soviet Union, with which it was closely aligned, the level of support that would have permitted seizure of Quemoy despite American threats of escalation. The apparent unwillingness of Moscow, both in 1954 and 1958, to give more than verbal support—in contrast to the direct military assistance, in the form of the Seventh Fleet, extended by the United States to its ally on Taiwan—must have contributed to the PRC's increasing disillusionment with the Soviet Union in the late 1950s. With the defusing of the Quemoy crisis of 1958, tensions between Peking and Washington eased, although intermittent shelling of Quemoy continued until the full normalization of relations in 1979. Differences with respect to Taiwan were to remain unresolved into the 1980s.

## RELATIONS WITH THE SOVIET UNION: THE "NEW LOOK"

In its policy toward the Soviet Union the Eisenhower administration sought to develop a political-military strategy based on the capability to respond decisively to aggression, while leaving the adversary uncertain as to the precise form the response would take. The "New Look," as the Eisenhower administration's national security policy was termed, was an expression of American nuclear superiority as it existed in the 1950s. While avoiding protracted intervention in conflicts that were deemed to be peripheral to the national interest, the Eisenhower administration served notice on the Soviet Union and China that it would maintain the means for "massive atomic and thermonuclear retaliation," as Dulles put it in an address to the Council on Foreign Relations in January 1954 and an article published in *Foreign Affairs* three months later.

The policy of the United States was not based on the implied threat to engage in such escalation in the case of all threats to its security. Instead, Dulles called for the "flexibility and the facilities which make various responses available," together with the "means for responding effectively on a selective basis when it chooses." The possession of such means was to be combined with an extended system of alliances in which the tangible expression of an American security commitment would serve to deter the Soviet Union and China from taking aggressive action. In this sense, the Eisenhower administration extended to a global scale the idea of containment developed by its predecessor and further revised it by declaring in advance that an adversary must expect a range of retaliatory responses. American strategy, and the capabilities to support it, Eisenhower reasoned, must be based on the assumption that the United States would never start a major war. However, the responses available to the United States after an attack on itself or on an ally should not be limited to the same kind, or level, of force.

The death of Stalin in March 1953 had led Prime Minister Churchill, on May 11, 1953, to call for a summit conference with his successor. At the end of his long political career, Churchill undoubtedly saw such a meeting as a fitting capstone and as an opportunity perhaps to test and even influence the policies of the Soviet Union. Eisenhower, however, took a more cautious view of such a meeting, understandable in light of the acrimony and partisan recrimination that had followed the summit conferences in the final months of World War II—at Yalta in February 1945 and at Potsdam in July 1945. As the essential conditions for such a meeting, the Eisenhower administration demanded tangible evidence of Soviet readiness to engage in constructive negotiations. Integrating the threat of military force and the use of diplomacy, the Eisenhower administration sought to deter Soviet expansion, while embarking on the first of several attempts at a form of détente, or relaxation of international tensions. In fact, the achievement of a stable U.S.–Soviet relationship based on reduced friction and a quest for peace became a central element of the policy of the Eisenhower administration. Although this administration was successful—to an extent far greater than either Truman's before it or Kennedy's after it—in limiting American military involvement overseas, its two terms ended without the achievement of the relationship sought by Eisenhower.

The president had sought to challenge the Soviet Union's post-Stalin leadership to work constructively for disarmament. In response to Premier Georgi Malenkov's "peace offensive" of March 1953, Eisenhower made a speech to the American Society of Newspaper Editors on April 16, 1953. He called for limits on weapons of mass destruction, German reunification on the basis of free elections, the international control of atomic energy, the conclusion of a peace treaty with Austria, and the establishment of an armistice in Korea. Eisenhower asked rhetorically if the Soviet Union would agree to free elections in Eastern Europe. The extent to which the Soviet Union was prepared, by acts rather than simply by rhetoric, to reach agreement on such issues would determine the future course of the U.S.–Soviet relationship and, in particular, the willingness of the administration to participate in a summit conference with Moscow.

### Eisenhower's "Atoms for Peace" Concept

These themes would be reiterated in the months that followed. The president was deeply concerned about the destructive potential of the hydrogen bomb. On November 1, 1952, almost on the eve of his election, the United States had tested its first thermonuclear device, to be followed by the Soviet detonation of a hydrogen bomb less than a year later, in August 1953. The approach to nuclear arms control chosen by the administration was embodied in the "Atoms for Peace" proposal put forward by Eisenhower in a speech to the United Nations

General Assembly on December 8, 1954. Developed with the help of Lewis Strauss, head of the Atomic Energy Commission and Eisenhower's personal adviser on nuclear issues, the idea that evolved from deliberations that included the Special Assistant for National Security Affairs, Robert Cutler, and C. D. Jackson, the president's speechwriter, was a simple one. Both the United States and the Soviet Union, as well as Britain, would donate uranium and other fissionable materials from their stockpiles to an International Atomic Energy Agency to be established under the auspices of the United Nations. Materials contributed would be made available for peaceful uses in such fields as agriculture and medicine, as well as for the generation of electrical power in energy-deficient areas of the world.

Eisenhower saw the Atoms for Peace idea as a first step in the development with the Soviet Union of a program to reduce nuclear armaments and to extend collaboration to other areas of mutual interest. Although it was taken as an exercise in public relations, it evoked widespread praise in the United States and abroad. However, Eisenhower's purpose must be viewed in the broader context of his perception of the need to develop with Moscow a greater level of trust, which in itself would supposedly enhance the prospects for a peaceful world. Such a view represented a simplification of the complex problems facing any American president in relations with the Soviet Union. The Atoms for Peace idea confronted one of the difficult problems of arms control: the asymmetrical capabilities and interests of nations. At the time of the proposal, the United States had far larger stockpiles of fissionable materials to make available to an international authority than the Soviet Union had. For this reason, Moscow could not have been expected to have as much interest as the Eisenhower administration in the Atoms for Peace idea. Accordingly, the Soviet response was negative.

From an American perspective, nevertheless, the proposal was ingenious insofar as it skirted the issue of inspection, which had contributed to the failure of the Baruch Plan in the late 1940s. The Soviet Union had not been prepared to accept international inspection of its territory which would have been necessary to ensure compliance under the Baruch Plan. Under Atoms for Peace, a far more modest concept, such inspection was not considered to be necessary. Although the Atoms for Peace proposal did little for U.S.–Soviet relations, it led to the creation in 1957 of the UN's International Atomic Energy Agency, together with a program for the development of peaceful nuclear technologies.

### The Geneva Summit Conference of 1955

The Soviet Union's decision to end one postwar occupation and to sign the Austrian State Treaty that led the Eisenhower administration to agree to a summit conference. The Austrian State Treaty, signed on May 15, 1955, had been preceded by the formation on May 14, 1955, of the Warsaw Pact. In the West, the longstanding questions of German rearmament and the admission of the Federal Republic of Germany to NATO were both resolved in the same month. Thus, a decade after the end of World War II, the division of Europe into two security blocs took formal shape.

The summit conference that convened in Geneva in July 1955 was the first since World War II and the only four-power meeting of its kind (including Britain and France as well as the United States and the Soviet Union). It was the forerunner of a series of meetings between U.S. and Soviet heads of government, but it produced little in the form of specific results, not even the heightened sense of trust that Eisenhower had envisioned. Soviet Premier Nikolai Bulganin offered as his principal proposal a system of collective security for Europe, which would later be reiterated and repackaged in various forms by successive Soviet leaders. Bulganin called for the dissolution of alliance systems—NATO and the Warsaw Pact—and the withdrawal of all "foreign" forces from Europe. This would have resulted in the removal of American capabilities, since all other states, except Canada, were European, including the Soviet Union. Under the circumstances, the USSR would have emerged as the dominant military power, casting its political shadow across Western Europe. Bulganin saw no prospect for German reunification, another item on the conference's agenda, as long as the Western allies proceeded with the rearmament of the Federal Republic of Germany and its integration into NATO.

The principal proposal put forward by the United States provided for aerial inspection of military installations. "Open Skies," as the concept was called, involved the exchange of detailed information about the location of military installations, agreement on which facilities (such as airfields and military detachments) would be observed, and decisions about the flight patterns and frequencies with which aerial surveillance would be conducted over each country. To the Eisenhower administration, Open Skies represented not only a constructive effort to minimize the possibility of surprise attack, but also an exercise in psychological warfare, in keeping with Washington's effort to place Moscow on the defensive. Aware of the historic Russian penchant for secrecy and Moscow's commitment to the preservation of a closed society, the members of what was called the Quantico Vulnerabilities Panel, headed by Nelson Rockefeller, had developed the Open Skies proposal both as a means of exploiting one such vulnerability and as a genuine attempt to penetrate the Iron Curtain in order to lessen the danger of the surprise use of nuclear weapons by the Soviet Union. The Soviet response, given by Nikita Khrushchev, secretary general of the communist party and soon to emerge as the undisputed Soviet leader, was a rejection of the U.S. proposal as an espionage exercise against the Soviet Union.

Nevertheless, in the years that followed, each side developed sophisticated means for aerial surveillance of the other's territory, first aircraft such as the U-2 shot down over the Soviet Union in 1960, and subsequently satellites that could take and transmit detailed pictures. In restrospect, Open Skies would have codified in treaty form the aerial reconnaissance that was eventually to become a routine part of the intelligence activities of both countries and a necessary component of the strategic arms limitation agreements of the 1970s. With an Open Skies accord, the U-2 incident of 1960 need not have taken place.

The hope that détente would emerge from the Geneva summit—the "spirit of Geneva," it was termed—was quickly dissipated in the harsh realities of the international political environment of the mid-1950s. Events in the Middle East demonstrated clearly the limits of any improved U.S. relationship with the Soviet Union. Within months of the Geneva Conference, which had left unresolved all the major issues that it had addressed, the first large-scale entry of the Soviet Union into the troubled affairs of the Middle East was to add yet further tension to relations between the Soviet Union and the Western allies.

## THE SUEZ CRISIS AND AMERICAN POLICY IN THE MIDDLE EAST

Initially overshadowed by problems facing the United States elsewhere, the Middle East formed an increasingly important focus of American foreign policy in the Eisenhower administration. Like other Third World regions, the Middle East was the scene in the 1950s of surging forces of nationalism, which embodied a large element of anticolonialism directed against Britain and France. Between 1953 and 1958 the United States moved from the position of a peripheral actor, far behind Britain and France, which had historic interests in the region, to the role of leading Western power in the Middle East. This transformation was symbolized, first, by the failure of Britain and France to impose their will on Egypt by military means in the Suez crisis of 1956 (with the United States opposing the use of force) and, second, by the enunciation in 1957 of the Eisenhower Doctrine and the Lebanon crisis of 1958 with the United States now the principal actor, as it would remain in the decades to follow. Successive administrations would find themselves confronted not only with the seemingly intractable problems directly associated with relations between Israel and its neighbors, but also with several other conflicts in the region.

### Iran Leans Toward the United States

In 1946, Iran had been the point of confrontation between the United States and the Soviet Union, with President Truman demanding that Moscow withdraw its forces under the Tripartite Anglo–Soviet–American Agreement of 1942. The strategic importance of Iran had derived from its location as a corridor for the transshipment of lend-lease materials to the Soviet Union for the war effort against Hitler's Germany. But in the early 1950s Iran, rich in oil revenues, posed for the West a far different kind of problem. On May 2, 1951, the Iranian government had nationalized the oil industry, including the huge Anglo-Iranian Oil Company, of which the British government was the principal stockholder. In retaliation, the British shut down the large refinery in Abadan. Oil exports from Iran ceased for two years. Premier Mohammed Mossadeq (who was considered eccentric because he conducted affairs of state in public wearing pajamas) refused to negotiate a settlement of the dispute with Britain, despite the loss of oil revenues that had accounted for as much as 30 percent of Iran's national income and more than half its foreign exchange. Early in 1953 Mossadeq had pushed the constitutional monarch, Mohammed Reza Shah Pahlavi, to announce that he would abdicate. However, the Shah's supporters clashed with his opponents in the streets of Teheran and elsewhere in Iran. There were also disturbing reports that

Mossadeq was seeking economic support from the Soviet Union, with the Communist Tudeh party of Iran taking a more conspicuous role in the rioting that was sweeping the country.

In this situation, the Eisenhower administration supported the Shah. The Iranian military turned against Mossadeq, who was overthrown. With the Shah safely installed in power, the Eisenhower administration extended nearly $85 million in economic aid to Iran in 1953–54. The oil dispute between Britain and Iran was settled. Until the late 1970s, when the power of the Shah once again crumbled, the United States had in Iran what it regarded as a stabilizing force in the Persian Gulf, as well as an important exporter of oil at a time when industrialized economies—those of Western Europe, Japan, and the United States—were consuming larger amounts of oil and, in the case of Western Europe and Japan in the 1950s and the United States after 1970, were increasingly dependent on oil imports from the Persian Gulf region.

### The Suez Crisis of 1956

The second, and far more important, Middle Eastern issue to face the Eisenhower administration resulted from the clash between rising Egyptian nationalism and the residual security interests of Britain, focused in this case on the Suez Canal. Built principally with French capital and opened in 1869, the Suez Canal had represented for Britain the "lifeline of the Empire," a strategically important waterway linking Britain and its imperial possessions in the Asian Pacific. British forces had been deployed on Egyptian territory since 1882 to protect the Suez Canal, which, under the terms of the Constantinople Convention of 1888, was to be kept open at all times to commercial shipping and naval craft.* Under the terms of the Anglo-Egyptian Treaty of 1936, Britain had constructed a huge military base, housing as many as 80,000 troops, along the banks of the canal. General Mohammed Naguib's seizure of power in July 1952 strengthened Egypt's nationalist impetus to regain full control of Egyptian territory and to end the British military presence. In Egypt, as elsewhere, Britain had recognized the need to accommodate a new age of nationalism in the Third World. In 1954, Britain and Egypt reached agreement on a phased withdrawal of British forces to be completed in 1956, with Britain retaining the right to return if regional stability and the security of the canal should be threatened.

The Suez Crisis of 1956, which was to preoccupy the Eisenhower administration for several months and to produce deep fissures in the Atlantic Alliance, must be seen in the broad context of Middle East politics of the time, as well as of the evolving policies of the Soviet Union and the Western powers. Not unlike the Moscow Summit Conference of 1972, the Geneva Conference of 1955 was followed by Soviet actions in the Middle East that, viewed from Washington, presented growing threats to American interests. By the autumn of 1955, it had become evident that the Soviet Union was embarking on initiatives in the Middle

---

*The signatories of the Constantinople Convention were Britain, Austria-Hungary, France, Germany, Italy, the Netherlands, Russia, Spain and Turkey.

East. In October Czechoslovakia and Egypt signed an arms agreement providing for the exchange of Egyptian cotton for weapons. Not only did this deal represent the entry of the Soviet Union, via Czechoslovakia, into the region, but it also marked the beginning of an era of far greater complexity in maintaining an arms balance between Israel and the neighboring Arab states—a balance to which the United States, together with Britain and France, was committed. The immediate result, as on numerous subsequent occasions, was that Israel requested additional arms assistance from the United States. The initial American reaction was to deny Israel such military aid, although the level of arms shipments to Egypt in 1955–56 threatened to upset the balance of power and weighed heavily in Israel's decision to attack Egypt at the time of the Suez War in 1956. It should be pointed out that, in February 1955, Gamal Abdel Nasser, who had succeeded Naguib as Egypt's prime minister in 1954, had approached the United States for arms. The Department of State had attempted to discourage Nasser by requiring payment in cash rather than barter, knowing that Egypt lacked the necessary foreign exchange. Thereupon, Nasser had approached communist sources. The signing of the Czech–Egyptian agreement was followed by a Soviet offer of arms to Israel, which the Israelis quickly rebuffed.

With arrangements for withdrawal from the Suez Canal Zone completed, Britain took steps to complete a defensive alliance with Turkey, Pakistan, Iran, and Iraq, which form a geographical barrier separating the Soviet Union from other lands in the Middle East and Southwest Asia. This Baghdad Pact had the full support of the United States, which itself did not become a full member, although it would be represented on the military committee. Other states of the Middle East, especially Egypt, saw the Baghdad Pact not as a means of halting Soviet penetration, but as a device for preserving the position of Western powers in the region. Nasser unleashed propaganda against remaining pro-Western Arab states, especially Iraq, where the pact had been signed.

At this time, as in later years, the United States confronted the seemingly intractable dilemma of reconciling, on the one hand, its interest in limiting Soviet encroachments in a vital region and, on the other hand, developing relations with smaller states in a region such as the Middle East having far more immediate and more narrowly defined security perceptions and needs involving conflicts with each other. Moreover, in the mid-1950s American policy-makers had problems that stemmed from the hostility toward Western European allies, especially Britain and perhaps to a lesser extent France, felt by Nasser and other anticolonial nationalist leaders. In supplanting Britain, which in any event no longer possessed the economic or military means to underwrite traditional interests, the United States might help to thwart Soviet penetration of the Middle East by virtue of its own superior capabilities, while simultaneously moderating a virulent pan-Arab nationalism, since the United States had no imperial legacy in the Middle East. Accordingly, the United States placed some distance between its Middle East policies and Britain's. This gap became evident in the formation of the Baghdad Pact, in U.S. arms shipments to Israel, and, to an even greater extent, in the major difference between Anglo–French policy and the Eisenhower administration's stance at the time of the Suez crisis.

Nasser's accession to power had brought the Middle East a leader determined, it seemed, to play off the United States and the Soviet Union against each other, a situation that further complicated the emerging Middle East policies of the Eisenhower administration. Having just seen the Soviet Union, through its Czechoslovakian surrogate, gain entry into the sensitive and dangerous Middle East situation, the United States attempted in late 1955 to find another basis for restricting the expansion of Moscow's involvement. Nasser had as a major goal the building of the Aswan High Dam, which would harness the Nile River and irrigate lands desperately needed to increase Egypt's agricultural production for its rapidly increasing population. The Aswan project was also designed to furnish hydroelectric power for a country which at that time had no known oil resources. The Aswan High Dam could be built only with technical and financial help from abroad. Initially, the Eisenhower administration saw the Aswan High Dam as a means for engagement extending beyond simply the maintenance of an arms balance in the region.

In December 1955, Undersecretary of State Herbert Hoover, Jr., with the representatives of Britain and the World Bank, began discussions with Egypt about the project. Britain and the United States offered to underwrite the foreign-exchange costs of constructing the dam. Instead of accepting, Nasser announced that he was considering a Soviet offer of aid to build the dam. By mid-1956, the Eisenhower administration had concluded that Nasser's efforts to engage the Soviet Union in the project, apparently to extract further concessions from the United States, had made American participation a proposition of dubious value and one that, in any event, was unlikely to obtain the necessary congressional or popular support. Therefore, on July 19, 1956, Dulles informed Egypt's ambassador that the Anglo–American offer was being withdrawn.

Nasser's response was to make a long public denunciation of the United States and to nationalize the Suez Canal Company on July 26. Its revenues and assets would enable Egypt to finance the Aswan Dam. Although Nasser offered compensation for the seized property, Britain and France were outraged; Britain placed its forces in the Mediterranean on alert. The governments of Anthony Eden and Guy Mollet were ready to employ military means against Egypt but the Eisenhower administration, though it agreed that the Suez Canal had to be kept open to international shipping, refused to condone force. As long as Nasser did not close the canal, Eisenhower reasoned, military action should not be used against Egypt. The Eisenhower administration's objective, keeping the canal open, would be defeated by a resort to arms. British and French policy, however, extended beyond that of the United States to include the overthrow of Nasser, which it was felt could be accomplished only by the use of force.

In the weeks that followed the nationalization announcement, a number of steps were taken, including the formation of a Middle East Emergency Committee, composed of representatives of governments and the oil companies, to plan for contingencies that might arise from the interruption of oil supplies, and the convening in London in August of a Twenty-Four Nation Conference, where Dulles proposed an international authority to operate the canal, a proposal quickly rejected by Nasser. This abortive U.S. effort at compromise was followed by another proposal put forward by Dulles for a Suez Canal Users Association, which received an equally negative reaction from Cairo.

By October 1956, the limits of American support had become apparent to Britain and France, who entered into a secret agreement with Israel to attack Egypt. For Israel, a military strike across the Gaza Strip into the Sinai Peninsula would eliminate terrorists who had conducted raids across the border into Israeli territory. An Israeli military operation against Sharm el-Sheikh, at the entrance to the Gulf of Aqaba, would give Israel access to the Indian Ocean, important because Israel, since its founding, had been denied use of the Suez Canal. Because the Suez Canal Company had helped to enforce the Egyptian ban on Israel's use of the Suez Canal, its nationalization evoked little sympathy in Israel for Britain and France. Instead, Israel's decision to attack Egypt was related both to the feared consequences of the Soviet–Egyptian arms buildup and to the need to stop terrorist attacks from the Gaza Strip into Israel. On October 29, 1956, Israel launched its attack against Egypt. The next day Britain and France gave Egypt and Israel 12 hours to withdraw to a point ten miles from the Suez Canal. This ultimatum was designed to permit Anglo–French occupation in accordance with a secret agreement that Britain and France had concluded with Israel just before the attack on Egypt. The United States had not been consulted about this accord. In fact, the Eisenhower administration had placed before the UN Security Council a resolution requesting all members of the United Nations to refrain from the use of force in the Middle East, which both Britain and France had vetoed, together with a Soviet resolution requesting Israel to withdraw from Egyptian territory. As Israeli forces raced across the Sinai toward the Suez Canal, British aircraft launched bombing raids against Cairo and other Egyptian targets. By November 4, Israel had occupied the Sinai. Landings of British and French combat units and military action continued until November 7, the day after the presidential election in the United States. Britain and France had deployed a total of 22,000 troops in Egypt by the time of the cease-fire. Nevertheless, the Suez Canal had been blocked by the Egyptian sinking of ships after hostilities began. In addition, an oil pipeline running from Iraq had been sabotaged.

With a new electoral mandate, the Eisenhower administration, in keeping with its basic approach of separating its Middle East policy from that of its major Western European allies, achieved a cease-fire and rebuffed a proposal by the Soviet Union for joint U.S.–Soviet military intervention in Egypt. Having seized the area along the Suez Canal but failed to keep it open, British and French forces were withdrawn before the end of December 1956. The Eisenhower administration put into operation a plan to supply oil to Britain and France, but only after London and Paris had agreed to an unconditional withdrawal from Egyptian territory. The gap between U.S. and allied policies greatly strained NATO.

Although Israel had withdrawn from the Sinai, its forces remained in possession of the Gaza Strip, from which it refused to pull back without strong guarantees against future commando raids and other attacks launched from that territory. Furthermore, Israel sought guaranteed freedom of passage through the Gulf of Aqaba as the price for withdrawing forces from Sharm el-Sheikh. The solution favored by the United States was the formation of a United Nations force, or what became the United Nations Emergency Force (UNEF), to patrol a demilitarized Gaza Strip and a commitment by the United States to ensure international access, including passage for Israel, through the Gulf of Aqaba. The administration soon found itself in diplomatic confrontation with Israel, which initially refused to exchange territory won in combat as a security perimeter in return for vague international guarantees. Although from Israel's perspective, as a small state surrounded by hostile neighbors, territorial gain provided an additional zone for security, it appeared to the Eisenhower administration to run counter to another U.S. interest: preventing the drift of Arab states toward alignment with the Soviet Union. Therefore, in early 1957, the United States pressured Israel to accept the American proposal for a United Nations presence and international guarantees in the zone of recent conflict. Nasser had made Israeli withdrawal from the remaining territory occupied in the Suez War the condition for completing the work of raising the ships that had been sunk in the canal.

The failure of Britain and France at Suez not only symbolized their military decline and the waning of their once commanding position in the Middle East but also illustrated the growing status of the United States as a global power. Unlike its Western European allies, the United States had no major historic interests in the Middle East. The formation of the state of Israel in May 1948, with the strong support of the Truman administration, had given the United States an important interest and an enduring political commitment in the region. The Soviet Union's entry as a major actor in the Middle East in 1955 had given the United States yet another set of interests and problems. Support for Israel had to be weighed against the exigencies of relations with Arab factions ranging from conservative oil-producing sheikdoms to the pan-Arab and other nationalist movements that were beginning to sweep the region. These were the circumstances that led to the formation of the Eisenhower Doctrine, which represented an effort to bring greater stability to the Middle East in the late 1950s.

## The Eisenhower Doctrine

The immediate problem facing the United States at the time of the Suez War was to prevent the Soviet Union from exploiting the conflict to enhance its influence in the region. In the Suez crisis the United States had sought to loosen Nasser's links with the Soviet Union by opposing Anglo–French policy. Nasser's behavior in the months following the Suez crisis provided no evidence that the attempt had succeeded. Nasser remained committed to the overthrow of remaining pro-Western governments in the Middle East, while continuing to receive arms from the Soviet Union, with which Egypt maintained close relations. The Eisenhower Doctrine was based on a two-point request to Congress on January 5, 1957. The administration called, first, for military aid and $200 million in economic assistance to help preserve the independence of countries in the region; and, second, for authorization to use American military power in the event that the Soviet Union or its clients posed a direct threat of aggression to any country of the Middle East. Congress passed a joint resolution embodying the Eisenhower Doctrine.

The doctrine's significance lay in the fact that, for the first time, the United States identified the Middle East as vital to its national security. States that were the object of armed aggression or internal subversion could expect to receive assistance from the United States if they requested it. It was not Nasser himself, but the Soviet Union, reasoned the Eisenhower administration, that could pose a threat to American interests in the Middle East. The Suez crisis had come about for a variety of reasons, including Nasser's increasing boldness as he contemplated the possibilities of more Soviet arms assistance, Moscow's help in building the Aswan High Dam, and the strengthening of relations with other Arab states in opposition to the residual influence of Britain and France, as well as of the United States. Nasser's objective, it seems in retrospect, was to assert Egypt's independence of all foreign influence, even if he had to resort to Soviet help in the process. Such were the complex conditions in which Eisenhower, and the doctrine that bore his name, had to operate in the years following the Suez crisis.

The first test of the Eisenhower Doctrine came in Jordan, where, in the spring of 1957, King Hussein faced a threat to his rule. In opposition to cabinet changes made by Hussein, including the dismissal of the pro-Soviet, pro-Nasser premier, Nasser had launched a propaganda campaign against the king. There was a general strike, together with rioting, that seemed but a prelude to the ouster of Hussein. Faced with such domestic disorder, Hussein imposed martial law and formed a new government. With Jordan having abrogated its agreement with Britain, which had provided a direct subsidy, the United States was called upon to help prevent the fall of the Hashemite monarchy, which, it was feared, would have led surrounding states to seize territory with the likelihood of renewed conflict in the Middle East. The Eisenhower administration gave Jordan an emergency grant totalling $10 million and shifted the Sixth Fleet to the eastern Mediterranean as a demonstration of American commitment to the preservation of stability in Jordan. By the end of April 1957, this crisis had passed and, with it, the Eisenhower Doctrine seemed to have passed its first test as the United States moved to prevent the emergence of a power vacuum resulting from the sharp reduction in the British presence and influence in Jordan.

Nasser's ambitions extended beyond Jordan to neighboring countries. In February 1958 Egypt formed a union with Syria called the United Arab Republic. Having outlawed the Communist party in Egypt, Nasser moved to dissolve Syrian political parties, including the Communist party. Appointments to the Syrian government were to be controlled from Egypt. Elsewhere, Egypt made a major effort to destabilize the Iraqi government until the pro-Western Baghdad government was overthrown and replaced by a left-leaning regime in July 1958. Syria's neighbor Lebanon seemed to offer inviting prospects for Nasser because of its internal conflict between Muslims forming a close relationship with the United Arab Republic and Christians supporting the preservation of Lebanon's independence and a pro-Western political orientation.

At the end of World War II Lebanon had been granted independence by France. The new state's political system divided power between the two roughly equal groups in the population: the Maronite Christians and the Sunni Moslems.

Under such a formula, the Christians held the presidency and foreign ministry, while the Moslems controlled the offices of prime minister and speaker. Lebanon's president, Camille Chamoun, had supported the Eisenhower Doctrine, although for the most part Lebanese foreign policy since independence had been neutralist. By 1957, Lebanon had become the target of a barrage of propaganda from Radio Cairo, urging the Muslim population of Lebanon to overthrow Chamoun, while arms flowed across the Syrian frontier to Nasser's supporters. Nasser's objective was not only the ouster of Chamoun but also the expansion of the United Arab Republic to include Lebanon. The immediate catalyst for the events leading to the Lebanon crisis of July 1958 and for the second test of the Eisenhower Doctrine was Chamoun's announcement in April 1958 that he would seek a second eight-year term as president, a step that would require an amendment to the constitution. The Eisenhower administration regarded Chamoun's decision as a political mistake, for it led to an outbreak of violence between rival political factions. It seemed to the United States that an escalating civil war in Lebanon would provide fertile ground for exploitation, by Nasser and the Soviet Union. However, the internal strife had subsided by June, with the Lebanese army helping to bring the situation under control. The United Nations sent a military investigation team to Lebanon in response to the Lebanese government's complaint to the Security Council that Egypt and Syria had been shipping arms into the country. By early July 1958, Chamoun had avowed that he would leave office when his present term expired.

The Lebanon crisis was rekindled by a coup in Iraq on July 14, 1958, which overthrew the monarchy, and by the murder of its pro-Western leaders, including King Faisal and Prime Minister Nuri al-Said. For the United States the significance of this event was profound, because Iraq had been regarded as the central element in the northern-tier alliance. The fall of the pro-Western Iraqi government seemed to be the prelude to further violence, especially in Jordan and Lebanon, with U.S. officials having fresh in their minds the recent Egyptian efforts toward political destabilization in both countries. Jordan had joined Iraq in what was called the Arab Union in February 1958, just after the formation of the United Arab Republic. It appeared that the forces that had overthrown the Iraqi government might move quickly against King Hussein. President Chamoun requested that the United States and Britain send military forces to Lebanon within 48 hours. In keeping with the Eisenhower Doctrine, the United States dispatched units of the Sixth Fleet eastward in the Mediterranean, and U.S. forces landed on the beaches of Lebanon on July 15, 1958. They were followed by British forces sent to Jordan at the request of Hussein, with airlift provided by the United States. The United States deployed just under 15,000 troops in Lebanon, all of whom were withdrawn by October 25, 1958. Eisenhower saw the intervention as a demonstration of resolve to Arab leaders and the Soviet Union and, specifically, as a deterrent to the escalation of violence that it seemed would follow the overthrow of the Iraqi government. The intervention also demonstrated to Arab states the limits of Soviet power, for Moscow was reduced to verbal condemnation of the action taken by the United States and Britain after having issued the hollow threat to send "volunteers" to the Middle East.

   Although he had eliminated local Communist parties within both Egypt and Syria because they would have posed a threat to his own rule, Nasser sought to use the Soviet Union, including the promise of support from Moscow, to augment his own position. In 1956 it was the United States, not the Soviet Union, that had saved Nasser. In 1958 it was again the United States that played the leading role as outside power. In both instances, although Nasser perhaps did not fully realize the fact, the United States had helped to shape the course of events in the region. The policy of the Eisenhower administration in 1956 had been based on the presumed need to work with, and thus modify, in ways compatible with U.S. interests, the emerging Arab nationalism that Nasser represented. In 1956 the principal instrument in support of this policy had been diplomacy. In 1958, the United States chose the limited, discrete application of force to restrain what appeared to be a rampant nationalism that threatened to engulf the Arab states in an anti-Western frenzy. In 1956 Britain and France had intervened militarily in Egypt against Nasser and, in doing so, had incurred the opposition of the United States. Having replaced its Western European allies as the principal external guarantor of stability in the Middle East, the United States engaged in a more limited use of military capabilities at the request of a state threatened by indigenous forces supplied and encouraged from Nasser's Egypt. Although the Eisenhower administration's view of Nasser had altered as his attacks against groups supported by the United States intensified, the framework within which force was committed in 1958 differed fundamentally from the circumstances in which the Eisenhower administration had helped to thwart the Anglo-French Suez intervention of 1956.

## THE HUNGARIAN CRISIS

The inherent limits of the American concept of liberation became clear as the Hungarian crisis unfolded in 1956. As the British–French–Israeli invasion of Egypt was being mounted, the Soviet Union faced a threat to the continuation of the Hungarian regime that had been imposed in the wake of the Red Army's advance across Central Europe as World War II drew to an end. In Hungary there were manifestations of growing opposition to Soviet domination in the years following Stalin's death. In June 1953 the Soviet Union had dealt with demonstrations against its rule in East Germany by quickly crushing opposition with the use of military power, including tanks deployed in city streets. In Poland a dispute erupted with Moscow over the composition of the Communist regime. In the first years of Communist rule after World War II, the secretary general of the Polish Communist party had been Wladyslaw Gomulka, who had also held the post of vice premier in the Polish government. Although he had been ousted from his official positions and imprisoned for alleged pro-Tito sympathies in 1949, Gomulka had been "rehabilitated" after Stalin's death and invited back into the government in April 1956 in an effort to broaden domestic support for the Polish Communist party. Gomulka demanded that the Russian Marshal Konstantin Rokossovsky, who had been Poland's minister of defense since 1949, be removed from office. In addition, Gomulka demanded membership for himself in the

Party Secretariat. In the last two weeks of October 1956, there was a showdown between Poland and the Soviet Union. Nikita Khrushchev, accompanied by other Soviet officials, descended upon Warsaw in an abortive effort to pressure the Polish Communist party into retaining Rokossovsky as minister of defense. Anti-Soviet demonstrations spread to Polish cities, with marchers demanding the withdrawal of Soviet forces and a relationship of equality, not subordination, between Poland and the Soviet Union. Gomulka became first secretary of the party's Politburo, a post that he was to hold until 1970, and Rokossovsky was removed.

What differentiated the Hungarian crisis from these events in Poland was its threat to the basis, or legitimacy, of Communist rule. In Poland the immediate issue had been the composition of the government and, in the case of Rokossovsky, the degree of direct and open control to be exercised from Moscow. The apparent success of Poland in modifying its relationship with the Soviet Union inspired the demonstrations that broke out in Hungary in late October 1956. Hungarian students, workers, and intellectuals called for the withdrawal of Soviet troops and the return to power of Imre Nagy, who had been premier in the first years of the post-Stalin period from 1953 until 1955, when he was replaced by two Stalinists. Mátyas Rákosi and Ernö Gerö. On October 24 Soviet troops entered Budapest with artillery and armored vehicles to crush the "counterrevolutionary" forces. Soviet military units opened fire on demonstrators, with the result that tensions and demonstrations increased dramatically, with Hungarian military units joining in action against the Soviet forces.

As large parts of Hungary fell under the control of anti-Soviet forces, Nagy became premier and took steps to include in his government the noncommunist leaders who had held power just after World War II, before the Communist party had consolidated its power in Poland. Nagy then announced that Hungary was renouncing the Warsaw Pact in favor of a foreign policy based on neutrality, with an appeal to the United Nations to support this new status. Having first promised the Hungarian government that its forces would be withdrawn, the Soviet Union sent as many as 200,000 troops into Budapest to overthrow the Nagy government. Hungary was quickly reoccupied by Soviet forces, and Nagy was taken into custody, tried secretly, and summarily executed. Thousands of Hungarians were reported killed, but a UN investigating group was denied entry.

The beginning of the Soviet assault, on November 4, 1956, coincided with the Suez military operation. The outcome of the two crises that simultaneously confronted the Eisenhower administration contrasted sharply. The Soviet Union succeeded in its effort to prevent the defection of Hungary from the Warsaw Pact, while Moscow acted equally decisively to restore the position of the Communist party as the only major political force in Hungary. Janos Kadar, placed in power in 1956, remained as premier of Hungary into the 1980s. At no time during the Hungarian crisis was the United States prepared to extend more than resolutions and humanitarian aid to the opponents of Soviet rule in Hungary. Nothing could have demonstrated more clearly the limits of the liberation concept in American foreign policy.

## RELATIONS WITH WESTERN EUROPE: NATO
## AND EUROPEAN INTEGRATION

In the 1950s the United States developed unprecedented interests and commitments as a global power. The priority that the United States accorded the Middle East during the Suez crisis—even above relations with Britain as America's closest ally and France as its oldest ally—illustrated the growing importance of regions outside the North Atlantic area in U.S. foreign policy. Although the Eisenhower administration extended American alliance commitments to other countries and regions, its policies toward Western Europe were constructed on the foundations established by its predecessor. It could hardly have been otherwise, for Eisenhower, as chief of staff of the U.S. Army between 1945 and 1948 and as supreme Allied commander in Europe between 1950 and 1952, had participated in the execution, if not the formulation, of policies on which rested the European–American relationship of the early 1950s. When the Eisenhower administration came to office, the Federal Republic of Germany was more than three years old. Decisions to rearm West Germany in a proposed European Defense Community, to strengthen the conventional military capabilities of NATO after the outbreak of the Korean conflict, and to follow up the Marshall Plan for postwar economic recovery with European integration, had all been made before the Eisenhower administration took office.

### The European Defense Community

By 1953 the Atlantic Alliance had been strengthened by the formation of the integrated command structure of which Eisenhower had been the first supreme Allied commander. The first of the European Communities to be formed in the 1950s, the European Coal and Steel Community, had been founded in 1952. Plans had been made for the creation of a European Defense Community. Like the ECSC, the EDC was envisioned as a means of harnessing the resources of Germany and preventing a resurgence of the destructive nationalism that had resulted in the devastation from which Western Europe had only recently recovered. On May 26, 1952—less than a year before the beginning of the Eisenhower administration—the United States, Britain, France, and the Federal Republic of Germany had signed the Bonn Convention, which restored Germany's sovereignty. The Bonn Convention would take effect upon the ratification of the Treaty of Paris by all of its signatories. The Treaty of Paris, creating the European Defense Community, had been signed the day after the Bonn Convention. It was at this point that Eisenhower had resigned his command to return to the United States to become a presidential candidate. Thus his administration came to office fully committed to the principal elements of an Atlantic Alliance policy for defense and containment.

The immediate problem that faced the administration, and that would ultimately lead to the failure of the EDC, was the reluctance of France to accept German rearmament. The French harbored vivid memories of three German invasions (in 1870, 1914, and 1940) which had cost so much in blood, treasure, and national pride. French opposition to the EDC was reinforced by the view that, with the death of Stalin, the prospects for a relaxation in tensions with the Soviet Union should be explored before German rearmament was undertaken. Shortly after his inauguration, Eisenhower had sent Dulles and Harold Stassen to Europe for discussions on the EDC, European unity, and German rearmament. At times Eisenhower suspected that France, aware of the strong American commitment to its success, would use the EDC to bargain for U.S. support in the Indochina War. With the fall of Dien Bien Phu and the decision of the Mendès-France government to seek an immediate withdrawal of remaining French forces by July 20, 1954, whatever hopes France might have had for linkage between the two issues were dashed.

France was not the only reluctant European power. Great Britain, too, was not prepared to join the EDC, even though Churchill himself had proposed an integrated (Continental) European army in 1949. If Britain had agreed to join as a full member, it would have become more difficult for France to remain outside. Without Britain, France argued, its armed forces would be merged with those of a rearmed Germany. Once again, France might find itself the weaker of the two major Western European Continental powers. In an effort to assuage French sensitivities, Britain signed an association agreement with the EDC members on April 13, 1954, pledging to maintain forces on the Continent on a permanent basis. The United States agreed to keep ground forces in Europe, and specifically on the NATO Central Front in Germany, if the EDC treaty was ratified. On June 17 Mendès-France announced in his first speech as premier that he would seek amendments in the treaty before consenting to ratification.

In the summer of 1954, moreover, the Soviet Union embarked on a propaganda campaign designed to forestall ratification of the EDC treaty. On August 4, the Soviet Union called for a meeting with the foreign ministers of Britain, France, and the United States on European security issues. Several days later, the Soviet government announced its willingness to take part in a conference on an Austrian peace treaty, perhaps to head off the EDC and German rearmament.

The EDC ceased to have relevance for the Austrian peace treaty, however, when its prospects suffered a fatal setback in the French National Assembly on August 30, 1954. With this rejection France, which had originated the Pleven Plan for the EDC, eliminated any practical possibility that the integrative impetus established in the Coal and Steel Community could be extended to the defense sector. The creation of a supranational authority for defense would have created the need, in turn, for the integration of sectors directly related to defense, such as foreign policy. Precisely because the implications of defense integration would have touched issues central to the concept of the sovereignty of the nation-state, the EDC was an idea for which Western Europe, even at the high point of support for integration in the 1950s, was not ready. Instead, the development of supranational institutions was to be confined to the economic sector. Henceforth, whatever political unity and defense collaboration would be achieved among Western European states would have the nation as its principal unit.

**The Western European Union**

Still committed to finding an appropriate framework for German rearmament and NATO membership, the Eisenhower administration accepted a British initiative led by Foreign Secretary Anthony Eden. This provided for the admission of Germany to the Brussels Treaty Organization, which had been created in 1948 as a Western European defensive alliance that had been eclipsed by the formation of NATO in 1949, but which was viewed by Britain as the forerunner of an Atlantic Alliance that would include the United States. Now the Western European Union (WEU), as the British initiative was called, was assigned another role. Germany, with Italy, would join the Brussels Treaty Organization, which would establish the levels of Continental European contributions to NATO. The Federal Republic of Germany would be prohibited from manufacturing atomic, biological, or chemical weapons. Germany would join NATO and contribute twelve divisions to the Central Front. By international agreement, there would be no independent German military capability. This formula furnished the basis for German rearmament and for admission of the Federal Republic to the Atlantic Alliance. NATO gained both the territory and the forces that were essential to any concept of "forward defense" in Europe. The Federal Republic of Germany achieved what had been a fundamental objective of Chancellor Konrad Adenauer: the restoration of sovereignty, via the formal end of occupation a decade after the defeat of Hitler's Third Reich, together with the integration of the Federal Republic of Germany as a democracy into a Western European community of nations and NATO. Viewed from the vantage point of the defeat and devastation of 1945, this was a remarkable achievement indeed both for Adenauer and for the allies of the Federal Republic in the Atlantic Alliance.

**The Creation of the European Economic Community**

The failure of the EDC led not only to the refurbishing of the Brussels Treaty Organization as the basis for a German contribution to the collective defense of the West, but also to a decision to try to integrate Western Europe in the economic sector, where the prospects seemed more promising than in defense. Less than a year after the defeat of the EDC treaty, the same six continental European states held a meeting in May 1955 in Messina, Sicily, at which they agreed to draft a treaty for the creation of a customs union. From this conference came the Rome Treaty, signed on March 25, 1957, in which Belgium, the Federal Republic of Germany, France, Italy, Luxembourg, and the Netherlands agreed to eliminate, over a 12 to 15-year period, internal barriers to trade among themselves and to establish a common external tariff around the European Economic Community in place of the differing national tariffs of its member states. The founders of the EEC foresaw the development of common policies on the movement of labor, the eventual adoption of a common monetary and fiscal policy, including interest rates and taxation, and even a common currency. The free flow of trade within the "Common Market" would include agricultural products as well as industrial goods and services. As the leading agricultural producer of the EEC, France would gain access to what previously had been the nationally protected farming sectors of other member states. In return, the Federal Republic of Germany, the largest industrial state of the Community, would obtain in effect a "domestic" market that extended throughout the European Community. While increasing agricultural trade by eliminating discriminatory subsidies and price supports among its members, the Community would erect barriers against imports of competitive farm products from outside countries, a policy that would later give rise to friction with the United States because of the large American agricultural-export markets in Western Europe.

The Suez crisis had occurred between the decision to draft the Rome Treaty and its signing, with the obvious implication that, by themselves, individual Western European states could not act independently of the United States even in what they regarded, rightly or wrongly, to be an issue of vital national importance. The inference to be drawn was, first, that henceforth Western European military capabilities would be designed almost exclusively for the protection of interests in Europe and that, as circumstances permitted or necessitated, more distant commitments would be reduced or abandoned. The view gained increasing currency in Western Europe that only an economic unit larger than the existing nation-state could compete successfully with the United States, which enjoyed the advantages of a huge domestic market for its goods and services. To be sure, this perspective was not as widely shared in Britain in the 1950s as it was within the Continental Six founding members of the European Community. Even in Britain, which, despite the failure at Suez, clung to the idea of global-power status, the view emerged that increasing links should be forged with the dynamic economies of its Continental Western European neighbors. Thus the formation of the European Economic Community, which came into existence on January 1, 1958, coincided with the long period of economic growth and broadening prosperity experienced by Western Europe beginning in the early 1950s with the completion of postwar recovery. For the United States, the formation of the European Community seemed the fulfillment, at least in part, of the belief long expressed on this side of the Atlantic that Western Europe must unite in order to transcend the conditions that had produced past conflict. Therefore, the United States welcomed the progress toward unity represented by the creation of the EEC, which provided yet another framework for linking the Federal Republic of Germany as fully as possible with its European neighbors to the west.

### France's Influence on the Atlantic Alliance

The European Community not only represented the fulfillment of a vision long held by West German Chancellor Konrad Adenauer but also was compatible with the idea of a unified Western European bloc of nation-states—*Europe des patries* (Europe of Nations)—that was a central element of Charles de Gaulle's grand design. It was only six months after the initiation of the EEC that de Gaulle had returned to power as the leader of the newly formed Fifth Republic in France. He had been called back to office by a revolt of military officers and other proponents of the preservation of French rule in Algeria. Algeria had been settled after 1830 by French *colons* and had legally been a *département* of France since 1871. It was predominantly Muslim in population, and its National Liberation Front ultimately wrested independence from France. After the Algerian conflict, de Gaulle sought, first and foremost, to reassert for France a position of independence by restoring internal political cohesion and national pride. The weak parliamentary system of the Fourth Republic was replaced with a government based on a strong presidency, occupied by de Gaulle himself.

De Gaulle's priorities would be the strengthening of the French economy, which had already made great strides since World War II, and the modernization of France's military capabilities, with heavy emphasis on the construction of a national nuclear force. The political rationale for the French nuclear *force de dissuasion* (deterrent force) lay in the need, as de Gaulle saw it, for France to achieve a position of equality with Britain in the Atlantic Alliance. Since his World War II experience as the leader of Free France, with his headquarters in London after the Nazi occupation of his country, De Gaulle had felt the humiliation that flowed from the subordination of the weakened French state to the Anglo–American relationship—the close wartime links between Churchill and Roosevelt. By 1958, not only had France recovered economically from the ravages of war, but its economy had moved forward to unprecedented levels of industrialization and technological sophistication. France was developing an infrastructure that would eventually be able to sustain the development of thermonuclear weapons and the aircraft and submarines from which to launch them. France's future, de Gaulle reasoned, lay not in the perpetuation of the debilitating and divisive colonial policies of the past, but in the extrication of France from outposts such as Algeria. This task he undertook, while pressing first for the revision of France's status within the Atlantic Alliance and later, in the 1960s, for France's removal from the integrated command structure formed as a Western response to the Korean War in 1950–51. In de Gaulle's view, the military threat of a massive Soviet land attack that had compelled the creation of an integrated command structure in the early years of the alliance had diminished by the late 1950s. In the 1950s the principal threats to Western interests emanated from regions outside Europe. Therefore, de Gaulle proposed in a letter to Eisenhower in 1958, France, Britain, and the United States should form, within the Atlantic Alliance, a directorate to coordinate their policies in all parts of the world. This idea de Gaulle repeated to Eisenhower during the latter's visit to France in 1959. Eisenhower reacted as he had in earlier diplomatic dealings with Britain in the period leading up to the Suez crisis. He believed that such a tripartite agreement would be resented by Third World states whom the United States sought to influence and might even have divisive effects on the Atlantic Alliance, whose other members would be excluded. Eisenhower's rejection killed the directorate idea.

In the years ahead French and American policies on other important issues would diverge. A generation after de Gaulle's proposal, when the coordination of Western policies would be proposed again, the French position would echo that espoused by Eisenhower. France would seek to avoid too close an identification with American policy, a position not dissimilar to that taken when Eisenhower placed distance between the Third World policies of his administration and those of Western European allies, principally Britain, in regions such as the Middle East.

The differences between France and the United States—in fact, between France and NATO—that would dominate the politics of the Atlantic Alliance in the 1960s began to emerge in the last years of the Eisenhower administration, just after de Gaulle's return to power. In keeping with his deeply held views about national independence, de Gaulle asserted that each nation in the alliance must take as full responsibility as possible for its own defense. Such a need was especially compelling in an era of nuclear weapons. By 1958, the global strategic environment had been changed by the new Soviet capability to strike targets in the United States. As American cities became vulnerable to nuclear attack, de Gaulle reasoned, it would be increasingly difficult, perhaps even impossible, for an American president to invoke a credible threat to use nuclear weapons against the Soviet Union in response to any attack by Moscow on Western Europe. As long as it was the only possessor of nuclear weapons, the United States could threaten with impunity to retaliate against Soviet aggression. In the changed circumstances of the late 1950s, however, would the United States be prepared to risk the destruction of New York in defense of Paris? As long as the nation-state continued to be the only entity responsible for the defense of its citizens from outside attack, logic dictated that the nation-state must possess adequate means for its defense. To France, this meant the acquisition of nuclear weapons. So broadly based became the national consensus in support of an independent nuclear force in France—initiated in the Fourth Republic under the Socialist Premier Guy Mollet—that it not only survived de Gaulle and his immediate successors but extended to the socialist Mitterrand presidency in the 1980s as well.

To delegate the defense of the nation to a multinational organization—to inform the citizens of France that NATO rather than France itself was responsible for their defense—would drain the national morale and will for effective defense. To make tangible his commitment to this view, de Gaulle acted in 1959 to remove the French fleet from the authority in wartime of the Supreme Allied Commander, Europe (SACEUR), although he declared that the French fleet, under France's national command, would cooperate with NATO in the event of war. He also forbade the stationing of Allied nuclear weapons on French territory unless France had veto power over their use. Clearly, de Gaulle saw nuclear weapons as having a central place in the French military establishment of the future, but only if they were owned, commanded, and controlled by France, rather than by a multinational organization or by another power such as the United States.

In practice, Eisenhower too had acknowledged the importance of nuclear weapons in his New Look strategy. De Gaulle, in effect, was paying him a compliment by emulating him. As the Algerian War came to an end, de Gaulle reduced the size of the French conventional military force in order to substitute firepower for manpower. French defense spending as a percentage of GNP could decline as a more compact military establishment based on nuclear weapons took the place of the conventional armies of the past. Similar changes had been made in the structure of Britain's defense capabilities after the Suez crisis. Britain demobilized conventional forces, ended conscription, and placed increased emphasis on a national nuclear force—in this case, however, to be built with technologies acquired in part from the United States and to be targeted in conjunction with the American Strategic Air Command.

With the Eisenhower administration's New Look in defense policy, as well as the burgeoning labor-short economies of NATO members as catalysts, the Atlantic Alliance adapted its forces in the mid-1950s to take account of perceived changes in the security environment. If the threat of a massive Soviet invasion with land forces no longer seemed to present a clear danger, the fact remained that the Soviet Union was acquiring atomic weapons that could be launched against Western Europe and, to a much lesser extent at that time, against the United States itself. NATO had built a conventional-force capability in Europe in the 1950s, augmented by the admission of the Federal Republic of Germany to NATO and German rearmament to the authorized level of 500,000 troops assigned to the alliance. Nevertheless, a conventional-force posture on the NATO Central Front was still seen as a "trip wire," designed to halt invading armies temporarily before all of Western Europe, and initially the Federal Republic, could be overrun and occupied. The principal deterrent to invasion was the American nuclear force. A Soviet–Warsaw Pact attack would be met with American nuclear retaliation, unless it could be halted immediately by the forces-in-being on the NATO Central Front.

The Western response to the launching by the Soviet Union of its Sputnik earth-orbiting satellite in October 1957, together with other mounting evidence of the development of Soviet nuclear capabilities, was to establish stocks of nuclear warheads in Europe and to agree, at the first NATO summit conference in December 1957, to provide sea-based intermediate-range ballistic missiles to SACEUR. The NATO leaders also agreed that their countries' foreign ministers would meet with Soviet representatives to discuss disarmament. For NATO in the late 1950s, the deployment of nuclear weapons in Western Europe was seen as a means of strengthening deterrence. The presence of nuclear weapons close to a potential battle zone might have a greater deterrent effect than would the threat of a U.S. nuclear response to a Soviet attack on one or more members of NATO. Thus the means for nuclear deterrence in the Atlantic Alliance, in the Eisenhower administration, extended from battlefield capabilities to the U.S. Strategic Air Command.

## KHRUSHCHEV'S BERLIN ULTIMATUM

In the 1950s the United States retained superiority in its vast military power and technological know-how, despite the strides being made by the Soviet Union in rocketry, space satellites, and nuclear weapons. The dynamic economies of Western Europe as they united in the Common Market stood in sharp contrast to the stagnant economic systems of the East. At the same time that the Soviet Union was suppressing the uprising in Hungary, the Rome Treaty for the formation of the Common Market was being drafted. To the extent that it represented a potential forerunner to a politically unified Western Europe, the Common Market would form not only a formidable obstacle to Soviet expansion, but might even hold magnetic appeal to populations living under Communist domination in Eastern Europe. Already Moscow faced the specter of large numbers of people, dissatisfied with life in East Germany, leaving in pursuit of political freedom and economic opportunity in the West. Movement from East Germany to the Federal Republic, via West Berlin, was relatively easy. The prosperity of the Western sector of Berlin, contrasted with East Berlin and the surrounding East German state, together with the location in West Berlin of powerful transmitters for beaming radio programs into the East, increased Moscow's already formidable problems with restive peoples under its rule. Khrushchev described Berlin as a "bone in his throat."

For nearly a decade since the end of the Berlin crisis of 1948–49, the former German capital had been relegated to the background of East–West relations. Nevertheless, Berlin remained for the Western powers an outpost, in itself militarily indefensible, located 110 miles behind the western frontier of the German Democratic Republic and vulnerable to unilateral Soviet action. On November 10, 1958, Khrushchev took such a bold step by declaring that he would sign with East Germany a "peace treaty" whose effect would be to terminate Allied rights in Berlin. At this time none of the Western occupying powers of Berlin gave diplomatic recognition to the German Democratic Republic. If Khrushchev carried out his threat, then the United States, Britain, and France would have to depend on negotiations with East Germany to ensure continued access to Berlin—which would be tantamount to diplomatic recognition. If the Western powers refused to deal directly with the East German regime and were then denied access to Berlin, they would have to use force against East Germany. In this event, the Soviet Union declared, Moscow would provide direct assistance to the German Democratic Republic. Because they remained committed to the eventual reunification of Germany and regarded the East German regime as simply a puppet government of the Soviet Union, the Western powers viewed Khrushchev's decision to sign a peace treaty as a thinly veiled device for obtaining international recognition for the German Democratic Republic. Khrushchev declared the postwar occupation of Berlin to be out of date, since East Berlin was the capital of the German Democratic Republic, with which the Western powers should begin negotiations for the full withdrawal of Allied garrisons from the city. Khrushchev proposed that the Western sectors of Berlin should become a "free city" under United Nations auspices after Allied forces had been removed. Unless the West agreed to such terms within six months, the Soviet Union would proceed with its plan for a peace treaty with East Germany.

The Soviet Union repeated an earlier proposal for German reunification based on a confederation of the two states. In practical terms, such a proposal was not feasible; the state-owned economy of the East and the private-sector economy of the West could not be merged without fundamental changes in one or the other. The Soviet reunification proposal represented a ploy to entice the Federal Republic into talks with the East and thus, in keeping with the peace-treaty proposal, was a means of gaining recognition for the German Democratic

Republic. In short, the Soviet Union did not favor German reunification on terms that provided any basis for compromise with the West.

The Eisenhower administration interpreted the Soviet announcement as a challenge not only to the Western position in Berlin, but also to the broader interests of the United States and its allies in Europe. Although the occupying powers stationed only token forces in Berlin and thus could not defend the city in the event of a Soviet–East German invasion, the withdrawal of those troops would leave the city vulnerable to political, military, and psychological pressures. The presence of even a small military garrison provided a tangible link to the much larger capabilities of the West that, in the event of a move on Berlin by the Soviet Union, could be brought to bear elsewhere. A demonstrated inability or un- willingness to stand up to Khrushchev's pressure would cast doubt on the broader commitment of the United States to NATO. If he could clearly provide evidence of such Western irresolution, Khrushchev would transform the Berlin problem from a source of possible instability in Eastern Europe to a distinct advantage; at the same time he would gain for the German Democratic Republic not only diplomatic recognition and hence the legitimacy of a political system imposed by Moscow but also a formalization of the postwar territorial status quo in Central Europe.

Thus the issues confronting the Eisenhower administration were more complex than they had been in the Berlin crisis a decade earlier. At that time the United States, with its nuclear monopoly, could upset Stalin's calculations by supplying West Berlin via a massive airlift. In this choice of response, rather than forcing its way across the land corridors that had been closed by the Soviet Union, the West had placed on Stalin the onus of escalating the crisis to the actual use of force. So long as the Soviets did not shoot down Allied aircraft flying within the legally designated air corridors to and from Berlin, the airlift could proceed. Any Soviet use of weapons would carry with it the likelihood of further escalation by the United Stats which enjoyed strategic superiority.

By 1958, this condition was changing as the Soviet Union developed its own strategic-nuclear capabilities. In any event, the situation facing the Eisenhower administration differed in that the Soviet Union did not block access routes, although there was sporadic interference after Khrushchev's East German peace-treaty announcement. Even without the use of force, which nevertheless remained an ultimate sanction in support of the Khrushchev ultimatum, the West could be forced into a retreat that would be devastating, especially for the Adenauer government and its firm commitment to the West. The Federal Republic would face the immediate effects of the withdrawal of the Western presence from Berlin: Adenauer had based his policy on the security relationship between Bonn and Washington, within the multilateral framework of the Atlantic Alliance, as the indispensable guarantor of his country's interests and as the best hope of eventual German reunification through strength on terms satisfactory to the West and to the Federal Republic.

Ultimately, the Eisenhower administration's response to Khrushchev's challenge was to communicate to the Soviet Union that, since the Four Power agreements governing the postwar status of Berlin could be changed only by mutual consent, the United States would hold the Soviet Union responsible for fulfilling its obligations in and around Berlin. In other words, the United States would not deal with any East German officials who performed the duties for which the Soviet Union itself was responsible, notably the monitoring of the movements of the Western powers to and from Berlin. If the East Germans interfered with traffic along the land corridors, the United States would attempt to send a convoy with armed protection through the checkpoint, although force would not be used unless the East Germans first opened fire on the convoy. Contingency plans were made for gradual escalation in the use of force although the Administration decided, in the event of a blockade, to place principal emphasis on diplomacy, including efforts at the United Nations.

As part of its effort to defuse the crisis, the United States called for a meeting of the foreign ministers of the Four Powers to be held in mid-April, several weeks before Khrushchev's ultimatum expired on May 27, 1959. In February 1959 British Prime Minister Harold Macmillan, who had succeeded Anthony Eden when he resigned after the Suez crisis in January 1957, had visited Moscow for what turned out to be a stormy meeting with Khrushchev, who reiterated his various threats before informing Macmillan that the May 27 deadline was not intended to be an ultimatum. Shortly after this meeting, Khrushchev sent a note to the Western powers proposing a summit conference, although Moscow was also prepared to attend a Four Power foreign ministers meeting, provided that it was confined to a discussion of the German peace treaty and the status of Berlin.

The Eisenhower administration, however, saw the purpose of a foreign ministers' meeting to be the discussion not just of Berlin but also of other issues associated with Germany, including reunification. The administration believed that the future of Berlin could be decided only in the context of German reunification and that for any such agreement to be made on terms satisfactory to the West, and specifically to Chancellor Adenauer—including free all-German elections—the rights of the Western allies in Berlin must not be abridged. Having witnessed the ephemeral results of the 1955 Geneva Summit, Eisenhower was not prepared to enter another conference with the Soviet leadership unless there were clear expectations of success. For Eisenhower, the principal condition to be met by the Soviet Union was assurance that Western rights in Berlin would not be restricted and that no ultimatum hung over the heads of the Western powers. The United States also sought progress at the foreign ministers' meeting in the field of cultural exchange and initial steps toward the banning of nuclear tests, which had first been discussed with the Soviet Union at a meeting of the United Nations Disarmament Subcommittee in London in January 1957. In March, yielding to pressure from Prime Minister Macmillan, who favored an early Four Power summit meeting, the United States agreed to enter negotiations with the Soviet at the foreign-ministers level, which would also include Britain and France. After Macmillan visited Moscow, he reported to Eisenhower that Khrushchev had hinted that the May 27 date was not an ultimatum. With the foreign ministers' conference, which began in Geneva on May 11, 1959, Khrushchev's May 27 deadline lost all significance, for the meeting dragged on until August, with the

Soviet Union conceding nothing that would justify another Four Power summit meeting but taking no action in support of its threat to sign a peace treaty with East Germany. The United States was represented by Christian A. Herter, who had succeeded as Secretary of State several weeks before the death of Dulles in late May 1959.

Eisenhower's approach to diplomacy with the Soviet Union contained, on the one hand, a determination to avoid euphoric expectations that would be dashed on the rocks of reality following a summit conference and, on the other hand, the conviction that he might use all the charm and persuasion at his command to penetrate the minds and hearts of the Soviet leadership in pursuit of peace. The belief that he could communicate directly to Stalin's successors the sincerity of his commitment to a peaceful world had led Eisenhower to the Geneva Summit of 1955, just as it had given him hope immediately after the Soviet leader's death that new contacts should be opened at the highest level with Moscow.

In this context Eisenhower invited Khrushchev to visit the United States in September 1959 and to meet with him. Although Eisenhower wanted to make progress at the foreign ministers' conferene in Geneva a condition for a visit by Khrushchev to the United States, this stipulation was erroneously left out of the invitation to the Soviet leader. After a ten-day tour of the United States, Khrushchev held discussions with Eisenhower at Camp David, the principal result of which was that the Soviet leader formally renounced any suggestion of a deadline on issues related to Berlin, thus paving the way for American agreement to a summit conference. Khrushchev's "concession" was the removal of a threat that he himself had created to Western rights as occupying powers in Berlin. This was a contrived crisis which nevertheless could have escalated beyond simple diplomatic verbiage. That it did not do so may be a tribute to the policies of the Eisenhower administration. Yet Eisenhower had been placed by Khrushchev in the position of agreeing to a summit conference without prior tangible evidence of progress toward the resolution of substantive issues, which the United States had set as a condition for such talks.

## THE UNITED STATES AND ARMS CONTROL IN THE LATE 1950s

Although it produced only one arms limitation treaty—the Antarctica Treaty of 1960, providing for inspection among countries engaged in exploration and barring the deployment of weapons on that continent—the Eisenhower administration considered the control of weapons to be an important element in its relationship with the Soviet Union. Both in his first Inaugural Address and in numerous other speeches as president, Eisenhower called for mutual reductions in armaments. In addition to the Atoms for Peace proposal, which led to the formation of the International Atomic Energy Agency, the Eisenhower administration put forward the "Open Skies" proposal at the Geneva Summit Conference in 1955, which the Soviet Union rejected. In 1954, Eisenhower appointed former Minnesota Governor Harold E. Stassen as his special assistant for disarmament, with duties that included evaluation of the interdepartmental positions on arms limitation within the U.S. government and representation of the United States on the five-nation disarmament subcommittee formed in 1954 as a working group within the United Nations Disarmament Commission.

### Disagreement over Inspection

The principal obstacle to arms limitation agreements in the 1950s was inspection. With the growing lethality of weapons and the speed with which they could be launched, the Eisenhower administration saw the need to minimize the possibility of surprise attack. Thus arose the term "confidence-building measures," which survives in the arms control lexicon. It was apparent that the gap between the two nations' capabilities, as well as the time needed to mobilize their forces, would decrease as a result of the advanced technologies then available or soon to be introduced. This realization had contributed to the Open Skies proposal, since it would make it impossible for either state to take the necessary steps to launch an attack without being observed by aerial photography. The existence of Open Skies inspection safeguards would "build confidence" that the other side was living up to an arms-control agreement and not preparing to launch a surprise attack.

While rejecting the U.S. proposal, the Soviet Union in 1955 set forth a scheme for observation posts to be located at communications and transportation centers—a proposal that U.S. policymakers deemed unsatisfactory, since the Soviet Union might still mobilize its forces clandestinely. Such an approach could be a supplement to, but not a substitute for, the more extensive inspection contained in aerial surveillance by mutual agreement. Another Soviet approach, which the United States also found inadequate, provided for the conclusion of friendship treaties, nonaggression pacts, and pledges to reduce conventional weapons and even to engage in "general and complete disarmament." Such accords seemed meaningless to the United States, since they did not provide for mutual inspection to verify compliance.

Thus, as long as the issue of inspection remained unresolved, it would be impossible to conclude arms limitation agreements that respected American national-security interests and needs. Because the United States, with its extensive debate on military programs, weapons systems, and defense budgets, made available detailed information about its armaments, it would have far more difficulty than the Soviet Union, with its historic penchant for secrecy, in concealing any violations of an arms limitation agreement. Hence the United States showed, then as in the decades to follow, far greater concern than the Soviet Union about the problems of arms-control inspection.

One solution to the problem of inspection, which would be applied in the arms-control agreements of the 1960s and 1970s, was verification carried out exclusively by the means available to the United States, including the technical capabilities afforded by monitoring stations not located on Soviet territory and by the increased reliability of aerial photography, first by manned aircraft such as the U-2, which began reconnaissance flights of the Soviet Union in 1956 for the specific purpose of observing Soviet missile installations and other armaments and then by the orbiting satellites launched with increasing frequency by both powers since 1960.

## Toward a Nuclear Test-ban Treaty

In the mid-1950s a series of arms-control proposals for Central Europe had been put forward. These included a plan for cuts in military forces in East and West Germany proposed by Poland's foreign minister, Adam Rapacki, and known as the Rapacki Plan. Although the idea attracted support in Britain, it encountered opposition both in France and in the Federal Republic of Germany. Whereas Soviet military units withdrawn from East Germany would have been redeployed only a few hundred miles away in the Soviet Union, American forces that left the NATO Central Front would be removed to the United States, nearly 4000 miles away. The Soviet Union's preponderance of conventional forces in Europe would have been increased, while it would appear to European allies that the United States was diminishing the commitment to forward defense and deterrence embodied in its military presence on the NATO Central Front. Hence the Rapacki Plan, as well as other proposals offered in the mid-1950s for disengagement in Central Europe, were viewed by the Eisenhower administration as infeasible because of the geographic asymmetries between the Soviet Union as a European power in close proximity to any likely zone of conflict in Europe and the United States as an Atlantic power committed to the preservation of freedom in Western Europe. Last but not least, the opposition of the two Western European allies most directly affected by any disengagement proposal—the Federal Republic of Germany and France—effectively doomed any such proposal, for the United States was not prepared to weaken the cohesion of the Atlantic Alliance in pursuit of what, in any event, seemed to be a dubious arms-limitation concept.

Instead, the arms-control focus of the Eisenhower administration in its second term was the banning of nuclear testing, an issue that Adlai Stevenson had raised in the 1956 presidential campaign. At that time Eisenhower, rejecting Stevenson's proposal, had argued that a presidential campaign was not the appropriate forum for such a sensitive and technically complex issue. The test-ban issue was stimulated by growing public concern, shared by Eisenhower himself, about the potentially harmful effects of radioactive fallout, although there was debate within the scientific community whether atmospheric testing in fact produced serious health hazards. During his first administration Eisenhower had issued orders that such tests be kept to a minimum.

In January 1957 the United States announced that it was willing to discuss methods for limiting and eventually halting all nuclear tests. The Eisenhower administration, moreover, called for an arms-control agreement that would

encompass earth-orbiting satellites, intercontinental missiles, and space platforms, all of which represented weapons of the future. This was followed by a
proposal put forward by the Eisenhower administration on August 21, 1957, for
the suspension of nuclear testing for a period of up to two years. At the same time
the U.S. approach called for a halt to the production of weapons-grade fissionable
materials, with inspection procedures to be worked out. The Soviet Union
rejected both aspects of the U.S. proposal.

In April 1958 the Soviet Union accepted a U.S. suggestion for an international meeting of technical experts to study the problems of detecting nuclear
explosions under various conditions by such means as seismic waves, radio
signals, and the collection of radioactive debris. With the report of this group in
hand, the Eisenhower administration in August 1958 proposed a one-year
moratorium on nuclear tests, which would be renewed on a year-by-year basis if
there was sufficient evidence of progress toward a permanent agreement that
satisfied American criteria for international inspection. That the test suspension
depended on similar action by the Soviet Union in itself placed a burden on the
capacity of the United States to verify Moscow's compliance, and there were not
then, nor were there to be in later years, the technical means to detect all nuclear
tests conducted by the Soviet Union.

With the Soviet acceptance of the American proposals and a moratorium in
effect, negotiations toward a test-ban treaty began on October 31, 1958. Once
again, the chief obstacle to a treaty was verification of compliance. The Soviet
Union objected to the establishment of control posts to monitor compliance with
the treaty, especially to differentiate underground nuclear explosions from
earthquakes and to investigate events that might constitute treaty violations.
Although the Eisenhower administration did not succeed in concluding a test-ban
agreement, the basis was established for the treaty signed by its successor in 1963.

In 1959 and 1960 the United States suggested a limited ban, permitting tests
to be conducted in environments—namely, the atmosphere, the oceans, and
space—where they could be monitored by the United States by its own technical
means. The underground environment presented the most complex problems,
because there it was possible to conduct certain types of low-yield nuclear tests
that could not be detected. The Eisenhower administration insisted that those
categories of underground nuclear tests that could not be reliably verified by the
United States would have to be excluded. The moratorium on U.S. nuclear testing
remained in force until the end of the Eisenhower administration, while a seismic
research program was undertaken to identify and to narrow the zone of uncertainty in monitoring nuclear explosions underground.

By the end of the Eisenhower administration, therefore, the verification of
compliance with an arms-control agreement by essentially national technical
means had been substituted for the concept of inspection by an international
authority. The principal problem that remained to be resolved was the
development of the necessary technical means for this purpose. The corollary to
this national approach to verification was that the terms of arms-control
agreements would be strictly limited to those for which it was possible to devise
adequate national means for assuring compliance.

## THE ABORTIVE PARIS SUMMIT CONFERENCE

As the Eisenhower administration entered its final year in office, it had fallen short of concluding a test-ban treaty, and the Berlin issue had been only partly defused. The very nature of Berlin in the context of East–West relations afforded little latitude to the United States and its Western allies for compromise, while for the Soviet Union into the early 1960s, Berlin as the point of exodus for growing numbers of disaffected East Germans continued to be a source of acute political embarrassment and testimony to the deficiencies of communist systems. With the agreement to convene a summit conference as part of the *quid pro quo* for the withdrawal of Khrushchev's Berlin ultimatum, preparations went forward for the Four Power meeting to be held in Paris in May 1960. Although Khrushchev had repeated in the spring of 1960 his threat to sign a peace treaty with East Germany, he had not included another deadline.

Despite the cautious approach that his administration had taken to the idea of a second summit conference, Eisenhower looked forward to the meeting as his final opportunity as president to achieve some form of breakthrough in East-West relations. Against this objective the administration weighed the need to gather information about Soviet military capabilities. The first Soviet ICBM installation had been detected during a U-2 flight over the Soviet Union in early April 1960. Eisenhower authorized a final flight to gather further intelligence before the summit conference. Although the U-2s flew at an altitude of 60,000 feet—beyond the range of Soviet aircraft or ground defenses—the Soviet Union was able to track them on radar. For whatever reason, the Soviet government had not revealed to the outside world its knowledge of the U-2 overflights of its territory. On May 6, just days before the summit conference was to open in Paris, Khrushchev announced that a U-2 had been shot down, presumably after a malfunction in its oxygen system and that its pilot, Francis Gary Powers, together with much of his reconnaissance equipment, had been captured by the Soviet Union. There followed a series of bellicose statements from Khrushchev, together with an admission by Eisenhower that he had authorized the U-2 flights in order to monitor Soviet weapons deployments and to guard against surprise attack on the West.

Although each of the principals went to Paris, the summit conference never took place. Khrushchev demanded an apology from Eisenhower for the flights over Soviet territory. This Eisenhower refused to give, in light of what he regarded as the need for U.S. reconnaissance to balance the espionage conducted by Soviet agents operating freely in the United States. Khrushchev stormed out of the meeting, not only ending any prospect for the Paris Summit Conference itself but also deferring until a new administration the next moves in U.S.–Soviet relations.

## HEMISPHERIC POLICIES AND CHALLENGES

Although relations with other states in the Western Hemisphere did not occupy a central place in its foreign policy, the Eisenhower administration nevertheless confronted problems that, on a larger scale, would endure to frustrate its successors. As noted in Chapter 1, the hemisphere had been virtually free of intrusion by outside powers, although the residual dependencies of Britain, France, and the Netherlands, located for the most part in the Caribbean and Central America, remained.

### A New Instability in the Hemisphere

The political systems of the states of Latin America were, by U.S. standards, unstable. The emphasis on rule by a narrowly based oligarchy, with governmental change the result of coups rather than of elections peacefully contested by competing political parties, shaped the American image of Latin America. Such political systems had emerged in societies, many of which had huge Indian populations, in which the gap between the wealthy and poor, between the educated modernizing elite and those still living in a traditional society, remained wide indeed. Because of the large nucleus of people of Indian origin and of people, especially in the Caribbean, who traced their ancestry to Africa, it is by no means accurate to refer to the southern reaches of the Western Hemisphere as "Latin" America, although the Portuguese and Hispanic political tradition transplanted across the Atlantic did ensure that the postcolonial states that emerged in the nineteenth century would differ fundamentally from the United States and Canada in their political practices and socioeconomic structures. Widespread illiteracy, maldistribution of wealth, lack of capital for investment in a broadly based program of modernization, grinding poverty, excessive dependence on exports of one crop or natural resources, characterized the states of Central America and South America. As producers of natural resources needed by industrialized states and of agricultural products such as sugar, coffee, and fruit, these states became the object of heavy investment from the United States.

All these ingredients formed the basis for many of the problems that the United States would face in the twentieth century in its relations with its neighbors to the south. Beginning with President Franklin Roosevelt's Good Neighbor Policy, each administration would seek solutions to these problems. It was the Eisenhower administration's lot to confront the phenomenon known as the "revolution of rising expectations" that in the 1950s swept across the Third World. Simultaneously, for the first time in this century, the Western Hemisphere became vulnerable to the intrusion of a hostile outside power as the Soviet Union began to look at states in Central America and South America—with their political and socioeconomic cleavages and their latent, and often overt, resentment of the dominant role of the United States—as fertile ground for exploitation.

Despite its preoccupation with the problems and crises of Europe, the Middle East, and Asia, the Eisenhower Administration found it necessary to give greater attention to Latin America than Truman had. Eisenhower appointed his brother, Dr. Milton S. Eisenhower, president of Johns Hopkins University, to be his personal representative with the rank of ambassador to study and report to him on issues directly related to Latin America.

## Fending Off Soviet Intervention in Guatemala

It was Guatemala that quickly engaged the attention of the Eisenhower administration. In the years since the Guatemala Revolution of 1944, which had resulted in the overthrow of General Jorge Ubico as authoritarian ruler, there had been a rise in Communist activity, including the infiltration of labor unions. Such activity seemed to increase after 1950, when Jacobo Arbenz Guzmán, a military officer, took control of the country. In 1953 Arbenz nationalized large tracts of unused lands owned by the United Fruit Company, offering compensation that amounted to expropriation. There was increasing contact between the Arbenz government and the Soviet Union, including not only visits by Guatemalan officials to Moscow, but also support for the Soviet contention that the United States had used bacteriological weapons in Korea—which the Eisenhower administration denied, and which could never be substantiated.

The United States sought and received condemnation of the Arbenz regime at the Tenth Inter-American Conference of the Organization of American States (OAS), which met in Caracas Venezuela, in March 1954. The basis for this censure was the threat to the independence of states in the hemisphere posed by the intervention of an outside power, and specifically by Communist subversion directly supported by the Soviet Union.

The administration concluded that immediate action was necessary when it learned that arms were being shipped from Eastern Europe to Guatemala. A Swedish ship chartered by a British company was loaded at Stettin, Poland, "bound" for Dakar with Skoda arms from Czechoslovakia. Although the hand of the Soviet Union was not directly visible behind all these proxy forces, Moscow's control over Poland and Czechoslovakia was so tight that no such transaction would have been possible without the direct complicity of the Soviet Union.

Concluding that such arms exceeded any legitimate security needs of the Arbenz regime, the United States considered intercepting the arms shipment on the high seas. Ultimately abandoning this idea, the Eisenhower administration instead gave military support to an exiled Guatemalan colonel, Carlos Castillo Armas, who invaded his country with a small band of supporters. With the defection of the Guatemalan army from Arbenz and the delivery of U.S. arms, including two P-51 fighter-bombers, Castillo Armas toppled Arbenz in late April 1954 and replaced his regime with an anticommunist government. Working with local forces opposed to Arbenz, while possessing the military capabilities to prevent the inflow of Soviet-bloc arms into Central America, the Eisenhower administration was able, to a far greater extent than would henceforth be possible, to thwart intervention by an outside power in the hemisphere.

## Increasing Technical and Economic Aid to Latin America

The Latin American policies of the Eisenhower administration included both increases in technical assistance and support for the establishment of new lending institutions. The latter included the International Finance Corporation, founded in 1956 to make loans to private companies, and the International Development Association, created in 1959 to make loans that could be repaid in local currencies because of the shortage of convertible foreign exchange; both agencies were formed within the framework of the World Bank. In 1959 the Inter-American Development Bank was established, with the United States furnishing nearly one half the initial $1 billion in capital funds. The flow of governmental and private capital from the United States to Latin America increased from $232 million in 1953 to a peak of $1.6 billion in 1957. U.S. assets and investment in Latin America, which totalled $7 billion in 1952, had nearly doubled by 1960. The greatest growth in capital flow from the United States to Latin America in the 1950s took place in the private sector. The Eisenhower administration supported the formation of common markets and other regional economic associations to promote trade, together with agreements on commodity-price stabilization that were intended to reduce wild fluctuations in the prices of primary products that had often produced cycles of boom and bust in one-crop countries.

### Castro's Revolution in Cuba

Although these programs were useful, they were not sufficient to attenuate the increasing antagonism that the United States faced in Latin America from the late 1950s onward. In May 1958 an angry mob surrounded the car in which Vice-President Nixon was traveling in Caracas, Venezuela, during an official visit to Latin America. Anti-American feeling was so intense that the administration flew troops to Puerto Rico and Guantánamo Bay in Cuba in case they were needed to evacuate Nixon and his party from Venezuela. This demonstration coincided with Anti-American riots in other parts of the world.

Even more disturbing to the Eisenhower administration was the revolution that transformed Cuba from an oligarchy headed by Fulgencio Batista to a Communist regime under Fidel Castro. In 1958, while the focus of U.S. attention in Latin American was elsewhere, Castro mounted a guerrilla offensive. The tactics used by Castro's forces were skillfully adapted to local circumstances by Ernesto ("Che") Guevara, an Argentinean physician who had been associated with Arbenz in Guatemala. Castro termed his struggle the July 26th Movement, commemorating the date in 1953 when he and a small band of followers had failed in their attempt to seize the Moncado Barracks in Santiago de Cuba. Exiled to Mexico, Castro returned to Cuba and established a base of operations in the remote Sierra Maestra region, from which he launched guerrilla operations of increasing intensity as his forces gathered strength and support. In accordance with the tactics of guerrilla warfare, Castro extended his control to the rural countryside and by 1958 was able to challenge and defeat Batista for control of urban centers as well. Parts of Batista's forces defected to join Castro, who enjoyed increasing support among the Cuban population and in the United States as well. For example, *New York Times* correspondent Herbert Matthews, after interviewing Castro, hailed him as a figure who promised social, political, and economic reform to his backward country.

For its part, the Eisenhower administration, in sharp contrast to the steps that it had taken to topple the Arbenz regime, seized arms exports destined for Castro wherever possible and in March 1958 suspended its own shipments of weapons to Batista. Not until December 1958 did the Eisenhower administration begin to fear that Castro might be something other than simply an agrarian reformer.

With Castro's triumphant entry into Havana on January 1, 1959, his forces moved rapidly to consolidate their control over all of Cuba. This was soon followed by the execution or imprisonment of Castro's political enemies, and the legalization of the Communist party, which moved quickly into all sectors of Cuban life. When Castro came to the United States at the invitation of the American Society of Newspaper Editors, which he addressed in April 1959, and met with U.S. officials, he did nothing to dispel the view that Cuba was slipping into the Communist camp. Castro denounced the United States for 50 years of intervention in Cuba, nationalized the private business sector, expropriated U.S. investments, and aligned his foreign policy with that of the Soviet Union.

In its last year, the Eisenhower administration pondered a series of measures against Castro, ranging from a quarantine of Cuba to the curtailment of sugar imports to the strengthening of opposition forces within Cuba and the arming of his enemies for a possible invasion. Yet, as the administration recognized, unilateral action against Castro risked opposition elsewhere in the hemisphere—where, despite the evidence of his affiliation with Moscow, Castro was still viewed as a folk hero, an opponent of the privileged classes and a champion of the poor and politically powerless masses. In the summer of 1960, Khrushchev threatened to protect Cuba from U.S. attack when the Eisenhower administration cut Cuba's quota for sugar exports to the United States. The Soviet threat was backed by the beginning of the arms flow into Cuba that in the decades to follow was to pose serious security problems for the United States.

In its last months in office, the Eisenhower administration made further increases in U.S. economic assistance to Latin America, while encouraging the region's governments to speed up social and economic reforms in the interest of creating or strengthening democratic political institutions, a concept that was embodied in the Act of Bogotá adopted by the OAS in September 1960. All these efforts toward reform helped set the stage for the Kennedy administration's Alliance for Progress and for the other challenges that hemispheric relations, especially vis-à-vis Cuba, would pose for U.S. foreign policy in the 1960s.

## OTHER THIRD WORLD ISSUES

By the end of the 1950s, the transformation of the European empires in the Third World into new states—a process that had begun with Britain's granting of independence to India, Pakistan, and Ceylon (now Sri Lanka) in 1947—was reaching its climax. In the years after Ghana became in 1957 the first black state under British rule in Africa to achieve independence, a similar status would be conferred on all the remaining European-ruled states south of the Sahara. Before 1957 all of sub-Saharan Africa except for Liberia, Ethiopia, and South Africa was ruled by Belgium, Britain, France, or Portugal. Within the next decade all overseas European dependencies in Africa, except those of Portugal, would become independent states. Their independence movements would be centered on Western-educated elites, living in societies whose dominant characteristics included tribalism, traditional value systems, and agrarian economies. The nationalism with which the leaders of independence movements were imbued was based, first and foremost, on a desire to rid their countries of Western rule. The concept of the nation had not penetrated deeply into the consciousness of the mass of the population, many of whom lived outside a moneyed economy, often owing primary allegiance to tribal chiefs. Aside from English and French, the languages of the principal European rulers, there was no local or indigenous African *lingua franca*. As a result of language differences, communication was even difficult within the political entities on which the new states were to be based.

Compared to the European empires in the Western Hemisphere or in Asia, those established in Africa were of recent origin. They had been created in the third and final great wave of West European imperial expansion that took place between 1890 and the outbreak of World War I in 1914. The boundaries of African states reflected not so much the linguistic-tribal divisions of the continent as the requirements of the European states, which carved out empires in Africa in keeping with the perceived needs of the balance of power in Europe. Although in many cases they laid the basis for economic growth with an infrastructure of ports and communications systems, with a civil service and educational system, the process of preparing peoples for independence was far from thorough, and in certain sectors and territories it was to prove woefully inadequate. In the aftermath of the granting of independence, most states onto which European political institutions had been grafted by the imperial powers were transformed into regimes ruled by authoritarian, often military governments.

In Africa, unlike Latin America, the United States traditionally had no vital interests at stake. Thus the independence process, while strongly supported by the United States and especially by those Americans who traced their origins to black Africa, was managed almost exclusively by Western European powers. Although a total of 17 Africa states gained independence without major repercussions in 1960, the imminent independence of the Belgian Congo triggered tribal warfare, rioting, looting, and the secession of the resource-rich Katanga Province, which contained the bulk of Belgian investment. When the Congo (later called Zaire) was granted independence on July 1, 1960, chaos ensued. After the African *Force Publique* revolted against its Belgian officers, the Belgian government sent troops into the Republic of the Congo, an action denounced by Patrice Lumumba, the new premier of the Congo. The Eisenhower administration, in support of a United Nations Security Council resolution, provided airlift and supplies for an international peace-keeping force consisting of Moroccan and Tunisian troops sent to help restore order until the Congo government could train its own forces for this purpose. At this point, the Soviet Union denounced the Eisenhower administration's actions and threatened, as on other occasions, to send its own forces into the Congo. This warning was followed in September 1960 by the dispatch of Soviet technicians and military equipment to support the Lumumba government. However, Lumumba was dismissed as premier by President Joseph Kasavubu, who appointed as his successor Joseph Mobutu. This led to the closing of the Soviet embassy and the sharp curtailment of any influence that Moscow had developed during Lumumba's short tenure. In the years to follow, the Congo crisis was to escalate as civil war between the central government and secessionist Katanga Province, led by Moise Tshombe, increased in intensity, with the intervention of a large United Nations force whose mandate was to restore a semblance of unity to the Congo.

By the end of the Eisenhower administration, the Third World was an arena of intensifying conflict and generated problems unprecedented in their magnitude for the United States, whose traditional preoccupations had been elsewhere. In the aftermath of European imperialism, new states faced the problems of reconciling traditional socio-political structures with the needs imposed by contact with the industrially and politically advanced societies of the West. Rapidly increasing populations, insufficient agricultural production, excessive dependence on one or a few exports, social and economic pressures resulting from rapid urbanization, a tendency to substitute one-party rule for the pluralistic political systems bequeathed by the colonial power—all posed problems both for the new states themselves and for relations with the West.

Such conditions led the United States in the 1950s to build on the programs of economic assistance that President Truman had first advocated in "point four" of his Inaugural Address in January 1949 as a logical extension of the highly successful programs of American postwar aid to Western Europe and Japan. If the results of such efforts in the Third World paled in comparison to the restored, robust, industrial Western European and Japanese economies, the problems facing Third World states were far more complex. To the extent that the United States emerged as a principal actor in the Third World as the power of Western European colonial states waned, the foreign-policy problems facing the Eisenhower administration became both more numerous and multifaceted than those that had confronted any previous American government, except perhaps in wartime. The administration had begun its tenure with an effort to build a series of alliance systems that would form a barrier to the extension of Communist power and to provide a form of global containment. By various means, by the end of the decade, the Soviet Union had leapfrogged the containment barrier by seeking to exploit anticolonial, anti-Western, and, in the case of Latin America, anti-U.S. sentiment. In the 1950s a series of nonaligned states, epitomized by India under the leadership of Prime Minister Nehru, had emerged and were striving to exert influence beyond the direct sphere of either the United States or the Soviet Union. Although the Eisenhower administration—committed as it was to the development of alliances along the rim of Asia—encountered criticism at the time for its alleged insensitivity to the concept of nonalignment, the fact remains that Eisenhower sought, as at the time of the Suez crisis, to separate American policy from that of the erstwhile colonial powers of Western Europe. In this respect, the administration was not entirely successful. Then, as now,

American interests dictated a policy designed, on the one hand, to encourage the emergence of moderate, modernizing forces and, on the other, to thwart the formation of revolutionary regimes aligned with the Soviet Union, such as those the United States faced first in Cuba and subsequently in North Vietnam.

## CRITICISMS OF EISENHOWER'S DEFENSE POLICY IN THE LATE 1950s

The New Look in defense strategy and forces introduced by the Eisenhower administration had enabled the United States to reduce the size of the United States Army from 1.5 million in 1952, at the height of the Korean War, to 870,000 at the end of the Eisenhower administration. U.S. defense appropriations for fiscal year 1953, when the Eisenhower administration entered office, totalled $46.6 billion. Eight years later the defense budget had been lowered to $41.2 billion, with Congress having added $500 million more than Eisenhower had requested in his last year in office. The principal saving had come from sharp reductions in the U.S. Army's conventional capabilities and from the Eisenhower administration's emphasis on nuclear weapons as against conventional weapons and manpower.

In its final years in office, and especially after the launching of the first Soviet orbiting satellite in September 1957, the administration encountered increasing debate about this nuclear emphasis. The criticisms seemed to some to be confirmed by the way Eisenhower managed the Berlin crisis precipitated by Khrushchev in 1959. The critics alleged that nuclear weapons were not plausible instruments of deterrence of warfare except in situations of threat to the most vital national interests. This condition obtained especially in the changing strategic environment of the late 1950s when the Soviet Union was acquiring the means, seemingly at an alarming rate, to threaten the United States with nuclear weapons. If both sides possessed atomic capabilities, critics asked, could either side deter anything beyond the nuclear weapons of the other? As long as the United States had been the sole possessor of nuclear weapons, as at the time of the first Berlin crisis in 1948–49, it could threaten with probable impunity to escalate hostilities beyond any level available to the Soviet Union. But with each side able to devastate the other with nuclear forces, would not the inherent advantage accrue to the side that had superior conventional capabilities? It was the local superiority of conventional forces around Berlin that had given credibility to the threat posed by Khrushchev in 1959.

Furthermore, it was argued, in the "brushfire wars" of the time—what Khrushchev termed "wars of national liberation"—the decisive military capability would not be nuclear, but instead the ability to fight using even primitive weapons and guerrilla tactics such as those employed successfully by Castro. This situation argued for the building of a more balanced American military capability, in which nuclear forces would be modernized but conventional forces would be strengthened, both for nonnuclear contingencies in Europe and for counterinsurgency operations in more remote parts of the world.

As the election of 1960 approached, the Eisenhower administration was being criticized on two fronts simultaneously: for having neglected conventional defense capabilities and for having allowed a nuclear "missile gap" to develop in favor of the Soviet Union. What had seemed to be adequate conventional forces in the years after the end of the Korean War represented an apparent deficiency in light of the altered security environment eight years later. Although the next administration took steps to augment conventional forces, Eisenhower's emphasis on nuclear capabilities and on research in strategic-weapons technologies had resulted in the deployment of the first of the Polaris class of nuclear-powered submarines, capable of launching ballistic missiles against the Soviet Union. At the same time, the United States had nearly completed research and development on the Minuteman land-based missile, which would become a central element in the American strategic deterrent in the 1960s. Although the United States, in fact, entered the 1960s with a substantial missile gap in its favor, the Soviet Union's capacity and propensity for intervention, particularly in the form of arms shipments, in regions from which it had previously been excluded namely the Caribbean–Central America and the Middle East, had grown dramatically.

Beyond its New Look in defense strategy and force levels, the Eisenhower administration obtained legislation designed to reduce interservice rivalries and to strengthen civilian control, specifically that of the president and the secretary of defense, over military planning and operations. In addition, the Defense Reorganization Act of 1958 was designed to unify, and thereby to simplify, the military command structure. The act stipulated that all military forces, regardless of which service branch was in the field, would be directed by a commander of the overall theater of operations. This commander, in turn, would be directly responsible to the "national command authority" consisting of the president as commander-in-chief and the secretary of defense. The Joint Staff was enlarge in order to enhance the Joint Chiefs' ability to assist the Secretary of Defense in the operation of the new command structure. Finally, the position of director for defense research and engineering, at the same level as the secretaries of the army, navy, and air force, was created to sharpen the focus on development of advanced defense technologies. As the United States moved toward the space age, the Eisenhower administration in 1958 established two parallel structures; the Advanced Research Projects Agency (ARPA) for military projects and the National Aeronautics and Space Agency (NASA) for peaceful applications of technology for space. Thus the organizational basis was created for the programs that, just over a decade later, would place an American astronaut on the moon.

## THE FOREIGN-POLICY ORGANIZATIONAL STRUCTURE UNDER EISENHOWER

Although Truman had signed the National Security Act of 1947, it remained for the Eisenhower administration to make extensive use of the National Security Council as an interdepartmental coordinating device within the White House for shaping foreign policy. Eisenhower's approach to the decision-making process differed substantially from that of his immediate predecessors and from that of the Kennedy and Johnson administrations as well. Whereas Truman had met infrequently with his cabinet as whole, Eisenhower regarded cabinet meetings as a centrally important forum both for communicating policy decisions and for developing options for presidential decision. In keeping with this outlook, Eisenhower viewed the National Security Council as a kind of mini-cabinet consisting of those highest appointed officials having a direct concern with national-security policy-making. In the 1952 presidential campaign, Eisenhower had declared that the formulation of a "national strategy for the cold war" would make necessary the "selection of broad national purposes and the designation within purposes of principal targets." To achieve this objective, Eisenhower stated, his administration would take steps to "bring the dozens of agencies and bureaus into concerted action under an overall scheme of strategy." Like the cabinet, the National Security Council met on a regular basis during the Eisenhower administration. In addition to the president, vice-president, secretary of state, secretary of defense, director of the Office of Civil and Defense Mobilization, the chairman of the Joint Chiefs of Staff, and the chairman of the Atomic Energy Commission, the National Security Council meetings were attended by the heads of the Central Intelligence Agency and the United States Information Agency (established in 1953). In keeping with his belief that economic factors must be taken as fully as possible into account in the development of a coherent and integrated strategy, Eisenhower brought into the National Security Council the secretary of the treasury and the director of the Bureau of the Budget.

Among the tasks given to the National Security Council was the review of the defense and foreign policies inherited by the Eisenhower administration from its predecessor, as well as the consideration of other policy issues as they arose during the Eisenhower administration itself. The discussions that took place within the National Security Council were based on policy papers prepared by a staff headed during most of the Eisenhower administration by Robert Cutler, who was the first special assistant for national-security affairs and, as such, was given membership on the National Security Council. Central to the National Security Council process during most of the Eisenhower administration, moreover, was General Andrew Goodpaster, who not only briefed Eisenhower on current developments on an almost daily basis but also organized the flow of information among the various departments and agencies. In fact, the position of national-security adviser, as it evolved in subsequent administrations, encompassed in one position the duties performed respectively by Cutler and Goodpaster. The discussion papers were prepared under Cutler's direction by the NSC Planning Board, which was actually the "senior staff" concept of the Truman administration.

The NSC Planning Board consisted of senior officials—assistant secretaries or undersecretaries—below the National Security Council level, from each of the departments having a direct concern with foreign policy. The board was charged with developing policy papers containing recommendations for discussion by the

National Security Council. Although an effort was made to develop unanimous positions on issues, the NSC Planning Board apparently did not set forth compromises that simply concealed differences. The work of the Planning Board generated a large number of policy splits for discussion at National Security Council meetings, over which Eisenhower presided. Although Planning Board members from the respective departments and agencies represented on the National Security Council were expected to reflect to some extent institutional and bureaucratic biases, they had specific presidential instructions to encompass in their thinking a much broader perspective. In addition, the work of the NSC Planning Board was shaped by the president's special assistant for national-security affairs and his staff. The small professional staff that worked directly with Cutler represented in itself an innovation of the Eisenhower administration as part of an effort to base policy choices on comprehensive staff work conducted according to carefully defined procedures. In those cases where the Planning Board could not reach agreement, the special assistant for national-security affairs had the responsibility to present such differences to the National Security Council for debate and discussion. The consensus of the National Security Council became the basis for official policy after Eisenhower himself had made necessary modifications. In addition, Eisenhower met frequently with smaller groups of advisers, sometimes after formal NSC meetings, to consider important national-security issues. Termed "special NSC meetings," they foreshadowed what was called the "Ex Comm" in the Kennedy administration. The decision-making process employed by Eisenhower thus had greater flexibility than was implied in the formal structure, whose purpose was to bring greater order and integration to the complex task of foreign-policy formulation.

If the Planning Board was the options-formulation part of national-security decision making, the other side of the process was the examination of chosen policies. For this purpose, the National Security Council system of the Eisenhower administration contained what was called the Operations Coordination Board. Like the Planning Board, but with policy implementation rather than formulation as its function, the Operations Coordination Board was designed to translate decisions into specific policies to be carried out by the various departments and agencies having responsibility for national security. The Operations Coordination Board, like the Planning Board having representation at the cabinet level from each of the departments and agencies represented on the National Security Council, had the responsibility of monitoring within the executive branch the implementation of the national-security policies of the Eisenhower administration.

Although its decision-making structure for national-security policy was elaborate and comprehensive, in sharp contrast to the informality of its predecessors, Eisenhower relied heavily on John Foster Dulles, whose power derived more from his close working relationship with the president than from the fact that he was secretary of state. In fact, the Eisenhower administration represented a period in which the Department of State experienced a sharp decline in influence, faced as it was with the growing importance of a large number of other actors in the national-security decision-making process. From time to time Eisenhower augmented the White House national-security structure with special assistants in such fields as foreign economic policy, arms control, and psychological warfare, but none of these appointees overshadowed Dulles, who clearly remained, as long as he held office, the principal adviser and presidential spokesman on foreign policy.

Although Eisenhower retained ultimate presidential control, often modifying or even drastically altering policies advocated by his secretary of state, Dulles had broad latitude both in the formulation of foreign policy and in the conduct of diplomacy. Both within and outside the formal national-security structure, Eisenhower spent more time in consultation with Dulles than with any other cabinet member. In sharp contrast to the Nixon administration, the special assistant for national-security affairs served more as a coordinator of policy options and a facilitator of decisions than as a conceptualizer. This latter role was reserved principally for Dulles, whose long experience in foreign affairs—at the Hague Peace Conference of 1907, the Versailles Peace Conference of 1919, the founding of the United Nations at the San Francisco Conference in 1945, and the negotiation of the peace treaty with Japan in 1951—had established him in Eisenhower's estimation as a person of unique experience and knowledge.

Thus what emerges from an analysis of the decision-making process of the Eisenhower administration is a picture of a formal structure designed to prevent the president from becoming involved in bureaucratic battles that could be resolved at lower levels and thus to preserve his energy and time for the larger issues that can be resolved only by the president himself. Eisenhower put into place, both in domestic policy and in foreign affairs, a structure that would enhance the prospects for full consideration of all facets of the complex issues that preoccupied policy-making officials. Accustomed to formal procedures in a military career whose assignments had included the organization of the largest amphibious military operation in history—the D-Day landings in Normandy in June 1944—Eisenhower brought to the presidency a penchant for formal organizations and clearly defined procedures for policy planning. At the same time, Eisenhower favored the practice of ad hoc meetings with select groups from the larger National Security Council and the use of various special assistants and other experts drawn for shorter or longer periods into the administration to help cope with immediate or long-term problems. Finally, the relationship between Eisenhower and Dulles, whose role as secretary of state was not to be approximated again until Henry Kissinger was appointed to that position in the second Nixon administration, demonstrated vividly the unique combination of formal structure and informal practice that combined in the Eisenhower administration to produce foreign-policy decisions.

## CONCLUSIONS

By comparison with the decades that preceded and followed it, the Eisenhower years seem in retrospect to stand out as a period of calm both in American foreign policy and in domestic affairs. Eisenhower's administration spanned most of a decade in which the interests and commitments of the United States were extended around the globe. Although American military power contracted in quantitative terms, the United States retained a qualitative advantage that helped to sustain its position as a world power. The 1950s saw vast global economic growth especially in economies of the United States and its allies in Western Europe and Japan. Without engaging American forces in armed combat after the Korean armistice in 1953, the Eisenhower administration nevertheless surmounted successive crises in Southeast Asia, the Middle East, and Europe. By the end of the decade, threats had mounted in the Western Hemisphere and Africa. It had inherited from its predecessor a series of difficult issues, many of which it resolved, but the most important of them—tensions with the Soviet Union—remained intractable, with the result that the Eisenhower administration bequeathed to its successor a complex agenda made even more challenging by the changing security environment in the world of the 1960s.

# chapter 5

# The Foreign Policy of John F. Kennedy:
Years of Idealism

John F. Kennedy was elected president in 1960 after a campaign in which the incumbent Eisenhower administration was criticized for a lack of dynamic leadership, an alleged "missile gap" in favor of the Soviet Union, a do-nothing policy on Cuba, a loss of initiative in the technological race for space, declining world confidence in the dollar, and failure to break out of a purely reactive pattern of policymaking in response to critical problems of the cold war and of relations with allies and the less developed countries. Every incoming presidential team likes to convey the impression that it has a mandate to make all things new and put all things right. True to form, one of Kennedy's slogans had been, "It's time America started moving again."

Apart from Jefferson and Adams, we do not usually associate the presidency with profound intellects. But Kennedy, a voracious reader, was somewhat like the energetic Theodore Roosevelt, who made heavy demands upon himself to be well-informed on a wide range of subjects. Kennedy's mental agility often made him impatient with people in the power structure (beyond those he had hand-picked) on whose advice he sometimes had to rely in foreign and defense policy. A man who revelled in dramatic paradoxes and contrapuntal sentence construction, it was his lot to suffer the most humiliating setback and to enjoy the most elegant triumph experienced by any postwar president up to that time. Both events centered on Cuba.

In the weeks prior to the inauguration, the problem of Cuba did not seem as urgent as that of foreign economic policy or the threats to Laos and Berlin. Kennedy had 10 weeks—72 days—between the election and the inauguration to organize the government for the conduct of foreign affairs by making the principal appointments. Yet five weeks passed before a secretary of state was chosen. Pressures from the worsening balance of payments and the consequent gold drain—resulting from the cost of U.S. overseas military commitments and stiffening trade competition from the European Economic Community—forced Kennedy to assign top priority to selecting a secretary of the treasury, members of the Council of Economic Advisers and a director of the Budget Bureau. In an effort to restore confidence in the international soundness of the dollar, the president-elect looked for someone from the financial community with diplomatic experience. He sought a bipartisan consensus in view of his own narrow electoral margin and the many new challenges then emerging to confront the nation within the global system. He appointed as the head of the Treasury Douglas Dillon, a liberal Republican, well-connected in Wall Street, who had served as undersecretary of state for Eisenhower. Kennedy apparently was ready to offer any of the three top cabinet posts—State, Treasury, or Defense—to Robert A. Lovett, who had been assistant secretary of war under Roosevelt and undersecretary of state and secretary of defense in the Truman administration, but Lovett declined for health reasons. Lovett did, however, recommend Robert McNamara (who had just been elected president of the Ford Motor Company) for Defense and Dean Rusk for State.

Many observers at the time assumed that Kennedy, somewhat more interested in foreign than domestic affairs, wished to be his own secretary of state. That, of course, was impossible. No president, however brilliant and industrious, can keep track of U.S. foreign relations with more than 100 governments,* much less supervise the operations of the State Department. He wanted a competent administrator to run the department and to carry on the vast business of routine diplomatic matters, budgets, and detailed legislation, while reserving the option of taking the reins in his own hands for creative judgments and initiatives on the more important issues, somewhat as FDR had done after 1937. In selecting Rusk, Kennedy passed over other, more obvious nominees: Adlai Stevenson, internationally the most prestigious Democrat, partly for that very reason and also for his reputed indecisiveness; the liberal Chester Bowles; and Senator J. William Fulbright (at one point favored by Kennedy, who had to be reminded that the Arkansan's voting record on segregation would render him suspect with the new states emerging from colonialism in black Africa). On December 12, 1960, Rusk, a former Rhodes scholar and intelligence officer in Asia during World War II, assistant secretary for Far Eastern affairs and deputy undersecretary in Acheson's State Department, and later president of the Rockefeller Foundation, was appointed. Bowles was named undersecretary; the eloquent Stevenson became ambassador to the United Nations; and McGeorge Bundy, a Republican Harvard dean and son-in-law of Henry L. Stimson, was chosen as special assistant for

---

*In 1961 there were 104 states with membership in the United Nations. The United States had relations with all except Cuba, and with four nonmember governments—the Federal Republic of Germany, Switzerland, South Korea, and South Vietnam.

national-security affairs, with M.I.T. economist Walt W. Rostow as his deputy for a time.

Rusk, a seasoned diplomat who believed devoutly in the doctrine of containment, was known for his patience, soft-spoken manner, diplomatic intelligence, practical wisdom, and tact. But he was not self-assertive. On many of the most critical issues in foreign affairs, he tended to defer to the views of three more dynamic figures who were usually closer to and more influential with the president—Attorney General Robert Kennedy, Defense Secretary McNamara, and National Security Assistant Bundy. Rusk grew into his administrative role with competence and graciousness, but he did not have the leadership qualities of Byrnes, Marshall, Acheson, or Dulles. Kennedy occasionally complained that he was not sure what Rusk was thinking. The Georgian, who seemed a bit reticent in dealing with the Bostonian president, his "Charles River Gang" from Harvard and M.I.T., and his "Irish Mafia," would later emerge as a somewhat more distinct figure during the presidency of Lyndon B. Johnson, who genuinely liked, trusted, and relied on him.

## FIRST STEPS TOWARD THE NEW FRONTIER — *his slogan*

Kennedy was less experienced in international affairs than Vice-President Richard M. Nixon, whom he narrowly defeated in the 1960 election. His basic attitude toward communism and the cold war did not differ significantly from that of his Republican rival. As a Harvard-educated intellectual of Irish ancestry, however, he was given to a much more liberal, lilting, catchy, and at times humorous or whimsically utopian rhetoric, which exemplifies the tone of his presidency (see box). He was anticolonial, sympathetic toward "the revolution of rising expectations" (Rostow's phrase) in the Third World, and strongly attracted to peace and disarmament themes even though determined to improve the nation's deterrence and defense capabilities. To signify that his presidency marked a historic threshold, he chose "New Frontier" as its slogan.

Generally speaking, Kennedy exuded an attraction to youth everywhere in this country and around the world. Having worked briefly as a reporter, he knew many newspapers and journalists, and he knew how to create the most favorable media image. Aware that the televised debates with Nixon had played a crucial part in his election campaign, he learned to use TV with great effect. He knew that he, his wife, and his family were photogenic, charming, and terribly interesting to the media here and abroad, and he sought to extract maximum political advantage from the quality that become famous as "Kennedy charisma." Coming into office with a reputation in many circles as an anti-Communist ideologue, he nevertheless quickly induced student, intellectual, and labor groups in foreign countries to tone down their anti-U.S. rhetoric. By supporting the aspirations underlying the UN's Decade of Development (which in the end did not prove very successful), he improved the image of the United States within the United Nations, thanks partly to the articulate contribution of Stevenson. His determination to reassert the technological leadership of the United States over the Soviet Union on the new frontier of space by proclaiming a U.S. landing on the moon within a decade as an urgent national priority made him look indeed like a leader with a clear vision of the future.

### Excerpts from Kennedy's Inaugural Address

Let the word go forth from this time and place, to friend and foe alike, that the torch has been passed to a new generation of Americans, born in this century, tempered by war, disciplined by a hard and bitter peace, proud of our ancient heritage, and unwilling to witness or permit the slow undoing of those human rights to which this nation has always been committed. . . .

Let every nation know, whether it wishes us well or ill, that we shall pay any price, bear any burden, meet any hardship, support any friend, oppose any foe to assure the survival and the success of liberty. . . .

To those new states whom we welcome to the ranks of the free, we pledge our word that one form of colonial control shall not have passed away merely to be replaced by a far more iron tyranny. . . .

To those nations who would make themselves our adversary, we offer not a pledge but a request: that both sides begin anew the quest for peace, before the dark powers of destruction unleashed by science engulf all humanity in planned or accidental self-destruction. . . .

So let us begin anew, remembering on both sides that civility is not a sign of weakness, and sincerity is always subject to proof. Let us never negotiate out of fear, but let us never fear to negotiate. . . .

Let both sides seek to invoke the wonders of science instead of its terrors. Together let us explore the stars, conquer the deserts, eradicate disease, tap the ocean depths, and encourage the arts and commerce. . . .

And if a beachhead of cooperation may push back the jungle of suspicion, let both sides join in creating a new endeavor, not a new balance of power, but a new world of law where the strong are just and the weak secure and the peace preserved. . . .

Now the trumpet summons us again—not as a call to bear arms, though arms we need; not as a call to battle, though embattled we are; but a call to bear the burden of a long twilight struggle, year in and year out, "rejoicing in hope, patient in tribulation," a struggle against the common enemies of man: tyranny, poverty, disease, and war itself. . . .

Kennedy was all for reducing poverty, unemployment, malnutrition, and the inadequacy of health and educational programs in the United States, but he had no desire to focus exclusively on domestic issues. Since the poorer lands of the Third World were becoming the arena of political and economic competition between the two major philosophical bases for the organization of society, Kennedy thought that improving the quality of American life would not by itself be sufficient. In his view, there had to be an increase in the flow of economic assistance to those unfortunate countries which had been called, in turn, "backward," "underdeveloped," "less developed," and finally "developing" (even though the industrially advanced nations were developing, too, and at a much more rapid rate).

## Revamped AID and "Food for Peace" Programs

The Kennedy administration would reorganize a variety of ongoing overseas assistance programs under the aegis of a new Agency for International Development (AID), headed by David Bell, in an effort to reverse a slow decline in public and congressional support for foreign-aid appropriations. Older programs designed by the Agriculture and State departments to help American farmers sell their surplus crops abroad were given a higher budgetary priority and a new name (long urged by Senator Hubert Humphrey of Minnesota) in Public Law 480 instituting "Food for Peace" shipments, which were administered under George McGovern before his election to the Senate in 1962. During Kennedy's tenure those shipments averaged nearly $1.5 billion annually, benefiting the American farmer while averting widespread starvation in India, Egypt, and other countries which were then unable to feed their populations adequately.

## The Peace Corps

One of Kennedy's most cherished projects, a key symbol of his New Frontier, was the Peace Corps, which had also been promoted by the altruistic Humphrey. As early as 1910, the philosopher William James, in his famous essay "The Moral Equivalent of War," had called for a national effort to divert into peaceful, constructive, and humanitarian channels against poverty, disease, ignorance, and war those forces of youthful idealism, zeal, energy, dedication, and impulse to self-sacrifice which in all times and cultures have produced the noblest warriors and finest soldiers. Franklin Roosevelt had tried to tap these forces, and simultaneously alleviate the frustrations of unemployed youth during the Depression, by creating the Civilian Conservation Corps (CCC). The Peace Corps volunteers, directed by the president's brother-in-law, Sargent Shriver, were fresh from colleges and universities, high-minded and unpaid conduits of development on a people-to-people basis. It was to be their function to facilitate the transfer of skills—to be carriers of knowledge about education, sanitation, basic medicine, nursing, agronomy, carpentry, and the utility of cooperation in solving local problems in areas deprived of most modern amenities.

The Peace Corps provoked domestic and foreign criticism. Eisenhower dubbed it a "juvenile experiment." Nixon feared it might attract draft dodgers. Moscow condemned it as an instrument of capitalist exploitation and espionage. Foreign governments already disposed to think the worst of the United States made it clear that the volunteers would not be welcome, and Washington made it equally clear that they would enter a country only by invitation. From the first project with 30 volunteers in Tanganyika, the Peace Corps expanded by 1963 to about 9000 volunteers serving more than 40 countries. Some of the volunteers suffered severe culture shock and depression at what they perceived as their lack of tangible progress they brought about in their host countries. On the whole, however, they were goodwill ambassadors of the American way at a grass-roots level impenetrable by diplomats. Their experience abroad probably had more effect on the Peace Corps volunteers than they had on their host countries.

## KENNEDY'S EMPHASIS ON LATIN AMERICA

One of the central areas for Washington's attention was to be Latin America. A favorite theme throughout Kennedy's campaign had been the urgent need to alleviate the poverty of that region and to reverse what he regarded as a long period of neglect in U.S. policy toward the countries south of the border. The Truman and Eisenhower administrations, preoccupied with Soviet and Chinese challenges in Europe and Asia, had devoted little concern and few resources to Latin America. Despite complaints about the failure of the United States to provide substantial economic assistance, there lingered from the days of FDR's Good Neighbor Policy a sufficient spirit of hemispheric cooperativeness to make it possible for the Organization of American States (OAS) to function as a damper of intraregional political conflicts, especially among the Caribbean states, despite what appeared to them as the heavy-handed approach of John Foster Dulles and the CIA's effort to overturn the pro-Soviet Arbenz regime in Guatemala. With increasing frequency, the United States was accused of being indifferent to nationalist stirrings and desires for socioeconomic reform in Latin America. Prior to Castro, "revolutions" in the Western Hemisphere (with the notable exception of Perónism in Argentina) had typically been military coups that would quickly win the support of the vested interests and posed no direct threat to American investments, security, and political values. American liberals had long berated their government for relying too heavily on private investment to bring about the needed development and for tolerating right-wing military regimes that fostered a climate favorable to business, instead of actively supporting progressive democracy. Between 1958 and 1960, the United States and its neighbors to the south had worked together, along with the UN Economic Commission for Latin America, to lay the foundations for the cooperative effort that Kennedy wished to emphasize at the outset of his term.

During the election campaign, Kennedy wanted an idea akin to FDR's Good Neighbor Policy, but one symbolizing a better set of economic relationships than those of the past. His advisers came up with *Alianza para el Progresso*—the Alliance for Progress. Kennedy's inaugural address contained the following passage:

> To our sister republics . . . we offer a special pledge: to convert our good words into good deeds, in a new alliance for progress, to assist free men and free governments in casting off the chains of poverty. But this peaceful revolution of hope cannot become the prey of hostile powers. Let all our neighbors know that we shall join with them to oppose aggression or subversion anywhere in the Americas. And let every other power know that this hemisphere intends to remain the master of its own house.

Less than two months later, on March 13, 1961, Kennedy, speaking to the Latin American diplomatic corps, called for a ten-year plan for the Americas, "a vast cooperative effort, unparalleled in magnitude and nobility of purpose, to satisfy the basic needs of the American people for homes, work and land, health and schools." The three goals of the new Alliance for Progress were: to speed up the rate of economic development; to encourage changes in the economy and social institutions (especially patterns of taxation and land ownership); and to support political democracy by throwing U.S. weight against dictatorships of the left or the right. Before the *Alianza* could show any progress, however, something happened that left many Latin Americans and others confused about the true direction of U.S. foreign policy.

## The Bay of Pigs Fiasco

Kennedy's dream of a new era of idealism in American history was almost shattered within three months of his inauguration. His first Cuban crisis, which was a foreign-policy fiasco and a human tragedy, illustrated both the problems of maintaining continuity of foreign-policy planning and execution in the American democratic system and the vulnerability of any new leadership in Washington to erratic performance. During the campaign, Kennedy had vacillated between the thesis that Castro should have been recognized and treated as a Communist from the start and the view that Eisenhower was to be criticized for having supported the Batista dictatorship as long as he did and for having failed to aid the non-Batista Cubans opposed to Castro's tyranny. Kennedy insisted, however, that the U.S. government should extend only moral and psychological, not military, support to those seeking a restoration of democracy.

Shortly after the election, the president-elect, in a briefing from Allen Dulles and Richard Bissell of the CIA, learned that President Eisenhower had decided earlier to authorize the CIA to organize a broad anti-Castro coalition and to train and equip Cuban exiles for a possible action against Castro, in which it was specified that U.S. forces would play no direct part. By November, 1200 Cubans, recruited largely in Florida from among disaffected Cuban refugees, were being trained by the CIA in the Sierra Madre of western Guatemala. Many of these had cheered the overthrow of the Batista dictatorship and the triumphal entry of Fidel Castro's forces into Havana at the beginning of 1959. Most of them considered themselves victims rather than enemies of the revolution—or, more precisely, of what the revolution had become. In their eyes Castro was less a convinced Marxist than a power-seeking opportunist who had betrayed their liberal democratic revolution by turning it over to the Communists.

Within a year of taking Havana, Castro proclaimed himself a Marxist-Leninist, railed against *Yanqui* imperialism, and initiated a rapid, ruthless system of summary justice and execution for Batistianos who could not escape to Florida. This was a bloodletting unprecedented in the history of Latin American revolutions. At the same time, he began to build up an army of 250,000 troops and supply it with Soviet equipment. Controversy has raged over the question of whether the Eisenhower administration, by instituting a boycott of Cuban sugar instead of granting economic aid, had driven the fledgling government into the arms of the Soviet Union. The historical evidence does not support this hypothesis. The United States had cut off arms shipments to the Batista regime in March 1958 and had promptly recognized the Castro government in the spring of 1959.

Though the State Department was willing to discuss economic assistance, Castro displayed no interest whatsoever. Influenced by his brother Raul and by

Che Guevara, both of whom had long maintained close relations with the Soviet Union, Castro seemed determined from an early date to break away from the traditional pattern of hemispheric security under the protection of the United States, to repudiate American capitalist aid, and to harness his revolution to that of the Soviet Union. Although the anti-Batista upsurge was originally an essentially liberal bourgeois movement, it encompassed many people on the social-democratic left who were anxious to bring about a substantial change in Cuba's social structure. One of the leftist leaders was Manuel Ray, who had organized the underground revolutionary resistance in Havana. Ray, alienated from Castro's methods, resigned from his government in November 1959. Several prominent spokesmen of the Latin American democratic left, including Romulo Betancourt of Venezuela, Haya de la Torre, head of the Peruvian Aprista party, Alberto Lleras Camargo of Colombia, and Jose Figueres of Costa Rica, turned sour on the Castro experiment months before centrists and liberals in the United States did.

Having inherited from his predecessor's administration an initiative that now had momentum, Kennedy was confronted with a serious dilemma. If he went forward with the exile-training project at the very beginning of his term, he ran the risk of provoking a Latin American outcry against a revival of *Yanqui* imperialist interventionism, thereby jeopardizing the success of his *Alianza para el Progresso.* If he cancelled it and ordered the dispersal of 1200 or more anti-Castro Cubans, most of them extremely frustrated after their hopes had been raised so high, he would be accused not only of a failure of nerve but also of giving comfort to Fidelistas throughout the region and of actively promoting communism in the hemisphere. The president temporized. While clearly reserving for himself the final decision to stop or go to make up to 24 hours ahead of time, he tentatively approved the plan for the CIA to proceed with its training program. He also instructed the departments of State and Defense, as well as the Joint Chiefs of Staff, to scrutinize the project carefully for its political and military feasibility. Kennedy strongly reiterated Eisenhower's ground rule against any overt U.S. military role. He authorized the CIA to train and equip an all-Cuban invasion force that would make a landing on the island, establish a beachhead, proclaim itself the provisional government, link up with rebel units already operating in the Escambray Mountains, and inspire a popular uprising against the oppressive regime of Castro.

The final execution of the plan, however, bore little resemblance to its original conception. Although Kennedy wanted the exile organization to be, or at least appear to be, as liberal and authentically revolutionary as possible, the CIA was unable or unwilling to alter the conservative complexion of the enterprise. Some of the leaders of the group being trained in Guatemala looked upon the philosophy of Manuel Ray and his followers as *Fidelismo sans* ("without") *Fidel.* Furthermore, the CIA was familiar with the personnel already in place and probably feared that it might lose control over the operation if dynamic new elements were introduced.

In order to salvage the project from the mildly skeptical criticism of Kennedy's inexperienced advisers, those who had a vested interest in carrying it through kept acquiescing in bureaucratic modifications of the plan that cumulatively eroded its chances of success. The planned landing site was shifted from Trinidad, far from Castro's growing army and easily accessible to the Escambray Mountains, to Cochinos Bay (the Bay of Pigs), 100 miles closer to the source of Castro's military strength and further removed over a more hostile route from the Escambrays. The Joint Chiefs preferred the Trinidad site, yet they offered no objections to the change because they regarded the project not as a military one but as a clandestine political enterprise of the CIA. The success of such an operation was predicated upon large-scale popular resistance, presumably spontaneous because it was never an integral part of the planning. Yet estimates of the prospect for such an uprising grew progressively dimmer without producing any adjustments in Kennedy's plans. Despite frequent reminders from the Oval Office that there should be no directly identifiable action of U.S. military forces, the Cubans later insisted that they had received assurance: Once the U.S. government made a commitment to go ahead with the invasion, it could not be allowed to fail. Not a few high-ranking U.S. policymakers proceeded on the same assumption. Those individuals who had doubts hesitated to express them or to challenge the confident expertise of those in charge. All around, hopes were higher than the quality of the decision making warranted.

From the start, the president had shown little enthusiasm for the operation and he frequently expressed misgivings, but at no point did he exercise decisive leadership by reversing the inexorable drift toward tragedy. Throughout his political career he had led a charmed life, and to his White House associates he seemed incapable of a major blunder. There may have been a vague expectation that luck would carry him through again, even though his political instincts should have warned him away from the approaching shoals. The plan would have succeeded either with a widespread popular uprising or with direct U.S. military support. The former was no longer expected; the latter was never authorized.

At the moment of crisis, in mid-April 1961, Kennedy's strategy was one of limiting the damage. Almost everything that could possibly go wrong did. The intelligence estimates proved woefully inadequate. The Cuban brigade, not well prepared for the night landing in outboard motor boats, was quickly overcome by Castro's forces, which were much stronger, better equipped, and readier than anticipated. The president had previously called off a second air strike, on which the Cubans and their American mentors had depended. There was no spontaneous popular upheaval in Cuba. The only role assigned to U.S. naval and air forces was to rescue as many of the brave Cubans as possible. Not many could be rescued, however. More than 80 percent of the brigade, which finally numbered 1400, were captured by Castro's forces. Fortunately, the casualties numbered only a few hundred, fewer than there might have been.

The Bay of Pigs fiasco was certainly one of the most ignominious episodes in the history of American foreign policy. Although the president had wanted it to appear as a purely intra-Cuban affair and had refused U.S. military support at the crucial juncture, the United States was subjected to diplomatic criticism from many capitals and especially at the United Nations, where an unwitting and skeptical Adlai Stevenson was allowed to vouch for a deceptive cover story concerning the first air strike, which had accomplished nothing except to alert

Castro of the impending invasion. The United States was also vilified, more than was Kennedy himself, for this latest instance of "ruthless American imperialist intervention" into the internal affairs of a small country. While privately blaming the mess on the incompetence of the CIA and the Joint Chiefs, Kennedy sought to profit from a bitter and costly lesson by frankly acknowledging his administration's naiveté and lack of experience in dealing with a foreign-policy crisis. On April 19, 1961, after the three-day tragicomedy was over, Kennedy quite remarkably was able to win public sympathy by shouldering the blame himself. "There's an old saying," he remarked at his press conference, "that victory has a hundred fathers and defeat is an orphan. . . . I am the responsible officer of the government. . . ." That was not only the politically shrewd thing to say, but also the courageous, proper, and wise thing to do, for it preserved the country from an enervating period of finger pointing and self-recrimination.

### The Alliance for Progress

After the Bay of Pigs, Kennedy turned to the OAS for assistance in the task of isolating Castro and curbing his ability to export revolution to the rest of Latin America. For this, however, he had to deliver on his earlier promise of substantial U.S. funding for hemispheric development under the Alliance for Progress. By moving quickly on this plan, he managed with surprising resilience to rebound from the adverse consequences of the dismal Cuban venture. He demonstrated his adeptness by sending several credibly articulate representatives—Adolf Berle, Arthur Schlesinger, Jr., Richard Goodwin, Adlai Stevenson, and others—to persuade the Latin Americans that a new day in hemispheric relations truly had dawned. Moreover, although his domestic legislative record was never very good, Kennedy managed to win congressional support in the way of funding for his Alliance goals. His administration dispatched energetic, idealistic young members of the Peace Corps to Latin America, increased Food for Peace shipments under P.L. 480, selected the Puerto Rican leader Teodoro Moscoso as Alliance for Progress coordinator within the Agency for International Development, and undertook other programs designed to arouse the expectations of impoverished segments of the population in a region where the upper 2 percent owned more than half of the wealth.

At the Conference of the Inter-American Economic and Social Council held at Punta del Este, Uruguay, in August 1961, democratic leaders pledged to strengthen democratic institutions, accelerate social and economic development, provide decent housing for all people, encourage agrarian reform, ensure fair wages and satisfactory working conditions, wipe out illiteracy, promote health and sanitation, reform tax laws, and take other steps to transform unjust social structures and redistribute the national income to benefit those most in need. In return, the United States promised to provide "a major part of the minimum of 20 billion dollars, principally in public funds, which Latin America will require over the next ten years from all external sources in order to supplement its own efforts."

Although the *Alianza* was designed to ensure the eventual triumph of democratic forces against rightist and leftist tyrannies, its projected benefits were extended to the dictatorial regimes of General Alfredo Stroessner in Paraguay and François Duvalier ("Papa Doc") of Haiti. The Kennedy administration deemed it possible to wean right-wing systems away from oppressiveness and toward a more benign posture, even if not toward real democracy because, unlike Castro's Cuba, they were not under the increasingly tight control of Moscow-oriented Communists. The determination to preserve national independence was a principal criterion of eligibility for U.S. assistance. At one point Kennedy expressed a willingness to aid socialist, Marxist-leaning regimes such as that of Dr. Cheddi Jagan in British Guiana provided that they would (like Yugoslavia) jealously guard their national independence and would remain committed to the parliamentary institutions that were part of their political heritage.

When Rafael Trujillo of the Dominican Republic was assassinated in May 1961 after more than 30 years of despotic rule, the hemisphere watched to see whether democracy would sprout up or whether his son Ramfis, who controlled the army, would try to perpetuate the family tyranny. The democratic opposition agreed to support the moderate Joaquin Belaguer (who had been a puppet president under Trujillo) only if Ramfis Trujillo would leave the country. The latter's apparent preparation in November 1961 to restore the dictatorship prompted Kennedy to dispatch eight ships and 1800 Marines to the waters off the coast of Santo Domingo in a show of support for the democratic forces that ultimately led to the departure of the younger Trujillo. This unusual display of "gunboat diplomacy" on behalf of nationalist and democratic aspirations brought cheers from virtually all the Latin America capitals except Havana, which denounced it. A month later, Kennedy and his wife Jacqueline undertook the first of their three annual grand tours to exert their charm on admiring Latin American crowds. Kennedy drew the most animated applause when he admitted past U.S. mistakes in the region and called upon Latin American landowners, business interests, and ruling elements to admit their own errors.

In December 1962 the Dominican people in their first democratic election chose a prominent literary figure, Juan Bosch, to head the government. His problems typified those facing moderate democratic left leaders throughout the southern part of the hemisphere. Convinced that the best way to combat the threat of Marxism-Leninism was to alleviate the plight of the poverty-stricken masses, they came under domestic attack from Communists and reactionaries alike. In a polarizing situation, the sensible middle way is invariably the hardest to follow. Unfortunately, the democratic left leaders proved more effective in frightening and alienating the upper classes than in winning the trust and allegiance of the lower classes.

The Alliance for Progress had some undisputed successes. These included the construction of low-rent public housing, meal and textbook programs for schoolchildren, the creation of long-range planning mechanisms, and modest improvements in land use and distribution, tax laws, and public administrative efficiency. About half of the 19 OAS members taking part surpassed the GNP growth goals set by the Alliance. For the most part, however, both the administration and the OAS found that the task of significant socioeconomic development was much more difficult than the rhetorician-architects of the

*Alianza* had expected, for it required profound cultural changes that could occur only at a glacial pace. No real agrarian or tax-structure reform was achieved. Whenever the United States attempted to press for faster progress, conservative vested interests sought to arouse nationalist resentment by accusing the U.S. government of intervening in the country's internal affairs. Most of the countries in the Alliance felt the adverse effects of a decline in the world prices of their products, and balance-of-payments deficits prevented them from importing much of the capital equipment needed for development. Other obstacles included: the opposition of U.S. private investors to the administration's policy of granting aid to governments that nationalized industries; population increases that cut into the per-capita GNP growth rate; bureaucratic inertia, inefficiency, and corruption that prevented incoming aid funds from being converted into assistance for those who needed it most; and unstable political leadership.

## COMMUNIST INSURGENCY IN SOUTHEAST ASIA

Kennedy, an anticolonialist at heart, was sympathetic to the new forces of nationalism stirring through the world. After a trip to Indochina in 1951, he had come to favor independence from France for that region. In 1954, when Dulles and Nixon were disposed toward U.S. intervention on behalf of the beleaguered French at Dien Bien Phu, Kennedy as a young senator had spoken against the idea. In 1957 he had attracted considerable attention with a major address in the Senate strongly criticizing French policy in the Algerian insurgency. (The selection of his targets made it seem that his anticolonial sentiments were directed solely against France.) Kennedy, however, was also an anticommunist in his determination to prevent newly independent states or democratic governments in older states from falling under the domination of foreign Communist capitals—Moscow, Peking, or Havana.

### Dealing with the Pathet Lao in Laos

On the day before his inauguration, Kennedy met with Eisenhower and showed greater concern over Laos than over any other problem he was about to inherit. The outgoing president warned him that a Communist takeover of the strategically pivotal Mekong Valley would put "unbelievable pressure" on Cambodia, Thailand, and South Vietnam. Kennedy apparently did not hesitate to subscribe to the "domino theory," which suggested that the fall of one country to the Communists would lead inevitably to the toppling of its weak neighbors. Eisenhower said that action by SEATO was preferable, but Britain and France, unwilling to become involved militarily, favored the neutralist solution under Souvanna Phouma, who had fled to Cambodia. Eisenhower and Dulles had always opposed Souvanna Phouma, regarding him as a pro-Soviet neutralist. Eisenhower cautioned his successor not to bring the Pathet Lao into a coalition: that proposed solution, he noted, had led to the failure of Marshall's mission to China. Kennedy did not want to provoke a debate over "who lost Laos?"

Kennedy knew that he could not sit back and allow the Communist Pathet Lao insurgents to take over because of the implications of such an outcome for U.S. commitments to the rest of Southeast Asia. However, he was determined to avoid a futile effort to dispatch an American expeditionary force to shore up the Royal Laotian Army, most of whose soldiers were Buddhist pacifists, as a bastion of freedom against the world's two principal Communist powers, which were still widely presumed to be allies, at least in their opposition to the West. (In April 1961, General MacArthur advised Kennedy never to commit American ground troops to the Asian mainland.) The president chose, therefore, to pursue through negotiations the kind of neutral Laos that the Eisenhower administration had rejected.

When the National Security Council discussed sending a small U.S. force into the Mekong Valley as a deterrent to the Pathet Lao and a bargaining counter for negotiations, the Joint Chiefs opposed this as a halfway measure, urging either an all-out effort or none at all. Faced with problems in Cuba, Berlin, the Congo, and Vietnam, Kennedy was reluctant to send troops into a country that did not seem worth a major conflict. Yet he felt he had to "look tough" in order to achieve his goal of a cease-fire and neutralization. U.S. forces in the South China Sea, Okinawa, and Thailand were alerted, strengthened, resupplied, and redeployed closer to Laos during the latter part of March. In response to a request from Kennedy, India's Nehru supported the idea of a cease-fire. Britain's Macmillan agreed to back U.S. military intervention if it should prove unavoidable, but France remained recalcitrant. Kennedy was walking a tightrope, trying to portray himself as willing to accept a truly neutral Laos if diplomacy could produce it but prepared, if necessary, to carry out a military intervention.

While the Pathet Lao was overrunning the country, Averell Harriman urged Kennedy to line up behind the neutralist solution of Prince Souvanna Phouma, the premier of Laos. Just at that point the president was compelled to divert his attention to the Bay of Pigs. Prior to that debacle, the Joint Chiefs had said they were willing to dispatch 60,000 troops to Laos. Afterward, they insisted that it would take 140,000, equipped with tactical nuclear weapons. It was becoming clearer by the day that no detailed contingency plans for a Laotian intervention existed and that public opinion, congressional leaders, and defense officials did not want U.S. ground forces committed in Asia.

Kennedy continued to order demonstrative military moves. In a dramatic news conference he publicly staked his prestige on the outcome of a test of wills—neutralization or substantial intervention. Apparently he somehow managed against all odds to persuade Khrushchev that the United States meant business when it really did not. Perhaps Khrushchev concluded that Kennedy simply could not accept another serious setback in Southeast Asia a week after the Bay of Pigs. He probably did not want to send Soviet troops to Laos and risk direct embroilment with U.S. forces. He was also sure, as he had predicted, that Laos would eventually "fall into our laps like a ripe apple." It was already certain that the Communist Pathet Lao would remain the dominant element in a "neutral" Laos; nothing could alter that fact. A cease-fire was negotiated on May 1. Three weeks later, an International Control Commission, consisting of representatives from India, Canada, and Poland, arrived to work out a neutralization agreement. Kennedy and Khrushchev added their formal blessing at Vienna in June—the one substantive result of their summit meeting.

All of Southeast Asia was fertile ground for what U.S. strategists of the 1950s called "brushfire wars" and what Khrushchev on January 6, 1961, had dubbed "wars of national liberation." The president had long been convinced that guerrilla insurgency represented a much more complex threat to the free world than conventional military aggression and that neither the government nor the army was prepared to cope with it. Counterinsurgency operations could not be conceived in narrow military terms, but required a subtle combination of political, military, social, economic, and psychological programs designed to win the hearts and minds of the people—who are, to paraphrase Mao Zedong, the sea in which the Communist guerrilla swims freely. Kennedy ordered that efforts be immediately undertaken on a broad front to improve U.S. counterguerrilla capabilities. Traditional institutions, however, do not readily change direction. After having been reminded countless times that politics should be left to political leaders and diplomats, the U.S. Army did not take to the idea that it should engage in democratic nation building and socioeconomic development while waging war against guerrilla revolutionaries.

### The Viet Cong Gathers Strength in Vietnam

The administration now had to shift its attention to South Vietnam, where more was at stake and the conflict was on a larger scale. The situation in Vietnam was deteriorating, but at a less disastrous rate than it had been in Laos. In less than 16 months the number of Viet Cong (VC) guerrillas had jumped from 4400 to 12,000.* At least half the territory of South Vietnam was under Communist control, especially at night. The VC had been engaged for more than a year in an intensive campaign of infiltration, subversion, sabotage, brutal terror, and assassination, killing an average of six local leaders per day in 1960, thereby decapitating the non-Communist elite. Favorite targets were teachers and schools; hospitals, malaria-control centers, and health workers; agricultural agents and research centers; rural police, priests, and village elders. Kennedy needed to reassure Ngo Dinh Diem in South Vietnam and Thanarat Sarit in Thailand that he had no intention of allowing all of Southeast Asia to go down the drain. The domino theory had taken on validity insofar as Southeast Asian government leaders believed in it, and they were deeply upset by developments in Laos.

Kennedy decided to reaffirm the U.S. commitment by sending Vice-President Lyndon B. Johnson in May 1961 on visits of reassurance to Chiang Kai-shek in Taipei, Diem in Saigon, and Sarit in Bangkok. After the trip, Kennedy and Johnson agreed that Southeast Asia need not inevitably be lost, but

---

*Viet Cong guerrillas were recruited mainly from two sources: North Vietnamese who had once lived in the south but who had gone north after the partition of Vietnam in 1954; and South Vietnamese leftists and nationalists who sympathized with Ho Chi Minh's struggle against Western imperialism. VC arms came from Communist sources and from Diem's armed forces.

could be saved from Communist totalitarianism with the proper mix of policies, military, economic, and political. Johnson wanted no troop involvement beyond training missions, backed up with substantial political and economic reforms.

Unfortunately, the U.S. commitment to South Vietnam, originally made by Eisenhower and Dulles, had become a commitment to a one-man regime to which the loyalty of the Vietnamese people had been eroded. Diem had come to power as a traditional patriot with a strong character, a feudal authoritarian anxious to raise the moral and socioeconomic standards of his people, who, in his view, owed him respect, allegiance and obedience, but to whom he was not responsible in any democratic sense. From 1960 onward, Diem became more repressive and paranoid, and increasingly a focus of resentment among intellectual, political, and military elites. At U.S. urging, he promised reforms that he never bothered to pursue. A swelling chorus of criticism from American journalists helped considerably to undermine his position both in the United States and in his own country, pushing him closer to absolutism.

General Maxwell Taylor and Walt Rostow (then moving to State as head of policy planning) were dispatched to Vietnam, and reported back that the massive flow of military aid from the north had to be stopped. They realized that the war could be won only by the Vietnamese themselves, with American help, but the South Vietnamese were not inspired by Diem. Buddhists who felt discriminated against by the Catholic, French-educated upper class demonstrated against the regime and drew fire from government troops, whereupon a number of Buddhist monks began to dramatize their case by engaging in self-immolation. These *bonzes* (fiery suicides), which furnished sensational pictures for the world press, became a powerful stimulus for anti-Diem feeling. The objective of the United States was to foster the conditions necessary to preserve freedom of choice for the South Vietnamese, not to plant seeds of liberal parliamentary democracy in soil where they could not sprout, much less grow. Not a few journalists seemed to assume that Diem's heavy-handed methods justified the goals of the Viet Cong. Ho Chi Minh, who did not have to brook any criticism for his repression in the north, was often portrayed as the George Washington of Vietnam, while the degree of freedom which the people of the south indisputably enjoyed was generally ignored in a reporting process that became increasingly one-sided.

Kennedy's response to this tense situation was to send 100 military advisers and 400 Special Forces troops, known as Green Berets. By the end of 1961, U.S. military personnel in Vietnam numbered 2000; a year or so later, 11,000. During 1962, the strengthening of the Military Assistance Advisory Group, the influx of helicopters, and the expansion of a highly touted "strategic hamlet" program (borrowed from British experience in the Malayan "emergency" and designed to protect civilians from Viet Cong by fortifying their villages) appeared to turn the tide. Even the Communists conceded that it had been Diem's year. In Washington, optimistic statements began to issue from Rusk, McNamara, Taylor, U. Alexis Johnson, and Kennedy himself in his State of the Union Message in January 1963.

From May 1963 onward, however, several key members of the Kennedy administration began to blame the lack of progress in the struggle on Diem and even more on his brother Nhu and his sister-in-law, Madame Nhu. Nhu was seen as the prime architect of failure in the strategic-hamlet program, which bogged down in corruption and aroused opposition from the peasant villagers it was supposed to insulate against VC terrorists. He also headed a uniformed youth corps and a clandestine organization that hunted Communists and other enemies of Diem. Madame Nhu, *femme fatale* of the Saigon regime, was increasingly accused of being a meddling power behind the throne who despised the Buddhists and urged the persecutions that aroused such adverse reactions throughout the Western world. Diem, aloof in manner and isolated by lifestyle from his people, allowed himself to be manipulated by his family, whose members identified the best interests of Vietnam with their own personal objectives.

The U.S. ambassador to South Vietnam from March 1961 to August 1963 was Frederick ("Fritz") Nolting, who had been dispatched to Saigon by Kennedy to support the Diem government in its struggle against communism. During the summer of 1963, several of Kennedy's policy advisers, notably Averell Harriman and Roger Hilsman, became convinced that the United States must withdraw its backing from the Ngo family if the war against the Communists was to be won. Hilsman, the former director of State Department intelligence and research who had recently become assistant secretary for Far Eastern affairs, contended that the attacks against Buddhists by a Catholic ruling elite were a disastrous mistake because, while the officers of the South Vietnamese Army were for the most part Catholic, the NCOs and foot soldiers were Buddhists.

Since Nolting could not suddenly turn against Diem or deliver a warning that he would be in deep trouble if he did not dismiss the Nhus (that is, his brother and his brother's wife), it was decided that Nolting should be relieved of his post. The president chose as his successor Henry Cabot Lodge, who had been defeated by Kennedy as a candidate for senator from Massachusetts in 1952 and by the Kennedy-Johnson ticket as a candidate for vice-president in 1960. The desirability of having a prominent Republican involved in any impending disaster in Vietnam was obvious.

Lodge arrived at his post not long after Diem, flagrantly reneging on a promise to seek reconciliation with the Buddhists, had allowed the secret police to attack their pagodas, arresting hundreds of priests and killing many. Back in Washington, on Hilsman's initiative, a controversial cable was written on Saturday, August 24, directing Lodge to pass the word that the United States could no longer support a government that included the Nhus. The message, drafted by Hilsman, Ball, and Michael Forrest of Bundy's staff, was supposed to be circulated for approval by Rusk, McNamara, McCone, and Taylor. The last three could not be reached on the weekend, although Rosewell Gilpatric, undersecretary of defense, and Richard Helms, deputy director of the CIA, were contacted by phone.

Kennedy later became furious when he learned that some of his leading advisers—especially McNamara, McCone, and Taylor—were expressing reservations about the cable after it had been dispatched. Everyone had proceeded on the assumption that there was a consensus on the proposition that a change of government in Saigon was essential, but such a consensus did not exist. The next time all the principals got together, the president stared icily at each and asked whether the cable should be changed. Everyone seemed to conclude that the cable must have reflected Kennedy's thinking; no one recommended a change. It takes much intelligence and courage to suggest that a president may have embarked on the wrong course.

The advocates of the anti-Diem coup had apparently contemplated a bloodless coup in which Diem and his family could be guaranteed safe conduct out of the country. No one condoned the assassination of Diem and Nhu as they came from church on November 1, 1963. It is clear that the Vietnamese officers who planned the coup would have been afraid to act without a sign from the United States that it looked with favor upon their efforts and would readily shift its support to them after they succeeded. Lodge, who became a champion of the coup, had informed Washington that a suspension of U.S. aid would be sufficient to topple Diem and his cohort. Kennedy had given Lodge the power to cut off the aid and thereby set the course of U.S. policy in Vietnam. During the last few weeks before the coup, the Kennedy administration oscillated in confusion between determined certainty and gnawing second thoughts. At times it was not clear who was really in charge of events out there—Lodge, Harkins, or the CIA—and whether anyone was sure that the coup would succeed. If it did, would the succeeding regime be better or worse than Diem's? Johnson later gave his opinion that it is better to deal with the devil you know than the devil you don't know. Four days after the coup, Lodge said that it "would not have happened as it did without our preparation."*

## THE VIENNA MEETING WITH KHRUSHCHEV

Kennedy and his team of foreign-policy advisers came to Washington convinced that Nikita Khrushchev, who had met Eisenhower on three occasions (at Geneva, the United Nations, and Camp David) would be eager to test their mettle and probe their intentions. They were right. In February 1961 the Soviet leader made an overture through the U.S. ambassador in Moscow, Llewellyn Thompson. Kennedy and Rusk were generally opposed to summit meetings as arenas for conducting diplomacy. Nevertheless, on this occasion Kennedy was willing to meet Khrushchev in Vienna in June in order to give the two leaders an opportunity to size each other up on a personal, informal basis so that each might form better judgments about the other's statements, policies, actions, and intentions. Kennedy wanted an exchange of views on Laos, the proposed nuclear test ban, and the Berlin crisis, as well as on a broad range of political and ideological questions affecting the relations between the two powers.

Kennedy had been determined to sound just as tough as his Soviet counterpart, but in actuality he was less garrulous and aggressive and more courteous than Khrushchev, who was more skillful in ideological dialectics and more colorful in the use of barnyard language. At several points the president was

*Seven months later, however, in June 1964, Lodge took the position that the overthrow of Diem was purely a Vietnamese affair.

anxious to stress the need for mutual understanding and restraint, and the heavy responsibility that the two leaders had for avoiding situations in which one side would challenge the vital interests of the other, thereby creating a direct confrontation. The great danger, he said more than once, was that of miscalculation by one side of the fundamental interests and likely responses of the other, until neither could back down before war erupted. Khrushchev disliked Kennedy's use of the term "miscalculation," for to him it implied a belief on Kennedy's part that the propagation of communist ideas must stop at the Russian frontier. Kennedy, he said, failed to understand that the communist revolutionary process is the normal course of the world's historical development.

On the three substantive issues discussed at Vienna, limited progress was made on only one. Following an acrimonious debate as to which side was intervening unjustly in Laos, the two leaders agreed that the small Southeast Asian country was not worth going to war over and pledged to work on a cease-fire. With regard to the nuclear test ban and the problem of detecting underground tests and distinguishing them from earthquakes, Khrushchev was willing to tolerate three on-site inspections per year, but deemed any higher number—the United States had called for 20 and later came down to 12—as tantamount to espionage. Whereas Kennedy stressed the potential of a test-ban treaty as a means of inhibiting the proliferation of countries possessing nuclear weapons, Khrushchev did not regard it as the best way to begin the disarmament process, but gave an assurance that the Soviet Union would not be the first to end the three-year moratorium by resuming nuclear tests. That assurance was broken less than three months later.

## THE BERLIN CRISIS OF 1961

Berlin was the focal point of contention at Vienna. Months earlier, on January 6, Khrushchev had pointedly noted the vulnerability of the Western position in Berlin and said that unless his demands were met, he would take unilateral action. Not long before the Vienna summit, he hinted to Ambassador Thompson that the issue of Berlin, muted since the U-2 crisis, was about to heat up again because his prestige was at stake and he had waited patiently for two and a half years since his original six-month ultimatum of November 1958. The contrast between the prosperous western and the drab eastern part of the former German capital was an increasing embarrassment to the Communists. Between 1949 and 1961, 2 million East Germans had "voted with their feet" by moving westward. Nearly all had executed their escape through the subways of Berlin. At Vienna, Khrushchev complained that the situation was no longer tolerable. If a general peace settlement for Germany could not be reached, he himself would take the necessary steps to end the state of war by signing a separate peace treaty with East Germany. Thus the fate of West Berlin, which would be declared a "free city," would be handed over to a sovereign German Democratic Republic, with whom the three Western allies could renegotiate their occupation and access rights.

Kennedy made it clear that the legal right of the United States, Britain, and France to keep occupation forces in Berlin, like that of the Soviet Union, was based on conquest and could not be abrogated by one power. Beyond the legal niceties, said Kennedy, Berlin was vital to Western security. If the United States acquiesced in the erosion of its position there, the credibility of its commitment to the whole of Western Europe would be undermined. Therefore America would not accept an ultimatum on Berlin. Kennedy had more than once expressed the view that negotiation could not take place in an atmosphere of threat. Before departing, Khrushchev set December 31 as the deadline for either a Four Power peace treaty terminating all Western occupation rights inside East Germany or a separate Soviet–East German treaty. Kennedy was aware that the Soviet leader was using the Berlin issue to test his nerve and Allied unity.

Kennedy had asked Acheson to head a study of NATO and German problems. Acheson, a hard-liner, recommended that when a crisis over Berlin came, the Allies must display their determination to defend their position in Berlin by force if necessary. He also recommended a series of military counter-measures, culminating in the sending of a U.S. armored division down the autobahn (Germany's superhighway) to reassert Western rights. The British foreign secretary, Lord Alec Douglas-Home, and several of Kennedy's advisers—including Bundy, Schlesinger, Kissinger, Thompson, and Harriman—thought that Acheson was focusing attention too early and too exclusively on the ultimate military response while bypassing the possibility of interim political-diplomatic initiatives that might avert a crisis. Acheson, however, was convinced that it would be futile to negotiate before the test of wills had shown Khrushchev that the West would not concede its rights merely because it seemed to be more afraid of the prospect of nuclear war than the Soviet leadership was. Besides, he did not think that there was much to negotiate, because German reunification on terms acceptable to both sides was out of the question, and it would be demeaning for the Allies to go hat in hand to Moscow, seeking new guarantees on Berlin from a bullying power that was now reneging on long-standing agreements.

The two months following the Vienna meeting were tense and gloomy ones in Washington. Voices were raised in favor of a massive military buildup, the proclamation of a national emergency, the activation (or at least the alert) of reservists, higher taxes to pay for defense, and the institution of wage and price controls. Since the strategy of massive retaliation inherited from the Eisenhower administration appeared to limit Kennedy's response options, there was a good deal of speculating, debating, and war-gaming during the summer as to whether the armored column that was to be sent down the autobahn must be equipped with conventional weapons only or could display nuclear weapons as well. Kennedy and his White House advisers were anxious to avoid a precipitate, dramatic move that would paint Khrushchev into a corner from which he could escape only by engaging in dangerous one-upmanship. While taking steps to improve U.S. military capabilities, they kept demanding fresh creative dip-lomatic initiatives to neutralize Moscow's propaganda offensive, but these were not easily produced.

Shortly after midnight on August 13, 1961, East German military and police units began sealing off East Berlin from the rest of the city. Within a few days, they had built an ugly structure known as the Berlin Wall, which quickly became a concrete, barbed-wire, and broken-glass symbol of the dividing line between Western democracy and Communist totalitarianism. The barricade aroused fear and fury, but it did not lead to any overt confrontation. Khrushchev had devised a carefully calculated solution to his dilemma: a tourniquet to stop the flow of lifeblood from East Germany without directly violating Western rights in West Berlin. No responsible statesman in the West was ready to risk a confrontation, and perhaps war, over the erection of the Berlin Wall, even though large segments of elite and public opinion wanted bulldozers to level this insult to human freedom. Both President Kennedy and West German Chancellor Konrad Adenauer were willing to exhibit restraint. To allay the apprehensiveness of the West Berliners, Kennedy sent Vice-President Johnson to reassure the population of the beleaguered city that the U.S. commitment was unshakable. He also ordered the 1500-man First Battle Group of the Eighth Infantry from West Germany to reinforce the U.S. contingents in West Berlin, and appointed as his personal representative in that sector General Lucius Clay, who had been a tower of strength during the 1947–48 Berlin blockade. Gradually the crisis subsided. In mid-October Khrushchev dropped his December 31 deadline for a peace treaty.

## THE MISSILE GAP AND U.S. DEFENSE POLICY

In the late 1950s strategic analysts in the United States were beginning to express concern about the continued effectiveness of the nuclear deterrent and America's general readiness to meet the kinds of security threats it would probably confront in the 1960s. Albert Wohlstetter of the RAND Corporation was pointing out that nuclear deterrence was not a condition to be achieved once for all time. While it was true that the numbers of nuclear weapons in the arsenals of the two principal powers made the outbreak of war unlikely, nevertheless in an age of constant, dynamic changes in military technology, the United States had to make sure that it would always possess an invulnerable, survivable second-strike capability that would prevent the Soviet leaders from thinking that they could carry out a surprise strategic nuclear first strike, and absorb the U.S. retaliatory attack.

The problem had been recognized for years as one of imposing limits on war by possessing the ability to control the escalation process at all levels. That meant, in effect, strategic nuclear superiority, an advantage that the United States had clearly enjoyed since the dawn of the atomic era. Nuclear superiority by itself was not sufficient. A whole range of capabilities for fighting limited war, both conventional and, as a last resort, nuclear, had to be developed. The problem was seriously complicated by the emergence of a dual threat posed by the Soviet Union—the development of rocketry and a policy of preference for reserving the use of missiles for purposes of propaganda and political blackmail, while at the same time supporting anti-Western guerrilla insurgencies in Asia, Africa, and Latin America.

The election campaign of 1960 featured a lively debate over the alleged missile gap, which the Kennedy team sought to exploit to advantage in the contest with Nixon. Kennedy and the Democrats did not invent the missile gap. For more than two years after the USSR launched the first Sputnik in October 1957,

Khrushchev bombastically exaggerated Soviet long-range missile capabilities. Many U.S. military officers and civil-defense officials were worried about the vulnerability of the U.S. strategic bomber force at a time when the United States was still in the planning stage for the deployment of intercontinental missiles. Only a few of the Strategic Air Command's bomber bases were "hardened"; most were vulnerable to a surprise missile attack. The United States had intermediate-range Jupiter and Thor missiles in Turkey and Italy, but these liquid-fueled "hot launch" missiles had to be kept above ground. They were, therefore, similarly vulnerable. Moreover, since they could not survive a first strike, they had the provocative appearance of being first-strike weapons themselves.

A coming missile gap had been postulated in a secret report by the Gaither Committee in 1957. Eisenhower's secretary of defense, Neil McElroy, told the House Appropriations Committee in 1959 that by 1962 the Soviet Union would probably be able to convert its rocket throw weight lead into a 3-to-1 margin in intercontinental ballistic missiles (ICBMs). The hypothesis of an impending gap came to be taken for granted by many Democratic and Republican congressmen, defense and other officials, scientists and nonpartisan journalists. The debate was characterized by a certain amount of ambiguity and confusion as to whether the gap was present or future, whether it referred to rocket thrust only or to overall quantitative and qualitative superiority, and whether it pertained to ICBMs only or to all nuclear missiles, including sea-based ones, which seemed incredible.

The apprehension prevailing at the time was not surprising. To many observers, the Soviet Union seemed to be surging ahead in some crucial technological sectors. Khrushchev was boasting that Soviet factories were mass-producing ICBMs—"like sausages." The 1960 U-2 flights, however, had obtained photographic evidence that Khrushchev had been bluffing. Finding their first ICBMs too clumsy and vulnerable, the Soviet planners shifted their priority to developing a better ICBM. Meanwhile, recognizing the close political, economic, and cultural relationship between the United States and Western Europe, they realized that they could gain substantial deterrent leverage over the former by bringing the latter under the gun. This they were able to do by deploying more than 600 intermediate-range ballistic missiles (IRBMs—SS-4s and -5s) aimed at targets in Western Europe. In the light of the latest intelligence reports, the Eisenhower administration reduced its estimate of the Soviet ICBM threat. In the rhetorical heat of the campaign, some Democrats insinuated that the Republicans were acting out of budgetary and political image considerations harmful to national security. Kennedy himself did not go this far, but said; "If we are to err in an age of uncertainty, I want us to err on the side of security."

Within a few months, Kennedy and McNamara were certain that there was no actual missile gap, and that none need be allowed to open provided that new plans were carried out. The new administration quickly became aware of a different kind of gap—that between the strategic doctrine of massive retaliation and the urgent need for operational military capabilities to cope with the real challenges short of nuclear war that the Soviet Union and allied Communist forces were likely to pose to the West. Kennedy wanted alternatives between holocaust and humiliation, between catastrophe and surrender. In short, he sought the means to make a controlled, flexible response to the threats that might be posed not directly to the security of the United States—threats that could be deterred by nuclear weapons—but rather to the security of U.S. allies in Europe and, less directly but nevertheless significantly, to the security of U.S. and allied vital interests in other regions of the world.

Defense Secretary McNamara was appalled at what he regarded as the unreadiness of U.S. military forces for less than all-out war. His team of "Whiz Kids," systems and operations analysts, war-games theorists, advocates of linear and dynamic programming, cost-effective economists, and computer experts made statistical studies and constructed abstract models of the nation's capabilities for meeting various military contingencies and found them to be deficient. The numbers of combat-ready divisions, armored personnel carriers, fighter bombers, self-propelled howitzers, and tactical missiles, as well as the available ammunition stocks and airlift capacity for overseas reinforcement, were all woefully low—in many cases as much as half, two-thirds or three-quarters below the levels required for fighting a war.

Eisenhower the general-president had not been worried, but the Harvard-M.I.T. scientists and the Ford Company management types who rejected the Eisenhower-Dulles strategy were. They were particularly determined to expand and improve the nation's ability to parry the Communist threat of guerrilla insurgency in view of the fact that on January 6, 1961, just two weeks before Kennedy's inauguration, Khrushchev in one and the same speech ruled out the possibility of nuclear war but pledged full Soviet support for "just wars of national liberation," practically all of which were anti-Western and pro-Marxist or Communist-influenced in some form.

## U.S. POLICY TOWARD AFRICA AND THE CONGO CRISIS

Although the United States had long been interested in North Africa,* American interest in black Africa had been minimal until the late 1950s. Because Africa had been under European colonial domination for such a long time, American business had scarcely invested in the continent. It was only in 1957 that a Bureau for African Affairs was established in the Department of State. In that year, there were fewer Foreign Service officers in all of Africa than there were in the Federal Republic of Germany alone. Washington was forced to increase its attention to that part of the world when, in the latter half of 1960, 16 former colonial territories became nominally independent, sovereign states and members of the United Nations. When Kennedy was chairman of the African Subcommittee of the Senate Foreign Relations Committee, he developed a reputation as a supporter of African nationalist, anticolonial movements. During the 1960 presidential election campaign, he criticized the Eisenhower-Nixon administration for having ignored the needs and aspirations of the African people. As president, his first State Department appointment was of former Michigan governor G. Mennen

---

*Morocco had been among the first nations to recognize the independence of the United States. In 1787, the two countries signed the Treaty of Marrakech, instituting the longest unbroken agreement of peace, friendship, and commercial relations in U.S. history.

Williams, an ardent proponent of civil rights, as assistant secretary for African affairs. Kennedy himself was hailed throughout Africa as a friend and champion.

Kennedy dispatched to the new states relatively young and vigorous ambassadors, who in several instances were more liberal than he was. Williams' remark that Africa was for the Africans did not go over well in Allied capitals with those conservatives who thought that the Europeans, even if they had exploited Africa for its economic resources, had also brought to the Africans much in the way of political, legal, administrative, economic, technical, and sociocultural development. Apologists for Europe's imperialist record in London, Paris, and Brussels often noted that the two most backward states in sub-Saharan Africa, Liberia, and Ethiopia, were the only two that had not experienced European colonialism. Kennedy went out of his way during his three years in office to convince upwards of 25 visiting African heads of state that he was more on their side than on that of the European ex-colonial powers, thereby pleasing the Africanists but unnerving the pro-NATO elements in the State Department. The United States in March 1961 supported a UN resolution calling for an end to Portuguese colonial rule in Angola, thus sparking anti-American outbursts in Lisbon and arousing fear in the Pentagon that the United States might lose access to its air base in the Azores. A few months later, when Tunisia tried to expel the French from their base at Bizerte, the French responded with crushing military force, and the matter came to the UN General Assembly. This time, Kennedy, who appreciated the difficulties facing de Gaulle in his effort to work out a solution to the bloody Algerian conflict, ordered a U.S. abstention. When Algeria became independent in 1962, the first major foreign trip of its radical nationalist-socialist leader, Mohammed Ben Bella, was a friendly visit to Kennedy—just before going to Havana and joining Castro in a communiqué demanding U.S. withdrawal from its naval base at Guantánamo!

### Approaches to Guinea and Ghana

In a period of growing U.S.–Soviet competition for influence in Africa, Kennedy tried to use his personal charm and U.S. foreign aid to woo two prominent West African leaders—Sékou Touré of Guinea and Kwame Nkrumah of Ghana—away from pro-Soviet Marxism toward nonalignment, if not a pro-Western position. He succeeded with the first but not the second.

Guinea had been the only former colonial territory to renounce membership in the French Community in 1958, prompting de Gaulle to sever all ties immediately. As a consequence, Touré received the cold shoulder from the Eisenhower administration but a warm embrace from Moscow. There was a tendency also in the new administration to write him off as a Communist, particularly after he blamed Kennedy for the death of Patrice Lumumba (see next page) and was awarded the Lenin Peace Prize. The Soviet economic assistance program in Guinea, however, soon bogged down in inefficiency, and Kennedy seized the opportunity to lure Touré away from close ties to Moscow with offers of American aid. Having at first launched a blistering attack on the Peace Corps, Touré now invited it into his country. Before the end of 1961, following a clumsy

Soviet effort to intervene in Guinea's domestic politics, Touré expelled the Soviet ambassador.

Kennedy's effort to wean Ghana's Nkrumah away from Moscow proved a dismal failure, despite the readiness of the United States to allocate a sizable portion of its African aid funds to the Volta Dam project. In the face of much congressional criticism, Kennedy approved the allocation anyway.

Subsequently, rather than risk losing the Azores base, Kennedy placed NATO needs ahead of the cause of Angolan independence, and became more supportive of Portugal in the United Nations. His willingness to explain his dilemma to moderate African leaders such as Félix Houphouët-Boigny of the Ivory Coast and Julius Nyerere of Tanganyika (now Tanzania) met with some success because they approved the basic thrust of his African policy, especially after the United States in August 1962 announced an embargo on the sale of arms to South Africa so long as its racist *apartheid* policy remained in effect.

### The Threat of Civil War in the Congo

The most difficult of all the policy problems faced by Kennedy in Africa arose in the Congo (now Zaire), which had been poorly prepared for the independence suddenly thrust upon it by Belgium in June 1960. The secession of the mineral-rich province of Katanga produced such political and economic chaos throughout the country that the young leftist prime minister of the Congolese Republic, Patrice Lumumba, called on the United Nations for assistance to prevent national dissolution. A Security Council resolution declaring that the UN was to be the exclusive channel for military forces and equipment flowing to the Congo was vetoed by the Soviet Union, which was anxious to exert its own influence on the worsening conflict and thereby gain a foothold in the heart of Africa. In the General Assembly, however, the neutral states voted overwhelmingly with nearly all Western states for such a declaration, with only France, South Africa, and the Communist bloc abstaining. The neutrals did not want armed intervention by either of the cold war antagonists, but they did want to halt the momentum toward a bloody civil war, and consequently they themselves provided most of the 20,000 troops in the United Nations Congo Force (ONUC), airlifted in U.S. planes.

The Soviet Union blamed the new actively interventionist stance of the United Nations on its secretary-general, Dag Hammarskjöld, who was determined to use "preventive diplomacy," and force if necessary, to avert a civil war. Disagreements between Congolese President Joseph Kasavubu and Prime Minister Lumumba over the role of UN forces, the handling of the Katanga secession, and the possibility that Lumumba might obtain Soviet military aid led to the latter's dismissal in September 1960. Only weeks after Kennedy's inauguration, Lumumba was murdered while being held prisoner in Katanga. Several states began withdrawing their units from the UN force, but when the Soviet Union called for the complete withdrawal of UN forces, it received no support. A compromise resolution authorized UN troops to use force to avoid civil war and urged the Belgians to pull out all of their military personnel. The

USSR stepped up its atacks on Hammarskjöld and demanded that he be replaced by a *troika*—a three-person UN secretariat (one Western, one Communist, and one neutral, each empowered to veto UN operations). This would have paralyzed the UN so far as its ability to carry out peacekeeping operations opposed by Moscow was concerned. The Soviet Union and France refused to pay their share of ONUC's operating costs, precipitating not only a substantial financial deficit but also the most serious constitutional crisis in the history of the international organization.

Everyone recognized that the secession of Katanga was the principal cause of the crisis and that the danger of civil war could not be removed until the entire country was unified under the control of a central government. That was quite clear to President Kennedy and to the man he had chosen as ambassador to the Congo, Edmund Gullion, a professional Foreign Service officer whose judgment the president had come to respect. They were joined by Undersecretary of State George Ball, who viewed the secessionist province as an enclave of colonialism, financed by the white capitalist mining firm Union Minière. All three realized that the leader of Katanga, Moise Tshombe, was regarded by the new African elites as a neocolonialist agent, and by supporting the Leopoldville central government's effort to reunify the country, they hoped to appeal to African nationalist sentiment. Strong reactions to Lumumba's murder led to negotiations between his followers and Kasavubu, which produced a more moderate government in August 1961 under Cyrille Adoula, who had the backing of the CIA.

The Kennedy administration threw its weight behind Adoula and against Tshombe and his Katangan army. For pursuing this policy, Kennedy was criticized in France, Belgium, and even Britain, and openly pilloried by conservative and right-wing elements within the United States, where the pro-Katanga lobby sought to equate the struggle of the foreign-financed mercenaries with that of the Hungarian freedom fighters five years earlier.

At the height of the crisis, Hammarskjöld was killed in a plane crash in Rhodesia while en route to the Congo. Kennedy encouraged his successor, U Thant of Burma, to continue using the UN troops to bring about Congolese unification. The goal proved extremely elusive. Efforts by U Thant, George McGhee of the State Department, and representatives of the European allies to work out a plan of reconciliation were constantly thwarted by Tshombe. Kennedy, however, thought that the United States had already made too large an investment in the United Nations peacekeeping operation to allow it to fail under the weight of mounting international criticism and opposition—much of it the result of Soviet agitation and propaganda. Reinforced by the knowledge that Kennedy was ready to accept large risks to terminate the conflict, U.S.-equipped UN forces under Indian command captured Kolwezi and crushed the Katanga resistance in January 1963.

To most Africans, the Kennedy policy seemed to be an appropriate reflection of the values with which the majority of Americans preferred to be associated within the United Nations and the developing regions of the world. It gave rise, however, to serious questions as to how far the governments of the leading powers wanted the UN's peacekeeping mandate to extend. None wanted it to go further; most thought it had already been stretched too far. In any event, there was a noticeable retreat from such active, preventive diplomacy within the United Nations from 1963 onward.

## KENNEDY'S STRATEGIES FOR DETERRENCE AND DEFENSE

As we have seen, Kennedy faulted the Eisenhower administration for bequeathing to him a military establishment inadequate to meet the full range of threats that the Communist powers, with their growing capabilities, could pose to the United States and its NATO allies. The new administration adopted a two-pronged strategy to cope with the threat of anti-Western revolutionary insurgency. To harness the forces of emerging Third World nationalism to peaceful democratic revolution, it developed the Peace Corps, the Alliance for Progress, and other aid programs of modernization and nation building, including flood control, irrigation, agricultural assistance, sanitation, transportation, and communication. On the military side, the Green Berets were organized and trained, along with native police and home-guard units in threatened countries, for counterinsurgency operations. These developments were to prove significant, for they provided a necessary condition to large-scale U.S. military involvement in Vietnam in the mid-1960s.

### Defense Buildup

To make certain that no missile gap would open and that the nuclear deterrent would remain impressively survivable, the president speeded up the Minuteman missile and Polaris submarine programs begun by his predecessor. Requesting an immediate $3 billion supplemental appropriation for defense, he declared that the nation could not afford to allow arbitrary budget ceilings to dictate arms availability; rather, defense levels should be determined by actual strategic requirements. For improved readiness to handle limited wars overseas, he ordered an increase in airlift capacity. McNamara sought to reduce duplication by ordering a new TFX aircraft for the Navy and the Air Force. The president and his secretary of defense emphasized the principle of civilian control, as well as the importance of tightening command, control, and communications ("$C^3$") procedures at all levels to minimize the risk of accident, unintentional war, and unlimited escalation, and also to preserve the ability to select from a variety of responses suited to whatever situation might arise.

The Kennedy administration was determined to prevent any use of tactical nuclear weapons by a field commander without an explicit authorization from the president. To this end, a "firebreak" was introduced between nuclear weapons and conventional weapons in Europe: the two categories were separated by geography and command, and nuclear weapons were locked into a special technical system of "permissive action links." Following the Bay of Pigs debacle, when it was so hard to tell who was responsible for letting things go awry, Kennedy was anxious to bring military operations under his direct supervision. Some military officers criticized him for bypassing the regular chain of command and meddling in detailed decisions better left to the military. His reputation in this regard was not enhanced by the fact that he brought General Maxwell Taylor into the White House as his personal adviser on professional military matters, thus inserting a kind of buffer between himself and the Joint Chiefs of Staff.

### Enhancement of Civil Defense

More than any other president in the nuclear age, Kennedy was a strong advocate of civil defense. Feeling responsible for the lives of Americans, recognizing that nuclear deterrence might conceivably break down someday, and realizing that preparations could be made that might save millions of lives in nuclear war even though millions of others would be lost, he urged the adoption of a program of "survival insurance" in the form of civil-defense fallout shelters. His summons to the people to think realistically about the consequences of nuclear war was made in late May 1961, just before the Vienna summit and the expected coming to boil of the Berlin crisis. His address on the subject stirred fears and a certain amount of hysteria, setting off a wave of panic planning, digging, building, and hoarding stocks for backyard shelters. Ethicians debated the burning moral issue of the day: When the unthinkable happened, was the sensible head of a family who had prudently constructed and supplied a shelter morally justified in using a gun to ward off irresponsible neighbors who had failed to make any preparations?

Within the government, there was much disagreement and confusion over the civil-defense program. Who would have ultimate responsibility for getting such a program started? (It was finally assigned to the secretary of defense.) Would passive defense (that is, shelters) be linked to active defense (that is, antimissile missiles)? Should the nation depend on individuals to build shelters, or should the government provide public shelters? What was to be the purpose of the program—to strengthen deterrence, to show that the Americans were just as tough as the Russians (who made much of civil defense), to save lives in case of an actual nuclear war, or what? Should shelters be built to protect against blast as well as fallout? Should plans be made to evacuate urban populations to the countryside in time of crisis?

In the end, no policy was ever developed or implemented to integrate a civil-defense program coherently into an overall national strategy. Kennedy continued to think that a civil-defense program was needed, but he came to regret the part he had played in provoking a nationwide controversy before the administration knew what it ought to do. Civil defense gradually drifted to a lower priority, and Congress was ultimately asked only to fund a modest program to provide federal incentives for the construction of shelters in schools, hospitals, and libraries. The crash program was abandoned.

### Strategic Flexibility

Defense plans initiated by the Eisenhower administration ensured that the United States would have sufficient ICBMs, nuclear submarines, and bombers in the early 1960s to continue to enjoy a comfortable margin of strategic superiority.

The growth of Soviet nuclear capabilities, however, forced the McNamara team to ask hard questions about U.S. strategic doctrine, because a deterrent must be operational in order to be credible. Yet to many analysts nuclear war seemed unthinkable. Kennedy, seeking a range of options between humiliation and all-out war, emphasized the need for "controlled" or "flexible" response rather than massive retaliation. There was a desire to break out of the assumption that nuclear war could only be a cataclysm, with both sides firing everything in their arsenals at each other's urban populations. That assumption was perhaps a natural consequence of World War II, in which the obliteration bombing of cities had played such a prominent role (whether decisive or not). In a speech in Ann Arbor, Michigan, in June 1962, McNamara enunciated a "no-cities" doctrine:

> The United States has come to the conclusion that, to the extent feasible, basic military strategy in a possible general nuclear war should be approached in the same way that more conventional military operations have been regarded in the past. That is to say, principal military objectives . . . should be the destruction of the enemy's military forces, not of his civilian population.

No one was sure even then that nuclear war could be limited and controlled; weapons and delivery systems were crude, less accurate and less "discriminating" than they would later become. McNamara was expounding the view that if restraint was conceivable in conventional war, as had sometimes been demonstrated in history, then it should also be possible in nuclear war, when the motives to keep the conflict limited might be even stronger. He was anxious to dispel the notion that the basically defensive ethos and "second-strike" strategy of the United States required this country, if forced into war, to absorb the full destructive power of the foe's offensive capabilities before striking back. He wanted to make it clear that the United States would act quickly against enemy military installations in order to limit the damage that might otherwise be inflicted on the American population. It was in that context that interest in civil defense reached its highest point.

There can be little doubt that the United States has always possessed "counterforce" as well as "countercity" capabilities, regardless of fluctuations of emphasis in the public enunciation of strategic doctrine. Within a year of the Ann Arbor speech, however, McNamara was veering toward the conviction that damage limitation would become increasingly chimerical as higher levels of nuclear arsenals on both sides would render it more difficult for the United States to exploit its superiority by setting limits on a nuclear exchange and making them stick. The problem of reconciling a doctrine of limited counterforce warfare with an essentially second-strike strategy proved insurmountable. By 1963, McNamara had gradually relegated the damage-limitation objective to a lower priority than the doctrine of "assured destruction." This entailed an invulnerable U.S. strategic capability to inflict on the Soviet Union (regardless of what the latter might do in a first strike) an "unacceptable level of damage" in retaliation. This level was variously described as the destruction of one-quarter to one-third of the population and one-half to two-thirds of the economic-industrial base of the

USSR. That, thought McNamara, would be quite sufficient to deter Moscow from ever seriously considering a surprise attack. The doctrine, which later became known as "mutual assured destruction" (MAD) as Soviet nuclear forces expanded, was designed to eliminate both the high costs and the possibly destabilizing consequences of an effort to build a credible counterforce capability. Despite the fact that the MAD doctrine was subsequently condemned as politically irrational, militarily absurd, and morally monstrous, it appeared to be both logical and effective as the basis of deterrence under the technological, political, and strategic circumstances prevailing at the time.

## THE CUBAN MISSILE CRISIS

The Cuban missile crisis has been characterized by Harold Macmillan as "one of the great turning points in history" and by Walt Rostow as "the Gettysburg of the cold war." Later, contradictory statements would emanate from Havana and Moscow as to whether the initiative for placing Soviet ballistic missiles on the island was a Cuban, Soviet, or joint one. The most logical explanation is that Castro wanted to be defended by the Soviet Union against the possibility of a more effective U.S. action than the Bay of Pigs effort had been. Such a purpose would not have required the installation of nuclear missiles, so that was very probably a Soviet idea, designed to serve Soviet strategic objectives rather than Cuban defense needs. (See the box on pp. 173–174 for a chronology of the crisis.)

### Why Were the Missiles Installed?

Perhaps a clear picture of Khrushchev's motives will never be obtained. Undoubtedly, he wanted to demonstrate Soviet ability to protect the world's newest adherent of Marxism-Leninism against putative attack from the stronghold of imperialism. There were signs that Republican senators Homer Capehart, Kenneth Keating, Everett Dirksen, and Barry Goldwater were getting ready to make the Cuban threat a major issue in the upcoming congressional elections. But it must be emphasized that conventional arms would have been sufficient to protect Cuba, and the USSR was in a position to supply ample amounts from its massive stocks—enough to make the cost of a U.S. invasion much higher than in April 1961. It was inconceivable that the United States would ever employ nuclear weapons against Cuba, so there was no need for a nuclear deterrent. Why, then, did Moscow "up the ante" so dramatically? Several theories have been offered:

1. *The strategic "quick fix."* The Kennedy administration had concluded early in 1961 that no missile gap existed. Furthermore, the United States was moving ahead of the USSR in the deployment of operational ICBMs and submarine-launched ballistic missiles (SLBMs). According to this theory, the availability of Cuba as a missile base provided a golden opportunity for the Soviet Union to double, within a short time, its capacity for striking targets in the United States.
2. *The bold revolutionary image.* Beijing had often charged Moscow with timidly abandoning its commitment to the support of the world

revolution and consorting with bourgeois powers because of a fear of nuclear weapons. Proponents of this explanation argued that Khrushchev was under pressure to act more boldly to speed the pace of global revolution. (Ironically, after the crisis ended, Beijing criticized Khrushchev for having engaged in reckless adventurism!)

3. *The Jupiter tradeoff.* During the Eisenhower period, the United States had deployed "soft," above-ground Jupiter missiles in Turkey and Italy. The secretary of defense and the Joint Committee on Atomic Energy had long been calling for their withdrawal. Such weapons did not fit into the strategy of assured destruction, which required an invulnerable second-strike capability. If Soviet planners were aware that their American counterparts regarded the Jupiters as obsolescent and likely to be pulled out within a year or two, they probably would not risk a dangerous confrontation with the United States merely to get them out earlier in a tradeoff. Khrushchev and his advisers probably expected to carry off their surprise successfully before the American political system could react on the eve of a congressional election. In any event, a missile tradeoff does not seem to have been the compelling motive, although McNamara apparently thought it was.

4. *Reheating Berlin.* It is possible that Moscow may have wanted to gain revenge for the many times it had issued ultimatums concerning the divided city, only to be forced ignominiously to postpone the showdown in the face of unified Western determination. As the missile crisis unfolded, many in Washington saw it as another test of wills not unrelated to a revival of the Berlin crisis, after the USSR had turned the political-strategic tables on the United States.

There is no need to select a single explanation. Perhaps Khrushchev saw his chance to blunt his Chinese critics, placate his military chiefs, improve the Soviet Union's strategic position, brighten its revolutionary image, put the United States on the political defensive in Berlin and elsewhere, and let the Americans feel how it felt to be "under the gun" (as he ostensibly did vis-à-vis the missiles in Turkey)—all in the guise of protecting a weak, impoverished socialist ally. Once the strategic decision was made, Moscow's principal problem was a tactical one: how to make the maneuver look like one designed solely for the defense of Cuba, even though its more fundamental purpose was to furnish a shield for the subsequent arrival of offensive weapons capable of hitting U.S. targets. This was accomplished with careful planning and preparation, by sending first purely defensive, surface-to-air and coastal-defense missiles.

## Debate over the U.S. Response

The United States suspended aerial reconnaissance over western Cuba for five weeks prior to October 14, by which time the construction of a missile base at San Cristobal could be detected in the photographs.* Once the missiles had been

---

*Prior to that date, there had been numerous reports from Cuban refugees in Florida that the Soviet Union was bringing large missiles into the island. Government officials dismissed these as wild and inaccurate rumors, and in fact there was no hard evidence to substantiate them.

photographed, Kennedy called for intensified surveillance and imposed the strictest secrecy. Publicly, everything was to proceed normally so that the suspicion of the press would not be aroused. To assess the threat and sketch out a preliminary spectrum of responses, an ad hoc group of approximately 15 advisers known as the Executive Committee (ExComm) of the National Security Council* began a round of meetings that would continue for 13 days. The principal question was how to cope with the danger most effectively and most safely before the missiles became fully operational. Should there be an air strike, a direct approach to Castro, or a summit meeting with Khrushchev, an OAS inspection, a full-fledged military invasion, or something else? Reliance on the United Nations was quickly ruled out because of the Soviet veto in the Security Council.

The urgent need for secrecy—to avoid panicking the American people and precipitating Soviet counteraction before the United States even decided what it intended to do—precluded consulting with allies, calling up reserves, and convening conspicuous gatherings of high-level officials in an atmosphere of emergency. The Pentagon, however, was instructed to alert U.S. forces to be ready for any contingency.

Attorney General Robert Kennedy and Defense Secretary McNamara played key roles in formulating the final decision. The Joint Chiefs and some of the civilian advisers, including Dean Acheson, proposed a "surgical" air strike against the missile sites and the airfields where bombers were housed. Robert Kennedy and several other State and Defense officials marshaled an array of arguments against such a strike: by killing large numbers of Russians, it could provoke war; by killing large numbers of Cubans, it would alienate the Latin Americans; it would appear excessive to the Europeans and would weaken their confidence in the United States as a responsible leader of the Alliance—indeed, it might frighten some of them into "wanting out"; a military move against Cuba might lead to a retaliatory Soviet move against Berlin, where the Soviet Union enjoyed the same wide margin of conventional superiority as did the United States in the Caribbean; worst of all, it might well bring on the nuclear war that everyone wished to avoid. Even those who were sure that Khrushchev would never place the Soviet homeland at supreme risk over Cuba feared that in the fog of confusion that clouds every war a "surgical" air strike, regardless of how efficiently executed, might fail to destroy all the missiles and bombers before some could be launched toward targets in the United States. The Air Force conceded that no 100 percent guarantee was possible.

McNamara suggested a naval blockade to cut off all further Soviet missile deliveries to the island. Advocates of the air strike contended that a blockade did not address the threat of the missiles already in Cuba, would invite a renewed Soviet blockade of West Berlin, and forfeited an opportunity to get rid of Castro once and for all. State Department lawyers, with an eye on the traditional

---

*ExComm meeting attendees were not always the same. The principal ones were Robert Kennedy, Robert McNamara, Dean Rusk, Undersecretary of State George Ball, Deputy Undersecretary U. Alexis Johnson, Llewellyn Thompson, Deputy and Assistant Secretaries of Defense Roswell Gilpatric and Paul Nitze, CIA Director John McCone, McGeorge Bundy, Dean Acheson, Robert Lovett, and Adlai Stevenson.

| | |
|---|---|
| July 1962 | Minister of the Cuban armed forces visits Moscow. Soviet military equipment in the form of surface-to-air and coastal-defense missiles begins to arrive at Havana. Initially the unloadings are conducted in secrecy at night, but as time passes, the operation becomes more conspicuous. |
| September 4 | President Kennedy assures the U.S. public that the equipment being delivered to Cuba from the Soviet Union is purely defensive and presents no threat to the security of the United States. |
| September 9–10 | A Nationalist U-2 plane is shot down over Mainland China. Since the U-2 incident of May 1960, U-2 flights had required presidential authorization. The Committee on Overhead Reconnaissance, chaired by McGeorge Bundy and with Secretary Rusk in attendance, notes that Soviet surface-to-air missiles in Cuba are already or soon will be operational. Fearing a popular outcry if another U-2 is shot down, the committee directs that photographic flights over that part of Cuba be avoided. |
| September 13 | Kennedy repeats his assurance, and adds that any Soviet effort to build up an offensive capability would raise a grave challenge to this country. In the days following, Soviet officials disavow any intention of placing offensive surface-to-surface missiles in Cuba as a threat to the United States. |
| September 19 | The United States Intelligence Board unanimously approves an intelligence assessment that Moscow will not introduce nuclear missiles into Cuba because the likelihood of discovery and adverse reaction is so high; because such action would be inconsistent with the caution always exercised by the Soviet Union in nuclear matters (for it had never placed nuclear weapons outside Soviet borders, not even in the adjacent and easily controlled Eastern European satellites); and because Soviet communications with Cuba were long, hazardous, and vulnerable to American interdiction. |
| Early October | It is estimated that since July more than 100 shiploads of arms have come from the Soviet Union to Cuba. Deliveries have included 144 surface-to-air missile launchers with four missiles per launcher and 42 MiG-21 fighter aircraft and cruise missiles, as well as patrol boats capable of carrying cruise missiles. All of these could be taken as intended for defensive purposes. In addition, the Soviet Union puts ashore a total of 42 medium-range ballistic missiles (with an estimated range of 1100 miles), 12 intermediate-range ballistic missiles (with an estimated range of 2200 miles), and 22,000 Soviet troops for assembling, operating, and defending the weapons. It is not asserted by official U.S. sources that nuclear warheads are actually delivered or installed, but it was not doubted that they are or soon will be available close to the missile sites. |
| October 15 | U-2 photos indicate that within two weeks the Soviet Union would probably have in readiness from 16 to 24 IRBMs capable of reaching Dallas, St. Louis, and Washington. Kennedy calls for intensified surveillance. |
| October 16 | The Executive Committee of the National Security Council begins its extraordinary series of meetings. |
| October 17–21 | New U-2 photos reveal preparations for the installation of IRBMs, which could, when ready in December, target almost any part of the |

|              | continental United States except the Far West and Northwest. Soviet Foreign Minister Andrei Gromyko meets President Kennedy at the White House. |
| --- | --- |
| October 22   | Kennedy goes on television and radio to take his case to the public. |
| October 24   | Soviet ships heading for Cuba slow down, awaiting further instructions. |
| October 26–27 | White House is confused about Soviet communications and intentions. |
| October 28   | Moscow Radio announces that Chairman Khrushchev accepts President Kennedy's terms. |

principles of international law, the United Nations Charter, and the Rio Treaty, added their legal briefs to the voices of those who proposed restraint on political and humanitarian grounds. The lawyer strongly favored self-defense measures of war rather than invasion, as well as measures that would readily command the assent of nearly all OAS members, thereby giving the U.S. response the character of a regional collective defense instead of a unilateral U.S. action. Acheson deemed considerations of unilateral self-defense quite sufficient and opposed the overture to the OAS as an unnecessary complicating and perhaps delaying factor. The president himself liked the idea of a naval blockade. It was a halfway step between inaction and war, and gave Khrushchev time to think and back off before it was too late.

A naval blockade, it was thought, would keep open the option of military action if that should prove necessary later, but the advocates of an air strike denied this, arguing that a blockade would alert the foe and waste time while the danger to national security grew day by day. Robert Kennedy was opposed to either an air strike or an invasion, saying that he did not want his brother to go down in the history books as the "Tojo of the Caribbean," plotting a Pearl Harbor–style attack.

The final ExComm vote was 11 to 6 for a naval blockade, now renamed a naval "quarantine" for legal reasons. Kennedy, anxious to win OAS support, instructed Assistant Secretary of State Edward Martin to obtain Latin American approval of a resolution endorsing the U.S. response as an act of hemispheric self-defense, although he made it clear that he wanted no reference to the Monroe Doctrine in the legal documentation. To inform (rather than consult with) the major Western European allies concerning an East–West confrontation in North Atlantic waters, which had been defined in the 1949 treaty as part of the area to be defended, the president entrusted Dean Acheson with a mission of special delicacy to de Gaulle, Macmillan, and Adenauer. All proved strongly supportive, but the British press expressed a great deal of skepticism as to whether the administration's response was really necessary. Adlai Stevenson was sent off to present the U.S. case in the United Nations, which he did with such superb eloquence that he demolished the claim of Moscow's propagandists that the Soviet missiles were purely defensive.

What had irritated Kennedy perhaps more than anything else, even more than Khrushchev's unexpected effort to emplace offensive missiles, was Soviet dissembling. Much would later be said about the strategic symmetry of U.S. missiles in Turkey and Soviet missiles in Cuba. Politically, however, the two deployments were vastly different. The United States had placed missiles in Turkey in the wake of a freely conducted and open debate within NATO, followed by the approval of freely elected executives and parliaments (which Turkey clearly enjoyed at the time). The Soviet Union, by contrast, sought to put missiles in Cuba suddenly and clandestinely. When Soviet Foreign Minister Andrei Gromyko met Kennedy in the White House on October 18, he made no mention of offensive weapons in Cuba but focused on Berlin, reinforcing Kennedy's expectations that the missile buildup was a prelude to a new, more serious Berlin crisis. Gromyko, not knowing how much Kennedy knew, reiterated that his government's intention was only to contribute to Cuba's defense against the threat of U.S. invasion.

### The U.S. Response: Readiness and Quarantine

Meanwhile, the United States was building up in Florida and other southeastern states the most formidable invasion force assembled since World War II. There were more than 100,000 troops in Florida alone. Two airborne divisions were placed on alert, fighter aircraft were redeployed to Florida air bases from all over the country, and 14,000 reserve airmen were called up to fly and service troop transports. The White House knew that the corps of reporters, ever eager to uncover what was hidden, would soon penetrate the curtain of secrecy.

The president had several more bases to cover before taking his case to the public on Monday, October 22. While revising drafts of his speech to the nation to achieve maximum legal, political, and strategic effect, he was simultaneously coordinating policy vis-à-vis the OAS, the United Nations, the NATO allies, and governments in other parts of the world; preparing to brief congressional leaders (who had to be flown back to Washington from their campaign trips on short notice); ordering all ambassadors to return to their posts; and making sure that State and Defense were prepared to cope with worst-scenario contingencies in Berlin, Guantánamo, and elsewhere. He checked and double-checked to make certain that U.S. military forces were properly and controllably poised to do whatever they were directed to do in the greatest test of deterrence to which they had yet been put in the nuclear age. When he took to the air that Monday evening, he spoke calmly but firmly:

> The purpose of these bases can be none other than to provide a nuclear strike capability against the Western Hemisphere.
>
> This action . . . contradicts the repeated assurances of Soviet spokesmen, both publicly and privately delivered, that the arms buildup in Cuba would retain its original defensive character, and that the Soviet Union had no need or desire to station strategic missiles on the territory of any other nation. . . .
>
> Neither the United States of America nor the world community of nations can tolerate deliberate deception and offensive threats on the part of any nation, large or small. We no longer live in a world where only the actual firing of

weapons represents a sufficient challenge to a nation's security to constitute maximum peril. Nuclear weapons are so destructive and ballistic missiles are so swift that any substantially increased possibility of their use or any sudden change in their deployment may well be regarded as a definite threat to peace.

For many years both the Soviet Union and the United States . . . have deployed strategic nuclear weapons with great care, never upsetting the precarious status quo. . . . Our own strategic missiles have never been transferred to the territory of any other nation under the cloak of secrecy and deception. . . .

But this secret, swift, and extraordinary buildup of Communist missiles—in an area well known to have a special and historical relationship to the United States and the nations of the Western Hemisphere, in violation of Soviet assurances, and in defiance of American and hemispheric policy—this sudden, clandestine decision to station strategic weapons for the first time outside of Soviet soil is a deliberately provocative and unjustified change in the status quo which cannot be accepted by this country if our commitments are ever to be trusted again by either friend or foe.

The president then announced what was being or would be done:
1. A strict quarantine on all offensive military equipment under shipment to Cuba was being initiated. Ships carrying such cargo, but not those carrying only food and other necessities, would be turned back.
2. Close surveillance of Cuba and the military buildup was increased. If the military buildup continued, further action would be justified. The armed forces were directed to prepare for any eventualities.
3. "It shall be the policy of this nation to regard any nuclear missile launched from Cuba against any nation in the Western Hemisphere as an attack by the Soviet Union on the United States, requiring a full retaliatory response upon the Soviet Union."
4. The naval base at Guantánamo was reinforced and U.S. dependents there were evacuated.
5. The OAS was being convoked to consider the threat, and allies around the world had been alerted.
6. The United States was requesting an emergency meeting of the UN Security Council, aimed at the dismantling and withdrawal of all offensive missiles under UN supervision before the quarantine would be lifted.
7. Khrushchev was urged to eliminate the reckless and provocative threat to world peace and to join in an historic effort to end the perilous arms race.

Reaction to the speech was highly favorable throughout the United States. The crisis, however, far from ending, worsened. Some two dozen Soviet or Soviet-leased merchant vessels were still heading toward Cuba on the second day after the speech, while a larger number of U.S. cruisers and destroyers, an antisubmarine aircraft carrier, and other ships were deploying to enforce the quarantine. Ships carrying food, medicine, and other nonmilitary cargo were still excluded from the quarantine; even petroleum, oil, and lubricants were allowed to go through in spite of their potential military utility. Navy orders were to turn back only ships carrying offensive weapons—first by firing a warning shot across the bow, and then by firing to cripple the rudder but not to sink the ship. Averell Harriman advised the president that Khrushchev did not want war and was looking for a face-saving way out. This evaluation was later proved to be correct, but it was hard to believe throughout the week after the speech, when work on the missile sites seem to be speeded up. Once the missiles were operational, Khrushchev could be a much tougher bargainer. David Ormsby-Gore, Kennedy's close friend and British ambassador in Washington, suggested that the quarantine line be pulled back closer to Cuba in order to give Khrushchev more time to deal with the consternation in the Kremlin that Kennedy's unexpected response had undoubtedly created. Advocates of the air strike and invasion argued that time was running out.

### Resolution of the Crisis

By Friday, October 26, signals were being received through Valerian Zorin at the United Nations and the American Broadcasting Company's State Department correspondent, John Scali, that Moscow would consider a deal—withdrawal of the missiles in return for a public U.S. pledge not to invade Cuba. This, combined with the fact that the missile-carrying ships had stopped, apparently to await further instructions, made the ExComm members breathe more easily on Friday night, especially after Kennedy received, through a private correspondence channel established after the Vienna summit, a meandering, contradictory but on the whole desperately conciliatory letter from Khrushchev. Everyone was utterly exhausted. Dean Rusk was thought to be close to a physical and mental breakdown.

On Saturday morning the new optimism was shattered when another message was received from Khrushchev, more strident in tone, proposing that Soviet missiles in Cuba be exchanged for U.S. Jupiters in Turkey. ExComm members were confused by the two messages, debating the sequence of their composition and transmission, as well as the possibility of a split between Khrushchev and Kremlin hard-liners, while the conviction grew that the SAM sites would have to be attacked early Sunday morning if the impasse could not be broken. Robert Kennedy suggested that the ExComm focus on the earlier letter and ignore the later, harsher one. The president acted on that advice, replying to Khrushchev that work must cease on offensive missile bases in Cuba and all offensive weapons on the island must be rendered inoperable and removed under appropriate United Nations observation and supervision. The Soviet Union must also halt the further introduction of such weapons. In return, the United States would end the quarantine and give an assurance against an invasion of Cuba. On Sunday morning word came from Moscow Radio that Khrushchev had accepted Kennedy's terms. Kennedy hailed Khrushchev's statesmanlike decision as a constructive contribution to peace. Recognizing that it would be counterproductive to add to Khrushchev's humiliation, he ordered his advisers not to indulge in public gloating.

The confrontation over Soviet missiles in Cuba quickly became a classic model of the international crisis that is supposed to be a recurrent characteristic of global politics—a sudden, unanticipated encounter between rival powers, involving a high-stakes test of wills with a foreshortened decision time before the diplomatic threat of force turns into actual use of force. The motives, actions, and decision-making methods of the leaders and bureaucracies of both sides have been exhaustively analyzed. More than any other episode since World War II, the behavior of the superpowers during those 13 days convinced most observers that Washington and Moscow could control international crisis in the nuclear age—that they were capable of calm, rational choices even when on a collision course because both were aware of the potentially catastrophic costs of any direct military embroilment that might escalate to the nuclear level. From 1962 onward, "crisis management" became a common term in the international strategic lexicon. Americans perhaps became unduly optimistic, at least for a time while they enjoyed unquestioned strategic superiority, about the nation's ability to dominate in its relationship with the Soviet Union. Questions would subsequently be raised, especially by conservatives, as to just how elegantly the crisis had been handled and whether the U.S. gains were more permanent or more ephemeral than those of the USSR. The latter not only obtained a secure client state in the Caribbean but also was led to appreciate more than ever the advantage of possessing both strategic nuclear and local conventional superiority in a crisis. Kennedy himself realized this, as well as the fact that the Soviet Union's national security was not at stake in America's backyard. Moscow, having a weak case in the United States and Latin America, could withdraw without establishing a behavioral pattern for every critical confrontation in the future.

## ARMS-CONTROL NEGOTIATIONS

No real progress had been made in the direction of disarmament or arms limitation, whether nuclear or conventional, since the end of World War II. The Eisenhower years, however, had witnessed the opening of an intensive international debate over the possibility of banning nuclear-weapons tests. For some years India, Japan, and other nations had been severely critical of the United States for conducting nuclear tests in the atmosphere over the Pacific, but scarcely critical of the Soviet Union, which was able to confine its testing to its own vast territorial expanse. The Western powers were under increasing pressure at the United Nations to suspend tests both as a cause of radioactive fallout and as a trigger of the arms race.

An international conference of experts on verification and control problems undertook discussions in Geneva with Eastern-bloc representatives in the summer of 1958 on the technical requirements of policing a test ban. The most difficult problem pertained to the means of detecting underground tests and distinguishing them from earthquakes. The technical experts had reached tentative agreement on a global network of approximately 180 monitoring posts, but Moscow and Washington were never able to arrive at a compromise regarding the number of on-site inspections needed to check out "doubtful events." During 1958, first the Soviet Union and later the United States and Britain, without the concurrence of France (which was still preparing for its first test), had announced that they would suspend tests on a voluntary basis, pending progress toward the establishment of a workable verification system. This "Big Three" nuclear moratorium was still in effect when Kennedy and Khrushchev met in Vienna in June 1961 and the latter said that the Soviet Union would not be the first to resume testing.

The debate over nuclear testing and a test ban intensified in the summer of 1961. Fears of radioactive fallout in the form of strontium-90 grew. The president sent Arthur Dean to Geneva with a draft of a new test-ban treaty, but Khrushchev, soured by the United Nations intervention in the Congo, declared that the Soviet Union could never trust "neutrals" on a control commission and demanded a *troika*, or three-way veto system, for all forms of international cooperation. Meanwhile, Kennedy was under pressure from Congress, the Defense Department, and the public to order a resumption of tests, lest the United States fall behind the USSR in the technology of very large nuclear weapons and knowledge of their electromagnetic pulse (EMP) effects on the military environment, and especially on the operational effectiveness of electronic communications and the workability of all military equipment with electrical parts in a nuclear attack. Kennedy suspected that Moscow was seeking to induce the United States to be the first to terminate the voluntary suspension (which either side was legally free to do). On August 30 the Soviet Union began a two-month series of atmospheric tests, including weapons at least as large as 50 megatons. (Khrushchev himself boasted of 100-megaton weapons, five times the size of the largest U.S. H-bomb explosion.) The White House immediately denounced this form of "atomic blackmail," which posed hazards to world health and peace. One week later, on September 5, the president ordered a resumption of underground tests. Hoping that enough could be learned from underground detonations, he held off a decision on atmospheric tests, but told the Atomic Energy Commission to prepare for them under carefully controlled conditions in case they should prove absolutely necessary. He was blamed by some for doing too much too soon by way of reaction, by others for doing too little too late. Reluctantly, he permitted atmospheric tests to be carried out in April 1962.

At the height of the crises over Berlin, Soviet nuclear testing, the United Nations intervention in the Congo, and the Soviet demand for a UN *troika*, Kennedy addressed the General Assembly. Under prodding from Adlai Stevenson, who feared that the Soviet Union was seizing the initiative in the battle to influence world public opinion and putting the United States on the defensive with regard to the disarmament issue, the president on September 25, 1961, unveiled a new U.S. proposal for "general and complete disarmament in a peaceful world." The plan was only a bit less utopian than the one Khrushchev had presented to the United Nations two years previously. The utopian character of both the Soviet and the American blueprints consisted in the goal of comprehensive disarmament, which would radically transform all nation-states and the international system itself. None of the older and more powerful states was prepared then or now to exchange the dangers of a familiar world for the dangers of an unfamiliar one.

It took strategic analysts in the West very little time to demonstrate the impracticability of the concept of general and complete disarmament under existing circumstances. A number of studies showed the technical, strategic, and political obstacles to be virtually insuperable. The Soviet Union was at that time precipitating a constitutional and financial crisis within the UN over the Congo peacekeeping operation. Two nuclear states, France and China, refused to take part in arms negotiations. Several important states were becoming increasingly convinced of the effectiveness of nuclear deterrence in preventing not only strategic nuclear war but any conventional war (especially in Europe) that might escalate to nuclear war, and they were not eager to dismantle that structure.

For more than four years, the Big Three had tried in vain at Geneva to draft a satisfactory treaty on the discontinuance of *all* nuclear-weapons tests. Their efforts always broke down on the issue of on-site inspections for an underground ban. After both sides, however, perceived how dangerous their confrontation in the Cuban missile crisis was or might have become, the Soviet Union showed interest in more practical, limited measures of "arms control," a concept previously criticized by Communist spokesmen as a "Wall Street deception." In December 1962 the two rivals, recalling the difficulties of communicating during the Cuban emergency, began to examine the possibility of establishing a direct communications link between their two capitals. The agreement to set up a "hot line" (consisting of duplex wire telegraph and radiotelegraph circuits) was signed in Geneva on June 20, 1963.

A few weeks later, the Big Three undertook negotiations to outlaw nuclear tests in the three environments where they could be easily monitored by existing detection systems—in the atmosphere, in outer space, and under water. It took only ten days to draft and sign a treaty to that effect on July 25, 1963—a treaty which, it was plausibly assumed, could have the effect of slowing the process of nuclear-weapons proliferation to states not already possessing them. The limited test-ban treaty was undoubtedly the most important arms agreement concluded by the United States and the Soviet Union up to that time. In a way, it can also be looked upon as the first international treaty drafted in response to genuine worries over the impact of human technological activities on the human environment. Despite the misgivings of some American military leaders that it would inhibit U.S. efforts to learn from larger atmospheric tests what the Soviet Union may already have learned about the effects of EMP, the Senate, by a vote of 80 to 19, consented to ratification on September 24, 1963.

## KENNEDY, EUROPE, AND THE WESTERN ALLIANCE

Kennedy attached great importance to the Atlantic Alliance. By reason of education and friendship, notably with Harold Macmillan and David Ormsby-Gore, he felt closest to Britain. The two English-speaking allies disagreed over recognition of Communist China. NATO strategy, nuclear testing, the desirability of additional summit meetings with Khrushchev and the cancellation of the Skybolt missile program. Nevertheless, the president assumed that when the chips were down, he could count on British cooperation. He was less at ease in dealing with French and West German leaders and diplomats.

## Kennedy and de Gaulle

Whereas Kennedy met Macmillan a total of seven times, he met de Gaulle only once, while en route to Vienna for the summit talks with Khrushchev. The young president recognized the older one as an historic figure who had dealt with the wartime Big Three leaders, and he admired de Gaulle's determination to restore France's national grandeur and pride, but he found him irritating, conceited, and stubborn. De Gaulle, for his part, understood well that the U.S. commitment to defend the Federal Republic of Germany gave him a military shield and a political flexibility that he proved quite adept at exploiting.

French and American policy diverged at many points. Paris and Washington pursued opposing approaches to European unity—the former preferring a Europe of traditional nation-states under French leadership to the functionally integrated Europe favored by the architects of the Economic Community headquartered at Brussels and strongly supported by the United States (even though it caused increasing problems of competition for American business). De Gaulle made no effort to disguise his resentment of American political-military domination of European affairs, the "invasion" of the European economy by giant American corporations, the special relationship between Britain and the United States, and Washington's encouragement of London's application for entry into the Common Market. De Gaulle backed Kennedy's firm stand on Berlin and assured him that Khrushchev did not want war. On Southeast Asia, however, he warned against U.S. "entanglement without end" in that "bottomless political and military quagmire," as if to suggest that the Americans would be naive to become involved in a regional situation that the more experienced French had been unable to control. He also opposed the UN peacekeeping intervention in the Congo.

## NATO and Nuclear Cooperation

Among the recurring periods of tension that have marked the internal history of the Western alliance, one of the most serious was that of late 1962 and early 1963, for it brought to a convergence political, economic, and military disagreements that reflected two not entirely compatible approaches to Atlantic unity: the quest for an American–European partnership of equals in the economic realm and the strategic requirement for U.S. domination with regard to nuclear deterrence. Ever since the early 1950s, succesful efforts had been under way, led by Jean Monnet, Robert Schuman, and Konrad Adenauer, to enhance Europe's competitive status in the world economy by carrying out integration through the Coal and Steel Community and the Common Market. Altering Europe's dependent status in the defense sector was a much more difficult matter. In fact, the European Community governments of the Federal Republic of Germany, Italy, and the Benelux countries refused to endorse de Gaulle's thesis that a self-respecting nation-state can never entrust its ultimate military security to a foreign power with a different set of national interests. Even when tempted to think that the French president might be correct, and to doubt the credibility of the U.S. nuclear guarantee in the years of Soviet missile growth ahead, most Western European governing elites realized that the Allies had no choice but to place their faith in the U.S. commitment because Western Europe, for a variety of reasons, more political than technical, could not create an effective deterrent of its own. De Gaulle himself apparently believed that European deterrence and defense could not be completely detached from the military capabilities of the United States. He probably had less difficulty than other Western European leaders in identifying with Kennedy's somewhat vague "Declaration of Interdependence," delivered at Independence Hall, Philadelphia, on July 4, 1962, in which Kennedy suggested the possibility of a military as well as an economic partnership between America and Europe. Most Europeans saw the proposal as uplifting but unrealistic rhetoric. They paid more attention to the Ann Arbor speech of June 1962 in which Defense Secretary McNamara fired his salvo against national nuclear deterrent forces:

> There must not be competing and conflicting strategies to meet the contingency of nuclear war. We are convinced that a general nuclear war target system is indivisible, and if, despite all our efforts, nuclear war should occur, our best hope lies in conducting a centrally controlled campaign against all of the enemy's vital nuclear capabilities. . . .
>
> Limited nuclear capabilities, operating independently, are dangerous, expensive, prone to obsolescence, and lacking in credibility as a deterrent.

The Europeans were disturbed by shifts in American strategic thinking during the Kennedy years. Although they had harbored misgivings over the Eisenhower-Dulles doctrine of "massive retaliation," they nevertheless had a basic confidence in the military judgment of a president who had been the first NATO commander. So long as Eisenhower thought that his strategy would protect Europe, that was sufficient for most Europeans, especially when no one doubted the fact of U.S. nuclear superiority. Kennedy, however, was impressed by the arguments of academic, military, and other strategic theorists—William Kaufmann, Henry Kissinger, James Gavin, Maxwell Taylor, Herman Kahn, Paul Nitze—who worried about how long massive retaliation would remain a credible strategy for NATO as Soviet nuclear missile capabilities grew. The recurring Berlin crises rendered the problem acute. Kennedy, who deemed massive retaliation a highly inappropriate response for Soviet conventional aggression in Europe, demanded a range of military options "between holocaust and surrender." U.S. officials, especially but not exclusively in the Arms Control and Disarmament Agency (which came into being in September 1961) called for a reduced reliance on nuclear strategy in NATO and tightened restrictions on nuclear weapons in Europe—separation by geography and command, "two-key" systems, electronic release controls, and the like—along with the buildup of conventional forces by the European allies.

Kennedy's emphasis on a strategy of "flexible response," as it came to be known, aroused misgivings in Western Europe, especially in the Federal Republic of Germany. NATO strategists across the Atlantic were much more interested in nuclear deterrence, with all its theoretical difficulties, than in an operational conventional defense. For one thing, it was much cheaper to deter war with nuclear weapons than to try to match Warsaw Pact conventional forces. If the gradual accumulation of nuclear stockpiles kept war "unthinkable," then why waste resources on large standing armies and why develop strategies for actually fighting a war? Adenauer and his advisers did not deem it wise to let Moscow conclude that the West, heavily dependent on a strategy of nuclear response, was more frightened by the specter of nuclear weapons than the Soviet Union was. They wondered whether the Western shift of emphasis from nuclear deterrence to conventional defense might tempt Soviet planners in a future crisis to test the will of the NATO allies with a limited conventional military probe. Worst of all, they feared that any military conflict in Europe would contain powerful built-in pressures to become nuclear sooner or later. They feared nuclear war as much as anyone, but they did not want a war to be confined to Central Europe, and they perceived a tragic irony in the possibility that responding to the fear with a conventional buildup might weaken deterrence and increase the likelihood that the dreaded nuclear war would occur. They were not at all receptive, therefore, to Undersecretary George Ball's repeated calls for increased defense expenditures and large non-nuclear capabilities. The allies did no more than the absolute minimum needed to comply with Washington's exhortations. De Gaulle resisted all efforts to change the official NATO strategic doctrine from massive retaliation to flexible response. In the end, the Kennedy administration found that its ability to reduce reliance on a nuclear strategy in Europe was quite limited.

The issue of nuclear cooperation and sharing within NATO became acute in the early 1960s. The United States, under a 1958 amendment to its Atomic Energy Act, had aided Britain's nuclear-weapons program, largely because British scientists had worked with American scientists on the wartime Manhattan Project. De Gaulle would have welcomed similar aid, without any strings attached. At the same time, he probably suspected that technical assistance from abroad meant political dependence on the foreign supplier and concluded that France could be assured of an independent national nuclear deterrent only by acquiring it through its own efforts. He was irritated, nevertheless, by the preferential treatment accorded to Britain and hardly concealed his disdain for the "independence" of the British deterrent. He was even more chagrined by McNamara's avowed contempt for France's fledgling *force de frappe* ("strike force").* Throughout Kennedy's presidency, de Gaulle's ardor for NATO grew cooler. He still wanted a tripartite (American–British–French) directorate of NATO, which he had formally proposed in 1958 and which Eisenhower had dismissed without so much as a letter of reply. Kennedy agreed with him, at least perfunctorily, on the need for reorganizing NATO, but when he asked the general for suggestions, the replies were vague. De Gaulle undoubtedly would have liked

---

*Many British Laborites, to cast doubt on the Conservatives' deterrent policy, argued that McNamara's Ann Arbor speech had strengthened their case for abolishing the British deterrent, but a few days later McNamara stated explicitly that he had not been referring to the British deterrent because it was integrated with that of the United States in NATO.

a voice in the formulation of America's global strategy, but it was never clear that he really wanted to strengthen the Alliance's military organization—in fact, quite the contrary, as later developments showed.

### Britain Applies for Membership in the Common Market

In the summer of 1961, the Macmillan government carried out a diplomatic revolution when it announced its intention to seek entry into the European Economic Community (EEC). For a decade Britain had shied away from the European integration movement because of its traditional political and economic ties with the British Commonwealth nations. Within recent years, British preferential trade with the Commonwealth as a whole had declined, while the Common Market had become increasingly significant to British industry, both as buyer and as international competitor. Britain's effort to cushion the impact of the dynamic EEC by taking the lead in organizing the European Free Trade Association (EFTA) had not proved sufficient to insulate itself against the logic of necessary historical change. London knew that the adjustment would be difficult, but it was determined to obtain the best possible arrangements—special protocols, escape clauses, and gentlemen's agreements—to ease the transition problems of Commonwealth members dependent on the United Kingdom market. Harvard economist John Kenneth Galbraith warned Kennedy that U.S. support for an enlarged European Community, with its rising tariff wall against nonmembers, would eventually hurt U.S. trade (in both European and other markets) and compound the already serious balance-of-payments problem. Kennedy, however, thought that the political benefits of British entry would outweigh its economic costs to Americans: Britain's steadying diplomatic hand would be good for the Continent's move toward unity. Many in the United Kingdom were unsure of their ability either to hold their own against European competition or to exert a moderating political influence. The Labor party, suspicious of the free market philosophy pervading much of the EEC, feared a dilution of hard-won social-welfare programs; the Conservatives, suspicious of written federal constitutions, feared the erosion of Britain's historic prerogatives as a sovereign, independent nation.

The European federalists could not at first make up their minds whether to welcome or dread the overtures of the Macmillan government. Some thought that British nationalism would buttress Gaullist antifederal tendencies. But since London's application for entry had Kennedy's full backing, the "Europeanists" concluded that on balance Britain's entry would be a gain. De Gaulle, aware that the Anglo–American group was far from sympathetic toward his vision and that the federalists who wanted to see the British come in were determined to subordinate the "European idea" to Atlanticism, began to suggest that England was not yet really ready to join Europe. Would the British, for example, upon coming into Europe, bring their nuclear weapons with them? Throughout the spring of 1962, the semi-official weekly, *The Economist*, hinted broadly that the British government should consider "some sort of *entente nucleaire*, a bilateral Anglo–French arrangement to replace the bad example the two countries are currently setting with their separate, national, atomic forces."

## Cancellation of the Skybolt Missile Program

Kennedy's "grand design" for the Atlantic Alliance was temporarily shaken in the wake of the Cuban missile crisis, when the Skybolt program was cancelled by an administration which failed to foresee the consequences of its action. At a Camp David meeting in 1960, Eisenhower and Macmillan had agreed that the United States would provide, when developed, the two-stage Skybolt missile for Britain's V-bombers. London at that time preferred Skybolt to Polaris for purposes of strategic deterrence, because the United States promised to pay the research and development costs for Skybolt, which would make for a more independent deterrent than Polaris missiles on British submarines placed under NATO command. In turn, Britain undertook to make the naval base at Holy Loch available to American Polaris submarines.

In November 1962, McNamara recommended that Skybolt be cancelled for reasons of technical difficulty and cost-ineffectiveness. Although there had been warnings that the program was not progressing well, the British were shocked by the news. The Macmillan government had depended heavily on the promise of Skybolt for the future of their deterrent, and the public furor that resulted threatened to bring down the Conservatives and produce a serious rift in Anglo–American relations. The British press accused the United States of treating an ally with insensitivity, heavy-handed methods, and tactlessness. Neither Washington nor London had been prepared to handle the matter intelligently by proposing an acceptable alternative before the storm broke, but the greater fault lay with Washington.

## The NATO Multilateral Force

When Kennedy and Macmillan met at Nassau in December 1962, the former offered several alternatives that failed to satisfy the latter. If Skybolt could not be salvaged—which seemed the case, especially after Kennedy had branded it a failure on television—Macmillan wanted Polaris. The Kennedy administration was reluctant to make a deal on submarine-launched missiles except within the framework of a NATO multilateral force (MLF), which had been under discussion since 1959. The MLF, an internationally staffed fleet designed to solve the nuclear sharing problem, went through several planning models (submarines at first, later surface ships) during the early 1960s, but met with active opposition or only the most grudging approval in Europe and in the U.S. Congress and the Pentagon. It was supposed to give the West Germans a share in NATO's nuclear strategy. Observers wondered whether it would satisfy the Germans' desire for equality or whet their appetite for nuclear weapons of their own. Some people in the administration argued that an outright gift of Polaris to the British would offend the French, provoke the Soviet Union, contravene U.S. interests in nonproliferation, and complicate the problem of nuclear disarmament.

Kennedy, who later complained that no one had warned him how politically explosive the Skybolt scuttling would be in Britain, wanted to help Macmillan out of an awkward domestic situation, lest he be succeeded by an anti-American cabinet. Moreover, he did not want to see the agreement on the use of the Holy Loch base jeopardized. The State and Defense departments, however, were not prepared with a detailed Polaris-transfer proposal. The result was a hastily concocted and ambiguously worded agreement ostensibly calculated to reconcile the idea of a national deterrent with centralized NATO command and the "indivisibility" of Western nuclear defense. The United States agreed to make Polaris missiles (without warheads) available to the United Kingdom, and the latter agreed to assign them to NATO,* reserving the right to withdraw them only when "supreme national interests are at stake."

It was decided that a similar offer should be made to de Gaulle, and this was done without fanfare. The French president seemed initially interested in receiving more information about what was involved, but he apparently concluded that acceptance would mean reversing his policy of gradually placing distance between France and NATO's integrated military command, so he declined the offer. Policymakers in Washington who regarded the MLF as a "military Rube Goldberg scheme" and a political charade had been hoping that de Gaulle would accept. With Britain and France both committed to the more realistic NATO multinational force, they thought the idea of a multilateral force (which the Admiralty Office in London called "crazy") would collapse. There remained, nevertheless, the problem of giving the Federal Republic of Germany some sense of participating in NATO nuclear strategic planning, and the American proponents of the MLF sold this solution to an originally skeptical group of officials in the Adenauer Government. Consequently, the idea of the MLF survived for another three years as a source of disagreement within both the U.S. government and NATO.

Meanwhile, on January 14, 1963, just a few weeks after Nassau, de Gaulle held the most famous of his semi-annual press conferences, in which he pointedly criticized the efforts of the United States to maintain a virtual monopoly on nuclear-weapons control in the West, reaffirmed his intention to oppose military integration and achieve a national defense capability, and vetoed the British application for admission to the Common Market. British entry, he declared, would transform the character of the EEC until "finally it would appear as a colossal Atlantic community under American domination and direction."

Kennedy realized that disagreements were inevitable in a defensive coalition of democratic governments. Each was bound to view its security problems, however common to all, from its own national perspective. Each would seek to preserve its self-esteem. The task of the Alliance leader was often the most delicate, for its very strength would make it seem arrogant no matter what decisions it took unilaterally. He concluded that it was therefore advisable for the United States to pursue its own national interest as the other allies did, but in a way to advance what it, as leader, perceived to be in the security interest of all. Aware that NATO could not always preserve a united front vis-à-vis Central Africa, the Middle East, Southeast Asia, or the People's Republic of China, he was satisfied

---

*The Nassau Communiqué provided that Britain might use the missiles either in a multinational force of nationally organized contingents assigned to NATO (from which withdrawal would be possible) or in the mix-staffed MLF (from which withdrawals would not be possible).

to see it hold firm on Berlin or any other direct challenge from the USSR in Europe.

Kennedy's moment of greatest personal glory came during his triumphal visit to Europe in the early summer of 1963. Still basking in the Cuban missile crisis victory and fresh from his American University speech on arms control, in which he held out the olive branch to the Soviet Union, he was eager to show the younger members of European societies what he had meant when he said at his inaugural that the torch had been passed to a new generation. He was already the hero of the European democratic left and of the advocates of a united Europe within an Atlanticist rather than a Gaullist framework. Kennedy was confident that he could eventually come to terms even with de Gaulle, whose leadership mystique he never ceased to admire. But above all he wanted to take advantage of his own vitality and contagiously optimistic outlook, in contrast to the aging conservative leadership of Western Europe, to project to European youth the image of a dynamic, progressive America. He also wanted to reassure those who were doubtful, nervous, and insecure. At the Bonn Airport, he said: "Your liberty is our liberty; and any attack on your soil is an attack upon our own. Out of necessity, as well as sentiment, . . . our fortunes are one." The following pledge came two days later in Frankfurt: "The United States will risk its cities to defend yours because we need your freedom to protect ours." Then on to Berlin, where he was frightened by the combustive interplay of his own eloquence and the emotions of a half-million Germans:

> There are many people in the world who really don't understand, or say they don't, what is the great issue between the free world and the Communist world. Let them come to Berlin!
>
> There are some who say that communism is the wave of the future. Let them come to Berlin!
>
> And there are some who say in Europe and elsewhere we can work with the Communists . . . *Lass sie nacht Berlin Kommen*! Let them come to Berlin!
>
> All free men, wherever they may live, are citizens of Berlin, and therefore, as a free man, I take pride in the words, *"Ich bin ein Berliner!"*

He reflected later that if he had urged his listeners to march on the Berlin Wall and tear it down, they probably would have done so. That speech may have been the last Western clarion call, the last summons to an ideological crusade that could safely be made in a world of two nuclear powers. He himself probably did not expect it, nor want it, to be heeded.

## EAST ASIA AND THE MIDDLE EAST

No president can attend constantly to all regions of the world. There is, fortunately, a certain slowly pulsing rhythm to international relations. Not all parts of the globe are sufficiently in ferment or movement to require urgently the problem-solving capabilities of those who make foreign policy. During his three years in office, Kennedy was compelled to focus his energies on the Soviet Union,

Latin America, Western Europe, Africa, and Southeast Asia, as the foregoing pages have shown. These were the areas of critical developments.

Two other important regions—East Asia and the Middle East—posed no acute crises during these years. Relations with Japan did not preoccupy Kennedy at all. As for China, he considered the Eisenhower–Dulles policy of nonrecognition of the Peking government a bit irrational, but he shied away from the domestic furor a U.S. policy shift would cause. Besides, although Khrushchev performed his annual ritual of calling for the PRC's admission to the United Nations, the slowly widening Sino–Soviet rift and budding U.S.–Soviet détente made the issue less irritating in U.S.–Soviet relations, while China's aggressive behavior against India's northern boundaries in 1962 made the American position seem less unreasonable in the eyes of the neutral bloc in the General Assembly.

### Sukarno's Indonesia

Between East Asia and the Middle East, Indonesia constituted a source of concern. This archipelago, with a population of more than 100 million, which had gained independence from the Dutch in the early 1950s, was ruled by the intensely egocentric Achmed Sukarno. His "guided democracy" was a euphemism for a dictatorship, based on a synthetic Marxist-Western nativist ideology, which failed to take economic advantage of the country's rich natural resources. Sukarno was more interested in unifying his people by "liberating" West Irian (West New Guinea) from Dutch control than by concentrating on modernizing development programs. Kennedy, determined to head off the necessity of additional U.S. intervention in a Southeast Asian war, put heavy pressure on the Dutch to negotiate a transfer settlement so that Indonesia could increase its economic ties with American oil companies and business interests in the Netherlands and other countries. After gaining West Irian with U.S. support, however, Sukarno embarked on a new "confrontation" to prevent the transition of Malaya and the Crown Colonies of Sarawak, Brunei, and North Borneo into a new Malaysian Federation. Kennedy's effort to divert Sukarno from external jingoistic adventures to the tasks of internal economic development failed.

### Nasser's Egypt

Comparable overtures to Gamal Abdel Nasser of Egypt seemed a bit more promising for a while. Although Soviet assistance on the construction of the Aswan High Dam continued, relations between Moscow and Cairo were cooling. The disintegration of the United Arab Republic (Egypt's merger with Syria) left Egypt somewhat isolated, and Nasser's brand of Arab nationalism suffered a setback. Since Egyptian–Israeli tensions were not at a crisis point, the situation seemed propitious for a warming trend in U.S.–Egyptian relations.

Despite his penchant for face-to-face encounters with foreign leaders, Kennedy never met Nasser. The two did, however, carry on a relatively cordial correspondence. Kennedy indicated a desire to pursue an even-handed Middle East policy between U.S. interests in the Arab world (namely, oil) and continued

U.S. support for Israeli democracy (which was a matter both of national moral-political responsibility and of domestic politics). His administration sought to persuade Nasser, as it did Sukarno, that he should de-emphasize regional imperialism in favor of internal economic development, for which Egypt possessed a more competent elite than Indonesia. The United States stepped up the flow of food aid to Egypt under P.L. 480.

An effort was also made to work out through the UN Palestine Conciliation Commission a humanitarian solution to the problem of the 1.2 million Palestinian refugees on the basis of repatriation and compensation for property. According to one plan, Israel would readmit up to 200,000 and the rest would permanently relocate in Arab states. Distrust ran high, and both sides were afraid to make the necessary concessions. After eighteen months, the negotiations collapsed. In the meantime, the administration decided to calm Israeli misgivings by selling it some Hawk anti-aircraft missiles. Nasser appreciated Kennedy's diplomatic courtesy of writing him a personal letter of information and explanation concerning the projected sale. In late December 1962 Kennedy gave Israeli Prime Minister Golda Meir an assurance of U.S. aid against invasion that went farther than any previous U.S. commitment to Israel and told her that the United States "has a special relationship with Israel in the Middle East really comparable only to that which it has with Britain over a wide range of world affairs."

U.S.–Egyptian relations took a turn for the worse in 1962, when Nasser, competing with Syria for leadership of the radical Arab nationalist movement, began sending Egyptian troops to Yemen to assist revolutionary republican forces against a Saudi-backed royalist government. Before that intervention ended five years later, the number of Egyptian forces in Yemen would rise to an estimated 70,000 to 80,000. Kennedy himself in 1963 began to feel some concern for the security of Saudi Arabia and its oil. Tensions arose within the region, but would not reach the crisis point until June 1967.

## KENNEDY AS DECISION MAKER

Although many observers took it for granted that Kennedy wanted to be his own secretary of state, and for that reason avoided appointing to the post anyone with a strong political base and popular personality who might upstage him, that was neither an entirely accurate assessment of the situation nor a feasible alternative. It is true that he passed over such prominent likely candidates as Adlai Stevenson and Chester Bowles (former governor of Connecticut and ambassador to India), but that was perhaps less because they might be independent-minded than because neither had supported Kennedy before the Democratic Convention and both were too predictably liberal and idealistic (for example, on the United Nations and complete disarmament) for Kennedy and his entourage. Kennedy was not attracted to the hard-nosed realism of a Dean Acheson, but having defeated Richard Nixon by only 119,000 votes (and by fewer than 10,000 votes in ten states), the man from Massachusetts did not deem it prudent at the height of the cold war to deviate from a centrist foreign policy by naming an idealistic liberal to the top post at State.

The president must try to be in ultimate control of foreign policy. At the beginning of the 1960s, the international system was rapidly becoming much more complicated as a result of numerous developments: decolonization and a doubling in the number of independent states since the late 1940s; the emergence of nationalist and revolutionary movements among the less-developed regions of the world; the acquisition of missile technology by the two principal nuclear powers; and the fissures that were beginning to appear in what had previously been regarded as a monolithic Communist bloc. The United States could no longer focus foreign-policy efforts almost exclusively on Europe and East Asia, with occasional involvement in the Middle East or Southeast Asia only during times of acute crisis. Most of the older Latin American republics and of the 40 new postcolonial African states were clamoring for sustained political attention and economic aid in various forms. Kennedy was convinced that if he was to stay on top of the foreign-policy planning process, he had to reorganize it and centralize its coordination in the White House, not to weaken the role of the State Department but because without centralization there could be no efficient leadership and control over the increasingly sprawling, labyrinthine bureaucracy that formulates and executes foreign and defense policy.

Walt Rostow has pointed out that the making of external national policy has to be organized in a manner congenial to the operating style of an incumbent president, who inevitably has preferred methods of receiving information, dealing with subordinates, resolving personality, policy, and "turf" disputes among them, establishing priorities among competing claims for attention and resources, weighing the quality of advice, assessing the pros and cons of proposed alternative courses of action, and finally arriving at decisions. All this must be done by way of pursuing the putative national interest within the context of a perceived and incompletely understood international setting, amidst the relentless ongoing duties of being president and the influx of contradictory domestic pressures from a variety of governmental sources and special-interest groups.

Dean Rusk, who had been nearly everyone's second choice for secretary of state, proved to be a fine professional technician in the conduct of routine diplomatic business. He was invariably dignified and impressively competent in his appearances before congressional committees and in international conferences, meetings of foreign ministers, and consultations with ambassadors. He was an able chief administrator of the department and the Foreign Service, monitoring the flow of critically important cable traffic. He had not chosen most of his key subordinates, and he did not always know what was going on at the highest policymaking levels, but he was usually well-prepared to brief the president on foreign situations and render his advice when asked. He was readier to say what he thought in one-to-one meetings, which were not very frequent. In larger meetings at the White House, he shied away from debating people who were known to be more influential with Kennedy.

Kennedy, though temperamentally ill-disposed toward the use of military force, nevertheless realized that credible deterrence and defense capabilities were an indispensable underpinning of an effective foreign policy. He reposed a great deal of trust and authority in Robert McNamara to run the Pentagon and the entire military establishment. Unlike Rusk, McNamara was allowed to pick his own team. The president, who was much more interested in the subtle political and psychological texture of foreign-policy problems than in the nuts and bolts of defense technology, did not closely monitor the reorganization of the Pentagon or the detailed revision of American strategy beyond the basic guiding principles on which he and his defense secretary were agreed. Actually, Kennedy was not at ease with the military mind. The Bay of Pigs experience had made him distrustful of military advice, at least until his protégé, Maxwell Taylor, became chairman of the Joint Chiefs of Staff in October 1962. Even then, he was less impressed with the quality of the recommendations from the uniformed services than with that of McNamara during the Cuban missile crisis. The secretary and his "whiz kids" were masters of operations analysis and calculations of cost-effectiveness in managing the defense budget and reformulating strategy. That was the plus side. On the minus side, efficiency in the realm of economics and business production came to be equated with efficiency not only in the procurement of military equipment (which was highly desirable) but also in the entire dimension of strategy (which was undesirable). Strategy must strive toward the achievement of objectives with maximum efficiency—that is, with maximum certainty and at minimum costs—but it must be analyzed primarily in a political rather than an economic framework.

To ensure the integration of many different strands of foreign and defense policy, Kennedy strengthened the role of the special assistant for national-security affairs. That office was filled by McGeorge Bundy, who might have been a stronger candidate for secretary of state had he been older. Bundy and the White House staff* were assigned numerous related tasks:

1. Seeing to it that the president was kept fully informed on all aspects of foreign and defense policy, as well as of the international situation, that required his attention.

2. Coordinating into a coherent whole, if possible, the work of the various departments and agencies that make up the far-flung external affairs establishment—State, Defense, CIA, AID, Treasury, Agriculture, and so on.

3. Monitoring the foreign-affairs bureaucracy to overcome the effect of bureaucratic compromise politics at lower echelons that would seek to limit the president to options that cause minimum disturbance to the bureaucrats' interests; bringing all relevant points of view forward to the president; and offering their own suggestions.

4. Assisting the president in carrying on an active role in diplomacy—

---

*Kennedy at first thought of Walt W. Rostow as head of Policy Planning at State, but Rusk scored one of his rare appointment successes by persuading the president that the post should go to George McGhee. For nearly a year Rostow served as Bundy's deputy until he took over Policy Planning when McGhee became deputy undersecretary.

correspondence, audiences with visiting foreign dignitaries, speeches, trips abroad, and so on.

5. Following through constantly to make sure that presidential decisions were being executed.

Kennedy presided crisply over foreign policy when the international system was passing through political, economic, and technological changes that no single power, however dominant, could control, much less prevent. His principal success was psychopolitical, flowing from his personality. He was able to project to the world the image of a forward-looking, creative leader. In his public utterances he was anticolonialist, in favor of nationalism and antipoverty development in the Third World, proponent of the Alliance for Progress, the Peace Corps, and Food for Peace, and an eloquent advocate of a movement away from cold war rigidities toward détente and nuclear-arms control, even though he was more skeptical than Chester Bowles, Hubert Humphrey, and Adlai Stevenson concerning the United Nations and general disarmament. His worst foreign-policy failures were the Bay of Pigs and, in hindsight, Southeast Asia. His performance in Africa and the Middle East received only mixed reviews; perhaps no one could have done better. His most conspicuous successes, besides the Cuban missile crisis, were the U.S. military buildup, his handling of the threat to Berlin, his face-to-face diplomacy, the negotiation of the Partial Nuclear Test Ban Treaty, the change of tone in U.S.–Soviet relations during 1963, and his reinfusion of spirit into the Atlantic Alliance. A staunch defender of NATO, he worked hard to make sure that his support for anticolonial causes, his détente overtures to Moscow, and transatlantic disagreements over strategy would not substantially weaken the Western Alliance. He was, thanks to his intelligence, wit, charm, and overall political style, the last president to enjoy throughout most of his term the generally friendly and often admiring support of the media as well as of a substantial majority of the American people for his handling of foreign policy.

# chapter 6

# The Foreign Policy of Lyndon Johnson:
From Tragedy to Disillusionment

Lyndon Baines Johnson assumed the presidency under the most unfavorable circumstances—as a result of the assassination of John F. Kennedy. The nation was in a state of shock and tragic gloom. The incoming president, whose personality and political style contrasted strongly with those of his predecessor, requested all of Kennedy's principal appointees to remain with him. He needed them if he was to convey a sense of continuity, to ensure an efficient transition to a new administration, and to link himself, if possible, with the Kennedy legend. Most of the Kennedy team did agree dutifully to stay on for at least a year, until after the 1964 election.

Kennedy as president had always treated his vice-president with fairness and consideration, but some of his closest associates in the White House had been known to regard Johnson with contempt and ridicule, if not animosity, and those attitudes were now amplified. Ever since the 1960 Los Angeles Convention, when Robert Kennedy had tried to block the Texan's nomination for second place on the ticket, the relationship between the two was one of antipathy. By 1963, LBJ had come to believe that Bobby was trying to dump him as his brother's running mate in 1964. Nevertheless, despite the mutual hostility, Johnson asked the attorney general to stay on, and the latter with great difficulty agreed to do so. For the last six months of John Kennedy's presidency, Robert was so preoccupied with civil rights that he withdrew from active involvement in foreign-policy matters. (He was not consulted on the overthrow of the Diem regime.) Kennedy never became a trusted adviser to President Johnson. In fact, the views of the two men on foreign policy increasingly diverged, especially with regard to Latin American and nuclear-arms control. Throughout the early months of 1964, there

**193**

was talk of a Johnson–Kennedy ticket, but that never became a realistic possibility. Johnson, anxious to be elected without invoking the Kennedy name, did not want Bobby as a running mate, and the latter, uncertain whether he should make a serious bid, finally decided that he would be in a more influential position to carry on his brother's legacy as senator from New York. Among other principal Kennedy carryovers, Rusk served Johnson loyally until the end of his tenure, and McNamara until he became head of the World Bank in 1968. McGeorge Bundy remained as special assistant for national-security affairs until March 1966. Walt W. Rostow chaired the Policy Planning Council until April 1, 1966, when he moved to the White House as Bundy's replacement.

## JOHNSON'S BACKGROUND AND PHILOSOPHY

Lyndon Johnson was ambitious, energetic, and determined to succeed as a brilliant practitioner of politics in the American democratic system. He was not an intellectual—far from it. Having grown up in the wide and open hill country of Texas, and having gone to rural schools where the quality of education fell far below his brain power, he possessed none of the polished manners or urban erudition of Kennedy's Cambridge crowd. In fact, he often shocked his listeners with his crude or vulgar comments. His spontaneous public statements seldom soared above the commonplace. (He sincerely regretted the departure of Theodore Sorensen, Kennedy's speechwriter.) His awareness of the difference in style between his predecessor and himself probably increased both his resentment at invidious comparisons and his tendency to portray himself as a man of the people and a product of that rural environment from which America's most fundamental moral values and patriotic virtues spring. Yet he had a shrewd ability to manipulate the levers of power, as he had amply demonstrated when he was Senate majority leader. His three years as vice-president also showed that he could be loyal, disciplined, and self-abnegating while accepting a role of increasing obscurity. Bill Moyers called him "a great horse in a small corral." He had long wanted to be president, but because the nation, as he himself once mused, was "not far enough from Appomattox," probably not even a New Deal Southerner could have reached the White House except under the unusual combination of circumstances of 1960 and 1963.

Once in office, Johnson, although he felt like a usurper, undoubtedly wanted to go down in history as a good, a strong, a great president. As president, Johnson remained more interested in domestic issues and social problems of the type to be solved with his Great Society programs—civil rights, Medicare, education, antipoverty assistance, and so on—than he was in international affairs. This was due partly to his experience as a politician from an "isolationist" section of the country, partly to his New Deal heritage. To the extent that he did become concerned with foreign affairs, he was more comfortable dealing with Latin American and Asian than with European or African questions.

In contrast to Kennedy, he had little tolerance for protocol, ceremony, and the endless parade of diplomatic dignitaries, whom he diverted to Rusk whenever he could. The philosophy of foreign policy that he brought to the office was relatively uncomplicated. Aggression must always be stopped in its tracks and turned back. The United States should uphold international law, but also make it clear to the world that it had a tough-minded view of its national interests and was ready at all times to protect them. In the final analysis, the United States could not depend on collective security action by international organizations. Nevertheless, in Johnson's view, the United Nations did help to serve some long-range constructive purposes; it deserved U.S. support and should be used insofar as possible to serve its stated purposes, which coincide with U.S. values and policy goals. Johnson was, of course, a strong advocate of NATO because the security of Europe was a vital interest of the United States. Finally, Johnson maintained, within the U.S. constitutional system the president makes foreign policy, but cannot pursue objectives that arouse the sustained opposition of Congress. At least the tacit acquiescence of that body is required. Remembering Truman and the Korean War, Johnson was convinced that foreign policy was more likely to lose than to win an election.

## TROUBLE SPOTS IN LATIN AMERICA

The Kennedy administration, as we have seen, had launched the *Alianza* para el Progresso in the hope of sounding a new note in U.S.-Latin American relations. It had sought to treat the right-wing dictators with cool detachment, to woo the leaders of the democratic left and encourage them to pressure the privileged ruling classes to accept reforms aimed at hunger, poverty, disease, and illiteracy, and to shift emphasis in the development process from private investment to governmental action. That was to be the strategy for changing an extremely lopsided social structure (particularly in land ownership) and improving national patterns of income distribution. The Alliance, however, had failed because of the intractability of the socioeconomic situation. The privileged classes remained rigidly opposed to reform. Some modest increases in production were realized, but annual gains in GNP growth were neutralized by a population growth rate in excess of 3 percent. Advocates of Castroism and communism worked overtime to exacerbate the popular discontentments swelling throughout the region and to channel them into an anti-American, Marxist, and if possible pro-Cuban, pro-Soviet direction.

Kennedy and those around him gradually became disenchanted as the gap between their hopeful rhetoric and the reality of widespread misery failed to narrow appreciably. Kennedy himself blamed Castro for being a spoiler insofar as he rendered the leaders of the moderate democratic left in Latin America suspect in the eyes of U.S. business executives and conservatives, and for forcing his administration to be wary of foreign influences in all "revolutionary" movements. Less than a week before he was assassinated, he had warned: "We in this hemisphere must . . . use every resource at our command to prevent the establishment of another Cuba in this hemisphere." Johnson would later have occasion to quote that line with relish.

## Nationalist Unrest in Panama

The first flareup occurred in Panama, when Johnson's presidency was scarcely six weeks old. He was hoping that 1964 would bring no major foreign-policy problems so that he could concentrate on domestic legislation prior to the election campaign. The executive bureaucracy under Kennedy had prepared some progressive proposals for tax reduction, civil rights—particularly the Voting Rights Act—and Medicare. But during his 34 months in office, Kennedy had not been successful in steering his programs through Congress. This was Johnson's forte: he had earned a reputation as a masterful majority leader in the Senate. But he needed time to cajole his former colleagues. It would be helpful, therefore, if the countries of the world would stay on their good behavior for a while.

Under its 1903 treaty with Panama, the United States maintained sovereignty "in perpetuity" over the canal and the ten-mile-wide Canal Zone. The United States had agreed to pay Panama $10 million and, beginning in 1913, $250,000 annually. (In 1921 the Senate gave consent to a treaty that provided for the payment of $25 million to Colombia, and in 1939 the annuity to Panama was increased to $430,000.) The United States fortified and administered the canal. Approximately 27,000 American "Zonians" lived in the strip, and they were well-off, superpatriotic, and alienated from the native population and culture. After World War II, Panamanian nationalist sentiment began to simmer, and the American enclave astride Panama's territory became the natural focal point of discontent, with the flag as the most emotional symbol. Within the Zone, only the Stars and Stripes could be flown. Bands of local students tried to cross the border and plant their national flag there. In 1959 several Panamanians had been killed in an invasion skirmish. A year later, Eisenhower ordered one Panamanian flag to be hoisted in the Zone as a sign of "titular sovereignty."

The Kennedy administration undertook a series of exploratory conversations with the government of President Roberto F. Chiari in 1962, but, fearing domestic political repercussions in the United States, it declined to open the question of renegotiating the basic 1903 treaty. In July 1963 the two presidents issued a communiqué announcing improved wages and benefits for Panamanian employees in the Canal Zone and providing that the flags of both countries would henceforth fly side by side at the 50 sites where only American flags had previously flown. Later, American civilian authorities, in an effort to minimize potential flashpoints for conflict, decided to phase out flagpoles.

In January 1964 a flag incident occurred at a high school, sparking three days of riots and leaving 20 persons (including three U.S. soldiers) dead, hundreds injured, and much property in the Canal Zone damaged. Panama, charging the United States with "unjustifiable aggression," severed diplomatic relations. President Johnson, in a telephone conversation that violated protocol in those circumstances, told President Chiari, who faced an election in four months, that he understood his situation and that he was prepared to work toward a solution once the violence came to an end. Chiari agreed, but also insisted that a new treaty must be negotiated. Johnson refused to accept conditions dictated by Panama. He was anxious, however, to avoid any appearance of *Yanqui* intransigence and dispatched a fellow Texan, Thomas C. Mann, former ambassador to Mexico, to Panama City to undertake problem-solving talks within the framework of the Organization of American States.

For several weeks the two governments were at an impasse over whether they should prepare to *discuss* or to *negotiate* a new treaty. On March 15 the OAS announced that concurrence had been reached on "discussions and negotiations," but Johnson, warned by conservative senators not to appear weak, formally contradicted the OAS statement, declaring that the United States had not committed itself to a revision of the 1903 treaty. A week later he reaffirmed the long friendship of the two countries and noted that Chiari's claims were based on "a deeply felt sense of the honest and fair needs of Panama." While not promising to negotiate a new treaty, he offered to review any issue Panama wished to raise, and he did not rule out renegotiation. A joint declaration in early April restored diplomatic relations and called for the prompt elimination of the causes of conflict "without limitations or preconditions of any kind." By December 1964, a month after his landslide victory over Republican candidate Barry Goldwater, he said that the United States intended to negotiate an entirely new treaty on the Panama Canal to serve the interests of both countries, while at the same time exploring with Panama and other interested governments the possibility of constructing a second interoceanic canal in Central America or Colombia. The negotiations would not be completed until the 1980s, during the Carter administration.

## U.S. Marines in the Dominican Republic

A more serious disturbance occurred in the Dominican Republic in April 1964. Eighteen months after the right-wing tyrant Rafael Trujillo was assassinated, Dr. Juan Bosch, a political liberal and prominent writer, had been chosen as president in a free election, and the republic seemed to be on the road to democratic development. Bosch, however, a better poet than politician, was incapable of coping with the problems inherited from the previous regime. After only seven months in power, he was overthrown in mid-1963 by a military coup. The military leaders brought in a civilian triumvirate backed by right-wing parties that feared the growth of communist influence under Bosch. The Kennedy administration, which had counted on Bosch to build "a showcase for democracy," cut off foreign aid to the Santo Domingo junta, headed by Dr. Donald Reid y Cabral. This compounded the island republic's economic woes, for the price of sugar exports, on which the republic heavily depended, had dropped to a low point.

Reid y Cabral, a moderate despised by the extreme left and right as well as by Bosch's followers, tried to institute reforms and austerity measures to restore soundness to the economy. His efforts were thwarted by strikes, drought, spreading unemployment, and falling revenues. An attempted coup, accompanied by popular demonstrations of discontent, led to the collapse of the junta in April 1965. The officers of the armed forces divided into older elements loyal to the army traditions and younger rebels who wanted Bosch back in power. The latter were reported to be handing out weapons in the streets to civilians who were shouting antigovernment slogans. Fighting between the factions broke out in the capital. As the situation deteriorated, confusion mounted and reports became garbled. When the army failed to support Reid, he resigned. The rebels proclaimed a Bosch supporter provisional president, pending Bosch's return from the United States. The "loyalists," thinking Bosch would be soft on communism, swung into action against the "rebels." Law and order broke down in Santo Domingo. Johnson ordered the Atlantic Fleet to prepare to evacuate American citizens, and Washington received requests from other governments to help evacuate their nationals from a capital increasingly terrorized by trigger-happy mobs.

The U.S. ambassador, W. Tapley Bennett, hurried back to his post from his home in Georgia. Both the embassy staff in Santo Domingo and State, Pentagon, and CIA officials were afraid that Bosch's restoration would open the way for a Communist takeover. On April 28 Bennett cabled Washington: "American lives are in danger. . . . I recommend immediate landings." The president responded quickly by sending in 500 U.S. Marines, and within two weeks he had built up the force to more than 21,000. In a television address, he told the American people that he had taken the action to protect the lives of hundreds of Americans and to escort them safely back to the United States. A few days later, referring to an international conspiracy, he indicated that the prevention of a Communist seizure was the primary motive for the intervention. There was not necessarily a contradiction between the two explanations. The smaller Marine force was sent in to protect lives. The larger force was ordered in a full day later to prevent a takeover by a rebel movement which, as moderate officers began giving up, came increasingly under the influence of three Communist organizations, one oriented toward Moscow, another toward Beijing, and a third toward Havana—none of them very large but all highly disciplined, well armed, and led by professional revolutionaries.

Johnson undoubtedly exaggerated the degree of danger to American lives. On May 3 he misquoted Bennett's cable as saying; "American blood will run in the streets." Reminiscing at a news conference six weeks later, he spoke of 1500 innocent people murdered and beheaded, and of the American ambassador telephoning him from under his desk while bullets were being fired through his windows. Many innocent people were indeed killed. Red Cross investigators later estimated the number at 1300. Some of the killings were quite savage; a few headless corpses were sighted. None of the American residents, however, were among the fatalities, and Bennett subsequently denied that the U.S. Embassy had been attacked or that he had ever telephoned Washington from under his desk. Nevertheless, Americans were besieging the Embassy, clamoring to be evacuated. On the morning of the 28th, Bennett cabled that the situation did not warrant landing the Marines at that time, but he wanted them to stand by offshore. A few hours later came the cable reporting that the situation was deteriorating rapidly and that American lives were in danger, after the chief of the Dominican police told Bennett that he could no longer protect the road over which the evacuees were moving. Johnson then decided to send in the Marines to protect the lives of Americans and nationals of other countries requesting help. He ordered Rusk to inform all the Latin American ambassadors and the OAS. That evening, the leaders of Congress backed the president's action.

When Ambassador Ellsworth Bunker informed the OAS Council of what had happened, a lengthy, emotional debate ensued. Members voiced bitter criticism of unwarranted intervention, the hasty U.S. resort to military force, the reversion to a form of imperialist gunboat diplomacy not seen since 1925 (in Nicaragua), and the violation of OAS principles by the United States, which acted unilaterally without consulting the organization in advance. In some cases, there was a marked discrepancy between what the ambassadors were saying in Washington and what their colleagues were saying in Santo Domingo. Reflecting later on the OAS debate, Johnson wrote:

> The interchange underlined the difficulty of persuading representatives of twenty governments to agree on a course of action or to act quickly in a crisis, especially when they are far removed from the scene and depend largely on news accounts for information. There were many expressions of regret but few proposals for effective reaction to Dominican developments. The OAS Ambassadors would not commit their governments to anything without thorough consultation.

While the OAS met, the situation in Santo Domingo continued to deteriorate. Bennett urged armed intervention that would go beyond protection of Americans, seek to re-establish order, prevent a Communist takeover, overcome critical shortages of food and medicines, and interpose U.S. forces between the opposing factions so that the OAS could be asked to negotiate a political settlement. Johnson ordered more forces into the island republic. According to Walt Rostow, the situation had changed markedly since the earlier decision to send in 500 Marines, because Communist leaders had become dominant in the rebel citadel in the center of the capital after the moderate pro-Bosch rebel leaders fled. Although many in Latin America and the United States insisted that the Communist threat had been overestimated, Johnson never budged from his conviction on that score. Conceding that the number of Communists was small—no more than 4000—he justified his assessment by noting that power is relative and that a small, disciplined group can prevail when it faces no effective opposition.

Did the United States have any legal grounds for acting unilaterally? The administration based its action on the Punta del Este decisions of January 1962, which declared communism to be "incompatible with the principles of the inter-American system" and urged OAS members "to take those steps that they may consider appropriate for their individual and collective self-defense." After the collapse of the pro-Bosch provisional government, a hastily formed military junta whose announced goals were peace and preparation for free elections had called for U.S. aid. This was a weak legal reed on which to lean, but the junta was the only group with any semblance of authority, and its request for U.S. intervention was reasonable. OAS members charged that it amounted to unilateral intervention, which is expressly forbidden by Article 15 of the Charter. American forces did not occupy the republic. They did not attack the rebel citadel or take sides, but isolated the citadel to achieve a cease-fire through the papal nuncio and create the conditions for negotiating an interim government that would arrange for a free, inspected election.

In late May the OAS established for the first time in its history a temporary inter-American peacekeeping force from seven nations under the unified command of a Brazilian general. This force assumed military responsibility in Santo Domingo, and the reduction of U.S. forces began. Protracted and complex negotiations involving the United States, the OAS, and rival Dominican factions led in September to an interim government under Provisional President Hector Garcia Godoy. On June 1, 1966, representatives from 18 OAS countries observed a democratic election in which Joaquin Belaguer, a moderate who had been president when Trujillo was assassinated, won by a decisive margin over Bosch and a conservative candidate.

Robert Kennedy and those who had originally participated in putting the Alliance for Progress together became increasingly disenchanted with Johnson's Latin American policy. They did not like the way he handled the Panamanian affair in January 1964, and when Brazilian generals carried out a coup against João Goulart three months later, they thought that Johnson showed himself too eager to recognize the military regime. They were furious over the Dominican intervention. They were convinced that Thomas Mann, first as LBJ's assistant secretary of state for Latin American affairs and later as undersecretary for economic affairs, was bent on radically altering the Allianza by deemphasizing two of its goals—social reform and political democratization—while stressing the role of private corporations in development.

Robert Kennedy, by then a senator, warned on May 6, 1965, that U.S. determination to halt communism in the hemisphere "must not be construed as opposition to popular uprisings against injustice and oppression just because the targets of such popular uprisings say they are communist-inspired." Later in that same year, when Kennedy visited Peru, Chile, Brazil, and Venezuela, he went out of his way to establish rapport with left-wing university students. Both his behavior and his speeches were widely interpreted as an endorsement of the Latin Americans' indignation over the Dominican intervention, a pointed criticism of Johnson's concept of the Alliance for Progress, and a thinly disguised effort to put distance between himself and the president, as though he was getting ready to be a candidate himself in 1968.

It is difficult to avoid the conclusion that the OAS was weakened as a result of the Dominican intervention. Many moderate Latin Americans who opposed communism felt misgivings over the Johnson Doctrine, proclaimed on May 2, 1965: "The American nations cannot, must not, and will not permit the establishment of another communist government in the Western Hemisphere." They did not disagree with the substantive idea; but in view of what had happened, they feared that future decisions would be unilateral, not multilateral.

## U.S.–SOVIET ARMS-CONTROL AGREEMENTS

During President Kennedy's funeral, Johnson spoke with Soviet Deputy Premier Anastas Mikoyan and assured him that his administration would work for the easing of world tensions. Later, in his book *The Vantage Point,* Johnson wrote: "Throughout my administration we avoided personal attacks on Soviet leaders and avoided using such phrases as 'captive nations' and 'ruthless totalitarians.' This was not a major breakthrough, but I thought that it might calm the waters." Addressing the United Nations in December 1963, he said that the United States wanted to see an end to the cold war, to prevent the dissemination of nuclear weapons to nations not already possessing them, and to make progress on arms control and reduction.

Ten days before the opening of the Geneva Conference of the Eighteen-Nation Disarmament Committee (ENDC) in mid-January 1964, Johnson announced in his State of the Union Message that the United States would close four plutonium plants, thereby cutting production of fissionable materials for weapons purposes by one-fourth. In April, Khrushchev said that the Soviet Union would halt the scheduled destruction of two new atomic reactors for producing plutonium and would also, "during the next few years," reduce substantially the production of uranium 235 for nuclear weapons. The more ambiguous character of the Soviet promise stemmed from the fact that the USSR had been producing fissionable material for a shorter time and from a smaller number of plants than the United States. Both powers seemed interested in modestly curtailing their defense budgets. Early in 1964, Moscow announced a 4 percent cut, Washington a 2 percent cut; at the end of the year, Moscow announced a 2 percent cut for 1965, Washington a 4 percent reduction. Arms controllers spoke of these as "reciprocal unilateral measures" of a "confidence-building" nature. They were erased by the end of 1965, however, due to a speed-up in Soviet strategic programs and the expansion of the U.S. commitment in Vietnam. The Soviet defense budget went up by 5 percent; that of the United States from $49 billion to $57 billion, of which $10 billion was allocated to the Vietnam conflict. In succeeding years, the budgets of both powers kept rising. The bulk of the Soviet increases during the late 1960s went to strategic nuclear forces, while virtually the entire U.S. increase went to conventional and counterinsurgency equipment and manpower costs.

Johnson had long been interested in the U.S. space program. As chairman of the Preparedness Subcommittee of the Senate Armed Services Committee, he urged intensified U.S. technological efforts after the Soviet Union launched Sputnik in October 1957. Later, in June 1958, as head of a special Senate committee, he played a key role in the passage of legislation establishing the National Aeronautics and Space Administration (NASA) as a civilian rather than a military agency and declaring that space activities should be devoted to peaceful purposes. Prior to his inauguration, Kennedy readily acceded to Johnson's request to be assigned responsibility for overseeing the space program.* As president, LBJ was willing to think of space as a dimension not only of strategic rivalry but also of cooperation with the USSR. During the Kennedy–Khrushchev period of arms-control détente after June 1963, there were signals from the two

---

*Kennedy in April 1961 requested Congress to amend the Space Act to replace the president with the vice-president as chairman of the Space Council. Johnson selected James Webb as first administrator of NASA and chaired the study that recommended a moon landing as a goal to be achieved before the end of the decade.

space powers that they did not regard the deployment of nuclear weapons in space, although technologically feasible, as desirable on either political or military grounds and that neither one was anxious to allocate resources to such a dangerous form of competition. In October 1963 the UN General Assembly called on all states to refrain from placing nuclear or other weapons of mass destruction in space. Before that time, the United States had often expressed concern over the verification problem, but it supported the UN resolution because it was content to rely upon its own space-tracking and other capabilities, as well as a presumed mutuality of interest between the two countries.

Three more years were to pass, however, before a formal treaty could be negotiated. The Outer Space Treaty, signed on January 27, 1967, prohibited the placing in orbit, installing on the moon or other celestial bodies, or stationing in outer space nuclear or other weapons of mass destruction. Outer space was declared free for exploration and use by all states, and not subject to national appropriation by claim of sovereignty or occupation. No military bases or installations may be established on any celestial body, but the use of military personnel for space activities was not prohibited. Signatories assumed international responsibility for their operations in space. In spite of heightening international tensions over Vietnam, the Senate on April 25, 1967, gave unanimous consent to ratification.

The most important arms-control agreement reached with the Soviet Union during the Johnson administration was the Nonproliferation Treaty (NPT). After the conclusion of the Partial Nuclear Test-Ban Treaty of 1963, a principal target of arms-control diplomacy was to prevent or discourage the acquisition of nuclear weapons by other would-be possessors. In spite of occasional suggestions by some writers that a world of several nuclear powers might be more stable than a world of a few and that entrance into the "nuclear club" might compel a militant power (such as China) to behave with greater caution and responsibility, most arms-control analysts took it for granted that a world of 12 or 15 nuclear states would be more dangerous than a world of four or five, because it would pose a higher statistical probability not only of premeditated aggression but also of technical accident, unauthorized use, strategic miscalculation, or escalation from conventional to nuclear war. France had become the fourth state to acquire a nuclear capacity in 1960. Just around that time, Khrushchev was reported to be withdrawing Soviet technical assistance from China's nuclear program. The power of the Soviet premier appeared to decline somewhat after the Cuba missile crisis, at the same time that the Sino–Soviet dispute was becoming more acrimonious. He was removed from leadership by the team of Brezhnev, Kosygin, and Podgorny on October 14, 1964, just one day before China conducted its first nuclear test. Aside from the problem of Chinese representation at the United Nations, this meant that the world's five nuclear powers were the same as those named in the UN Charter as permanent members of the Security Council. The atom bomb and the veto had been married, as it were. The PRC entered the UN in 1971.

The question in the mid-1960s was whether it was possible to create by treaty an international regime limiting to five the number of states with nuclear weapons. It was presumed that the privileged five were not motivated to dilute their nuclear prestige by helping others to join their ranks. A treaty promise not to transfer nuclear technology and know-how was hardly necessary to make them refrain from doing what it was not in their interest to do. But what about all the others? Why should they adhere to a treaty that distributed the benefits and burdens so unevenly? A nonproliferation treaty would require them to renounce an option that might someday be essential to their security. Recognizing that nuclear weapons provide unprecedented power available in no other form, and that they alone could deter a nuclear-equipped opponent, several governments remained as unimpressed as the French with McNamara's logical arguments against national nuclear forces. Most states, of course lacked the economic and technological base for acquiring nuclear weapons; it would be to their interest to sign. They constituted the UN General Assembly majority that favored the NPT. But a dozen or more states—including Argentina, Belgium, Brazil, Canada,* Czechoslovakia, the Federal Republic of Germany, the German Democratic Republic, India, Israel, Italy, Japan, Poland, South Africa, Spain, and Sweden—were at or near the capacity to go nuclear.

Nonaligned nations, especially Third World countries in the process of industrializing and determined to have access to nuclear power for peaceful uses, were highly skeptical of the treaty. India led the opposition, contending that the treaty represented "an effort by the armed to disarm the unarmed." The Indian government kept asking whether the nuclear powers were willing to extend credible security guarantees to states forswearing nuclear weapons. India was worried about the possibility of nuclear aggression or blackmail by China. The United States, the Soviet Union, and Britain were willing to do no more than reaffirm their obligations under the UN Charter to deal with threats to the peace, and that did not satisfy India. New Delhi also resented the fact that Beijing prestige in the international system had been enhanced as a result of its acquisition of nuclear weapons. Several less-developed countries dependent on the growth of civilian nuclear-energy programs joined India in complaining that the proposed treaty would discriminate against them by subjecting their reactors, but not those of the nuclear-weapons states, to international inspection. To meet this objection, the United States offered to open its nonmilitary nuclear-power plants to international inspection, but the Soviet Union refused to follow suit. Finally, the "have-nots" were bitterly critical that they were being relegated to second-class citizenship within the international system and that the proposed treaty was aimed only at "horizontal proliferation" among states, while doing nothing about the "vertical proliferation" of nuclear-weapons stockpiles by the nuclear powers. To deal with that issue, the two principals had to draft a provision in the treaty (Article VI) pledging to make progress toward nuclear disarmament.

Industrially advanced states allied with the United States or the Soviet Union were in a different category. Such people's republics as Czechoslovakia, East Germany, and Poland posed no problems, for Moscow would never permit them to acquire their own nuclear weapons. The allies of the United States,

---

*Canada had the capacity to go nuclear, but had tacitly given up the option early in the nuclear age.

however, were independent states. Even if they regarded the American pledge to defend them as credible at that time, as they generally did, they were not certain that it would always be dependable. That was why there was so much discussion of "nuclear sharing" within the Atlantic Alliance in the early 1960s and why there were proposals for a NATO multilateral force (MLF), which was discussed in Chapter 5. Whereas the United States looked upon the MLF as an antiproliferation measure, especially if it would head off West German acquisition of nuclear weapons and lead to the integration of the British and French strategic nuclear forces, the Soviet Union condemned the MLF as an instance of proliferation on the grounds that it would broaden "the right to participate in the ownership, control, or use" of nuclear weapons in NATO, particularly by admitting the Germans to a role. It proved impossible for Washington and Moscow to make progress toward negotiating the NPT until Dean Rusk assured Andrei Gromyko in September 1966 that the United States would rule out the "transfer" of any of its nuclear weapons to joint NATO ownership. That major concession alleviated Soviet concern, but it aroused West German misgivings.

U.S. allies required additional assurances on several other counts. Japan and the Federal Republic of Germany were unwilling to subject themselves to any system of international inspection that entailed a risk of industrial espionage. The members of the European Community (including the Federal Republic) insisted on collectively negotiating with the International Atomic Energy Agency (IAEA) an agreement guaranteeing that no fissionable materials would be diverted to weapons manufacture in violation of the treaty and at the same time preserving the interests and prerogatives of the European Atomic Energy Community (Euratom). In effect, the Western Europeans held out for the right to inspect themselves under regional agreements that had been in effect since 1954 (under a protocol to the Western European Union Treaty). At the insistence of the NATO allies, the United States agreed to interpret the treaty as applying only to nuclear weapons but not to delivery systems; not to prohibit NATO consultation and planning on nuclear defense nor ban deployment of U.S.-owned and U.S.-controlled nuclear weapons on the territory of nonnuclear NATO members; and not to preclude "succession by a new federated European state to the nuclear status of one of its members." The Soviet Union did not challenge these unilateral U.S. interpretations.

The Nonproliferation Treaty, described by President Johnson as "the most important international agreement since the beginning of the nuclear age" up to that time, was signed on July 1, 1968. Walt Rostow called it essentially "a constitutional arrangement for the organization of the noncommunist world." It cost the Soviet Union practically nothing, but it placed serious strains on the cohesiveness of NATO while it was under discussion from the early 1960s onward and during the 18 months it was being negotiated. Furthermore, the neutral and less-developed nations opposed to the treaty, egged on by Peking, vented most of their spleen on the United States, while Moscow escaped criticism. The United States paid the price for assuming international responsibility on the proliferation issue. France and China did not sign the treaty, but they indicated—the former more clearly than the latter—that they had no intention of helping other states to acquire nuclear weapons. Other states refusing to sign the treaty included

Argentina, Brazil, India, Israel, Japan, Pakistan, South Africa, and Spain.* On the day the treaty was opened for signature, the two principals announced that they would soon enter into Strategic Arms Limitation Talks (SALT), but the Warsaw Pact invasion of Czechoslovakia in August 1968 forced a postponement of the SALT negotiations until December 1969.

## DEFENSE ISSUES

Defense questions loomed large in the 1964 presidential campaign. Republican nominee Goldwater charged that the administration was failing to make certain that the United States would not fall behind the Soviet Union strategically within a few years. He specifically objected to the fact that the Pentagon under McNamara was planning to phase out strategic manned bombers by 1970 and to rely on less dependable and "unrecallable" missiles, thereby eliminating about 90 percent of the nation's deliverable megatonnage in nuclear firepower. By way of rejoinder. McNamara pointed out that the projected long-range missile force of more than 1700 delivery vehicles (1000 Minuteman I and II ICBMs, 656 Polaris SLBMs, and 54 land-based Titan IIs) would more than suffice for the United States to remain ahead of its adversary and to ensure its capacity to survive any conceivable surprise first strike, to limit damage by destroying the enemy's remaining missiles, and to inflict "an unacceptable level of damage" in retaliation on the foe's population and economic base. The defense secretary also insisted that the Strategic Air Command would keep 700 bombers operative at least through 1969 and many of them beyond that normal planning horizon. He denied that a large missile force and a new missile-carrying strategic bomber would be needed by 1970.

Another debate flared when Goldwater, criticizing NATO's "permissive action link" system, under which no NATO field commander could fire a nuclear weapon until it had been released or "unlocked" by a coded electronic signal from the White House, argued that SACEUR, the American commander of NATO, should have the discretionary authority to order the use of tactical nuclear weapons in a military emergency. Johnson, unwilling to weaken deterrence, declined to clarify what he meant by "presidential control," which everyone agreed was required in some form.

In his 1965 defense report to Congress, McNamara said, "It may be that as long as we maintain the kind of forces that would make global nuclear war and even local wars unprofitable for the Soviet Union and Communist China, we can deter them from starting such conflicts." He added that the Communists had been prompted to shift their efforts to wars of national liberation, and that the United States still had a long way to go in devising effective countermeasures to such threats. At the beginning of 1966, 40 prolonged insurgencies were being waged throughout the world.

*The members of the European Economic Community signed the treaty within a few months, but they all waited to deposit their ratifications until May 1975, after they were satisfied that their basic interests were secured under inspection agreements negotiated with the IAEA in Vienna. Japan signed the treaty in 1970 but did not ratify until 1976.

Although congressional appropriations for defense increased by about $10 billion to $12 billion per year from 1966 onward, the GNP had also been growing, and military expenditures ran just over 8 percent of GNP, lower than in the three Kennedy budgets. Congress in 1966 voted funds for the development of a new bomber by the mid-1970s; the development of the Air Force's Manned Orbital Laboratory (MOL); the hardening of underground silos for Minuteman missles; the development of multiple, independently targetable re-entry vehicles (MIRVs); procurement of additional Polaris A-3 missiles and development of advanced Poseidon missiles, both for nuclear submarines; and the development of penetration aids to help missiles and bombers overcome enemy defenses. Congress and the Air Force deemed McNamara's plans for the development of a new strategic manned bomber inadequate. But the most bitterly debated issue in the mid-1960s had to do with ballistic missile defense (BMD), or the antiballistic missile (ABM).

BMD or ABM—similar acronyms at that time—provoked one of the most persistent and bitter debates over defense technology between strategic analysts and advocates of arms control throughout the 1960s. Defense Secretary McNamara was opposed to it, for a number of reasons: in his view, the existing technology could not provide an impenetrable shield; it would be relatively easy to defeat a missile defense system by saturating it with additional warheads or dummy decoys and other penetration aids; if the United States were to deploy a "heavy" ABM system, the Soviet Union would be motivated to increase its offensive capability to cancel the U.S. defensive advantage; and after each side had spent many billions, the strategic nuclear balance would remain essentially the same, with neither side enhancing its security. Yet in September 1967 McNamara announced that the administration had decided to go forward with the deployment of a "thin" ABM system, not oriented against the Soviet threat—which he deemed both technically and economically futile and strategically unnecessary under the American doctrine of assured destruction—but oriented prudently against the threat of an irrational Chinese nuclear attack.

The three military services—Army, Navy, and Air Force—all supported the deployment of ABM, for different reasons and with certain reservations. Missile defense was the only area in which the Army could play any role with regard to strategic nuclear forces. The Navy supported land-based ABMs in return for Army support of sea-launched ballistic missiles. The Air Force was not happy about having its land-based ICBMs protected by the Army, but to preserve the principle of unanimity in the Pentagon's presentation of service procurement budgets, the Air Force supported the Army's Nike-Zeus ABM so long as it did not divert funds from strategic offensive forces.

The civilian side of the Pentagon was less united than the uniformed services. The director of defense research and engineering, John S. Foster, was in favor of the ABM program because he was more optimistic than McNamara about its technical feasibility and because he wanted to prevent the breakup of the scientific research and weapons laboratory teams on which advanced technology defense depended. The Office of Systems Analysis, headed by Alain Enthoven, saw in ABM a means of reducing demands for new strategic offensive missiles, bombers, and submarines. Paul Warnke, assistant secretary of defense for international security affairs (ISA), joined the U.S. Arms Control and Disarmament Agency in arguing that ABM would be strategically destabilizing, speed up the arms race, dim the prospects for arms control, and waste defense funds that could be used to better purpose. McNamara himself contended that for a "damage-limiting" program designed to save lives, a nationwide program of fallout shelters would be more cost-effective.

Secretary of State Rusk, who often deferred to McNamara's judgment, agreed with him on this issue also and opposed ABM deployment, but for reasons of diplomacy. European elite and public opinion was far from friendly to the idea of missile defense. American advocates of ABM contended that, once the cases were properly presented, the Western Europeans ought to welcome it because it would enhance the credibility of the U.S. deterrent and the U.S. pledge to NATO. But the Europeans did not want anything at that time to disturb the progress then being made, however ambiguous, in U.S.–Soviet détente and in West Germany's embryonic *Ostpolitik*, or policy of opening toward Eastern Europe. Moreover, with the United States becoming increasingly preoccupied with Asia, there was a nervous misapprehension that Americans might lose interest in Europe. Many Europeans, therefore, looked askance at a program that might eventually leave the Americans protected but their allies unprotected. Conversely, if the Americans insisted on providing a NATO umbrella, the Europeans would have to raise their defense budgets substantially to pay for it. Strategic analysts in Britain and France speculated that the deterrent value of the national strategic nuclear forces of their own countries, which were not terribly impressive at the time, would be further degraded if the two superpowers should acquire ABM capabilities.

In the end, domestic political considerations played a significant role in the ABM decision of 1967. Advocates of the system argued that it was technically possible and that even though it might be only 50 or 60 percent effective rather than 100 percent, it could still save tens of millions of lives that would otherwise be lost. Moreover, the Soviets were known to be working on missile defense and to have deployed ABMs around Moscow; the field should not be forfeited to them. Congress had never rejected a unanimous Joint Chiefs recommendation for a major strategic-weapons program deemed vital to national security. Besides, many in Congress thought that U.S. strategic-weapons programs had been put on the back burner during the Vietnam War. President Johnson, not wishing to give the Republicans a "defense gap" issue in the 1968 election year, decided to head off the possibility with the modest Sentinel ABM program.

## EUROPE AND THE ATLANTIC ALLIANCE

Although Johnson was preoccupied throughout most of his presidential term with Southeast Asia, from time to time he and his administration were compelled to attend to serious problems in Europe and NATO. A few of them—such as the Greek–Turkish dispute over Cyprus, the withdrawal of France from the Alliance's integrated military command, and the invasion of Czechoslovakia by Soviet and other Warsaw Pact forces—reached critical proportions. Most of the problems, however, were of the more subtle and slowly developing type. By and large, they pertained to changes in the attitudes of publics, in the thinking of elites, and in the policies of governments seeking to negotiate a continuing consensus with regard to their security and political and economic interests during an era of precarious East–West détente in Europe. There were recurring doubts about the credibility of the American commitment to defend Europe and nervous fears that the deepening U.S. involvement in Asia might mean a decline of interest in Europe. Many Europeans disputed the arguments occasionally made by some administration spokesmen that if the United States did not stand firm in Southeast Asia, the Western European allies would suffer a loss of confidence in Washington's determination to honor its Atlantic Alliance obligations. Hue and Da Nang, they said, are not Berlin and Paris.

## The Cyprus Dispute

Tensions rose sharply on the southern flank of NATO during 1964, when serious violence erupted on the island of Cyprus, which had changed from a British crown colony to an independent republic in August 1960. Cyprus had long been a source of conflict between two NATO allies—Greece and Turkey. Greek Cypriots (77 percent of the population) had always wanted *enosis* (union) with Greece; Turkish Cypriots (18 percent) demanded partition. All through the 1950s, life on the island had been marked by Greek Cypriot guerrilla warfare aimed at ousting the British. The secretary-general of NATO had urged the three allies to work out their problems peacefully within an Alliance framework. Britain and Turkey had been willing, but not Greece, probably because Athens feared that within NATO it would be at a disadvantage. There would be two NATO allies against one, for British and Turkish interests coincided against those of Greece, and the United States would be likely to assign greater strategic weight to Britain and Turkey. The Greeks preferred to carry their case to the United Nations General Assembly, where struggles for national self-determination were much more popular than Western strategic interests. Nevertheless, in 1959 the three principals had arrived at a delicate compromise. Greek Cypriots renounced their demand for *enosis,* and the Turks their demand for partition. Cyprus became an independent republic with a Greek president (Archbishop Makarios III), a Turkish vice-president, and a joint guarantee of independence by Britain, Greece, and Turkey.

The historical passions involved made the settlement fragile and potentially explosive. It was not long before guerrilla attacks and counterattacks resumed. By the spring of 1964, it was necessary to dispatch a UN peacekeeping force of 7000 troops to the island to police a truce. In June President Johnson, concerned over the adverse effects the conflict was having on NATO and suspicious that the Soviet Union would not be able to resist the temptation to meddle in the eastern Mediterranean, invited the prime ministers of Greece and Turkey, Georgios Papandreou and Ismet Inonu, to confer with him in Washington. They came, separately, but his efforts produced no success. Anti-American resentment was expressed in Greece, and there were signs that both antagonists were becoming more neutralist in their attitude toward NATO. For the United States,

Greek–Turkish hostility and the Cyprus dispute constituted a no-win situation. The Soviet Union and Czechoslovakia shipped arms to the island at the same time that Moscow was intensifying efforts to forge closer diplomatic and trade ties between the Eastern bloc and Turkey. The UN force remained on Cyprus, but Greece and Turkey came close to open war in 1967, until Johnson's special envoy, Cyrus Vance, helped to work out an agreement under which the bulk of Greek and Turkish forces were to be withdrawn from the island. The conflict was temporarily subdued, but it would continue to smolder and to plague NATO planning on the southern flank.

## De Gaulle and NATO

Throughout 1964 and 1965, de Gaulle pursued his policies of strengthening French national independence, disengaging piecemeal from NATO, criticizing the American approach to Vietnam (which he thought should be neutralized), opposing the projected NATO multilateral force (MLF), and calling upon the Europeans to become, under France's leadership, a "third force" between the United States and the Soviet Union. His statements drew severe criticism from the Federal Republic of Germany, where Ludwig Erhard had succeeded Konrad Adenauer as chancellor in 1963. Franco–German relations, which had become quite warm as a result of the *rapprochement* achieved by de Gaulle and Adenauer, underwent a distinct cooling in 1964 and 1965. The Bonn government, professing itself to be both Atlanticist and Europeanist, resented having to choose between two major allies who were becoming involved in acrimonious controversy over issues fundamental to the Alliance and the defense of Europe. When de Gaulle would insinuate that the closer integration of Europe was not compatible with dependence on military links to the United States and would warn of the danger of a split between the two principal members of the European Economic Community, Bonn would retort somewhat testily that its policy was dependent neither on Washington nor on Paris. That was not true, of course. Because of its geographical location, the Federal Republic, of all the Atlantic allies, was most heavily dependent on the United States for its military security and its political stability. If forced to choose between a chimerical European collective defense and the U.S. deterrent, there was no question as to which way Bonn would lean.

De Gaulle realized that, but probably deemed it useful to employ the dilemma of Atlantic versus European unity as a means of applying pressure on Erhard for economic reasons. Erhard was a weaker, less self-confident chancellor than Adenauer had been. Adenauer in his prime was a match for de Gaulle, and the latter did not try to play games with him. De Gaulle was interested in improving the economic benefits to France of membership in the Common Market, especially with regard to agricultural products. De Gaulle probably concluded that he had to rely on political bluffs and threats to obtain what he wanted for French farmers (see "The Economics of the Atlantic Community" below). Erhard had little choice but to take him seriously. De Gaulle had, after all, demonstrated his independence in several ways that had not been to Bonn's liking—recognizing Communist China early in 1964, accepting the

German–Polish boundaries as permanent (whereas the Federal Republic and the United States insisted that boundary questions should be reserved until a peace settlement), and ordering government studies concerning the impact on France of decisions to leave the EEC and NATO.

Nearly all of de Gaulle's foreign policies irritated the U.S. government: his recognition of Beijing, his proposals for the neutralization of Vietnam, his call—regarded as quaint and archaic by most economists—for a return to the gold standard as the basis of the international monetary system, and his barrage of criticism against all things tending toward "supranational" integration in the political, economic, or military order, such as majority voting in the EEC or a NATO MLF. While he railed against the efforts of U.S.-based multinational corporations to "leap over" the rising common external tariff wall of the EEC by investing directly in new manufacturing plants in Europe, thereby trying to bring France under the domination of an "invading" American capitalism, Pentagon officials peppered the fledgling French national nuclear *force de frappe* (or *force de dissuasion,* the term for deterrence) with disparaging comments.

France's disengagement from NATO occurred over a long period of time, not suddenly. France's Mediterranean fleet had been withdrawn from NATO command as early as 1959, a year after de Gaulle returned to power, and its Atlantic fleet in 1963. In April 1964 French naval officers were removed from the Alliance's integrated command organizations in the Mediterranean and the English Channel. President de Gaulle, in a letter to President Johnson on March 7, 1966, announced France's complete pullout from the integrated command—NATO—but not from the Atlantic Alliance itself. That is, France would remain a North Atlantic Treaty partner, but would sever all ties with the Organization (the "O" in NATO). All French land and air forces assigned to NATO, as well as five submarines and military staffs still in NATO, were withdrawn by July 1. Supreme Headquarters, Allied Powers, Europe (SHAPE) and Allied Forces, Central Europe (AFCENT), along with the NATO Defense College, were required to leave France by April 1, 1967. The North Atlantic Council relocated SHAPE to Casteau, Belgium, and AFCENT to the Dutch province of Limburg. The NATO Defense College moved to Rome. U.S. and Canadian forces stationed in France, given the choice to depart or submit to French authority, departed. The Allies lost the right to overfly French territory except with specific permission, to be granted or withheld on a monthly basis. In order to symbolize its adherence to the political side of the Alliance, France was willing to keep the North Atlantic Council in Paris. Among the Allies there was some sentiment in favor of this, lest France became isolated within the West, but in the end the council took up residence in Brussels.

Johnson reacted rather philosophically to the French withdrawal. Adjusting to the situation, he rejected the advice of those who wanted him to resist or punish de Gaulle, for he thought that a vindictive approach would not only further inflame French nationalism but also exacerbate the strained relations between France and Germany and harden the stalemate in the EEC. Western strategic analysts attempted to minimize the impact of the French withdrawal on the validity of the basic NATO deterrence-and-defense concept. They derived some comfort from the fact that France continued to grant the Allies overflight rights. They hoped that the departure of an obstreperous de Gaulle would enable the Alliance to improve its military cooperation and planning and to shift its official doctrine at long last from "massive retaliation" to "flexible response." They also realized that de Gaulle was not immortal and that France might someday return to the fold. Even if France after de Gaulle pursued the course of national independence, its adherence to the treaty reflected a basic realism in policy and boded well for a future in which the imperative of protecting the national interest would probably impel France to cooperate in NATO's logistical and other efforts.

### West Germany: Nervous Ally

The Federal Republic of Germany experienced the Johnson years as a period of nervous uncertainty. Neither the Christian Democrats of Ludwig Erhard nor the Social Democrats (SPD) of Willy Brandt wanted East–West tensions to increase. Both parties welcomed the mood of relaxation resulting from the shift toward a mixture of cold war and détente, but the waning government of Chancellor Erhard had more misgivings than the SPD, which was gaining in self-confidence as it rose in popularity, about U.S.–Soviet arms-control negotiations that might lead to "deals" at Germany's expense. Having been sold on the idea of the MLF by persuasive advisers in the Kennedy administration, Erhard feared—correctly, as events proved—that the Johnson-McNamara team might abandon plans for the MLF in order to obtain a nonproliferation treaty with the Soviet Union. Bonn had been the only NATO capital to give solid support to the MLF proposal, not as a means of parrying either official or popular West German desires for a national nuclear force (for there were no such desires), but merely because the Federal Republic was inclined to go along with whatever Washington wanted in the early 1960s and West German participation in such a force would reduce the political stigma of inequality and discrimination, to which the Germans were sensitive, as the only NATO member pointedly excluded by international agreement (the WEU Protocol of 1954) from direct access to nuclear weapons. The West Germans did not want their own nuclear force; they wanted a voice in NATO nuclear strategy, so that they would not look like second-class allies. The MLF had ostensibly been designed to provide precisely that, under collective arrangements that would have kept all nuclear weapons under the control of the president of the United States.

    The Soviet Union mounted an intensive propaganda campaign against German militarist revanchism and against the MLF as a device to give Bonn a finger on the nuclear trigger (which it was not). Erhard did not want the United States to scuttle the MLF merely to placate Moscow. Washington had other credible reasons for letting the MLF die a quiet death. Congress was not happy about the MLF, and several U.S. military leaders sniped at it. No European ally other than the Federal Republic showed any enthusiasm, and the British were actively opposed, preferring their own proposal for an Atlantic Nuclear Force with a quite different structure. When Erhard saw Johnson in Washington in

December 1965, the two appeared to be putting the projected MLF on a back burner. Erhard remained filled with apprehension. The foreign policy that he had inherited from Adenauer was apparently coming apart at the seams. He was caught between two major allies, both of whom were embarked on courses which took them further away from each other and from Germany: France was leaving NATO, and the number one protecting power was becoming bogged down militarily in Asia.

In the United States Mike Mansfield, the Senate majority leader, was beginning to build support for a resolution calculated to reduce the drain on U.S. gold and to stimulate greater defense efforts on the part of the NATO allies by substantially reducing the number of U.S. troops permanently stationed across the Atlantic. Moreover, as will be discussed below, the European integration movement was stalled. The Hallstein Doctrine, under which it was West German policy to shun or sever diplomatic relations with any government (apart from that of the Soviet Union) recognizing East Germany, was coming to be regarded as anachronistic at a time when West Germany was interested in developing closer ties with Eastern Europe. An Arab version of the Hallstein Doctrine was applied to West Germany in 1965: after Bonn initiated diplomatic relations with Israel, ten Arab states retaliated by breaking relations with West Germany.

Throughout 1966, Erhard's problems grew worse and his governing position weakened. In September 1966 Secretary Rusk and Foreign Minister Gromyko, meeting at the United Nations, apparently reached an understanding that the proposed MLF would be dropped by the United States if the USSR would abandon its opposition to the "two-key system" in NATO,* and the right of a politically united European Community, if one should ever develop, to become the legal successor to Britain and France as a nuclear power. These understandings paved the way for the negotiation of the Nonproliferation Treaty.

They also aroused profound misgivings in the Federal Republic. Although many West Germans who had originally supported the MLF now wondered whether its political and military advantages were being exceeded by the political cost of the divisions to which it had given rise, leading figures in all major parties had the uncomfortable feeling that Washington and Moscow were reaching a bilateral agreement on a question vitally affecting Germany's future. A beleaguered Chancellor Erhard, stung by charges that the decision to shelve the MLF had been a serious blow to the Federal Republic's prestige, responded sharply: "We are not a satellite of Washington."

Erhard's government fell in October 1966. Kurt Kiesinger, who assumed the leadership of the Christian Democrats, decided that the domestic and international situations had become so delicate and complex that the time was ripe for a "Grand Coalition" (*Grosse Koalition*) of the two major parties. The Johnson administration was aware that, having buried the MLF, it had to do something about nuclear sharing in NATO, especially with regard to the Bundesrepublik. McNamara recommended a set of new consultative structures

---

*Under that system, nuclear weapons based in Europe could not be fired without positive assent by both the United States and the host country.

within the Alliance, including a Nuclear Planning Group (NPG) which was approved by NATO's defense ministers in December 1966. The NPG was to have seven members (with Germany assured of always being a member) and was expected to consider questions related to strategic nuclear missiles, ABM systems, tactical nuclear systems, and improved consultation between the United States and host countries where nuclear weapons were deployed. The NPG held its first meeting in Washington in April 1967, and the new arrangements proved to be remarkably satisfactory. The long, acrimonious debate over the MLF soon subsided, even though it was not quickly forgotten.

## The Soviet Invasion of Czechoslovakia

The Grand Coalition of Kiesinger, with Brandt as his foreign minister, accelerated the pace at which West Germany was forging trade links with the countries of Eastern Europe. Bonn's policy of "building bridges," a forerunner of what Willy Brandt as chancellor would subsequently call his *Ostpolitik*, inevitably produced a change in the political, economic, and social-psychological climate of the people's democracies, particularly Czechoslovakia. Since the 1948 Prague coup, no Soviet-bloc country had been more rigidly subservient to Moscow than Czechoslovakia under Antonin Novotny. In January 1968 Novotny was ousted by the Czech Communist party and a younger idealist, Alexander Dubček, took over as party secretary. Dubček initiated a series of reforms aimed at "giving socialism a human face." He introduced freedom of the press, assembly, and religion, the right to strike, the right to travel abroad, and freedom of debate and secret elections at all levels of the party organization. The new regime also undertook some experiments in the economic order based more on the ideas of a free market than on those of rigid Marxist socialist orthodoxy. Moscow was not at first disturbed, trusting Dubček as a disciplined party member who had been brought up and trained in the USSR. Dubček reaffirmed Czechoslovakia's loyalty to the Soviet Union, arguing that his reforms would strengthen rather than weaken communism. But as the "Prague Spring" came into full bloom, the Kremlin became frightened at the prospect of a strategically vital satellite in the heart of Central Europe spinning out of orbit.

As Soviet propaganda became shriller in tone, observers in Western Europe noted unmistakable preparations for a military crackdown on the "counterrevolutionary" element in Prague. Warsaw Pact members scheduled maneuvers to take place in Czechoslovakia in June, obviously to warn the Czech leaders that they were courting disaster. In mid-July Moscow issued an unambiguous ultimatum, and the capitals of Western Europe concluded that, with a major crisis in the offing, only the United States could deter a move by the Soviet Union to crush the most serious political threat to the Soviet empire since 1956.

Deeply mired in Vietnam, the United States was in no mood to confront the Soviet Union in Eastern Europe. Johnson's advisers hoped for the best—that Moscow would be deterred by an assessment of likely consequences, such as the inflammation of public opinion, especially in the West, and a setback to

U.S.-Soviet détente in Europe. Ever since September 1966, relations between Washington and Moscow had seemed to be improving vis-à-vis the contested terrain of Europe. Détente had been derailed in the Middle East as a result of the Six-Day War, and there was nothing resembling détente in Southeast Asia; but the demise of the MLF had smoothed the way for a Nonproliferation Treaty, and the Johnson administration was interested in opening talks on offensive and defensive missiles. The president and Soviet Premier Alexei Kosygin had held a hastily arranged and personally friendly summit meeting at Glassboro, New Jersey, for two days in late June 1967, at which they had discussed the situation following the recent Six-Day War, Vietnam, the Nonproliferation Treaty, and the prospects for curbing the arms race by fixing a ceiling on missiles. The ensuing year had seen the successful conclusion of negotiations for the Nonproliferation Treaty, which had been opened for signature on July 1, 1968.

Nevertheless, on August 20, 650,000 troops from five Warsaw Pact states—the USSR, Poland, Hungary, Bulgaria, and East Germany—carried out an extremely well-organized and overwhelmingly powerful invasion of Czechoslovakia, a bloodless affair because the Czechs recognized the futility of resistance. The invasion shocked Europe and plunged it into despondency and anxiety, for it not only reversed five years of a slowly developing and fragile détente but also presented NATO's Central Front with a heightened security threat. German defense analysts were the most worried of all. The Soviet Union alone had suddenly moved ten additional divisions into Czechoslovakia, yet NATO's forces had not even gone on alert. Within the previous two years, there had been a tendency in discussions of NATO strategy and force postures for British and American planners to play down the danger of an overwhelming westward Warsaw Pact attack. The rotation of some military units out of Germany, they said, could be done without seriously endangering NATO area security, since there probably would be "political warning" and intelligence of military movements prior to actual aggression. That theory was badly damaged by the events of August 20. Western analysts now concluded that NATO's earlier loss of French territory and air space, combined with the latest Soviet deployments in the heart of Central Europe, rendered it all the more unlikely that the Alliance would be able to reduce its dependence on nuclear weapons in favor of a conventional strategy.

The foreign-policy and defense elites of other countries farther removed from the zone of forward defense were less worried than those of West Germany about the immediate danger of attack, but they were nevertheless deeply disturbed by the invasion. The French were worried about a possible Soviet crackdown in Romania, which had not taken part in the invasion. The British and the Italians were apprehensive that Moscow would later attempt to apply what was quickly dubbed the "Brezhnev Doctrine"—the right of the Soviet Union to employ force to crush "counterrevolutionary" elements within the socialist camp. The British especially feared that, even though the United States might respect the de facto spheres-of-influence distribution tacitly acknowledged at Yalta, post-Tito turmoil in Yugoslavia might lead to a tragic Soviet miscalculation, a Soviet effort to reestablish its control over that country (which had broken loose in 1948)—tragic because it could trigger World War III.

All the Allies were irritated and frustrated by what seemed to them to be a lack of any rigorous response on the part of Washington. On the evening of August 20, Soviet Ambassador Anatoly Dobrynin went to the White House and read to President Johnson a lengthy statement purporting to justify the military intervention of the Soviet Union and its socialist allies to combat the "conspiracy of the external and internal forces of aggression against the existing social order in Czechoslovakia" and expressing the hope that "current events should not harm Soviet–American relations." Many European commentators were of the opinion that those relations had barely been disturbed. Johnson had been considering another summit meeting with the Soviet leaders to work out initial guidelines for the impending strategic arms limitation (SALT) talks and had also been contemplating calling the Senate into special session to act on the Nonproliferation Treaty, until he was persuaded by his advisers that the political climate was not propitious for either step. He agreed to postpone both and wait for the atmosphere in Europe to calm down. The European allies were generally dismayed by the bland reaction of the United States. They certainly did not want military action. In fact, they were not sure what they wanted from the United States, apart from a firmer display of leadership. Some of them murmured that the United States, by refraining from issuing a clear diplomatic warning to the USSR prior to August 20 and preferring instead to hope for the best, had therefore made it too easy for Moscow to calculate the costs of snuffing out the Prague Spring, as if the Johnson administration had tacitly signaled the Soviet leaders: We know that you will do what you think you must do; there is not much that we can really do to prevent it; get it over with as quickly and painlessly as possible, and accept the adverse political costs in world opinion; then we can both return to the more important items on our agenda.

### The Economics of the Atlantic Community

During most of the Johnson era prior to the Soviet invasion of Czechoslovakia in 1968, economic difficulties competed strongly with the political and military problems of security as the chief concern of the Atlantic Community. With politicians and diplomats emphasizing détente and arms control, the sense of threat in Europe had declined markedly since the Cuban and Berlin crises, not least because of the widening breach between Moscow and Beijing. Whenever democratic publics think that "peace has broken out," the promotion of prosperity, business, and lower taxes becomes a more popular cause for politicians to espouse than expenditures for defense, and a military alliance begins to lose some of its solidarity.

During 1966, the issues of "burden sharing" and offsetting the costs of keeping British and American troops in Germany moved toward the top of the Atlantic economic agenda. When at full strength, the British Army of the Rhine (BAOR) totalled 55,000 and added more than $200 million a year to the drain on the British balance of payments. U.S. forces numbered about 240,000, and they contributed more than $800 million a year to West German's foreign-exchange balance. (These were the amounts that British and U.S. soldiers spent on themselves and their dependents living in the Federal Republic.) In July 1966

British Prime Minister Harold Wilson's chancellor of the exchequer, James Callaghan, informed Bonn that some British troops would have to be recalled to Britain unless the full foreign-exchange costs were offset.

This demand was quite serious, for a British withdrawal of troops would be likely to generate additional American support for the Mansfield Resolution, introduced in August 1966, declaring that "a substantial reduction of U.S. forces permanently stationed in Europe can be made without adversely affecting either our resolve or ability to meet our commitment under the North Atlantic Treaty." Prior to that time, Bonn had been offsetting the foreign-exchange costs of American troops by purchasing military equipment from the United States. As the conflict in Asia expanded, the military services were under pressure to redeploy some troops from Germany to Vietnam. In April the United States had announced its intention to withdraw some experienced units from the Seventh Army and to replace them with new recruits for a net reduction of 15,000. The Johnson administration began to link the remaining force of 225,000 to Germany's fulfillment of the $1.35 billion offset agreement signed in 1965. When Chancellor Erhard visited Washington in September, he gave an assurance that the Federal Republic would live up to that agreement, but served notice that a future agreement would cover only about half the exchange costs. The United States, Britain, and West Germany decided to carry on tripartite discussions on costs, burden sharing, and NATO force needs, with a view to determining whether NATO strategy would be compatible with troop reductions. Britain deemed some reductions possible in the less tense European climate. The United States, focusing more on known Soviet capabilities than on putative and change-able Soviet intentions, argued against a reduction in conventional forces, es-pecially on the European side, before adequate airlift was available to reinforce NATO quickly in a crisis.

Johnson had concluded that multilateral negotiations on exchange-cost offsets would be less divisive than two sets of bilateral talks. During the transition from the Erhard cabinet to the coalition government under Kiesinger, the United States helped to ease Wilson's exchange deficit by offering to purchase $35 million worth of military equipment from Britain. By April 1967, a settlement was reached that constituted a temporary solution of what would be a continuing problem. The Germans agreed to purchase $500 million worth of medium-term U.S. government bonds. Bonn and Washington agreed jointly to assist the British with purchases. The Federal Republic also promised to reduce the gold drain on the United States by holding dollars instead of converting them into gold. Finally, the Pentagon worked out a "dual-basing" rotation plan under which U.S. combat brigades and air wings would be moved on a regular basis to the United States without impairing their combat-readiness. Since the troops would be spending their dollars at home, they would not be adding to the foreign-payments im-balance, but this arrangement did involve higher operational expenditures.

The negotiations between the United States and its European allies over tariffs and trade were longer and more difficult. The Trade Expansion Act of 1962 authorized the president to go beyond the Roosevelt-Hull Reciprocal Trade Agreements Act of 1934 to cut existing tariffs up to 50 percent with reciprocation and to abolish entirely duties of less than 5 percent. This legislation was designed to enhance the flexibility of the United States in the upcoming talks with an increasingly competitive EEC, which was then raising its common external tariff wall while lowering customs duties on the flow of goods within the Community. It was hoped that these negotiations, known in succeeding years as the "Kennedy Round" and carried on within the framework of the multinational General Agreement on Tariffs and Trade (GATT), would stimulate world commerce and prosperity, not only in the Western industrial nations but also in developing countries that were economically linked to them. This could be achieved, however, only if the United States, Western Europe, and later Japan could bring themselves to act more like cooperative partners than cutthroat rivals pursuing "beggar-my-neighbor" policies. Since 1959, Europe itself had been divided between the six Common Market countries and the European Free Trade Association (EFTA), composed of Austria, Britain, Denmark, Norway, Portugal, Sweden, and Switzerland, with Finland as an associate member.* Many Europeans were worried about the splitting of the region into two trading groups and about the deepening of the rift after de Gaulle vetoed Britain's application for entry into the EEC early in 1963.

American foreign-policy makers feared that, since members of the Atlantic Alliance were found in each bloc, the economic division of Europe would have adverse effects on the cohesion of NATO. That furnished an additional reason, besides the protection of U.S. business and agricultural interests, for attaching great importance to the Kennedy Round. Britain and its EFTA trading partners generally favored the U.S. initiative, undertaken in the 1962 Trade Expansion Act, to work toward cutting tariffs among the Western industrial nations in half. The task was extremely complex, however, and required two years of preparations and three additional years of formal negotiations from 1964 to 1967.

The United States was especially anxious to make sure that American farmers would not be excluded from selling in the Common Market. Progress on this issue proved to be painfully slow because of the impasse that de Gaulle created in the EEC over trade in agricultural products. The French president was convinced that West German business had gained much more than French farming during the seven years since the Rome Treaty had gone into effect. As a result of progressive lowering of internal barriers, tariffs on industrial goods were down to only about 40 percent of what they had been prior to 1958. Intra-EEC customs on agricultural products had not been reduced nearly as much. French farmers were disappointed and resentful, for they had been promised from the beginning that they would become the "grocers" of the Economic Community and that a system of price supports in the EEC would give them "parity" with other producing groups. On July 30, 1964, a common agricultural policy (CAP) did go into effect for dairy products, beef, and rice, but a stalemate had been reached on the harmonization of grain prices.

In October 1964 de Gaulle threatened French withdrawal from the EEC unless a settlement could be reached with West Germany to extend the CAP to grains. For that, he was accused by many in the United States, Britain, and

---

*A free-trade area differs from a common market in that the former moves to eliminate tariffs among members but does not erect a common tariff wall against nonmembers.

Western Europe of trying to wreck the Common Market. West Germany was in a stronger economic position than France at that time, and Erhard, a former successful economic minister, knew it. De Gaulle knew it, too, and that was why he shifted to a political threat. In all probability de Gaulle did not really intend to pull France out of the EEC. The French economy had already become so thoroughly enmeshed with the Common Market that the economic dislocation resulting from such a drastic separation would have been enormous. But de Gaulle understood the utility of political threat in the bargaining process. The fact that he was already in the process of disengaging from NATO in 1965 made his threat of disengagement on the economic front more credible than it might otherwise have been. He boycotted all consultations with the EEC until further integration was halted. He demanded that the Council of Ministers, in which each member government wielded a veto, be given greater authority than the EEC Commission in Brussels, in which some economic decisions could be made by majority vote. He also insisted that the European Parliament in Strasbourg, which was not yet fully in operation, be denied any authority to control the budget. In the end, de Gaulle achieved his objectives. The CAP was extended to grain trading, and the process of integration was brought to a standstill.

Negotiators in the Kennedy Round encountered another obstacle in de Gaulle's opposition to Britain's application for entry into the EEC, which Wilson renewed in May 1967 with the approval of Britain's EFTA partners. This involved a reversal of policy on the part of the Labour party, which had previously opposed British membership on the grounds that the Common Market was too wedded to the principles of free-market competition and therefore posed a threat to Labour's social-welfare programs. Despite serious misgivings with the ranks of both Labourites and Conservatives, the Wilson cabinet concluded that with Commonwealth ties and the special Anglo–American relationship growing weaker and with British trade being oriented more toward the Continent, membership in EFTA was no longer enough. By 1966 the Franco–German stalemate had been resolved, and it was clear that the Common Market would achieve a full customs union and common agricultural policy by 1968. The longer Britain remained aloof, the higher its price of admission to the EEC and the more painful the adjustment would be. The Wilson government decided, therefore, that the best course of action was to apply for membership once again, seeking not only the best possible terms for Britain, especially in regard to higher food prices, but also favorable arrangements for those EFTA partners which were expected to follow Britain's lead, as well as cushions for Commonwealth countries, such as New Zealand, which depended heavily on trade with the United Kingdom.

The Johnson administration, like that of Kennedy, supported the British application. So did the "friendly five"—the Federal Republic of Germany, Italy, and the Benelux states. The major obstacle was de Gaulle, whose distrust of *les Angle-Saxons* was not diminished. He reiterated his objections: Britain was not really "European"; it was still too closely linked to the United States; with its preference for low food prices, it would not be able to accept the Common Agricultural Policy, which involved export subsidies, the maintenance of higher levels of farm-product prices, and payments to finance investments in agriculture modernization; Britain would want to preserve its special trade arrangements with certain Commonwealth countries; and its application would bring new ones from several other European states, admission of which would dilute the consensus already carefully worked out among the Six. It appears that he simply did not want London (perhaps with Bonn's backing) to compete with Paris for domination of the Community. In November 1967 he announced that Britain's entry would be incompatible with the best interests of the Common Market. The view of many that this second veto sprang from de Gaulle's deep feeling for France and against Britain, rather than from economic considerations or solicitude for the EEC, seemed plausible in light of the fact that during a visit to Canada during the summer of 1967 he had shouted *"Vive le Quebec libre!"* to the French-speaking population of Montreal and cancelled his scheduled visit to Ottawa when the Canadian authorities expressed their shock over what appeared to them to be such bad diplomatic form.

Ministers representing 56 GATT member countries took part in the Kennedy Round negotiations. The EEC acted as a single entity. The aim was to replace agreements on a commodity-by-commodity basis with across-the-board cuts covering all industrial goods, with exceptions held to a minimum. At U.S. insistence, agricultural products were included in GATT talks for the first time. The EEC members adopted a tough negotiating stance, arguing that since their tariffs were already lower and more uniform than those of the United States, a 50 percent cut across the board would be inequitable to them. Most of the detailed haggling was over the lists of products to be exempted from the cuts. The United States and the EEC tabled approximately equal lists of dutiable imports to be excluded from tariff reductions. Before agreement was reached in May 1967, the EEC, the United States, the U.K., and Japan all had to make substantial concessions. The ensuing outcries from protectionist groups within all countries concerned demonstrated once more that tariff walls are usually matters of domestic politics more than foreign policy, and serve subnational better than national interests.

The 50 percent cut was to apply to such items as autos, washing machines, typewriters, tape recorders, tires, machinery, precision instruments, and chemicals—the last one only after Congress repealed the law setting the American selling price rather than the import price as the valuation for tariff purposes. The results of the Kennedy Round were somewhat disappointing to American farmers, who did not gain the access to the European agricultural market for which they had hoped, and to Third World countries, on whose primary products only the most limited tariff-reduction progress was made. Nevertheless, on the whole the GATT negotiations did lead to an expansion of world trade among the industrialized states.

## JOHNSON, THE ARAB WORLD, AND THE SIX-DAY WAR

Throughout the five years of the Johnson administration, the Arab world remained divided between the more radical states (Algeria, Iraq, Syria, and the United Arab Republic), which subscribed to a variety of revolutionary and socialist ideologies, and a more conservative grouping (Morocco, Tunisia, Lebanon, Jordan, Libya—then still under King Idris—and Saudi Arabia and the Persian Gulf sheikdoms). With the latter group, U.S. relations were for the most part friendly, except for the Arab–Israeli conflict, and the United States furnished military aid to several of its members. U.S. relations with the radical group, which received weapons from the Soviet Union, usually varied from cool to strained to bitter, depending on the mercurial swings of Arab ideology, rhetoric, and foreign policy. U.S. ties with Algeria, for example, improved somewhat after Colonel Houari Boumedienne, in a coup, succeeded Ben Bella and seceded from the close connection with Castro. There was also a temporary warming trend between Washington and Cairo in 1965, when Nasser terminated his military aid to the Congolese rebels in Leopoldville and appeared to reach agreement with Saudi Arabia by promising to withdraw Egyptian troops from the civil war in Yemen. Following the announcement of that agreement, the United States renewed arrangements for the sale of food grains to the UAR in return for "soft" currency. At other times, relations with the radical Arab states deteriorated.

All Arab governments, the conservative ones in less inflammatory terms, criticized or condemned the United States for giving economic and military assistance to Israel. Yet the Arabs themselves were never able to achieve, except ephemerally, the degree of unity against "Zionist imperialism" to which they aspired. They failed to coordinate their policies effectively against Israel's effort to divert Jordan River waters to the Negev Desert. Tunisia's Habib Bourguiba issued a call for a settlement of the Palestine problem on the basis of principles that both sides respected. All Arab states except Tunisia cut their diplomatic ties with Bonn when the Federal Republic recognized Israel, but within a year some of them were wondering whether they had lost more economically than they had gained politically. Syria and Iraq, as a result of coups by revolutionary *Ba'ath* socialist elements in 1963, appeared ready for the new merger efforts with Nasser's UAR, but despite recurring announcements of a unified Arab military command, which naturally aroused Israel's defensiveness, nothing came of the plan until May 1967. Nor was any real progress made toward a resolution of the Egyptian–Saudi conflict over Yemen or toward a pullout of Egyptian troops. In June 1966 the United States did not renew the agreement to ship food to Egypt under P.L. 480.

The most serious problem that Johnson had to face in the Middle East was the Six-Day War of June 1967. Early in that year, tensions had been rising along the border between Syria and Israel. Syria had long been taunting Nasser to employ Egypt's military strength, the greatest in the Arab world, against the common enemy. Syria became increasingly active in sponsoring raids into Israel by bands of *Al-Fatah* and Palestine Liberation Organization (PLO) guerilla. Israel's prime minister, Levi Eshkol, announced on May 12 that his government would choose the time, place, and means to retaliate against the provocative attacks by guerrillas based in Syria. One day later, Moscow warned Nasser that Israel was massing forces along the Syrian border in preparation for an attack. Israel vehemently denied this rumor. Nasser, under mounting pressure from Arab nationalists and the press in several Arab capitals to do something, began to move his armed forces eastward into the Sinai. Despite the fact that his troops were still bogged down in Yemen, he concluded that he had to make a dramatic response if he was to retain his image as the leader of the Arab world.

Facing a much larger Arab population on its immediate borders, Israel was in no mood to engage its foes in guerrilla combat, preferring instead to rely on its technologically superior conventional forces. This meant that after a dozen or so *Al-Fatah* raids, Israel would retaliate against the cumulative provocations with a large-scale reprisal by conventional and commando units, which would then evoke from an already anti-Israel United Nations majority resolutions much more condemnatory of Israel than of the Arabs. Thus in the spring of 1967 the Israelis had no confidence in the United Nations as an impartial arbiter to which they could look for fair treatment. Eshkol may have hoped that his warning to Syria, and similar statements by other Israeli officials, might induce the Soviet Union to rein in its Syrian clients. Whatever the intent, such warnings from Tel Aviv inflamed the Arabs to believe that an anti-Syrian plot was being hatched in "imperialist and Zionist quarters" and made it easier for Moscow to disseminate its charges of Israeli plans for aggression.

For nearly a year, Nasser had been urged by militants to remove the United Nations Emergency Force (UNEF) that had been stationed in the Sinai along the UAR–Israel border and at Sharm el-Sheikh after the 1956 Suez crisis. They wanted Nasser to close the Strait of Tiran to Israeli ships bound through the Gulf of Aqaba to the port of Eilat. On May 16 the Egyptian commander-in-chief sent a message to the UNEF commander informing him that his forces must be withdrawn from the Sinai border. In New York, UN Secretary-General U Thant told the UAR representative that the request was unacceptable: UNEF could not merely redeploy to allow the Egyptian army to move troops to the border with Israel: UNEF must remain where it was or else withdraw completely. The secretary-general gave the assurance that if the UAR should request withdrawal, he would comply immediately. Nasser formally requested the withdrawal of the UNEF, and it departed the next day.

Several international law-and-organization authorities have argued in an abstract way that, since UN peacekeeping forces operate only with the consent of the host state, U Thant had no choice but to comply. The UNEF had originally been created as a result of delicate negotiations among several other interested parties, none of whom was consulted concerning Nasser's request. The secretary-general knew full well that immediate compliance would precipitate a major international crisis. It did. In acting as he did, legalistically, U Thant certainly did not serve the cause of peace.

The UNEF unit had been a small one, designed to serve as a stabilizing buffer and guarantor of the cease-fire. Under no circumstances could it have undertaken a combat role and resisted the advancing Egyptians, but consultation would probably have slowed the pace of events. Rapid, fundamental change in an area of high tension is always a harbinger of crisis. Nasser himself perhaps had not expected the scenario to unfold as fast as it did. Amazed at his own success, he may have been swept along by an emotional tide surging through the Arab world, and he may have begun to act more on the basis of impulse than of careful planning. He was buoyed by the knowledge that he enjoyed the backing of the Soviet Union. Ever since 1964, the Soviet fleet had maintained a presence in the Mediterranean. During May 1967 its surveillance and intelligence-gathering activities vis-à-vis the U.S. Sixth Fleet were noticeably intensified. Early in June, as Middle East tensions approached the breaking point, Moscow augmented its naval presence in the Mediterranean with reinforcements from the Black Sea until more than 50 Russian military vessels were deployed between Gibraltar and the Turkish Straits—the largest number in history. All Western strategic analysts interpreted this as an unmistakable demonstration of support for Nasser, which emboldened him to take unprecedented risks. The Soviet fleet was not sufficient to challenge the U.S. naval presence in the Mediterranean, but it added to Israel's fear of hostile encirclement.

On May 22 Nasser closed the Gulf of Aqaba to Israeli shipping. President Johnson wrote in his memoirs that the action was probably taken independently of the Soviet Union. Five days earlier, on May 17, Johnson had sent a cable to Prime Minister Eshkol urging restraint: "I cannot accept any responsibilities on behalf of the United States for situations which arise as the result of actions on which we are not consulted." On the day of Nasser's Aqaba decision, but before he learned of it, the president reminded Soviet Premier Alexei Kosygin that the harassment of Israel by elements based in Syria, with its attendant consequences, had brought the area close to war and that U.S. and Soviet ties to nations in the region "could bring us into difficulties which I am confident neither of us seeks." He expressed the hope that each side would use its influence in the cause of moderation. At the same time, he sent a message to Nasser assuring him of America's friendship for the Egyptian people and his own understanding of their pride and aspirations. He offered to dispatch Vice-President Hubert Humphrey to search for a solution.

Johnson inquired of Eisenhower what kind of understanding had been reached with Israel early in 1957 concerning passage through the strait and the gulf. The former president informed him that Israel's right of maritime access had definitely been part of the U.S. commitment when Israel agreed to withdraw from the Sinai Peninsula in favor of UNEF. Johnson, calling the blockade illegal, concluded that the United States had an obligation to uphold the principle of free passage. He also reaffirmed U.S. support for maintaining the political independence and territorial integrity of all states concerned.

The United States was determined to keep Aqaba open to all ships as an international waterway, but Congress made it clear that if any action had to be taken, it should be multilateral, not unilateral. Washington sounded out Paris and London on their position with regard to the Tripartite Declaration of 1950, under which the three principal Western powers pledged themselves to resist any effort to alter by force the existing borders in the Middle East. Between Truman and Johnson, Eisenhower and Kennedy had reiterated U.S. adherence to the Tripartite Declaration. The French government thought it would be a mistake to invoke the declaration and seemed uninterested in any joint response. The British were willing to cooperate. They proposed a public reassertion, by as many maritime states as possible, of the right of free passage in the Gulf of Aqaba and the creation of a naval task force to break the blockade. Israel's Foreign Minister Abba Eban flew to Washington and informed the president that Israeli intelligence was warning of UAR preparation for an all-out attack. McNamara and Johnson gave their opinion, based on CIA reports, that an attack was not imminent but that if the UAR did start a war, it would be badly defeated. Eban, however, was rendered somewhat skeptical by the stress Johnson placed on the importance of trying to see first what could be accomplished through the United Nations and of working to make certain that the Executive did not get too far out in front of Congress. Johnson cautioned that Israel should avoid responsibility for any outbreak of war. "Israel will not be alone," he said, "unless it decides to go alone." That was on May 26.

Four days later, Prime Minister Eshkol indicated that a consensus had been reached on May 26 and that Eban's conversation with Johnson had influenced Israel's decision to await developments for a little longer. He said, "It is crucial that the international naval escort should move through the strait within a week or two." The Johnson administration took that to mean that it had two weeks—at least until June 11. As June began, it looked as though four countries were committed to the naval task force: the United States, Britain, the Netherlands, and Australia.

For Israel, it was more than a matter of freedom of navigation alone. There were seven UAR divisions in the Sinai. At the end of May, King Hussein of Jordan joined the Arab cause. He signed a defense pact with Nasser, placed his forces under the command of a UAR general, allowed UAR commando units to enter Amman, and granted passage to an Iraqi armored division to cross the eastern frontier of Jordan and head toward the West Bank of the Jordan. Never in its 19-year history had Israel experienced such a feeling that its survival was being threatened through coordinated encirclement by the well-equipped forces of the UAR, Jordan, Iraq, and Syria. The Israeli cabinet, deciding that it could wait no longer, chose preemptive war.

The war, which began on June 5 and lasted exactly six days, produced one of the most decisive military victories in modern history. Israeli forces demonstrated conclusively the strategic advantages of the first lightning strike. The air forces of the UAR, Jordan, Syria, and Iraq were virtually wiped out before most of the planes could get off the ground. The seven UAR divisions in the Sinai were decimated, losing 10,000 soldiers. A substantial portion of the UAR's armor, artillery, and naval equipment was destroyed or captured. Israeli forces, which suffered light casualties, occupied the West Bank (populated by 750,000 Arabs), the entire city of Jerusalem, Sharm el-Sheikh, and the Golan Heights (formerly held by Syria).

On the second day of the war, Cairo Radio, picking up an erroneous report from Jordanian radar stations that carrier-based planes were approaching from the west, announced that U.S. planes were taking part in the attack on Egypt. Six Arab states—the UAR, Algeria, Syria, Iraq, Sudan, and Yemen—broke off diplomatic relations with the United States on the basis of that false announcement the UAR accepted a cease-fire on June 8, but Israel still had to deal with Syria, which was a special protégé of the USSR. That same day saw the only American casualties of the war. The U.S. Navy communications ship *Liberty* was torpedoed in error by Israeli gunboats. Ten Americans were killed and 100 wounded. Israel expressed profound regret over the tragedy.

The Six-Day War created an extremely delicate situation for the United States and the Soviet Union. The United States was the chief protector of Israel; the Soviet Union had long been committed to Nasser because of his prominent anti-Western stance and in spite of his "bourgeois nationalist" suppression of communism in Egypt. It was essential, therefore, that Washington and Moscow avoid becoming too publicly committed to their friends while the war was on. Fortunately for the United States, the conflict was over quickly. The United States was under no compulsion to become involved, while the Soviet Union, which always moves slowly and cautiously, had very little time to take concrete steps in support of the UAR or Syria. There was considerable use of the hot line, which until then had been activated only for testing and for the exchange of holiday greetings. Johnson was bent on persuading Kosygin that the United States was not a participant in hostilities and that both powers should exert their influence to bring the war to an early end. On the last day of fighting, June 10, Kosygin sent a tough message: A "very crucial moment" was approaching, one involving a risk of "grave catastrophe." Israel must halt operations against Syria within a few hours, or else Moscow, in an "independent decision," would take "necessary actions," clearly including military ones. Johnson, taking no chances, ordered the Sixth Fleet moved closer to the Syrian coast, not long before Israel subscribed to a cease-fire with Syria.

The Soviet Union played a part in bringing on the 1967 crisis with its propaganda, warnings, ship movements, and diplomatic maneuvers in the United Nations and elsewhere. The Kremlin probably wanted not a major international crisis, but a more limited local scare to shore up its client Syrian regime. The Soviet leaders may have expected only a hesitant, equivocal response from the West in support of Israel and a political victory by Nasser. If so, their assessment of the West may have been closer to the mark than their estimate of Israeli capability and Arab incompetence. Israel emerged from the war in a stronger strategic position than ever, despite the fact that it politically alienated much of the Third World, where the Israeli reputation for aggressive behavior was strengthened. Moscow recouped its position in the Arab world in a surprisingly short time. By early 1969 the air, tank, and naval forces of Egypt, Syria, and Iraq had been restored to their prewar levels or better as a result of Soviet resupply shipments. Soviet naval deployments in the Mediterranean remained inferior to those of the U.S. Sixth Fleet, but the psychological consequences of the new situation were significant, especially in Turkey, which now faced the Soviet navy on its northern and southern coasts. Having routinized unobstructed passage of its vessels through the Turkish Straits, the Soviet Union no longer found it necessary to press for revision of the Montreux Convention, as it had in 1945–1947.

## THE VIETNAM QUAGMIRE

John F. Kennedy had bequeathed to Lyndon Johnson a Vietnam policy that, even in the eyes of some Kennedy admirers, appeared retrospectively to be contradictory. On the one hand was the ever-increasing political commitment and military involvement of the United States; on the other hand was a projected (or at least vaguely hoped for) phased withdrawal of American forces. When Kennedy took office, there were 685 U.S. military advisers in Vietnam. By October 1963 the number had risen to more than 16,700. Kennedy definitely appeared to subscribe to Eisenhower's domino theory: "For us to withdraw," he said in July 1963, "would mean a collapse not only of South Vietnam, but Southeast Asia. So we are going to stay there."* He insisted that the United States must provide advisers, trainers, equipment, supplies, and other forms of aid. But he was against committing American combat forces to fight in Vietnam. It was "their war," and "they," not "we," had to win it.

Kennedy had been warned early in 1961 by two eminent generals—MacArthur and de Gaulle—never to be drawn into a war on the Asian mainland. Nevertheless, he allowed himself to be sucked in bit by bit through a series of compromises, which he said he did not like but to which he consented. *The New York Times, The Washington Post*, and other influential newspapers were all in favor of resisting communism in Vietnam. The Joint Chiefs were calling for more effective military action to turn the tide. His dilemmas were compounded by the division between those who viewed the conflict largely as a case of external international aggression and those who conceived of it as an internal civil war, and as part of a "nation-building" process. The former faction, headed by General Earle G. Wheeler, later chairman of the Joint Chiefs of Staff, and General Paul Harkins, head of Military Assistance Command—Vietnam, saw the threat as primarily military, to be met with conventional forces using high technology. The latter group—Averell Harriman, Walt Rostow, and Roger Hilsman of State Department Intelligence and Research—favored a counterinsurgency approach, with heavy emphasis on guerrilla-type operations, socioeconomic programs (including designation of "strategic hamlets" in a program designed to insulate villagers against the Viet Cong), and political and diplomatic initiatives (including the reform of Diem's authoritarian regime).

According to Arthur M. Schlesinger, writing nearly 15 years after Kennedy's death, Kennedy said privately on several occasions that he wanted to extricate himself and the United States from what he had increasingly come to look upon as a quagmire, but he did not know how that could be done. Certain that he could not do it before the November 1964 election without extremely adverse effects on his chances for reelection, he is said to have instructed McNamara as early as July 1962 to proceed on the assumption that South

*Earlier, in March 1963, he had extended the domino theory, noting that the fall of Southeast Asia would inevitably affect the security of India and "begin to run perhaps all the way to the Middle East." In response to a direct question in a television interview with David Brinkley and Chet Huntley in September 1963, Kennedy asserted three times that he accepted the domino theory.

Vietnamese troops would be sufficiently well trained to carry on their own war effort to permit the phased disengagement of U.S. military personnel by the end of 1965. That would be possible after his reelection, but he had to win the election first. He could not, however, speak publicly about his plan, for that would produce devastatingly demoralizing consequences in Southeast Asia. Meanwhile, his own rhetoric and that of all the spokesmen for his administration reinforced the political commitment of the United States to Vietnam, as the flow of military and economic assistance enlarged the American presence there by undramatic increments. Secretary of State Dean Rusk, in an oral-history interview with Merle Miller, noted that he and Kennedy had discussed Vietnam "hundreds of times," but the president had never even hinted at withdrawal. If he had decided to take the troops out only after the 1964 election, said Rusk, it would have meant leaving Americans in uniform and in a combat situation for domestic political reasons—something no president could do. In any event, as George W. Ball pointed out, "escalation was proceeding fairly rapidly before Johnson took office." Johnson certainly had no doubt that he was inheriting a strong Kennedy commitment to prevent a Communist takeover of Southeast Asia. He also inherited all of Kennedy's principal advisers.

On the question of whether the United States should favor a coup against Diem, Johnson's views had not been solicited by Hilsman or Ball, for the vice-president was known to be, along with Nolting, General Harkins, and others, a staunch supporter of Diem. In April 1961, when Kennedy had asked Johnson to undertake a trip to Southeast Asia to calm the neighbors of Laos about what was happening in that country, the vice-president, not at first very happy about the risky trip, had gradually warmed to the task, had come to admire Diem, whom he called "the Winston Churchill of Southeast Asia," and had given him the firmest possible assurance of U.S. support. With that commitment, he had pledged his own word, and where Johnson came from, a man's word was better than his bond. In the early fall of 1963 Johnson had been upset by talk that the United States should countenance a coup against Diem. He regarded Hilsman and others in the White House and the State Department who appeared bent on abandoning Diem as his own personal enemies, and dealt with them accordingly after he became president.

### Steps Toward Deepening U.S. Military Involvement

Diem and Kennedy were assassinated twenty-one days apart. Johnson inherited a Vietnamese situation that was rapidly deteriorating toward chaos. Diem was succeeded by generals who were even more incompetent. The problems of corruption, confusion, and social instability worsened. Vietnamese youth grew more skeptical of and alienated from their leaders by the month. By the spring of 1964, several American officials in Vietnam, both civilian and military, began to think that the tide was turning against the United States. Johnson, convinced that Southeast Asia had become the crucial arena of the global struggle against communism and anxious to keep faith with the Vietnamese, said that his administration would hold "steady on course." McNamara and Taylor were sent back to Saigon in March 1964. McNamara, analyst *par excellence* of complex systems and calculator of cost-effectiveness, had no doubt that the country could do anything it really wanted to do so long as it was willing to invest adequate resources, but he reiterated the Kennedy thesis that the war could be won only by the Vietnamese. He advised Johnson that the United States should be able to withdraw its forces by the end of 1965, provided that the Vietnamese could reestablish political order so that military operations could proceed efficiently. Several officials began saying what they assumed Johnson wanted to hear. Others were saying one thing in public, in order to keep up the appearance of a united front, but something else in private to the president. Few doubted that it would be a "long and arduous war."

Hilsman and Harriman, the original advocates of the anti-Diem coup, were among the few Kennedy people to be dropped by Johnson early in 1964. Hilsman was replaced as assistant secretary of state for Far Eastern affairs by William P. Bundy, brother of the special assistant for national-security affairs, son-in-law of Dean Acheson, and up to that time assistant secretary of defense. When Lodge resigned as ambassador to seek the Republican presidential nomination in 1964, Johnson selected Maxwell Taylor, chairman of the Joint Chiefs of Staff, to replace him, with the top-ranking diplomat U. Alexis Johnson as his deputy. At the same time, he named Lieutenant General William C. Westmoreland to succeed Harkins as head of the U.S. Military Advisory Group. All the leading figures in the administration realized how much importance Johnson attached to Vietnam.

Early in 1964 Walt Rostow suggested that it would be useful to obtain from Congress a bipartisan resolution giving the president discretionary authority to conduct war in Asia, similar to the one Eisenhower had obtained early in 1955 to meet Chinese Communist threats to Taiwan and the offshore islands of Quemoy and Matsu, and to preclude the possibility that Peking might try to play off one branch of government or one political party against another in Washington. William Bundy, who favored carrying the war to North Vietnam, also supported the plan for a congressional resolution and proceeded to draft one in May for floor debate in June. By mid-June, however, Johnson decided to postpone the request for such a resolution until after the November election, because he did not want to appear eager in the eyes of the electorate to have his powers to use military force expanded.

South Vietnamese army volunteers trained by the CIA had for years conducted covert raids into North Vietnam to carry out sabotage, propaganda, and intelligence-gathering activities in retaliation for Ho Chi Minh's subversion in the South. During 1964, William Bundy and Pentagon officials started to make contingency plans for the bombing of North Vietnam. Ho, anticipating the escalation of the war, sought and received anti-aircraft missiles and radar stations from the Soviet Union. Aware of these developments, the U.S. Air Force and Navy intensified their surveillance activities with high-altitude U-2 flights and the cruising of electronic-intelligence vessels in the Tonkin Gulf. The situation under the international law of territorial waters was hopelessly confused in the gulf, and Ho probably preferred to keep it that way.

## The Tonkin Gulf Resolution

Partly because of this confusion, the U.S. destroyer *Maddox*, cruising beyond seven miles from the coast and four miles from adjacent islands on August 2, was pursued by three North Vietnamese patrol boats. Fearing an imminent torpedo attack, the U.S. destroyer fired and missed. When the three pursuing boats attempted to torpedo the destroyer but failed, the *Maddox*, aided by planes from the carrier *Ticonderoga,* sank one patrol boat and badly damaged the others.

Three months before the election, Johnson shunned the image of both warmonger and appeaser. Since no American had been hurt, he ordered no reprisals against North Vietnam. He used the hot line to assure Khrushchev that the United States did not seek to widen the conflict, and would not if the North Vietnamese would refrain from attacking U.S. vessels in international waterways. He did, however, direct naval forces in the Tonkin Gulf to defend themselves against any attack and sent a warning note to Hanoi. Rusk alerted his staff to dust off the proposed congressional resolution drafted a few months earlier but shelved temporarily. The Joint Chiefs, who had already developed a list of targets in North Vietnam, sent additional U.S. fighter-bombers to South Vietnam and Thailand. On August 4 the commander of the *Maddox* again sensed an imminent assault by Communist patrol boats, but no tangible evidence of aggression was ever produced. Nevertheless, Johnson announced that U.S. destroyers had been attacked and said that he would ask for a resolution that would permit U.S. retaliation. At that point, Johnson was concerned about looking indecisive if he failed to act. Although the "second deliberate attack" later became a matter of considerable controversy, Johnson authorized bombing raids on four North Vietnamese patrol-boat bases and a large fuel-storage depot.

The situation gave Johnson an opportunity to obtain from Congress a free hand to "take all necessary measures to repel any armed attack against the forces of the United States and to prevent further aggression." This Tonkin Gulf Resolution was adopted by a vote of 466 to 0 in the House and 88 to 2 in the Senate, with only Earnest Gruening of Alaska and Wayne Morse of Oregon dissenting. The man who was most helpful in securing passage in the Senate was J. William Fulbright, who later became a severe critic of U.S. policy in Vietnam. At the time, there was practically no dissent in Congress. Years later, during the 1970 debate on the war powers in Congress, several members of both houses said in effect that they had been duped or misled, or had not understood the significance of the resolution, and had had no idea that it might lead to several years of warfare. Yet the wording of the resolution quite clearly asserted the president's power to do whatever he saw fit in Southeast Asia and placed no time limit on him.

During 1964, the number of U.S. forces in Vietnam rose from 16,000 to 22,000 and the number of casualties from 105 to 245. The American public scarcely yet felt the effects of the conflict. Johnson during the election campaign had said, "We are not about to send American boys nine or ten thousand miles away from home to do what Asian boys ought to be doing to protect themselves." As desertions from the South Vietnamese army multiplied, the Viet Cong grew bolder, carrying out its first major attack against an American military installation at the Bien Hoa air base. An outraged Ambassador Taylor urged Washington to order bombing runs against selected North Vietnamese targets. The Joint Chiefs wanted more massive bombing. It was now, however, only two days before the election. Johnson waited until his reelection was a fact, and then directed the bureaucracy to study the options. Some policymakers, perceiving disaster resulting from deepening military involvement, called for a political solution—neutralization. Others thought that the United States was too committed to Vietnam to accept a neutralization that would be tantamount to abandonment and gradual Communist takeover.

Rostow favored a massive demonstration of force to show that the United States was prepared to accept whatever degree of escalation was necessary to break the will of the Communists. Some strategic theoreticians thought that the United States, having demonstrated its strategic nuclear superiority in the Cuban missile crisis, might now take advantage of an unprecedentedly favorable opportunity to confront Lin Piao's strategy of protracted guerrilla warfare. They generally agreed with William Bundy that Beijing was the main backer of Communist insurgency in Southeast Asia, despite a centuries-old enmity between the Chinese and the Vietnamese. They assumed that General Vo Nguyen Giap, Ho's military genius, was a believer in Lin Piao's plan of "surrounding the cities from the countryside." If that strategy could be defeated once and for all, it would reduce the probability of a later large-scale embroilment that might bring on World War III. McNamara, speaking to the House Armed Services Committee in February 1965, said that "the Chinese Communists have made Vietnam the decisive test of their theory" and that "the outcome of this struggle could have grave consequences not only for the nations of Southeast Asia but for the future of the weaker and less stable nations everywhere in the world."

### The U.S. Military Buildup and Growing Domestic Opposition

In 1965 came the turning point in the war, when the U.S. personnel stopped being only "advisers" and became major participants in combat operations. Frequently during the 1964 election campaign Johnson had contrasted his own firm but cautious policy with that of those who wanted to "start dropping bombs around" and involve American boys in a war with China. After the election, however, he had to react to stepped-up pressure. As the Viet Cong intensified their attacks in the South, with increased aid from Hanoi, Johnson ordered bombing raids on North Vietnam in February 1965, primarily against roads, bridges, rail lines, and military installations—close to the border of South Vietnam at first, but soon over a wider area.

The spring and summer months saw a large-scale buildup of U.S. forces in Vietnam, with whole Marine and Army divisions arriving on the scene. By the end of the year, the earlier strategy of letting South Vietnam do the fighting to avoid any appearance of a "white man's war" in Asia had been abandoned. Large numbers of American soldiers were involved in helicopter-supported search and destroy missions. The number of American casualties in 1965 rose to more than 2400, nearly ten times as many as the year before.

The American military buildup continued, until by December 1966 there were 380,000 troops on the ground, another 60,000 on ships offshore, and an additional 35,000 in Thailand. More than 4000 Americans lost their lives in 1966. The total American force commitment to Southeast Asia by December 1966 was 40 percent greater than in Korea at the height of that war. (Australia, New Zealand, and South Korea also had fighting units in Vietnam by 1966.) McNamara's bombing plan for 1966 called for a greater tonnage of bombs than was dropped in the entire Pacific theater during World War II.

The cost of prosecuting the war—$1 billion per month—was beginning to have a dislocating impact on the U.S. economy, adding to the growing domestic discontent over an apparently futile yet deepening involvement. There were bitter debates within the United States over alleged shortages of equipment and bombs, the inadequacy of training facilities and programs, the failure of the president to call up reserves, and the fairness of the Selective Service system. To avoid alienating the middle class, Johnson allowed college students to be deferred, which gave rise to charges that the burden of conscription was being unjustly shifted to lower-income groups, especially blacks. Opposition to the war, particularly among students as campus "teach-ins" multiplied, became merged with the civil-rights movement, pushing both groups toward greater militancy.

Strains appeared within the Atlantic Alliance as Allied criticism of U.S. bombing of North Vietnamese urban areas was met with spreading complaints among Americans about the failure of the Europeans to contribute toward the containment of communism in Asia. The Europeans not only perceived no threat to their own interests there but feared that U.S. preoccupation with Vietnam might either diminish security in their own region or compel them to bear a larger share of the defense burden in NATO. Among the European allies, only the British government provided any semblance of diplomatic support for U.S. policy.

**The U.S. Search for a Way Out**

From 1965 onward, the United States sought in vain a basis for negotiating an end to the conflict that would yet preserve South Vietnam's independence. In April 1965, speaking at Johns Hopkins University, Johnson offered to enter unconditional discussions with the governments concerned, not merely with the National Liberation Front (the political arm of the Viet Cong), and offered to allow North Vietnam to take part in a billion-dollar regional development plan for all of Indochina. The Mekong Valley Project, Johnson thought, would be an Asian TVA, and he could use it as a bargaining instrument to obtain a satisfactory settlement of the war. "Old Ho can't turn me down," he said on one occasion. Pope Paul VI, UN Secretary-General U Thant, and others appealed for efforts toward a negotiated peace. At no point did Ho Chi Minh display the slightest interest in entering negotiations, neither when the bombing raids were intensified nor when they were suspended. In October 1966 Johnson traveled to Australia and New Zealand and took part in a seven-nation conference (United States, Australia, New Zealand, Philippines, Thailand, South Korea, and South Vietnam) in Manila, at which the allies pledged to remove their forces from South Vietnam within six months after the other side withdrew its forces to the north. The

Communist states immediately denounced the Manila offer as worthless. Ho and Giap were determined to fight on to victory for 10, 20, or 50 years, if necessary.

It is not possible to present here a detailed history of the course of the war, diplomatic or military, for the remainder of the Johnson presidency. Suffice it to say that the entire situation continued to deteriorate. American and Vietnamese casualties mounted steadily. Targets in the Hanoi-Haiphong area, previously off-limits, were subjected in 1967 to heavy bombing, but that seemed only to stiffen North Vietnam's resistance rather than bringing it closer to the conference table. The Army, the State Department, the CIA, and AID squabbled endlessly in Saigon and Washington over intelligence estimates, types of aid needed, strategy and tactics, and the degree of progress or regress to be reported.

The massive movement of guerrillas and conventional military forces with their equipment from North to South Vietnam along the Ho Chi Minh Trail through "neutral" Laos led to fiercer fighting in the South and set the stage for some of the bloodiest and most intensive engagements in the history of warfare. The presence of from 2 million to 3 million Vietnamese uprooted from their homes, combined with runaway inflation of food prices, made the difficulties of carrying out land reforms and other essential socioeconomic reforms insuperable amidst the chaos of war. Even under less terrible conditions, reform could not have been achieved by the unstable, corrupt, and incompetent governments of Nguyen Cao Ky and Nguyen Van Thieu. Buddhist demonstrations and self-immolations against the Ky–Thieu regime and the Americanization of the war were revived. Incidents of terrorism abounded. American and European correspondents became increasingly skeptical of every official statement emanating from Saigon and Washington.

In September 1967 Johnson announced that the United States was willing "to stop all aerial and naval bombardment of North Vietnam" if Hanoi would give assurances that such a step would "lead promptly to productive discussions" and would promise not to take military advantage of the bombing halt during the discussions. Ho Chi Minh dismissed the offer out of hand. The growth of opposition to the war in Congress and the American press, as well as the spread of antiwar demonstrations, some violent, served to reinforce the intransigence of Ho, who was confident that the antiwar protest was isolating the Johnson administration from the American people and the European allies.

From early 1966 onward, McNamara—despite his rosy public statements concerning the progress of the war effort—began to have second thoughts about whether the bombing raids against North Vietnam could end the war or induce Hanoi to negotiate. Becoming a "closet dove," he was willing to send more troops if the bombing could be reduced. His advisers doubted that a basically subsistence agricultural economy could be driven into submission by attacks on its relatively few industrial targets, which its manpower-intensive military forces really did not need. North Vietnamese recruitment and infiltration had increased in spite of the bombing, which had the effect of strengthening the enemy's nationalist resolve.

The Joint Chiefs, however, believed that the bombing was hurting North Vietnam and should be intensified. They said that, given a free hand to do what military necessity required, they could bring the war to a successful conclusion by utilizing U.S. naval and air superiority. General Westmoreland, Admiral Ulysses Grant Sharp, Walt Rostow, and Dean Rusk, as well as Senator John Stennis, chairman of the Senate Armed Services Committee, were all in favor of pushing on to victory. During 1967, McNamara and his civilian aides at the Pentagon began to gravitate toward Senators Mike Mansfield and J. William Fulbright, who were looking desperately for a way out. Rusk had originally harbored reservations about the deepening involvement, but once the United States was committed to a large-scale war, he regarded it as a grave mistake to signal Hanoi too early that the world's greatest power was eager to get out of the war and to negotiate with a small nation of only 17 million people.

Johnson, caught between "escalators" and "de-escalators," temporized, compromised, and attempted to placate factions which were rapidly polarizing between optimism and pessimism across a widening ideological chasm. By the fall of 1967, McGeorge Bundy, George Ball, and Bill Moyers had all resigned, disenchanted over the war. McNamara, unable to admit that his confident projections had all gone wrong, became despondent, pessimistic, and less welcome to Johnson as a bearer of bad tidings. At the end of August McNamara presented a bleak picture to the Senate Armed Services Committee, noting that bombing the North was no substitute for an arduous ground war in the South. He said in effect that, since carrying the war to the foe had not been effective, it would be better to pursue the fight on our side of the Demilitarized Zone between North and South Vietnam. McNamara by then had so infuriated the military chiefs that Johnson decided to let him go. In late November 1967 it was announced that the defense secretary would accept the presidency of the International Bank for Reconstruction and Development (IBRD), or World Bank. His successor at the Pentagon was Clark Clifford. Meanwhile, Johnson became morose at the shattering of his dreams for the "Great Society" and turned bitter, sometimes even paranoid, in the face of increasingly vicious and unfair criticism. The president who had made such arduous efforts to woo the media now found himself accused of concealing or doctoring the truth. Never loved, he was now distrusted by many and despised by some.

As secretary of defense, Clifford initially favored a strategy of escalation. Probably to head off a punishing American offensive by those who appeared to have Johnson's ear after the departure of McNamara, Hanoi sent a signal at the end of 1967: a bombing halt might produce peace talks. Meanwhile, North Vietnam stepped up its preparations for a final massive assault—less directly against U.S. military power in Southeast Asia, where more than a half million troops were stationed, than against the weak government in Saigon and the fragmenting American political system. A truce had been proclaimed to celebrate Tet, the Lunar New Year holiday, from January 26 to February 2, 1968. After careful, deceptive preparations, 70,000 Viet Cong violated the truce and mounted a full-scale, simultaneous attack against five major cities, including Saigon, many towns, and more than 60 provincial capitals. The Communists expected to score such a stunning psychological victory with their surprise offensive (which included a daring attack on the American Embassy in Saigon) as to provoke a revolutionary uprising against the regime, to divide South Vietnam from the

United States, and perhaps even to knock a weary, divided America out of the war. Militarily, the Tet campaign was a disastrous failure for the Communists. U.S. and South Vietnamese suffered 2600 killed, compared to 60,000 Viet Cong and North Vietnamese killed. Despite 26,000 civilian casualties in the South and more than 600,000 refugees, the Saigon government was not overthrown.

## The U.S. Bombing Halt

Ho did win his victory against the U.S. political system. The president concluded that the optimistic statements issuing from General Westmoreland and from the White House were no longer having any effect except to widen the "credibility gap" and that it would not do to send another 100,000 troops, call up the reserves, or intensify the bombing. After Senators Eugene McCarthy and Robert Kennedy had made known their intention to seek the Democratic presidential nomination on antiwar platforms, Johnson announced on March 31, 1968, that he would not seek the presidency again—his hope being to place U.S. policy in Vietnam above divisive partisanship—and that he was ordering a cessation of the bombing over 90 percent of the area of North Vietnam.

Hanoi responded in three days, declaring its readiness to engage in peace talks even before unconditional cessation of bombing and other war acts. That marked a change in policy, which some policymakers attributed to Hanoi's desire to take advantage of the turmoil caused by the Cultural Revolution in China to reestablish an independent North Vietnamese foreign policy, free of Beijing's influence. Beijing condemned Johnson's offer as "a swindle," but it can only be conjectured whether the PRC was yet beginning to think of an end to the Vietnam War as containing any potential benefit to China in its dispute with the Soviet Union. During 1968 the Soviet Union had substantially increased its shipment of military aid to Hanoi in the form of surface-to-air missiles, anti-aircraft guns, radar equipment. MiG fighter planes, and ammunition, whereas the bulk of Chinese aid was in the form of food and other consumer goods, trucks, boats, small arms, and artillery.

Talks began in Paris in May, with Harriman leading the U.S. delegation, and were stalemated when North Vietnam demanded an immediate cessation of all bombing and other U.S. acts of war. No new step was taken until October 31, 1968, less than a week before the Humphrey–Nixon election, when Johnson ordered an end to all naval and aerial bombing and Hanoi agreed to allow South Vietnam to be a party to the Paris talks.

## Confusion and Controversy over U.S. Policy in Vietnam

The Vietnam War was the most traumatic foreign-policy experience in American history—the only one to generate such deep domestic divisions as to compel an incumbent president who was eligible for reelection to resign his candidacy. It had become the nation's longest and most frustrating war. The peninsular conflict on the opposite side of the globe produced at home an unprecedented alienation of intellectuals and youth from the institutions of government, the erosion of military service, a breakdown of social order, and a rise in the incidence of political violence in several U.S. cities. Moreover, substantial segments of the body politic experienced a strange mixture of emotional reactions, varying from a sense of failure or defeat to suspicions of betrayal to tendencies toward moral recrimination and psychological self-flagellation. All this happened less than a quarter of a century after the most decisive worldwide political-military victory ever scored by any nation. The age of American imperial grandeur seemed about to come to an early end.

The perplexity to which the Korean War had given rise was greatly compounded in the Vietnam War, in which there was much more confusion regarding the nature of the conflict, the national purpose for which blood and treasure were being spent, and the best political-military strategy for reaching that goal. The Johnson administration was simply unable to articulate to the American body politic that the United States was really involved in an international war, aiding a victim of Communist aggression, rather than intervening in a civil war that was none of its business. It never made clear whether the United States was acting out of a sense of commitment to its own moral, legal, political values (aiding helpless people, fulfilling a treaty obligation, or preserving a people's freedom of choice against the imposition of a communist system) or out of a realistic assessment of its own national interest—and if so, how that interest was defined.

Many U.S. military officers who fought in Vietnam agree that the strategy and tactics should have been different, but they also criticize the counterproductive role played by the press, which reported "Mr. Johnson's war" in a manner that turned a substantial segment of the American system, especially university professors and students, against the U.S. commitment. General Westmoreland accused the media of distorting the true outcome of the Tet offensive by converting a Communist military defeat into a psychological victory for Hanoi.

Finally, the critics faulted Johnson and his administration for failing to articulate a coherent rationale and set of strategic objectives and failing to mobilize the full support of the American people for the war effort, lest the president's domestic Great Society programs be jeopardized. Even after the Tet offensive, a majority of the American people still did not want a pullout, but favored a strategy of either victory or withdrawal. During his last two years in office, Johnson and his advisers seemed to be pursuing an experimental trial-and-error method of finding a compromise path between "too much" and "too little," between provoking large-scale Soviet and/or Chinese intervention and losing South Vietnam to the Communists. This was insufficient to bring the enemy to the breaking point. It underestimated the zealous tenacity of the enemy and the willingness and ability of its leadership to spill as much blood as was necessary to achieve its goal. The Johnson administration riveted its attention on the statistics that poured in daily from the battleground—sorties flown, tonnage dropped, targets hit, body counts, hamlets secured. Ho and Giap kept their eyes on Washington and the pages of the leading American newspapers. General Westmoreland was sure that his strategy of attrition would bring victory once the technologically superior U.S. forces were able to engage large North Vietnamese army units in conventional combat. He underestimated the North's staying power. David Halberstam has summed it up succinctly: The United States was a great but divided nation fighting a limited war; North Vietnam was a small but united nation waging total war.

## OTHER TROUBLE SPOTS

Like Kennedy, Johnson found himself unable to monitor the whole world carefully and to become personally involved in the details of foreign policy in all regions. Most of his attention, naturally, was devoted to Southeast Asia, and most of his travel abroad was related to the diplomatic conduct of that war. When Joseph Kasavubu, who had overthrown Moise Tshombe in the Congo, was in turn ousted by Joseph Mobutu in 1965, the Johnson administration scarcely reacted to the change in a country whose leadership problems had absorbed Kennedy for weeks.

A much more decisive event took place in Asia in October 1965, when the Indonesian Communist party, which was made up largely of Chinese and pro-Chinese elements, attempted to carry out a coup in the world's fifth most populous nation, probably with the concurrence of the dictator-like president, Sukarno. A number of high-ranking Indonesian officers were ambushed and killed in what appeared first to be a successful coup, but enough nationalist officers survived to rally the army for a counterblow. During the preceding three years, U.S. relations with Indonesia had fallen to a low point. At Sukarno's insistence, the staff at the U.S. Embassy had shrunk to a small group; the United States played no part in the countercoup. President Johnson was convinced, on the basis of subsequent conversations with Asian leaders, that the Indonesian turnaround, which constituted a major political disaster for communism in Asia, probably would not have occurred if the United States and its allies had not appeared to be increasing their military and political commitment to the containment of communism in that region and to be making gains in Southeast Asia.

Johnson was capable of some subtle diplomatic maneuvering in complex situations, alternating between toughness and reasonableness, as his approach to Moscow showed. Soviet Premier Khrushchev's fall from power in October 1964 was interpreted in Washington as a possible signal of a hardening in the Soviet line in both the dispute with China and détente with the United States. Increasingly preoccupied with the war in Vietnam, Johnson wanted to avoid being drawn into a direct conflict with either Moscow or Beijing. The United States had no formal relations with the PRC, but carried on communications through the American and Chinese missions in Warsaw. U.S. policymakers, as we have seen, assumed that China was the ideological and strategic mentor of the North Vietnamese. They also realized that the Soviet Union was in a better position than China to supply Hanoi with moden weapons. From 1964 through 1968, therefore, Johnson and his administration worked harder to cultivate good relations with Moscow than with the PRC, whose admission to the United Nations Washington continued to block.

In September 1965 Johnson tacitly cooperated with Alexei Kosygin through the United Nations to bring about a fragile cease-fire between India and Pakistan when conflict erupted between them in the Punjab. Neither one of the principal powers wanted China to intervene on the side of Pakistan, since that would have made matters much worse. Speaking at the United Nations, Secretary of State Rusk praised the Soviet Union for its constructive attitude and warned China against meddling. It was reported that the administration had transmitted a similar warning though the Warsaw channel. In January 1966, when Kosygin traveled to Tashkent to arrange a settlement between Ayab Khan of Pakistan and Lal Bahadur Shastri of India, Johnson orchestrated U.S. diplomacy to facilitate Kosygin's task and allowed him to take the credit for a successful negotiation to end the conflict. Johnson was later occasionally heard to say, "I couldn't be seen, but I was at Tashkent."

Walt Rostow had recorded that Johnson's "most painful exercise in self-restraint" came in the weeks following the seizure of the U.S. electronic intelligence ship *Pueblo* and its crew of 83 by North Korean patrol boats on January 22–23, 1968. The incident occurred after months of heightened tension between the two Koreas and frequent clashes between North Korean infiltrators and U.S.–ROK forces south of the Korean DMZ. It was integrally related to an attempt by 31 Communist guerrillas, infiltrated from the North, to slip into Seoul with the mission of assassinating South Korean President Park Chung Hee. U.S. policymakers also assumed that the crisis in Korea was timed as a diversionary operation just a few days prior to the Tet offensive in Vietnam, aimed at drawing Washington's attention and perhaps U.S. air and naval forces away from Southeast Asia at a crucial moment. North Korean Radio broadcast an alleged "confession" by the *Pueblo's* commander that he had been in North Korean territorial waters. The United States insisted that the vessel had been 25 miles off North Korea's coast and demanded the immediate release of the *Pueblo* and its crew. U.S.–North Korean negotiations began in early February at Panmunjon. South Korea complained about being excluded from the negotiations, since its own vital security interests were at stake. University students in Seoul and other cities demonstrated against American "appeasement" of the North and called on their government to bring back 40,000 South Korean troops from Vietnam.

Johnson, concerned about reducing the chances that North Korea might be tempted to open a second front, ordered that U.S. air and naval strength in the vicinity of Korea be built up without weakening the American military posture in Southeast Asia. Air capabilities were thought to be particularly important because of North Korea's superiority over the South in that dimension. After considering a range of alternatives from rescue operations to threats of retaliation, Johnson concluded that there was no way to get the *Pueblo* crew back alive except through tortuous diplomatic negotiation.

The South Koreans were deeply disturbed by what appeared to them to be U.S. passivity in the face of gross provocation. Cyrus Vance, former deputy assistant secretary of defense, was dispatched to Seoul to try to convince the South Koreans that U.S. inaction in the *Pueblo* case was due to concern for the lives of Americans and did not mean the slightest weakening of American determination to defend the ROK. Vance urged the South Koreans to derive satisfaction from the fact that they were rapidly outdistancing the North in economic development. The week Vance spent in Seoul turned out to be a very rough one. The government there was not reassured. Johnson and his advisers had to wait more than ten months before the members of the ship's crew were finally released in December 1968, and then only after the United States formally admitted that the ship had been engaged in espionage activities within North Vietnam's territorial waters. The United States immediately, officially, and categorically repudiated this admission once the prisoners, who had been subjected to barbarous treatment in clear violation of customary international law, were free and safe.

## JOHNSON AS DECISION MAKER

Much has already been said about Lyndon Baines Johnson as a foreign-policy decision maker. He retained many of the important people he inherited from Kennedy, not necessarily because he liked or trusted them but rather because he thought he needed them to invest his administration with an aura of legitimacy, respectability, and continuity with the administration elected in 1960. He came to depend on a few of them—Rusk, McNamara (until late 1967), McGeorge Bundy (until he left voluntarily in 1966), Maxwell Taylor, and Walt Rostow. Some he disliked and distrusted intensely—Robert Kennedy, Roger Hilsman, Averell Harriman (most of the time), and those he regarded as "cookie pushers" in the State Department. Although he was a man of passionate feelings, he had sufficient self-control to be able to work pragmatically with anyone who could make a contribution toward the advancement of his policies. This was not purely a matter of personal ambition, jealousy, or vindictiveness. He had reason, for example, to dislike Lodge as a Boston Brahmin who had advocated the anti-Diem coup. When Lodge resigned in mid-1964 to seek the Republican nomination, Johnson replaced him with Taylor. A year later, however, he sent Lodge back to Saigon as a successor to Taylor. Having dumped Harriman in 1964 for his anti-Diem proclivities, Johnson nevertheless selected him to initiate talks with the North Vietnamese in Paris in May 1968. When it served his policy purposes, Johnson was a good executive who could, regardless of personal chemistry, appoint to a post anyone with the skills to do what he wanted done.

President Johnson inherited not only the personnel but also the foreign-policy machinery of the Kennedy administration and did not substantially overhaul it, although he had his way of making sure that it worked to his liking. From the time he became president, he knew better than Kennedy the strengths and weaknesses of the people who filled the principal posts. No less than Kennedy did Johnson entertain suspicions of the professionals in the State Department who were always calling for diplomatic solutions and seemed pusillanimous about the use of force, and also of the Joint Chiefs and their Pentagon staffs who thought that most conflicts were to be resolved by giving the enemy "a whiff of grape shot." The difference was that Johnson distrusted the former group more and the latter group less. He conceived of himself as a tough, patriotic American who knew how to follow the middle of the road between his advisers on the two extremes. He had a great capacity for hard work and almost infinite patience when it came to listening to recommendations from all points of the compass, but during meetings he would interject such questions or comments as to signal to his advisers the direction of his current thinking and the shape of the consensus he would like to see emerge. He did not make up his mind quickly, and he was not a shooter from the hip. He never doubted that the State Department cable of August 24, 1963, containing instructions to Ambassador Lodge concerning Diem, had been "hasty and ill-advised." As president, he wanted to make certain that the crucial foreign-policy decisions would be his; he refused to be manipulated or preempted by subordinates by being placed in a situation where he was faced with a *fait accompli* or a commitment undertaken without his consent.

Examples of his reluctance to be rushed into action may be drawn from his record in late 1964. Following Viet Cong attacks on the air base at Bien Hoa and the Christmas Eve bombing of the U.S. officers' billets in Saigon, Ambassador Maxwell Taylor and the Joint Chiefs urged Johnson to permit retaliatory bombing against North Vietnam. He turned down the requests on both occasions, probably because he wanted to appear self-restrained rather than trigger-happy in the eyes of his intellectual critics at home and abroad, to whose views he was more sensitive than he cared to admit. In early 1965, when it was no longer possible to postpone critical decisions to respond to stepped-up North Vietnamese aggressive activity—decisions authorizing the bombing of North Vietnam and the buildup of U.S. forces in South Vietnam—he met several times with the National Security Council and elicited unanimous or nearly unanimous consensus.*

In July 1965 Johnson outlined five available courses for the United States to pursue in Vietnam:

1. Use the Strategic Air Command to bring the enemy to its knees.
2. Pack up and go home.
3. Stay in a holding pattern and suffer the consequences in loss of territory and casualties—an alternative that no parent with a soldier in the field would choose.
4. Request great sums of money from Congress, call up the reserves, increase the draft, go onto a war footing, and declare a state of emergency—a course of action likely to bring increased aid to North Vietnam from China and Russia.
5. Give our commanders in the field the troops and supplies they say they need.

---

*Secretary Rusk was either out of town or ill during some of the meetings. He and the following regular or ad hoc participants in the National Security Council were among the 1965 consensus advisers: Robert McNamara, General Earle G. Wheeler, Cyrus Vance, George W. Ball, Llwellyn Thompson, McGeorge Bundy, William P. Bundy, John McCone, Richard Helms, John McNaughton, Douglas Dillon, General Andrew Goodpaster, Henry Fowler, Carl Rowan, Nicholas Katzenbach, Richard Goodwin, and Clark Clifford. Apparently the only person who ever attended these meetings and dissented from the consensus was Senator Mike Mansfield.

After listening to all the arguments and counterarguments concerning each possible line of action, Johnson concluded that the United States should do whatever was necessary to resist aggression without becoming "overly dramatic" and causing tensions that might lead to a major war. For five years he sought the middle course between abandoning South Vietnam and provoking a larger war. It has been suggested that with the passage of time he may have begun to think of himself as a combination of some of the great strategic thinkers of history—Sun Tzu, Machiavelli, and Clausewitz—who would be able to calibrate and orchestrate various applications of force and strands of diplomacy to bring about the kind of negotiated settlement for which he undoubtedly yearned. Perhaps his greatest failure, as Hans Morgenthau has hypothesized, stemmed from the fact that he had been a brilliant politician in the American political system and in the Senate, where he had an uncanny ability to maneuver and make political deals, to bribe, threaten, and cajole his colleagues to support his cherished legislative goals, which were usually enlightened, just, and good for the American people. Perhaps—like a great many Americans in high places—he did not clearly understand that the international system is *essentially different* in its operational characteristics from the American democratic system. The political leaders of the totalitarian states that take their turns in becoming mortal enemies of the United States do not think at all like American politicians and do not rise to the top according to the rules of the American political game.

# chapter 7

# The Nixon/Ford Administration and a New Structure for World Peace

The Nixon administration came to office at a time of deepening division over foreign policy within the United States. The debate of the late 1960s involved the priorities to be attached to domestic and foreign policy and the nature of U.S. foreign policy in a world that was in the midst of structural change, with the emergence of a large number of new actors. As Henry Kissinger put it,

> The postwar period was the first in which *all* the continents interacted. In 1945, the world community comprised fifty-one nations; by 1968 it had more than doubled, to nearly one hundred thirty. Modern communications transmitted news and ideas instantaneously. Events that used to be local—news, rivalries, scandals, domestic upheavals, natural tragedies—suddenly began to assume global significance. When the Nixon Administration entered office all the elements of international relations were in flux simultaneously.

The new administration confronted a world in which the military power of the United States, relative to the Soviet Union, was diminishing just when the consensus that had sustained American foreign policy since the late 1940s seemed to have been shattered in Vietnam. The Nixon administration had been elected, among other things, to achieve "peace with honor" in Vietnam and to extricate the United States from what would soon become the longest war in its history. The tasks facing the United States encompassed the management of a global rivalry with the Soviet Union under conditions of emerging military parity; the development of support for whatever would be the foreign policy of the administration; and the adjustment of American diplomacy, capabilities, and commitments in light of changes that were unfolding in the international system in the last third of the twentieth century.

By the late 1960s, many of the assumptions on which American foreign policy in the preceding generation had been based had become the object of criticism. Although Nixon himself had been identified with such assumptions—especially what liberal critics saw as an excessively rigid anticommunism—the Nixon administration embarked upon approaches to foreign policy that, in certain essentially important dimensions, represented a fundamental break with the recent past (although in retrospect there remained significant continuity in American foreign policy between the Nixon administration and its post–World War II predecessors). Although Nixon's own approaches to foreign policy had evolved between his unsuccessful first presidential bid in 1960 and his victorious 1968 campaign, his administration could have rebuilt a foreign-policy consensus, it would be argued, only by coopting some of the ideas of the critics of American foreign policy of the late 1960s. To some extent, it did so. The foreign-policy themes that characterized Nixon's campaign speeches in 1968, together with the ideas that were to emerge in the Nixon administration, had their intellectual antecedents in the critiques of the period: the emergence of a world of additional actors as a result of the diffusion of political and economic power; the need to exploit differences between, or among, Communist states; the reassessment of security burdens to be borne by the United States in light of the capabilities available to other states in a world of wider distribution of power; and the possibilities alleged to exist in the building of a less hostile relationship with the Soviet Union.

## THE NIXON DOCTRINE

As the Nixon administration began to develop a conceptual framework for American foreign policy, such ideas were given a prominent place. The Nixon Doctrine had its debut in what was first called the Guam Doctrine, set forth by President Nixon on July 23, 1969, on a round-the-world trip that included visits to Guam, the Philippines, Indonesia, Thailand, South Vietnam, India, Pakistan, Romania, and Britain. Whereas it had been past American policy to furnish U.S. personnel *and* weapons, as in the Korean conflict and subsequently in Vietnam, Nixon declared that in the future the United States would supply only military and economic assistance to those states prepared to make available the soldiers to defend themselves. Nixon rejected the interpretation that this new doctrine would lead to a total American withdrawal either from the Asian Pacific or from other parts of the world. In his mind, the Nixon Doctrine was "not a formula for getting America *out* of Asia, but one that provided the only sound basis for America's staying *in* and continuing to play a responsible role in helping the non-Communist nations and neutrals as well as our Asian allies to defend their independence."*

*Richard Nixon, *RN: The Memoirs of Richard Nixon* (New York: Grosset and Dunlap, 1978), p. 395.

The intellectual foundations of the Nixon Doctrine were deeply rooted in the balance-of-power concept, specifically in the assumption that security is to be found in international equilibrium. The basis for world peace in the late twentieth century lay in the development of an international system in whose preservation all states would have an interest. Viewed from the perspective of Europe's classical balance of power, and especially the Congress of Vienna (the study of which had been Henry Kissinger's doctoral dissertation), the task of diplomats at that time was the restoration of an international system based on legitimacy, or procedural consensus, stated in the contemporary terminology of political science. That is to say: the issues that divide states would not include the structure of the international system itself.

The Nixon administration envisioned an international system in which the United States and the Soviet Union, as well as Japan, China, and Western Europe, would be the principal actors. Such a system would provide the focus for an American foreign policy whose strength was based not only on military power but also on partnership, or at least more mature relationships, with other states, especially Japan and the nations of Western Europe, that were capable of assuming greater responsibility for their own security; and on negotiations with adversaries, notably the Soviet Union, designed to transform a condition of confrontation to one of détente. The Nixon Doctrine was founded on the belief that it would be possible to alter over time the behavior of the Soviet Union by offering or withholding various rewards. At the same time, the United States would gain leverage over the Soviet Union by exploiting the schism that by 1969 was manifest in the deteriorating Sino–Soviet relationship. As early as 1969, the United States had signaled to the Soviet Union that it would oppose any military action by Moscow that would weaken China, which, in keeping with the classical balance-of-power theory, had become an "essential actor" in the five-power international system conceptualized by the Nixon Administration. The United States would develop a strategic relationship with China that would strengthen Beijing (Peking) against Moscow, while simultaneously seeking to minimize differences with the Soviet Union. Thus a central element of the Nixon Doctrine would emerge: what was termed a triangular strategic-political relationship, encompassing the United States, China, and the Soviet Union.

Although Nixon spoke in 1972 of the eventual evolution of five "economic superpowers," the pentapolar system of the Nixon Doctrine contained three major economic powers (the United States, Western Europe, and Japan), together with two military superpowers (the United States and the Soviet Union) and two huge land powers (China and the Soviet Union). Only the United States possessed both vast economic *and* enormous military capabilities. China not only ranked far behind the other major powers in economic capabilities but was further weakened by the domestic power struggle known as the Cultural Revolution. Western Europe was not a unified political entity capable of conducting a cohesive foreign policy or maintaining an integrated defense capability. Japan's self-defense forces were minuscule in comparison with those of the superpowers. Hence the pentapolar international system existed more as a concept than a reality. Its five members were asymmetrical in their capabilities.

Its relative strengths in both economic and military terms placed only the United States within each of the two hypothesized triangular relationships: a strategic-political triangle encompassing the United States, China, and the Soviet Union and an economic triangle (or what came to be called a trilateral relationship) that included the United States, Japan, and Western Europe. Such a structure was clearly an American creation, for only the United States could provide its central element.

Another fundamental difference existed between the Nixon Doctrine and the policies of preceding American administrations. The pursuit of balance-of-power politics depended on a foreign policy characterized by surprise and flexibility—the ability to shift alignments quickly in pursuit of equilibrium—as Secretary of State Kissinger demonstrated at the time of the October 1973 war, when the United States first resupplied Israel with massive amounts of military equipment until Israeli forces had penetrated deeply into Egypt, at which time Kissinger embarked upon his effort to restrain Israel and to achieve a cease-fire and to build for Washington a new relationship with Egypt. His idea was related to two principles that became part of the Nixon Doctrine: the quest for moderation in foreign policy and the avoidance of the humiliation of a defeated state in order to allow maximum latitude for diplomatic efforts to attain a political settlement.

Unlimited pursuit of national interest, Kissinger enjoined, would contain the seeds of international conflict, for the greater the quest for security by one state, the more it must be encroached upon the security needs of other states. Therefore, central to the operation of the global structure for peace envisioned in the Nixon Doctrine was the pursuit by as many states as possible of national interest based on limitations. By the structure itself, and in particular by the manipulation of the strategic-political triangular relationship, the United States would enhance the likelihood of moderation in the behavior of the other members, notably the Soviet Union. The strengthening of partnerships with allies would further enhance the development of a world of pluralism. The more actors were involved, the more likely it was that the international system would be characterized by norms of moderation in the practice of statecraft.

## THE U.S.-SOVIET-CHINESE TRIANGLE

By the end of the 1960s, the Soviet Union was on the verge of attaining strategic-nuclear parity with the United States. At the same time, Moscow was seeking to advance its influence in the Third World, especially in the Middle East but also in South and Southeast Asia. Against these major gains for the Soviet Union had to be weighed the fragmentation in the world communist movement resulting from the deepening schism between China and the Soviet Union. The fracturing of what had once been a monolithic Sino–Soviet bloc led to the conclusion that, especially for the People's Republic of China, ideology had been subordinated to the exigencies of forging a strategic relationship with other states against the Soviet Union. With the Soviet Union, in turn, the Nixon Doctrine had as a premise the possibility of negotiated agreements based on mutual interest.

### The Concept of "Linkage" Vis-à-Vis the Soviet Union

Although the term "détente" had often been used in connection with the U.S.–Soviet relationship during previous administrations, it became the principal concept in American diplomacy toward the Soviet Union in the Nixon administration and, by the end of the Ford administration, the basis for much of the deepening criticism of American foreign policy that emerged in the 1970s, notably in the 1976 presidential campaign. According to Kissinger, détente was regarded as a search for a more constructive relationship with the Soviet Union based on a balance of mutual interests between the superpowers. It should be possible, the Nixon administration posited, to reach agreement across a broad spectrum of issues, with progress in one area enhancing the prospects for advancement elsewhere. In this perspective, no single agreement would stand in isolation from other issues confronting the United States and the Soviet Union. Because of the range of issues that impinged upon one another and upon the overall relationship between Washington and Moscow, it would be both possible and necessary to link the outcome of one set of negotiations to other problems of importance. Thus, there was said to be "linkage" among seemingly discrete, but nevertheless closely related, issues confronting the United States and the Soviet Union. The Nixon administration sought to develop with the Soviet Union a standard, or code, of international conduct based on the mutual interests that would be embodied in a widening web of linked agreements. It was anticipated that the Soviet Union would acquire a vested interest in an evolving network of relationships with the West that would be sufficiently strong and durable to render a return to hostility less likely.

Furthermore, the problems confronting the superpowers cut across the lines that, in the generation since World War II, had constituted the boundaries of East and West. These transcendent global issues of the late twentieth century included maintaining energy supplies, sustaining adequate levels of economic growth, providing food for increasing populations, preserving the environment and enhancing the quality of life, cooperating in scientific and medical endeavors, and regulating the utilization of the seabed and resources of the oceans. Such problems could be addressed more fully, the Nixon administration reasoned, if the tensions that had divided the United States and the Soviet Union for more than a generation could be eased.

In this approach the Nixon administration had gone far toward incorporating into its foreign-policy agenda both assumptions and prescriptions that had formed important components of the critiques of the preceding administration. On the threshold of the 1970s, in the Nixon administration's quest for a new American foreign-policy consensus, economic and political issues were given at least as much weight as the threat of war and the use of military force. Among the guiding principles of the administration was a conception of security interests deeply influenced by the needs of a multipolar political structure. This meant a reduction in certain once-prominent threats to U.S. interests. The Johnson administration had based its military action in Vietnam in large part on the need to contain Chinese expansion into Southeast Asia. With the United States soon (in the early 1970s) to attempt to forge a new relationship with China as a counterpoise to growing Soviet power, its military commitment in Vietnam would come to have less significance for the United States. Thus the United States embraced a concept of national interest related specifically to a geopolitical conception of the world and to the triangular relationship seen to be emerging among Washington, Beijing, and Moscow. These sets of strategic relationships existed within the broader Alliance interests of the United States and the nonstrategic, global economic-political issues of increasing importance in the late twentieth century.

In its relationship with the Soviet Union, the Nixon administration faced the formidable task of relating its conceptual framework to major issue areas. Although the United States and the Soviet Union had agreed during the Johnson administration to initiate Strategic Arms Limitation (SALT) Talks in 1968, the Soviet invasion of Czechoslovakia, together with the change of administrations in Washington, had resulted in their postponement until November 1969.

For the Nixon administration the limitation of competition over strategic weapons was considered to be the most important component of its evolving policy toward the Soviet Union. At the end of the 1960s, the basis for strategic-weapons limitations was considered to lie in the belief, voiced in the United States more than by the Soviet leadership, that any decisive military advantage conferred by the possession of nuclear weapons could be achieved only by enormous efforts. Kissinger reasoned that the levels of expenditure and investment of resources not only would be prohibitive but would be matched by an adversary, so that equilibrium would be restored—and at an even higher level of strategic capabilities. If no decisive military or political advantage was possible under such conditions, both sides would come to the conclusion that negotiated arms-control agreements were in their interest, for otherwise they would each have spent vast sums for only marginal increments in their overall security. The necessary caveat for American defense policy, according to the Nixon administration, was the maintenance of overall strategic parity, or "strategic sufficiency," as it was termed, in nuclear forces with the Soviet Union. Although in 1974 Kissinger was to question rhetorically the meaning of strategic superiority, he acknowledged that the appearance of inferiority in strategic-nuclear forces could have adverse political consequences for the United States. While the United States remained resolute in its desire to prevent nuclear war, an effort should be made to limit the levels of strategic nuclear capabilities available to both sides. In keeping with its concept of linkage, the Nixon administration held that unrestrained armaments efforts by the Soviet Union would be incompatible with a détente relationship.

The emergence of the Soviet Union as a superpower having rough strategic parity with the United States created a series of problems with which the Nixon administration had to cope. The United States could hope to build necessary domestic support for its defense programs at a time of major domestic opposition only if it could be clearly demonstrated that efforts were being made to achieve negotiated limits on weapons. Without such negotiations, the Soviet programs would continue unchecked, while the United States remained unable, in a period of emphasis on the reordering of priorities from international to domestic politics,

to maintain the military equilibrium deemed necessary for peace, and in particular would be unable to pursue the U.S.–Soviet relationship envisioned by the
Nixon administration. Thus the United States sought to build a framework within
which to restrain the Soviet arms buildup that, as the 1970s unfolded, assumed
proportions that were alarming to many.

There was a direct relationship, here as in the other features of the Nixon
Doctrine, between domestic factors influencing American foreign policy and the
international strategic-political environment of the times. During the Nixon
presidency, defense programs were subjected by Congress to appropriations cuts
at an annual level of $6 billion between 1969 and 1975, while at the same time
nondefense spending increased each year by an average of $4.7 billion. In the first
half of the 1970s, the percentage of U.S. GNP devoted to defense declined, despite
the efforts of the Nixon administration to appease Congress by making its own
defense-budget reductions and by fashioning a foreign policy whose purpose was
to restore public support. The United States did embark upon the development
of the B-1 bomber (subsequently cancelled by the Carter administration in 1977
but revived by President Reagan in 1981), the Trident submarine, the cruise
missile, and the MIRVing of the Minuteman III, but there were severe cutbacks
in U.S. conventional forces, some of which were the result of the withdrawal of
American forces from Vietnam. U.S. Army and Marine Corps divisions were
reduced from 23 in fiscal year 1968 to 16 by 1974. The U.S. Navy shrank from 976
ships to 495, with further reductions to come in the 1970s, so that by the end of the
decade the Navy was at its lowest level since U.S. entry into World War II.
Although the U.S. Navy retained a *qualitative* edge, by the early 1970s the Soviet
Union was emerging as a maritime power capable of deploying naval units in all
the world's oceans.

### The Strategic Arms Limitation (SALT) Talks

This was the domestic political, and the global strategic, context in which the
United States entered negotiations with the Soviet Union for strategic-arms
limitation in 1969. After having initially rejected the idea of a limitation on
ballistic missiles at the Glassboro summit conference in 1967, the Soviet Union
pressed for an anti-ballistic missile (ABM) treaty with the United States. Although the United States had become apprehensive that the Soviet Union
was developing a more sophisticated ABM to upgrade a system already deployed
around Moscow, the United States, by the end of the 1960s, had developed an
ABM capability that, in retrospect, the Soviet Union sought to restrict by means
of an ABM treaty. By 1970 the United States had become committed to the
negotiation of an arms-control agreement that included both a limitation on
strategic defense in an ABM treaty and ceilings on offensive strategic forces,
notably land- and sea-based ballistic missiles. In May 1971 the United States
and the Soviet Union achieved a breakthrough that enabled them to negotiate
the ABM Treaty sought especially by the Soviet Union, but also by important
proponents of arms control in the United States. At the same time, it was agreed
that talks would be completed for an Interim Agreement on Offensive Missiles

sought by the United States to place limits on the rapidly increasing levels of Soviet strategic missiles that, if unrestrained, would eventually pose a counter-force threat to the United States, specifically to the fixed, land-based elements of its strategic-nuclear force.

From the perspective of the Nixon administration, the logic of its SALT policy lay in the need to place effective restraints on the Soviet Union's deployment of offensive strategic systems targeted against the United States if at the same time an agreement were to be signed with Moscow that would restrict the capacity of the United States to defend such targets, by means of an ABM capability, from such attack. From its perspective, the Soviet Union had an interest in an ABM treaty that prevented the United States from emplacing a system of strategic defense against the emerging ballistic missile forces then, or about to be, deployed by Moscow. For the United States, SALT represented part of a continuing effort to preserve strategic-nuclear deterrence between the superpowers. Of crucial importance, from the U.S. perspective, was the capacity of American strategic forces, or a significant portion of them, to survive any Soviet attack and to be able to retaliate in sufficient strength to inflict "unacceptable" levels of devastation on the adversary. In the early 1960s this condition for strategic stability had increased in complexity as the Soviet Union acquired larger numbers of ICBMs. It would become even more formidable in the view of American policymakers and the broader strategic-military community in the United States in the 1970s. The problem was stated succinctly by President Nixon when he suggested that no president, in a nuclear crisis, should be left with the prospect that the Soviet Union might be able to threaten the destruction of the land-based U.S. strategic-nuclear force, leaving the United States principally with its sea-based force to retaliate against Soviet cities. Under such circumstances, the United States would confront residual Soviet strategic forces, superior in numbers, that could inflict vast levels of devastation on remaining targets in the United States.

By the early 1970s the United States had begun to deploy MIRVed ICBMs, a total of 550 Minuteman III missiles, each with three warheads, which were designed to penetrate any ABM system that the Soviet Union would then have deployed. In the SALT accords the United States called for the limitation of each side's ABMs to 200 launchers (later reduced in 1974 to 100 launchers) and thus the preservation of a form of deterrence based on a theory of mutual assured destruction. By making the destructive consequences of nuclear war so great by reducing strategic defense, it was assumed that deterrence could be preserved. The ABM Treaty, signed on May 26, 1972, at the Moscow summit conference by President Nixon and Soviet Chairman Leonid Brezhnev, was to be of indefinite duration.

Because agreement on offensive missiles had proven far more difficult to achieve, the result of this first round of SALT talks was an interim agreement limited to a five-year period extending to October 3, 1977. This agreement froze the number of ICBMs and SLBMs possessed by both sides at their existing levels: 1619 ICBMs and 740 SLBMs for the Soviet Union and 1054 ICBMs and 656 SLBMs for the United States. Excluded from the interim agreement were strategic bombers, in which the United States in 1972 had a numerical advantage over the Soviet Union (460 to 140). In effect, the United States had traded a Soviet advantage in numbers of missiles for an American edge in technology, especially in accuracy, warhead design, rocket propulsion, and submarine construction. However, both sides, within the SALT framework, could make qualitative improvements within the quantitative totals contained in the interim agreement. The Soviet Union could be expected to take full advantage—as it in fact did—of the broad latitude permitted for such advances. What was not fully anticipated by the American officials was the speed with which the Soviet Union moved to deploy new-generation strategic systems, including several new launchers called the SS-17, the SS-19, and the SS-18. The last-named missile has five times the throw weight of the U.S. Minuteman III. The Soviet Union had been unwilling in the Interim Agreement to agree to U.S. efforts to include a definition of "heavy missile" that would have prohibited the deployment of a weapon as large as the SS-18.

Thus the effect of the interim agreement was to codify a form of strategic parity at levels of existing or impending strategic capabilities on both sides, while even giving an incentive to the signatories to pursue R&D programs—in the case of the Soviet Union, to narrow the American lead and, in the case of the United States, to preserve whatever margin of technological advantage it then had. The ratification of the SALT I accords by the U.S. Senate in the autumn of 1972 provided the occasion for passage of a resolution introduced by Senator Henry Jackson of Washington to the effect that the interim agreement should be replaced by a treaty specifying equal aggregates of strategic forces for the United States and the Soviet Union. The problems inherent in the development of a framework for equal aggregates were to prove formidable indeed, since the size and composition of U.S. and Soviet strategic forces differed in several fundamentally important respects, including the deployment during the ten years after 1972 of at least 300 SS-18s, each of which, even under the terms of the SALT II treaty, could have deployed as many as ten MIRVed warheads. Such problems were to confront each of the successors to the Nixon administration.

The summit conference at which the SALT I accords were signed provided the setting for other Soviet–American agreements, including a series of principles designed to guide superpower conduct. Just as the Geneva summit conference of May 1955 had been the high point of the U.S.–Soviet relationship during the Eisenhower administration but was followed in 1956 by growing Soviet military assistance to Nasser's Egypt and the Suez crisis of October–November 1956, within as many months after the May 1972 summit conference, the Arab–Israeli war of October 1973 broke out. Although the circumstances differed, in both cases it was quickly apparent that superpower summitry could not obscure profound political differences in such volatile regions as the Middle East. Nevertheless, at the May 1972 conference, President Nixon and Chairman Brezhnev signed a declaration in which the United States and the Soviet Union agreed to

do their utmost to avoid military confrontation and to prevent the outbreak of nuclear war. They will always exercise restraint in their mutual relations, and will be prepared to negotiate and settle differences by peaceful means.

> Discussions and negotiations on outstanding issues will be conducted in a spirit of reciprocity, mutual accommodation, and mutual benefit. Both sides recognize that efforts to obtain unilateral advantage at the expense of others, directly or indirectly, are inconsistent with these objectives.

From the U.S. perspective, this effort to establish a structure for peace on the basis of principles of peaceful coexistence embodied the idea of linkage. In signing the SALT accords, the United States had enabled the Soviet Union to achieve formal acceptance and codification of the new strategic-military parity. In return, it was hoped, Moscow would be prepared to forego the temptation to seek "unilateral advantage" in the various conflicts endemic to the Third World, especially to the Middle East. At no time was the Soviet Union prepared to accept such a form of linkage. In 1973 the Agreement for the Prevention of Nuclear War, affirming as a shared goal efforts to remove the danger of nuclear conflict and the use of nuclear weapons, was signed.

The other incentive toward détente that was offered the Soviet Union consisted of trade and technology transfer. Because all industrialized states were developing trading relations, it was clearly impossible for the United States to isolate or boycott the Soviet Union. For the Soviet Union, as Kissinger saw it, increased commercial exchanges with the advanced industrial states of the North Atlantic area and with Japan would help to counter the effects of declining industrial growth rates, the repeated failures in agriculture, and slackening labor productivity. The Soviet Union needed access to Western capital markets for investment in its natural resources, especially oil and natural gas. The Soviet Union lagged far behind the non-Communist industrialized states in such fields as electronics, microminiaturization and computers, and petrochemicals. In the 1970s, half a century after the Bolshevik Revolution of 1917, the Soviet Union, unlike Tsarist Russia, was unable to feed its population without huge imports of agricultural products, especially grain, from the United States and other farm producers (a condition that is basically unchanged in the 1980s).

For the West, the incentives were to be found in the expanded markets for exports that the détente policy might generate. Although Kissinger acknowledged that economic relations cannot be isolated from their political context, he maintained that the normalization of political relations would be accompanied by a similar process in the commercial sector. Accordingly, the United States negotiated parallel sets of political and economic agreements in the early 1970s. These included the settlement of the Soviet lend-lease debt outstanding since World War II; the extension on a reciprocal basis of "most favored nation" trade status to the Soviet Union; the development of various practical arrangements for the conduct of business with the Soviet Union by American industry, including making available the credit facilities of the U.S. government; and a maritime agreement for the transport of exports and imports. Such agreements were designed to provide the framework for a strengthened commercial relationship if and when the political context became more favorable.

As it turned out, the Nixon administration soon confronted international and domestic constraints that cast a lengthening shadow over its unfolding trade policy with the Soviet Union. The deteriorating political relationship of the mid-1970s, together with the efforts of Congress, spearheaded by Senator Jackson, to establish another form of linkage spelled the end of the Nixon administration's efforts to make trade a vital component of U.S.-Soviet relations. In the 1970s the idea of greatly increased trade, which held appeal for business interests in the United States (many of them the supporters of a Republican administration), became once again a mirage on the horizon that receded in direct proportion to the steps taken toward it. The clash of opposing interests within the Nixon administration became apparent in the efforts of the Departments of Agriculture and Commerce to resist linkage between trade and political behavior. In the summer of 1972 the United States sold to the Soviet Union large quantities of grain at bargain prices, the effect of which was an increase in food costs for American consumers. This was followed by the negotiation of an accord by which the United States agreed to sell grain to the Soviet Union on an annual basis. If the development of increased commercial relations with the Soviet Union enjoyed a natural domestic agricultural and business constituency, it confronted opponents in other segments of U.S. public opinion. In the final analysis, those who opposed increases in trade, except in exchange for political concessions that Moscow was unprepared to make, carried the day. Nevertheless, in the meantime, the Nixon administration did not succeed in establishing linkage policy that was adequately coordinated throughout the large bureaucracy of the U.S. government.

### Nixon's Opening to China

The other crucially important element in the triangular relationship of the Nixon Doctrine was the opening to China. In the 1960s the United States, in the Kennedy and Johnson administrations, had held informal talks with the People's Republic of China, principally through the Chinese Embassy in Warsaw. However, the Vietnam War and the Cultural Revolution in China had made impossible, or even undesirable, any concerted effort to alter the deeply rooted hostility that existed between China and the United States.

However, in keeping with the conception of the world implicit in the Nixon Doctrine, with national interests as the deciding factor in identifying threats, the United States embarked on a reassessment of its China policy. The deepening tensions between China and the Soviet Union, dramatically revealed in the Sino–Soviet border clashes along the Ussuri River in March 1969, contributed decisively to the changed circumstances that beckoned American policymakers toward Beijing in the opening years of the 1970s. By the time President Nixon visited China in February 1972, the Soviet Union had replaced the United States as the principal enemy of the PRC. Furthermore, the Nixon administration had sent unambiguous signals to the Soviet Union that the United States could not acquiesce in any effort that might be made by Moscow to destroy China's nascent nuclear-weapons capability. In keeping with the balance-of-power concept of the Nixon Doctrine, the United States regarded China as an "essential actor" in the emerging international system of several power centers—essential in the efforts of the United States to develop an effective counterpoise to the increasing military capabilities of the Soviet Union.

For China, the disengagement of American military power from Southeast Asia decreased whatever threat the United States might have posed and, by the same token, increased the Soviet Union's potential for becoming a power in the Asian Pacific. Under such circumstances, the development of a strategic relationship with the United States would serve the security interests of China. President Nixon's indication that U.S. interests could be served by the establishment of normal relations with China, followed by the American table-tennis team's visit to China (the first by any U.S. group since 1950), and the secret meetings in China between Kissinger and Premier Zhou Enlai, culminated in the surprise announcement on July 15, 1971, that Nixon would visit China and that, if circumstances permitted, the United States was prepared to establish full diplomatic relations with China.

This normalization process ultimately spanned three American presidencies, being concluded only in late 1978 by the Carter administration. President Nixon's visit provided the opportunity for lengthy discussions, the main purposes of which were to identify issues and areas of common or parallel interest, to discuss the numerous differences that separated the erstwhile adversaries, and to lay the basis for the building of a new relationship.

Paramount among the differences separating Beijing and Washington was the future of Taiwan, with which the United States in 1972 maintained a treaty of defense against Mainland China. Taiwan was regarded by Beijing as still a part of China. Because the Nationalist regime on Taiwan likewise considered Taiwan to be a part of China but regarded itself as the legal government of all China, the basis was laid for the reduction of differences over the future of Taiwan. On February 27, 1972, at the end of President Nixon's historic visit, the Shanghai Communiqué was released, in which the United States reaffirmed its defense commitment to Taiwan but agreed to remove gradually all its military forces from the island and to support the "peaceful settlement" of differences between Mainland China and Taiwan. Set in the broader strategic context of the interests of China and the United States, the Shanghai Communiqué stated the opposition of both signatories to the hegemony of any power in Asia, thus making a clear reference to the Soviet Union and reaffirming the basis for the emerging relationship between China and the United States.

## U.S. RELATIONSHIPS WITH THE ATLANTIC ALLIANCE AND JAPAN

Indispensable to the structure for peace envisioned in the Nixon Doctrine was the formation of closer trading partnerships by the United States with Japan and Western Europe, which by the end of the 1960s had become economic giants, even surpassing the American economy in certain indicators of production. What was termed a trilateral relationship had emerged among the three principal economic units of the non-Communist world. Especially as a result of the economic resurgence of Japan and of other states, especially in the Asian Pacific, it was no longer possible to consider the economic issues confronting industrialized states on a strictly transatlantic basis. Therefore, the United States, in the late twentieth century, confronted the need to supplement the existing security structure, which was based on the defensive actions of the post–World War II era, with broader concepts encompassing the major economic issues of a more complex and heterogeneous world. Although the Soviet Union had become a military superpower, there had been a diffusion of economic power such that Japan and Western Europe now constituted economic entities of growing importance. The question confronting the Nixon administration was the role that such allies might play in the hypothesized multipolar world of the late twentieth century. Japan and Western Europe might be expected gradually to assume a greater portion of the burden for their defense, thus enabling the United States to refocus its energies and resources in keeping with a changed consensus on domestic and foreign policy.

## Greater Independence within the Alliance

To a far greater extent than any of its predecessors, the Nixon administration was politically and philosophically attuned to the foreign-policy tenets and techniques employed by President Charles de Gaulle. Although the French quest for independence in defense had met with opposition in the United States less than a decade earlier, the Nixon administration acknowledged that the Gaullist approach, including the concept of a French national nuclear force, accorded with its own views of Alliance relationships based on greater independence on the part of member nations. Previous American administrations had supported a strengthened Common Market as the basis for an eventual European political entity that would be tightly knit, perhaps on federalist principles. In sharp contrast, the Nixon administration acknowledged, as de Gaulle had, that Western Europe was unlikely soon to develop a high degree of political integration. Whatever unity emerged would be based on cooperation among the existing nation-states—as in fact began to appear in the 1970s with increasing consultation and concentration of policy among the foreign ministries of members of the European Community. Coming to office within months of de Gaulle's resignation in June 1969. President Nixon had made France a major stop on his initial trip to Europe as president in February 1969. Like de Gaulle, Nixon practiced a form of diplomacy based on flexibility, in which tactical differences were exploited in accordance with classical balance-of-power principles. De Gaulle had preceded the United States in such approaches, especially to Eastern Europe and to China. De Gaulle had loosened France's links with NATO, had opposed American policy in Southeast Asia and the Middle East, and had acted independently with respect to the Soviet Union. Whatever may have been their perceived merits from a French perspective, these tactics had deepened transatlantic tensions in the 1960s.

The problem that confronted the Nixon administration in the early 1970s was the extent to which the United States could pursue diplomacy based on surprise, flexibility, and maneuverability—especially with the adversary against which the Atlantic Alliance had been formed—without incurring the suspicion and opposition of other Alliance members. In short, the Nixon administration confronted the dilemma of reconciling the pursuit of negotiations with the Soviet Union and the strengthening of partnerships with allies.

**Ostpolitik under Brandt**

The early 1970s was a period in which parallel efforts were made, on both sides of the Atlantic, to normalize relations with the Soviet Union. The Nixon administration undertook to increase contacts with Eastern European states. This effort included Nixon's visit to Romania in August 1969 (the first trip by an American president to a Communist state in Eastern Europe), a visit to Yugoslavia in 1970, and a brief stop in Warsaw en route home in 1972. The Ostpolitik launched by the Federal Republic of Germany, under Chancellor Willy Brandt in 1970, represented another aspect of the evolution of East–West relations anticipated in the Nixon Doctrine. The Brandt government had altered the Ostpolitik begun under the Christian Democratic Party governments of Erhard and Kiesinger, which had emphasized the development of closer links with Eastern European states other than the Soviet Union. The Brandt government made simultaneous approaches to the Soviet Union and to other Communist states. Bonn formally accepted the post–World War II frontiers of Eastern Europe as part of a broader economic and political normalization. In August 1970 the Federal Republic of Germany concluded a nonaggression treaty with the Soviet Union, with both parties pledging to "respect without restriction the territorial integrity of all states in Europe within their present frontiers." Thus the Federal Republic of Germany officially recognized the loss to Poland and the Soviet Union of German territory held before 1945. In December 1970, Brandt signed a treaty with Poland in which the Oder/Neisse line was recognized as the Polish–German frontier.

These treaties were followed by the Four Power Agreement of September 3, 1971, in which, for the first time, the United States, Britain, France, and the Soviet Union, as occupying powers retaining a presence in Berlin, formally agreed to permit Western access across territory of the German Democratic Republic to the encircled city. This agreement took effect after an accord was signed in December 1971 between the East and West German governments for the implementation of its provisions. It governed road traffic and telecommunications to and from West Berlin and granted access for West Berliners to East Berlin and to the German Democratic Republic. With this agreement, the contentious Berlin issue, which had twice given rise to international crises and had culminated in the building of the infamous Berlin Wall, had been resolved. In subsequent evaluations of East–West détente diplomacy, this agreement was among the most tangible benefits on the balance sheet of accomplishments and failures. With its aging population and declining industrial base, West Berlin received a new lease on life.

With the establishment of diplomatic relations between the Federal Republic of Germany and Poland, the Brandt government reached another agreement that gave formal recognition to the postwar territorial status quo in Europe. In December 1972 the Federal Republic signed an accord with the German Democratic Republic that normalized relations and achieved official international acceptance for the Soviet-sponsored East German regime. Such recognition had long been an objective of Moscow but until then had been resisted by successive West German governments and by the United States. With this normalization in what was termed a framework providing for "two German states within one German nation" came the admission of both Germanies to the United Nations in 1973 and the development of expanded intra-German trade, together with substantial increases in the 1970s of West German exports and loans to the Soviet Union and to other Eastern European states.

### The Helsinki Conference

The West German bilateral discussions for Ostpolitik provided the context for the Conference on Security and Cooperation in Europe (CSCE) in Helsinki, Finland, which represented yet another effort in the 1970s to provide a normalization of East–West relations. The Soviet Union had pressed for such a conference as a means of achieving an international acceptance of the postwar territorial and political status quo in Europe. Unless and until the Federal Republic of Germany was prepared to relinquish claims to lost territories, the CSCE was an idea whose time had not come. The accords signed by the Federal Republic between 1970 and 1972 constituted the prerequisites for the CSCE.

The Nixon administration attempted to give practical effect to the concept of linkage by making Soviet agreement to the convening of negotiations for "mutual and balanced force reductions" (MBFR) an essential condition for the CSCE conference. Although the idea of MBFR had first been endorsed at the NATO ministerial meeting held in Iceland in 1968, it was not until the Moscow summit conference of May 1972 that East–West agreement was reached to proceed with both sets of negotiations. Whatever hopes the United States may have entertained about linkage between CSCE and MBFR were unfulfilled, for the former negotiations moved along more rapidly than the latter.

The Helsinki Conference of August 1975, the largest meeting of heads of government since the Congress of Vienna in 1815, was not a peace conference, but instead symbolized multilateral acceptance of the postwar II boundaries of Europe. The signatories agreed that none would attempt to change existing frontiers by force. The CSCE provided a forum not only for the discussion of security but also for the consideration of economic and cultural issues. Western countries pressed the Soviet Union to sign a document that would contain a pledge to observe principles of human rights and to provide for the freer exchange of ideas, the movement of persons, and the increase of economic relations. The Helsinki Final Act, often called the Helsinki Accords, was signed in 1975 by 34 states, including all NATO and Warsaw Pact members, Spain, Switzerland, and Yugoslavia. Only Albania refused to sign.

The CSCE produced a series of agreements for exchanges and cooperation that lacked enforcement mechanisms. With the five-year review conferences—the first of which was convened in Belgrade and the second in Madrid—the CSCE had gained a forum for the discussion of the application of the principles contained in the Helsinki accord. Much of the discussion at such meetings was to focus upon Western allegations of Soviet human rights violations and efforts by the United States and its allies to secure a greater commitment from Moscow to cultural and human contacts.

In the early 1970s, the Nixon administration confronted domestic challenges to its alliance policies and, in particular, to the preservation of U.S. ground forces in Europe. While calling for the withdrawal of American military units from Southeast Asia, the administration staunchly resisted Congressional initiatives, led by Senator Mike Mansfield, to mandate reductions in troop strength committed to NATO by the United States. But for the vast array of Soviet-Warsaw Pact capabilities in Europe, the logic of the Nixon Doctrine concerning the provision of ground forces principally by the state whose security was endangered might have been considered applicable to Western Europe. In the absence of a unified West European political entity that could furnish a military counterpoise to Soviet-Warsaw Pact forces, the efforts of individual West European states could not be aggregated in integrated fashion. Therefore, an American military commitment, within the Atlantic Alliance, remained indispensable to the security of Western Europe. Could Western Europe be encouraged to build the necessary level of political unity and defense integration by the withdrawal, gradual or rapid, of U.S. forces deployed as part of NATO's forward defense? This question was still being asked in the early 1980s. Western European allies sought to keep U.S. forces committed in Europe as a tangible expression of the American security guarantee. The United States wished to have Western European allies shoulder a greater part of the burden of conventional defense. In turn, the Allies were reluctant to do so out of fear that a greater commitment on their part would only encourage U.S. force withdrawals. In the absence of an expressed willingness in Western Europe to do more for conventional defense, the case of those in the United States calling for American force reductions was strengthened. A transatlantic dialogue often took place in which neither side addressed adequately the concerns of the other or was prepared to take actions that would alter the prevailing defense commitments and contributions.

In this context, the MBFR negotiations were useful both to the Nixon administration and to the European NATO members. In 1971 the administration had narrowly defeated a resolution introduced by Senator Mansfield calling for U.S. troop withdrawals. Part of the administration's rationale was that unilateral U.S. force withdrawals would have jeopardized the prospect for negotiated reductions of both U.S. and Soviet forces that were called for in the MBFR concept. In this respect, Brezhnev's announcement in June 1971 that the Soviet Union might enter such negotiations strengthened the administration's case against unilateral reductions in U.S. forces stationed in Europe. If the MBFR could be used in negotiations between the executive branch and the U.S. Congress, it could also provide a vehicle for Western European allies both to seek to minimize U.S. force reductions and to ensure that, in any such cuts, both American and European NATO forces would be included in any agreement with members of the Warsaw Pact. If the United States was prepared to negotiate reductions in its forces stationed in Western Europe, the Allies reasoned, it would become necessary for them also to cut troop strength committed to NATO. Not unlike the United States, Western European governments faced domestic political and economic pressures for defense reductions. In this sense, MBFR was incompatible with U.S. efforts to obtain a more equitable sharing of transatlantic defense burdens, unless it resulted, as intended, in proportionate reductions in Soviet–Warsaw Pact forces—an objective that the negotiations clearly failed to attain. Instead, during the 1970s, Soviet–Warsaw Pact forces increased both in quality and in quantity, while NATO faced the prospect of reduced warning time (to as little as 48 hours) of a possible attack. However, the growth of Soviet–Warsaw Pact military forces occurred in the context of a political détente within Europe.

### Japan Begins to Come into Its Own

In the Japanese–American relationship the Nixon administration faced problems that in certain respects were similar to those of the Atlantic Alliance but in other ways differed substantially. If Japan was seen as an emerging power center in the Nixon Doctrine, the contribution of Japan to its own defense, in GNP percentage terms, lagged far behind that of NATO members in Europe. The prospects for substantial increases in Japanese defense spending were remote. Unlike the Federal Republic of Germany, whose rearmament effort had been undertaken in the multilateral framework of NATO, with the consent of the Allies, there was no comparable mechanism in the Asian Pacific whereby Japan, even if it had wished to do so, could have achieved the official support of its neighbors, many of whom, like Germany's neighbors, had been the victims of aggression in World War II. No domestic, regional, or international consensus existed on acceptable levels or types of defense forces that would have enabled Japan to undertake security burdens heretofore borne by the United States. But the United States could not realistically withdraw military capabilities from Northeast Asia as it might have been able to do in Western Europe. In the Republic of Korea the United States maintained only 40,000 military personnel, who, along with approximately 635,000 South Korean forces, guarded the Demilitarized Zone separating the two Koreas. In Japan and Okinawa the United States had stationed 72,000 troops, and in the Western Pacific the United States maintained a major maritime presence.

Instead of considering troop withdrawals, the administration needed to fashion a balance of power in the Asian Pacific that would help sustain the global configuration set forth in the Nixon Doctrine. Viewed in broad geostrategic perspective, Northeast Asia represented the point of intersection of three of the global power centers that the administration envisioned: China, the Soviet Union, and Japan. Nixon's opening to China had helped bring into existence a quadrilateral power relationship in the region, in which the Soviet Union might be balanced by China, Japan, and the United States. Depending on the magnitude of the Soviet military buildup in the years ahead, this emerging political configuration might be adequate to check the expansion of Soviet influence.

Japan faced the immediate dilemma of having patterned its own relations with China after those of the United States. The sudden American announcement on July 15, 1971, that President Nixon would visit China had caught the government of Prime Minister Kakuei Tanaka by surprise. Nevertheless, Japanese policy moved quickly in the wake of the U.S. decision, with Tanaka visiting China in the fall of 1972 in order to offer apologies for past Japanese aggression against China and to establish full diplomatic relations with the PRC. This diplomatic initiative coincided with the growth of Japanese interest in increased commercial relations with the Soviet Union, which, especially as the energy crisis of the 1970s loomed larger, included the exploitation of oil and natural gas reserves in Siberia, in which Japan sought to enlist U.S. participation as a partner.

The effect of the Nixon Doctrine, despite initial Japanese consternation, was to lessen the American tutelage over Japan that had been a legacy of World War II. Japan was even encouraged to develop a normalized relationship with China, which, in turn, would enhance somewhat Japan's flexibility with respect to the Soviet Union. A strengthened Sino–Japanese relationship, which did evolve after 1972, would presumably give added leverage to Tokyo in diplomacy toward Moscow, although not sufficient to obtain return of the Japanese Northern Territories seized at the end of World War II. At the same time, Japan retained the security relationship that had been forged with the United States since the early 1950s, which in the emerging East Asian security environment of the 1970s still furnished a defensive shield behind which Tokyo could maximize a diplomacy of flexibility with respect to Peking and Moscow. Japan also maintained the pace of its trade expansion and economic growth, until the energy crisis intervened to reduce growth rates to more modest proportions.

In the Japanese–American relationship of the early 1970s there were other manifestations of the end of Japan's subordinate status. The Nixon administration completed negotiations with Japan for the reversion of Okinawa, occupied by the United States since its seizure by U.S. forces during World War II. Under the terms for its return to Japanese sovereignty, which took place on May 15, 1972, the United States retained access to military bases in Okinawa. At the same time, the Nixon administration faced increasing domestic pressure, especially from the American textile industry (much of which was located in Southern states whose electoral support Nixon had obtained in 1968) to restrict Japanese exports to the United States. Well before the early 1970s, the booming Japanese economy had produced chronic balance-of-payments deficits with the United States. Japan's exports to the United States far exceeded U.S. exports to Japan. The textile issue proved to be a principal irritant in the Japanese–American relationship. It was not until October 15, 1971, that agreement was reached to restrict Japanese textile exports, with the United States threatening to invoke import quotas by executive order under the terms of the 1917 Trading with the Enemy Act. The United States was to face further problems with Japan and with other industrialized states with whom it shared strategic interests but was in economic competition.

## THE U.S. DISENGAGEMENT FROM VIETNAM

Like Eisenhower, President Nixon had come to office in the midst of an Asian war in which American military participation had become increasingly unpopular at home. During the 1968 presidential campaign, Nixon had pledged to end direct American involvement in the Vietnam War, but without specifying how this would be accomplished. The Guam formulation of the Nixon Doctrine applied to Southeast Asia, rather than to NATO-Europe. Between 1969 and 1972, the withdrawal of American ground forces that had begun in the final months of the Johnson administration was all but completed. For the Nixon administration, Vietnam assumed a significance that contrasted sharply from the outlook of its predecessor, which had viewed American participation as necessary for a bulwark against Chinese southward expansion. The deepening Sino–Soviet conflict, together with the new relationship that the Nixon administration was beginning to forge with China, removed this central premise of American participation in the Vietnam War.

What remained, however, was what Nixon administration spokesmen termed the need to achieve "peace with honor." For this purpose, it was essential that the American withdrawal be undertaken on terms that safeguarded the residual interests of the United States and its Vietnamese allies. It was feared that a too-rapid withdrawal of U.S. forces would cause the collapse of Nguyen Van Thieu's government in Saigon, undermining the credibility of the United States as a reliable ally in other parts of the world, jeopardizing détente with the Soviet Union, and weakening the administration's position in its reconciliation with China. Having already made great sacrifices both in military casualties and in economic resources, the United States would do everything possible to ensure the survival of non-Communist forces in Vietnam as American power was withdrawn.

Thus the twin concepts of prestige and power influenced greatly the timing and the methods by which the United States disengaged from Southeast Asia. The basic strategy employed by the administration was to negotiate a political settlement with, while applying direct military pressure against, North Vietnam and at the same time to strengthen the defensive capabilities of the Saigon government in order to achieve what was called "Vietnamization" of the war. Presumably, the forces that had been supported by the United States would be strong enough to withstand political and military pressures from their opponents after the U.S. withdrawal of ground forces had been completed. Presumably, the phased reduction in U.S. troop strength would erode public opposition to the Vietnam War in the United States. The dilemma facing the administration was to ensure that the withdrawal of U.S. forces coincided with the strengthening of South Vietnamese military capabilities. This goal eluded the architects of American policy in Vietnam.

The South Vietnamese were being asked to accomplish what the United States had failed to achieve with half a million military personnel. In a major test of Vietnamization, the South Vietnamese army failed to repel a North Vietnamese attack across the Demilitarized Zone in the spring of 1972, launched by massed conventional forces with heavy armor and tanks. Without the American ground forces, most of whom by this time had been withdrawn, South Vietnam lost its northern provinces and confronted the Nixon administration with another dilemma: whether the planned Moscow summit conference of May 1972 would have to be cancelled if the United States now escalated the war once again by air and naval action. Nixon correctly concluded that the United States could blockade and bomb North Vietnamese ports in order to slow the influx of arms because the opening to China had enhanced the incentive of the Soviet Union to meet with the United States. Moscow's interest was undoubtedly strengthened by the prospect that the summit conference would result in a SALT treaty, the effect of which would be to codify the Soviet Union's status as nuclear superpower under conditions of parity with the United States—clearly a major accomplishment after the Soviet humiliation in the Cuban missile crisis in October 1962.

The Vietnam strategy of the Nixon administration was clearly evident in the decision arrived at on April 30, 1970, to extend the war into neighboring Cambodia for six to eight weeks in order to destroy North Vietnamese military positions, especially along border areas, from which attacks had been launched against South Vietnam. This decision followed the overthrow of Cambodia's Prince Norodom Sihanouk and his replacement by a regime headed by a former protégé, Lon Nol, who was not prepared to accept North Vietnam's use of Cambodian territory as a military supply line into South Vietnam. The Cambodian incursion by South Vietnamese and U.S. forces unleashed a storm of domestic opposition that overshadowed the administration's announcement on April 20, 1970, that 150,000 U.S. soldiers would be withdrawn by the end of the spring of 1971, on top of the 50,000 that had been taken out of Vietnam over a four-month period ending in April 1970.

The risk that the administration faced was that its negotiating posture would be weakened by the progressive withdrawal of U.S. forces before the achievement of an acceptable political settlement, unless there was evidence that Vietnamization was succeeding. Henry Kissinger had undertaken a series of secret negotiations in Paris with North Vietnam beginning on February 20, 1970. During these meetings it had become clear that Hanoi was unwilling to end the war unless the United States withdrew support from the Thieu regime and unconditionally removed all American forces from Vietnam. Such terms remained unacceptable to the United States, although by the spring of 1972, when the stepped-up bombing and mining of North Vietnamese ports and harbors were undertaken, the Nixon administration had modified its position considerably. It offered a cease-fire in place, thus leaving North Vietnamese forces in South Vietnam, together with the withdrawal of all American forces within four months after hostilities ended. This U.S. proposal simply called for a political settlement among the various Vietnamese factions, with no specific reference to the survival of the Thieu government. The Nixon administration had compromised its position as far as it deemed possible under the circumstances, short of formally abandoning the Thieu government.

It was only the approaching presidential election of 1972, which Nixon was heavily favored to win, that apparently led Hanoi to modify its earlier terms for a settlement, perhaps in the belief that Nixon, reelected for a second term with an overwhelming mandate, would be less inclined to negotiate a settlement satisfactory to North Vietnam. The terms included total American force withdrawal within a two-month period after the beginning of a cease-fire to be internationally supervised, with an exchange of prisoners of war. The terms also left President Thieu in control of most of the country, including all military centers. Nevertheless, Thieu balked at the terms of the settlement, demanding that his government's authority over all of South Vietnam should be recognized and the 145,000 North Vietnamese troops withdrawn.

Although Thieu was unsuccessful in altering the terms of the settlement, the final agreement was not concluded until January 1973. The Paris peace accords ended only direct American military involvement, not the war itself, which dragged on after the departure of the last American combat forces. The United States had 57,000 dead and 100,000 injured in the Vietnam War.

Domestic political factors would continue to influence decisively the nature and level of U.S. support for South Vietnam in the years that remained before Thieu's regime finally collapsed in April 1975. The settlement that the Nixon administration had achieved was based on the assumption that the United States would continue to supply military aid to South Vietnam, just as the Soviet Union would do for Hanoi, and that South Vietnamese forces would be able to prevent any advance by hostile units into territory under Saigon's control. It was assumed, furthermore, that the United States would resume bombing missions over Vietnam in the event of a renewed North Vietnamese offensive. But the progressive embroilment of the Nixon administration in the Watergate affair, with the attendant weakening of the chief executive in foreign policy during what remained of Nixon's tenure, rendered impossible the continuation of American support for South Vietnam.

Whether the Thieu government could have provided the basis for an independent South Vietnam with the sustained levels of American support anticipated at the time of the Paris peace accords will never be known. In any event, the North Vietnamese had about 160,000 troops in South Vietnam in January 1973. In violation of the Paris agreement calling for no new units to be introduced into South Vietnam, North Vietnam sent in an additional 300,000 men, together with a large amount of modern equipment supplied for the most part by the Soviet Union. With these augmented capabilities, the North Vietnamese forces launched a series of offensives. In the midst of the Watergate crisis, which coincided with the period of national self-doubt and preoccupation with the limits of power occasioned by the Vietnam experience, Congress was in no mood to give continued support to direct, or even indirect, American involvement in Vietnam.

In November 1973 Congress had passed the War Powers Resolution as part of an effort to limit the president's ability to commit the United States to military action in the future. The president can authorize the use of military forces in an emergency without seeking a declaration of war from Congress, the War Powers Resolution stipulates, but he must inform the Congress immediately. After 60 days, the forces must be recalled unless Congress has authorized their continued use. Fearful of the resolution's effect on the ability of the executive branch to act effectively and decisively in foreign policy (it was enacted at the time of the crisis resulting from the October 1973 war in the Middle East), Nixon had vetoed it, only to have Congress override his veto. Thus the United States was legally unable to threaten to reintroduce forces into Vietnam for most of the period that intervened between the signing of the Paris peace accords and the collapse of South Vietnam in April 1975.

In 1974 Congress reduced U.S. military and economic aid to South Vietnam, and in early 1975 it signaled that all such assistance might be terminated. After becoming president on August 10, 1974, upon Nixon's resignation as a result of Watergate, Gerald Ford requested $1.4 billion in military aid for South Vietnam and Cambodia, of which $1 billion was authorized but only $700 million actually appropriated by Congress. Here, it should be recalled that Ford came to the White House not only as an unelected president but also without even having been elected to the vice-presidency. He had succeeded Spiro Agnew as vice-president in October 1973. Thus Ford lacked whatever mandate might have been available to an elected president. Although he enjoyed substantial goodwill as he became president, probably no amount of popular support would have been sufficient to enable him to surmount the Vietnam trauma of the mid-1970s. In April 1975 Ford asked Congress for $722 million in military assistance, together with $250 million in humanitarian and economic aid, to South Vietnam. By this time, however, no amount of American financial assistance, it seemed, could stem the tide. Ford's request was refused. Troops of the Khmer Rouge took control of Phnom Penh, the capital of Cambodia, on April 17. In Vietnam additional provinces had been lost by the end of March 1975 as the forces loyal to the Saigon government withdrew. It remained only for the United States to complete the evacuation of Americans remaining in South Vietnam, together with as many South Vietnamese refugees as possible, as Communist forces entered Saigon.

The aftermath of the Vietnam War was to include, by the late 1970s, a tightening Vietnamese alignment with the Soviet Union, to the dismay of the People's Republic of China, which nevertheless had supported North Vietnam in the war and which itself invaded North Vietnam briefly in early 1979 to "teach the Vietnamese a lesson." In the years that followed the Vietnam War, forces loyal to Hanoi would invade Cambodia, or Kampuchea as it was to be called. Persecuted by their new rulers, thousands of South Vietnamese "boat people" would take to the seas, hoping to find asylum in neighboring countries and creating yet another formidable and tragic refugee problem.

## THE MIDDLE EAST

It was the Middle East, rather than Vietnam, which seemed to the Nixon administration to present the greatest risk of confrontation between the super-powers. Peace in the Middle East was central to the global structure embodied in the Nixon Doctrine, but the deeply rooted conflict between Israel and its neighbors could be resolved only within a framework acceptable to the principal protagonists in the region. The prospects for a reduction of tension in the region did not seem promising, since successive American presidents since World War II had failed to make such a breakthrough.

### The United States Negotiates an Uneasy Cease-Fire

The Middle East was to be a major focus of Nixon and Kissinger's foreign policy. The administration confronted a situation in the Middle East in the early 1970s in which the protagonists did not even officially communicate directly with each other. The Soviet Union was deeply involved in the region, especially as a supplier of arms and other direct assistance to several states, notably Egypt, Syria, and Iraq. Between 1969 and early 1971, therefore, American diplomacy was based on an effort to engage the Soviet Union and other interested powers in the development of a comprehensive political solution. In this respect, U.S. policy had two distinctive phases.

First, the United States embarked on an active diplomacy that included Four Power discussions with other permanent members of the United Nations Security Council having an interest in the Middle East (Britain, France, and the Soviet Union), together with a series of bilateral talks with the Soviet Union in Washington. The Four Power discussions were designed to provide ideas about a settlement that might be useful to the efforts of the United Nations secretary general's special representative, Ambassador Gunnar Jarring. Since 1968, Jarring had been attempting to achieve a political settlement in accordance with Security Council Resolution 242 of November 22, 1967, calling for Israel's withdrawal from territories occupied during the Six-Day War of June 1967, in return for "secure and recognized boundaries free from threats or acts of force."

Second, beginning in mid-1970, the United States made an effort on its own to halt what by then was a spiraling level of violence and drift toward war in the Middle East by diplomatic pursuit, not of a comprehensive settlement—which seemed impossible under the circumstances—but of an interim agreement, which might furnish the necessary momentum for productive negotiations on remaining issues. The need for an interim agreement was heightened by the deteriorating political situation in the region and by the evident divergence of interests between the superpowers. Moscow's cooperation was vital to the achievement of a comprehensive settlement, but it was evident to the administration by mid-1970 that the Soviet Union was not prepared to assist in its attainment. The Soviet Union not only had shown no interest in the deescalation of tensions that was the prerequisite for such a settlement, but was actually engaged in a large-scale arms-supply effort in the region.

By 1970 a war of attrition was being waged along the Suez Canal, which separated Israeli and Egyptian forces. The Soviet Union had deployed in Egypt at least 80 surface-to-air missile installations and large numbers of personnel for their operation, together with several squadrons of combat aircraft with Soviet pilots. With several thousand advisers and technicians in Egypt, the Soviet Union seemed to be making every effort, as it had in the previous two decades, to exploit to its advantage the tragic political divisions between Israel and its neighbors. In the spring of 1969 the cease-fire that had existed between Egypt and Israel since the Six-Day War had broken down. Hostilities resumed between Egyptian and Israeli forces across the Suez Canal. This included exchanges of artillery fire by both sides and deep air strikes into Egypt by Israel's air force. At the same time, fedayeen (Palestinian guerrilla) attacks were launched against Israel from Jordan and Lebanon. Israeli reprisals followed, together with fighting on the Golan Heights between Israel and Syria.

For its part, the Nixon administration had come to office with a philosophical commitment to an "even-handed" Middle East policy, which meant that it would be less inclined than its predecessor to support the policies of Israel. On December 9, 1969, Secretary of State Rogers delivered a speech calling for "recognized political boundaries" that should "not reflect the weight of conquest and should be confined to insubstantial alterations required for mutual security." In the case of Egypt and Israel, this would mean the return of virtually all territory that Egypt had lost in the June 1967 war. Containing proposals that had been rejected by both sides, the Rogers Plan evoked opposition from the Arab states and from Israel. In early 1970, in another manifestation of even-handedness, the administration held in abeyance Israel's request for additional Phantom and Skyhawk jet fighters in the hope that the Soviet Union might exercise comparable restraint with Egypt.

The most important accomplishment of American diplomacy in this second phase of the Nixon administration's Middle East policy was the negotiation of a cease-fire between Egypt and Israel, which took effect on August 8, 1970. Conceivably, Nasser accepted the cease-fire because he feared another Israeli preemptive attack, or because it could offer a cover for the strengthening of Egyptian positions on the Suez Canal—which in fact the Soviet Union later attempted to accomplish. Although the cease-fire lasted until the October War of 1973, it was marred by Soviet-Egyptian violations of the provision that activities within the zone extending 50 kilometers to the east and west of the cease-fire line would be confined to the maintenance of existing installations, with the introduction of new installations prohibited. The deployment by the Soviet Union of numerous new sites for SA-2 and SA-3 ground-to-air missiles in violation of the agreement led the Nixon administration to seek a major supplemental appropriation for military assistance to Israel, as well as more modest arms aid to Lebanon and Jordan in order to maintain a military balance in the region.

The purpose of the cease-fire was not only to halt the deteriorating political and military situation but also to provide a basis for the negotiations for a settlement that the Nixon administration sought to achieve. In 1971 the United States pressed for a step-by-step approach that would begin with a limited withdrawal of Israeli forces and the reopening of the Suez Canal. This approach, pursued by Secretary of State Rogers during the summer and fall of 1971, foundered on the basic issue of the relationship between an interim agreement and an overall peace settlement. Other issues also constituted stumbling blocks: the scope of the withdrawal of Israel troops; the extent of the Egyptian presence in territory to be evacuated by Israel; the timing of Israel's use of the Suez Canal; and the duration of the cease-fire.

While the United States was engaged in an effort to achieve an interim, step-by-step deescalation, Ambassador Jarring was pursuing the idea of an overall peace settlement. Both approaches encountered insurmountable obstacles. Israel insisted that substantial changes in its pre-1967 borders were necessary in order to achieve secure frontiers, while Egypt maintained that it could not enter into peace negotiations, even for an interim agreement, unless Israel was prepared to withdraw to the boundaries existing before June 1967. Jordan, too, had accepted the principle of a peaceful settlement, but only if the West Bank was returned by Israel and Jordanian sovereignty was restored in Jerusalem. In the absence of tangible guarantees of its security, Israel was not prepared to give up the territorial zone of safety that it had acquired by war in 1967. Without such explicit assurances from Israel, Egypt was not willing to take steps that could be interpreted as a surrender of sovereignty over the territories occupied by Israel.

In the autumn of 1970, civil war had broken out in Jordan between the government of King Hussein and *fedayeen* guerrillas who were launching raids against Israel from Palestinian refugee camps. Although the Palestine Liberation Organization (PLO), founded in 1964 and claiming to represent Palestinian nationalism, had established its leadership in Beirut, Lebanon, it sought in 1970 to seize power in Jordan. In what came to be called "Black September," the PLO mounted its effort against Hussein. In 1972, moreover, the PLO had claimed responsibility for terrorist actions against Israeli athletes at the Munich Olympic Games, as well as the hijacking of three airplanes with hundreds of passengers to Jordan, and in 1973 the assassination of two American diplomats in Khartoum. King Hussein attacked PLO guerrilla units in his country, together with 17,000 Iraqi troops who had been occupying territory in eastern Jordan since the 1967 war. The presence of these forces posed a threat to the existence of Hussein's regime, the overthrow of which would have further destabilized the region. The crisis deepened with the intervention of Syrian armed forces. The United States augmented the Sixth Fleet in the Mediterranean, and Israel mobilized for a possible strike into Jordan and strengthened its forces on the Golan Heights as a threat to the Syrian flank. Syria withdrew its armed units from Jordan, and Hussein expelled from Jordanian territory the guerrilla units that had operated against Israel. By 1970, the Palestinians had become a quasi-independent force in Jordan and Lebanon. After its expulsion from Jordan, the PLO would continue its campaign for an independent Palestinian state from Lebanon.

Although Secretary of State Rogers was initially the principal administration policymaker on the Middle East, Kissinger eventually asserted his primacy here as elsewhere. Building upon the 1970 cease-fire, Kissinger promoted a step-by-step approach in which the easier issues would be resolved first and the more intractable problems, such as a Palestinian state, would be left for last. Of equal importance in the Kissinger framework was the demonstration that only the United States, not the Soviet Union, held the key to the achievement of the goals of the moderates in the region. Therefore, American policy was designed to demonstrate that neither the Arab radicals nor the Soviet Union could obtain the return of territory lost to Israel. Once this fact was clearly shown, Kissinger reasoned, the Arab moderates would abandon the Soviet Union for a closer association with the United States. At that moment, the United States could move decisively toward a diplomatic settlement.

After the death of Nasser on September 28, 1970, Anwar Sadat had come to power in Egypt. Sadat had failed to elicit from the Soviet Union the arms supply that he sought during his visit to Moscow in February 1972. The statement emanating from the May 1972 U.S.–Soviet conference to the effect that no more than minor border changes were possible in a Middle East settlement left Sadat feeling abandoned by the Soviet Union. In April 1972, moreover, a secret channel of communication had been opened between Washington and Cairo in the wake of Sadat's increasing dissatisfaction with the Soviet Union. On July 18, 1972, Sadat announced that he was expelling 4000 Soviet military advisers and 12,000 Soviet soldiers from Egypt, with all military equipment installed by the Soviet Union to become Egyptian property. Soviet personnel numbering 2000 remained.

### The October War

If the United States alone could help Sadat to recover lost territory, the expulsion of the Soviet military presence in itself contributed little toward the attainment of this objective. It was essential, Sadat may have reasoned, to launch an attack across the Suez Canal, if only to achieve strictly limited and temporary military gains that nevertheless would form the psychological basis for negotiations. Sadat chose, therefore, to attack Israel on October 6, 1973. This strike across the Suez Canal, coordinated with an attack by Syria in the Golan Heights, took Israel by surprise on its holiest of days, Yom Kippur, the Day of Atonement in the Jewish calendar.

At the June 1973 summit conference, Brezhnev had hinted at the possibility of a new Middle East war. In September, Soviet Foreign Minister Andrei Gromyko had delivered a similar warning to the White House. On October 3 the Soviet ambassador in Cairo, officially informed of the impending attack, evacuated his staff, together with units of the Soviet fleet in Alexandria and Port Said. Whether or not there was direct Soviet collusion, Moscow did not attempt to prevent the attack and moved rapidly to deliver huge amounts of arms to both Egypt and Syria. At the same time, the Soviet Union expressed support for the oil embargo announced by the Organization of Petroleum Exporting Countries (OPEC) against the United States. In response to large-scale Israeli losses of equipment during the opening phase of the war, the United States mounted a massive airlift to Israel. The Israelis drove back Syrian forces from the Golan Heights and crossed to the west bank of the Suez Canal, thus trapping on the east bank the Egyptian forces that had staged the assault against Israel.

Although Sadat had demonstrated the capability for temporary military gains, he would have faced ultimate defeat at Israeli hands but for the decision of the United States to press for a cease-fire and the eventual separation of forces. Although the Soviet Union threatened to send in military units and the United States placed its armed forces on worldwide alert, it was American diplomacy that brought the fighting to an end on terms that held promise of recovering lost territory for Egypt as part of an overall settlement with Israel. Cairo could see that the United States, not the Soviet Union, could produce a political settlement in the region. The Soviet Union had supported Egypt and Syria in a military confrontation in which they could not prevail.

The way was now open, Kissinger concluded, for the diplomatic effort that he had hoped for. At a crucial moment, the United States had chosen to pressure the Israelis to agree to a cease-fire and then to begin the slow process of disengagement of forces that would eventually provide the basis for the Camp

David Agreement of the Carter administration. Kissinger negotiated first a disengagement of forces in the Egyptian Sinai and on the Golan Heights. This was followed by an agreement for the withdrawal of Israeli military units from two strategic points in the Sinai. An early warning system operated by American technicians was established between Egyptian and Israeli forces. In 1976 Sadat denounced his 15-year treaty of friendship with the Soviet Union as Egypt's relationship with the United States grew warmer.

In its relationship with the Soviet Union, the Nixon administration confronted in stark reality the inherent limitations of détente. From Washington's perspective, the Soviet Union had clearly violated the principle of the U.S.–Soviet agreement signed at the Moscow summit that neither side would seek "unilateral advantage" in regional conflicts such as that in the Middle East. Increasingly, the Soviet Union placed its support behind the more militant foes of Israel in Syria and the PLO, while denouncing Kissinger's diplomatic efforts and the policies of Sadat's Egypt.

## ENERGY DEPENDENCE AND ALLIANCE ISSUES

As the October War unfolded, the United States faced simultaneously a five-fold increase in oil prices and an embargo on oil exports from OPEC. Although the effects of the embargo were short-lived, the raising of oil prices engendered an inflationary spiral that, in turn, led to the worst recession in industrialized, oil-importing states since the Great Depression of the 1930s. Oil-producing states found that they could use oil as a weapon in order to obtain from Western Europe and Japan foreign-policy positions compatible with their interests, while at the same time rapidly increasing their revenues from rising oil prices.

### The Impact of Rising Oil Prices on the Atlantic Alliance

In 1970 the United States, for the first time, had become a net importer of petroleum. The spectacular economic growth of Western Europe and Japan in the 1960s had been underwritten by the availability of cheap energy imports. Throughout the decade the cost of energy, in real terms, had declined relative to the prices of most other commodities. By 1973 Western Europe as a whole imported 70 percent of its energy from the Middle East. As its dependence on oil imports from the Persian Gulf increased, the West's influence on events in the region diminished. By the end of 1971 Britain had completed its military withdrawal from the Persian Gulf. Although the United States maintained close ties with major oil-producing states in the region, especially Saudi Arabia and Iran, the interests of leaders such as the Shah of Iran were not identical with those of the United States. Sharing a belief in the need for regional security and, in particular, for the exclusion of Soviet influence, these leaders foresaw tangible economic rewards that would result from higher oil prices (such as the ambitious and ill-fated modernization program of the Shah's Iran). What they faced, however, was the danger that oil revenues would bring not only the modernization desired by Western-educated elites but also a reaction in the form of

Islamic fundamentalism, which rejected the imposition of values and mores imported from the West and corrosive of Moslem traditions. From the perspective of the early 1970s, however, Iran represented one of the regional emerging power centers with which the United States shared security interests in the Persian Gulf.

The issue of energy dependence, in the context of the October War, had immediate implications for relations between the United States and its allies in Western Europe. It had been widely recognized that the military disparities between the superpowers, on the one hand, and Western Europe, on the other, were vast. But it appeared that Europe had emerged by the early 1970s as a powerful economic bloc increasingly in competition with the United States. The United States looked upon the European Economic Community with growing concern as American balance-of-payments deficits mounted. However, one effect of the Middle East crisis was to diminish greatly the economic basis on which a European center of power in a multipolar global structure for peace might eventually evolve. Europe's economic problems became manifest in the frenzied efforts of political leaders not only to work out bilateral deals with oil-producing states but also to accommodate to political pressures from the Arab world. Europe appeared to be neither a partner of the United States, as originally envisioned in the Nixon Doctrine and a decade earlier during the Kennedy administration, nor an emerging center of power, but rather a series of weak states attempting individually and collectively to work out whatever deals might be possible with the oil-producing states.*

In April 1973, Kissinger delivered his "Year of Europe" speech in New York in an effort to strengthen the transatlantic relationship, which had suffered under the rigors of the administration's triangular diplomacy. Even before the October War, Western European allies had responded to the "Year of Europe" idea with a mixture of confusion and suspicion, if not outright hostility. Kissinger's proposal for a new Atlantic declaration, as the basis for establishing a transatlantic consensus for the 1970s, was criticized for having been issued without adequate consultation with European allies. The year closed with the Alliance having confronted its most severe crisis since the formation of NATO in 1949. The United States and its major Western European allies engaged in a transatlantic verbal exchange unprecedented in the history of the Atlantic Alliance. This included reciprocal recriminations about the lack of consultation on Middle East issues, with Western Europe accusing the United States of taking an excessively pro-Israeli stance and the United States expressing displeasure with the lack of consultation by the European community in the formation of a "European" approach to the Middle East. According to Kissinger, Western Europe strove for an "identity" measured, it seemed, by the distance of the "European" policy from the United States. At the time of the Suez crisis of 1956, another example of the

---

*Japan was also heavily dependent on oil imports and far less able to cope with the energy crisis than the United States. Although not a formal member of the Western alliance, Japan was a major economic power dependent on the United States for security. From the 1973 energy crisis onward, the United States and its European partners had to start treating Japan, for all practical purposes, as a "Western industrial state."

inability of the Alliance to reach agreement on extra-Atlantic security issues, Britain and France had been aligned with Israel against Nasser's Egypt. Yet the growing dependence of Western European economies on Middle East oil had coincided with a shift from pro-Israeli to pro-Arab policies. The transatlantic divisions had been sufficiently deep that the United States encountered difficulties, and often outright opposition, from its European allies during the massive American airlift to resupply Israel during the October War.

In an effort to dampen Alliance tensions, the United States invited Britain, Canada, the Federal Republic of Germany, France, Italy, Japan, Norway, and the Netherlands to attend an energy conference in Washington. From the meeting came agreement on an energy-policy coordinating group composed of major consuming nations, which led to the formation of the International Energy Agency. This was clearly a victory for the United States, which had sought cooperative policy arrangements for energy conservation; for the allocation of oil supplies in times of emergency and severe shortages; for the accelerated development of energy sources in order to diversify supply; and for an increase in energy research and development programs through international collaborative efforts. In the aftermath of the October War and the energy crisis, moreover, relations between the United States and Western Europe improved as their Middle East policies became less divergent. The growth of American influence in the Arab world in the aftermath of the October War, symbolized by President Nixon's visit to Egypt, Saudi Arabia, and Syria in June 1974, together with Kissinger's "shuttle diplomacy" and the achievement of disengagement agreements between Israel and Egypt and between Israel and Syria, served the interests of Europe and other oil-importing states such as Japan at least as much as those of the United States.

### Upheaval in Portugal

In the first half of the 1970s, the United States confronted other problems in Europe as well. Although during the October War in 1973 Portugal had cooperated fully with the United States, permitting Lajes Air Base in the Azores to be used in the refueling of U.S. aircraft carrying military equipment to Israel, events in 1974 were to cast temporarily into doubt the future of the Portuguese relationship with NATO. In April 1974 a group of officers, radicalized by the guerrilla insurgency in the southwest African colony of Angola, ousted the authoritarian government that had ruled Portugal for more than half a century. Although by the late 1970s Portugal had emerged as a state with a multiparty system, governed first by a left-of-center anti-Communist regime, followed by a right-of-center coalition in the early 1980s, the prospect loomed that the Portuguese Communist party, backed by the Soviet Union, would come to power in the chaos of the mid-1970s. When the Communist party failed to attract more than 12.5 percent of the popular vote in a national election, Communists, together with radical officers, seized control of many of the instruments of power, including municipal governments, newspapers, trade unions, and even large tracts of land in the countryside. At the same time, Portugal undertook a rapid withdrawal from its vast overseas territories that resulted in polarization among rival tribal, regional, and political factions. The Soviet Union exploited the ensuing civil war in Angola. Moscow sent not only large amounts of military equipment but also military advisers and a Cuban force of more than 12,000 men to support the Popular Movement for the Liberation of Angola (MPLA), which was winning against forces sympathetic to the West, far less abundantly supplied by the United States and France. By 1975 the Ford administration, its foreign-policy prerogatives having been weakened in the aftermath of Watergate and Vietnam, faced with hostility in Congress toward the idea of American aid, was powerless to counter Moscow's massive assistance. In December 1975 the U.S. Senate voted to block any further American military aid to Angola. Although the Ford administration had no intention of sending U.S. ground forces to southern Africa, the effect of the Senate's action was to concede to the Soviet Union the right to aid local forces of its choice and to deny the United States the opportunity to protect its own interests in the area.

Both in Angola and in Portugal, the Soviet Union had taken full advantage of opportunities that had suddenly become available. Having established a potential bridgehead on the south Atlantic coast of Africa, the Soviet Union at the same time was intervening with funding and advice to the Communist party of Portugal, a member of the Atlantic Alliance. However, the anti-Communist Portuguese Socialist party, under the leadership of Mario Soares, with support from the ECC other social-democratic parties in Western Europe and the United States, was able to defeat the Communist bid for power and gradually to create the basis for a pluralistic political system.

### Communist Electoral Gains in Western Europe

Although the Portuguese Communist party was avowedly entirely pro-Soviet, Communist parties in France and Italy in the mid-1970s took steps to gain greater electoral acceptance on the basis of their supposed independence from the Soviet Union on certain categories of issues. Although such parties remained hierarchically centralized in their internal leadership, they sought to portray themselves as champions of freedom of speech, press, religion, and association and tolerant of a pluralistic political system. Especially as coalition partners in France and Italy, Communist parties hoped to come to power via the ballot box. In France's presidential election of 1974, the Communist party, in coalition with the Socialist party, had come within one percentage point of victory. In the Italian general election in June 1976, the Communist party increased its vote to 34.4 percent from 27.2 percent in 1974.

In sharp contrast to its approach to the Sino-Soviet relationship—seeking to exploit divisions between Beijing and Moscow—the Nixon/Ford administration attempted to forestall the entrance of what were called Euro-Communist parties into European governing coalitions by announcing in advance that such governments would be incompatible with political pluralism and with the democratic principles of the West. The Communist parties of Western Europe continued to rely on the Soviet Union for financial backing. However much they might quarrel with Moscow on certain issues, their accession to power would represent a grave weakening of the Atlantic Alliance. The Communist parties of Western Europe remained united in their goal to bring about the triumph of communism throughout Europe, to sever the political-military links between Western Europe and the United States, and to create economic systems basically incompatible with those of the West.

## THE THIRD WORLD IN STRATEGIC PERSPECTIVE
## DURING THE NIXON/FORD YEARS

Although American foreign policy in the first half of the 1970s had as its strategic focus the triangular relationship with China and the Soviet Union, as well as the security treaties and other understandings between allies, the Third World remained an important arena for action, both in economic affairs and in actual military confrontation. The problems with which American policymakers had to deal emanated not only from Southeast Asia and the Middle East but also from South Asia, Africa, and Latin America. The Nixon Doctrine, applied in Southeast Asia, held implications for American foreign policy elsewhere in the Third World. Although the administration foresaw a world of five major power centers, its structure for peace contained ample scope for lesser states within their respective regions. It was anticipated that regional powers, of which Iran represented one example, would become increasingly able to provide not only for their own defense but also for their own economic well-being. The diffusion of technology, for both military and civilian purposes, together with high levels of economic growth, would contribute to the evolution of an international structure containing a series of greater and lesser powers.

The Nixon Doctrine represented, in this sense, a response and an antidote to the perceived tendency of past administrations to seek to do too much with foreign aid. If it was not within the means of the United States to remake other societies in its own image, it nevertheless remained possible to support efforts undertaken principally by such societies themselves. American military and economic tutelage was to be replaced by a philosophy of self-reliance. While continuing to furnish economic aid at the governmental level, the Nixon/Ford administration placed increasing emphasis on the private sector. Reporting on U.S. economic policy in Africa in his last Report to Congress in May 1973, President Nixon had written:

> In the economic sphere, while the United States was able to maintain the level of its governmental assistance, the most promising sources of capital to finance African development were now trade and private investment. The means of American support for African development would thus necessarily be more diverse, and the first responsibility for mobilizing energies and resources would clearly rest on the Africans themselves.*

*Richard M. Nixon, *U.S. Foreign Policy for the 1970s: Shaping a Durable Peace.* A Report to the Congress, May 3, 1973, p. 153.

Compared to the Soviet Union, in strictly military terms, the ability of the United States to influence events in Africa, small to begin with, diminished as Soviet power, in the form of large quantities of military equipment and advisers, and Cuban and other proxy forces, grew, as we have seen in Angola.

Although the United States condemned the apartheid policies of South Africa, the Nixon/Ford administration was equally firm in rejecting the use of violence to effect change in the region. The United States continued to enforce an embargo on arms shipments to southern Africa, to condemn the racist regime of Ian Smith in Rhodesia, and to adhere to the United Nations program of economic sanctions. In keeping with its approach to foreign policy, however, the administration held that whatever changes might occur in southern Africa should be the result of actions taken by the peoples and states of the region, rather than pressure from outside.

## Another Soviet Threat in Cuba

In 1970 the United States found evidence that the Soviet Union was constructing a naval base at the Cuban port of Cienfuegos to accommodate submarines armed with nuclear ballistic missiles. This facility violated the U.S. interpretation of the 1962 Kennedy–Khrushchev understanding concerning the withdrawal of Soviet offensive missiles in exchange for U.S. assurances that it would not invade Cuba. At the same time tension was rising in the Middle East, especially in Jordan. To make matters worse, the United States detected a flotilla of Soviet ships en route to Cuba. The United States warned the Soviet Union that it would not tolerate any attempt to circumvent the agreement under which the Cuban missile crisis of 1962 had been ended. If the Soviet Union was testing American resolve, the U.S. response was sufficient to make Moscow back down and withdraw its naval units and to halt construction of the base itself.

## Election of a Marxist Government in Chile

If in Western Europe in the 1970s the prospect of the popular election of Marxist governments was remote, it was in the Western Hemisphere, in Chile, that such a possibility became a reality in September 1970. Salvador Allende, a Marxist committed to a radical transformation of Chile's economic and social structure and to violent revolution in the Western Hemisphere, was narrowly elected president. With 36.2 percent of the vote, contrasted with 62.7 percent divided between his two opponents, Allende came to power as a minority president.

Allende announced his intention to revise the Chilean Constitution and to place restrictions on opposition parties and the media. As a founder of the Organization of Latin American Solidarity, Allende called for armed struggle and revolution against the United States and its supporters in the hemisphere. Shortly after assuming power, Allende had granted amnesty to imprisoned members of the Movement of the Revolutionary Left (MIR), a terrorist organization dedicated to the use of violence to seize power, and had admitted to Chile several thousand persons thought to be members of militant groups in other Latin American countries and the core of a paramilitary force to be formed in Chile.

Allende quickly moved to seize control of Chile's private economic sector. Basic industries and foreign companies, including copper mines, were nationalized. Back taxes that often exceeded payments for nationalization were levied on such corporations. In 1971 Chile defaulted on most debts to overseas creditors, including the United States government and private financial institutions. Falling domestic productivity and governmentally mandated increases in wages produced a spiraling inflation which, by 1973, exceeded 350 percent per annum, with disastrous consequences for the Chilean middle class.

Preoccupied as it was with the more immediate issues of Vietnam and the Middle East, as well as the Cienfuego submarine base, the Nixon administration had given little attention to Chile or to the rest of Latin America in the last half of 1970. Nevertheless, in the preceding Chilean presidential election in 1964, and again in the congressional elections in 1968, the United States had made available substantial amounts of money in an effort to thwart the electoral ambitions of Allende and his supporters. In 1970 the efforts of the Nixon administration were less extensive, and far more belated, than had been the programs of its Democratic predecessors. This may have been attributed not only to the problems and crises that simultaneously faced the United States elsewhere, but also to the State Department's underestimation of the prospects for a three-way split that would bring Allende to power. Nevertheless, Nixon, no less than his predecessors, considered the accession to office of a Marxist government in Chile as a threat to U.S. interests in the hemisphere. The Soviet Union would now have a base for the stockpiling of weapons to be used in subversion against other states, especially Argentina, Bolivia, and Peru, with which Chile shares borders. Although Allende had financial and other support from Cuba, the United States had failed to give more than token "covert" support, said not to exceed several thousand dollars, to the democratic candidates in the 1970 election—far less than funds channeled to Chile from the United States in the 1964 election.

Although American policy, including alleged efforts to "destabilize" Chile, became the object of intense criticism, especially in Congress, in fact the United States did not play a decisive role in the events that led to Allende's assassination in September 1973. Although Allende had taken over American-owned companies, Chile nevertheless remained, on a per capita basis, among the largest recipients of foreign aid from the United States during Allende's rule. This included $16.8 million in the Food for Peace program, U.S. support for Inter-American Development Bank loans of $11.5 million to two Chilean universities, $42 million in military assistance, and the rescheduling of $250 million of Chile's overseas debt. During Allende's rule, Chile received $950 million in new credits from all sources, of which $600 million came from Communist countries.* During Allende's presidency, the United States had made available financial support totalling several million dollars for opposition political parties and media in Chile. This included funds for democratic parties in the March 1973 congres-

---

*Henry A. Kissinger, *White House Years* (Boston: Little, Brown, 1979), pp. 681–682.

sional elections. Just as the far greater sums that were received from Communist sources were not sufficient to stave off the coup that toppled Allende in September 1973, it should be remembered that in the 1970 presidential election, with far less American support to his opponents than in 1964, Allende came to power with a lower percentage of the total vote cast than he had received in 1964. In each instance, it was the internal dynamics of Chilean politics that proved decisive in effecting the changes that occurred. Nevertheless, the Nixon administration argued that its assistance to opposition groups was justified as a contribution to their survival during a difficult period.

Allende was followed by a military junta headed by Augusto Pinochet, which proceeded to destroy the cadres that had supported Allende and to take steps to reduce the rampant inflation and restore the Chilean economy. Because it did not restore freedoms enjoyed before 1970, the Pinochet regime, although less repressive than Allende's and not so stridently anti-American in its policies, was deprived of all aid by the U.S. Congress by 1976. This congressional action foreshadowed the approach to foreign policy of the Carter administration, and the recurrent theme of human rights standing in contrast to, and sometimes in conflict with, the geopolitical interests of the United States. In another sense, the United States seemed to hold rightist regimes to a higher standard of domestic political conduct than governments of the left.

### Secession of East Pakistan

Elsewhere in the Third World the Nixon administration attempted to create or to maintain a series of power balances as part of its global geopolitical perspective. In South Asia the United States had an alliance with Pakistan that dated from the Eisenhower administration, although its nonaligned adversary India had long enjoyed support in the United States. Upon partition in 1947, Pakistan had been established as a state containing most of the Moslem population of the Indian subcontinent, while India, with its predominantly Hindu composition, emerged as the dominant state both in territory and in numbers of people. Pakistan consisted of two Moslem territories separated by 1000 miles of Indian territory. By the end of the 1960s, demands for independence had arisen in East Pakistan. As secessionist pressures mounted in East Pakistan, accelerated by inadequate relief efforts in the wake of a devastating cyclone in November 1970, the West Pakistan government of Yahya Khan attempted unsuccessfully to impose military rule on the 75 million people of East Pakistan and arrested Sheikh Mujibur Rahman, leader of the East Pakistan independence movement, called the Awami League. In the weeks following the West Pakistani intervention, millions of refugees fled from East Pakistan to India and thousands of persons were killed.

At this point the Nixon administration faced a dilemma. It could not condone the repression being carried out by Pakistani military units. However, the United States at this time was using the Pakistan government as its communication channel to the PRC in arranging the opening to China that culminated in President Nixon's visit in February 1972. China had been informally aligned with Pakistan against India, with Beijing having gone to war with New Delhi in 1962 over border disputes.

The politics of the Indian subcontinent were further complicated by mounting tensions in 1971 between India and Pakistan, with Prime Minister Indira Gandhi publicly warning the government of Yahya Khan that Indian forces would take military action against Pakistan. The Soviet Union expressed support for Indian operations into East Pakistan and offered India protection against reprisals from China. On August 9, 1971, India ended its era of non-alignment by signing with the Soviet Union a twenty-year Treaty of Peace, Friendship, and Cooperation which followed the evolution of a closer relationship between the two countries during the 1960s. Thus the regional politics of the subcontinent and the global system had become closely linked, with the Soviet Union attempting both to exploit to its own ends the deeply rooted divisions between India and Pakistan and to demonstrate in advance of the Sino–American rapprochement that, together, China and the United States could not assist West Pakistan to retain control over its eastern territory. India invaded East Pakistan, and West Pakistan retaliated on December 3. This conflict raised the possibility that India, with its superior military forces, would turn on West Pakistan after completing the dismemberment of East Pakistan. If that happened, all of the Indian subcontinent would eventually be reunified under New Delhi's rule.

American policy was designed not to prevent the establishment of an independent state in East Pakistan, for this was seen in Washington as inevitable even without India's military intervention, but to prevent India from taking advantage of what seemed to be a historic opportunity to dismember West Pakistan as well. In 1971 the United States moved naval units to the Indian Ocean, pressed the Soviet Union to exercise restraint or place in jeopardy the planned 1972 summit meeting, and cut off economic aid to India—similar action having already been taken against Pakistan after its repression in the East. American policy "tilted" toward Pakistan in an effort to preserve what remained of a power balance on the Indian subcontinent, for the relationship with Pakistan was seen in broader geopolitical terms as ultimately related to the diplomatic bonds that the United States was forging with China and with the Soviet Union.

## THE NIXON DOCTRINE AND THE FAILURE OF "LINKAGE"

While the relationship between the United States and China was gradually and steadily strengthened, both by the Nixon administration and by its successors, the U.S. policy of seeking détente with the Soviet Union was short-lived. The confrontation with Moscow at the time of the October War, together with the Soviet propensity to exploit other issues to its own advantage, produced growing opposition in the United States to what was seen as a one-sided policy favoring the Soviet Union. In Nixon's second term a critique of the détente policy emerged that encompassed liberals and conservatives.

### The Liberal Critique

For liberal critics, the focus was the behavior of the Soviet regime in quelling dissidence and in preventing oppressed groups, especially Jews, from emigrating. The Nixon administration was accused of having paid too little attention to human-rights issues in its eagerness to build détente. In the absence of evidence that Moscow was prepared to ease domestic oppression, no basis could exist for a long-term, broadly based relationship between the United States and the Soviet Union. This critique embodied a long-standing normative element of American foreign policy that had been enshrined in the concepts of Wilsonian idealism—namely, that the prerequisite for a more peaceful world is the existence of states with representative governments. While the Soviet Union was hardly expected to transform itself into such a political system, the harassment of dissidents—including author Alexander Solzhenitsyn and physicist Andrei Sakharov, to mention only the most eminent (both were Nobel Prize winners)—was seen to be incompatible with a détente policy. The administration faced criticism for not having used détente to change the Soviet domestic political structure to conform more closely to the democratic values of the United States.

The Nixon administration had attempted to establish linkages among the major international issues in its relationship with the Soviet Union. By 1973–74, the administration faced mounting criticism for having failed to utilize linkage to gain concessions on issues of Soviet domestic policy. Nowhere was such opposition more manifest than in the effforts made in Congress to link East–West trade with Jewish emigration from the Soviet Union. The Soviet Union had greatly increased the numbers of persons permitted to leave—from 400 in 1968 to nearly 35,000 in 1973. Kissinger attributed to the quiet diplomatic efforts of the administration and to the general improvement in U.S.–Soviet relations at that time. In 1972 the United States concluded with the Soviet Union a trade agreement that provided for the settlement of World War II lend-lease debts to the United States in return for granting the Soviet Union status as a most favored nation (MFN). Before the trade agreement could be ratified by the Senate. Senator Jackson first pressed successfully for removal of the Soviet's newly imposed exit tax on emigrants and then introduced an amendment to link MFN status to an explicit Soviet commitment to increase Jewish emigration. Despite the Nixon administration's efforts to defeat the Jackson-Vanik Amendment, it was adopted in the House of Representatives on December 11, 1973, by an overwhelming vote of 319 to 80. The administration blamed this congressional inititive not only for the failure of its trade policy but also for the ensuing sharp reduction in the number of Jews permitted to emigrate from the Soviet Union, down to 12,000 in 1974.

### The Conservative Critique

The administration's détente policy also encountered opposition among conservative groups. Some saw efforts to negotiate agreements with Moscow as essentially fruitless, and some believed that the Soviet Union was utilizing the SALT process as a means of achieving strategic-military superiority. The Nixon administration had wanted to link SALT with Soviet geopolitical conduct. In fact, the United States had attempted to elicit from Moscow a commitment to restraint in the exploitation of tensions in the Third World at the Moscow summit conference of 1972, in return for the codification of superpower strategic parity, with the international prestige thereby conferred on the Soviet Union. When it became apparent that Moscow did not acknowledge any such linkage, a part of the political foundation for the SALT process had crumbled. Under conditions of an improving overall U.S.-Soviet relationship, it would have been easier for the United States to accept the deficiencies that it perceived in the SALT process.

By 1973–74, not only were such political conditions unfulfilled but the Soviet Union was developing four new missiles. These included the SS-17, with four warheads, and the SS-18, which could carry at least 10 MIRVed warheads. These missiles could be launched by a new technique called a "cold launch," being lifted from their silos before their rocket engines ignited, which meant their silos could be reused. By 1973 a third Soviet missile, the SS-19, had been tested; it could carry as many as six MIRVed warheads. With such a strategic arsenal, the Soviet Union, it began to be feared, would eventually be able to destroy, in a surprise attack, the fixed, land-based portion of the U.S. triad of strategic forces, notably the Minuteman.

The Soviet Union's deployment of such strategic forces made it more difficult for the United States to achieve the "strategic equivalence" stipulated by the Jackson Resolution of 1972, to which in principle the United States was committed in SALT II. By 1973 the United States had deployed 350 MIRVed Minuteman missiles out of a planned total of 550. (Each Minuteman III carries three MIRVed warheads.) At this time the Soviet Union had not yet begun to deploy its MIRVed systems. The United States proposed equal aggregates and a freeze on the MIRVing of all land-based missiles. Since the United States had planned to deploy only 600 more MIRVed warheads on its remaining 200 Minuteman III missiles, while the Soviet Union was building land-based launchers capable of carrying as many as 7000 warheads, the U.S. proposal was rejected by Moscow.

In the strategic environment of the 1970s, the United States found itself in a dilemma on strategic systems: to insist on equal aggregates would confer an advantage on the Soviet Union unless restrictions were placed on the number of MIRVed warheads. The levels of equal aggregates at which the United States could achieve Soviet agreement were higher than the United States had, or even wished to have, available in its own arsenal. Therefore, an agreement specifying equal aggregates in itself gave the Soviet Union a de facto superiority in numbers. Moreover, the larger size of its new systems, especially the SS-18, gave the Soviet Union the potential to deploy a larger number of MIRVed warheads than the United States. Even to reduce the number of launchers, however, without constraining their size and throw weight, would pose formidable problems for the United States. Thus the problem of strategic equivalence was immensely complicated by the fundamental asymmetries between the U.S. and Soviet strategic forces—and the problem was only to increase in complexity beyond SALT II and into the early 1980s. The key issue confronting the SALT negotiations in 1973–74 was the MIRV totals both sides would be permitted to have.

In an effort to achieve what he termed a "conceptual breakthrough" in Moscow in March 1974, Kissinger proposed two options: the first called for a temporary agreement restricting the deployment of MIRVs to an equal aggregate of missile throw weight for both the United States and the Soviet Union, with the interim agreement of 1972 to be extended for three years beyond its October 1977 expiration date. This option Brezhnev rejected. Kissinger then suggested that, in addition to extending the interim agreement, as in the first option, the United States would be allowed to deploy MIRVs on more missiles, while the Soviet Union could MIRV a larger total of its missile throw weight—in effect placing more MIRVed warheads on fewer larger missiles, while the United States placed fewer MIRVed warheads on a greater number of missiles, in keeping with the fundamental differences between the nuclear arsenals of the superpowers. This proposal, too, was rejected by the Soviet Union.

The MIRV-limitation issue remained unresolved at the end of the Moscow summit conference, held between June 25 and July 3, 1974. In this, the last such U.S.-Soviet meeting—with Nixon's power rapidly slipping away in the Watergate affair and his resignation only weeks away—the two sides agreed to abandon the quest for a permanent treaty in 1974 and instead to attempt to conclude an eight-year agreement to begin in 1977. It was left to the Ford administration, in the Vladivostok summit conference, to reach agreement on the basic framework for a SALT II treaty. The United States abandoned its attempt to include limitations on missile throw weight in the treaty. Each side would be permitted to deploy 2400 strategic launchers, of which 1320 could be MIRVed. The Soviet Union withdrew its demand that account be taken of U.S. NATO systems capable of striking Soviet territory or that British and French nuclear forces be counted as part of the Western total that Moscow could match. For its part, the United States accepted the principle of equal aggregates, even though the Soviet Union was deploying significantly larger systems, both in size and in numbers, within the agreed-upon aggregates. Strategic bombers were included in the 2400.

The development of a satisfactory formula for counting MIRV warheads in a SALT II accord had been given increased urgency as a result of the deployment by the Soviet Union of its first MIRVed missile in January 1975. After suggesting that MIRVed ICBMs be restricted to specified missile fields in the Soviet Union and the United States, respectively, the administration finally reached agreement with the Soviet Union on the verification issue in talks between Ford and Brezhnev during the final session of the Helsinki conference, held between July 30 and August 2, 1975. The agreement represented an acceptance by the Soviet Union of an earlier U.S. proposal that all strategic launchers capable of carrying MIRVed warheads be counted within the aggregate levels agreed upon at Vladivostok.

Far more difficult, however, were the twin issues of the cruise missile and the Backfire bomber. The United States had developed technologies for the eventual production of a cruise missile having counterforce-potential accuracy and an advanced propulsion system. The cruise missile could be deployed on a variety of launch platforms, including submarines and surface ships, as well as aircraft and land launchers. Flying at low altitudes, the cruise missile could evade enemy radar and other early warning systems. Flying at subsonic speeds (approximately 650 miles per hour), the cruise missile could not be considered a first-strike weapon because of the greater time, relative to a ballistic missile, that it would need to reach any designated target. If weapons having great potential for a first strike because of their speed and accuracy could be regarded by arms-control advocates as "destabilizing," then the cruise missile, with its subsonic speed, might stabilize the strategic balance as a weapon only for retaliatory strikes. Nevertheless, the cruise missile, because of the multiplicity of platforms from which it could be launched, presented its own verification problems. The United States pressed for the exclusion of the cruise missile from the Vladivostok aggregates, which, in the American view, applied only to ballistic missiles.

While seeking to include the cruise missile, the Soviet Union wished to omit from the SALT II strategic-force levels its new Backfire bomber, whose range clearly made it capable of striking targets in Western Europe and in East Asia, of landing in a third country such as Cuba, and even of delivering nuclear weapons against the United States itself. The Ford administration wanted the Backfire bomber to be counted as part of the Vladivostok aggregate strategic-force levels.

The result was U.S.–Soviet discord on both these issues. In January 1976 in Moscow, Secretary of State Kissinger attempted to resolve the disputes over the cruise missile and the Backfire by proposing limitations of 2500 kilometers on the range of cruise missiles, which would be counted within the 1320-MIRV ceiling, while the Soviet Union would be asked to place constraints on the forward deployment of the Backfire at bases that would give it maximum range and to make other assurances that the Backfire would not threaten the United States. Thus the Backfire augmented the Soviet Union's already vast nuclear capability targeted against states on its periphery. In this sense, the issue was no longer the NATO forward-based systems capable of hitting Soviet territory, but the growing capability possessed by the Soviet Union—first in the Backfire and then, by the late 1970s, in the SS-20 ballistic missile—against targets in Western Europe, China, and Japan. To argue, as the Soviet Union did, that the Backfire was configured principally for shorter-range missions rather than against the United States, and therefore should be excluded from SALT, was to heighten Western European suspicions that the security of the United States was divisible from that of the rest of the Atlantic Alliance. The cruise missile and Backfire issues remained unresolved during the remainder of the Ford administration. Although the SALT process continued, it was subjected to increasing criticism as domestic support for détente eroded.

## THE FOREIGN-POLICY DECISION-MAKING
## PROCESS UNDER NIXON AND FORD

Before becoming president, Nixon had promised to "restore the National Security Council to its preeminent role in national security planning." As vice-president during the Eisenhower administration, Nixon had observed and participated in a decision-making structure in which the National Security Council had served as a mechanism for producing policy positions to be presented for final presidential decision. Eisenhower had a strong secretary of state in John Foster Dulles, whose effectiveness was directly proportional to the confidence reposed in him by the president. Nevertheless, Eisenhower had developed within the White House a National Security Council structure that, if dominated by Dulles, nevertheless was based more on his close association with Eisenhower than on the fact that he was secretary of state.

## The Primacy of the National Security Council

Because Nixon sought to exercise close presidential control over the conduct of foreign policy and viewed with suspicion the entrenched bureaucracy, especially that of the Department of State, he moved swiftly to put into place a system that reflected his preference for a centralized decision-making process. Nixon modified the Eisenhower structure in three ways: (1) he enhanced the importance of policy options set forth in papers prepared for presidential decision; (2) he established a strong National Security Council staff both to integrate policy options for his final decision and to obtain from the various governmental departments and agencies the studies and memoranda needed for the analyses of policy options to be submitted for his decision; and (3) he created a series of interdepartmental committees headed by the national-security adviser.

The utilization of the National Security Council, with a professional staff reporting to the national-security adviser, represented for Nixon a realization that none of the existing departments could perform an equivalent function. The Department of State would be perceived by Defense as having an undue advantage if State were the chosen instrument for policy coordination and integration. With its own bureaucratic interests and perspectives, State would be both resented by the other departments and agencies and not fully trusted by the Nixon administration. Nixon insisted on having, not a series of options based on the preferred policies of each of the departments and agencies, nor an agreed-upon position constructed out of what he regarded as an empty bureaucratic consensus, but instead clearly developed alternatives on which presidential choices could be based. In his Report to Congress on American foreign policy issued in 1970, Nixon declared that he did "not believe that Presidential leadership consists merely in ratifying a consensus reached among departments and agencies." If foreign policy, in its substance, was to have coherence, it must be based on a decision-making structure that permitted orderly deliberation.

Because the Nixon administration attempted to evolve a foreign policy that substituted creativity and systematic planning for simply reacting to events as the basis for its "new structure for world peace," it needed to be able both to integrate present policy within a global strategic framework and to fashion long-range policy. The most pressing issues were not necessarily the most fundamental problems facing the United States. Therefore, the decision-making process must permit problems to be considered before they become crises. The administration would attempt to shape, rather than allow itself to be shaped by, issues and events. Hence an inextricable relationship was forged between the decision-making structure and the policies that would create and reinforce the various elements of the Nixon Doctrine.

In place of what were viewed as the flexibility and occasional disarray of the Johnson administration and the formality and somewhat rigid framework of the Eisenhower period, Nixon sought a decision-making process that combined the best elements of both. This included an organizational structure for systematic development of policy positions and a series of procedures that would bring the alternatives before the president without simply restating bureaucratic preferences. The result was the creation or reorganization of interdepartmental committees that could be instructed to study a particular foreign-policy issue. In the Nixon administration interdepartmental groups (IGs) replaced the interdepartmental review groups (IRGs) of the Johnson administration, although they continued to be chaired by assistant secretaries from the Department of State. The Senior Interdepartmental Group (SIG) that had been created by the Johnson administration in 1967, composed of the highest officials just below cabinet level—for example, the undersecretaries of state and defense—was disbanded. In place of the SIG, which had been chaired by the undersecretary of state, the Nixon administration created what was called the Undersecretaries Committee (USC), headed by the undersecretary of state. The crucial difference between the committee structure of the Nixon and Johnson administrations was that, under Nixon, the various committees reported to the Senior Review Group, chaired by Kissinger as national-security adviser. In short, the Senior Review Group, also consisting of the undersecretary of state, the deputy secretary of defense, the director of central intelligence, and the chairman of the Joint Chiefs of Staff, formally reviewed the studies prepared at lower levels and integrated by the National Security Council staff, and then presented them to the president for policy action.

In 1969 four other interagency committees were established, with Kissinger as chairman; by the end of Kissinger's term as national-security adviser a total of nine such committees had been formed. In addition to the USC and the Senior Review Group, they included the Washington Special Actions Group (WSAG), whose task was to develop contingency plans and policy during international crises such as those that preoccupied the administration in Southeast Asia and the Middle East; the Verification Panel, organized to perform "technical" analyses needed to develop options for the SALT talks, the MBFR negotiations, and other arms-control issues; the Vietnam Special Studies Working Group, whose charge was to bring together and analyze data about the Vietnam War, especially those factors directly related to the security implications of the various cease-fire proposals of the day; and the Defense Program Review Committee, whose purpose was to integrate the strategic, political, and economic dimensions of defense programs and to relate military needs to budgetary constraints and other national priorities. The other two interagency committees created during the Nixon administration were the International Energy Review Committee, established at the time of the energy crisis of 1973-74, and the Intelligence Committee, formed to set policy for the intelligence community, consisting principally of the Central Intelligence Agency, the National Security Agency, and the Defense Intelligence Agency.

### Kissinger's Dominance in the Decision-making Process

At the apex of the National Security Council structure, operating on behalf of, and reporting directly to, Nixon, was Kissinger as national-security adviser. The various IGs and departments received their assignments from the National Security Council in the White House in the form of national security study memoranda, or NSSMs, as a means of developing policy choices and assessing their implications for ultimate decisions at the highest level. An effort, not always successful, was made to produce clearly defined options based on rigorous analysis, rather than simply presenting the president with one plausible policy choice and two or more straw men not worthy of serious consideration. The position of national-security adviser was enhanced by the fact that studies produced in response to the NSSMs were submitted to the Senior Review Group headed by Kissinger. Kissinger had originally viewed himself more as a conceptualizer than as an operative, as a provider of creative ideas rather than a bureaucrat. Increasingly, however, by reason of his proximity and unlimited direct access to Nixon, he became the most influential presidential adviser in any administration since World War II. After Nixon appointed him secretary of state in August 1973, Kissinger kept his official position as national-security adviser until November 1975, when Ford relieved him of this latter job. During this period Kissinger retained direct control over the interdepartmental committee structure, which led to public criticism that the foreign-policy machinery was excessively concentrated in the hands of one person.

In the final analysis, Kissinger's dominance resulted not so much from the organizational arrangements as from the professional relationship that he managed to develop first with Nixon and later with Ford, whose foreign-policy knowledge and experience were less extensive than Nixon's. As secretary of state, Kissinger managed to dominate the White House National Security Council structure in somewhat the same way Dulles had. Kissinger's position was reinforced by his appointment as secretary of state, although his influence, like Dulles's, transcended the office that he held. The strength of the Nixon–Kissinger foreign-policy decision-making structure lay in its effort to develop an integrated approach to foreign policy based on an understanding of the relationship between longer-term and immediate issues.

Paradoxically, the concentration of power as a basis for integrated decision making had unintended negative effects. The pressure of events rendered difficult, if not impossible, the detached development within the National Security Council of longer-term policy options. Responses to the many NSSMs, filtered through the national-security adviser to the president, encountered the inevitable delays that result from limitations on time. Under such circumstances, the issue of the day received principal attention while other problems that were not necessarily pressing, but were nevertheless important, were neglected. Another effect, not always unintended, was the exclusion of key bureaucratic actors, including even Secretary of State Rogers, from important decisions such as the opening to China in 1972. If the decision-making process was highly centralized within the Nixon/Ford administration, it followed necessarily that problems of consultation with allies, a perennial area of divisiveness, would be exacerbated. Moreover, the concentration of power in the hands of one presidential adviser, while it enhanced his own standing, diminished that of his subordinates because they did not have direct access to the president; and Kissinger, given the many pressing demands on his time to serve immediate presidential policy needs, could not always have adequate levels of contact with National Security Council staff members whose own bureaucratic strength would have flowed from their perceived links with him. If Kissinger could speak effectively for the president, his subordinates could not equally claim to act directly on his behalf. The result was the attrition through resignation of a substantial part of the strong staff that Kissinger had assembled at the beginning of the Nixon administration.

Like its predecessors and successors, the Nixon/Ford administration represented an imperfect effort to achieve coherence and integration of perspective in foreign policy within a vast bureaucratic decision-making structure. If the administration did not find the optimal solution to this enduring problem, they nevertheless brought to an unprecedented level of development the White House structure provided by the National Security Council and combined with it the variables of personality in support of longer-term goals and immediate foreign-policy needs.

## THE NIXON/FORD ADMINISTRATION AND FOREIGN POLICY: A CRITIQUE

The late 1960s was a time of deep division within the United States in foreign policy. Even before the end of the Nixon/Ford administration, the limitations of the Nixon Doctrine, with its emphasis on a global structure for peace within which relations with the Soviet Union could be managed, had become apparent. The October War of 1973 had shown vividly the vulnerability of allies of the United States to international forces, notably energy price increases and supply interruptions over which they had no control. The implications were twofold. First, the basis for the Atlantic Alliance was eroded by conflicting interests as allies attempted to work out their own deals with energy-producing states to forestall anticipated shortfalls in supply. The Nixon Doctrine did not furnish a framework within which the United States could evolve with allies a collaborative relationship in issue areas outside the North Atlantic. Second, the efficacy of a global structure containing Western Europe and Japan as power centers was undermined by the patent weakness of allies faced with economic and political pressures from oil-producing states. Western Europe and Japan remained heavily dependent on the United States for their defense. The gap between the Nixon Doctrine's call for greater self-reliance and the actual capabilities of allies, relative to the Soviet Union, was no narrower at the end of the Nixon/Ford era than it had been in 1969.

At best, the concept embodied in the structure for peace was premature in the real world of the 1970s. Although economic power and military capabilities, especially at the conventional level, were being diffused to a large number of states (and even to nonstate elements), the international system still contained two superpowers far surpassing all other states in overall military capabilities. By the early 1970s the Soviet Union had achieved, for the first time, the strategic parity codified in the SALT I accords. At worst, the Nixon Doctrine was built on an illusion about both the structure of the international system and the capacity of the United States to transform its relationship with the Soviet Union from confrontation to negotiation, from the exploitation of opportunities for unilateral gain to the exercise of mutual restraint. Indispensable to the creation of a global structure for peace would have been the acceptance by *both* superpowers of a shared vision of the nature of that framework and the limits of actions that either state could take in support of its national objectives. As Kissinger himself wrote in *A World Restored*, the major achievement of the Congress of Vienna had been the restoration of a framework based on a balance of power in which disputes were focused not on the legitimacy of the structure itself, but rather on substantive issues.

However, so long as the Soviet leadership remained the captive of Marxist-Leninist ideology, the Soviet Union would continue to be committed to the creation of a world order fundamentally opposed to the principles that guided American statecraft in the Nixon Doctrine. To abandon Marxist-Leninist principles would be tantamount to casting away the mandate by which the Communist party of the Soviet Union retained its monopoly of power. Although the Soviet Union might conclude agreements for the sake of a tactical advantage, the Soviet leadership was explicit in pointing out that its ideological struggle with opposing political systems would continue undiminished.

Faced with such an adversary, the United States could not expect to use transfers of trade and technology as inducements. To have been able to bribe the Soviet leadership to alter its behavior with such blandishments would have represented a monumental achievement that would have been possible only in the absence of deeply rooted conceptions of Russian national interest and a Marxist-Leninist world view. In any event, the material inducements available to the United States could not begin to approximate the other values on which the foreign policy of the Soviet Union was based. In the early 1970s the Nixon Doctrine represented for the United States a basis for rebuilding a shattered domestic foreign-policy consensus in a changed world in which the administration strove to establish a framework for global stability. As Kissinger acknowledged, the task confronting the United States was to restrain the Soviet Union in what was termed the imperial phase of its history. Historically, Russia, of course, had been an imperial power, since the sixteenth century working to extend its control over contiguous lands, which then became the outer zone for further expansion across a vast portion of the Eurasian land mass. By the early 1970s the United States, in the Nixon Doctrine, saw the need to contain a Soviet Union whose military capabilities were growing at a time when those of the United States, in relative terms, were declining—and this at a time when the capacity and will of the United States to influence events in the Third World, increasingly the battleground for confrontation, had diminished. In the Nixon/Ford era the need for the United States to pursue limited objectives with limited means explicitly influenced foreign policy. The same could not be said for the Soviet Union. Under such circumstances, the basis for the formation of the global structure for peace envisioned in the Nixon Doctrine was fatally flawed.

# chapter 8

# The Carter Administration:
## World-order Politics Beyond Containment

During the presidential campaign of 1976, Democratic candidate Jimmy Carter criticized the Ford administration, and by inference the Nixon-Kissinger foreign policy, for its allegedly excessive preoccupation with East–West issues, and specifically with the security threat posed by the Soviet Union. In his first speech on foreign affairs after he became president, Carter expressed satisfaction that his administration had rejected "the inordinate fear of communism which once led us to embrace any dictator who joined us in that fear." Instead, Carter pointed to the emergence of a new world, which the United States could help to shape by a foreign policy based on "constant decency in its values and on optimism in our historical vision."

### CARTER'S FOCUS ON THE THIRD WORLD AND HUMAN RIGHTS

In Carter's view, the United States faced, in the remaining decades of the twentieth century, a series of problems whose focus and remedy lay outside the security relationship between Washington and Moscow. These included economic development, international trade and investment, energy, overpopulation, nuclear proliferation, international monetary systems, arms transfers, environmental damage, and—above all—the need to strengthen respect for human rights in countries around the world. The failure of the United States and other nations to cope satisfactorily with these problems would, it was feared, result in growing disorder that threatened to unleash conflicts whose effects ultimately might extend to war involving the United States and other nuclear powers. While the United States, as in years past, would find it necessary to manage its security relationship with the Soviet Union, the changed circumstances of the global system of the late twentieth century—the new world to which Carter referred—called for the development of a diplomacy for the management of change, with specific emphasis on the Third World. However complex the issues facing the United States in its relationship with the Soviet Union, the agenda of problems for the non-Communist world contained a larger number of issues, the finding of solutions to which represented what the Carter administration saw as the proper focus of American foreign policy.

Indispensable to the resolution of the great global issues of the late twentieth century, contended Carter and his followers, was the deepening of the trilateral relationship among the three great non-Communist industrial power centers: Japan, Western Europe, and the United States. Together, these powers encompassed the capital, human resources, technologies, and political-administrative skills that might enhance the prospects for a more humane world order. Having himself been a member of the Trilateral Commission, from whose ranks his administration had drawn many of its senior national-security personnel, Carter saw a need to engage the industrially advanced democracies in systematic efforts toward closer political cooperation and to create the basis for enhanced economic coordination in as many of the world's issue areas as possible. Therefore, the Carter administration envisioned collaborative arrangements with the industrialized allies of the United States as indispensable, in a world of enhanced social, political, and economic interdependence, to increase cooperation with Third World states.

Trilateralism was to be supplemented by other types of links with emerging Third World states, and especially with those entities which, by virtue of resource wealth or regional power, illustrated the transformation that was said to be sweeping the international system of the late twentieth century. The diffusion of capabilities—military, political, and economic—to such states, together with the growing urgency of issues associated with, and contributing to, greater global interdependence pointed to the need for new policy priorities and, reasoned the Carter administration, a more effective framework for cooperation. Henceforth, states such as Brazil, Nigeria, India, Venezuela, Saudi Arabia, Indonesia, and Iran would play a role of greater importance in their respective regions. In this sense, the Carter administration's approach differed from the Nixon-Kissinger diplomacy in attaching appreciably less emphasis to such states as part of a regional power balance while giving greater emphasis to economic issues and to the strengthening of human rights. Here the Carter administration faced an internal division that seemed never to have been fully resolved between an emphasis on national interest and a desire to enhance the prospects for human rights. The dilemma was to become acute at the time of the Iranian crisis, for the Shah had been seen in the Nixon/Ford administration as a surrogate for American power, although his government was criticized for its abridgement of human rights. Differences within the Carter administration focused principally on the disputes that erupted from time to time between Secretary of State Cyrus Vance and National Security Adviser Zbigniew Brzezinski. To a greater extent than Vance, or even Carter himself, Brzezinski, with increasing support from

Secretary of Defense Harold Brown, pressed for the restoration of American military capabilities as a prerequisite for the achievement of the humane goals cherished by Carter.

If American foreign relations just before Carter were alleged to have been too narrowly rooted in a U.S.–Soviet geopolitical struggle, Carter sought to base his administration's policy on a greater empathy for the aspirations of Third World peoples. Specifically, the Carter administration saw the need for a more explicit American condemnation of the apartheid policies of South Africa and for a more rapid transition to black majority rule in southern Africa. As the United States achieved a closer identification of its policies with the goals of Third World peoples, reasoned the Carter administration, hostility toward the United States and the appeal of the Soviet Union would be diminished. Because such an emphasis accorded with basic American values, it held the prospect of helping to restore the consensus that any administration needed in sustaining support for an adequate conception of national security.

In the mid-1970s, the scars of Vietnam and Watergate remained on the American body politic. Their effect had been both to lower drastically the confidence of Americans in their elected leaders, specifically in the president, and to circumscribe the president's latitude in the formulation and conduct of foreign policy. These factors, together with an historic propensity to prefer openness to secrecy in foreign policy, had resulted in increased congressional oversight in the decision-making process. In part because Nixon and Kissinger had been remarkably successful, given the political environment engendered by Vietnam, in maintaining secrecy in the formulation of foreign policy, Carter had pledged an "open" administration.

No less than in his emphasis on Third World issues and human rights, Carter attempted at the outset of his administration to make use of the policy process itself as a consensus-building device. In calling for "world order politics," which he contrasted with the geopolitical, balance-of-power preoccupations of the recent past, Carter sought to appeal to the American idealistic tradition as a means of building public support. Thus an emphasis on human rights accorded both with Carter's own deeply held religious views and with his apparent conception of what would be necessary in the prevailing circumstances for the formulation of a consistent foreign policy.* An emphasis on the application of human-rights standards to friendly and hostile states flowed logically from the Wilsonian principle of the universal applicability of democracy.

This is not to suggest that the Carter administration, any more than Woodrow Wilson, did not recognize that, even under the best of circumstances, the gap between the ideal world and present reality would remain substantial.

---

*The human rights violations, a pattern of which rendered foreign governments ineligible for U.S. economic aid, included the following: suppressing opposition parties; assassinating opponents; muzzling the media; abolishing or rigging elections; persecuting or grossly discriminating against religious, ethnic, linguistic, or other groups; arbitrarily arresting dissidents and subjecting them to punishment without a fair trial; detaining or imprisoning people for extended periods without bringing charges against them or informing their families of their whereabouts; employing terroristic methods of rule; and otherwise depriving persons of those political and civil liberties which Western democratic societies take for granted.

Nevertheless, in pressing for the observance of human rights, the Carter administration would link its foreign policy to ideals that had been closely identified with the Founding Fathers, who had enshrined them and given them universality of potential application, in the Declaration of Independence and the Constitution. A world in which the prospects for the freedom that was basic to human rights could flourish would accord with the most fundamental aspirations of millions of people around the world, whose interests would then be closely identified with those of the United States. In keeping with the political ideals of Woodrow Wilson, a global system with states having governments founded on principles that accorded with American democratic values would be more stable than a world containing authoritarian or totalitarian states. The human-rights focus of American foreign policy thus had a basis for the Carter administration both in political pragmatism and in historical principles and basic values.

However, the world beyond the borders of the United States and of its politically pluralistic allies provided little prospect for the realization of the human-rights standards espoused by the Carter administration. Instead, fundamentally different historical circumstances and conceptions of relations between ruling elites and the governed, together with the nature of perceived national interests and resulting security needs, shaped the environment in which the Carter administration, like its predecessors, had to conduct foreign policy. Inevitably, there would be a fine line between helpful prodding of oppressive regimes toward greater respect for human rights and pressures against other governments that might either result in their downfall (as may have happened in Iran and Nicaragua) or lead to a backlash in the form of even greater domestic repression (as seems to have been one of the effects in the case of the Soviet Union). What was deemed to be necessary in the process of consensus formation within the United States for the conduct of foreign policy ran counter to the prevailing political and social structures of a large number of other states.

## THE U.S.-SOVIET RELATIONSHIP IN THE LATE 1970s

Although the Carter administration attempted to devise a broader focus for American foreign policy beyond containment, the relationship with Moscow remained, of necessity, a principal preoccupation for two reasons. First, the administration needed to reduce the competitive aspects of the U.S.–Soviet relationship if the United States was to focus its energies on the global issues of the late twentieth century. Specifically, this meant the achievement of an arms-control agreement with the Soviet Union in the form of a SALT II treaty and the conclusion of other arms-control accords, notably the Comprehensive Test Ban Treaty and progress in the negotiations for mutual and balanced force reduction (MBFR) to limit levels of Soviet–Warsaw Pact and NATO forces in Europe. Second, the administration confronted a Soviet foreign policy that was backed by increasing armaments and that saw Moscow showing a greater propensity in the late 1970s to project its power and influence into regions as remote as Vietnam, Ethiopia, southern Africa, and Central America, as well as to Afghanistan, with which the Soviet Union shares a frontier. In its quest for an arms-control agreement with the Soviet Union, the Carter administration had no greater success than its predecessors in restraining Moscow's military buildup. At the same time, the Carter administration evoked from the Soviet Union the accusation that the American human-rights policy was designed to undermine the Soviet political system. Whereas Ford had refused to receive Alexander Solzhenitzyn at the White House for fear of endangering the SALT II negotiations, Carter went so far as to write to Andrei Sakharov, a leading Soviet dissident who had played a major role in the development of the Soviet hydrogen bomb. Carter sought not only to press the Soviet Union toward observance of human rights, but also to achieve with Moscow an arms-control agreement that went substantially beyond the SALT II treaty under negotiation by the Ford administration. In both contexts, the achievement fell far short of initial expectations.

The Carter administration had inherited SALT II treaty negotiations that had produced agreement on all the most important issues except the contentious questions of whether the Soviet Backfire bomber should be included in strict SALT limitations, and of what range limitations should be placed on the cruise missiles that the United States would deploy in the early 1980s. After its initial review of the SALT II treaty, the Carter administration had decided to attempt to move substantially beyond the final negotiating position of Ford and Kissinger. Carter himself held to a conception of nuclear deterrence based on considerably lower numbers of strategic nuclear launchers than existed in the arsenals of either the United States or the Soviet Union. In briefings with the Joint Chiefs of Staff before his inauguration, for example, Carter had asked whether nuclear deterrence could be sustained if both superpowers cut their numbers of launchers to 200 each.

In March 1977 Secretary of State Vance took to Moscow two American SALT proposals. The first "preferred option," as it was called, provided for reductions in total strategic force levels from the 2400 launchers and 1320 MIRVed systems established at Vladivostok in 1974 to an aggregate of 1800 to 2000 launchers and 1100 to 1200 MIRVed systems, with a range limitation of 2500 kilometers for the cruise missile. The second "comprehensive proposal," as it was termed, also provided for a reduction in heavy missiles, possessed only by the Soviet Union, from the 308 agreed on at Vladivostok to a total not to exceed 150. The American proposal contained a prohibition on the building of any new ICBMs, which would have precluded the deployment by the United States of the MX (a mobile missile to be deployed in a multiple-basing mode so that it could be shuttled around to escape precise targeting in a first strike,) even though the Soviet Union by 1977 had deployed three new classes of ICBMs, while the last American Minuteman launcher had been deployed a decade earlier.

In calling for deep cuts in strategic forces, the administration was responding not only to Carter's own penchant for lower numbers of systems, but also to the need to place restrictions on Soviet heavy ICBMs, especially the SS-18s, which posed an increasing threat to the fixed, land-based Minuteman ICBM, as a result of the accuracy of and large number of warheads deployed on the Soviet systems. Analysts of the strategic-nuclear balance and arms control, such as Senator Henry Jackson, concerned about the growth of Soviet forces, favored deep cuts principally as a means of reducing the threat posed by Soviet heavy systems, which seemed to have no other purpose than to furnish a surprise first-strike capability against the United States strategic forces, notably its land-based missiles. In fact, Jackson had sent Carter a memorandum stating his opposition to the Vladivostok aggregates and calling for deep cuts, especially in heavy missiles. If arms-control agreements could not constrain this emerging Soviet threat, it was doubtful what useful purpose they could serve. To those committed to arms control as a manifestation of substantially lower levels of forces, in this case Carter himself, the deep cuts proposal held attraction. Thus the Carter administration's preferred option had the merit of uniting, momentarily at least, a broad spectrum of thought, from those whose principal concern was the impending threat to American ICBM survivability posed by the Soviet nuclear buildup to those committed to arms control as a process whereby reductions in superpower nuclear capabilities could be obtained.

The question of what sufficed, or was indispensable, for American domestic consensus on arms control, somewhat analogous to the human-rights problem already discussed, was debated in a sharply different international context. The Soviet Union quickly rejected both the comprehensive, or deep-cuts, proposal and a second U.S. proposal that accepted the Vladivostok ceilings and deferred the cruise missile and Backfire issues. The Soviet Union sought to retain its advantages in land-based systems, including heavy missiles, while drastically restricting the options available to the Carter administration for the deployment of cruise missiles, in which Soviet technology in propulsion and guidance systems lagged behind that of the United States. In subsequent years the opponents of the SALT II treaty were frequently to point to the deep-cuts proposal as an appropriate standard against which to judge the SALT II treaty that eventually emerged from the negotiations. They would also criticize the Carter administration for having cancelled the B-1 bomber in June 1977 without having gained any concession from the Soviet Union in the SALT II negotiations. The argument used by the Carter administration against the B-1 was that the B-52, armed with the cruise missiles shortly to be deployed, could perform the strategic missions of the bomber leg of the U.S. strategic triad at substantially lower cost than the B-1. Critics of the Carter administration contended that not only had the United States gained nothing from the Soviet Union in the form of concessions in SALT, but that the aging B-52 was older than most of the pilots who flew it. The Carter administration eventually sought to soften the impact of the B-1 cancellation by revealing during the 1980 presidential campaign the technological feasibility of developing, before the end of the century, an advanced-technology "stealth" bomber that could penetrate highly sophisticated Soviet air defenses at low risk of being detected.

Faced with obdurate Soviet opposition, the Carter administration eventually revised its position that the Soviet Union cut sharply its heavy ICBM systems in return for a subceiling by the United States on heavy bombers carrying air-launched cruise missiles (ALCMs). Rejecting the U.S. effort to link these issues, the Soviet Union maintained—successfully, it turned out—that the Ford administration had agreed to count the ALCM-carrying bombers in the 1320

MIRV total. The final SALT II treaty permitted the Soviet Union to deploy all the proposed 308 SS-18 launchers, each of which could carry as many as ten warheads, while the United States was obligated to count each heavy bomber with cruise missiles as part of its 1320 MIRV aggregate. In late 1977, moreover, U.S. and Soviet negotiators reached agreement on a subceiling of 820 on deployments of MIRVed ICBM launchers, substantially more than the 550 figure set forth in the March 1977 American comprehensive proposal. A compromise was also reached reducing the overall Vladivostok ceiling of 2400 to 2250. Thus by the end of 1977 the United States and the Soviet Union had reached agreement on all but a few issues: cruise-missile range limitations, permissible new types of inter-continental missiles, restrictions on the improvement of existing missiles, and the encoding of telemetry of tests of Soviet missiles—the latter an issue of importance because the United States relied on techniques that it had developed to monitor radio signals emitted by Soviet missiles during testing as a means of verifying compliance with arms-control agreements. Last but not least, until the SALT II treaty was concluded to replace it, both sides would continue to observe the SALT I Interim Agreement on Offensive Systems, which had been scheduled to expire on October 3, 1977, until a new accord could be concluded.

## REGIONAL TURBULENCE IN AFRICA

If the Carter administration sought to focus American foreign policy on the global issues of the Third World, which supposedly transcended the U.S.–Soviet rela-tionship, it was the transfer of the superpower competition to such geographically remote regions as Africa and Southeast Asia that contributed to a further political deterioration between Washington and Moscow in the second half of the 1970s. At the beginning of his administration, Carter believed that an East–West geopolitical security relationship between the United States and the Soviet Union could be separated from the broader global North–South context. The Soviet Union would either exclude itself from the global agenda developed by the Carter administration or, better yet, might somehow find it advantageous to involve itself constructively in such issues. The Carter administration set out consciously to differentiate its approach to Soviet–American relations from that of the Nixon/Ford administration. The SALT II treaty was viewed as a desirable objective in itself without explicit linkage to other issues. Perhaps because the United States, in association with other non-Communist industrialized states, held the key to the emerging global agenda, a policy of linkage with the Soviet Union was considered by the Carter administration to be unnecessary. Nevertheless, in the late 1970s the Soviet Union stepped up a policy designed to inject its presence and influence into unstable Third World states from Southeast Asia to southern Africa. Although it operated on substantially different premises, the Carter administration was no more successful than its immediate predecessors in foreclosing the Soviet Union's options in the Third World.

In the final analysis, Soviet political-military expansionism, which included the use of Cuban surrogates and culminated in the Soviet invasion of Afghanistan in 1979, had a kind of reverse linkage. Whereas the Nixon-Ford-Kissinger foreign policy sought Soviet compliance with principles of coexistence in the Third World with SALT as an incentive, the Carter administration, having rejected such linkage, found Moscow's behavior in Afghanistan and Africa as fatal impediments to U.S. Senate ratification of the SALT II treaty. In retrospect, as Zbigniew Brzezinski declared, "SALT lies buried in the sands of Ogaden."

### The Horn: Ethiopia and Somalia Dispute the Ogaden Territory

Shortly after it assumed office, the Carter administration faced a challenge to its conception of relations with the Soviet Union as a result of shifting Soviet-Cuban alignments in the Horn of Africa. For several years Somalia had allowed the Soviet Union to use the port facility at Berbera, located on the strategically important Gulf of Aden athwart the maritime passage between the Indian Ocean and the Red Sea leading to the Suez Canal, in return for Soviet supplies of weapons. Somalia used such Soviet assistance in the irredentist war being waged against Ethiopia by pro-Somali forces in the Ogaden territory. By the middle of 1977, however, the Soviet Union had shifted sides to support Ethiopia, which was engaged in a struggle to defeat the secessionist movement in the Ogaden. The realignment of the Soviet Union appears to have been motivated by a calculation that Ethiopia, because of a larger population, its geographic location on the Red Sea, and its anti-American Marxist government headed by President Mengistu Haile Mariam, had more to offer Moscow than Somalia.

The broader geopolitical significance of the Soviet presence in the Horn of Africa stemmed from the proximity of the region to the Arabian Peninsula and, specifically, to oil-rich Saudi Arabia. With the establishment of a Soviet-sponsored regime in South Yemen, just across the Red Sea from Ethiopia, the Soviet Union appeared to some, though by no means all, in the Carter administration to be positioning itself for the eventual domination of oil supplies on which the United States and its industrialized allies were dependent.

The Carter administration faced a dilemma: it did not want to be seen as supporting a Somali invasion of the Ogaden, which legally was the territory of Ethiopia. At the same time, the extension of Soviet influence in the region, with Ethiopia as its spearhead, was contrary to American interests. As the Soviet involvement with Ethiopia quickened with the signing of two arms agreements and the deployment of Cuban forces on behalf of Moscow's interests, the Somali government sought to enlist the United States to replace the Soviet Union as its supplier of weapons. By January 1978 several thousand Cuban mercenaries had been sent to Ethiopia to repel the Somali invasion of the Ogaden. The response of the Carter administration was to limit American military aid to Somalia while seeking the withdrawal of all foreign forces and mediation of the conflict by other African states.

Within itself the Carter administration faced fundamental differences: was the Soviet Union merely exploiting to its advantage a local conflict, with Moscow's presence likely to diminish after the war over the Ogaden ended? Or was the Soviet Union attempting to establish a permanent presence on both sides of the Red Sea—in South Yemen and Ethiopia? Vance saw the conflict as essentially a local matter, while Brzezinski viewed the Soviet-Cuban involvement as part of a broader geostrategic ploy by Moscow to gain direct access to the Persian Gulf. The leverage available to the administration in the Horn of Africa itself was severely limited, for the United States had maintained a self-imposed restraint in arms assistance to Somalia, while the Soviet Union had become deeply committed to Ethiopia. The U.S. leverage over Somalia to force a withdrawal from the Ogaden was not great; hence little could be done to induce Soviet-Cuban restraint in Ethiopia. This left principally the question of linkage between the Horn of Africa and the broader U.S.–Soviet relationship. Since the administration was committed to SALT as a process considered to be valuable on its own merits without direct reference to other dimensions of Washington's relationship to Moscow, it was not possible to exploit linkage between super-power arms-control agreements and such Third World security issues as the Ethiopian–Somali war. Nevertheless, the increasing Soviet-Cuban presence in Ethiopia cast a lengthening shadow over the U.S.–Soviet relationship, for it was accompanied by other manifestations of Moscow's heightened propensity in the late 1970s to exploit Third World turbulence and to project military power into geographically remote states.

### Central Africa: Insurgency in Zaire and Angola

In the center of Africa disintegrative forces reasserted themselves in the early months of 1977. Shortly after independence in 1960, the mineral-rich Katanga Province had seceded from the Congo. In the ensuing civil war the United States had strongly supported the multinational United Nations force that intervened to prevent the breakup of the new state. Although Katanga Province was brought back under the rule of the Congo central government, secessionist sentiment remained strong. In March 1977 Katangan opponents of President Mobutu Seko of Zaire (formerly the Congo) invaded Shaba (formerly Katanga) Province from neighboring Angola.

The Angolan government of President Agostinho Neto had come to power with Soviet and Cuban military support. Cuban troops fought on behalf of the Popular Movement for the Liberation of Angola (MPLA) in the civil war that had followed the end of Portuguese rule in 1974. Even after Neto's forces had seized power, low-intensity warfare continued in Angola, with some support from Shaba Province. Seemingly in retaliation for covert aid to the Angolan insurgency provided by President Mobuto of Zaire, Neto had allowed, and perhaps encouraged, the incursion from Angola into Shaba.

Here again, the Carter administration faced an African issue that had broader implications. The detachment of Shaba from Zaire, especially if it was accomplished with the support of a Soviet-Cuban backed Angola, would enhance Moscow's position in central Africa. The government of Mobuto Seko, which was friendly to the United States, would have been destabilized by an Angolan-sponsored detachment of Shaba from Zaire. The Carter administration confined its support to Zaire to the shipment of rifle ammunition and, more important, provided Morocco with the airplanes it used to send a combat unit to Zaire with French assistance. In April 1977 the invasion was repelled and thus the territorial integrity of Zaire was preserved.

### South Africa: The Drive toward Black Majority Rule

However important both in a specifically African context and in a broader geopolitical setting may have been the problems of the Horn and central Africa, the Carter administration's interest was focused far more intensely on the problems of southern Africa, particularly Rhodesia (later Zimbabwe) and the territory of Southwest Africa (Namibia). A foreign policy in southern Africa that pushed more vigorously for black majority rule would strengthen U.S. links with the forces represented by the tide of African nationalism that had swept across the continent at the end of the European imperial era. The narrowly strategic interest of the United States in the precarious "stability" furnished by white minority regimes was to be subordinated to the achievement of rule by black governments. It was necessary, the Carter administration reasoned, to remove the legacy of past American support for forces whose principal function seemed to be to insulate South Africa from the full impact of the black nationalism to the north. However, the Carter administration, despite pressures within it (notably from Secretary of State Vance), stopped short of granting diplomatic recognition to the Neto government as long as Cuban forces remained in Angola.

Nowhere more than in southern Africa did the Carter administration seek to differentiate its Third World policies from those of its predecessors, although in its final years the Nixon/Ford administration had moved toward policies, in both Rhodesia and Namibia, similar in many respects to those of its successor. At the outset, the Carter administration, in its quest for more accommodating North–South relations, set for itself the ambitious goal of achieving a transfer of power in Rhodesia to black majority rule by 1978, the partial dismantling of apartheid in South Africa, and the sharp reduction in, if not the elimination of, the Soviet-Cuban military presence, as well as in arms transfers by both the United States and the Soviet Union, in the African continent by 1980. At the same time, the Carter administration sought major progress toward the independence of Namibia. Such policies were related, of course, to Carter's conception of the importance of human rights, which, he reasoned, would have credibility only if the United States matched words with deeds.

In Rhodesia, a white minority government headed by Prime Minister Ian Smith had been established in 1965 after Smith and his followers had declared independence for the colony from British rule. Although Rhodesia had survived the economic sanctions imposed by the United Nations, the guerrilla war mounted by black nationalists under the leadership of Joshua Nkomo and Robert Mugabe in 1972, together with the end of Portuguese rule in neighboring Mozambique, had begun, by the middle of the decade, to sap the energies of the increasingly beleaguered Smith government. In 1976 the Ford administration had announced its support for black majority rule in Rhodesia, and Kissinger had developed a framework for transition that included formation of an interim government with negotiations about its composition between Ian Smith and black political representatives. Kissinger's initiative had led to a conference in Geneva in December 1976, but the meeting ended in a stalemate because each side sought to obtain a dominant position during the transitional period, with Smith seeking a lengthy transfer and the black nationalists wanting to assume full control as soon as possible. In early 1977 Smith developed what was termed an "internal solution" that excluded both Britain and the most radical of the black liberation factions in favor of a coalition between whites and more moderate blacks. Smith wanted to entice Joshua Nkomo into this coalition and thus to abandon his tactical alliance, in what was called the Patriotic Front, with Robert Mugabe. Mugabe's political base was the Shona tribe, which accounts for about two-thirds of the population of Zimbabwe and which, during the war against Smith's government, had received backing from the People's Republic of China. Nkomo led the Matabele tribe, which makes up the remainder of the black population of Zimbabwe. Although Nkomo was supported by the Soviet Union in the war, Moscow shifted to Mugabe after he emerged as the leader of Zimbabwe.

Before the settlement and elections that brought Mugabe to power, Smith made an effort to accommodate moderate black groups. Central to Smith's proposed multiracial approach was Bishop Abel Muzorewa, head of the African National Congress (ANC), and another black leader, Ndabaningi Sithole. In effecting such a settlement, Smith faced a formidable, and eventually insurmountable, problem resulting from the fact that the Patriotic Front, unlike Bishop Muzorewa and the ANC, waged increasingly successful guerrilla warfare from bases in neighboring Mozambique, with military equipment furnished by the Soviet Union and with the active support of other neighboring "Front-Line" African states, including Zambia and Tanzania. Because Muzorewa was prepared to work toward a peaceful solution with Ian Smith, he was rejected by Front-Line states in favor of the Nkomo-Mugabe forces, who were said to represent a more authentic form of African nationalism. Specifically, Nkomo had the support of President Kenneth Kaunda of Zambia, while Mugabe was aided by President Julius Nyerere of Tanzania and by President Samora Machel of Mozambique.

The Carter administration worked closely with Britain to produce a peace plan based on a British-administered transition government, together with a constitution providing for universal suffrage, an internationally supervised cease-fire, free elections, the integration of guerrilla forces into a post-independence army, and constitutional rights, including legislative representation, for the white minority. However, Smith reached his own agreement with Muzorewa and his followers to form a government providing for direct black participation. With Britain under James Callaghan's Labor government pressing for a settlement based on the Anglo–American peace plan of 1977, the Carter administration confronted pressures in Congress to take a more flexible approach toward the Rhodesian problem, especially if Muzorewa formed a multiracial government.

Although Muzorewa formed a government with himself as prime minister in April 1979 based on elections in which blacks received 72 of the 100 seats in the parliament, the internal solution was unable to bring the Patriotic Front into its ranks or to entice Nkomo to defect from his alliance with Mugabe. The British election of a Conservative government headed by Margaret Thatcher in May 1979 failed to produce the basic change in British policy that Smith and Muzorewa had hoped for. Instead, the new British foreign secretary, Lord Carrington, together with the Carter administration, continued to press for a settlement that would include Nkomo and Mugabe and would of necessity be based on a framework such as the Anglo–American peace plan of 1977. With neither Britain nor the United States prepared to recognize the Muzorewa government and with both London and Washington pushing Nkomo and Mugabe into direct negotiations with Muzorewa's government, the basis for a settlement with the Patriotic Front was reached in early August 1979. A conference convened in London with all parties in attendance produced an agreement on elections, which were held in February 1980 and produced a sweeping political victory for Mugabe, who became prime minister; Zimbabwe achieved final independence in April 1980. Initially appearing to adopt moderate policies toward the white minority, Mugabe's role in the following years was marked by increasing frictions both with the followers of Ian Smith and with Joshua Nkomo. The stable, prosperous, and independent Zimbabwe envisioned by the Carter administration did not emerge from the tangled politics of independence.

The second objective of the Carter administration's policy in southern Africa was the achievement of a satisfactory formula for the independence of Namibia, which since the end of World War I had been administered by South Africa, first as a League of Nations Mandate and later as a United Nations Trust Territory. Namibian independence would represent an important step toward the evolution desired by Carter in the Republic of South Africa itself. Furthermore, the Carter administration viewed the withdrawal of South African military units from Namibia as a prerequisite to the ending of the Cuban armed presence in neighboring Angola. As in the case of Rhodesia, Washington feared that escalation of the conflict in Namibia would result in the direct involvement of Cuban forces. The United States sought also to preclude South African military action in Angola or Rhodesia, fearing the implications that such action would have for further racial polarization in southern Africa.

In shaping its own policy, the Carter administration built on the initiative of its predecessor. Kissinger had pressed the adoption by the United Nations Security Council of a resolution calling for the end of racial discrimination in Namibia, the release of political prisoners and repatriation of exiles, internationally supervised elections, and the withdrawal of South African forces. By 1976 South Africa faced in Namibia an insurgency, but on a much smaller scale than the unrest encountered by the Smith government in Rhodesia. In Namibia the guerilla war was mounted by the black nationalist Southwest Africa People's Organization (SWAPO), headed by Sam Nujoma, who had established a revolutionary government in neighboring Angola. Tensions between South Africa and Angola had been exacerbated by South African raids on SWAPO camps inside Angola. South Africa provided covert assistance to insurgents led by Jonas Savimbi against the Neto government and the 20,000 Cuban troops deployed in Angola.

As an alternative to SWAPO, in 1978 South Africa had itself developed a proposal for Namibian independence based on the Democratic Turnhalle Alliance (DTA), a coalition named after the building (*turnhalle* means gymnasium in German) in which it was formed. The DTA brought together tribal-ethnic groups other than the Ovambo tribe, upon which SWAPO was based. Because the Ovambo tribe constituted just over 50 percent of Namibia's population, it was feared that, if it attained power, it would dominate the remaining tribal-ethnic groups. With Soviet and UN support, SWAPO, viewing itself as the authentic spokesman for the Namibian people, saw no need for elections. The Turnhalle conference produced a program for Namibian independence by the end of 1978 from which SWAPO would have been excluded. Such a solution, of course, was unacceptable to the Carter administration, committed as it was to a form of black majority rule that was acceptable to the front-line states to the north. Protracted negotiations failed to produce a formula satisfactory to the various parties. South Africa was not prepared to withdraw its military forces from Namibia without a total cease-fire. The Carter administration was unable to dissuade South Africa from holding elections in December 1978 in which the DTA won nearly all the seats in the Constituent Assembly, but in which SWAPO did not participate. Thus by the end of the Carter administration, its goal of Namibian independence based on UN-supervised elections with a government containing all tribal-ethnic factions remained unrealized. In fact, the prospect for a mutually acceptable framework for independence—encompassing SWAPO and Turnhalle—that could form the basis for a lasting solution to the complex Namibian question confronted numerous formidable obstacles and remained unfulfilled into the 1980s.

## THE PANAMA CANAL TREATIES AND LATIN AMERICA

If black majority rule in southern Africa was crucial to the Carter administration's policies in Africa, the conclusion of the Panama Canal treaties was considered to be indispensable to American foreign policy in Latin America. The Carter administration held that in the absence of treaties changing the status of the Panama Canal, anti-American sentiment would increase throughout Latin America. Just as in Africa, American policy was to be designed to accommodate the rising forces of nationalism and, to the extent possible, divert them from policies hostile to the United States and prevent the Soviet Union from exploiting them for its own purposes. The Panama Canal, having been built in an era of American overseas expansion, symbolized the dominant position of the United States in the Western Hemisphere. Latin American nationalism, in this respect not unlike nationalism elsewhere, sought relationships on the basis of equality. It was to such aspirations that the Carter administration sought to appeal in its Third World policy. For this reason, Carter placed the Panama Canal treaties at the top of his policy agenda in the Western Hemisphere.

The "colonial" relationship that the Carter administration was determined to change was based on the 1903 treaty that had given the United States full sovereign rights in perpetuity over the Panama Canal and a zone of territory across the narrow isthmus between the Atlantic and Pacific oceans. When anti-American riots had broken out in Panama in 1964, the Johnson administration, with Cyrus Vance as the special presidential emissary, had decided to begin negotiations for a new treaty. Although a draft treaty had been negotiated by 1967, it had never been submitted to the Senate for ratification and, in any event, had been rejected by Panama after General Omar Torrijos came to power in a military coup in that year. The Nixon/Ford administration continued to negotiate with Panama for a new treaty. In fact, in February 1974, Kissinger and Panama's foreign minister, Juan Tack, had reached agreement on a series of principles that furnished the basis for the treaties to be concluded during the Carter administration. Any new treaty would be for a fixed term, thus satisfying Panama's position that the idea of perpetuity should be abandoned. During the life of the new treaty, the United States would retain the right to operate and defend the canal, although the Canal Zone would be returned to Panamanian jurisdiction. Both Panama and the United States committed themselves to the permanent neutrality of the canal after the fixed time period.

What remained for the Carter administration, therefore, was essentially the resolution of two important issues: the duration of the treaty and the defense of the Panama Canal after the treaty expired. The United States demanded the right to defend the canal at any time in the future, unilaterally and with military force if necessary, while Panama opposed granting the right to the United States to intervene on its sovereign territory. From negotiations conducted in the first several months of the Carter administration, two draft treaties emerged, which were signed on September 7, 1977, by Carter and Torrijos. In the first treaty the United States reserved the right to operate and defend the canal until the end of the year 2000. The second treaty, which provided for the permanent neutrality of the canal, conceded to the United States the right to ensure its neutral status, interpreted by the Carter administration to include the use of force if necessary. Under the new arrangements, the United States was granted expeditious passage for its ships ahead of other vessels in a national emergency.

Having pushed the canal negotiations to a successful conclusion with Panama, the Carter administration still faced the difficult task of obtaining Senate ratification and necessary public support. There was skepticism, especially among treaty opponents in the Senate, about whether the United States had a clear right to take unilateral action in order to keep the canal open. If so, the language contained in the Neutrality Treaty should be strengthened. Before ratification could be completed in the spring of 1978, it was necessary to insert language that satisfied a sufficient number of the Senate critics and at the same time to assuage Panamanian sensitivities. These problems were resolved in the insertion of wording that affirmed explicitly the right of the United States to intervene only for the purpose of keeping the canal "open, secure, and accessible, and shall not have as its purpose nor be interpreted as a right of intervention in the political affairs of the Republic of Panama, or interference with its political independence or sovereign integrity."

In the controversy that surrounded the Panama Canal treaties, the Carter administration, in addition to offering arguments in keeping with its basic approach to Third World issues, had contended that, faced with obdurate Panamanian opposition, the defense of the Panama Canal would be impossible for the United States. Panamanian nationalism directed against the canal, together with growing insurgencies and other turbulence in the Caribbean and Central America, would confront the United States with a series of insurmountable problems. Hence the Panama Canal treaties were regarded as an essential contribution to the stability of the region. To critics, however, the treaties represented yet another manifestation of the decline of the United States as a world power, even in its own backyard. As it turned out, the opposition to the treaty enabled the administration to persuade Panamanian officials that no agreement could be ratified that did not provide explicitly for the permanent neutrality of the Panama Canal by whatever means necessary.

## THE MIDDLE EAST AND CAMP DAVID

The Middle East came to represent one of the Carter administration's greatest foreign-policy achievements—namely, the Camp David accords providing for normalization between Egypt and Israel after decades of hostility and three wars. At the outset of his administration, Carter had decided to seek a comprehensive settlement of the issues that had long divided Israel and its neighbors that would encompass: (1) the withdrawal of Israeli forces from territory Israel had occupied since the Six-Day War of June 1967, building on the step-by-step approach that Kissinger had undertaken after the October War of 1973 for the disengagement of Israeli and Egyptian forces; (2) the development on the Israeli-occupied West Bank of a Palestinian state based on some form of self-determination; (3) agreement on the future status of East Jerusalem: and (4) the resolution of differences between Israel and Syria over the Golan Heights.

In the Six-Day War Israel had occupied the West Bank of the Jordan River, which previously had been Jordanian territory; had taken the Golan Heights from Syria to foreclose the possibility of continued Syrian attack mounted from this strategically important area; and had occupied East Jerusalem, which had subsequently been declared to be the capital of Israel instead of Tel Aviv. Like its immediate predecessors, the Carter administration faced the intractable problem of reconciling Israel's understandable quest for secure frontiers with the equally plausible Arab demand that territories seized by Israel in the wars of the preceding decade should be returned. Given the bitter legacy of the recent past, Israel could not be expected to withdraw from lands that it had occupied in order to obtain security unless it received full diplomatic recognition and guarantees that were more than mere words.

### The Quest for a Political Settlement

From Carter's perspective, the goal of American diplomacy was the achievement of a political settlement that would enable all parties to live in peace and security. Although Israel retained a large measure of military superiority, as long as there was no resolution of the problems separating Israel from its neighbors the prospect existed either for an Israeli preemptive strike, as had happened in June 1967, or for a surprise attack against Israel like that of the October War of 1973. Either contingency held the ominous possibility of escalation to involve the United States and the Soviet Union.

In addition to its potential contribution to the stability of the Middle East, a political settlement would form part of the Carter administration's broader strategy of building a peaceful world order. Without resolution of the endemic conflicts of the Middle East, the development of institutions and processes for peaceful change elsewhere, a goal of the Carter administration, would not be great. Having achieved a political settlement in a region of such turbulence, the reasoning went, the United States would have enhanced greatly the likelihood of peaceful change elsewhere. Kissinger, in his celebrated shuttle diplomacy, had concentrated on partial steps toward disengagement and eventual peace between Egypt and Israel and between Israel and Syria; in contrast, Carter set out to obtain a comprehensive settlement by convening in Geneva a conference to which the states of the Middle East directly involved in the conflict would be invited. Because no political settlement could endure without the support of Moscow, the Soviet Union was to be included.

In pressing for a conference in Geneva to negotiate a comprehensive settlement, the Carter administration ran up against the core issues that separated Israel and its neighbors. The Arab states sought a return to the borders existing before the Six-Day War and the establishment of a Palestinian state in exchange for an end of the state of war between them and Israel. Israel sought not merely the formal end of belligerency but also a treaty establishing peace and full normalization and allowing Israel to retain certain parts of the occupied territories as strategic buffers. Moreover, Israel preferred to negotiate separately with Egypt, Syria, and Jordan in the hope that some, if not all, of the issues could be settled. For Israel, peace meant not simply the absence of war, but full legal, political, and economic acceptance by the Arab states.

At the core of the Arab–Israeli dispute lay the Palestinian problem. Israel was not prepared to accept a fully independent Palestinian state on the West Bank dominated by the Palestine Liberation Organization, which it feared would become the base for a continued campaign to destroy Israel. In fact, Israel rejected any formal PLO participation in a Geneva conference, preferring Jordan and, specifically, the government of King Hussein as the representative of the Palestinian people. Refusing to deal directly with the PLO, to whom it sought to deny international recognition and political legitimacy, Israel was prepared to accept non-PLO Palestinians as part of the Jordanian delegation, while the Arab states wanted PLO representation. President Anwar Sadat of Egypt, King Hussein and, to a lesser extent, President Hafez Assad of Syria, saw the possibility of a Palestinian state linked constitutionally with Jordan. The achievement of such a solution depended on the creation of a viable political force other than the PLO on the West Bank. However, the PLO was unprepared to state clearly in advance of any political settlement its willingness to grant diplomatic recognition to Israel or to accept fully United Nations Resolution 242, adopted at the time of the Six-Day War in 1967, relating to the "right" of all states in the Middle East to "live in peace." The PLO, under Yasir Arafat, was not prepared, as the United States sought, to announce its full acceptance of Resolution 242. Instead, the PLO attempted to extract in advance political recognition from the United States. Failing to achieve a mutually satisfactory formula for Palestinian representation, the Carter administration faced the prospect of continuing construction of Israeli settlements on the West Bank, which seemed to some in Washington to represent a deliberate provocation that would further diminish the possibility for settling the Arab-Israeli dispute.

### Sadat's Peace Initiative

Much of the first year of the Carter administration was occupied with the effort to launch the Geneva conference for a comprehensive settlement. It was in this setting that Sadat made his historic and dramatic trip to Israel in November 1977, an initiative that stunned the Carter administration and governments elsewhere. Speaking to the Israeli Knesset (parliament), Sadat offered Israel peace, security, and full diplomatic relations in return for Israeli withdrawal from Egyptian territory occupied since 1967 and the eventual achievement of a comprehensive settlement. Although Carter, in this respect not unlike Sadat himself, continued to hold onto the ultimate goal of a comprehensive settlement, henceforth emphasis was placed on a bilateral agreement between Egypt and Israel, together with an interim solution to the problem of a Palestinian homeland in the West Bank and Gaza.

The immediate effect of Sadat's bold initiative was to split the Arab states, several of which—Syria, South Yemen, Algeria, and Libya, together with the PLO—formed a "rejectionist bloc" in opposition to Sadat. With Sadat having made his move, the task of developing a negotiating process fell to the United States. The best, and perhaps the only real, hope for achieving a peace treaty between Egypt and Israel lay in the active participation of the United States in the negotiations.

In the months following Sadat's journey to Israel, the United States held a series of high-level consultations with all the parties. The essence of the Carter administration's diplomatic strategy at this time was to use Sadat's initiative as the basis for pressing Israel to make concessions, especially on the West Bank question, in order to preserve a peace treaty whose effect would be to strengthen the overall American position in the Middle East. Israeli policy was based on the perceived need to achieve with Egypt a peace treaty that left as intact as possible Israel's dominant position in the West Bank. From the Egyptian perspective, the concept of Palestinian autonomy meant a phased transition, including Israeli withdrawal, with the ultimate goal being some form of Palestinian self-determination. Menachem Begin's government saw Palestinian autonomy as a limited form of internal self-government in which Israel retained overall control over the West Bank and Gaza.

The formidable task confronting the United States was to reconcile these fundamentally different approaches to the future status of the West Bank and Gaza. The greater the success of Israel in separating the West Bank issue from the peace process, the greater would be Sadat's isolation, and by inference the United States' isolation, from the rest of the Arab world. Hence the American interest, as an active participant in the negotiations, in a peace treaty that did not exclude the West Bank. Under such circumstances, differences between the Carter administration and the Begin government inevitably clouded the negotiations. The Carter administration saw a need to bolster Sadat's sagging position in the Arab world by giving him a justification for a separate peace with Israel. This could be accomplished only by enabling Sadat to claim credibly that his bold initiative represented the only practical means to achieve a mutually acceptable accommodation on the West Bank and Sinai issues.

### The Camp David Accords

By midsummer 1978, it had become apparent to the Carter administration that the only hope for pressing the negotiations to a successful conclusion lay in the convening of a summit conference. With the invitation to Begin and Sadat to meet with him at Camp David, the presidential retreat in Maryland, Carter undertook the role of "full partner," as it was termed. Not since the convening of the conference that led to the Treaty of Portsmouth after the Russo–Japanese War (1903–1905) had the United States played such a dominant role in the mediation of differences between two former adversaries. At that time, President Theodore Roosevelt was not himself an active participant in the negotiations. In sharp contrast, Carter took a direct and continuing part in all phases of the negotiations that shaped the Camp David accords.

The outcome of the Camp David meetings, held in September 1978, was agreement between Egypt and Israel to conclude a peace treaty within three months based on the framework that had just been developed in the marathon negotiations. Israel had agreed to withdraw all its military forces from the occupied Sinai within three years. Within nine months of the signing of the peace treaty, a partial interim pullback of Israeli forces would take place. After this troop withdrawal, full diplomatic relations would be established between Egypt and Israel. Freedom of passage would be established through the Strait of Tiran, and an international police force would be placed on the Egypt–Israel border with necessary security zones and monitoring stations. Central to the Camp David accords were the provisions for the West Bank and Gaza. Negotiations were to be conducted among Israel, Egypt, Jordan, and representatives of a Palestinian authority as part of a transitional phase toward self-government for the West Bank and Gaza.

In short, then, the achievement of Camp David was the formulation of a timetable for Israeli withdrawal from the Sinai in return for Egyptian agreement to full normalization of relations with Israel. The contentious issues associated with the West Bank and Gaza, and the future of a Palestinian state, remained unresolved. Thus the Camp David accords, signed at the White House on September 17, 1978, represented (1) a commitment by Egypt and Israel to sign a peace treaty, and (2) a framework for negotiating transitional arrangements for the West Bank and Gaza.

Only after several months of high-level negotiations, extending well beyond the three-month timetable contained in the Camp David accords, were Egypt and Israel prepared to sign a peace treaty. The climax of the negotiations, which were punctuated by periods of despair and pessimism, was the exercise in summit shuttle diplomacy by Carter, who went to Cairo and Jerusalem in March 1978 in order to press the parties toward the resolution of remaining issues so that the peace treaty could finally be signed. This phase of the U.S. peace effort in the Middle East coincided with the deterioration of the political situation in the Persian Gulf resulting from the Iranian crisis (discussed later in this chapter).

After meeting successively with Sadat and Begin, and finally again with Sadat, Carter produced the agreement that led to the historic signing of the first peace treaty between an Arab state with Israel on March 25, 1979, in Washington. The issues that had to be resolved before the peace treaty could be signed had included: the establishment of economic relations, with provision for the sale of Sinai oil and guarantees by the United States to make oil available if Israel could not purchase it in sufficient quantities elsewhere; provisions for the exchange of ambassadors between Egypt and Israel; and arrangements for talks on autonomy for the West Bank and Gaza.

On this last issue, Egypt and Israel had agreed, in a joint letter attached to the peace treaty, to enter negotiations within a month after the signing of the peace treaty, with Jordan and mutually acceptable Palestinian representatives being included. A "self-governing authority" was to be established by negotiations leading to "full autonomy" in the West Bank and Gaza. Although the Palestinian-autonomy talks began as stipulated, they quickly became bogged down. The PLO continued its terrorist acts against Israel, which maintained its policy of establishing new settlements in the West Bank territories that Begin called by their biblical names of Judea and Samaria. Although Egypt and Israel had agreed that their peace treaty represented part of a quest for "comprehensive peace" in the Middle East, the Camp David accords fell short of such a political settlement, for the issues associated with Palestinian autonomy were more complex and contentious than the bilateral relationship between Egypt and Israel that had just been codified.

## AMERICAN RELATIONS WITH CHINA

Among the goals that the new Carter administration had established for itself was the completion of the normalization process with the People's Republic of China begun by the Nixon/Ford administration. In a speech at Notre Dame University in May 1977, Carter stated, in words that could equally well have described Nixon's original approach to relations with China, "We see the American–Chinese relationship as a central element of our global policy, and China as a key force for global peace." A secure China represented an important contribution to global equilibrium. In this respect, not unlike its immediate predecessors, the Carter administration, especially National Security Adviser Brzezinski, saw Sino–American normalization as enhancing the ability of the United States to maintain better relationships with both China and the Soviet

Union, than either could have with the other. Although the Carter administration sought to minimize the idea that the Sino–American relationship was directed against the Soviet Union, the growth of American interest in normalization had coincided with the deterioration in relations between Washington and Moscow. Thus, official statements notwithstanding, there was a "strategic" element in the Sino–American normalization process that spanned and extended beyond the Nixon/Ford and Carter administrations. The greater the tension between Washington and Moscow–which by 1978 included not only differences over the SALT II treaty and rising American concern about the Soviet strategic-military buildup but also fundamental cleavages resulting from Soviet-Cuban activities in the Horn of Africa and Southern Africa–the more inclined the United States was to see a strategic advantage in Sino-American normalization.

Here the Carter administration, however, was divided within itself, more on the timing and manner of the normalization than on the perceived need to complete the process begun by Nixon. There were differences within the Carter administration over the emphasis to be placed on a strategic relationship with China. Vance argued for an "even-handed" policy toward both China and the Soviet Union in which similar relations, namely the granting of most favored nation status to both, would be developed with Beijing and Moscow, but from which military issues would be excluded. Brzezinski and Secretary of Defense Harold Brown contended that, because China was so much weaker than the Soviet Union and posed no military threat to the United States, the PRC's security needs should be given sympathetic consideration. This included possible Chinese access to technology having both civilian and military applications. Previously, the United States had applied equal restrictions to China and the Soviet Union to prevent the transfer of high technologies that had military uses.

In short, Vance and the State Department feared the establishment of a diplomatic relationship with China; Brzezinski and Brown saw the need for a security relationship with China. The case was put by Brzezinski for the strengthening of links with China in order to place pressure on the Soviet Union to improve its own relationship with the United States. In contrast, Vance was inclined to attribute increased friction with the Soviet Union over the SALT II treaty in the winter of 1978–79 not only to the strengthening of the Sino–American relationship itself but also to the timing of the announcement that full diplomatic relations would be established as the SALT negotiations were nearing a conclusion. Nevertheless, the Carter administration was engaged in the practice, with Moscow and Beijing, of a form of triangular diplomacy whose mark of success would have been the simultaneous conclusion of a SALT II treaty with the Soviet Union and agreement with China for full normalization. Ideally, the United States could have "played the China card" (a phrase never used officially by the administration) to extract concessions from the Soviet Union on the most contentious issues of SALT II.

Of course, things did not work out this way. Sino–American normalization could not shape a SALT II treaty that would be acceptable to the increasingly vocal critics of the arms-control and defense policies of the Carter administration. The momentum of the Soviet strategic-military buildup had strengthened the case within the Carter administration for completion of normalization, while at the same time diminishing the prospects for a SALT II treaty that would do little more, in the words of a growing number of critics, than codify a strategic-military balance tilting ominously in favor of the Soviet Union.

In formulating its China policy, the Carter administration had not only to accept the framework of the Nixon/Ford administrations but also to resolve several remaining contentious issues. Although in the Shanghai Communiqué of February 1972 the United States had accepted the Chinese position that there is one China and Taiwan is part of it, the Carter administration faced the task of finding a mutually acceptable formula for retaining a residual relationship with Taiwan while phasing out remaining direct American defense links and at the same time establishing an official diplomatic relationship with Beijing. With the PRC leadership the Carter administration opened a series of channels that included visits by Vance and Brzezinski.

However, until the spring of 1978, relations with China did not form a principal preoccupation of the Carter administration, whose attention was focused instead on SALT II, the Panama Canal treaties, and the Middle East peace process. The completion of the Panama Canal treaties, together with the apparent efforts of the Soviet Union to strengthen its geopolitical position in and around the vital oil-producing states of the Persian Gulf—in Ethiopia and South Yemen—increased the need, perceived especially by Brzezinski, to put countervailing pressure on the Soviet Union. In discussions in Beijing in May 1978, Brzezinski sought to emphasize to the Chinese leadership an American commitment to oppose Soviet expansionism and to counter Moscow's military buildup. The visit provided the occasion for a series of direct signals that the United States was prepared to move swifty toward full normalization with China: the United States would further reduce its military presence on Taiwan; the administration would look favorably on the development and expansion of scientific, economic, and cultural exchanges and cooperation; and the United States would seek to develop with China security concessions in opposition to Soviet intrusion into the Third World, notably the Horn of Africa, Southern Africa, South Asia, and Southeast Asia. China was asked for a commitment to the promotion of stability in the Korean peninsula.

The completion of the negotiations leading to Sino–American normalization coincided with the events leading to the signing in October 1978 of the Sino–Japanese Treaty of Peace, Reconciliation, and Friendship that formally ended the era of Japan's invasion and occupation of China that had begun with the Manchurian Campaign in 1931 and ended only with Japan's defeat in 1945. In accepting an "anti-hegemonism" clause in the treaty—a Chinese code word for opposition to Soviet expansionism—Japan had appeared to abandon a policy of equidistance in its relations with China and the Soviet Union in favor of a tilt toward the PRC. With the Sino–Japanese treaty and the formal completion of Sino–American normalization, Japan and the United States had taken a major step toward the development in the Asian Pacific of an embryonic framework designed to symbolize and signal concern about, and opposition to, Soviet "hegemonism."

In the latter years of the 1970s, China seemed to be moving toward membership in what was termed a "united front," a coalition including the United States, Japan, and NATO-Europe standing in opposition to the expansion of Moscow's influence both in Europe and in Asia. In this Chinese global perspective, as officially articulated, the Soviet Union maintained a two-pronged strategy, one purpose of which was to isolate and encircle China by strengthening Moscow's position in South and Southeast Asia. The other prong of Soviet strategy, according to PRC statements, was to cut off Western Europe and Japan from their Persian Gulf oil supplies and to establish and consolidate Soviet influence in the Third World. Because China held down approximately one-quarter of Soviet military power on the long Sino–Soviet frontier, while an even larger number of Soviet forces faced NATO to the west, the Soviet Union had been effectively blocked in its expansion on both fronts. However, the Soviet Union was left with substantial resources to press to the south—into the rimlands of Asia, into Southeast Asia, and into Africa. Because the Soviet Union, it was asserted in Beijing, could not coexist in a relationship of equality with neighboring states, it was necessary that China develop closer links not only with the United States but also with Japan and with Western European countries. Last but not least, the PRC sought access to advanced Western technologies, usually in a form that would permit the construction of production facilities in China, as a means of modernizing a military capability that lagged increasingly behind Soviet forces positioned against China on the Sino–Soviet frontier.

The normalization agreement presented by the United States on December 15, 1978, provided for the termination of the defense treaty that had been signed in 1950 between the United States and the Republic of China, or Taiwan, at the height of enmity between Washington and mainland China. Remaining U.S. military forces on Taiwan were removed, although the United States reserved the right to engage in selective arms sales to Taipei for defensive purposes. Official U.S. diplomatic recognition of Taiwan was withdrawn, although the United States established a framework for unofficial ties. In effect, China and the United States had agreed to disagree on the Taiwan question in the interest of achieving a normalization agreement. The United States asserted publicly its commitment to the peaceful resolution of the question of the future relationship between Taiwan and the mainland, while Beijing declared that such issues were its own internal affair. Henceforth, from the U.S. perspective, arms sales to Taiwan would be calibrated to take account of the security environment prevailing on both shores of the Strait of Taiwan. Progress toward peaceful reconciliation would lead to a decline, and conceivably termination, of the sale of American arms to Taiwan. The evolving U.S. relationship with Taiwan was codified in the Taiwan Relations Act passed by Congress to establish the American Institute on Taiwan, which was the legal structure, in place of an embassy, for the conduct of unofficial relations with Taiwan.

In the last two years of the Carter administration the momentum generated by the normalization agreement was sustained by a series of such events affecting "parallel" interests, such as the increasing Soviet presence in Vietnam, the Soviet invasion of Afghanistan in December 1979, and the growing Soviet maritime presence in the Asian Pacific. In November 1979 the Soviet Union had signed a "friendship treaty" with Vietnam, an event that undoubtedly contributed to China's decision to launch limited military action across the border into Vietnam in February 1979 in order, as Premier Deng Xiao-ping put it, to "teach Vietnam a lesson." During a state visit to the United States in January 1979 to cap the normalization agreement, Deng had privately notified Carter of China's intention to attack Vietnam, which itself had invaded Cambodia, an action that China opposed because Soviet-sponsored Vietnamese domination of Indochina would enhance the Soviet encirclement of China. Successful Chinese military action against Vietnam would create for Hanoi a second front that would draw Vietnamese military capabilities away from Cambodia.

With Sino–American normalization having been completed, China, so it seemed in Washington, was playing its "American card." The closer the Sino–American relationship, the less Beijing would have to fear a Soviet retaliatory incursion into China along its border with the Soviet Union and the freer China might be to take action in support of its interests in Southeast Asia. The response of the Carter administration was to urge restraint on both China and the Soviet Union—to propose the simultaneous withdrawal of Vietnamese forces from Cambodia and Chinese military units from the border areas of Vietnam, and to indicate to the Soviet Union that, while the United States had not encouraged or supported the Chinese incursion, any stepping up of Soviet activity in Southeast Asia or along China's borders would lead to an American response of some kind. The withdrawal of Chinese forces less than a month after the beginning of their offensive left unanswered questions about their combat quality. Nevertheless, China's ability to take such action without strong Soviet countermeasures revealed that an ally of Moscow could be attacked without evoking the full support of the Soviet Union.

Although the Carter administration had attempted to prevent the Chinese military strike against Vietnam from interfering with its relations with either Beijing or Moscow, the Sino–American relationship evolved in 1979–80 toward a U.S. tilt toward China as relations between Washington and Moscow deteriorated. After the Soviet invasion of Afghanistan, the United States authorized the sale of certain types of "defensive" military technologies to China, including communication equipment, transport helicopters, electronic countermeasures, and air defense radar. Vice-President Walter Mondale's visit to China at the end of August 1979 provided the setting for the granting of most-favored-nation status to China, thus reversing U.S. policy that had applied the same restrictive trade policy to both China and the Soviet Union. Last but not least, China was declared to be a "friendly" nation, thus qualifying Beijing for commercial credits not available to the Soviet Union. Agreements were concluded with China for the opening of consulates, commercial airline service, and textile imports. Thus by 1980 the Carter administration had evolved with China a relationship having political-strategic and economic dimensions more in keeping with the original premises of Nixon's opening to China than with Carter's initial view of the world when he came to office. Now China formed an integral part of the administration's effort to develop a framework for the containment of an expansionist Soviet Union.

## U.S. SECURITY POLICY AND THE KOREAN PENINSULA

Since the Korean Armistice in 1953 the United States had maintained a residual military presence, including ground forces, in the Republic of Korea. By the mid-1970s U.S. forces stationed in South Korea numbered 42,000, of which 33,000 were U.S. Army units and the remainder were part of the U.S. contribution to air defense. Such military capabilities, minuscule compared to the South Korean force of 625,000, were intended to provide tangible evidence of a firm American commitment to the preservation of peace in the Korean peninsula. U.S. ground forces, stationed below the demilitarized zone between South Korea and North Korea, would be immediately engaged in any attack on the Republic of Korea from the north. Therefore, they represented the intent, stated by successive administrations since the Korean War, to escalate American involvement to levels needed to defeat any North Korean offensive.

Although the Republic of Korea had achieved spectacular economic growth rates, especially in the decade before the mid-1970s, that placed it in the ranks of a series of newly industrializing countries (with other political entities in the Asian Pacific such as Taiwan, Hong Kong, and Singapore), uncertainty remained about its ability to withstand another surprise attack launched from the North. Seoul, the capital and commercial center of South Korea, lies within 35 miles of the DMZ and can be reached within minutes by North Korean aircraft. During the 1970s North Korea, whose civilian economy lagged far behind that of South Korea, had built nevertheless a huge weapons-production capability whose effect was to lessen its dependence on arms supplies from China or the Soviet Union. Although contacts between Seoul and Pyongyang on the question of reunification had been initiated in the early 1970s, tensions had remained high. Sporadic incidents of violence had occurred, including the killing of several U.S. military personnel in the so-called tree-cutting incident of 1976. The discovery of tunnels dug from North Korea under the DMZ, through which military units and their equipment could be moved, lent further substance to South Korean fears that the North might be preparing to launch a surprise attack in order to achieve the forcible reunification of Korea. Geographically, South Korea had little territory to trade for time. Like NATO in Europe, South Korea had to deter, or prevent, an attack or to halt it at the earliest possible time. In the Republic of Korea, the object of the American guarantee was the defense of the southern end of a peninsula that was attached to the larger Asian land mass.

The strategic interest of the United States in stability in the Korean peninsula, strategically situated at the point of intersection of the three major powers of the region—China, Japan, and the Soviet Union—was complicated by certain concerns within the Carter administration about respect for human rights in the Republic of Korea. To be sure, however restricted from the perspective of the Carter administration, the levels of freedom in the South stood in stark contrast to the totalitarian Communist regime of North Korea. Here the Carter administration faced an inevitable dilemma between its commitment to human rights and the strategic interests of the United States in a world of imperfect political systems based on diverse cultural, social, and political traditions and values. In the case of China, the administration had not allowed its human-rights standards to cloud an unfolding conception of its security interests. The U.S. relationship with South Korea was damaged in the mid-1970s by what was called the "Koreagate" scandal, in which several members of Congress had been the object of a Korean influence-peddling scheme. This affair, together with the human-rights question, was detrimental to the U.S. relationship with Korea.

During the 1976 presidential campaign, Carter had stated his intention, if elected, to withdraw American ground forces from South Korea, a pledge that he reaffirmed shortly after the election. Viewed in the context of an American foreign policy designed to encourage the emergence of regional and local power centers that could survive without a U.S. military presence, one of the principles of the Nixon Doctrine, Carter's approach to the U.S.-Korea security relationship seemed to represent a basic policy departure. However, the withdrawal of American military power from Southeast Asia had been followed not by the demonstration of the capability of the United States' South Vietnamese ally to fend for itself, but instead by political and military collapse leading to the consolidation of a Communist state closely aligned with the Soviet Union. The reaction of allies in the Asian Pacific, including the Japanese government of Prime Minister Takeo Fukuda, to the proposed removal of U.S. ground forces from the Republic of Korea was negative. Despite growing opposition, both in the Asian Pacific and in Congress, Carter persevered in his policy decision until the summer of 1979, when he visited South Korea after attending the economic summit conference in Tokyo. Carter's visit evoked from North Korea a verbal attack on the president and a rejection of his call for talks for peaceful reunification between North and South Korea. This reaction, together with the release of new intelligence estimates revising substantially upward North Korea's military strength relative to that of South Korea, indicating that it might be possible for North Korea to attack across the DMZ without warning, led the Carter administration in July 1979 to suspend its plan to withdraw ground forces from South Korea.

## MANAGING ALLIANCE RELATIONS: NATO-EUROPE

To the Carter administration trilateralism meant the creation of a strategic, political, and economic relationship with Western Europe and Japan as a means of coping with the global issues of the late twentieth century. In fact, the achievement of higher levels of cooperation in the political and economic fields ranked at the top of its foreign-policy priorities. Certain organizational frameworks already existed for joint consultation and policy integration among the world's leading non-Communist industrialized states. Japan, the nations of Western Europe, and the United States, as well as Canada, were and are members of the Organization for Economic Cooperation and Development (OECD). Especially in the immediate aftermath of the 1973–74 energy crisis, with the formation within the OECD of the International Energy Agency (IEA), a broadening web of arrangements for consultation and coordination had been developed among industrialized states.

Symbolic of the perceived need for collaboration was the convening, on an annual basis after 1976, of summit conferences that included the heads of government of Britain, Canada, the Federal Republic of Germany, France, Italy, Japan, and the United States. Such meetings, devoted to economic issues, not only continued during the Carter administration but had been expanded to include political issues by the time of the Venice meeting of June 1980. With the revolution in Iran, growing instability in the Persian Gulf region, and the sharp rise in oil prices in 1979, there could be no useful separation of the economic and strategic-political issues associated with oil supply. Moreover, at the beginning of his administration, Carter had participated actively in the NATO summit conference held in London in May 1977. Such consultations were symbolic not only of the Carter administration's perception of the need to evolve a trilateral approach to global issues but also of the Nixon/Ford administration's belief that more mature relationships with allies should be forged. An era of American tutelage had come to an end. Together, the United States and its industrialized allies could develop the means to deal more effectively with an increasing array of complex issues.

Economic and defense issues transcended both a purely transatlantic framework and the bilateral relationship between the United States and Japan. However, no security framework in defense existed at a trilateral level, nor did the Carter administration seek to create an arrangement that would have linked industrialized and other states. NATO, or several if not all of its members, faced security threats emanating from regions, such as the Persian Gulf, outside the geographic perimeter of the Atlantic Alliance. Changes in the deployment of American forces to counter security threats outside the Western Pacific or the North Atlantic oceans, as in the Persian Gulf and Indian Ocean in the late 1970s, had important implications for the collective strength of the U.S. security relationships. Although Western Europe and Japan were far more dependent than the United States on imports of oil from less than stable countries and regions, only the United States maintained means that, in the final analysis, might be adequate to safeguard, or to help restore access to, such resources. Clearly there was a wide gap between the strategies and interests of the allies, on the one hand, and their capabilities, on the other.

In sum, no clear-cut distinction could be drawn between economic and political security issues, for the rapid increase in oil prices, first in 1974–75 and subsequently in 1979, had been triggered by political events in the Middle East and Persian Gulf—the Arab-Israeli war of October 1973 and the Iranian revolution of 1978–79. None of the existing alliances or security relationships was designed to cope with such contingencies, nor did frameworks exist for the full integration of the security and economic factors into a common strategy. For reasons associated with the diverse national perspectives of the United States, its NATO-European allies, and Japan, the prospects for achieving a form of trilateralism based on the transformation of existing arrangements into a global framework remained remote. Instead, the Carter administration had as the focus of its attention a series of immediate issues in the transatlantic relationship related directly to the original purpose of the Alliance: how to provide for the security of Western Europe in light of the Soviet–Warsaw Pact military buildup. Closely related was an issue that has had its counterpart in the U.S. relationship with

Japan: how to ensure that allies bear a greater portion of the burdens of collective defense. The importance of sharing the defense burden was heightened in the minds of American policymakers and Congress as a result of the fact that the United States, by the end of the 1970s, had assumed new security commitments in the Persian Gulf–Indian Ocean. It was reasoned that U.S. allies—the nations of Western Europe and Japan—should contribute more to the defense of their respective regions at a time when the United States was compelled to devote greater resources to the defense of interests—safeguarding oil supplies—that were of even greater immediate importance to Western Europe and Japan than they were to the United States.

At the London summit conference of May 1977, NATO members unanimously agreed to a long-term defense program to strengthen conventional and nuclear capabilities. Although the detailed steps to be taken to modernize NATO forces were left to a series of working groups, the Alliance reached agreement on an increase of 3 percent (in real terms after taking account of inflation) in annual defense spending in order to counter the Soviet–Warsaw Pact's advantage in force levels. The 3 percent increase, strongly supported by the United States, represented an effort both to increase burden sharing by Western European allies and to enable NATO forces to improve such military capabilities as antitank weapons and to develop integrated air defense systems.

### The Neutron Bomb Controversy

Among the technologies that could blunt, and perhaps halt, an armored assault against Western Europe was the enhanced radiation warhead (ERW), or neutron bomb as it came to be called. This warhead emitted radiation to penetrate Soviet–Warsaw Pact armored vehicles. It could be deployed on artillery and short-range tactical missiles against advancing forces. The neutron bomb could disable enemy tank crews without inflicting large-scale damage on surrounding property because, unlike other nuclear weapons, the ERW did not produce a large blast and heat. Civilians protected by intervening concrete walls would also not be affected. The ERW became simplistically characterized as "the weapon that destroys people but not property." The ERW, which had been under development for some time in the United States as part of the program to modernize NATO's aging battlefield nuclear weapons, was the subject of a *Washington Post* article in early June 1977 that was quickly picked up in the Western European press. Although Carter authorized the continuation of funding for development of the ERW, he was uncomfortable with the prospect of its deployment because of his deep commitment to arms control and aversion to the deployment of nuclear weapons.

The essential condition in Carter's mind of the stationing of the ERW in Europe was a clearly stated expression of willingness by NATO allies to accept it. For their part, Western European governments, long accustomed to American leadership, were not prepared to state in unambiguous terms their commitment to the ERW before the United States did. For the Federal Republic of Germany in particular, the neutron bomb posed a dilemma. Because of its location on NATO's Central Front, most of the stocks of the ERW would be based on West German territory. However, the Federal Republic of Germany did not wish to be the only European NATO member in which such weapons would be deployed. Chancellor Helmut Schmidt faced substantial domestic opposition as well as a mounting Soviet propaganda campaign designed to make any ERW deployment impossible. Schmidt's insistence on multilateralism in deployment was intended to blunt such opposition. With Britain and the Federal Republic of Germany, the United States worked out a formula in which NATO would forego deployment of the ERW if the Soviet Union would agree not to deploy the SS-20, an intermediate-range (500-kilometer) ballistic missile with counterforce accuracy carrying three 150-kiloton warheads. As the final details were being completed for the March 20, 1978, meeting of the North Atlantic Council, where this formula would have been announced, Carter himself decided against producing the ERW. With his visceral revulsion for nuclear weapons, Carter had overruled his closest advisers (Vance, Brown, and Brzezinski).

Having made a strenuous effort to build Alliance consensus in support of ERW deployment if arms-control negotiations to prevent the Soviet deployment of the SS-20 failed, the Carter administration, in reversing itself, projected an image of indecisiveness both to its allies and to domestic critics. The Bonn government, and especially Chancellor Schmidt, felt that they had expended considerable political capital to achieve even fragile support in the Federal Republic for ERW deployment in the absence of successful SS-20 arms-control negotiations, only to have the rug pulled out from under them without prior consultation by the Carter administration. Without a clearly stated Western European assent to deployment, without a willingness on the part of the United States to exercise Alliance leadership on this issue, the basis for stationing the ERW on NATO's Central Front did not exist. Notwithstanding NATO's failure to deploy the ERW, the Soviet Union proceeded with the SS-20, which it targeted against Western Europe and East Asia (principally China and Japan) at the rate of one new system every six days from 1977 onward.

### The Controversy over New Intermediate-Range Nuclear Missiles in NATO-Europe

The SS-20 was at the center of another issue that faced the Atlantic Alliance into the 1980s. As the Soviet deployment of the SS-20 proceeded, Western European concern about its implications increased, although without producing a readily discernible consensus about an appropriate NATO response. In a speech in London in October 1977, Schmidt had set forth a more broadly held European perspective. Because the SS-20, he pointed out, was excluded from the SALT II negotiations, the effect of a U.S.–Soviet treaty to limit intercontinental strategic systems would leave an imbalance in the European theater starkly in favor of the Soviet Union. Somehow, he pointed out, it would be necessary to remove "disparities of military power in Europe parallel to the SALT negotiations." In

1978 NATO established a High Level Group to address the issue of nuclear-force modernization and to develop an appropriate Alliance program for deploying new-generation intermediate-range nuclear forces (INF).

The result was the North Atlantic Council's unanimous decision on December 12, 1979, to deploy in the Federal Republic of Germany 108 Pershing II ballistic missiles with a range of 900 miles in place of the aging, shorter-range Pershing I. Moreover, NATO would deploy in the Federal Republic of Germany, as well as in Belgium, Britain, Italy, and the Netherlands, 464 ground-launched cruise missiles (GLCM), but would also withdraw a total of 1000 nuclear warheads from Western Europe, which would, when the NATO modernization program was eventually completed, represent a net reduction in warheads on Western European soil.

The Soviet Union condemned the idea of NATO deployment of these missiles. In October 1979 Brezhnev offered to remove 20,000 troops and 1000 tanks from East Germany in return for the nondeployment of nuclear systems in the NATO theater. While continuing its SS-20 deployment program, the Soviet Union mounted a propaganda effort of growing intensity designed to prevent any NATO nuclear-weapons modernization. Although the NATO "double-track" decision to deploy both Pershing II and cruise missiles had been the subject of protracted consideration among member governments, it had not been widely discussed by the general public. If there was not widespread popular support for the decision, neither was public opinion heavily predisposed against the modernization of NATO's nuclear forces. In the years after the decision, the public in Western Europe, especially in the Federal Republic of Germany, the Netherlands, and Britain, became polarized on the deployment issue. Although the reasons for opposition differed to some extent from one Western European country to another, one common denominator was fear of a heightened risk of nuclear war—a fear that seemed to increase in direct proportion to the level of Soviet SS-20 deployment. In the Federal Republic of Germany, Schmidt faced growing opposition from the left wing of his Social Democratic party and from the Greens, a new party that had originated as an ecologically oriented movement opposed to nuclear power plants and environmental pollution. Having focused the attention of the United States and other NATO members on the imbalance in nuclear forces in Europe resulting from the Soviet SS-20 deployment, Schmidt began to waver. In contrast to its behavior during the ERW controversy, the Carter administration remained steadfast in support of the NATO double-track decision, whose realization and full implications were bequeathed to its successor.

### Discord Between the United States and Its NATO Allies
Although tensions in the transatlantic relationship deepened during the Carter administration, their causes were rooted in changes that had taken place before the mid-1970s in Western Europe and the United States. One of the legacies of the Vietnam War had been the emergence of a counterculture in Western Europe not unlike that in the United States itself, opposed to American military action in Southeast Asia. In the United States such protests had as their focus the policy of

the administration then in office; in Western Europe they took the form of a more generalized anti-Americanism that should not, of course, be exaggerated.

Although fundamentally important strategic-political and economic interests remained, as did the shared intellectual and cultural heritage of Western civilization, Europeans and Americans had drawn apart in the 1970s. A number of trends heightened this discord: the tendency toward unilateralism in the Nixon administration's diplomacy, differing Western European and U.S. responses to the October War of 1973, the quest for economic unity based to some extent on European Community policies that restricted American access to Western European markets, and the need, perceived more strongly in Western Europe than the United States, to preserve the alleged benefits of détente.

As early as 1968, in the Harmel Report, the Atlantic Alliance had formally achieved a security consensus based on the preservation of adequate defense capabilities as a necessary condition for the pursuit of détente with the Soviet Union. By the time of the Carter administration, the gap was beginning to widen between the United States and at least certain of its allies (less, for example, with Britain after the election in May 1979 of the Conservative Thatcher government) about the priorities to be attached to defense and to détente. After the Soviet invasion of Afghanistan in December 1979, Western European governments showed decidedly less enthusiasm than the Carter administration in taking concrete steps to penalize Moscow, such as the American embargo on the export of grain, although verbal condemnations of the Soviet action were forthcoming at the official level. Public demonstrations in Western Europe against Soviet military action in Afghanistan paled in comparison to those that were made to protest plans for the installation of new NATO missiles.

In the late 1970s Western Europe's commitment to the deterrence of war remained, based on the guarantee implicit in the Atlantic Alliance to deter or prevent the outbreak of armed conflict by the threat to escalate, if necessary, to strategic-nuclear warfare. Nevertheless, the vast growth in the capacity of the Soviet Union to launch nuclear weapons against the United States, together with the emerging theater imbalance in Europe to which Schmidt had referred, increased uncertainty about how automatic the promised American escalation from the battlefield to the strategic-nuclear level would be in the event of attack. Opponents of the NATO double-track decision often alleged that the deployment of such systems, because they had ranges sufficient to strike targets in the Soviet Union, would enable the United States to avoid the use of nuclear forces launched from American soil. Under such circumstances. Europe would be devastated, but the United States would be unharmed. Thus the American strategic nuclear force, by this reasoning, was "uncoupled" from the deterrence of conflict in Europe. Therefore, the deployment of new-generation NATO missile systems might actually heighten the likelihood of war. This reasoning was the reverse of the logic on which the NATO double-track decision was in part based—namely, that the expressed willingness of the United States to launch theater nuclear weapons against the Soviet Union at an early stage in a hypothesized Soviet–Warsaw Pact attack reinforced the American commitment to escalation to whatever level might be deemed necessary as the basis for deterrence. Furthermore, as its official statements repeatedly suggested, the Soviet Union would not distinguish in its own nuclear targeting policy between American-controlled nuclear forces launched from Western European territory and those launched from the United States itself.

Finally, the Carter administration's human-rights policy evoked opposition in Western Europe as it applied to the Soviet Union rather than to rightist Third World governments, which themselves were frequently criticized, especially by left-of-center governments and their followers in Western Europe. The policy's application to the Soviet Union would have no appreciable effect on Soviet domestic policies but would endanger, once again, the tangible benefits to Western Europe seen to exist in détente. Western Europeans feared that any deterioration in relations between Washington and Moscow would have adverse consequences for their own national interests. In fact, the deterioration in the U.S.–Soviet relationship by the end of the Carter administration in itself had contributed to the heightening of transatlantic tensions. Although European allies have been wary of U.S.–Soviet agreements that do not take sufficient account of their interests (as in the exclusion of the SS-20 from SALT II and the resulting imbalance in theater nuclear forces), they have been equally apprehensive about the potential consequences for them of heightened tensions between Washington and Moscow.

## U.S. RELATIONS WITH JAPAN

In its policies toward Japan the Carter administration avoided "shocks" such as those which had marred the U.S.–Japanese relationship in the Nixon administration—the failure to inform or consult with Japan in advance of the surprise announcement of Nixon's visit to China in February 1972 and the first steps toward normalization of relations with China. If the Carter administration fell short of achieving a relationship with Japan based on the assumptions and principles of trilateralism, the problems of earlier years subsided as Japan moved rapidly to complete its own reconciliation with China and adjusted to the rapid rise in oil prices in the years after 1973. Although U.S.–Japanese relations improved during the Carter administration, two principal sets of issues confronted Washington and Tokyo: the trade imbalance and the need for Japan to share the responsibility for its defense.

### The Trade Deficit with Japan

By 1978 Japan had become the second-largest economic power of the non-Communist world, surpassed only by the United States. On a global basis, Japan ranked third in total GNP, with the United States and the Soviet Union in first and second place, respectively. From the devastation of World War II Japan had built an advanced industrial economy in which, by 1972, 65 percent of Japanese manufacturing facilities and equipment was less than five years old, in contrast to the United States, where an equal percentage of industry was more than ten years old. As a result, Japan had surpassed the United States and the nations of Western

Europe in total productivity in a large number of industries. Totally dependent on imports of raw materials, including energy, Japan had developed export industries such as automobiles, shipbuilding, and electronics that had achieved all but dominant positions in the domestic markets of a large number of other countries, including the United States.

The effect of Japan's rising productivity, based on its utilization of advanced technologies and its highly skilled and motivated labor force, was a surplus of exports over imports. In 1977, for example, Japan exported $9.7 billion more than it imported. In that year the United States had a $7.3 billion trade deficit with Japan. The European Community imported $4.5 billion worth of products more than it exported to Japan. Many Japanese exports competed directly with American products of the same kind. Whereas most American exports to Japan consisted of agricultural products and raw materials, for which Japan had no competitive domestic equivalents, Japan's exports of automobiles, electronics, and textiles cut deeply into sales of American products.

The result was the development of sentiment in the United States and Western Europe in favor of protectionism to reduce the growing trade imbalance. Although the Carter administration resisted domestic pressure from American labor unions and other groups for restrictions on Japanese exports, the United States and Japan worked out a series of "voluntary" Japanese quotas on certain types of exports such as automobiles. By the 1970s, moreover, there was a growing tendency both in the United States and Western Europe to attribute Japan's export success not only to its high product-quality control, managerial efficiency, marketing prowess, and good labor relations, but also to allegedly "unfair" trade practices. These included Japanese tariffs, quotas, and procurement policies, the cumulative effect of which was alleged to be the exclusion of U.S. manufactured exports from Japanese domestic markets. Japan was criticized for maintaining nontariff barriers, such as weight restrictions on automobiles, that discriminated against imports and for not permitting foreign banks to operate in Japan on terms that would reciprocate Japanese access to overseas financial markets. In the late 1970s Japan took a series of steps toward trade liberalization that included tariff cuts negotiated in the Tokyo Round of multilateral trade negotiations that were conducted between 1973 and 1979. The Carter administration pressed Japan to increase its import quotas for certain other U.S. goods. Nevertheless, the trade deficit continued to rise. One of its effects was to increase the perception that Japan, though it had become an economic giant, was not contributing its fair share to defense. Japanese spending in that sector remained just below 1 percent of GNP.

### Japan Increases Its Defense Budget

Japan's position as an "economic superpower" was fragile, for changes in the global economic system and military-security environment held far-reaching implications for Japanese prosperity. The loss of overseas markets as a result of the protectionism of others, the disruption of raw-material supplies, and changes in the relative military positions of the United States and the Soviet Union in the

Asian Pacific were recognized as having special significance for Japan. Under the Treaty of Mutual Cooperation and Security of 1960, the United States retained access to bases on Japanese territory and assumed an obligation to come to Japan's defense in the event of an attack, while Japan incurred no comparable obligation with respect to the United States. Thus the treaty was not "mutual," but, in contrast to the Atlantic Alliance, continued to be one-sided. It differed in another important respect from the Atlantic Alliance: NATO had provided a multilateral framework within which a consensus could be developed for a West German contribution to the common defense of the North Atlantic area, but there was no comparable multilateral basis for Asian Pacific consensus for Japan's rearmament in support of shared security interests. NATO had enabled the United States to avoid the friction and apprehension that would have arisen from a strictly bilateral security relationship with the Federal Republic of Germany. In its diplomacy toward Japan the Carter administration could only attempt, as it did increasingly after the beginning of the Iranian crisis and the Soviet invasion of Afghanistan, to nudge Japan to increase its defense spending, especially for maritime forces for the protection of sea lanes and for the strengthening of air defenses. The United States achieved substantial increases in the annual Japanese contribution to the cost of maintaining the U.S. force of 43,000 troops stationed in Japan. Steps were taken toward increased cooperation between Japan and the United States in the exchange of intelligence and in the command of joint defense forces under emergency conditions.

In the late 1970s there was a gradual shift in Japan toward support for a somewhat greater defense effort as a result of several changes in the international security environment. These changes included the substantial increase in Soviet maritime forces in the Western Pacific that coincided with the reduction in the American military presence in the aftermath of Vietnam and, specifically, with the redeployment of American naval units to the Indian Ocean at the time of the Iranian crisis. The increased Soviet military presence in Vietnam, including the use of bases once held by the United States, athwart the sea lanes to and from the Indian Ocean–Persian Gulf heightened Japanese concern about defense. The Soviet invasion of Afghanistan, the deployment of Soviet SS-20s targeted against Japan, and the military fortification of the territories seized by the Soviet Union in the closing days of World War II contributed to the Japanese perception of a changing security situation.

The result of such factors, combined with prodding from the Carter Administration, was Japan's decision in 1980 to undertake a steady growth in defense of at least 5.7 percent annually, allowing for inflation. This compared favorably with the NATO commitment in 1977 to real annual increases of 3 percent, although Japan continued, even with such increases, to allocate just under 1 percent of GNP to defense in contrast to substantially larger percentages in Western Europe and the United States. Because the Japanese Self-Defense Forces, totalling 240,000 troops, was incapable of assuming burdens borne by the United States in such vital missions as sea-lane defense, the argument persisted in the United States and elsewhere that Japan was enjoying a free ride—able to devote its talents to trade expansion and thus to take jobs from workers in the United States and elsewhere.

## THE CARTER ADMINISTRATION
## AND NONPROLIFERATION POLICY

Although every American administration has been committed to the prevention of nuclear proliferation, Carter had come to office with a deeply held concern about the possibility that nuclear technologies might be converted from peaceful to destructive purposes. In the nonmilitary applications of nuclear technology, American policy had been based on the framework created after the Eisenhower administration's Atoms for Peace proposal and further developed in the Non-proliferation Treaty of 1968. By the mid-1970s, however, the use of nuclear power as an energy source, which seemed likely to increase in the decades ahead as a result of declining supplies of fossil fuels, had heightened fears, especially in the Carter administration, that highly enriched uranium and plutonium from nuclear power plants could be converted to weapons. In 1974 India had made use of such materials from a nuclear reactor to detonate a "peaceful" atomic device that did not differ appreciably from a nuclear-weapon capability. Hence, the Carter administration concluded, the safeguards already in existence in the International Atomic Energy Agency to prevent diversion of enriched uranium and plutonium were inadequate.

The essence of the Carter administration policy that emerged was a call for an international moratorium on nuclear-energy development programs that might permit the production of weapons-grade materials. At the same time, Carter proposed a multilateral effort to evaluate the nuclear fuel cycle with the objective of achieving international agreement on adequate nonproliferation standards.

Far more heavily dependent than the United States on energy imports, several Western European countries and Japan had developed substantial nuclear power industries, including plants for the reprocessing of nuclear fuel. In some cases, as in the agreement signed between the Federal Republic of Germany and Brazil in 1975, European allies were engaged in the export of nuclear-reactor technology and the construction of atomic power plants both at home and in other countries. In earlier years the United States had concluded agreements with countries such as Britain, France, the Federal Republic of Germany, and Japan for the supply of nuclear fuel. Before spent fuel could be reprocessed, the prior agreement of the United States was needed. If applied stringently against reprocessing, the Carter administration's new nonproliferation policy, announced abruptly without prior consultation with allies, would cut deeply into the nuclear power programs of such states. In 1977 the Carter administration launched the International Nuclear Fuel Cycle Evaluation (INFCE), which eventually produced a report based on a consensus about strengthened safeguards.

The second component of the policy was the Nuclear Nonproliferation Act of 1978, which established licensing standards for the export of nuclear material and prohibited the supply of any nuclear fuel to countries that did not accept international safeguards for all their nuclear reactors and plants. Although the Carter administration persuaded France not to sell reprocessing plants to Pakistan and South Korea, the United States in 1980 sold nuclear fuel to India despite that country's refusal to accept international safeguards, a decision that seemed inconsistent with U.S. nonproliferation policy but was based on India's assurances of good faith. The effect of the Carter administration's nonproliferation policy was to scale back greatly the development of nuclear power in this country and, over time, to widen an emerging technological margin over the United States in favor of other industrialized states, especially France and Japan, but also potentially Britain and the Federal Republic of Germany, in the utilization and export of nuclear power plants and reactors.

## DETERIORATION IN U.S./SOVIET RELATIONS:
## THE FAILURE OF SALT II

The Carter administration's inability to use its human-rights policy to prevent the suppression of dissidence in the Soviet Union, together with Moscow's apparent success in the exploitation of Third World conflicts and its ongoing strategic-military buildup, cast a lengthening shadow over the SALT negotiations in the eighteen months before the SALT II treaty was signed in Vienna in June 1979.

### Internal Debate over Soviet Policy

Furthermore, the Carter administration seemed to be divided within itself on the strategies to be used in coping with the Soviet Union. The Department of Defense and National Security Adviser Brzezinski sought a tougher U.S. policy on issues such as the SALT II treaty and the transfer of technologies, while the Department of State, and particularly Secretary of State Vance and Paul Warnke, chief SALT negotiator and director of the Arms Control and Disarmament Agency (ACDA), favored greater flexibility to resolve remaining issues in order to bring the SALT II negotiations to a rapid conclusion. The former group believed that SALT II should be pursued as part of a broader strategic dialogue; the latter group held that SALT had intrinsic merit as an arms-control effort and as a basis for future improvement in relations with the Soviet Union on other issues of mutual interest. Increasingly, Carter seemed to identify with the Brown-Brzezinski position of a tougher policy as relations with Moscow worsened in the period that culminated in the Soviet invasion of Afghanistan in December 1979. In a widely quoted commencement speech at the U.S. Naval Academy in June 1978 devoted to relations with the Soviet Union, Carter had asked Moscow to choose "cooperation or confrontation." Both groups, however, favored the conclusion of a SALT II treaty, which remained the principal focus of the Carter administration's policy toward the Soviet Union in 1978–79. Having committed itself so fully to the SALT II treaty and having consciously avoided any effort to link arms-control accords to Soviet behavior elsewhere, the administration had little leverage to exert in order to minimize Soviet misconduct. In turn, the increasing evidence of Soviet policies detrimental to U.S. interests in the Third World and the continuing Soviet military buildup spilled back into the discussion of SALT itself. The effect was to undermine public support for the Carter administration's policies toward the Soviet Union, including the SALT II treaty when it finally emerged from the negotiations.

**Issues of Force Levels and Verification**

In the Carter administration the SALT talks were normally conducted at two levels: through formal meetings between the U.S. and Soviet delegations in Geneva and by means of an informal channel between Vance and Soviet Ambassador Anatoly Dobrynin in Washington, although talks took place between Vance and his Soviet counterparts in Moscow and with Soviet Foreign Minister Andrei Gromyko in Washington at various times. As in other national-security issue areas, the U.S. position was the result of a continuing process of consensus formation within the government that included not only ACDA but also the Departments of State and Defense and the National Security Council, which provided the framework for the development of U.S. policies. In April 1978 agreement was reached between the United States and the Soviet Union that the overall total of their strategic launchers would be placed at 2250 each, a modest reduction from the earlier Vladivostok aggregate of 2400. The total MIRV level for each side was to be 1200, another cut from the original Vladivostok figure of 1320.

In this phase of the negotiations, the issue of telemetry encryption was addressed. In order to verify Soviet compliance with a SALT II treaty, the United States monitored the radio signals emitted by Soviet missiles during their test phase. Such signals enabled the United States to determine many of the characteristics of the missiles, including qualitative aspects of ICBM modernization that were restricted in the SALT II treaty. In the late 1970s the Soviet Union had encoded such signals. The Carter administration sought, and obtained, in the SALT II treaty a commitment that encoding of telemetry needed for verification would be prohibited. The problem of SALT II treaty verification by home-based technical means increased for the United States as a result of the loss of two monitoring sites in Iran after the fall of the Shah in January 1979. Because of the secrecy that shrouds Soviet policy and the pervasive controls exercised by the Soviet government on all information about military programs, the United States would have much more difficulty verifying Moscow's compliance with an arms-control agreement such as SALT II than the Soviet Union would have monitoring American compliance. As is not the case in the Soviet Union, the minute aspects of U.S. defense budgets are subjected to detailed and continuing public and congressional scrutiny. Important defense decisions, such as the construction of new weapons systems and the proposed location of their deployments—such as new NATO intermediate-range nuclear systems and the MX intercontinental missile—are the subjects of protracted debate. The existence of a free press and a large number of groups having an interest in arms control in the United States contribute to a form of self-monitoring of defense policy, including compliance with arms-control agreements, that is absent in the Soviet Union. Therefore, the United States has sought arms-control agreements that permit sufficient verification to prevent cheating by the Soviet Union.

The SALT II treaty concluded by the Carter administration with the Soviet Union limited warhead numbers to ten per MIRVed land-based intercontinental system and to 14 per MIRVed sea-based missile. During the term of the SALT II treaty, which was to expire at the end of 1985, each side could build and deploy no more than one "new" ICBM with or without MIRVed warheads. Among the problems that faced the United States, which the debate about the SALT II treaty brought to public attention, was the fact that in the 1970s the Soviet Union had deployed several new strategic systems. These included the SS-17, SS-18, and SS-19, each of which could carry more warheads against targets in the United States than the American Minuteman land-based ICBM. The largest of the so-called fourth-generation Soviet ICBMs, the SS-18 had a throw weight of approximately 18,000 pounds, contrasted with the 4000 pounds in the Minuteman, which constituted nearly the entire American land-based strategic force. Since completing the installation of a total of 1000 Minuteman missiles in 1967, the United States had deployed no new generation of land-based ICBMs, although the warhead of the Minuteman had been modernized and MIRVed systems had been placed on the Minuteman. However, Soviet strategic capabilities, both in numbers of missiles and in warheads, had grown vastly since the late 1960s. In the SS-18 force alone, the Soviet Union was permitted, in the SALT II treaty, to deploy as many as 308 launchers, each of which could legally carry a total of ten warheads. The SALT II treaty would have prohibited the United States from deploying a similar system, even though there were no American plans to build a missile as large as the SS-18 (the throw weight of the new U.S. MX did not exceed 8000 pounds, less than half that of the SS-18). Moreover, the SALT II treaty excluded the controversial Backfire bomber from the aggregate launcher numbers, even though its more advanced version had intercontinental range if refueled. At the time of the signing of the SALT II treaty, the Soviet Union confirmed an American understanding that 30 Backfires were being produced each year. While the Backfire was left outside the strategic launcher restrictions, the United States was compelled to count every one of its aging B-52 aircraft, even those that were no longer operational, as well as any B-1 aircraft that might be built.

### Criticisms of SALT II's Terms

Critics seized on the SS-18 and Backfire provisions as support for their claim that the SALT II treaty was "unequal" because it conferred important unilateral advantages on the Soviet Union. Both in the case of the SS-18 and the Backfire, the SALT II treaty did little more, critics alleged, than to codify, or legitimize, the deployment by the Soviet Union of nuclear systems beyond the level necessary for strategic stability. On the one hand, the proponents of a strong U.S. defense policy contended that the SALT II treaty conceded to Moscow a strategic-nuclear force that was large enough (combined with vast increases in accuracy since SALT I) to pose a first-strike threat to the fixed, land-based Minuteman force of the United States. Furthermore, it was argued, the decade of SALT (1969–79) had coincided with the greatest buildup in nuclear forces in peacetime, undertaken by the Soviet Union without any comparable American effort in response. The effect of the Soviet buildup (the SS-18 force alone, if MIRVed in accordance with levels permitted in the SALT II treaty, could launch three warheads against each Minuteman silo) would be to open in the 1980s a "window of vulnerability" for the United States, which meant for Moscow a "window of opportunity." The Soviet Union, it was feared, would feel emboldened to step up its political-military operations, especially in unstable Third World regions. Superior Soviet military power, both in strategic-nuclear forces and in conventional capabilities, might cast before it the lengthening shadow of political influence. In such a perspective, Soviet actions in Ethiopia, South Yemen, and Afghanistan coincided with the growth of Moscow's military power.

On the other hand, the SALT II treaty encountered growing criticism even among those who were preoccupied with arms control. The aggregates, both for launchers and MIRVs, were said to be too high. This perspective, of course, accorded with the original "deep cuts" approach from which the Carter administration had hastily retreated after being rebuffed by the Soviet Union in March 1977. Acknowledging in 1979 the existence of strategic-military trends disadvantageous to the United States, the Carter administration held that the SALT II treaty represented a framework within which the Soviet Union was forced to retire as many as 250 systems (such as older bombers) to achieve the 2250 aggregate launcher level. Here, the critics countered that, having done so, the Soviet Union could simply replace most such systems with the uncounted Backfire bomber. Since the United States had fewer than the 2250 aggregate, the Carter administration argued, in turn, that only the Soviet Union was required to reduce the overall number of its strategic forces. The administration contended that, without the SALT II treaty, the Soviet Union could build an even larger strategic-nuclear force. To its opponents, the SALT II treaty seemed only to give formal sanction, as in the case of the Soviet SS-18 and Backfire, to what the Soviet Union planned to deploy by the mid-1980s anyway.

Although the Carter administration, in this respect like its successor, did not plan to build American nuclear forces to the aggregate of 2250 launchers permitted in the SALT II treaty, it saw the need for strategic-force modernization. Having cancelled the B-1 in 1977, it proceeded with research and testing of the cruise missile, to be deployed on the B-52. Within the SALT II treaty, the United States was permitted to deploy a total of 120 aircraft, each equipped with as many as 20 cruise missiles. Just before the signing of the SALT II treaty, the Carter administration made the decision to deploy as many as 200 MX missiles, although controversy surrounded the question of an appropriate basing mode. In view of the vulnerability problems associated with the fixed, land-based Minuteman, it was considered to be necessary to find alternative means to enhance MX survivability.

Increasingly in 1979, steps toward the modernization of strategic-nuclear forces became the essential condition for the development of domestic consensus, and in particular for the Senate votes that would be needed for ratification of the SALT II treaty. This modernization should be compared with NATO's double-track decision of December 1979, in which the conduct of arms-control negotiations became the prerequisite for the deployment of modernized theater nuclear forces. In both cases defense policy and arms control were inextricably linked. In the SALT II debate, however, the result was the public perception that the United States needed to increase its military capabilities in light of adverse trends in the U.S.–Soviet military balance and to adopt a more assertive political stance to counter Soviet expansionism. Although the SALT II treaty faced formidable and increasing opposition as the debate on the adequacy of U.S. defense capabilities unfolded in the last months of 1979, it was a broader set of issues, related more to the U.S.–Soviet political relationship than to specific military considerations, that eventually doomed it.

### Cuba as a Soviet Surrogate

The Carter administration had as one of its early objectives the improvement of relations with Castro's Cuba as a means of undercutting Soviet influence in Havana. If successful, such an initiative, it was reasoned in Washington, might reduce the Soviet military presence in Cuba and might lessen Moscow's use of Cuban military units as surrogates for Moscow in Africa and elsewhere. In early 1977 the Carter administration established with Cuba the first official diplomatic contacts in more than 15 years, which led to agreements on fisheries and maritime boundaries and to the opening, on September 1, 1977, of diplomatic interest sections, or small offices, in Washington and Havana, which stopped short of the establishment of full diplomatic relations. Such steps had no discernible effect on the Soviet–Cuban relationship. Instead, in 1977 the use by Moscow of Cuban proxy military forces in Ethiopia and Southern Africa increased.

Moreover, in the fall of 1978 the Carter administration became aware of an increased Soviet military presence in Cuba that included the stationing of MiG-23s. If such aircraft were carrying nuclear weapons—and they were capable of doing so—the Soviet Union would be in violation of the understanding reached in 1962 after the Cuban missile crisis, when the Soviet Union had agreed to station no nuclear weapons in Cuba. Perhaps because it was anxious not to inflame the U.S.–Soviet relationship or to endanger the SALT II treaty, the Carter administration accepted Soviet assurances that the Mig-23 aircraft in Cuba did not have nuclear weapons.

In mid-1979, however, public attention began to be attracted to Soviet military deployments in Cuba. At a hearing on the SALT II treaty in July 1979, Senator Richard Stone of Florida suggested that the Soviet Union had stationed a brigade of combat troops in Cuba. Stepped-up U.S. intelligence activity furnished evidence in support of Stone's contention. This information soon became public, although controversy remained about the actual combat capability of the Soviet unit and how long it had been in Cuba. The effect of these revelations was to diminish support for the SALT II treaty even among some of the Carter administration's allies in the Senate, including the chairman of the Senate Foreign Relations Committee, Frank Church, then waging an uphill reelection campaign, in which his support for the SALT II treaty was an issue and which he eventually lost.

The Carter administration suggested to Moscow that, unless the Soviet brigade was withdrawn from Cuba, the prospects for ratification of the SALT II treaty were remote. The Soviet Union merely declared that the unit was a "military training center" that had been in Cuba since 1962, and therefore Moscow had no intention of withdrawing it. Although the Carter administration accepted the Soviet explanation and the brigade issue faded from public attention, it damaged the prospects for ratification of SALT II.

## The Soviet Invasion of Afghanistan

More than any other event, however, it was the Soviet invasion of Afghanistan, which began on December 25, 1979, that sealed the fate of the SALT II treaty. Having rejected the idea of political linkage between arms control and other aspects of the U.S. relationship with the Soviet Union, the Carter administration was unable to avert the consequences for the SALT II treaty of the deterioration in the overall state of U.S.–Soviet relations. Thus there was a kind of reverse linkage, with the SALT II treaty having become hostage to Soviet behavior on other issues—most of which, from the sands of Ogaden, to which Brzezinski had referred, to the Khyber Pass in Afghanistan, were centered on the Third World.

In the decade since Britain's withdrawal from the Indian subcontinent in 1947, Afghanistan, initially poised politically between the United States and the Soviet Union and receiving aid from both, had drifted gradually into the shadow of Soviet power. In April 1978 any pretense that Afghanistan was a buffer between the Soviet Union to the north and Iran and Pakistan to the south disappeared with the overthrow of the civilian government of President Mohammed Daoud by radical leftist military elements and the installation of a regime headed by Nur Mohammed Taraki. Although the Carter administration had no evidence of direct Soviet complicity in the coup, Taraki represented a pro-Soviet faction in Afghanistan.

In the months following the coup, there was widespread opposition that culminated in a fatal attack on Taraki in September 1979. Several months before Taraki's death, Hafizullah Amin, the foreign minister and one of the leaders of the April 1978 coup, had taken charge of the campaign against the opponents of the regime, who occupied much of the countryside. Dissatisfied with Amin's lack of success in quelling dissident forces, the Soviet Union launched a massive invasion of Afghanistan. Amin was killed and his government overthrown.

Whatever may have been the immediate motives in the Soviet decision to intervene, its effect was to pose the possibility that Soviet military power, deployed in Afghanistan, would lie within 300 miles of the strategically important Strait of Hormuz. It appeared that Moscow was contemplating moves that would eventually place it in a position of dominance astride oil-producing states of the Persian Gulf that would enable it to interdict the flow of oil to Western Europe, Japan, and the United States.

In response to the invasion, Carter withdrew the SALT II treaty from Senate consideration on January 3, 1980, although he did not abandon all hopes for eventual ratification and stated that the United States would observe the terms of SALT II. The Carter administration took other steps to give tangible expression to its opposition to the Soviet invasion of Afghanistan: the imposition of an embargo against U.S. grain exports to the Soviet Union; a halt in the sale of certain high-technology products; and a U.S. boycott of the 1980 Olympic Games in Moscow.

Although the Soviet Union had used military power on a large scale in East Germany in 1953, in Hungary in 1956, and in Czechoslovakia in 1968, the invasion of Afghanistan represented the first case since World War II of such action by Soviet forces against a country formally outside the Soviet bloc. Coming less than a year after the fall of the Shah and the collapse of American influence in neighboring Iran, the Soviet military action in Afghanistan led the Carter administration to consider the need to strengthen U.S. capabilities to protect its interests in Southwest Asia. Its response was the Carter Doctrine, enunciated in early 1980, after not only the Soviet invasion of Afghanistan but also the Iranian revolution and the sharp decline in American influence in the Persian Gulf dramatized by the seizure of 51 members of the U.S. Embassy staff in Teheran on November 1, 1979. (The Carter Doctrine is discussed later in this chapter.)

## THE IRANIAN CRISIS

Especially in the Nixon/Ford administration, but also in the 1977–78 period of Carter's presidency, Iran represented a perceived source of stability in the oil-rich, strategically important Persian Gulf. Under the authoritarian rule of Shah Mohammed Reza Pahlavi, who had been in power since 1952, Iran seemed to be modernizing rapidly. Iran had been the recipient of large-scale arms sales, principally from the United States. Viewed by the United States and the governments of Western Europe as an emerging regional power and by the Nixon Doctrine as a surrogate whose military capabilities would reduce the need for a direct American presence, Iran under the Shah had evolved increasingly close relations with successive administrations in Washington. Although in retrospect benign by comparison with the regime of the Ayatollah Ruhollah Khomeini which replaced him, the Shah evoked criticism in the United States on human-rights issues. During the Middle East War of 1973 and the subsequent sharp increase in oil prices, the Shah had refused to join the Arab oil embargo or to use oil as a political weapon, though he had supported the rise in oil prices for the increased revenues that would contribute to his ambitious program for the modernization of Iran.

Not fully understood in the United States (and perhaps even by the Shah himself) was the narrow, and narrowing, base of domestic political support on which his government rested. By the 1970s the Shah's modernization program was encountering mounting opposition from the powerful fundamentalist Islamic clergy and from landowners whose interests were threatened. The Islamic fundamentalist movement represented an amalgam of forces determined to turn back the assault on traditional values that was represented by the modernization programs of the Shah. Because such economic development brought with it Western practices, institutions, and technologies most fully embodied by the United States, Islamic fundamentalism was suffused with anti-Westernism and, specifically, anti-Americanism. Although Carter had visited Iran at the end of 1977, the full impact of the revolutionary forces that would soon topple the Shah was not readily discernible in Washington until the late autumn of 1978.

### The Overthrow of the Shah

Sporadically, but with increasing intensity, demonstrations broke out that pitted the followers of the Ayatollah Khomeini against the Shah's policies and internal-security forces. As leader of the Shi'ite Islamic sect in Iran, Khomeini had long been recognized as a dedicated enemy of the Shah. In 1963 the opposition movement led by Khomeini had been crushed and the Ayatollah exiled first to Turkey, then to Iraq, and finally to Paris. In responding to the rising tide of demonstrations, the Shah faced a dilemma: the more he attempted to use the security forces to quell disorder, the more the mullahs, the Islamic clergymen who followed Khomeini, seemed to succeed in organizing new protests.

The signals to the Shah from the Carter administration seemed ambiguous. The U.S. Embassy in Teheran and the Department of State argued for a process of reconciliation between the Shah and his political opponents and resisted the idea, supported by National Security Adviser Brzezinski, that greater force, including a crackdown by the Iranian military, should be employed. The Carter administration confronted a difficult dilemma in which its commitment to human rights clashed with the strategic interest of a beleaguered ally. The suppression of the challenge to the Shah could be accomplished only with force that would eventually produce great bloodshed. The failure to quell the opposition would bring to power a government that was xenophobic, anti-American, and capable of far greater human-rights violations and brutality against its opponents.

As the Carter administration, in the fall of 1978, moved from the Camp David accords to the eventual conclusion of the peace treaty between Egypt and Israel, completed negotiations for normalization of relations with China, and met with the Soviet Union on the SALT II treaty, the regime of the Shah moved rapidly toward disintegration. Despite the mounting unrest, the approach chosen by the Shah was the continuation of a liberalization program begun in 1977 in an abortive effort to divide the opponents of his regime, combined with the use of restraint designed to prevent further violence in the streets. Although he stopped short of full use of the military (which itself became increasingly divided about his rule), the Shah declared martial law in the cities where unrest was the greatest. In November the Shah had appointed the chief of staff of the Iranian military as prime minister, while retaining civilian control of the rest of the government. In January 1979 the Shah formed a new government headed by Shapour Bakhtiar, a leader of the National Front, an opposition political grouping. In a last-ditch effort to find an alternative to Khomeini, the Shah sought a compromise based on rule by moderate opposition elements and the Shah's departure from Iran for an extended period.

The Shah's departure—which turned out to be permanent—on January 16, 1979, had little effect on the political chaos in Iran. The Carter administration sent a message to Khomeini, still in exile in Paris, urging that an effort be made to bring together a coalition of the diverse forces, including the Islamic fundamentalists, the moderate political opposition to the Shah that Bakhtiar and the National Front symbolized, and the military—an impossible task given the interests, values, and goals represented by such diverse and hostile contenders for power. Any hope that the National Front, the military, and Khomeini's fundamentalists could work together soon gave way to the realities of the Iranian revolution. The National Front had long been opposed by the military. Moreover, the Communist Tudeh party, with close links with the Soviet Union, was a force of increasing importance in Iran. The Islamic fundamentalist followers of Khomeini despised both the National Front, itself the product of the political values of the West, and the military, which had been nurtured and amply sustained as a critically important element of the Shah's regime. In early February much of the Iranian military establishment disintegrated, with some units even declaring their support for Khomeini, whose cadres were already setting up a parallel government to the Bakhtiar regime. With the disintegration of the Iranian military went Brzezinski's hopes for a coup against Khomeini. Bakhtiar resigned and was replaced by a provisional government headed by Mehdi Bazargan, appointed by Khomeini, who had returned from exile to Iran on February 1, 1979.

### The Aftermath of the Iranian Revolution

During the Iranian revolution, the Carter administration had followed a course of moderation. While expressing support for the Shah, American policy had been directed toward encouragement of internal reforms designed to broaden domestic political support for the Iranian government. As the Shah faltered and then fell from power, the Carter administration, after having publically endorsed the short-lived Bakhtiar government, made cautious approaches to the Bazargan regime, which itself seemed to contain elements far more moderate than Khomeini and his Islamic fundamentalist zealots. Nevertheless, the conflicts among moderates in favor of a social-democratic government, the Islamic fundamentalists who sought a return to older religious and social-political values, and the disciplined Marxist-Communist forces, precluded any possibility of a strong, cohesive central government in the months after the departure of the Shah.

   Although seemingly removed from the daily conduct of government, the Ayatollah Khomeini emerged as the ultimate source of political authority. Below him battles raged among the politically radicalized groups of revolutionary Iran. The focus of their hatred was the departed Shah and by inference the United States, with which his government had been so closely linked. Supporters of the Shah faced persecution and death at the hands of the Islamic revolutionary regime of the Ayatollah Khomeini on a scale far exceeding the excesses of the Shah's government. There were mock trials and mass executions conducted systematically against known and suspected opponents of the Iranian revolution. Although followers of the Shah were the principal victims, acts of violence, including assassinations, took place among the various groups contending for power and against ethnic and religious minorities in Iran, including Jews. While protesting the violations of human rights that were occurring on a daily basis in Iran, the Carter administration sought to minimize frictions with the new rulers of Iran. The administration indicated its willingness to maintain mutually acceptable arms supplies, although it was evident in Washington that the previous era of a strong U.S.–Iranian relationship had ended with the fall of the Shah.

Although the forces that toppled the Shah were long in the making, the question lingered whether there was anything that the Carter administration could have done to help forestall the chaos that enveloped Iran. Could the United States, by unambiguously supporting the Shah's full use of his internal-security forces against opponents in the latter months of 1978, or a full military government after disturbances spread, have sustained the Shah in power? Alternatively, could the Shah have pursued modernization policies other than those that made enemies of the influential Islamic clergy and other groups whose land was taken in the Shah's reforms of the 1960s? Could political participation have been broadened to include at least some of the forces that eventually coalesced against the Shah? Would it have been possible to set in motion a modernization program that ensured the dominance of modernizing elements instead of creating dissatisfaction with the pace of political democratization and students and intellectuals, including a large number of persons who had received education in the United States and Western Europe, and fostering opposition to the socioeconomic implications of modernization for traditional values among the fundamentalist Islamic clergy? To ask such questions is to probe the "lessons" of the Iranian revolution for modernization programs grafted onto the traditional body politic of Third World states elsewhere, although no two situations are identical in all respects and must be examined, therefore, for their unique features as well as for shared characteristics.

One of the immediate results of the Iranian revolution was the second oil crisis of the 1970s. Amid the demonstrations against the Shah, a strike of oil workers broke out in late October 1978 and quickly reduced daily production in Iran from 5.8 to 1.9 million barrels of oil per day. As the effects of this severe cut in output were felt in world markets, the price per barrel of oil rose from the $12 established by OPEC in 1974 to an unprecedented $40 per barrel. In 1979 it was necessary for oil-consuming countries—wealthy industrialized powers and poor Third World consumers alike—to absorb a three- to four-fold increase in oil prices. The sharp curtailment of Iranian oil production, which was at less than half the level under the Shah, persisted into the 1980s, with no likelihood of a return to previous high levels.

Because it had no ambitious modernization programs to finance, the new Islamic Republic of Iran had no need for huge oil revenues. Previously, it had been conventional wisdom in the West to regard modernization as crucially important to any Iranian government and, hence, the production of oil at high levels as an interest that would transcend any specific government of Iran. Thus the value structure of the leaders of the Iranian Revolution was at odds with the assumptions contained in the interdependence concept that was central to the globalism of the Carter administration when it came to office. If the consuming states remained heavily dependent on Persian Gulf oil, it did not follow that all producers had equal need for oil revenues or that they shared Western values about the benefits alledged to accrue from modernization. Nevertheless, one of the immediate effects of the sharp rise in oil prices was increased balance-of-payments deficits especially for poor Third World countries as well as inflation and economic recession, with increasing unemployment, in industrialized oil-importing nations.

### The Hostage Crisis

It was not oil but hostages that most fully dramatized the increasing difficulty and frustration that the United States was having in influencing events beyond its own shores. Oil had been used by producers both as a political weapon and as a commodity to extract maximum economic gains. The 1970s was also the setting for the growing use of terrorism, hijacking, and the taking of hostages as political weapons. Such acts were perpetrated either against anonymous targets as a means of attracting attention to causes such as a Palestinian homeland or to gain a specific goal, such as the freeing of prisoners held in jails in another country in return for the release of hostages held after, for example, the hijacking of an airliner. The storming of the American Embassy in Teheran by militant followers of Khomeini on November 4, 1979, and their capture of 51 U.S. official diplomatic representatives did not conform fully to either of these rationales. Instead, the seizure of the embassy compound was precipitated by the decision, reluctantly made by the Carter administration, to admit the Shah to the United States for medical treatment for cancer. Having first accepted Sadat's hospitality in Egypt, the Shah had then spent time in Morocco, the Bahamas, Mexico, Panama, and finally back to Egypt, where he died in July 1980. In his later years in power the Shah's health had been deteriorating, a factor that may have contributed to the political indecisiveness that characterized the period just before his downfall. The effect of the decision, made more for humanitarian than political reasons, to admit the Shah to the United States provoked heightened anti-American demonstrations in Iran and the seizure of the hostages less than two weeks after the Shah's arrival.

The militants who captured and held hostage the U.S. embassy personnel demanded the return of the Shah to Iran to stand trial for alleged crimes and the restoration of the Pahlavi family's financial assets to the Iranian government. As it had in other phases of its relationship with Iran, the Carter administration sought to deal with more moderate elements in the Iranian government, while using whatever political leverage was available. However, Bazargan was forced out of office by the rising tide of Islamic fundamentalism within days of the seizure of the American hostages, and Khomeini, on whom any agreement for their release depended, refused to receive emissaries that the Carter administration proposed to send to Iran. The difficulties facing the United States in negotiating the release of the hostages were magnified by the fact that, after the collapse of the Bazargan government, political power in Iran was lodged in the Revolutionary Council, which included an assortment of clerics and secular militants who considered themselves to be the protectors of the Iranian revolution, but who were actually riding the crest of support from mobs who demonstrated in the streets against the departed Shah and the United States. The sanctions Carter imposed against Iran included the suspension of oil imports by the United States from Iran, the blocking of all Iranian assets in the United States, and official action to deport Iranians living illegally in the United States. Additional U.S. naval units were deployed to the Indian Ocean, while the Carter administration searched without success for ways to obtain the release of the hostages.

Initially buoyed in domestic support by his handling of the hostage crisis, the longer it dragged on, the more Carter came to be criticized as the presidential primaries and the election campaign of 1980 unfolded. In keeping with his penchant as president to delve personally into the minute details of foreign policy, and in this case morally repelled by the action of the Iranian militants, Carter elevated the release of the hostages to an urgent policy objective. Here the Carter administration faced a dilemma: the greater the importance attached to the hostages by the United States, the more valuable the hostages became to those who had seized them. In turn, the inability of Carter, despite his own personal political and emotional involvement, to achieve a satisfactory resolution inevitably raised questions about his leadership abilities. This factor, together with the symbolism of a declining, impotent United States that came to surround the hostage situation, contributed to Carter's defeat in the 1980 presidential election.

The image of an irresolute American policy, linked to a deficient military capability, came sharply into focus when the Carter administration launched an abortive mission to rescue the hostages in April 1980. After all other efforts had failed, a small U.S. force was sent to free the hostages in what was to have been a commando raid on the embassy compound in Teheran. Because of equipment failure in the desert staging area, the mission was called off. As the rescuers were departing, a helicopter and a transport plane collided, killing several military personnel. Secretary of State Vance, who had opposed the use of force to secure the release of the hostages, resigned, to be replaced by Senator Edmund Muskie of Maine. Throughout the presidential campaign and during the remainder of the Carter presidency, the hostage crisis continued. Although the Carter administration in its waning days finally negotiated the release, the departure of the hostages from Iran began only moments after Carter had relinquished the presidency to his successor, Ronald Reagan, on January 20, 1981.

## THE CARTER DOCTRINE AND U.S. DEFENSE POLICY

Whether the Soviet Union would have invaded Afghanistan if the Shah of Iran had remained the guardian of U.S. strategic interests in the Persian Gulf cannot be known for certain. What is apparent, however, is that the Soviet invasion of Afghanistan followed the Iranian revolution. The Soviet leadership may have viewed the severe setback for American policy represented by the fall of the Shah as affording a unique opportunity to extend Soviet power into Afghanistan and, specifically, to quell internal opposition to a Marxist regime aligned with the Soviet Union. By the end of 1979, moreover, domestic support for the Carter administration's foreign policy had diminished as a result of its inability to obtain the removal of the Soviet brigade stationed in Cuba. The fact that the Soviet military unit had been deployed in Cuba for several years without apparently arousing the concern of U.S. policymakers did little to bolster public confidence in the collection and analysis of intelligence information that would be essential for verification of Soviet compliance with the SALT II treaty.

### The Carter Doctrine Reaffirms Containment Policy

By the end of 1979, the Carter administration faced the need to furnish tangible evidence that its foreign policy was being adjusted in light of a series of formidable challenges posed by the Soviet Union and by political change in the Persian Gulf. Taken together, these events furnished the setting for what came to be called the Carter Doctrine. In his State of the Union Address of January 23, 1980, Carter announced that the United States would act as necessary to prevent the Soviet Union from establishing itself as the dominant power in the Persian Gulf: "Let our position be absolutely clear: An attempt by any outside force to gain control of the Persian Gulf region will be regarded as an assault on the vital interests of the United States of America, and such an assault will be repelled by any means necessary, including military force." Viewed from the perspective of American foreign policy since the Vietnam War, the Carter Doctrine was a dramatic departure from the recent past and from what, in the case of the Middle East, had been an episodic American interest and commitment of capabilities. Since the Eisenhower Doctrine, a number of trends—the completion of the withdrawal of European power from the region, and in particular from the Persian Gulf in the case of Britain; heightened Western oil-import dependence; the growth of political instability in the region; and the Soviet military buildup—had imposed a series of new security interests and burdens on the United States.

Having entered office with a commitment to substitute "world-order politics" for "balance-of-power politics" and to transcend East–West issues by focusing on the global agenda of the industrialized allies and the Third World, the Carter administration found itself forced not only to address the old agenda but also to take steps, including threatened military action, to prevent Soviet expansion into the vitally important Persian Gulf. Elected in the immediate aftermath of the fall of Vietnam and embodying in its initial foreign-policy perspectives the anti-Vietnam syndrome ("no more Vietnams"), the Carter administration had been forced by threats to U.S. security back to a concept of balance of power—to finding the means of countering Soviet capabilities positioned increasingly close to the Persian Gulf oil-producing states.

In the Carter Doctrine the United States extended the containment principle of earlier administrations, beginning with the Truman Doctrine of 1947, to Southwest Asia. The Eisenhower Doctrine of 1957 had symbolized the emergence of the United States as a power with vital interests in the Middle East, although the focus of attention of the Eisenhower administration had been the eastern Mediterranean and, specifically, the relationship between Israel and its neighbors (including Lebanon, Syria, Jordan, Egypt, and Iraq), rather than the Persian Gulf itself. Although the Eisenhower administration, in contrast to Carter, had successfully used military power on a limited scale (in Lebanon in July 1958), the effect of the Carter Doctrine was to set forth a major and continuing U.S. commitment to the security of the Persian Gulf from the external threat represented by the Soviet Union.

In a sense, the Carter Doctrine represented a reaffirmation of the continuity that has characterized American foreign policy in its quest to mobilize the means, by U.S. capabilities and by alliances, of containing the Soviet Union. In this respect, the efforts to strengthen NATO by the modernization of intermediate-range nuclear forces after the policy debacle represented by the neutron-bomb controversy, the emergence of a tentative strategic relationship with China, and the Carter Doctrine itself formed the central elements of an evolving policy of containment in the late 1970s. In the case of the China policy, the Carter administration's approach was shaped more by design than by events; in contrast, the Carter Doctrine seemed to have been more the product of events than of design. In any case, they formed a policy framework in which, whatever their motivating circumstances, they were fully consistent with the goal of containing the Soviet Union. Last but not least, the events leading to the Carter Doctrine, including this new dimension of the administration's foreign policy, signaled the formal end of the détente relationship nurtured by its two immediate predecessors and severely strained in the latter half of the 1970s.

## The Gap between Defense Commitments and Capabilities

If the immediate threat to the Persian Gulf stemmed, as Carter suggested, from the military capabilities available to the Soviet Union, it was deemed to be essential for the United States to develop necessary countervailing defense forces. Nevertheless, the Carter administration had come to office committed to a reduction in military spending. The immediate effect of the Carter Doctrine was to place in bold relief the considerable gap that separated American security commitments and U.S. military capabilities. The history of American foreign policy is replete with examples of situations in which there has been a major discrepancy between what the United States has been committed to defend and the means it has available to do so. Like the bank that does not keep on hand enough cash to meet the needs of its depositors because a contingency seldom arises in which they all wish to withdraw their money at the same time, it has been the normal practice for U.S. security commitments to exceed capabilities. The United States is not likely to be forced to defend commitments everywhere simultaneously. However, the effect of the growth of Soviet military power, together with the security commitments in the Persian Gulf–Indian Ocean assumed by the Carter administration, was to give added impetus to the debate about the adequacy of U.S. defense capabilities that had been sparked by the SALT II treaty.

The gap between increasing commitments and available capabilities that existed at the end of the Carter administration can be illustrated by reference to several sets of data about U.S. force levels and defense expenditures as when

Carter took office and when he relinquished the presidency in January 1981. In 1977 the U.S. government was authorized to spend $177.2 billion for defense; by 1981 this figure had risen to $200.3 billion. Actual defense expenditures in these two years totaled $157.9 billion and $177.8 billion, respectively. In 1977 U.S. defense spending accounted for 24.2 percent of the budget of the U.S. government, or 5.3 percent of GNP. In 1981, the comparable figures were 24.7 percent of the federal budget and 5.7 percent of GNP. The strength of the U.S. Army's 16 divisions in 1977 totalled 782,246, which decreased, but only slightly, to 781,419 in 1981. In 1977 the U.S. Navy consisted of 529,895 personnel on active duty, which grew to 540,504 in 1981. In 1977 the U.S. Navy had 414 ships; by 1981 this number increased to 423. U.S. Air Force personnel totalled 570,479 in 1977, organized into 76 tactical wings of aircraft, which totalled 2311; by 1981, the Air Force had 570,302 active duty personnel, organized into 78 tactical wings of aircraft, which had grown to 2442. In 1977 the number of U.S. military personnel deployed to NATO-Europe was 318,000; by 1981 this number had risen to 329,000.

Despite increases in defense spending during the Carter administration, such figures illustrate the essentially static quality of the defense capabilities of the United States in the latter half of the 1970s—a trend that nevertheless differed from that prevailing in the Nixon/Ford administration, when there was a sharp decline in most of these indicators as the United States completed force drawdowns as its military commitment in Southeast Asia ended. Thus the defense programs of the Carter administration essentially represented a transition from the overall cuts in spending of the first half of the decade, when the Nixon/Ford administration faced congressional opposition to extended security commitments and capabilities as a result of the Vietnam experience and at the same time were in the process of paring U.S. military capabilities after the withdrawal from Southeast Asia. The Carter administration therefore stood between the reductions of the Nixon/Ford period and the substantial increases initiated by the Reagan administration in an effort to narrow the wide gap between U.S. commitments and capabilities that had been accentuated by Carter's decision to increase the American security commitment in recognition of important interests in Southwest Asia.

### The Rapid-Deployment Concept

The principal effort of the Carter administration to meet the military requirements inherent in the Carter Doctrine was the formation of the Rapid Deployment Joint Task Force (RDJTF). Instead of increasing conventional forces to provide manpower for the RDJTF, the Carter administration decided to utilize units that were already a part of the U.S. force structure but which were committed to contingencies in NATO-Europe and the Western Pacific-East Asia. The RDJTF headquarters would train and plan for the rapid deployment of these units to the Persian Gulf in the event of Soviet action in the area. The Carter administration asked Congress to make appropriations for logistical ships and a new transport aircraft in order to enhance the mobility of the force. The goal of the Carter administration was to develop the means for the deployment within 35 days of a force totalling 100,000 to the Persian Gulf area. Several problems immediately became apparent. Because it shared a border with Iran, across which it could launch a large number of divisions (as many as 26 Soviet divisions were said to be stationed in proximity to Iran), the Soviet Union enjoyed the advantages of location, while the United States suffered the logistical disadvantages of distance. If the United States withdrew some of its forces committed to European/Asian contingencies and sent them to the Persian Gulf, the Soviet Union might be tempted to launch what was called "horizontal escalation," or an attack in another region or point of its adversary's vulnerability.

In U.S. security planning, the concept of deterrence had always taken account of the possibility that any local or regional military conflict between the forces of the superpowers might lead to escalation to the strategic-nuclear level. As long as the Soviet Union feared that such might be the outcome of a military engagement with the United States at the conventional level, it was reasoned that Moscow would therefore not engage its forces in places where U.S. capabilities were deployed, as in NATO-Europe. According to this logic, the RDJTF, insofar as it was designed to protect U.S. interests from Soviet attack, might best serve its purpose if it could be deployed before the arrival of Soviet forces in the Persian Gulf in the event of a crisis there. However, the preemptive positioning of a U.S. rapid deployment force would pose a deterrent to Soviet intervention only if the United States could threaten credibly to escalate to a higher level, including potentially strategic-nuclear forces. As long as the United States possessed clear strategic superiority, so the reasoning went, the threat of such escalation remained credible. In fact, the predominance of U.S. strategic-nuclear forces had helped to compensate for reduced conventional capabilities, especially during the Eisenhower administration, which had substantially cut conventional capabilities while emphasizing a nuclear strategy of massive retaliation. The cuts in conventional forces of the first half of the 1970s, after the U.S. withdrawal from Vietnam, had coincided with the codification of parity in strategic-nuclear forces between the United States and the Soviet Union, thus restricting the American capability to threaten nuclear escalation.

### The "Countervailing Strategy" of Nuclear Deterrence

Successive administrations, from Nixon to Carter, attempted to address this problem through the refinement of nuclear targeting concepts. Shortly after assuming office, the Carter administration had initiated a study of the targeting options available to the United States with the goal of reinforcing its ability to deter nuclear war. In the late 1970s there was a growing level of appreciation among official and academic strategic-military experts that the Soviet Union had embraced a nuclear doctrine substantially different from the principles that had long guided American policy. While the U.S. approach to deterrence was based on the notion that nuclear war could be prevented by mutual assured destruction, the Soviet Union held to a concept whose principal purpose was to ensure that in the event of nuclear conflict, the Soviet Union could eventually recover. Evolving Soviet strategic force levels, including the huge and increasingly accurate SS-18, seemed to accord with a Soviet nuclear strategy designed to destroy the U.S. land-based ICBM forces in a surprise attack and to retain sufficient forces and other military capabilities that would be protected from the effects of an American retaliatory strike. At all levels, the Soviet Union had a higher survival rate in hypothesized nuclear exchanges. Under such circumstances, an emerging level of Soviet advantage in nuclear force levels would lead to the self-deterrence of the United States. The result would be the decoupling of the escalatory threat at the nuclear level from the deterrence of superpower conflict at the conventional level.

This specter haunted those who addressed the problems associated with deterrence on the NATO Central Front and those who thought about the capacity of the United States, with a smaller RDJTF than opposing Soviet conventional capabilities, to control escalation in a Persian Gulf military contingency. Although it had cancelled the B-1 bomber, the important decisions made by the Carter administration to deploy the cruise missile, to maintain the Trident submarine-launched ballistic missile program, and to deploy the MX represented an effort to modernize the strategic nuclear capabilities of the United States and to maintain a diversified capability as the basis for deterrence.

The result of the Carter administration's strategic-targeting study was the "countervailing strategy" contained in Presidential Directive (PD) 59, issued in July 1980. The essence of PD 59 was the proposition, basic to deterrence theory, that there exists a calculus of risk versus gain with respect to the military action of an adversary. In order to influence this calculation to ensure that the enemy's risk clearly outweighs any possible gain, the United States must possess the means to place at risk, or to threaten credibly to retaliate against, the targets that are of greatest value to the Soviet Union. Such targets, as Secretary of Defense Brown stated in his 1981 Department of Defense Report, would "include not only the lives and property of the peoples of the Soviet Union, but the military, industrial, and political sources of power of the regime itself." These were precisely the types of targets needed by the Soviet Union both for the conduct of nuclear war and for its survival in the event of such a conflagration. Hence the targets that the United States should have the nuclear means to destroy consisted of the Soviet armed forces, the leadership structure, and the internal security network, as well as the communications, transportation, and industrial facilities vital to the successful conduct of military operations and to postwar survival and recovery. Possession of such means, it was concluded, would reinforce deterrence at the nuclear level and, by direct inference, would increase the calculus of risk versus gain for the Soviet Union. The result would be a reinforcement of the coupling between deterrence of superpower conflict at the battlefield level and the prevention of miscalculation by the Soviet leadership that it could with relative impunity engage in nuclear warfare. Under such circumstances, military conflicts between the United States and the Soviet Union could be prevented.

## FOREIGN-POLICY DECISION MAKING UNDER CARTER

In designing its foreign-policy decision-making system, the Carter administration sought to establish a clear distinction between its own practices and those of its predecessors. Carter had been critical of the "Lone Ranger" style of the Nixon/Ford administration, in which such great power had come to be wielded by Henry Kissinger. In contrast, Carter strove to develop a decision-making structure whose principal organizational characteristic was simplicity and which thereby could be made responsive to the control of the president himself. This philosophy resulted in the formation of only two interdepartmental policy-coordinating committees in the National Security Council. One was called the Policy Review Committee (PRC), charged with consideration of regional and functional foreign-policy issues (such as Europe or human rights); defense-policy questions; and international economic issues, such as oil, having direct implications for national-security policy. The Policy Review Committee usually met with the secretary of state as chairman and occasionally with the secretary of defense performing that function. The other interdepartmental coordinating committee was established to deal with intelligence policy, including budgets and such sensitive issues as covert operations; the formulation of SALT and other arms-control policies; and crisis management. The Special Coordination Committee (SCC), as it was designated, was chaired by the assistant for national-security affairs.

In the process of formulating policy options, what was termed a Presidential Review Memorandum (PRM) would be requested by the national-security adviser acting in behalf of the president. In the case of the Policy Review Committee, the PRM would be prepared principally by the department whose secretary would chair the meeting, whether Defense or State, although the purpose of the process was to produce policy options representing the integrated perspective not readily available in any single department or agency of the foreign-affairs bureaucracy. In the Special Coordinating Committee, the PRM was prepared by staff members of the National Security Council. Meetings of each of the two committees yielded either a unanimous recommendation or a series of alternative recommendations to be given to Carter for final decision. Another output of the two committees was a series of option papers for consideration at a National Security Council meeting (including as members the secretary of state, the secretary of defense, the secretary of the treasury, and the director of central intelligence). Reports from the PRC or SCC meetings or from the full NSC meeting to the president would be prepared by the staff of the National Security Council. Because these reports were submitted to the president directly by the national-security adviser, Brzezinski enjoyed access to presidential decision making at a critically important final phase of the process. In contrast to his predecessors, Brzezinski was given the status of cabinet member, although Carter strove, at least in the early years of his administration, to make Vance his chief foreign-policy spokesman. The outputs of the Carter administration's decisional structure came in the form of Presidential Directives (PDs) if the issue was of great importance or simply as decision memoranda on more routine questions transmitted usually under the signature of the assistant for national-security affairs. Carter himself signed those PDs that were of the greatest importance, such as PD 59, which marked a shift in U.S. strategic-nuclear targeting doctrine.

Continuous access, enhanced by the proximity of the office of the assistant for national security to the oval office, undoubtedly helps to account for the influence wielded by the national-security adviser. Although Brzezinski benefited from such an advantage in his relationship with Carter, the structural charac-teristics of the United States government contributed to his influence. Because Carter saw himself as a president deeply involved in the intricacies of foreign policy, he needed an assistant for national-security affairs who could integrate for him the complex policy issues confronting him. Such a presidential approach to foreign-policy decision-making almost of necessity enhances the role of those advisers most immediately available on a continuing basis to the president, while diminishing the influence of other actors in the policy process, including the secretary of state. Vance found himself not consulted on numerous occasions but instead presented with *faits accomplis.* His duties as secretary of state resulted in protracted trips abroad which removed him from the center of the decision-making process at critically important times, such as the completion of the negotiations for diplomatic normalization with China. However, the secretary of state had his own direct avenues to Carter. Vance submitted a daily foreign-policy briefing paper that did not pass through the NSC structure but instead went to Carter directly at the end of each day. In addition to his own frequent meetings with Carter, Vance participated, with Brzezinski and Brown, in a weekly breakfast meeting with Carter. There was another coordinating mechanism in the form of a weekly luncheon meeting, at which Brown, Brzezinski, and Vance exchanged ideas, made decisions, and settled policy differences without having to deal with cumbersome formal agendas or entrenched bureaucratic positions.

In his own style of presidential decision making, Carter was conspicuous in the extent to which he immersed himself in the minute details of the policy process. The knowledge that Carter expected to be kept fully informed and the assurances that he might, as in the case of the neutron-bomb controversy, even act contrary to the strongly held policy positions of his closest advisers, limited the latitude for independent, uncoordinated action by the various departments and agencies. Nevertheless, the effect of Carter's detailed attention was also to hamper the achievement of coherent, consistent policies. It was the proverbial problem of the person who, preoccupied with the trees, can't see the expanse of the forest. The greater the attention to detail in one issue area, as in the negotiations for release of the U.S. hostages in Teheran, especially in the final days of the Carter presidency, the less time available to deal effectively with other important issues and, in particular, the greater the difficulty in establishing broad policy priorities and frameworks, as well as specific goals and strategies.

Carter gave what seemed to be excessive attention to tactics, to the neglect of grand strategy. In doing so, he may have made himself the object of criticism that otherwise could have been absorbed by those subordinates most directly involved in the failure of a policy. As head of state, an American president holds a position that places him above the political battles of the day. Yet, as head of government, he is directly involved in the political process. The key to effective presidential leadership lies in the imagination and political ingenuity demonstrated by a president in combining these seemingly contradicting elements of his job description. To do so, a President must appear to separate himself from much of the day-to-day policy process without, of course, actually doing so. Under such circumstances, he can take credit for successes and minimize the direct onus he bears for failure, although in the final analysis the incumbent president is held accountable for the success or failure of foreign policy no less than of domestic policy. To cultivate the public perception of continuous presidential direct involvement in policies that do not succeed, as Carter did, is both to elevate those policies to a level that may exceed their actual importance or, as happened in the Carter administration, to reinforce the popular perception of a president lacking the necessary qualities of leadership. In Carter's case, the personal triumph represented by the Camp David accords, which probably could not have been negotiated without his own detailed and continuing participation, was outweighed by failures in Southwest Asia, including the seizure of the American hostages and the abortive rescue operation, and by the deteriorating political relationship with the Soviet Union.

## CONCLUSIONS ABOUT CARTER'S CONDUCT OF FOREIGN POLICY

Having entered office with a strong interest in reorienting American foreign-policy priorities from the East–West focus of previous administrations, Carter ended his term having enlarged the commitment of the United States to the containment of Soviet power in Southwest Asia. The Carter administration had developed a foreign-policy agenda whose principal focus was to be the engagement of American nonmilitary capabilities in the global issues of the late twentieth century, especially in the North–South arena. In this sense, the administration held, the assets available to the United States and to Western Europe and Japan, if linked more fully in a trilateral relationship, would furnish the basis for dealing with such issues as global development, trade, investment, overpopulation, and human rights. The Soviet Union faced the choice of either joining the industrialized states of the West and Japan in this eminently worthy endeavor or being bypassed by the sweeping tides of history. This approach, at least in the early days of the Carter administration, represented an effort to substitute "world-order" for "balance-of-power" politics, to diminish the importance of a strategic approach to foreign policy and to elevate to greater prominence the great global socioeconomic issues of the late twentieth century.

If the preceding administration had found it impossible to entice the Soviet Union into a global structure for peace founded on a multipolar framework in whose preservation Moscow no less than Washington would have a vital stake, the Carter administration confronted equally formidable obstacles in making a heterogeneous world conform to its assumptions, priorities, and goals. The Soviet

Union was no more prepared to accept the global policy agenda of the Carter administration than it was to abide by principles of coexistence calling for restraint or to forgo the opportunity for unilateral advantages, especially in Third World regions, that the Nixon/Ford foreign policy had attempted to elicit from Moscow.

Having faced differences within itself almost from the outset with respect to the relationship between its strategies and other policy priorities, the Carter administration was increasingly drawn back to an approach that emphasized the need to confront and contain an expansionist Soviet Union. This was the meaning of the Carter Doctrine, which represented a substantial expansion of U.S. commitments, more in a political than a legal sense, without a commensurate increase in means that, in any event, could not have been developed in the brief time then still available to the administration. The Carter administration's commitment to building relationships with Third World states based on greater empathy for their political and socioeconomic aspirations not only recognized the intrinsic importance of policies based on such values—compatible as they were with the political philosophy of Carter and his associates—but was also designed to reduce the potential for Soviet influence in the Third World. Yet the Carter administration faced its greatest challenges in the Third World in conflict situations that were local, or indigenous, in their origins, but in which the Soviet Union, usually with Cuba as a surrogate, played a major role. Having itself supported the successful effort to replace the oligarchic Somoza regime in Nicaragua with the revolutionary Sandinistas, the Carter administration reaped not gratitude but instead the beginning of a process of growing alignment by the new Nicaraguan government with Havana and Moscow and the political de-stabilization, whose roots to be sure were complex, that would become a major security-policy problem for the Reagan administration. If American military means seemed inappropriate to Third World conflicts, especially in the post-Vietnam phase of American foreign policy, it was equally apparent that the political fortunes of a large number of states, from Central America to Africa to Southwest Asia to Southeast Asia (and especially in Afghanistan and Vietnam), were being shaped by the use of armed force. Thus the debate in the United States about the appropriate relationship between the military and nonmilitary means of statecraft was far from settled. The Carter administration, and a growing constituency of Americans as the election of 1980 approached, came to the conclusion that greater U.S. military capabilities would be needed to meet the security commitments already undertaken and being assumed by the United States.

The task that faced the Carter administration when it assumed office was the reestablishment of a foreign-policy consensus in the aftermath of the Vietnam War and, in an even broader sense, the reconstruction of confidence in American political institutions that had been shaken by the trauma of the Watergate scandal. Such perceived needs formed important themes of both the Carter campaign in 1976 and the policy priorities and style of the Carter administration. Such a mandate was not rooted deeply enough to sustain the foreign policies fashioned by the Carter administration. Instead, Carter soon confronted an emerging American foreign-policy perspective, if not a full consensus, that called for a toughened approach to adversaries, and especially to the Soviet Union, as the challenges to the United States, especially in Southwest Asia, mounted and as the debate about the adequacy of U.S. defense capabilities occasioned by the SALT II negotiations unfolded. In this respect, the administration had to cope with a deterioration in the bases of its domestic support that reached shattering proportions in November 1980. This deterioration more or less coincided with a changing international strategic-political environment that differed profoundly from the perspectives that initially had guided much of Carter's thinking about foreign policy. The effect was to impel the Carter administration, in the final analysis, toward a reassertion of elements of continuity in strategic purposes that had been basic to U.S. foreign policy since World War II, but to do so in a world that, by 1980, had become far more complex and heterogeneous than ever before.

# chapter 9

# The Reagan Foreign Policy:
## A Quest for Restored Purpose and Strength

The Reagan administration came to office on a broad tide of dissatisfaction with the condition of the American economy—with high rates of interest and inflation, rising unemployment, and declining productivity—and a perception of incoherence and vacillation in the Carter presidency and its foreign policy. Just as Jimmy Carter, both in the 1976 campaign and in the early years of his administration, had epitomized the retrenchment in American capabilities and commitments that formed a central element of the post-Vietnam syndrome of the early 1970s, Ronald Reagan symbolized rising concern about the adverse implications for U.S. national security of a marked decline in power. The initial predisposition of the Carter administration had been that overseas commitments must be brought into balance with constrained capabilities. The apparent effects of a reduced level of effort at a time of heightened threats to national interest seemed unsettling to increasing numbers of Americans in the second half of the 1970s. The price of a slackened commitment of resources to foreign policy included the dangers flowing from a greater propensity on the part of adversaries to challenge the interests of the United States in the expectation that an American response would not be forthcoming. The Carter administration's decision in January 1980 to defend territory bordering the Persian Gulf, in what was termed the Carter Doctrine, only widened the gap between commitments and capabilities. If it was proving impossible and potentially dangerous to redefine vital interests more restrictively in keeping with a reduced American level of effort at a time of increasing Soviet military power, then capabilities must be increased to sustain commitments based on vital interests. Thus the Reagan critique of the post-Vietnam approach to foreign policy had as its focus the perceived dangers inherent in retrenchment. The world-order politics espoused by the Carter administration furnished a worthy but distant goal for American statecraft. Nevertheless, it remained essential to shape a power balance in which the U.S.–Soviet relationship formed the central element. Thus the election of the Reagan administration reflected, in part, widespread apprehension about the apparent ineffectiveness of recent American foreign policy.

## REAGAN'S RENEWED EMPHASIS ON CONTAINMENT

Whereas President Carter had decided only after the Soviet invasion of Afghanistan that his initial perceptions of the Soviet Union and its foreign policy had been faulty, the Reagan administration committed itself at the outset, fully and without reservation, to a foreign policy based on a recognition of the Soviet Union as the principal strategic threat confronting the United States. Although not all American foreign-policy problems were attributable to the Soviet Union, the security of the United States and its allies and other friendly states would be jeopardized if growing Soviet military power remained unchecked by appropriate U.S. countervailing capabilities. In a speech to the Chicago Council on Foreign Relations in March 1980, presidential candidate Reagan declared that, as a result of Soviet investment in strategic-military capabilities at a rate nearly three times that of the United States, and expenditures for conventional forces almost twice as great, "we now face a situation in which our principal adversary, the Soviet Union, surpasses us in virtually every category of military strength."

The approach of the Reagan administration would be to revitalize the U.S. effort to contain Soviet expansion, in this respect in keeping with the basic thrust of American foreign policy since the early post–World War II period. Although the United States could not assume global responsibility for all regional and local disputes, the Reagan administration's strategic approach to foreign policy had as a principal premise that no region lies beyond American interest if control or influence by a hostile power threatens the security of the United States. This concept had the advantage of the flexibility inherent in ambiguity. An adversary could not be certain that the United States, restored in military strength, would not intervene, while the administration was not forced to undertake new extended commitments that would have disrupted the fragile national-security consensus that had emerged in the United States by the early 1980s. This consensus entailed a broader support for increased defense capabilities, but a reluctance actually to use such strength in overseas engagements, least of all in those that would be protracted and whose outcome was uncertain—in short, conflicts like Vietnam. The greater the defense capabilities available to the United States, the Reagan administration reasoned, the more credible its diplomacy would become and the less likely it would be that such military means would actually have to be employed in support of vital interests.

American foreign policy in the early 1980s retained elements of the multilateral Atlanticism forged in the mid-twentieth century together with an emergent nationalist, or unilateralist, approach to strategy and foreign policy. The dilemmas inherent in multilateralism and unilateralism became apparent as the United States faced major constraints on available resources at a time of increased threats to national security, from Central America to the Persian Gulf, with extended security commitments from Western Europe to the western Pacific. In one ideal world the United States would have means sufficient to permit exclusive reliance on its own national capabilities (unilateralism). In another ideal world the United States could call on the capabilities of allies sharing its conception of vital interests and having similar perspectives on the appropriate strategy for achieving common security goals (multilateralism). It was necessary for the United States to devise a strategy that related means to ends in a national-security policy containing a combination of the elements of unilateralism and multilateralism.

Taken together and viewed in the context of the continuity of U.S. strategic interests in the twentieth century, the official statements of the Reagan administration yielded the basic concepts of American global strategy. Secretary of State Alexander Haig outlined an approach to foreign policy that was articulated as a series of goals, or "four pillars." These included the restoration of American and Western economic and military strength; the reinvigoration of alliances and other relationships with friendly states; the promotion of progress, in an environment of peaceful change, among less industrialized countries; and, last but not least, the development of a relationship with the Soviet Union based on Soviet restraint and reciprocity. In contrast to the Nixon Doctrine, the Reagan administration's policy eschewed identifying any single strategic concept, or analytic construct, of the international system. The foreign policy of the Reagan administration encompassed not only the rebuilding of military capabilities but also a rebirth of the American spirit in place of the national self-doubt of the Vietnam era. As the prerequisite for the restoration of purpose and power, the American economy must be strengthened by the release of the creative energies of the private sector from stultifying governmental regulation.

## THE PERIPHERAL VS. CONTINENTAL STRATEGIES

In the early 1980s two contrasting basic approaches to American strategy had asserted themselves. The "Peripheral Strategy" called for military capabilities based principally on strategic-nuclear forces, air power, and maritime supremacy, with a substantial emphasis on the assumption of greater defense burdens by allies. The Peripheral Strategy had antecedents in the Nixon Doctrine, in which allied burden sharing was a central element. Because the United States is constrained in its capacity to project military power simultaneously to all theaters of vital interest, its allies must make a greater commitment to defense. The United States would furnish increased capabilities to counter security threats emanating from outside the North Atlantic area and the western Pacific. Therefore, both Western Europe and Japan should assume a greater portion of the burden of defense within their immediate geographic regions in order to enable the United States to focus its defense energies on other regions such as the Persian Gulf, in which Western European and Japanese interests were deemed to be at least as great as those of the United States. A rational division of labor would provide for modernized European ground forces and a substantial increase in Japan's self-defense capabilities. U.S. military priorities would shift toward a larger navy and strengthened nuclear capability, together with greater mobility and firepower for remaining land forces.

The other approach, the "Continental Strategy," or forward-defense concept, posited the need for the United States, with a balanced-force posture, to maintain substantial ground forces both in Western Europe and Northeast Asia as a means of countering superior numbers of mobilized Soviet capabilities and of preserving deterrence. However desirable such burden sharing might be, this strategy held, the growth of Soviet capabilities made necessary a commensurate increase in the military forces of the United States and the maintenance of a forward defense. The withdrawal of American ground forces from Western Europe, in this perspective, would not necessarily be offset by a growth in Western European capabilities. In fact, it was suggested, an irreversible erosion of political will and defense commitments might take place. Western Europe would then become the object of increasing Soviet political pressure and influence as the military balance, both in conventional and nuclear forces, tilted toward Moscow.

The Reagan administration sought to evolve a strategy that embraced elements of both approaches in keeping with basic and continuing American conceptions of vital interest. It remained necessary to develop and preserve the means, within an appropriate strategy, for ensuring the denial to the Soviet Union and other hostile forces of both the core area of Western Europe and the maritime periphery, while attempting to emphasize the vulnerabilities of the Soviet Union. As National-Security Adviser William P. Clark stated in an address in May 1982, the Reagan administration sought to evolve a strategy that would force the Soviet Union "to bear the brunt of its economic shortcomings," and American strategy "must be forward-looking and active. . . . To secure the America we all want and the global stability and prosperity we all seek, we cannot sit back and hope that somehow it will happen. We must believe in what we are doing. That requires initiative, patience, and persistence. We must be prepared to respond vigorously to opportunities as they arise and to create opportunities where none have existed before."

## RELATIONS WITH THE SOVIET UNION

Although the Reagan administration had inherited a deteriorating political relationship with the Soviet Union and regarded Moscow, in Secretary of State Haig's words, as the "greatest source of international instability," its approach to the Soviet leadership resembled U.S. policy in the Nixon-Kissinger era in the perceived need to establish "linkage" among the major issue areas of foreign policy. A decade earlier the Nixon administration had tried but failed, under conditions of a militarily stronger United States relative to the Soviet Union, to obtain Moscow's compliance with the principles of coexistence negotiated at the May 1972 summit conference. In its first months in office the Reagan administration sent signals to the Soviet Union to the effect that Moscow faced a choice between an improved relationship with the United States and the political confrontation that would result from the continued Soviet exploitation of conflicts and expansion of influence in the Third World. The failed détente of the previous decade that had been a "one-way street" for the Soviet Union must be replaced by a relationship based on reciprocity.

The Reagan administration had moved quickly to attempt to open such a dialogue with meetings at many levels, including discussions between Haig and Soviet Foreign Minister Andrei Gromyko and with the Soviet ambassador in Washington, Anatoly Dobrynin. The principal theme of such discussions, from the American side, was that Soviet behavior must improve before it became too late to reverse the deterioration in the political relationship between Moscow and Washington. Specifically, the United States sought tangible evidence of Soviet restraint both in the crisis that was developing in Poland in 1981 and in the numerous Third World conflicts in which the Soviet Union was involved in some fashion. Thus the price for a U.S.–Soviet dialogue on issues such as arms control, technology transfer, and trade credits was a reduction in Soviet involvement in conflict situations as geographically separated as Poland, Cambodia, Yemen, Afghanistan, Africa, and Central America. In its early months the Reagan administration's policies toward the Soviet Union proceeded on essentially two levels: public rhetoric condemning Moscow for its misdeeds, coupled with attempts to engage the Soviet leadership in diplomacy on the numerous issues dividing the superpowers. It has proven far easier for the Soviet Union to restrict outside interference in the formidable problems that it faces in Eastern Europe than it is for the United States to take actions deemed necessary to thwart Soviet-Cuban support for leftist elements in Central America. This basic asymmetry between the United States and the Soviet Union confronted the United States once again in the early 1980s, despite efforts of the Reagan administration to develop a strategy designed to limit Soviet intervention in the Third World and to enable the United States to benefit from the numerous vulnerabilities of the Soviet Union.

## THE POLISH CRISIS

In 1980 Poland faced near economic collapse and food shortages. The failure of the industrialization policies of the previous decade, which had been financed largely by substantial loans from Western European and American banks, had caused the Polish economy to founder so badly that by 1981 it was on the verge of defaulting on its loan repayments. The economic failures of the previous decade provided fertile ground for the formation of the Solidarity trade union under the leadership of Lech Walesa, founded in the port city of Gdansk, in July 1980.

For Solidarity to have succeeded in its objectives would have established an ominous precedent in a country where the Communist regime was the exclusive repository of political power and authority. Within weeks of its creation, Solidarity had an estimated membership of 10 million. The immediate response of the ruling Communist party, guided by the Kremlin, was not repression, because of the likelihood of mass resistance. Instead the regime gave the deceptive appearance of accepting Solidarity's demands. In addition, the Communist authorities confronted a persistent and strengthened Polish nationalism symbolized in the Catholic Church, which was a dominant influence in Poland but which had maintained an often uneasy coexistence with the Communist regime.

## Reform and Repression

In contrast to its invasions of Hungary in 1956 and Czechoslovakia in 1968, this time Moscow opted for a more subtle policy of mobilizing military capabilities, but also bringing to bear economic pressures designed ultimately to weaken dissent within Poland. Moscow withheld its own economic assistance while offering no strenuous objections to Western credits and other aid to Poland. In 1981 Poland received massive shipments of food from the West, as well as an infusion of more than $9 billion, with the United States furnishing credits of $1.1 billion in order to meet Poland's immediate economic needs. After the Polish Communist Party Congress in July 1981, recently appointed First Secretary Stanislow Kania was ousted and replaced by the premier and defense minister, Wojciech Jaruzelski. The appointment of General Jaruzelski symbolized the decay of the Polish Communist party as an effective force capable in itself of reversing the reformist tide without Soviet military intervention.

In a move that was not widely anticipated either in the United States or Western Europe, on December 13, 1981, Jaruzelski declared martial law and made massive arrests that included nearly all members of the Solidarity leadership, whom it apparently also caught by surprise, with the Polish security forces and the army assuming the effective powers of control held in other Communist states by the party. The Soviet Union had achieved the goal that it desperately sought—the reversal of political reform in Poland—through the action of an indigenous Polish force in the form of the crackdown by the Jaruzelski regime without the damage to Moscow's broader international interests, especially relations with Western European countries, that would have resulted from a direct Soviet military intervention.

## The Reagan Administration's Response

In the Polish crisis the Reagan administration had essentially two objectives: to prevent a Soviet invasion and to preserve intact the reforms achieved by Solidarity. In keeping with the linkage concept revived from the Nixon-Kissinger era, the United States attempted to convince Moscow that a Soviet invasion would endanger the superpower relationship and make impossible new agreements with the Soviet Union in other areas of mutual interest. It was debated whether to allow Poland to default on its huge foreign debt, with principal and interest owed totalling $27 billion in 1981, as a means of demonstrating the economic failures of a Communist regime and expressing displeasure with the military crackdown. Western banks would have faced huge financial losses in the event of Polish default, however, and the financial communities of Western Europe and the United States had a greater vested interest in Poland than the Polish regime, or the Soviet Union, had in the West. Ultimately, the Western banks decided to postpone until 1986 Poland's debt repayment—and learned a valuable lesson about the risks inherent in large-scale loans to Communist states. Most of all, the Polish experience brought home again the inherent limits of political change in Eastern Europe.

If the default of the Polish debt would have proven at least as onerous to the lenders as to the debtors, what other options were available to indicate, both to the Soviet Union and to Poland, the displeasure of the United States and its allies? The course of action chosen by the Reagan administration was the imposition of a series of economic sanctions that included a trade embargo. However, the problem was complicated not only by the difficulty of ensuring that sanctions would hurt the transgressors more than the West but also by the perceived need to distinguish, on the one hand, between the Soviet Union and Jaruzelski's regime and, on the other, the Polish people, the majority of whom had supported or at least sympathized with the goals of Solidarity. At another level, the Reagan administration faced the problem of achieving consensus among members of the Atlantic Alliance, for the contemplated trade embargo against the Soviet Union and Poland would need to have the support of the countries capable of supplying embargoed items. The détente legacy of the previous decade, negative for the United States, had yielded gains for Western Europe, especially for the Federal Republic of Germany—gains in trade and inter-German normalization that Bonn and its Western neighbors were reluctant to sacrifice. For the Reagan administration, moreover, the normalization in Europe achieved by the Ostpolitik of the Federal Republic of Germany in the 1970s, together with the Helsinki Final Act of 1975, had symbolized a fundamental change, a new "framework of international relations," as Secretary of State Haig stated.

As sanctions, the Reagan administration decided either to suspend or not to renew licenses for several important technology transfers, including such high-technology products as computers and electronic equipment. This included pipe-laying machinery for the construction of the Soviet-Western European natural-gas pipeline that had been negotiated during the Carter administration. For Western Europe, the pipeline represented a response to the need, since the energy crisis of 1973, to diversify supply and, specifically, to obtain, over a 25-year period, as much as 30 percent of its natural-gas needs at current rates of consumption. Although Western Europe would pay the entire $15 billion cost of the pipeline, its industries would gain a large number of construction contracts and jobs from the project. In December 1981 the United States had banned participation by American companies in the construction of the pipeline.

The divergence between the United States and its Western European allies deepened with the decision by France in early 1982 to proceed, despite Reagan administration objections, not only with participation in the pipeline project but also with a new $140 million loan to the Soviet Union. In June 1982, after an unsuccessful attempt to reach a compromise at the Versailles summit meeting, the Reagan administration extended the prohibition to the subsidiaries and license holders of American companies in Western Europe, an action that would have prevented the export of critically important turbine technologies in which there was an American monopoly. In response to this application of extra-territoriality (the extension of U.S. law to the subsidiaries of American companies operating in other countries), Western European governments instructed such companies operating within their jurisdiction to defy the ban. The United States then forbade the companies to export embargoed technologies—in effect penalizing U.S.-based companies for the compliance of their European subsidiaries with instructions from European governments that ran contrary to American policy. In November the intra-Alliance gas pipeline controversy was resolved when the United States lifted all restrictions on American companies supplying technologies in exchange for a European commitment to end cheap commercial credits to the Soviet Union; to forego future huge projects like the gas pipeline that could be constructed only with below-market-rate credits; and to tighten restrictions on the export of technology to the Soviet Union. To Western Europe, the pipeline controversy was seen as a part of domestic industrial policy. To the Reagan administration it was an element of international strategy and that involved the basic issue of the extent to which the West should strengthen the economy and, by extension, the military capabilities of its principal adversary.

## REAGAN'S POLICIES TOWARD CENTRAL AMERICA

At the same time it was confronting the Polish crisis, the Reagan administration encountered another threat whose roots lay deeper in the history of the U.S.-Soviet relationship. By the late 1970s the endemic political, social, and economic problems of Central America were being exacerbated by the shipment of Soviet-Cuban arms and other forms of support for revolutionary forces of the left. Contrary to popular belief, the United States at the end of the decade was not supporting regimes of the far right in Central America. In fact, the Carter administration had sympathized with the leftist Sandinista revolution and had withdrawn support from the Somoza oligarchy in Nicaragua.

To a far greater extent than its predecessor, the Reagan administration viewed Central America, like other regions of the world, within a strategic context. The strategic importance of Central America and the Caribbean was grounded in the realization that Soviet control of all, or even a large part, of the region would pose formidable obstacles to American foreign policy elsewhere in the world. The United States could not fulfill security commitments in NATO-Europe or in the western Pacific if the Soviet Union or its proxies dominated the Caribbean basin. Most of American shipping to Western Europe, whether in peacetime or wartime, would flow from the U.S. ports on the Gulf of Mexico. Central America constitutes a strategic and geographical bridge between the Americas—between the oil fields of Mexico to the north and the petroleum reserves of Venezuela to the south. For the United States to be compelled to expend large amounts of resources in this region would probably make necessary the curtailment of extended security commitments elsewhere, with adverse consequences of immense proportions for the global security environment. If Soviet-Cuban intervention in the indigenous political instability of Central America and the Caribbean could not be halted, the United States and the moderate, reformist forces of the region—seeking to avert the stark alternatives of the authoritarian oligarchies of the past and totalitarian Communist regimes on the Cuban model—must have the opportunity to build modern societies. In the absence of a sharp curtailment in the violence spurred by Soviet-Cuban arms shipments, forces of moderation could not construct the necessary political, social, and economic infrastructures faster than they could be destroyed by Soviet-Cuban forces of the far left. Hence the Reagan administration's strategic approach called for steps to end Soviet-Cuban arms shipments and other forms of intervention as the prerequisite for the modernization of Central American states.

## Cuba as Moscow's Agent in the Region

For nearly a quarter of a century the Soviet Union had heavily subsidized the faltering Cuban economy and built Fidel Castro's military machine as an integral part of Moscow's power-projection capabilities in the Third World. With massive Soviet aid, Cuba had developed the largest military force in Latin America: an army of 225,000, an air force of 16,000, and a navy of 11,000. The cost of the Soviet subsidization of Cuba, said to total $11 million a day, was not excessive for Moscow if considered in the context of the global strategy of the Soviet Union, in which Cuban forces had been deployed in such distant places as Angola and Ethiopia in support of Moscow's interests. In Nicaragua by 1983 there were reported to be as many as 7000 Cuban troops and advisors, together with several thousand Soviet and other Eastern European personnel. The flow of Soviet weapons to Nicaragua for transshipment to support insurgent forces in El Salvador included armored personnel carriers, anti-aircraft guns, anti-tank rocket launchers, semiautomatic small arms, tanks, and mortars. Such capabilities supported a Soviet-Cuban "strategy of unification" based on what Castro termed "revolutionary armed struggle." Its tactics, refined in the years since Castro's seizure of power in 1959, included sabotage and armed attacks against the economy as well as the fomenting of disorder by the sporadic use of violence designed to provoke a crackdown by the incumbent government, which could then be accused of political repression and human-rights violations. The purpose of such tactics was to undermine the political legitimacy of the existing government. The strategy provided for covert or overt Cuban alignments with opposition groups and local leaders most closely identified with Soviet-Cuban Marxist goals, together with sustained assistance, including a steady flow of weapons.

## The Sandinista Revolution in Nicaragua

Having come to power in 1979, the Sandinista junta had reneged on its pledge to form a representative, pluralistic political system. Instead, the Sandinistas had moved quickly to establish a state security organization and system of neighborhood surveillance bearing an ominous resemblance to its counterparts in Cuba and other Communist states. Nicaragua built a military establishment totalling 50,000, the purpose of which—or so it seemed not only to the United

States but also to the governments of Honduras, Costa Rica, Guatemala, and Panama—was to assist in the establishment of a revolutionary regime in El Salvador as the base for further Communist expansion in the region. Opponents of the regime formed by the Sandinistas, including many of the regional supporters of the anti-Somoza revolution, were harassed. Although the Sandinista regime had not immediately put into place the pervasive controls characteristic of Cuba or Eastern Europe and the Soviet Union, it attempted, to a far greater extent than had Somoza, to restrict the activities of such groups as the independent press, the Catholic Church, opposition political parties, and trade unions. Their treatment of the Moskito Indians, a group of whom opposed the Sandinistas, was especially harsh; tens of thousands of tribe members were forcibly evicted from their lands bordering Honduras and resettled elsewhere. Other opposition coalesced around disillusioned veterans of the revolution, including former members of the Sandinista junta, and former supporters of Somoza, to form a guerrilla movement called the "*contras*." They began to attack the Sandinista regime from neighboring countries, from which the Sandinistas themselves had originally mounted their successful assault against Somoza.

### The Reformist Coup in El Salvador

The Sandinista victory in Nicaragua had given impetus to a reformist coup of a different kind in El Salvador. In October 1979 the ruling oligarchy was replaced by a junta consisting of military officers and civilian politicians. The Salvadoran military formed a government with the Christian Democrats, the largest political party in the country. In its final weeks in office, the Carter administration had renewed American military aid to El Salvador after receiving mounting intelligence information about Soviet-Cuban arms shipments to the Salvadoran guerrilla movement to overthrow the new government. Although the new Salvadoran government was committed to a potentially far-reaching economic program that included land redistribution, its standing in the United States continued to be tarnished by human-rights violations that included death squads operating against opponents.

The Reagan administration's dilemma quickly became apparent. Governments already burdened with a political legacy that differed substantially from that of the United States in safeguarding the individual were even less likely to champion human rights if they faced internal security threats heightened by Soviet-supplied advisors and weapons. The greater the threat of armed insurgency supplied from outside sources, the more difficult it would be for states such as El Salvador, Guatemala, and Honduras to develop the kind of democratic order favored by the United States. The failure, or inability, of states threatened by Soviet-Cuban insurgency to meet U.S. standards of conduct led, in turn, to demands in Congress for the further curtailment of American aid. In 1981 Congress voted to require the president to certify at six-month intervals that El Salvador was making progress in human rights, moving toward the holding of free elections, bringing about agrarian reform, and seeking a peaceful solution to the civil war.

In the early 1980s El Salvador confronted an insurgency of mounting intensity. Its economy, damaged by civil war, capital flight, and declining commodity prices, registered substantial negative growth. The immediate consequence of agrarian reform was to reduce export crops. Politically, El Salvador confronted not only the threat from leftist insurgency but also deep divisions within the junta that included the Christian Democratic leader, José Napoleon Duarte, and the rightist Roberto D'Aubuisson, president of the Constitutional Assembly, who enjoyed the support of one of the principal factions within the Salvadoran military. The Reagan administration cast its support toward the more moderate Duarte and pressed the Salvadoran junta to frame a new constitution and hold elections, which took place in March 1982 and again in March and May 1984, with Duarte emerging as president in 1982 and again in 1984.

### The Reagan Administration's Strategy of Symmetry

The Reagan administration's approach to events in Central America, specifically in Nicaragua and El Salvador, was based on an attempt at symmetry. If the United States was to press for elections in El Salvador, a similar standard for political legitimacy should be applied to Nicaragua. If the Sandinista regime was arming insurgents operating in El Salvador, the opposition groups in Nicaragua should be supported, at least to the extent of rendering Sandinista assistance to the El Salvador insurgency impossible, if not to the level that would be needed to topple the Nicaragua regime itself. Here the administration faced substantial differences with Congress. The dichotomy was symbolized by the Boland Amendment passed by the House of Representatives in 1982, which prohibited U.S. funding of groups whose purpose was the destruction of the Sandinista regime. Nevertheless, the administration was able to support a growing anti-Sandinista force whose goal was the destruction of the staging areas from which arms and other military supplies were being shipped from Nicaragua to El Salvador and other Central American states. Congressional and public discussion focused on whether the United States should give covert (as opposed to overt) aid to groups fighting the Sandinista regime. A strategy of symmetry had its limits not only in the restrictions on funding and activity imposed by a Congress bent on increasing its oversight of foreign policy but also in the different political conditions in Nicaragua and El Salvador. Attacking Sandinista outposts from bases in Honduras and Costa Rica, the opposition forces had not proven able to seize and hold substantial territory. In contrast, the insurgent units in El Salvador had expanded the territory under their control.

In an effort to build broader domestic support for its Central American policy, in 1983 the Reagan administration assembled a bipartisan presidential commission headed by Henry Kissinger. In its report, issued in January 1984, the commission stated a central premise that great gaps between rich and poor, increasing population, and declining economic growth, together with a massive Soviet- and Cuban-sponsored effort to exploit such problems, had combined to create a growing danger. Although the United States was already making available hundreds of millions of dollars of aid to El Salvador, Honduras, and

Costa Rica, the Kissinger Commission called for a huge increase in military and economic aid. Such a recommendation itself might represent a basis for consensus between those who believed that the problems of Central America flowed principally from social inequality and poverty and those who held that the causes of instability are to be found in Soviet-Cuban exploitation of such indigenous issues. "Unchecked," the Kissinger Commission concluded, "the insurgents can destroy faster than the reformers can build. One reason for this is that an explicit purpose of guerrilla resistance is to make matters worse."

The Reagan administration's policy in Central America had as major elements an effort to isolate and to bring effective pressure to bear against Nicaragua. Its principal objectives were to prevent the use of Nicaragua by the Soviet Union and Cuba for infiltration into other parts of Central America—an essential condition for the success of any major program of economic modernization—and the dilemma of differentiating between security assistance and economic aid to which the Kissinger Commission had referred. In keeping with the symmetry principle providing for multiparty elections in El Salvador and Nicaragua, the Reagan administration sought the transformation of the Sandinista regime into a government based on political pluralism. In an effort to promote Central American political groupings against Nicaragua, the Reagan administration encouraged cooperation among the military establishments of El Salvador, Honduras, and Guatemala, including joint exercises and training programs in Honduras.

Meanwhile, the Contadora Group, consisting of Mexico, Venezuela, Colombia, and Panama, was working to provide a framework for a negotiated settlement that might foreclose any possibility of a U.S.-sponsored invasion of Nicaragua and preserve the Nicaraguan revolution. With Nicaraguan support, the Contadora Group produced a peace plan that included the withdrawal of foreign military advisers and a pledge that other territory would not be used to stage attacks against neighboring or nearby states. The shipment of arms to insurgent forces across frontiers would likewise be prohibited. This proposal confonted the intractable problems associated with verification of a cessation of arms shipments from Nicaragua to El Salvador. The United States would be forced to halt arms exports to the government of El Salvador, whose survival was threatened by a mounting insurgency. Under prevailing conditions the Salvadoran government would probably be less able than the Nicaraguan Sandinistas to withstand the pressures, respectively, of guerrilla or *contra* forces operating against them. The result might well have been the defeat of the anti-Sandinista groups and the demise of the El Salvador government, with all the attendant consequences for American interests in Central America.

## THE UNITED STATES AND THE CARIBBEAN:
## THE GRENADA INCIDENT

Heavily dependent on primary products such as sugar as well as tourism, most Caribbean states had gained independence only as recently as the 1960s. By the time the Reagan administration entered office, the forces of nationalism that had swept across the Caribbean had transformed the former European (mostly British) dependencies in a variety of ways. If the Caribbean states shared the characteristic of weak economies dependent on the export of only one or a few products to industrialized states, they differed in political structures, which ranged from the rigid one-party Communist model of Cuba to the parliamentary party structures that had taken root in nearly all the former British dependencies, including Jamaica.

Jamaica had quickly caught the attention and support of the incoming Reagan administration. In October 1980 the Jamaican Labor party of Edward Seaga, committed to private enterprise and foreign investment and highly critical of Castro's Cuba, had defeated the ruling People's National party headed by Michael Manley. The Manley government had been socialist in political orientation and friendly toward Castro's Cuba. As the Reagan administration took office, Seaga visited the United States and Jamaica received foreign aid totalling $90 million, together with American support for a $600 million loan from the International Monetary Fund.

However compelling the economic problems of the Caribbean were, their solutions lay at best in the distant future. The more immediate issue confronting the Reagan administration was a Soviet military buildup in Grenada, a small island with a population of 110,000 that had been granted independence by Britain in 1962. In 1969 Grenada's post-independence government had been ousted in a leftist coup led by the New Jewel Movement of Maurice Bishop, who became prime minister and established a Marxist government with close links with Castro's Cuba. By 1980 work had begun on the construction of a huge airport with the assistance of several hundred Cuban workers and military personnel. If this facility had the potential to increase dramatically Grenada's capacity to receive tourists (provided other facilities such as hotels were eventually built), it could also be used as part of the logistical system for the transport of Cuban forces in support of Soviet interests outside the Western Hemisphere. The establishment of a Soviet-Cuban base in Grenada would threaten vital shipping lanes between the eastern Caribbean and the Atlantic.

In June 1983 Bishop visited the United States for meetings with administration officials, including National Security Adviser William P. Clark. Whether Bishop sought somehow to begin to extricate himself from a tightening web of Soviet-Cuban control may never be known. In any event, on October 13, Bishop was ousted in a coup led by a member of the Central Committee of the New Jewel Movement. On October 19 Bishop was executed by those who had arrested him. In the days that followed, several neighboring governments of former British colonies, members of the Organization of Eastern Caribbean States, requested outside intervention out of fear that the radicalized Grenadian regime, which was becoming a storehouse for Soviet-Cuban military equipment, posed a threat to them.

This request, together with an appeal from the governor-general of Grenada, Sir Paul Scoon, who had been placed under house arrest, contributed to the Reagan administration's decision to take military action that would topple the Marxist government and set in motion the machinery for elections. Of even greater immediate importance was the significance attached to intelligence reports that a group of about 1000 American students at a medical college in Grenada might be taken hostage, especially if the new Grenada regime perceived the evacuation of the students as the prelude to an American invasion. With the hostage crisis in Iran still fresh in his mind, Reagan moved quickly to prevent any such situation in Grenada. An American force landed in Grenada on October 25 and secured the controversial airport, made its way to the students, and freed the governor-general. U.S. forces uncovered Soviet-Cuban plans for the use of Grenada in broader political-military operations in the region. According to documents obtained by the United States in Grenada, the Soviet Union had signed military aid agreements providing for massive shipments of weapons, including 4000 submachine guns, 2500 automatic rifles, 7000 personnel carriers, and more than 10,000 military uniforms. Supplies of weapons were discovered that greatly exceeded U.S. intelligence estimates made before the invasion.

The United States sustained few casualties in Grenada, and all combat forces were withdrawn by December 15. The American intervention, swift, limited, and with a clear purpose, enjoyed widespread support both in Grenada and at home, but not in Western Europe. Nevertheless, as the events surrounding the Grenada intervention became clearer, Western European criticism subsided. Within the Caribbean basin itself, the immediate efffect of the American rescue operation was to lead Fidel Castro both to denounce the United States and to suggest that, in the event of such action by the United States in Nicaragua, the Sandinista regime could not count on automatic and decisive military assistance from Havana. Although the differences between the situations in Grenada and Nicaragua were profound, the Reagan administration, in achieving the dismantling of a Marxist regime in the former, had sent a signal that other such governments, especially if they faced internal breakdown, as Grenada had, might not be immune to similar pressure.

## SOUTH AMERICA AND THE FALKLANDS WAR

In the 1970s several Latin American countries had launched ambitious economic development programs with large amounts of capital borrowed from abroad. The debt of Third World countries totalled $500 billion by 1983, approximately one half of which was the result of borrowing by Latin American countries, with Argentina accounting for $85 billion; Brazil, $80 billion; and Mexico, $40 billion. With the worldwide recession at the beginning of the 1980s, the demand for the exports of these countries had declined and the variable interest rates on which most of the borrowing had been based had risen. As a result, the repayment of interest and principal on loans from banks in the United States and Western Europe consumed a rising proportion of declining foreign-exchange earnings. Increasingly, the threat of default hung like a dark cloud over the international financial community, with consequences as potentially disastrous for commercial banks in industrial countries as for the debtors themselves. The immediate course chosen was the rescheduling of payments on long-term loans, although in many cases new, short-term credit at higher interest rates was made available to meet the immediate financial needs of debtor countries. For Mexico, the Reagan administration authorized $3 billion in various arrangements that included advance payment on oil to be purchased for the American Strategic Petroleum Reserve. The United States extended other loans of more than $1 billion to Brazil. The International Monetary Fund made a loan of nearly $4 billion to Brazil to help stave off default on its huge external debt. Although such measures furnished a useful stopgap for the overextended economies of major Latin American and other Third World countries, the debt problem remained. The conditions for the bailout loans were the imposition of austerity programs, the effect of which was to reduce domestic consumption and employment. Would such declines, within economies already plagued by rising urbanization, population explosion, and grinding poverty bring to power radicalized governments prepared to repudiate foreign debt instead of paying it? In such a perspective the economic, social, and political futures of such countries were seen to be intertwined.

Amid the debt crisis, Argentina repudiated authoritarian government and returned to democracy with the election victory of Raul Alfonsín as president in 1984. The fall of the military junta that had ruled since 1976 was a direct result of Argentina's defeat by Britain in the Falklands War. Located in the South Atlantic 200 miles from Argentina, the Falkland Islands had been ruled by Britain since 1833. Argentina had long insisted that the Malvinas, as they designated the islands, were its territory. Successive British governments had attempted without success to negotiate a resolution of the Falklands dispute that would provide suitable safeguards for the less than 2000 inhabitants, mostly sheepherders.

At the end of March 1982 Argentina, then ruled by a military junta headed by President Leopoldo Galtieri, invaded the Falklands and quickly disarmed the few British defenders. The British response, to the surprise of Buenos Aires, was the rapid assembly and dispatch of a task force consisting of 35 ships on an 8000-mile voyage with uncertain prospects for success. The nearly three weeks needed for the force to reach its destination provided time for diplomacy, which included an exercise in shuttle diplomacy by Secretary of State Haig after President Reagan had failed in direct communications to dissuade Galtieri from the Falklands operation. The United Nations Security Council passed a resolution calling for the withdrawal of all forces, the end of hostilities, and negotiations for a permanent settlement between Britain and Argentina. The issues that remained irreconcilable by diplomacy included Argentina's demand that Britain concede sovereignty before entering negotiations over the future of the Falklands. Britain refused to accept any such condition which, under the circumstances, would have been tantamount to acquiescence in the use of force by Argentina. The Thatcher government insisted on the right of self-determination for the islanders, whose clear preference for British administration had been repeatedly stated.

With loss of lives and ships on both sides, Britain retook the islands in a war that ended on June 14, 1982. Seemingly anachronistic in the slowness with which military power was projected over the vast distances to the South Atlantic, the war nevertheless featured the use of some of the most advanced air-to-air and air-to-surface precision-guided missiles. In retrospect, it appeared that the Galtieri government had assumed that Britain would not fight to reclaim the Falklands and that the United States, given its commitments and interests in the Western Hemisphere, would not support any such British military action. It was reasoned in Buenos Aires that in themselves, the islands lacked any major strategic value either to Britain or to the United States. Undoubtedly, the Galtieri regime overestimated the support that it could receive from other hemispheric states.

Although other Latin American countries voted for resolutions favoring Argentina in the Organization of American States, the United States abstaining, there was uneasiness about the precedent that would have been established by the success of the Argentine attempt to seize the Falklands by force. In the late 1970s Chile and Argentina had gone to the brink of war over the Beagle Islands, which were claimed by Argentina but held by Chile. Similarly, a large part of the territory of Guyana was disputed by Venezuela. Although there was widespread support in Latin America for a peaceful settlement favoring Argentina's claim to the Falklands, the military action taken by Buenos Aires was regarded not only as a potentially dangerous precedent for analogous situations elsewhere but also as a violation of international law.

The Reagan administration shared these views. What distinguished U.S. policy, however, was the clear choice that was made in support of Britain, not only on legal and moral grounds of international law and the principle of self-determination for the Falklands population but also on broader geostrategic grounds. Britain remained a pivotal member of the Atlantic Alliance and America's closest ally, a country with which the United States had evolved a "special relationship." Aside from its implications for other countries faced with territorial claims, the defeat of Britain in the Falklands would have inflicted severe political and psychological damage not only on London but also on the transatlantic relationship, already contending with a variety of debilitating crises and disputes. Acknowledging the need for the United States to act unilaterally, if necessary, on behalf of vital interests, and facing Western European opposition or impotence, in the Falklands crisis the Reagan administration chose the Atlantic Alliance over solidarity with other states of the Western Hemisphere.

## THE TROUBLED TRANSATLANTIC RELATIONSHIP

In addition to the pipeline controversy discussed above, the Reagan administration confronted other divisive issues in the transatlantic relationship. The emphasis of the administration on rebuilding American defense capabilities was widely welcomed in Western Europe, but there was equal support for diplomacy designed to reduce East–West tensions. Although Reagan's rhetoric characterizing the Soviet Union as an "evil empire" was regarded as accurate by many in Western Europe, the deterioration in relations between Washington and Moscow sent tremors through the NATO-European political landscape. If there was apprehension at times of improved superpower relations that the two nuclear giants might reach bilateral accords detrimental to Western European interests, there was even greater concern about the potential implications of a breakdown in the relationship. In the early 1980s the Reagan administration's attempt to restore American power and influence within a globalist foreign policy based, if necessary and where feasible, on elements of unilateralism, reinforced neutralist tendencies in Western Europe.

### Economic Woes: High Interest Rates and Lingering Recession in Western Europe

There was discussion of an impending political "divorce" at the transatlantic level, with erstwhile allies seeming more and more to go their separate ways on the issues that divided them. Although such differences might be obscured in the anodyne communiqués issued at the end of the annual summit conferences held in Versailles (1982), Williamsburg, Virginia (1983), London (1984), and Bonn (1985) the problems resurfaced with amazing rapidity and frequency. They included perennial disagreements about the alleged effects of American economic policies, in particular higher interest rates, on sluggish Western European economies. The American economic recovery that got firmly underway in 1982 had begun to stimulate the lagging Western European economies, but the persistence of high interest rates in the United States not only attracted capital away from Europe but also added to the debt burden of the Third World states with which Western Europe traded. Although for the most part not prepared even to meet the 3 percent real growth in defense to which they had agreed in 1978, European governments criticized the Reagan administration for its high deficits—produced in part, it could be argued, by U.S. defense budgets, a substantial portion of which contributed directly to the defense of allies. Such deficits were said to account for high interest rates because the U.S. government financed its deficit with funds that otherwise would have been available for the private sector.

By the early 1980s, moreover, Western European economies faced formidable structural problems related to what were by American standards expensive publicly supported social-welfare programs, together with rising unemployment and a technologically obsolescent industrial sector. In the ten years before 1984 the United States, despite the recession and unemployment of the early 1980s, had added 13 million new jobs, while Western Europe had lost 3 million jobs. In the emerging technologies of the future, Western Europe seemed to be falling farther behind Japan and the United States and to have little prospect of catching up.

While the United States, a decade after the Vietnam trauma, was gaining a renewed sense of confidence in the future, the term "Europessimism" was coined to describe the prevailing mood in Western Europe. The United States and its European allies held divergent perspectives on technology transfer, interest rate structures, trade policy, and numerous issues directly related to foreign policy and national security, such as: the management of relations with the Soviet Union; the modernization of forces, nuclear and conventional, for the common defense; defense burden sharing; and the "out-of-area" issues such as crises in the Caribbean, Central America, and the Middle East.

## Continued Controversy over Nuclear-force Levels

Although each of these issues was fraught with danger for the transatlantic relationship, it was the Pershing II and cruise missile deployment that dominated the Alliance agenda in the early 1980s. As the Reagan administration took office, the Soviet Union was deploying SS-20s at the rate of one new system every six days. The effect was not a strengthened resolve and a broadened European consensus in support of the deployment of the Ground-Launched Cruise Missiles (GLCMs) and Pershing II systems upon which NATO had reached agreement in the "two-track" decision of December 1979, but instead to exacerbate a transatlantic crisis of political confidence. Simultaneously, apprehension grew in Western Europe that in the event of East–West military conflict, the United States would come to Europe's defense—or that it would not. The United States was seen as prepared either to fight a war in which American territory might be spared while Western Europe would be devastated or to disengage militarily and leave Western Europe to Soviet domination. In short, the effect of superpower strategic nuclear parity, together with the shifting military balance in Europe, diminished the credibility of NATO's deterrent capabilities. In the broader context of the transatlantic differences, the political trust among allies that was necessary to sustain public support for U.S. nuclear-force deployment on European territory had eroded significantly in the years since nuclear weapons were first stationed in Western Europe during the Eisenhower administration.

In 1982 Helmut Schmidt's West German government faced mounting challenges from the antinuclear left of the Social Democratic party and strident opposition from the Green/Alternative Movement. In October 1982 Schmidt's government fell and was replaced by the Christian Democrats, who had been out of office since 1969 and were returned with the support of the small Free Democratic party which had shifted its support from the Social Democratic coalition to the new government. In the federal election of March 1983 the Christian Democrats, headed by the new chancellor, Helmut Kohl, won a substantial victory in a campaign that was waged on economic issues and the missile-deployment question.

Elsewhere in Western Europe, especially in Britain and the Netherlands, there were large demonstrations against INF deployment. Although it had supported NATO nuclear modernization when in office before 1979, the British Labour party, under new leadership since its electoral defeat by the Conservative party, adopted a position favoring unilateral nuclear disarmament. In June 1983 the government of Prime Minister Thatcher, still basking in the afterglow of the Falklands success, won a resounding victory in an election in which the Labour party, whose base of support had been weakened by the emergence of the Liberal/Social Democratic Alliance, suffered its worst defeat since before World War II. In Belgium and the Netherlands, fragile coalition governments found it difficult to do more than indicate that, in principle, they continued to accept the double-track decision while hoping to postpone the actual deployment as long as possible.

In November 1983 the first cruise missiles arrived in Britain and Italy, and the Federal Republic of Germany began deployment of the Pershing II. Although there were demonstrations against the Euromissiles, the "hot autumn" of protests originally anticipated failed to materialize. The Green/Alternative Movement which strongly had opposed the NATO deployment of new generation inter-mediate range nuclear forces (INF), received 5.7 percent of the total vote in the German election of March 1983, thus qualifying for representation in the federal parliament for the first time. The Social Democrats at their party congress in November 1983 repudiated by an overwhelming vote their own party's former approval of the position held by Chancellor Schmidt when he was in office in support of INF deployment. Nevertheless, the Kohl government proceeded with deployment while simultaneously embarking on a policy to improve inter-German relations with large-scale loans and credits, which were reciprocated by the East German government's granting of exit permits to 26,000 persons wishing to emigrate to West Germany. In effect, the Kohl government, with its emphasis on creating in the two German States an "island of détente," had effectively removed one of the principal arguments available to its opponents. For the regime of the German Democratic Republic, increased contact with Bonn furnished a needed infusion of capital and technology and a safety valve to diminish dissent in the form of emigration for the dissatisfied.

The beginning of INF deployment came at the end of a series of arms-control negotiations that had proven fruitless. In November 1981 the Reagan administration had put forward the "zero-zero option," in which the United States would have foregone deployment of the planned 464 GLCMs and 108 Pershing IIs in return for the Soviet Union's dismantling of all its SS-20 and older SS-4 and SS-5 systems targeted against Western Europe. The zero-zero option had the virtue of simplicity in that it would have eliminated from Europe an entire modern generation of intermediate-range, highly accurate nuclear systems. The weakness of the zero-zero option was that it would have foreclosed the modern-ization of NATO nuclear forces that, it had been argued, was essential in order to preserve the coupling between battlefield and strategic-nuclear deterrence.

Although the zero-zero option was widely acclaimed in Western Europe at first, the Reagan administration came to face growing pressure to show greater "flexibility" in its arms-control policy. The Soviet Union had quickly rejected a U.S. proposal that would have meant the dismantling of already-deployed Soviet systems in return for U.S. capabilities yet to be deployed. The Soviet Union first announced, in March 1982, that it would freeze its deployment of SS-20s at the then-existing level of 300 in return for nondeployment on the NATO side. It then offered to cut its SS-20 force to 162 launchers, the total number of the British and French nuclear-missile force, leaving an overall total of about 420 warheads for each side. The effect of this second Soviet proposal would have been to prevent any INF deployment in the Federal Republic of Germany, while Soviet SS-20s would remain targeted against West Germany. Furthermore, it was argued, the British and French nuclear forces did not possess the accuracy levels of the SS-20, which could be used either as part of a surprise first strike against NATO-Europe or as a weapon of political intimidation. In contrast, the British and French nuclear forces were intended only to deter attacks on Britain and France, not on West Germany or any other NATO member. Besides, those submarine-launched ballistic missiles had been taken into account by the Soviet Union in the SALT I interim agreement in 1972. Hence the British and French nuclear forces, if they were to be discussed in future arms-control negotiations, should be considered in a more comprehensive forum than that of INF.

By the spring of 1983 the United States had modified its zero-zero option to call for a joint ceiling in warheads at a negotiated level between zero and the 572 total of the planned U.S. force. This proposal followed the widely publicized "walk in the woods" formula discussed in the late summer of 1982 by U.S. negotiator Paul Nitze and his Soviet counterpart, Yuli Kvitsinsky. On the Western side there would have been 75 cruise-missile launcher units, with a total of 300 warheads. The Soviet Union would have reduced its SS-20s to 75, each with three warheads. Although there were reservations about this formula in Washington because it restricted the United States to the subsonic cruise missile while permitting a monopoly Soviet deployment of supersonic ballistic missiles, it was Moscow that decisively repudiated the Nitze-Kvitsinsky proposal. In retrospect, the Soviet Union had attempted to use the Geneva negotiations as a forum for preventing any INF deployment on NATO territory, while the United States had sought first to dismantle Soviet systems already deployed and, as an alternative, to reach an agreed total at a lower aggregate level than already existed on the Soviet side. Having failed to achieve its objective with the beginning of INF deployment in Western Europe—whatever the original motive of Moscow in entering the talks—the Soviet Union withdrew from the negotiations in November 1983. By the time the negotiations were broken off, the Soviet Union had deployed nearly 378 SS-20 launchers, each with three warheads targeted against Western Europe and such East Asian countries as China, Japan, and the Republic of Korea.

## NATO's Dilemma over Its Conventional Forces

The Alliance was also troubled by the question of whether to rely more heavily on its nuclear deterrent or on conventional forces for its defense. The superiority of Soviet–Warsaw Pact forces in conventional weapons could be countered by nuclear capabilities only as long as the Soviet Union was inferior in such means. The acquisition of modern nuclear weapons in large numbers targeted by the Soviet Union against Western Europe and the United States raised fundamental questions about the adequacy of NATO conventional forces. If NATO could not halt a Soviet-Warsaw Pact attack by conventional means, escalation to the nuclear level would become necessary—and the outcome would be uncertain owing to the shift in nuclear capabilities in favor of the Soviet Union. If it had become increasingly difficult to contemplate NATO escalation to the nuclear level, the inference to be drawn was clear: in the absence of symmetrical reductions in military forces, NATO should devote a greater effort to modernization of its conventional forces.

Many unofficial proposals for a "no first use" policy were made. These quickly encountered the criticism that, as a defensive alliance based on a strategy of flexible response to an attack, NATO should retain its option to use whatever weapons might be necessary in order to repel an attack. To announce in advance that NATO would not resort to nuclear weapons if it was attacked by Soviet–Warsaw Pact conventional forces might even have the effect of encouraging an attack under circumstances Moscow perceived as favorable. In any event, there was no clear evidence that the Soviet Union adhered to a military doctrine that clearly delineated conventional and nuclear phases, even though the Soviet Union had built a formidable array of nuclear and conventional capabilities that gave it unprecedented flexibility.

In the Atlantic Alliance there was discussion, stimulated by its supreme allied commander in Europe (SACEUR), General Bernard Rogers, about conventional-force modernization designed to make possible "no *early* first use" of nuclear weapons. If the conventional military option of the Atlantic Alliance were to be increased, NATO would find it necessary to deploy new-generation weapons based on emerging technologies. Because of personnel constraints exacerbated by demographic trends toward lower birth rates, a greater reliance on conventional forces would create the need for military units that were less manpower-reliant and more firepower-intensive. The weapons of the future would be based on microelectronic technologies including advances in target acquisition, accuracy, surveillance, and speed of reaction.

Discussion of a need to raise the NATO nuclear threshold took place in the context of defense policies, in the case of Britain and France, in which paradoxically the modernization of national strategic nuclear forces placed increasing financial demands on limited defense budgets, with the likely prospect that conventional-force contributions to European security would be diminished, not increased, in the years ahead. The unwillingness of most European NATO members to meet the agreed goal of 3 percent annual real increase in defense spending, let alone the 4 percent yearly growth suggested by General Rogers to be the minimum needed for the acquisition of new conventional technologies, did not augur well for the Alliance. The result was to produce within NATO trends that included, on the one hand, reluctance to contemplate escalation to the nuclear level in a prevailing U.S.-Soviet and Eurostrategic balance adverse to the United States and, on the other hand, a continued emphasis, in the case of Britain and France, on nuclear weapons at the expense of conventional forces. A fracturing of the defense consensus in certain Western European NATO countries diminished support for NATO modernization, especially at the nuclear level. It also raised fundamental questions about the ability and willingness of European members to contribute to enhanced conventional defense.

## CONTINUED CONFLICT IN THE MIDDLE EAST

At the outset the Reagan administration's approach to the Middle East had as central elements the importance of Israel as a "strategic asset," the term used during the 1980 campaign, together with a quest for a "strategic consensus" that would have embraced as many Arab states as well. It was acknowledged that, after the disastrous experience of having relied on the Shah of Iran as a surrogate for American interests in the Persian Gulf, there was no substitute, in the final analysis, for U.S. power that could be deployed in the region in support of vital interests. Hence the Reagan administration placed greater emphasis than its predecessor on building maritime forces and on increasing the strength of the Rapid Deployment Force begun during the Carter administration. The task facing the United States in the early 1980s was to find a basis, by diplomatic means and adequate military capabilities, both for containing Soviet power and for lessening the dangerous conflicts within the Middle East. More than any other part of the world, the Middle East held the potential for escalation of indigenous conflict—between Israel and one or more of its neighbors and, more recently, between Iran and Iraq—to a military confrontation between the United States and the Soviet Union. The United States would temper unilateralism based on increased military power with an attempt to sublimate the profound political differences in the Middle East within a strategic consensus about the dangers posed both to Israel and to the moderate Arab states by the Soviet Union. Secretary of State Haig's effort, undertaken with a visit to the Middle East shortly after the Reagan administration came to office, recalled an effort by the Eisenhower administration to help build a "northern tier"—as a chain of states sharing a border or close proximity to the Soviet Union and a barrier of containment across the Middle East into southern Asia. The resulting Baghdad Pact had not survived the revolutionary forces that swept away the pro-Western governments of Iraq and Iran in the late 1950s. If there was to be a new framework based on a strategic consensus in the 1980s, its members would include states such as Israel, Egypt, Jordan, Saudi Arabia, and Oman, together with Turkey and Pakistan. The fact that only the latter two states survived from the "northern tier" concept of the past bespoke the decline in the overall strategic position of the United States and its allies since the 1950s.

It is a principal characteristic of global powers that their interests encompass, but also transcend, any particular region. What distinguishes them, aside from overall capabilities, from smaller states is the tendency to fit local or regional issues within a broader framework for policy. In contrast, the strategic preoccupations of smaller states are those of their immediate region. It was this basic structural difference in their foreign policies that separated the United States from those with whom it sought to develop common policies, not only in the Middle East but also in other regions, from Western Europe to the western Pacific. In the Middle East this principle was manifest in the local power balance that posed for the states of the region the most immediate security problem. Specifically, an increase in American arms transfers to Saudi Arabia in support of larger interests would affect the Israeli perception of security.

## Saudi Arabia's Pivotal Position

If Israel represented a crucially important strategic asset, Saudi Arabia was indispensable to American policy in the Persian Gulf, especially after the fall of the Shah. The strategic significance of Saudi Arabia arose not only from its status as the leading producer of oil but also from its links with the smaller oil-producing states in the Gulf and its leadership role in the Arab world. Its dominant position in the international petroleum market allowed Saudi Arabia to play a moderating role in OPEC's pricing policies. With the curtailment of oil exports from Iran and Iraq, the importance of Saudi oil production was heightened, despite the declining overall demand for petroleum in reaction to the price increases of the 1970s and the world economic recession at the end of the decade.

In any American effort to press forward the peace process, and in particular to deal successfully with the future of Palestine, it seemed to the Reagan administration, Saudi Arabia could play a pivotal role as a result not only of its relations with moderate Arab leaders, such as King Hussein of Jordan, but also of its links with the Palestine Liberation Organization. When the Reagan administration entered office, the Saudis provided financial subsidies to Jordan, Syria, and the PLO. Although Saudi Arabia had denounced Sadat for signing the Camp David accords, broken off diplomatic relations, and ended financial aid to Egypt, the Saudi monarchy, with its long-standing links with the United States, had an abiding fear of radical forces—whether communism or Islamic fundamentalism—and sought protection from them.

Although they had joined in the cutoff of oil exports in 1967 and 1973 in support of perceived Arab interests, the Saudi leaders viewed with concern the Soviet invasion of Afghanistan; the establishment of a Marxist state, the People's Democratic Republic of Yemen (South Yemen), on their border; Soviet gains in the Somali-Ethiopian conflict in the Horn of Africa; the Iran–Iraq war; and the revolutionary forces represented by Khomeini's Iran. The Reagan administration had pledged not to allow Saudi Arabia "to be an Iran," meaning apparently that the United States would protect Saudi Arabia both from internal and external threats—in this respect more precisely formulating the principles of the Carter Doctrine. To be sure, Saudi Arabia differed substantially from Iran. If the Shah of Iran had become increasingly isolated from the Iranian population, the Saudi royal family, with its nearly 4000 members, extended its tentacles throughout a state that, while larger geographically than Iran, held a much smaller population (an estimated 8 million, compared with 36 million in Iran). Although Saudi Arabia had embarked on a huge modernization program with oil revenues, the Saudi monarchy, with its close links with Islam, did not face the challenges from politically ambitious mullahs that had destroyed the Shah of Iran.

Although Saudi Arabia wanted a close relationship with the United States, it stopped short of a formal alliance or the stationing of American military forces and equipment. Such a strategic relationship with the United States would have been incompatible with Saudi conceptions of independence and nonalignment. Instead, the Saudis wanted American arms and training for their own military force. If such capabilities in Saudi hands could help restore a deteriorating political-military balance in the Gulf, they would also heighten Israel's perception of threat, for the Saudi regime had long regarded Zionism and communism as twin evils. Moreover, Saudi Arabia was strongly committed to the Palestinian cause and opposed Israeli policy in Jerusalem because of that city's religious importance to Islam. For the Saudis, the strength of their relationship with the United States was measured by the American willingness to sell them advanced military equipment. The controversial agreement of the Carter administration to make the F-15 available was followed by a decision that Reagan inherited from Carter to sell to Saudi Arabia airborne warning and control aircraft (AWACs) that could detect and track other aircraft at distances as great as 350 miles. If the AWACs sale was regarded as a test of American commitment in Saudi Arabia, it evoked the specter of a new threat to Israel. After the Reagan administration won a narrow victory in support of the AWACs sale in the Senate in October 1981, U.S. relations with Israel deteriorated noticeably as a result of the AWACs sale itself and also because of what were regarded in Washington as Israeli efforts to intervene against the administration's policy in the internal American debate on this issue. In June, moreover, Israel had overflown Saudi Arabia in a bold and successful operation to destroy an Iraqi nuclear reactor that, it was feared, would have the potential of producing weapons-grade nuclear material and eventually turning Iraq into an atomic power. Nevertheless, the United States joined in the resolution adopted by the United Nations Security Council condemning Israel for its military action. As it had in past cases of arms sales to Arab governments, the United States reaffirmed its commitment to maintain an Israeli "qualitative edge" in the region.

However illustrative the AWACs sale was of the dilemma facing the Reagan administration in reconciling its global strategic interests with the more immediate preoccupations of friendly states in the region, the conflict map of the Middle East contained several formidable problems in the early 1980s that had deeper roots in the history of the region. These problems included the future of the Egypt–Israel relationship with the final withdrawal of Israel from Egyptian territory, in keeping with the Camp David accords, in April 1982. Although Sadat, who had been the original architect of the Egyptian–Israeli peace process, had been assassinated in October 1981, his successor, Hosni Mubarak, had made a sufficiently persuasive commitment to carry forward the accords in order to induce Israel, despite the cloud over its relations with Washington, to complete the Sinai withdrawal on schedule.

### The Saudi Peace Initiative

A second issue area, also a legacy of Camp David, was the Palestinian question, with profound differences between Israel and Egypt on the meaning to be given to the principle of "full autonomy" contained in the agreements signed in 1979. Israel would remain in possession of the West Bank territories until a mutually acceptable definition of autonomy was worked out. Such a condition worked to Israel's favor by permitting it to establish settlements and administrative arrangements that would tighten its grip. By 1983, despite objections voiced by the United States, Israel had established nearly 100 settlements with as many as 27,000 Jewish settlers on the West Bank, with plans to build many more. The longer the Palestinian question remained unresolved, the less significant would be the "green line" dividing pre-1967 Israel from Judea and Samaria, the biblical names of the West Bank territories, as Begin referred to them.

As an alternative to the approach to the Palestine question contained in the Camp David accords providing for "full autonomy," Saudi Arabia proposed a "peace plan" in August 1982 that, after the AWACs vote in the U.S. Senate, attracted attention. The initiative, pressed by Crown Prince Fahd of Saudi Arabia, represented a reformulation of the Arab interpretation of United Nations Resolution 242 (calling for Israeli withdrawal from territory it had occupied since the Six-Day War of June 1967), together with a specific proposal for the creation of a Palestinian state on the West Bank and the Gaza Strip, with East Jerusalem as its capital. It was basically the proposal on Palestine that Anwar Sadat had taken to Jerusalem during his historic visit in October 1977. Even though unacceptable in its existing form either to Israel or to the United States, the Fahd Plan was regarded as useful by the Reagan administration because it might bring Saudi Arabia into the peace process in a positive role and furnish the potential for a diplomatic breakthrough. Although Israel was not mentioned by name, the Fahd Plan acknowledged specifically that all states in the Middle East had the right to live in peace.

The meeting of the Arab League convened in Fez, Morocco, to discuss the Saudi proposal, furnished renewed evidence of the deep divisions within the Arab world. Indicative of its opposition to the Fahd Plan, Syria did not participate in the Fez meeting; the PLO joined the rejectionist front of Arab states. The failure of the Fahd Plan also revealed the wide, and seemingly irreconcilable, differences separating Israel and the radical forces within the Arab world. Prospects dimmed for a revival of the Camp David autonomy talks. Partly in order to repair its damaged relations with Israel, the Reagan administration in late 1982 attempted to give substance to its policy of strategic cooperation with Israel by concluding an agreement reaffirming the exchange of intelligence information and providing for the stockpiling of American medical supplies in Israel for military contingencies in the Persian Gulf. Simultaneously, the Reagan administration pressed forward its defense cooperation with Egypt by participating in a joint exercise called Operation BRIGHT STAR, with U.S. military forces on Egyptian territory.

The improvement in Israeli–American relations was quickly reversed by the sharp reaction of the Reagan administration to the unanticipated action taken by Israel in December 1981 to extend Israeli civil law to the Golan Heights, representing in effect its assumption of virtual sovereignty over territory it had taken in June 1967. For Israel, control of the Golan Heights represented a strategically important geographic barrier to raids on Israeli settlements that had been launched from Syria before 1967. The United States suspended the recently concluded agreement on strategic cooperation and joined in the UN Security Council's resolution declaring null and void Israel's action on the Golan Heights.

## The Lebanon War

The chaotic situation in Lebanon formed an inextricable part of the Palestinian question not only because the PLO's stronghold was in Lebanese territory but also because Syria played an important role there. To the Syrian government of Hafez al-Assad, Lebanon seemed a logical extension of Syrian influence. To Israel, the Syrian military presence, together with the PLO infrastructure, represented a security threat. By the end of the 1970s, Lebanon had become the setting for several simultaneous armed conflicts among Christians and Moslems of various political orientations, including members of the Sunni, Shi'a, and Druse sects, as well as Palestinians, all contending in a state that lacked a central government capable of imposing order. Such chaotic conditions, wherever they exist, have usually provided either the incentive or the need for intervention by outside powers. Supported by Soviet arms, Syria harbored ambitions that included not only the destruction of Israel but also the establishment of hegemony over as much of Lebanon as possible. The PLO sought to use Lebanon as the base for the ultimate establishment of a Palestinian state incorporating the West Bank. Israel had cast its support with Christian forces who opposed both Syria and the PLO. Although one Christian force was positioned on Lebanese territory near the Israeli border, the principal Christian territory was to the north. As the Syrian military threat to Christian Phalangist forces rose, Israel threatened to take military action, including the destruction of surface-to-air missiles provided to Syria by the Soviet Union.

The Reagan administration's response to the escalating unrest was to send Philip Habib, a diplomat with long experience, to the Middle East in an attempt to prevent the outbreak of war. The Habib mission was broadened to include the increasing conflict between Israel and the PLO. The result was a cease-fire, arranged in July 1981, that furnished only a temporary respite. In the months that followed attacks were launched against Israeli territory by Palestinian forces operating from southern Lebanon, and Israeli citizens were attacked at home and abroad.

In the spring of 1982 Israel responded with air strikes against enemy strongholds in Lebanon. In retrospect, Israel appears to have decided to take decisive military action at an appropriate moment to eliminate the threat posed by Syria and the PLO and, in particular, to remove from Lebanese territory the Palestinian forces that posed a danger. The terrorist attack on the Israeli ambassador to Britain, in early June 1982, furnished such an opportunity, which Israel quickly seized, to launch an operation across the Lebanese border in what was called Operation PEACE FOR GALILEE. Its immediate objective was to establish a 25-mile buffer zone in southern Lebanon, from which hostile forces would be excluded. The Israelis sought the expulsion of the PLO from Lebanon in order to remove its influence in the determination of the future status of the West Bank and Gaza. They had as their objective also the shaping of a Lebanese state in which a peace treaty with Christian forces friendly to Israel could be signed and Syrian influence curtailed sharply. If such a unified Lebanon proved impossible, a de facto partition between Syria and Israel would represent an acceptable solution, provided forces hostile to Israel were removed, especially from southern Lebanon.

The Israeli military action had its immediate intended effect. Syrian forces and large amounts of their Soviet equipment were destroyed. Lebanese territory long held by the PLO was freed, with Israeli forces being initially welcomed by the local population. It appeared that Lebanon might finally have an opportunity to achieve the semblance of unity that the PLO had helped to undermine by its destructive presence. Although the Reagan administration had stated its opposition to the Israeli military operation in Lebanon, the United States played a major diplomatic role both in achieving a cessation of hostilities and in arranging for the departure of the PLO from Beirut, with Philip Habib shuttling among the various Arab capitals and Israel. Arrangements were made for an American, French, and Italian multinational force to be placed in Lebanon to oversee the PLO evacuation, which began in August 1982.

In the wake of Israel's military success, the Reagan administration launched its own diplomatic initiative in an effort to revive the stalled Camp David process. Conceivably, a battered and dispersed PLO might be more amenable to a political solution now that it was deprived of military options. Even with Soviet arms, Syria had proven no match for Israeli military prowess. With the PLO and Syria in retreat, Israel would have less to fear in working out a solution to the Palestinian question that it found acceptable. This was the context in which the Reagan administration put forward a peace plan in September 1982 providing for an interim period of self-government for the West Bank. Subsequently, negotiations would be conducted among Israel, Jordan, and the Palestinian Arabs to develop detailed plans for the ultimate political status of the West Bank. Central to the Reagan administration's plan, in the formulation of which Secretary of State George Shultz played a crucial role, was the idea of an association between Jordan and the West Bank and Gaza. The United States opposed the extremes of Israeli annexation and the creation of an independent Palestinian state. The Reagan administration sought the suspension of Israeli settlements and PLO recognition of Israel's existence, If Israel, in the American perspective, could not retain all its occupied territories, neither could it be expected to return to the pre-1967 status quo.

Jordan was pivotal to the Reagan peace initiative, and King Hussein was the indispensable actor in whom the administration reposed its hope for success. Hussein went so far as to meet with PLO leader Yasir Arafat and subsequently with President Reagan. The United States promised to supply Jordan with the sophisticated weapons, including F-16 aircraft, sought by Hussein. Moreover, the Reagan administration was developing with Hussein's government a plan for equipping a Jordanian mobile strike force for use in Persian Gulf contingencies.

In Washington and among Hussein and other Arab leaders, there were varying perceptions of linkage between the U.S. peace plan and the withdrawal of foreign forces from Lebanon. Thus the Reagan administration's peace initiative had become hostage to events in Lebanon. Israel could not be expected to withdraw all its forces unless Syria took similar action. In the continuing effort to strengthen its position in the West Bank, Israel announced the construction of new settlements. Arafat proved unwilling or unable to unify the deeply divided PLO. Among other things, the PLO would have had to abandon the 1974 Rabat decision of Arab states granting the PLO an exclusive right to represent all Palestinians in future negotiations. Such a Palestinian agreement was regarded by Hussein as indispensable to his active participation in the Reagan peace plan. With help from Habib, Lebanon and Israel reached agreement ending the state of war between them, establishing a framework for diplomatic relations, and setting a timetable for withdrawal of Israeli forces.

Syria remained the main stumbling block; its intransigence grew almost in direct proportion to the resupply of arms by the Soviet Union lost in the recent military engagements with Israel. The United States had given priority to the effort to forge an agreement between Israel and Lebanon in the hope that Syria would join the peace process at a later date. Originally opposed even to the Saudi peace plan, Syria used its influence to help destroy the Reagan initiative and set about repairing the damage Israel had inflicted on its position in Lebanon. Clearly, Syria could not be excluded from a settlement of the Palestinian question, which remained linked to the status of Lebanon. Syrian diplomacy included a successful effort in 1983 to bring under Syria's control a part of the PLO split away from Arafat, who, having returned to Lebanon, was again expelled. In short, the hostility of Syria dashed any hope that Hussein could play the constructive role desired by the Reagan administration. Without Hussein there was no basis for a settlement based on an association between Jordan and the West Bank and Gaza.

In September 1982, following the assassination of Bashir Gemayel, the newly elected president of Lebanon, Israel moved forces into West Beirut. At the same time, the Israelis gave permission to Christian-Phalangist forces to enter Palestinian refugee camps, ostensibly to search for Palestinian terrorists, but where instead they massacred hundreds of civilians. The resulting outcry, nowhere greater than in Israel itself, led to the formation of an Israeli commission of inquiry that issued a report criticizing Begin's government for negligence in light of the history of hostility between Lebanese Christians and Palestinians.

In Lebanon Amin Gemayel, brother of the slain president, was elected to take his place. In response to his request, the United States, France, and Italy, having just withdrawn the multinational force, agreed to its return, this time to help maintain order in the immediate aftermath of the refugee-camp massacre and with the expectation that they would leave Lebanon by the end of the year. The Reagan administration did not intend to involve its contingent of Marines in hostilities in Lebanon. Its mission was to assist the Gemayel government in maintaining order in and around Beirut. In the months that followed, Gemayel proved unable to impose the authority of the central government on the warring political and religious groups or to build an army capable of restoring order out of the disruption that had persisted since the civil war of 1975–77. The Reagan administration made available training and other assistance to the Lebanese army.

Such aid was far exceeded by massive shipments of weapons sent by the Soviet Union to Syria. By 1984 the Soviet Union had provided double the military equipment lost by Syria in 1982, as well as 8000 Soviet personnel to operate communications, air-defense installations and missiles, and help in training Syrian armed forces. If Israel sought a stable Lebanon under a friendly government with strong Christian-Phalangist influence, Syria's interest lay in a reconstituted regime in which Moslem factions would be dominant.

The deteriorating political situation in Lebanon led the United States to use naval power for bombardment of targets and to launch carrier-based air strikes against Syrian military positions in Lebanon. By March 1983 the Marines themselves had become the object of attack. In April a car bomb destroyed the U.S. Embassy in Beirut. In the subsequent months the United States and Israel moved back toward the strategic relationship that had abruptly been shattered at the end of the first year of the Reagan administration.

This improvement in relations coincided with both Lebanon's deepening problems and the threat to the broader peace process posed by Syria. The redeployment of Israeli forces from the Shouf Mountains to more defensible positions to the south in the latter part of 1983 created a military vacuum in which fighting erupted between warring Lebanese groups, including Christian Phalangist supporters of Gemayel, but whom he could not effectively control. Conflict between the Syrian-supported Druse militia and the Lebanese army, the latter rebuilt with American assistance, escalated to the level of civil war. While continuing to bolster Gemayel's waning strength with American offshore military power, the Reagan administration, with a new envoy, Robert McFarlane, who had replaced Habib, negotiated a cease-fire and an agreement providing for national-reconciliation talks among the warring Christian and Moslem factions. Despite talks held in Geneva in late 1983 and again in 1984, the dominant characteristic of the Lebanese national scene remained confrontation rather than reconciliation.

In the unaccustomed role of defending static positions around Beirut Airport, the U.S. Marines suffered casualties, culminating in terrorist bombing of their headquarters on October 23, 1983, with the loss of 249 lives, coinciding with a terrorist strike that inflicted a large number of casualties on the French contingent of the multinational force. Although the Reagan administration did not face a rising tide of opposition to the continuation of the Marine presence in Lebanon in the immediate aftermath of the attack, there were nevertheless increasing expressions of concern about the advisability of keeping U.S. forces in Lebanon. In its existing numbers and tactics, the force could neither protect itself from attack nor provide effective military support for the Gemayel government. With pressure from a Congress that had only reluctantly approved the return of the Marine contingent to Lebanon after the Palestinian refugee-camp massacre, the Reagan administration withdrew the 1200 Marines in February 1984; the remainder of the multinational force pulled out soon afterward. Gemayel undertook a diplomatic effort that included a meeting with Syrian President Assad, mediated by the United States and encouraged by Israel, to bring about a power-sharing arrangement based on political concessions among opposing groups.

## The Iran-Iraq War

When the Reagan administration took office, Iran and Iraq were engaged in a military struggle that had broken out in 1980. With its large Shi'ite population Iraq, to a greater extent than any other Moslem state, had been an effective target for Khomeini's Islamic fundamentalist propaganda directed against allegedly illegitimate regimes such as that of President Saddam Hussein in Iraq, based as they were on Western concepts of socialism and nationalism rather than cultural emancipation derived from the traditional teachings of the Koran. Although Hussein had few supporters in states such as Saudi Arabia, Kuwait, Jordan, and Egypt, he nevertheless received substantial military support because of shared fears about the threat posed by Khomeini's Islamic fundamentalism to existing regimes in the region. Undoubtedly, the Saudi monarchy, as well as other threatened political elites in the Arab world, recalled the attack mounted by Islamic fundamentalists on the mosque in Mecca in 1979. By 1984 Iraq had received economic aid totalling $30 billion from the Arab world, together with arms shipments, especially from France and the Soviet Union.

In what turned out to be a grievous miscalculation, the Iraqi government had assumed that Iran could easily be defeated as a result of factionalism in its military resulting from the purges and other disruptions caused by Khomeini's revolution. In contrast to Iraq's emerging economic strength, based on an ambitious modernization program and revenues from oil exports of about 3 million barrels a day, Iran faced severe dislocations in its economy. In a view shared by other Arab regimes, Hussein believed that Khomeini could be toppled by an attack against Iran. Having made a preemptive strike against Iran in September 1980 and having achieved early military victories, Iraq faced successive onslaughts by numerically superior Iranian forces that periodically threatened to overrun enough territory to destroy Hussein's regime. In the weeks following the outbreak of conflict, Iraq seized about 4000 square miles of Iranian territory: by the middle of 1982 Iranian counteroffensives had driven Iraq's armies from nearly all this conquered territory. The war then lapsed into a series of onslaughts by Iran against successive fixed military positions defended by Iraq.

Although the Soviet Union had originally supported Iran, the prospect of an Iranian victory, together with the anti-Soviet stand taken by Khomeini, who cracked down on the Communist Tudeh party in Iran, had led Moscow to give massive military assistance to Iraq in the form of armor, artillery, aircraft, and ammunition. In early 1984, moreover, with or without direct Soviet assistance, Iraq had used chemical weapons against entrenched Iranian forces. In an escalating move, Iraq attacked Iranian oil-production facilities with aircraft and Exocet air-to-surface missiles supplied by France. Iran responded by launching attacks against tankers and other surface shipping in the Persian Gulf and threatening to close the Strait of Hormuz. The United States, Britain, and France deployed naval forces in the Arabian Sea, while the Reagan administration warned that it would not permit the shipment of oil through the strait to be halted.

Although the war remained stalemated, the losses on both sides were enormous. By 1984 Iran's military casualties were estimated to be as high as 500,000. Iran's oil-production facilities had suffered extensive damage, though petroleum exports continued at a rate of about 2 million barrels a day. In contrast, Iraq had suffered as many as 150,000 casualties and a sharp curtailment in oil exports. Clearly, the war had a far worse effect on the smaller Iraqi economy than on Iran, which actually increased its foreign-exchange holdings in the early 1980s. Contrary to initial Iraqi expectations, the war had the apparent effect of strengthening popular and clerical support for the Khomeini regime.

For the Reagan administration, one of the results of the war was to reduce, but not eliminate, reservations about close military cooperation between other Gulf states and the United States and Western European countries. The dilemma facing such governments was simply that, although their survival might be threatened by the spread of the Iran–Iraq war, their political legitimacy would be undermined by the appearance of close military cooperation with the United States, regarded as it was by Islamic fundamentalism as an alien, hostile power. If they distanced themselves from the United States politically in order to bolster their legitimacy, such governments risked exposing themselves to the revolutionary forces represented by the Islamic fundamentalist movement. A partial way out of such a dilemma was the development of greater cooperation among threatened states along the littorals of the Persian Gulf, a pattern chosen by such governments in the early 1980s.

With its considerable geographic size and position, sharing a long frontier with the Soviet Union and a commanding position on the Persian Gulf extending to and beyond the Strait of Hormuz, Iran remained a country of immense strategic importance to the United States, notwithstanding the excesses of the Islamic fundamentalist regime of the Ayatollah Khomeini, by which the United States was regarded as "the great Satan." The interest of the United States lay in victory for neither Iran nor Iraq in this war. The replacement of the existing Iraqi government by an Islamic fundamentalist regime aligned with Khomeini's Iran would send additional shock waves to such states as Jordan and Egypt, as well as to Persian Gulf oil-producing states, including Saudi Arabia.

## AMERICAN POLICY IN AFRICA

As a vast continent containing 51 independent states, Africa presented for the United States a large number of foreign-policy problems, none of which ranked at the top of the agenda of the Reagan administration—whose stance toward Africa in this respect was not substantially different from that of its recent predecessors. In southern Africa there were continuing civil conflicts in Angola and Mozambique and tensions, sometimes marked by military encounters, between South Africa and neighboring states. Of special importance in southern Africa, both as a source of conflict and as an issue of diplomatic action with the United States playing a leading role, was the future of Namibia. Elsewhere there were persistent conflicts in Chad, in which Libya's leader, the mercurial Colonel Muammar el-Qaddafi, played a central role. Qaddafi's influence extended far beyond Libya, to Western Europe and the Middle East. His government was believed to support a range of terrorist activities. In the western Sahara a struggle by insurgent Polisario forces backed by Algeria and Libya continued against Morocco over control of the former Spanish Sahara, annexed by Morocco in 1975. In the Horn of Africa, strategically important because of its proximity to the Persian Gulf, the Reagan administration faced the need to assist Somalia against Soviet-supported Ethiopia, which, in the late 1970s, had occupied the Ogaden region claimed by Somalia.

The numerous conflicts in Africa, especially the war between Somalia and Ethiopia, had produced by the early 1980s more than 5 million refugees, about half of all of the world's refugees. In much of Africa economic conditions had deteriorated in what was already the poorest continent. The world recession at the beginning of the decade, high interest rates adding to the international debt burden of African states, depressed commodity prices and worsening terms of trade for African exports, lower levels of foreign aid, and internal misman-agement of available resources and corruption—all contributed to economic malaise in Africa. Increasing population, as well as long-term drought and resulting famine in parts of the Sahel, western and central Africa, the Horn, and southern Africa, took a heavy toll on African economies. Millions of people were dependent on donated emergency food supplies for survival. Since the early 1960s, when most African states gained their independence, food production had not kept pace with population growth. The need for food imports further strained economies already facing balance-of-payments deficits. Although the debt accumulated by African states did not pose for the international financial community problems as formidable as Latin America's debt did, it remained a heavy burden for countries with subsistence economies. Increasingly, African states resorted to loans from the International Monetary Fund to provide temporary financing for their balance of payments.

Despite its preference for private-sector investment rather than govern-mental aid, the Reagan administration, recognizing the limited appeal that Africa (except South Africa) had for foreign investors, maintained economic assistance at a level just under $1 billion a year and worked within financial institutions such as the International Monetary Fund and the World Bank to meet at least a small part of the staggering economic needs of African states. Neither private-sector initiatives launched from the United States and other industrialized countries nor massive infusions of governmental aid, even if they had been forthcoming, seemed adequate to resolve the seemingly insurmountable problems of much of Africa.

### Southern Africa: South Africa, Namibia, and Angola

The principal exception to the seemingly permanent African economic crisis was South Africa. In place of Carter's policy of "confrontation" with the white-dominated government, the Reagan administration hoped to establish with South Africa an approach based on what it called "constructive engagement." It was reasoned that nagging pressure from outside powers, including the United

States, had the unintended result of hardening South African attitudes both toward greater black participation in the political process and toward the settlement of the question of independence for Namibia. "Constructive engagement" accorded with the Reagan administration's preference for quiet diplomacy over public hectoring in attempts to encourage respect for human rights in other countries. The administration also sought an improved relationship with South Africa because of its strategic importance astride the vital sea lanes around the Cape of Good Hope between the Indian Ocean and the South Atlantic. The fact that South Africa possessed vast deposits of some of the most important minerals on which industrialized economies were heavily dependent enhanced its strategic importance to the United States. Therefore, the task confronting the Reagan administration was to effect a reconciliation between strategic needs and the various power struggles shaping southern Africa in the late twentieth century.

The focus of the Reagan administration's diplomacy was Namibia, whose independence the United States proposed, in a "two-track" policy, to link indirectly and ambiguously with the withdrawal of Cuban military forces deployed in Angola. South Africa, as the Carter administration had discovered, was not prepared to accept an independent Namibia dominated by the South West African People's Organization (SWAPO), which did not have the support of tribal groups constituting nearly one-half the total Namibian population or of the white minority. SWAPO had mounted its incursions into Namibia from neighboring Angola, whose Popular Liberation Movement of Angola (MPLA) government, in power since 1975, supported SWAPO.

The MPLA itself faced a continuing challenge from the rival National Union for the Total Independence of Angola (UNITA), headed by Jonas Savimbi, whose forces were strong enough to lead the government to impose emergency legislation on as many as seven central and southern provinces. UNITA insurgency forces staged operations within several hundred miles of Luanda, the capital of Angola, which faced increasing economic dislocation and political uncertainty in the early 1980s as a result. Cuban forces stationed in Angola had first arrived in 1975 in response to South African military operations in Angola. In the years that followed, South African forces entered Angola in an effort to interdict SWAPO's raids into Namibia from Angola. By 1982, as many as 30,000 South African troops (nearly one-third of them blacks from Namibia) patrolled the border between Namibia and Angola. South Africa effectively controlled a strip of territory about 30 miles wide in Southern Angola as a buffer with Namibia and as a base for support of operations by UNITA against the MPLA-dominated Angolan regime.

Under these circumstances, the basis for a settlement of the Namibian problem seemed to have as a principal element the withdrawal of Cuban forces from Angola in return for a pledge that South Africa would not stage military operations against the MPLA regime, together with a commitment by Angola to prohibit SWAPO from using its territory to mount offensives in Namibia in return for the suspension of South African assistance to the UNITA insurgency in Angola. This series of concessions, however attractive it might seem, encountered a formidable obstacle: the political orientation that an independent Namibia would take. Although South Africa appeared to have made major military advances in halting the SWAPO operations, while strengthening UNITA in Angola, the not-unjustified fear remained that an independent Namibia would be a Marxist state. South Africa viewed with misgivings tendencies toward one-party rule under Prime Minister Robert Mugabe in Zimbabwe, where tribal conflicts increased in the years after independence. Although criticizing American policy for allegedly encouraging South Africa to step up military actions to counter threats from neighboring states, Mugabe nevertheless maintained a balance between the radical demands of some of his followers and the need to avoid alienating sources of foreign aid and investment and the skilled whites who chose to remain after independence.

Beyond the broader strategic considerations, a prerequisite for a political settlement in Namibia was an agreed formula for a constitution that would accommodate the country's diverse interests. The Reagan administration developed a series of proposals, including formation of a constituent assembly that would approve, by a two-thirds vote, a constitution providing for a multiparty, nonracial state based on principles of representative government. Such a political framework would be placed into operation over a transitional period in which, in accordance with Resolution 435 of the UN Security Council, there would be a cease-fire and a UN peacekeeping force would be substituted for South African units in a demilitarized zone between Namibia and Angola. Among the obstacles remained such issues as the size and phasing of the United Nations force, the electoral system in Namibia, and, of course, the withdrawal of the Cuban forces from Angola.

### Northern Africa: Focus on Libya

In northern Africa the Reagan administration's attention was focused on Libya and the regime of Colonel Qaddafi. Libya was the recipient of large-scale Soviet arms transfers, with its bases being used as a point of transshipment for Soviet military aid. Just after seizing power in Libya in 1969, Qaddafi had begun to give aid to various groups in the civil war in Chad, which had broken out several years earlier. Until 1980 French forces had been deployed in Chad. After their departure, the Chadian government of Goukouni Oueddei had received Libyan military help, especially in an effort to defeat forces led by Hissen Habre, who had received military aid from the United States for the Chadian civil war. The civil war had resulted in the partition of Chad, with the northern third, adjacent to Libya, under the control of Goukouni and the remainder of the country controlled by Habre. Libya had territorial claims in northern Chad.

In 1983 France, wishing to prevent the Libyan-sponsored forces of Goukouni from moving beyond northern Chad, sent 3000 troops and several fighter planes to protect the Habre government. The Reagan administration mounted a military airlift in support of the Habre government. American assistance included AWAC reconnaissance planes and F-15 fighter bombers, which were deployed to Khartoum, the capital of the Sudan. The military positions of the principal parties to the Chad conflict, resulting in partition and stalemate, furnished an incentive for negotiations whose outcome was the withdrawal of French forces from Chad, although there was no assurance either that the protracted civil war would end or that Qaddafi's interest in the destabilization of neighboring states would be diminished.

## THE ASIAN PACIFIC

The Asian Pacific formed not only a vital strategic focal point for a global American foreign policy but also the setting for a number of dynamic economies with which the United States was developing commercial links that surpassed its trade with Western Europe. In 1982, for example, trade between the United States and the Asian Pacific would soon surpass that between the United States and Western Europe. While the economies of Western European countries stagnated by comparison, it became fashionable to refer to newly industrialized states in the Asian Pacific in such terms as "the other Gang of Four," meaning the Republic of Korea, Taiwan, Hong Kong, and Singapore. All these nations had achieved unprecedented economic growth as a result of economic structures based on a large private sector and the encouragement of investment from overseas. There was some uncertainty about the future of Hong Kong after its reversion in 1997 from Britain to China, but the Asian Pacific remained economically dynamic, with growth rates for most of its countries at or above 4 percent. In the most advanced technological sectors, moreover, the United States looked to Japan with a mixture of admiration, envy, and apprehension, as its chief contender for leadership in biotechnology, microelectronics, fine ceramics, and pace-setting innovations that would shape the information-based society of the future.

### Emphasis on Stability in Korea

Reagan pledged to keep American ground forces in the Republic of Korea as a deterrent against North Korean attack across the demilitarized zone. In 1983 the United States announced a five-year military-improvement program that included the purchase by South Korea of arms totalling $4.7 billion. With "quiet diplomacy" in place of the public criticism of human-rights violations voiced by its predecessor, the Reagan administration obtained the release of opposition political leader Kim Dae Jong. Although the South Korean government of President Chun Doo Hwan faced internal opposition that led to periodic protests and arrests, by the early 1980s the Republic of Korea had become the fifth richest country in Asia on a per capita basis, surpassed only by Japan, Hong Kong, Singapore, and Taiwan. In 1983 the South Korean economic growth rate stood at 9.3 percent, contrasted with economic stagnation in North Korea, which devoted about one-quarter of its GNP to military capabilities deployed for possible attack against South Korea.

With a population twice that of North Korea, and a growing economy, South Korea was gaining a military advantage over the North. In keeping with its support for South Korea, the Reagan administration opposed North Korean efforts to begin negotiations with the United States on the reunification of the Korean peninsula. In such a negotiating framework, North Korea's intention was to have itself acknowledged as the sole representative of all the Korean people, clearly a one-sided and unacceptable formula for the Republic of Korea, which would have been relegated to the subordinate status of observer. From the perspective of the Reagan administration, stability in the Korean peninsula remained an important ingredient in the preservation of broader American security interests in the Asian Pacific because of the proximity of the two Koreas to the major powers of the region.

### Relations with Japan in the Mid-1980s

The dual issues of defense burden sharing and trade not only beset the Reagan administration's relations with Japan as they had those of its predecessors but assumed dimensions of increased importance as a result of the changing international security environment and the expanding trade deficit facing the United States in the early 1980s. To an even greater extent than Carter had, Reagan pressed Japan to increase its defense spending to permit the safeguarding of sea lanes and air space within 1000 nautical miles of Tokyo as a supplement to American naval and air units in the western Pacific. There were recognized deficiencies in training and stockpiles in Japanese forces. In the early 1980s, perhaps as a result of U.S. prodding but more likely in response to a recognition in Japan of altered security needs created by the Soviet military buildup, Japanese spending for self-defense forces had risen by about 6 percent in real annual terms, exceeding overall budgetary growth in Japan and surpassing the rate of increase of all NATO members except the United States. Nevertheless, Japan's defense spending, which had started from a substantially lower point than that of NATO countries, remained just below the self-imposed 1 percent of GNP. This contrasted, in 1983, with 4.3 percent of GNP for the Federal Republic of Germany, 5.3 percent for Great Britain, and 4.1 percent for France. However, because Japan's real increases in defense spending each year were greater than the growth of GNP, it was likely that the 1-percent-of-GNP barrier would be broken by the late 1980s unless defense was slowed considerably in Japan.

The elevation in 1982 of Yasuhiro Nakasone as leader of the ruling Liberal Democratic party and thus as prime minister brought to office a leader who presented a sharp contrast to his predecessors in leadership style and a willingness to state views, controversial in Japan but welcomed in Washington, in support of increased defense burden sharing by Japan and the liberalization of Japanese trade policy. At the conference held in Williamsburg, Virginia, in 1983, Nakasone went further than any of his predecessors in endorsing the communiqué supporting the deployment of Pershing II and cruise missiles in Western Europe if the Soviet Union refused to conclude an agreement for SS-20 reductions satisfactory to Western security needs.

Within recent years, Japan has become concerned about the deployment of SS-20s in the eastern part of the USSR and has supported the U.S. effort to negotiate a global, and not merely a regional, European ceiling on intermediate-range nuclear missiles. Nakasone has emphasized the need for Japan to have air-defense capabilities to prevent the overflight of Soviet aircraft. None of these security capabilities seemed within Japan's reach under existing defense programs, even though by 1984 Japan ranked sixth among nations in defense spending. If it proved impossible to elicit from Japan desired burden sharing for the protection of sea lanes and air defense, there was increase defense cooperation in the early 1980s in the form of joint exercises and official studies of problems of maritime defense between Japan and the United States, as well as Japanese economic assistance to countries such as Egypt, Pakistan, and Thailand, each of which was important to overall American interests, in keeping with Tokyo's concept of "comprehensive security." This Japanese–American division of labor had inherent limits in the unwillingness of the United States to continue to give Japan a "free ride" in defense, while Japan specialized in the economic instruments of statecraft that both encompassed and encouraged export competition on terms seen as unfavorable to American exporters.

At the center of the burden-sharing problem was the American contention that the United States, on a per capita basis, spends ten times as much as Japan on defense, while at the same time facing a trade deficit that approached $20 billion in 1983—a year in which Japan enjoyed a record trade surplus of nearly $32 billion. In 1982 Japan exported nearly $141 billion worth of products, including automobiles, television sets and other home appliances, computers, ships, textiles, and steel. The protectionist sentiment that rose in the United States at the end of the 1970s was directed principally against Japan. Such direct American pressures produced "voluntary" restrictions on Japanese automobile exports to the United States, as well as demands from American manufacturers and labor unions for domestic-content legislation to ensure that products sold by Japan in the American market contained components manufactured in this country. Although Japan cut tariffs on a large number of imports, a variety of other barriers remained on a large number of products such as petrochemicals, fertilizers, pharmaceuticals, data-processing software, electronic equipment, citrus fruit, and beef. Japan argued that its industry was being penalized for its efficiency, innovation, and effective marketing techniques, while the United States and other exporting countries had not made an equivalent effort on a sustained basis to enter the Japanese market. Resentment in Japan had as one focal point the contention that their country was one of the world's largest importers of goods and services. Manufactured imports constituted a relatively small percentage of total Japanese imports because Japan, lacking natural resources, must obtain from abroad nearly all its raw materials.

Despite the friction in the areas of defense and trade policy, the Nakasone government developed a close working relationship with the Reagan administration. Although quotas on Japanese automobile exports to the United States were extended (despite the recovery of the American automobile industry), the Reagan administration faced a rising tide of sentiment for more protectionist trade policies. In turn, the Nakasone government reduced or eliminated tariffs on a large number of products, simplified other import procedures, and removed a ban on the export of defense-related technology to the United States. The United States and Japan had evolved a relationship whose scope and magnitude were unprecedented in world economic history, set within a mutual security context, acknowledged in Tokyo and Washington, that remained pivotal to American policy in the Asian Pacific.

### U.S. Relations with China

With the Reagan administration U.S. policy toward China underwent a change based upon the recognized need to preserve and strengthen cooperation where mutually beneficial, while also attaching somewhat less strategic significance to the PRC in the global power equation. The change was the result of several factors shaping American policy in the Asian Pacific. They included an assessment that, in overall terms, Asia had grown in importance within the global context of American foreign policy, but China was only one of the key Asian-Pacific actors whose interests the United States must take into account. The final years of the Carter administration had produced a closer Sino–American relationship that seemed to presage strategic cooperation, especially after the Soviet invasion of Afghanistan. The Reagan administration took a somewhat more detached approach to the potential and the limits of closer links between Beijing and Washington. For all its emphasis on human rights as a guiding foreign-policy principle, the Carter administration had been evolving with the unrepresentative Beijing regime a relationship of *realpolitik*, based on strategic interest. Paradoxically, the Reagan administration, committed to the restoration of American military strength and other necessary capabilities as a counterpoise to the Soviet Union, weighed the Sino–American relationship against other interests, including what Ronald Reagan, long before he became president, had regarded as an American commitment to Taiwan. During the campaign of 1980 Reagan had criticized the Carter administration for having concluded a diplomatic normalization agreement with Mainland China that discriminated unnecessarily against Taiwan. Specifically, Carter was said to have erred in agreeing to establish full diplomatic relations with Beijing without retaining some form of official links with Taiwan. Reagan's criticism was based in part on the ideological incompatibility between the PRC and the United States and in part on the need, as he saw it, to upgrade the "unofficial" relationship with Taipei and to sell weapons to Taiwan. In 1980 the Carter administration, in keeping with the Taiwan Relations Act of 1979, had resumed arms sales to Taiwan, despite the vocal opposition of the Beijing government. With the election of Reagan, American policy toward China entered a period of uncertainty, resulting only in part from the diminished perception of the significance of a strategic relationship.

By the early 1980s the Chinese leadership had stepped back from the idea expressed earlier by Deng Xiao-ping that China, together with Western Europe, Japan, and the United States, should form a united front in opposition to Soviet "hegemonism." The emergence of a defense consensus in the United States sufficient to bring to office the Reagan administration, committed to an American defense buildup and sharing many of the global strategic perspectives publicly enunciated by the PRC, had seemed to cool the ardor of the Chinese leadership for a close strategic relationship with the United States. A more powerful United States, standing in opposition to the Soviet Union, would enable China to establish a position of equidistance from both superpowers and thus maximize Beijing's independence from both Moscow and Washington. From the American perspective as well, certain features of the contemporary international landscape restricted the need for a more intimate diplomatic relationship with China. If the principal benefit derived from China for the United States was the stationing by the Soviet Union of about one-quarter of its military forces along the Sino–Soviet frontier—capabilities that therefore were not available for deployment elsewhere— the fact remained that such units had been there in large numbers before Sino–American normalization. In fact, the reported border clashes between China and the Soviet Union in 1969 had preceded the transformation of relations between China and the United States. Although it would be necessary for the United States to exercise whatever influence it had to help forestall a return to Sino–Soviet cooperation and friendship, the deeply rooted tensions resulting from the Sino–Soviet dispute were likely to lead Moscow to deploy large numbers of its forces adjacent to the border with China. The logical inference to be drawn from such an analysis was that the United States need not make major conces- sions, least of all the total abandonment of Taiwan, as part of a Sino-American strategic cooperation. Under prevailing circumstances China, in its own self- interest, would do more or less what it was already doing in global strategic terms. Given the vast military disparity that favored the Soviet Union, as well as China's economic backwardness, there was not much more, in strategic terms, that China could offer the United States.

Having placed reduced emphasis on the "China card," the Reagan ad- ministration nevertheless faced internal divisions in the evolution of its relation- ship with Beijing, with Secretary of State Haig favoring a coalition strategy comparable to that advocated successfully by Zbigniew Brzezinski in the final years of the Carter administration. Perhaps to balance differing internal views, the Reagan administration sought to quiet PRC opposition to plans to sell arms to Taiwan by expressing a U.S. willingness to respond favorably to Chinese requests for weapons on a case-by-case basis. Although the Reagan adminis- tration turned down Taiwan's request to purchase the advanced FX fighter aircraft as unnecessary for its defensive needs, Taipei was permitted to continue to coproduce the F-5E, a less sophisticated aircraft. China and the United States produced a document that reconciled by diplomatic ambiguity their otherwise divergent positions on arms sales to Taiwan. Without setting a precise cutoff date on such weapons sales, as Beijing desired, the United States nevertheless stated its intention to reduce such transactions over a period of time, depending presumably on the state of relations between Taiwan and the mainland. China answered that it would pursue reunification by peaceful means, reiterating a 1982 plan by which Taiwan, as an autonomous province of China, could retain its own armed forces, government, and economic structure. In short, the Reagan ad- ministration remained committed to the concept of one China, of which Taiwan formed a part, although the United States would resist efforts to incorporate Taiwan by force into the PRC. In the meantime, the United States would continue to make defensive military capabilities available to Taiwan at a level not to exceed, qualitatively or quantitatively, the levels supplied since the completion of Sino–American normalization.

As the Sino–American relationship improved and the United States managed at the same time to maintain arms sales to Taiwan, the PRC sought to strengthen its independence in foreign policy by entering normalization negotiations with the Soviet Union. In 1981, with the United States and China in disagreement over arms sales to Taiwan, the Soviet Union proposed the resumption of Sino–Soviet talks, which the PRC had suspended in the wake of the Soviet invasion of Afghanistan in 1979. Although the immediate Soviet goal was undoubtedly to exploit Sino–American differences on Taiwan, Moscow stood to benefit greatly from a normalization that would diminish tension with China and thereby release military and other capabilities for redeployment elsewhere. Conversely, the security burdens confronting the United States, in both Europe and the Asian Pacific, would be immensely greater if the Sino–Soviet conflict were replaced by reconciliation. From China's perspective, an improvement in relations with Moscow might enable the PRC to divert resources from military forces to economic modernization and benefit from limited restoration in technology transfer from the Soviet Union.

In October 1982 China and the Soviet Union began a series of talks, held at six-month intervals alternately in Beijing and Moscow. Faced as it is with Soviet forces deployed not only along the frontier but also in Afghanistan and Vietnam, China attached several conditions to normalization of relations with Moscow: a cessation of Soviet military assistance to Vietnam and the withdrawal of Vietnamese forces from Kampuchea; the withdrawal of Soviet forces from Afghanistan; the dismantling of SS-20s targeted against China; and a pullback of Soviet forces stationed along the Sino–Soviet frontier. In short, China sought from the Soviet Union a fundamental reduction in both levels and deployment patterns of Soviet military forces as evidence of Moscow's commitment to political normalization. Such Chinese security interests clashed with the perceived need of the Soviet Union to maintain large-scale forces on the Sino–Soviet border in order to protect sparsely settled territory containing immense untapped natural resources, including energy, in which Moscow planned to make substantial investments. The continued deployment of Soviet forces might be due to a fear that China would someday occupy Soviet territory as a result of the increasing Chinese population, even though population growth had not caused territorial expansion in modern times and Beijing was engaged in a drastic campaign to lower the birth rate. The talks conducted between Beijing and Moscow coincided with the continued buildup of Soviet capabilities, as well as forces supported by the Soviet Union, in each of the areas of contention outlined by China. Although trade between China and the Soviet Union grew rapidly in the early 1980s, from a low of $150 million in 1981 to just above $1 billion in 1984, the overall relationship between Beijing and Washington underwent an even greater development, despite the major issues dividing China and the United States and notwithstanding the effort by the PRC to achieve a more flexible and independent stance with respect to both superpowers.

In Southeast Asia, the gap between Soviet and Chinese policy illustrated the broader problems dividing Moscow and Beijing. A legacy of the Vietnam War, the close alignment between Moscow and the Democratic People's Republic of Vietnam was based both on Soviet strategic interests and goals and on Hanoi's historic fear of Chinese expansionism in Southeast Asia. Soviet subsidies, estimated at about $5 million a day, underwrote Hanoi's military operations in the neighboring states of Indochina. The Soviet Union made use of the American-built naval and air base at Cam Ranh Bay for a force of as many as 27 warships, including attack submarines, as well as aircraft deployed on a regular basis adjacent to vital sea lanes. This Soviet presence served as a shield against Chinese expansion both for Vietnam and for other Southeast Asian states.

China supported forces in Cambodia opposed to Vietnam, notably the infamous Khmer Rouge under the leadership of Khieu Samphan. In light of the Khmer Rouge's practice of genocide against hundreds of thousands of the population of Cambodia less than a decade earlier, it could command no broad international support against the Vietnamese invaders. In 1982 the Association of Southeast Asian States (ASEAN) had undertaken a diplomatic initiative consisting of an effort to put together a coalition of groups in order to reach a compromise acceptable to both Hanoi and contending forces in Cambodia to reduce, if not remove altogether, the Vietnamese military presence while leaving to Vietnam a large measure of political influence in Cambodia.

Although the United States retained links with all states except Vietnam, its leverage in Indochina was severely limited. The bitter legacy of the Vietnam War, the geostrategic interests of Hanoi in its security arrangements with Moscow, and the closer Sino–American relationship all made unlikely any immediate diplomatic reconciliation between Vietnam and the United States. Not the least of the results of the Vietnam War was the sharply diminished influence of the United States and the greatly enhanced leverage of the Soviet Union in shaping the political map of Indochina.

### Afghanistan and South Asia

By the early 1980s the Soviet Union had deployed as many as 105,000 troops in Afghanistan in a relentless effort to support its puppet regime headed by President Babrik Karmal against the freedom fighters, the Mujaheddin, who controlled as much as 80 percent of the countryside. The Mujaheddin remained split along tribal and religious lines, rendering all but impossible a concerted effort against occupying Soviet forces and military units loyal to the Karmal government. The Soviet Union mounted military action designed to maintain essential lines of communication, while the Mujaheddin attacked convoys and other military units and electrical power lines and other elements of the infrastructure. Soviet military power was used in savage attacks that probably included the use of biochemical weapons, or mycotoxins, against suspected centers of resistance in an effort to destroy the Mujaheddin and much of the local population. Despite a diplomatic effort, under United Nations auspices, to arrange a political settlement providing for the withdrawal of Soviet forces, the Soviet Union seemed prepared to maintain its military presence in Afghanistan for as long as necessary in order to destroy the opposition. The Reagan administration made available arms supplies and humanitarian aid to the Mujaheddin through Pakistan. Assistance to the Mujaheddin from other quarters, including Saudi Arabia and Egypt, flowed through Pakistan.

In 1981 the United States negotiated with Pakistan a $3.2 billion military and economic assistance agreement that provided for the transfer of F-16 aircraft, destroyers, and antiship missiles. Pakistan remained pivotal to American policy because it constituted a barrier to southward Soviet expansion into South Asia and because it was forging closer links with the oil-producing Persian Gulf states.

In turn the Reagan administration attempted to minimize the impact of its strengthened links with Pakistan on its troubled relationship with India. Resentful of U.S. military assistance and recalling the American "tilt" toward Pakistan at the time of the 1974 Indo–Pakistani War, India's ties with the Soviet Union led the New Delhi government to take a somewhat relaxed view of both the Soviet invasion of Afghanistan and the establishment under Vietnamese armed forces of a pro-Soviet regime in Kampuchea.

## THE REAGAN ADMINISTRATION AND THE SOVIET UNION:
## A QUEST FOR REALISM AND CONSENSUS

Unlike any of its predecessors, the first Reagan administration had to adjust to two changes of leadership in the Soviet Union. After 18 years in power, Leonid Brezhnev died in November 1982 and was followed by Yuri Andropov, who died in February 1984. The leadership of the Soviet Union then passed to Konstantin Chernenko, a protégé of Brezhnev who had originally lost out to Andropov in Kremlin succession politics. Despite this rapid turnover in leadership, Soviet foreign policy displayed elements of continuity that included an effort, through public statements and policy actions, to undermine support for the Reagan administration both in the United States and abroad. The Soviet Union could not be certain whether the policy orientation of the Reagan administration were a transient or long-term phenomenon. Perhaps just because the Reagan administration had argued for a defense buildup so that it could negotiate from a position of greater strength with the Soviet Union, Moscow was determined to convince governments and private citizens alike that it would not negotiate under such conditions. Instead, the Soviet Union would attempt to undermine the Reagan administration's support in the hope that its defense programs and other policies could not come to fruition before an election brought to office less anti-Soviet forces in the United States. By appealing to various constituencies in the United States and within the Atlantic Alliance, using a combination of threats and promises, the Soviet Union might weaken support for the Reagan administration and its policies. The extent to which Moscow succeeded in this strategy would depend on the depth of public support for the features of American foreign policy that were most disagreeable to the Soviet Union.

Where it suited Soviet interests, however, negotiations with the United States continued in the early 1980s. A new five-year agreement was concluded in 1983 for the sale of American grain to the Soviet Union, and arrangements were completed in 1984 for the modernization of the hot line to provide instantaneous communication between Moscow and Washington. The superpowers negotiated from June 1982 to December 1983 in the Strategic Arms Reduction Talks (START), which were conducted separately from, but coincided in time with, the INF in Geneva.

## The START Talks for Arms Reduction

Having declared during the 1980 presidential campaign that, in his view, the SALT II treaty was "fatally flawed," Reagan announced shortly after becoming president that the United States, nevertheless, would not "undercut" its provisions as long as the Soviet Union showed similar restraint. Among its principal deficiencies, according to critics within and outside the Reagan administration, the SALT II treaty placed no effective limitations on the number of heavy ICBMs and warheads that the Soviet Union, even within the terms of the treaty, could deploy against nuclear targets in the United States. With such strategic systems, the Soviet Union could pose a threat of increasing magnitude to the fixed, land-based strategic force of the United States. Although SALT II had codified strategic forces at the approximate levels anticipated to be deployed during the period it was in effect (until December 31, 1985), the unratified treaty would be observed if only because the United States would be worse off militarily if all constraints on the Soviet Union contained in the treaty were removed.

While abiding by the SALT II treaty's provisions, the Reagan administration would take necessary steps to rebuild American strategic forces and other defense capabilities and would enter negotiations with the Soviet Union for substantial symmetrical reductions in their respective nuclear arsenals. Central to the approach chosen by the administration for these negotiations was the substitution of the term "reductions" for "limitations," as indicated in the acronym START in place of SALT. Equally important was the need to develop an arms-control concept that bore a direct relationship to the broader strategic-military problem confronting the United States, which SALT II had failed adequately to address: the huge Soviet counterforce capability, which posed a threat to the United States both because of the size of its launch vehicles and the number and accuracy levels of its warheads. In the conceptualization and development of appropriate units of account, American arms-reduction policy should have as its focus a diminution in the increasing threat posed by such Soviet systems, for which the United States possessed no equivalent capability. Hence the emphasis in the Reagan administration on proposals that would require the Soviet Union to reduce the number of land-based warheads to a level far below that permitted in the SALT II treaty.

In keeping with its belief that negotiations with the Soviet Union for an arms-control agreement on strategic forces should follow, rather than precede, decisions about the scope of American strategic-force modernization, the Reagan administration used its first months in office to formulate a strategic-force program providing for: the deployment of 100 MX missiles (reduced from 200 planned by the Carter administration); construction of 100 B-1-B long-range combat aircraft (revived by the Reagan administration after having been cancelled by Carter); and acceleration in the deployment of the Trident ballistic-missile submarine with research and development to proceed on a new missile that would eventually give greater accuracy to submarine-launched ballistic missiles.

The original American START proposal, set forth in June 1982, had called for drastic cuts to 850 in the number of ballistic missiles as well as reductions in total warheads to 5000 for each side. According to the American proposal, limits on missile size, or throw weight, as well as on strategic aircraft, would be discussed in a second phase of the negotiations. The unit of account for START would be missiles and warheads rather than the launchers from which missiles and warheads could be fired, a change that in itself symbolized the far greater complexity in strategic-arms limitation since the time of SALT I. The Soviet reaction was that agreement to the U.S. proposals would require it to restructure its strategic force and that therefore such an arms-control concept was unacceptable. The Soviet Union criticized the American proposal for emphasizing ballistic missiles without placing comparable constraints on strategic aircraft and cruise missiles, both of which were important components of the American strategic-force structure.

The Soviet Union, for its part, put forward a START proposal that would have permitted each side a total of 1800 strategic delivery vehicles (ICBM launchers, submarine-launched ballistic missile launchers, and strategic bombers). Although this proposal represented a reduction in launchers to levels originally sought by the Carter administration in its March 1977 "deep cuts" initiative then rejected by Moscow, it was based on launchers as the unit of account. As such, it would have done nothing to constrain the threat posed by heavy ICBMs targeted with large numbers of warheads, although the Soviet Union expressed a willingness to discuss a limit in numbers of what they termed "nuclear charges," or missile warheads and nuclear weapons carried on launchers. Also in keeping with earlier Soviet SALT policy, the Soviet Union proposed a ban on all cruise missiles with ranges in excess of 600 kilometers, the effect of which would be to prohibit the deployment by the United States of any of the long-range cruise missile variants under development or already in production, including the ground-launched cruise missile, in accordance with the NATO "double-track" decision of 1979.

In its arms-control policy the Reagan administration faced a series of dilemmas. In order to obtain an arms-control accord that was in keeping with principal American strategic interests—namely, to lower the large number of Soviet highly accurate systems targeted against the smaller U.S. land-based strategic force—the United States found it necessary to put forward a START proposal calling for major changes in the configuration of Soviet strategic forces. When the Soviet Union rejected this proposal, the Reagan administration opened itself to allegations that it was not serious about arms control. To find an arms-control proposal that both restricted destabilizing Soviet strategic forces and was acceptable to the Soviet Union represented under the circumstances a probable contradiction in terms. Furthermore, the administration contended that, in the absence of resolve in the deployment of new systems to replace components of the aging American strategic force (of which a large proportion was more than two decades old, while a comparable proportion of the Soviet force was less than ten years old), the Soviet Union would have little incentive to enter serious talks to achieve effective reductions. The Reagan administration's critics responded that new deployments would simply fuel an arms race. Instead, these critics contended in the debate that unfolded in the United States in the early 1980s, both sides should freeze their nuclear arsenals at present levels as the first step toward reductions. To freeze nuclear systems under such conditions would reward the

Soviet Union for its vast modernization programs while preventing the United States from redressing deficiencies that had accumulated during the last decade. Applied to all nuclear-capable systems, the administration contended, a nuclear freeze would codify the imbalance in intercontinental strategic forces while thwarting a necessary American modernization program; a freeze would leave the Soviet Union with a monopoly position in highly accurate, land-based intermediate-range nuclear systems, the SS-20, targeted against Western Europe and the Asian Pacific. The MX, a larger land-based missile to be deployed as a replacement for the older Minuteman, became a focal point for criticism because of its cost as well as questions about its basing mode and therefore survivability under nuclear attack. Faced with congressional pressure to cut the MX from its strategic modernization program, the Reagan administration appointed a bipartisan presidential commission to study the question of deployment modes for the MX within the broader context of American strategic deterrence needs and arms-control policy. The Scowcroft Commission (after retired General Brent Scowcroft, who had been President Ford's national security adviser) recommended the deployment of up to 100 MX missiles (with as many as ten warheads each) in alternate basing modes, including super-hardened Minuteman silos. The commission also called for the development of a smaller, single-warhead ICBM termed Midgetman. One longer-term answer to the problem of missile vulnerability was said to lie in the deployment of a smaller missile in larger numbers but each with only a single warhead. If such a recommendation held implications for the future structuring of strategic forces, it would have equally important conceptual ramifications for the arms-control policy of the Reagan administration, linked as it was to the perceived requirements of nuclear deterrence and force survivability.

The effect of the Scowcroft Commission's report was to produce an American START proposal in June 1983 that was based on a revision upward of the proposal put forward a year earlier, limiting each side to a total of 850 ballistic missiles and an aggregate of 5000 warheads. Such a proposal would accommodate a total number of missiles, including the Midgetmen, larger than 850 while reducing the warhead total of 5000 permitted to each side by the earlier American START proposal. Furthermore, the United States offered to negotiate an agreement that, in its first phase, would limit all strategic systems rather than only ballistic missiles. This would include an equal ceiling for the United States and the Soviet Union on the number of heavy bombers and cruise missiles carried by such aircraft below the numbers permitted in the SALT II treaty. In the modified American proposal, the United States would trade its advantages in bombers and cruise missiles for Soviet superiority in ballistic missiles.

In addition to the recommendations of the Scowcroft Commission, the Reagan administration incorporated within its START proposal the "double build-down" concept originally put forward by two Republican members of the Senate, William Cohen and Charles Percy, and one Democrat, Sam Nunn. In the build-down idea, the United States and the Soviet Union would be required to retire at least one older nuclear weapon for each new one deployed, and two-for-one or three-for-two in some weapons categories. The U.S. proposal provided for a guaranteed annual build-down of approximately 5 percent. Although the

Soviet Union would have to make substantial cuts in its heavy, MIRVed ICBM force, as favored originally by the Reagan administration, there was considerable latitude for a compromise that would include limitations on American cruise missiles.

If the bipartisan consensus on which American START policy had been constructed all but ensured Senate ratification of a treaty negotiated within this emerging framework, it nevertheless met with Soviet rejection for much the same reason as the administration's original proposal: it would have the effect, according to a Soviet statement, of "emasculating" the strategic force of the Soviet Union. In December 1983 the START talks adjourned with the Soviet Union refusing to set a date for their resumption.

### The Strategic Defense Initiative ("Star Wars")

If technology, in the form of greater accuracy, held unsettling implications for the survivability under nuclear attack of the offensive retaliatory forces that constituted the basis for deterrence, could technology also produce a transformation in the superpower strategic relationship, from an emphasis on offensive missiles to reliance on a defense that would eventually render such capabilities obsolete? At the time of SALT I it had been concluded that strategic defense was not technologically feasible, since it would be possible to construct additional offensive missiles to saturate any defensive system that could be deployed. Because it might arouse fear on one side that the other might carry out a surprise attack while hoping to blunt the retaliatory blow, the deployment of a strategic defense was held to be destabilizing. The ABM Treaty of 1972, in SALT I, had prohibited the superpowers from deploying an effective strategic defense, placing equally stringent restrictions on the deployment of offensive forces capable of striking the targets whose defense was prohibited by the ABM Treaty.

In a decision announced on March 23, 1983, the Reagan administration proposed a research program to determine the technological feasibility of a defense against ballistic missiles. The Strategic Defense Initiative (SDI) informally and inaccurately referred to as the "Star Wars" defense, represented an effort to ascertain the prospects for a strategic posture that would compound the cost and uncertainty of a first strike. The SDI was hardly an American "initiative," since the Soviet Union had long been engaged in such research and, within the terms of the ABM Treaty, had deployed the world's only ABM system. If it proved possible to deploy such a strategic defense, the basis would have been created for a reduction in offensive systems because there would be little incentive to deploy missiles that would not be able to destroy targets protected by the strategic defense. Even if it proved impossible to build a fully leakproof ballistic-missile defense system for the protection of cities, the ability to defend such targets as command, communication, and control centers, as well as other elements of strategic forces, or at least to enhance greatly their survivability, would reinforce deterrence. In its Strategic Defense Initiative, the Reagan administration adopted an approach that sought to determine whether, in an evolutionary fashion, technologies could be developed for clearly defined categories of targets that would enhance deterrence.

Critics alleged that making nuclear war more survivable would actually enhance the prospects for conflict if one or both sides concluded that they could fight and survive, if not win, a nuclear war. Supporters of the Strategic Defense Initiative responded that such logic was as flawed as the assertion that, by wearing a seat belt, a motorist would be more likely to drive recklessly because his or her prospects for surviving a crash would be greater.

The Strategic Defense Initiative raised questions associated with security during the transition from an offense-dominant to a defense-oriented strategic environment; with the implications for conventional nuclear thresholds in the extended-security guarantees in alliances, in particular the Atlantic Alliance; and finally with its effects on arms-control negotiations. Critics of the Strategic Defense Initiative contended that the testing and deployment of a strategic defense system would require either the abrogation or amendment of the ABM Treaty. Proponents held that, in any event, the Soviet Union was developing its own technologies for strategic defense. Unlike the United States, the Soviet Union had the world's only deployed strategic-defense system under the ABM Treaty. The existence of a countervailing American research program might lessen the likelihood that the Soviet Union would seek to break out of the ABM Treaty with its own strategic defense. If the United States were unable quickly to counter any such Soviet deployment, Moscow might have an incentive to put into place a large-scale strategic defense, with enormous consequences for the strategic environment. In fact, it was suggested, the deployment by both superpowers of some form of strategic defense, reducing the possibility of surprise attack, would enhance the stability of their military relationship. Last but not least, the results of more than a decade of strategic arms limitation negotiations had shown the inherent inability of such talks in themselves to lower the numbers, lethality, and accuracy of offensive nuclear forces. Hence it would be necessary to utilize technology in the form of strategic defense potential to furnish the incentive for reductions in offensive capabilities. Ideally, under such circumstances, greater emphasis would be placed on the deployment of weapons that destroy weapons rather than weapons that destroy people.

At the time of SALT I, the Soviet Union had favored the signing of an ABM Treaty without equally rigid prohibitions against the deployment of offensive forces, which Moscow had continued to deploy at an unabated pace in the years that followed the signing of SALT I. In 1984 the Soviet Union pressed the United States to enter negotiations to prohibit the deployment in space of weapons that could be used against satellites or as part of a strategic-defense capability. Within days of the successful testing by the United States of a missile launched against an ICBM, intercepted about 100 miles from the surface of the earth, the Soviet Union reiterated an earlier call for a treaty against such weapons. The U.S. response was to accept the Soviet proposal, but to indicate that any discussion of weapons in space for strategic defense had to include offensive means as well—in short, a return in some form to the problems of offensive systems inadequately addressed from the American perspective in SALT II and in the negotiations suspended by the Soviet Union in 1983. At a meeting in Geneva in January 1985, agreement had been reached to hold negotiations under an "umbrella" framework containing three sets of talks—intercontinental systems, intermediate-range forces, and strategic defense.

In early 1984 the Reagan administration had called for the establishment of a "constructive and realistic working relationship" with the Soviet Union based on a dialogue about their differences in "troubled regions of the world" and reductions in the level of armaments. This approach followed the sharp deterioration that had marked U.S.–Soviet relations after the Soviet Union shot down Korean Airlines Flight 007 when it entered Soviet air space over Kamchatka and Sakkalin on September 1, 1983, with the loss of 269 lives. After initially refusing to acknowledge responsibility, the Soviet Union issued a succession of statements claiming that Moscow was fully justified in shooting down a "spy plane" that had entered its air space. The United States accused the Soviet Union of a "brutal disregard for life and truth." Moscow's rhetoric escalated in a denunciation of the Reagan administration for "foul-mouth abuse mingled with hypocritical sermons on morality and humanity." Notwithstanding such vituperative statements, the Soviet leadership remained prepared to do business with the Reagan administration whenever it suited Moscow's purposes. Indeed, even as the Soviet Union denounced the American condemnation of the Soviet destruction of the Korean airliner, Andropov stated that Soviet policy was based not on "emotions," but on "common sense" and "realism." This was the context within which the Soviet Union withdrew from arms-control negotiations that no longer served its perceived interests in late 1983, and subsequently came back to such talks in 1985.

## FOREIGN-POLICY DECISION MAKING UNDER REAGAN

At the outset, the Reagan administration attempted to put into place an organizational structure for foreign policy based on an American version of "cabinet government," a term that is commonly used to describe the collective responsibility of the cabinet and prime minister in Great Britain. In contrast to the British parliamentary system, there is no such collective responsibility in the relationship between an American president and the members of his cabinet. Unlike a British prime minister, the president of the United States can use the members of his cabinet, individually or collectively, in the official decision-making process as much or as little as he or she wishes. The Reagan administration entered office with the idea, based in part on Reagan's decision-making style as governor of California, that members of the cabinet would form a cohesive unit. The appointment to such positions of persons sharing Reagan's general political philosophy, capable of working together in support of agreed foreign-policy objectives, would make possible at least some decentralization of the policy-integration function that had been concentrated in the National Security Council staff in recent administrations.

Moreover, the approach to cabinet government initially preferred by the Reagan administration included a downgrading of the position of national-security adviser from the cabinet rank it had held during the Carter administration. Presumably, the relegation of the national-security adviser to a less exalted status would diminish discord of the type that had marred the relationship between Secretary of State Vance and National Security Adviser Brzezinski in the

Carter administration. Instead of having direct and continuing access to the president, the national-security adviser would report through a senior White House counselor to the president—although Reagan's first national-security adviser, Richard V. Allen, for the first several months of the administration continued his predecessors' practice of providing daily presidential briefings.

The National Security Council structure established early in the Reagan administration furnished further evidence of the decision-making system that was intended. Three Senior Interdepartmental Groups (SIGs) were formed: the first to deal with foreign-policy issues, to be headed by the secretary of state; the second to focus on defense policy, presided over by the secretary of defense; and the third to consider intelligence issues, under the director of central intelligence. These three SIGs replaced the Policy Review Committee of the Carter administration as the locus for the development and coordination of national-security policy. Below the SIGs were established a series of Interdepartmental Groups (IGs), which were designed to coordinate policy in each of the various regions, with assistant secretaries of state presiding over them. The IGs were another indication of the shift of the locus of decision making from the national-security adviser and his staff to the Department of State. Nearly all the approximately 30 IGs created in the Reagan administration were chaired by Department of State personnel. Despite the preponderance of State in such IGs, Secretary of State Haig did not develop a close working relationship either with Reagan or with Reagan's inner circle in the White House. Haig's aloofness stood in sharp contrast to the style of his successor, George Shultz, and to the experience of predecessors such as Kissinger and Dulles, during whose terms the State bureaucracy was largely excluded from the most important part of the decision-making process. Finally, in March 1981 a crisis-management committee headed by Vice President Bush was created, with the task of integrating resources in response to domestic and international emergencies. The failure of the Reagan administration to name the secretary of state as the head of this committee represented one of many issues of discord between Haig and the White House that culminated in his resignation in June 1982. Thus the National Security Council structure developed by the Reagan administration did not live up to expectations in minimizing bureaucratic in-fighting and battles for political "turf" in the decision-making process.

In early 1982 the Reagan administration embarked on a mid-course correction in its national-security decision-making personnel and structure. The resignation of Richard V. Allen was followed by the appointment of William P. Clark as assistant to the president for national-security affairs. Perhaps in light of the experience of the first year of the Reagan administration, when the national-security adviser did not have direct access to the president, and because of his long-term close association with Reagan, Clark worked directly with the president. The role of the National Security Council staff was strengthened. Additional IGs were created in support of the crisis-management committee, and a planning group was formed to develop contingencies for future crises. Furthermore, a Senior Interdepartmental Group for International Economic Policy was established, with the secretary of the treasury as its head. Other SIGs—on space, public diplomacy, technology transfer, and emergency preparedness—

were formed, with the assistant to the president for national-security affairs presiding, to integrate policy in these sectors. By the time Clark was succeeded, in late 1983, by his deputy, Robert McFarlane, the National Security Council had substantially increased its role in the decision-making process, not only because additional interdepartmental coordinating groups had been formed but also because it was supported by a staff that, while substantially smaller in number than at the height of the Kissinger era, included just under 50 persons divided about equally among academic, civilian governmental, and military personnel.

In the final analysis, the Reagan administration's foreign-policy decision-making process combined elements of a formal structure set forth in the various Senior Interdepartmental Groups and their subordinate elements with a competitive approach in which diverse groups set forth options for coordination at the highest level. Like Eisenhower, and in sharp contrast to Carter as well as Nixon, Reagan preferred to be relieved of the burden of decisions that could be taken at lower levels of government. The Reagan approach was based on what White House Counselor Edwin Meese described as a "participatory decision-making system for policy implementation with specific responsibility and accountability." In practice, this meant debate, and even division, at the levels below the president, with policy conflicts being brought to Reagan, as necessary, for final decision. The three most important SIGs—foreign policy, defense, and intelligence—remained under the control of the Department of State, the Department of Defense, and the Central Intelligence Agency, respectively. This gave rise to concern that the institutional interests and biases of the three bureaucratic structures most directly related would hamper the creation of an integrated policy perspective, to which the principal answer seemed to be the transfer of the leadership of such SIGs to the special assistant for national-security affairs.

## CONCLUSIONS ABOUT REAGAN'S CONDUCT OF FOREIGN POLICY

Like its predecessors, the Reagan administration confronted the need to define the limits of American foreign policy in a dynamic and rapidly changing global security environment and, above all, to relate its international commitments to existing and prospective capabilities in a fashion acceptable to the electorate. While devoting greater resources to defense, the Reagan administration sought to evolve a national consensus for the conduct of foreign policy.

Illustrative of this quest was the formulation by Secretary of Defense Caspar Weinberger, in late 1984, of a series of criteria for the future use of military power. In order to preclude the recurrence of the trauma of Vietnam, the United States, it was asserted, should be guided by six criteria in any decision to commit forces to combat areas: (1) the engagement should be clearly in the national interest; (2) the commitment should be wholehearted, with the clear intention of achieving victory; (3) political and military objectives should be precisely identified, with an appropriate strategy for using committed forces to attain them; (4) there must be a continuing reassessment of the relationship between means and ends after forces have been sent into action; (5) there must be a strong likelihood of support from both the American people and Congress; and (6) the utilization of U.S. military power in combat should be only a last resort.

Left unresolved in Weinberger's formulation was the precise identification of "the national interest," about which substantial differences remained between the Reagan administration and its Democratic opponents, as evidenced in the presidential campaign of 1984, in which sharp disagreement was expressed over the potential use of force of Central America and the Persian Gulf. If no bipartisan agreement existed on the possible application of military power in support of U.S. interests in these regions, it seemed unlikely that the necesary consensus could easily be forged for the use of force elsewhere. Thus, for better or worse, the legacy of Vietnam with respect to the employment of military power remained a compelling element in American foreign policy. If the commitment of the U.S. Marines to Lebanon had fallen short of the criteria established by Weinberger, the Grenada rescue mission had proven successful in both political and military terms and, as a result, had received widespread popular support in the United States. The limited intervention in Lebanon, with U.S. forces withdrawn after terrorist attacks and the crumbling of the domestic political situation in Beirut, illustrated the problems facing the Reagan administration in reconciling means with ends within a framework acceptable to the complex forces of domestic public opinion. The threats that the United States faced in the late twentieth century encompassed a variety of forms of low-intensity violence, including terrorism, for which the remedy was not easily discernible. In the absence of an ability to identify the exact target for retaliation and to take appropriate action, traditional principles of deterrence could not be applied. Here the Reagan administration, faced with attacks on American embassies and other installations abroad, could more easily devise security precautions for such facilities, itself a formidable task, than it could locate and retaliate against those who committed such acts.

The Reagan administration reflected, and to some extent shaped, a foreign-policy consensus that had as its principal characteristics apprehension about the military capabilities of the Soviet Union and a distrust of Soviet motivates, together with a belief that a dialogue with Moscow on security issues was nevertheless an essential ingredient of the superpower relationship. For all the polarized discussion about the state of U.S.–Soviet relations, the fact remained that, in its first term, the Reagan administration confronted no international crisis with the Soviet Union comparable to those faced by nearly all its predecessors. Instead, the U.S.–Soviet confrontation was waged largely at the rhetorical level. As the likelihood of an electoral victory for the Reagan administration grew in the autumn of 1984, the interest of the Soviet Union in the "constructive dialogue" offered by the United States early in 1984 quickened, thus setting the stage for the foreign-policy agenda that would preoccupy the administration in its second term in office.

# Selected Bibliography

Each year the government printing office publishes numerous volumes of official documentation on U.S. foreign policy. These include *The Public Papers of the Presidents of the United States; The Foreign Relations of the United States* (for the Department of State); *Documents on Disarmament* (for the Arms Control and Disarmament Agency); and hearings and reports of several committees and subcommittees of Congress, particularly the Senate Foreign Relations Committee; the House Committee on Foreign Affairs; the appropriations committees and armed services committees of both Houses; and other committees or subcommittees responsible for intelligence, foreign trade and economic policies, government operations, and related areas.

## U.S. DIPLOMATIC HISTORY AND FOREIGN POLICY: GENERAL

Bailey, Thomas A. *A Diplomatic History of the American People*, 10th ed., Englewood Cliffs, N.J.: Prentice-Hall, 1980.

Bemis, Samuel Flagg. *A Diplomatic History of the United States*, 5th ed., New York: Holt, Rinehart and Winston, 1965.

Blake, Nelson M., and Oscar T. Barck, Jr. *The United States in Its World Relations*. New York: McGraw-Hill, 1960.

Crabb, Cecil V., Jr. *The Doctrines of American Foreign Policy*. Baton Rouge, La.: Louisiana State University Press, 1982.

DeConde, Alexander. *A History of American Foreign Policy*, 2 vols., 3rd ed. New York: Scribner, 1978.

Ferrell, Robert H. *American Diplomacy: A History,* revised and expanded edition. New York: Norton, 1969.

Paterson, Thomas G., Clifford, J. Garry, and Kenneth J. Hogan. *American Foreign Policy: A History*. Lexington, Mass.: D. C. Heath, 1977.

Perkins, Dexter. *The Evolution of American Foreign Policy*. New York: Oxford University Press, 1966.

## U.S. DIPLOMATIC HISTORY 1776–1933: SPECIALIZED

Beale, Howard K. *Theodore Roosevelt and the Rise of America to World Power*. Baltimore: John Hopkins University Press, 1956.

Bemis, Samuel Flagg. *The Diplomacy of the American Revolution*. New York: Prentice-Hall 1935.

———. *John Quincy Adams and the Foundation of American Foreign Policy*. New York: Norton, 1973.

Burton, David H. *Theodore Roosevelt: Confident Imperialist*. Philadelphia: University of Pennsylvania Press, 1968.

Campbell, Charles S. *The Transformation of American Foreign Relations, 1865–1900*. New York: Harper & Row, 1976.

Combs, Jerald. *American Diplomatic History: Two Centuries of Changing Interpretations*. Berkeley, Calif.: University of California Press, 1983.

Dingman, Roger. *Power in the Pacific: The Origins of Naval Arms Limitation, 1914–1922*. Chicago: University of Chicago Press, 1976.

Dulles, Foster Rhea. *America's Rise to World Power, 1898–1954*. New York: Harper & Row, 1963.

Ellis, L. Ethan. *Frank B. Kellogg and American Foreign Relations 1925–1929*. New Brunswick, N.J.: Rutgers University Press, 1961.

———. *The General Pact for the Renunciation of War*. Washington, D.C.: U.S. Government Printing Office, 1928.

Ferrell, Robert H. *Peace in their Time*. New Haven, Conn.: Yale University Press, 1952.

Freidel, Frank. *The Splendid Little War*. Boston: Little, Brown, 1958.

Graebner, Norman A. *An Uncertain Tradition: American Secretaries of State in the Twentieth Century*. New York: McGraw-Hill, 1961.

Gregory, Ross. *The Origins of American Intervention in the First World War*. New York: Norton, 1971.

Kennan, George F. *American Foreign Policy, 1900–1950*. Chicago: University of Chicago Press, 1951.

La Feber, Walter. *The New Empire: An Interpretation of American Expansion, 1860–1898*. Ithaca, N.Y.: Cornell University Press, 1963.

Levin, N. Gordon, Jr. *Woodrow Wilson and World Politics*. New York: Oxford University Press, 1968.

Link, Arthur S. *Wilson: Confusions and Crises, 1915–1916*. Princeton, N.J.: Princeton University Press, 1964.

May, Ernest R. *The World War and American Isolation, 1914–1917*. Chicago: Quadrangle, 1959.

———. *American Imperialism: A Speculative Essay*. New York: Atheneum, 1968.

Minger, Ralph E. *William Howard Taft and United States Foreign Policy*. Urbana, Ill.: University of Illinois Press, 1975.

Morgenthau, Hans J. *In Defense of the National Interest*. New York: Knopf, 1951.

Munro, Dana G. *Intervention and Dollar Diplomacy in the Caribbean*. Princeton, N.J.: Princeton University Press, 1964.

Nevins, Allen. *The United States in a Chaotic World: 1918–1933.* New Haven, Conn.: Yale University Press, 1950.

Osgood, Robert E. *Ideals and Self-Interest in America's Foreign Relations.* Chicago: University of Chicago Press, 1953.

Owsley, Frank L. *King Cotton Diplomacy.* (1931) rev. ed. by Harriet C. Owsley. Chicago: University of Chicago Press, 1951.

Perkins, Dexter. *The Monroe Doctrine, 1823–1826.* Cambridge, Mass.: Harvard University Press, 1927.

Smith, Daniel M. *The Great Departure: The United States and World War I, 1914–1920.* New York: Wiley, 1965.

Varg, Paul. *Foreign Policies of the Founding Fathers.* East Lansing, Mich.: Michigan State University Press, 1963.

## THE ROOSEVELT ADMINISTRATION

Beard, Charles. *President Roosevelt and the Coming of the War.* New Haven, Conn.: Yale University Press, 1948.

Bullitt, Orville H., Ed. *For the President—Personal and Secret: Correspondence Between Franklin Roosevelt and William C. Bullitt.* Boston: Houghton Mifflin, 1972.

Burns, James M. *Roosevelt: The Lion and the Fox.* New York: Harcourt Brace Jovanovich, 1956.

_____ . *Roosevelt: The Soldier of Freedom.* New York: Harcourt Brace Jovanovich, 1970.

Cole, Wayne S. *Roosevelt and the Isolationists, 1932–1945.* New York: Columbia University Press, 1980.

Corwin, Edward S. *The President: Office and Powers.* Princeton, N.J.: Princeton University Press, 1948.

Freidel, Frank. *Franklin D, Roosevelt,* 4 vols. Boston: Little, Brown, 1952–1973.

Grew, Joseph C. *Ten Years in Japan.* New York: Simon & Schuster, 1944.

Hull, Cordell. *Memoirs,* 2 vols. New York: Macmillan, 1948.

Kimball, Warren F. *Franklin D. Roosevelt and the World Crisis, 1937–1945.* Lexington, Mass.: D. C. Heath, 1973.

Langer, William L., and S. Everett Gleeson. *The Challenge to Isolation: The World Crisis of 1937–1940 and American Foreign Policy.* New York: Harper & Row, 1952.

Lash, Joseph P. *Roosevelt and Churchill, 1939–1941: The Partnership That Saved the West.* New York: Norton, 1976.

Offner, Arnold A. *American Appeasement: United States Foreign Policy and Germany, 1933–1938.* New York: Norton, 1976.

Wiltz, John E. *From Isolation to War, 1931–1941.* New York: Harper & Row, 1968.

## WORLD WAR II AND ITS DIPLOMACY

Baker, Leonard. *Roosevelt and Pearl Harbor.* New York: Macmillan, 1970.

Beitzell, Robert. *The Uneasy Alliance: America, Russia, and Britain, 1941–1943.* New York: Knopf, 1972.

Churchill, Winston. *The Second World War.* 6 vols. Boston: Houghton Mifflin, 1948–1953.

Dallek, Robert. *Roosevelt Diplomacy and World War II.* New York: R. E. Krieger, 1970.

Divine, Robert A. *Roosevelt and World War II.* Baltimore, Md.: Johns Hopkins University Press, 1969.

Feis, Herbert. *The China Tangle*. Princeton, N.J.: Princeton University Press, 1953.

_____ . *Churchill, Roosevelt, Stalin: The War They Waged and the Peace They Sought*. Princeton, N.J.: Princeton University Press, 1957.

_____ . *The Road to Pearl Harbor: Warning and Decision*. Stanford, Calif.: Stanford University Press, 1962.

Leahy, William D. *I Was There*. New York: McGraw-Hill, 1950.

Lohbeck, Don. *Patrick J. Hurley*. Chicago: Regnery, 1956.

Murphy, Robert. *Diplomat among Warriors*. Garden City, N.Y.: Doubleday, 1964.

Neu, Charles E. *The Troubled Encounter: The United States and Japan*. New York: Wiley, 1975.

Prange, Gordon W. *At Dawn We Slept: The Untold Story of Pearl Harbor*. New York: Penguin Books, 1982.

Sherwood, Robert E. *Roosevelt and Hopkins: An Intimate History*. New York: Harper & Row, 1948.

Snell, John L. *Illusion and Necessity: The Diplomacy of Global War, 1939–1945*. Boston: Houghton Mifflin, 1963.

Tuchman, Barbara. *Stilwell and the American Experience in China*. New York: Macmillan, 1970.

## THE TRUMAN ADMINISTRATION

Acheson, Dean. *Present at the Creation: My Years at the State Department*. New York: Norton, 1969.

Bernstein, Barton J., Ed. *Politics and Policies of the Truman Administration*. Chicago: Quadrangle, 1970.

Byrnes, James F. *Speaking Frankly*. New York: Harper & Row, 1947.

Donovan, Robert J. *Conflict and Crisis: The Presidency of Harry S. Truman, 1945–1948*. New York: Norton, 1977.

_____ . *The Tumultuous Years, 1949–1953*. New York: Norton, 1977.

_____ . *Nemesis: Truman and Johnson in the Coils of War in Asia*. New York: Norton, 1979.

Druks, Herbert. *Harry S. Truman and the Russians, 1945–1953*. New York: Speller, 1966.

Goldman, Eric F. *The Crucial Decade—and after: America, 1945–1960*. New York: Knopf, 1960.

Heller, Francis H., Ed. *The Truman White House: The Administration of the Presidency, 1945–1953*. Lawrence, Kan.: University Press of Kansas, 1980.

Millis, Walter, Ed. *The Forrestal Diaries*. New York: Viking, 1951.

Moseley, Leonard. *Marshall: Hero for Our Times*. New York: Hearst Books, 1982.

Pogue, Forrest C. *George C. Marshall: Organizer of Victory, 1943–1945*. New York: Viking, 1973.

Truman, Harry S. *Memoirs*, 2 vols. Garden City, N.Y.: Doubleday, 1955–1956.

## THE KOREAN WAR

Clark, Mark W. *From the Danube to the Yalu*. New York: Harper & Row, 1954.

Collins, J. Lawton. *War in Peacetime: The History and Lessons of Korea*. Boston: Houghton Mifflin, 1969.

Goodrich, Leland M. *Korea: A Study of U.S. Policy in the United Nations*. New York: Council on Foreign Relations, 1956.

*Hearings on the Military Situation in the Far East.* Senate Armed Services Committee, 82nd Congress, 1st Session, 1951. Washington, D.C.: U.S. Government Printing Office, 1951.

Joy, Turner C. *How Communists Negotiate*. New York: Macmillan, 1955.

Leckie, Robert. *Conflict: The History of the Korean War*. New York: Putnam, 1962.

Marshall, S. L. A. *The River and the Gauntlet: Defeat of the Eighth Army by the Chinese Communist Forces*. New York: Morrow, 1956.

Osgood, Robert E. *Limited War: The Challenge to American Strategy.* Chicago: University of Chicago Press, 1957.

Paige, Glenn D. *The Korean Decision*. New York: Free Press, 1968.

Rees, David. *Korea: The Limited War*. Baltimore: Penguin Books, 1964.

Rovere, Richard H., and Arthur M. Schlesinger, Jr. *The General and the President*. New York: Farrar, Straus & Giroux, 1951.

Spanier, John. *The Truman-MacArthur Controversy and the Korean War*. New York: Norton, 1965.

## THE EISENHOWER ADMINISTRATION

Adams, Sherman. *Firsthand Report: The Story of the Eisenhower Administration.* New York: Harper & Row, 1961.

Alexander, Charles C. *Holding the Line: The Eisenhower Era, 1952-1961*. Bloomington, Ind.: Indiana University Press, 1975.

Ambrose, Stephen E. *Eisenhower, Vol. II: The President*. New York: Simon & Schuster, 1984.

Beal, John R. *John Foster Dulles*. New York: Harper & Row, 1956.

Branyan, Robert L., and Lawrence H. Larsen, Eds. *The Eisenhower Administration, 1953-1961: A Documentary History*, 2 vols. Westport, Conn.: Greenwood Press, 1971.

Divine, Robert A. *Eisenhower and the Cold War*. New York: Oxford University Press, 1981.

Eisenhower, Dwight David. *Mandate for Change*. Garden City, N.Y.: Doubleday, 1963.
_____ . *Waging Peace*. Garden City, N.Y.: Doubleday, 1965.

Eisenhower, Milton S. *The President Is Calling*. Garden City, N.Y.: Doubleday, 1967.

Greenstein, Fred I. *The Hidden Hand Presidency: Eisenhower as Leader*. New York: Basic Books, 1982.

Guhin, M. A. *John Foster Dulles: A Statesman and His Times*. New York: Columbia University Press, 1972.

Hoopes, Townsend. *The Devil and John Foster Dulles*. Boston: Little, Brown, 1973.

Hughes, Emmet John. *The Ordeal of Power: A Political Memoir of the Eisenhower Years*. New York: Atheneum, 1963.

Killian, James R., Jr. *Sputnik, Scientists, and Eisenhower: A Memoir of the First Special Assistant to the President for Science and Technology.* Cambridge, Mass.: MIT Press, 1977.

Kistiakowsky, George B. *A Scientist at the White House: The Private Diary of President Eisenhower's Special Assistant for Science and Technology*. Cambridge, Mass.: Harvard University Press, 1967.

Neff, Donald. *Warriors at Suez: Eisenhower Takes America into the Middle East*. New York: Linden Press/Simon & Schuster, 1981.

Rostow, W. W. *Europe after Stalin: Eisenhower's Three Decisions of March 11, 1953.* Austin, Texas: University of Texas Press, 1982.

_____. *Open Skies: Eisenhower's Proposal of July 22, 1953.* Austin, Texas: University of Texas Press, 1983.


## THE KENNEDY AND JOHNSON ADMINISTRATIONS

Ball, George W. *Diplomacy for a Crowded World.* Boston: Little, Brown, 1976.

Evans, Roland, and Robert Novak. *Lyndon B. Johnson: The Exercise of Power.* London: George Allen & Unwin, 1967.

Fairlie, Henry. *The Kennedy Promise: The Politics of Expectation.* Garden City, N.Y.: Doubleday, 1973.

Galbraith, John K. *Ambassador's Journal: A Personal Account of the Kennedy Years.* Boston: Houghton Mifflin, 1969.

Geyelin, Philip V. *Lyndon B. Johnson and the World.* New York: Praeger, 1966.

Goldman, Eric F. *The Tragedy of Lyndon Johnson.* New York: Knopf, 1969.

Hilsman, Roger. *To Move a Nation.* Garden City, N.Y.: Doubleday, 1967.

Johnson, Lyndon Baines. *The Vantage Point: Perspectives of the Presidency, 1963-1969.* New York: Holt, Rinehart and Winston, 1971.

Kalb, Madeleine G. *The Congo Cables: The Cold War in Africa—From Eisenhower to Kennedy.* New York: Macmillan, 1982.

Kearns, Doris. *Lyndon Johnson and the American Dream.* New York: Harper & Row, 1976.

Kern, Montague, Levering, Patricia W., and Ralph B. Levering. *The Kennedy Crisis: The Press, the Presidency, and Foreign Policy.* Chapel Hill, N.C.: University of North Carolina Press, 1983.

Miller, Merle. *Lyndon: An Oral History.* New York: Putnam, 1980.

Parmet, Herbert S. *JFK: The Presidency of John F. Kennedy.* New York: Dial Press, 1983.

Rostow, Walt Whitman. *Diffusion of Power.* New York: Macmillan, 1972.

Rusk, Dean. *Winds of Freedom.* Boston: Beacon Press, 1963.

Schlesinger, Arthur M., Jr. *A Thousand Days: John F. Kennedy in the White House.* Boston: Houghton Mifflin, 1965.

_____. *Robert Kennedy and His Times.* Boston: Houghton Mifflin, 1978.

Sidey, Hugh. *John F. Kennedy, President.* New York: Fawcett, 1963.

_____. *A Very Personal Presidency: Lyndon Johnson in the White House.* New York: Atheneum, 1968.

Sorensen, Theodore C. *Kennedy.* New York: Harper & Row, 1965.


## THE NIXON/FORD ADMINISTRATIONS

Ehrlichman, John. *Witness to Power: The Nixon Years.* New York: Simon & Schuster, 1982.

Evans, Rowland, and Robert Novak. *Nixon in the White House: The Frustration of Power.* New York: Random House, 1971.

Ford, Gerald R. *A Time to Heal.* New York: Harper & Row, 1979.

Hersh, Seymour M. *The Price of Power.* New York: Summit Books, 1983.

Joiner, Harry. *American Foreign Policy: The Kissinger Era.*

Kalb, Marvin, and Bernard Kalb. *Kissinger.* Boston: Little, Brown, 1979.

Kissinger, Henry A. *White House Years.* Boston: Little, Brown, 1979.

_____. *Years of Upheaval.* Boston: Little, Brown, 1982.

Liska, George. *Beyond Kissinger: Ways of Conservative Statecraft.* Baltimore: Johns Hopkins University Press, 1975.

Morris, Roger. *Uncertain Greatness: Henry Kissinger and American Foreign Policy.* New York: Harper & Row, 1977.

Nixon, Richard M. *Six Crises.* Garden City, N.Y.: Doubleday, 1962.

_____ . *RN: The Memoirs of Richard Nixon.* New York: Grosset & Dunlap, 1978.

Osgood, Robert E., Tucker, Robert W., Rourke, Francis E., Dinerstein, Herbert S., Martin, Laurence W., Calleo, David P., Rowland, Benjamin M., and George Liska. *Retreat from Empire? The First Nixon Administration.* Baltimore: Johns Hopkins University Press, 1973.

Safire, William. *Before the Fall: An Inside View of the Pre-Watergate White House.* Garden City, N.Y.: Doubleday, 1975.

Szulc, Ted. *The Illusion of Peace: Foreign Policy in the Nixon-Kissinger Years.* New York: Viking Press, 1978.

Wills, Gary. *Nixon Agonistes.* Boston: Houghton Mifflin, 1970.

## THE CARTER ADMINISTRATION

Brzezinski, Zbigniew K. *Power and Principle: Memoirs of the National Security Adviser, 1977–1981.* New York: Farrar, Straus & Giroux, 1983.

Carter, Jimmy. *Keeping Faith: Memoirs of a President.* New York: Bantam Books, 1982.

Johansen, Robert. *The National Interests and the Human Interest: An Analysis of U.S. Foreign Policy.* Princeton, N.J.: Princeton University Press, 1980.

Jordan, Hamilton. *Crisis: The Last Year of the Carter Presidency.* New York: Putnam, 1982.

Kissinger, Henry. *For the Record: Selected Statements, 1977–1980.* Boston: Little, Brown, 1981.

Mollenhoff, Clark R. *The President Who Failed: Carter Out of Control.* New York: Macmillan, 1980.

Sarkesian, Sam, Ed. *Defense Policy and the Presidency: Carter's First Years.* Boulder, Colo.: Westview Press, 1979.

Shogan, Robert. *Promises to Keep: Carter's First Hundred Days.* New York: Harper & Row, 1977.

Shoup, Laurence H. *The Carter Presidency and Beyond.* Palo Alto, Calif.: Ramparts Press, 1980.

Vance, Cyrus. *Hard Choices: Critical Years in America's Foreign Policy.* New York: Simon & Schuster, 1983.

## THE REAGAN ADMINISTRATION

*America and the World, 1981, 1982, 1983, 1984.* Special annual volumes of *Foreign Affairs,* the first three edited by William P. Bundy, the fourth by William G. Hyland. New York: Council on Foreign Relations, 1982, 1983, 1984, 1985.

Bark, Dennis L., Ed. *To Promote Peace: U.S. Foreign Policy in the Mid-1980s.* Stanford, Calif.: Hoover Institution Press, 1984.

Cannon, Lou. *Reagan.* New York: Putnam, 1982.

Greenstein, Fred I., Ed. *The Reagan Presidency: An Early Assessment.* Baltimore: Johns Hopkins University Press, 1983.

Haig, Alexander M., Jr. *Caveat: Realism, Reagan and Foreign Policy.* New York: Macmillan, 1982.

Kirkpatrick, Jeanne J. *The Reagan Phenomenon and Other Speeches on Foreign Policy.* Washington, D.C.: American Enterprise Institute, 1983.

Oye, Kenneth A., Lieber, Robert J., and Donald Rothchild. *Eagle Defiant: United States Foreign Policy in the 1980s.* Boston: Little, Brown, 1983.


## U.S.-SOVIET RELATIONS

Bell, Coral. *The Diplomacy of Detente: The Kissinger Era.* New York: St. Martin's Press, 1977.

Bohlen, Charles E. *Witness to History, 1929–1969.* New York: Norton, 1973.

Browder, Robert P. *The Origins of Soviet-American Diplomacy.* Princeton, N.J.: Princeton University Press, 1953.

Clay, Lucius. *Decision in Germany.* Garden City, N.J.: Doubleday, 1950.

Davison, W. Phillips. *The Berlin Blockade.* Princeton, N.J.: Princeton University Press, 1958.

Dulles, Eleanor W., and Robert Crane. *Detente: Cold War Strategies in Transition.* New York: Praeger, 1965.

Duncan, W. Raymond, Ed. *Soviet Policy in the Third World.* New York: Pergamon Press, 1980.

Feis, Herbert. *From Trust to Terror: The Onset of the Cold War, 1945–1950.* New York: Norton, 1970.

Fleming, D. F. *The Cold War and Its Origins, 1917–1960,* 2 vols. Garden City, N.Y.: Doubleday, 1961.

Fontaine, Andre. *History of the Cold War.* New York: Pantheon Books, 1970.

Gaddis, John Lewis. *Strategies of Containment: A Critical Appraisal of Postwar American National Security Policy.* New York: Oxford University Press, 1982.

George, Alexander L. *Managing U.S.-Soviet Rivalry: Problems of Crisis Prevention.* Boulder, Colo.: Westview Press, 1982.

Graebner, Norman A. *Cold War Diplomacy.* Princeton, N.J.: Princeton University Press, 1962.

Griffith, William E. *Cold War and Coexistence: Russia, China, and the United States.* Englewood Cliffs, N.J.: Prentice-Hall, 1971.

Halle, Louis B. *The Cold War as History.* New York: Harper & Row, 1967.

Kaplan, Stephen S. *Diplomacy of Power: Soviet Armed Forces as a Political Instrument.* Washington, D.C.: Brookings Institution, 1981.

Kuniholm, Bruce R. *The Origins of the Cold War in the Near East: Great Power Conflict and Diplomacy in Iran, Turkey and Greece.* Princeton, N.J.: Princeton University Press, 1980.

Maddox, Robert James. *The New Left and the Origin of the Cold War.* Princeton, N.J.: Princeton University Press, 1973.

Payne, Keith. *Nuclear Deterrence in U.S.-Soviet Relations.* Boulder, Colo.: Westview Press, 1982.

Pipes, Richard. *U.S. Soviet Relations in the Era of Detente: A Tragedy of Errors.* Boulder, Colo.: Westview Press, 1981.

_____. *Survival Is Not Enough: Soviet Realities and America's Future.* New York: Simon & Schuster, 1984.

Sobel, Lester A., Ed. *Kissinger and Detente.* New York: Facts on File, 1977.

Ulam, Adam B. *The Rivals: America and Russia since World War II.* New York: Viking Press, 1971.

———. *Dangerous Relations: The Soviet Union in World Politics, 1970-1982.* New York: Oxford University Press, 1983.

Yergin, Daniel. *Shattered Peace: The Origins of the Cold War and the National Security State.* Boston: Houghton Mifflin, 1978.


## STRATEGY, DEFENSE, AND ARMS CONTROL

Allison, Graham, T., Carnesale, Albert, and Joseph S. Nye, Jr., Eds. *Hawks, Doves and Owls: An Agenda for Avoiding Nuclear War.* New York: Norton, 1985.

*Arms Control and Disarmament Agreements: Texts and Histories of Negotiations.* Published for the Arms Control and Disarmament Agency. Washington, D.C.: U.S. Government Printing Office, 1982.

Aron, Raymond. *The Great Debate: Theories of Nuclear Strategy.* Trans. by Ernst Pawel. Garden City, N.Y.: Doubleday, 1965.

Blechman, Barry, M., and Stephen S. Kaplan, Eds. *Force without War: U.S. Armed Forces as a Political Instrument.* Washington, D.C.: Brookings Institution, 1978.

Brennan, Donald G., Ed. *Arms Control, Disarmament and National Security.* New York: Braziller, 1961.

Brodie, Bernard. *Strategy in the Missile Age.* Princeton, N.J.: Princeton University Press, 1959.

———. *War and Politics.* New York: Macmillan, 1973.

Brown, Harold. *Thinking about National Security: Defense and Foreign Policy in a Dangerous World.* Boulder, Colo.: Westview Press, 1983.

Bull, Hedley. *The Control of the Arms Race,* 2nd ed. New York: Praeger, 1965.

Burt, Richard, Ed. *A Strategic Symposium: SALT and U.S. Defense Policy.* New Brunswick, N.J.: Transaction Books, 1979.

Carnesale, Albert, Doty, Paul, Hoffmann, Stanley, Huntington, Samuel, Nye, Joseph, and Scott D. Sagan. *Living with Nuclear Weapons.* New York: Bantam Books, 1983.

Dougherty, James E. *How To Think about Arms Control and Disarmament.* New York: Crane, Russak, 1973.

Enthoven, Alain C., and K. Wayne Smith. *How Much Is Enough? Shaping the Defense Program, 1961-1969.* New York: Harper & Row, 1961.

George, Alexander, and Richard Smoke. *Deterrence and American Foreign Policy: Theory and Practice.* New York: Columbia University Press, 1974.

Hitch, Charles J., and Roland McKean. *The Economics of Defense in the Nuclear Age.* New York: Atheneum, 1965.

Huntington, Samuel. *The Common Defense: Strategic Programs in National Politics.* New York: Columbia University Press, 1961.

Jastrow, Robert J. *How To Make Nuclear Weapons Obsolete.* Boston: Little, Brown, 1985.

Kahan, Jerome H. *Security in the Nuclear Age: Developing U.S. Strategic Arms Policy.* Washington, D.C.: Brookings Institution, 1975.

Kahn, Herman. *On Thermonuclear War.* Princeton, N.J.: Princeton University Press, 1960.

———. *Thinking about the Unthinkable in the 1980s.* New York: Simon and Schuster, 1984.

Kaufmann, William, Ed. *Military Strategy and National Security.* Princeton, N.J.: Princeton University Press, 1956.

Kissinger, Henry A. *Nuclear Weapons and Foreign Policy*. New York: Harper & Row, 1957.

McNamara, Robert S. *The Essence of Security*. New York: Harper & Row, 1968.

Newhouse, John. *Cold Dawn: The Story of SALT*. New York: Holt, Rinehart and Winston, 1973.

Pfaltzgraff, Robert L., Jr., Ed. *Contrasting Approaches to Arms Control*. Lexington, Mass.: D. C. Heath, 1974.

Pierre, Andrew J. *Arms Transfers and American Foreign Policy*. New York: Council on Foreign Relations, 1980.

Smith, Gerard. *Doubletalk*. Garden City, N.Y.: Doubleday, 1980.

Talbott, Strobe. *Endgame*. New York: Harper & Row, 1979.

_____ . *Deadly Gambits*. New York: Knopf, 1984.

Tucker, Robert. *The Purposes of American Power: An Essay on National Security*. New York: Praeger, 1981.

## WESTERN EUROPE, NATO, AND THE EEC

Anderson, Terry H. *The United States, Great Britain, and the Cold War*. Columbia, Mo.: University of Missouri Press, 1981.

Baylis, John. *Anglo-American Defense Relations, 1939–1980*. New York: St. Martin's Press, 1981.

Buchan, Alastair. *NATO in the 1960s*. New York: Praeger, 1960.

Camps, Miriam. *Britain the European Community, 1955–1963*. Princeton, N.J.: Princeton University Press, 1964.

Cottrell, Alvin J., and James E. Dougherty. *The Politics of the Atlantic Alliance*. New York: Praeger, 1964.

Diebold, William, Jr. *The Schuman Plan*. New York: Praeger, 1959.

Fedder, Edwin J. *Defense Politics of the Atlantic Alliance*. New York: Praeger, 1980.

Griffith, William E. *The Ostpolitik of the Federal Republic of Germany*. Cambridge, Mass.: MIT Press, 1978.

Grosser, Alfred. *The Western Alliance: European-American Relations since 1945*. New York: Continuum, 1980.

Haas, Ernst B. *The Uniting of Europe*. London: Stevens, 1958.

Hanreider, Wolfram F., and Graeme P. Auton. *Foreign Policy of West Germany, France and Britain*. Englewood Cliffs, N.J.: Prentice-Hall, 1979.

Hoffmann, Stanley. *Gulliver's Troubles, or the Setting of American Foreign Policy*. New York: McGraw-Hill, 1968.

Ireland, Timothy. *Creating the Entangling Alliance: The Origins of the North Atlantic Treaty Organization*. Westport, Conn.: Greenwood Press, 1981.

Kaplan, Lawrence S. *The United States and NATO: The Formative Years*. Lexington, Ky.: University Press of Kentucky, 1984.

Kissinger, Henry A. *The Troubled Partnership*. New York: McGraw-Hill, 1965.

Kolodziej, Edward A. *French International Policy under de Gaulle and Pompidou*. Ithaca, N.Y.: Cornell University Press, 1974.

Kraft, Joseph. *The Grand Design: From Common Market to Atlantic Partnership*. New York: Harper & Row, 1962.

Lundestad, Geir. *America, Scandinavia, and the Cold War 1945–1949*. New York: Columbia University Press, 1980.

Meyers, Kenneth A., Ed. *NATO: The Next Thirty Years*. Boulder, Colo.: Westview Press, 1980.

Nee, Charles L., Jr. *The Marshall Plan: The Launching of Pax Americana*. New York: Simon & Schuster, 1984.

Osgood, Robert E. *NATO: The Entangling Alliance*. Chicago: Chicago University Press, 1962.

Pfaltzgraff, Robert L., Jr. *The Atlantic Community: A Complex Imbalance*. New York: Van Nostrand Reinhold, 1969.

_____ . *Britain Faces Europe*. Philadelphia: University of Pennsylvania Press, 1969.

Richardson, James L. *Germany and the Atlantic Alliance*. Cambridge, Mass.: Harvard University Press, 1966.

Schlaim, Avi. *The United States and the Berlin Blockade, 1948–1949*. Berkeley, Calif.: University of California Press, 1983.

Watt, D. Cameron. *Succeeding John Bull: America in Britain's Place, 1900–1975*. New York: Cambridge University Press, 1984.

Wexler, Immanuel. *The Marshall Plan Revisited: The European Recovery Program in Economic Perspective*. Westport, Conn.: Greenwood Press, 1983.

## EASTERN EUROPE

Braun, Aurel. *Romanian Foreign Policy since 1965*. New York: Praeger, 1978.

Dawisha, Karen, and Phillip Hanson. *Soviet-East European Dilemmas*. New York: Holmes & Meier (for the Royal Institute of International Affairs), 1981.

Fischer-Galati, Stephen, Ed. *Eastern Europe in the 1980s*. Boulder, Colo.: Westview Press, 1981.

Forster, Thomas M. *The East German Army: Second in the Warsaw Pact*. Winchester, Mass.: Allen & Unwin, 1981.

Holloway, David, and Jane Sharp. *The Warsaw Pact: Alliance in Transition?* Ithaca, N.Y.: Cornell University Press, 1984.

Hutchings, Robert L. *Soviet-East European Relations: Consolidation and Conflict, 1968–1980*. Madison, Wis.: University of Wisconsin Press, 1984.

Jones, Christopher D. *Soviet Influence in Eastern Europe: Political Autonomy and the Warsaw Pact*. New York: Praeger, 1981.

Kalvoda, Josef. *Czechoslovakia's Role in Soviet Strategy*. Washington, D.C.: University Press of America, 1981.

Lukas, Richard C. *The Strange Allies: The United States and Poland, 1941–1945*. Knoxville, Tenn.: University of Tennessee Press, 1978.

_____ . *Bitter Legacy: Polish-American Relations in the Wake of World War II*. Lexington, Ky.: University Press of Kentucky, 1982.

Mandel, Ernest. *From Stalinism to Eurocommunism*. London: NLB, 1978.

Molnár, Miklós. *A Short History of the Hungarian Communist Party*. Boulder, Colo.: Westview Press, 1978.

Singer, Daniel. *The Road to Gdansk: Poland and the USSR*. New York: Monthly Review Press, 1981.

Sodaro, Michael J., and Sharon L. Wolchik, Eds. *Foreign and Domestic Policy in Eastern Europe in the 1980s*. New York: St. Martin's 1983.

Wandycz, Piotr. *The United States and Poland*. Cambridge, Mass.: Harvard University Press, 1980.

Weschler, Lawrence. *Solidarity: Poland in the Season of Its Passion*. New York: Fireside/Simon & Schuster, 1982.

Woodall, Jean., Ed. *Policy and Politics in Contemporary Poland: Reform, Failure, Crisis*. New York: St. Martin's Press, 1982.

## LATIN AMERICA

Alexander, Robert J. *The Tragedy of Chile*. Westport, Conn.: Greenwood Press, 1978.

Ball, M. Margaret. *The OAS in Transition*. New York: Knopf, 1978.

Blaiser, Cole. *The Hovering Giant: U.S. Responses to Revolutionary Change in Latin America*. Pittsburgh: University of Pittsburgh Press, 1976.

Bonsal, Philip W. *Cuba, Castro and the United States*. Pittsburgh: University of Pittsburgh Press, 1967.

Draper, Theodore. *Castro's Revolution*. New York: Praeger, 1962.

Dreier, John C., Ed. *The Alliance for Progress*. Baltimore: Johns Hopkins University Press, 1962.

Duncan, W. Raymond. *Latin America: A Developmental Approach*. New York: Praeger, 1976.

Gantenbein, James W. *The Evolution of Our Latin American Policy*. Englewood Cliffs, N.J.: Prentice-Hall, 1955.

Gleijeses, Piero. *The Dominican Crisis: The 1965 Constitutional Revolt and American Intervention*. Baltimore: Johns Hopkins University Press, 1979.

Hayes, Margaret Daly. *Latin America and the U.S. National Interest: A Basis for U.S. Foreign Policy*. Boulder, Colo.: Westview Press, 1984.

Levesque, Jacques. *The USSR and the Cuban Revolution*. New York: Praeger, 1981.

Martin, John Bartlow. *Overtaken by Events: The Dominican Crisis from the Fall of Trujillo to the Civil War*. Garden City, N.Y.: Doubleday, 1966.

Mecham, J. Lloyd. *The United States and Inter-American Security, 1889-1960*. Austin, Texas: University of Texas Press, 1961.

Nystrom, John Warren, and Nathan Havestock. *The Alliance for Progress*. Princeton, N.J.: Princeton University Press, 1966.

Payne, A. J. *The Politics of the Caribbean Community, 1961-1979*. New York: St. Martin's Press, 1980.

*Report of the President's National Bipartisan Commission on Central America*. Foreword by Henry Kissinger. New York: Macmillan, 1984.

Wesson, Robert. *The United States and Brazil: Limits of Influence*. New York: Praeger, 1981.

Wyden, Peter. *Bay of Pigs: Untold Story*. New York: Simon & Schuster, 1979.

(For the Cuban missile crisis, see the section on Foreign Policy Decision Making.)


## THE MIDDLE EAST

Abdulghani, Jasim. *Iraq and Iran: The Years of Crisis*. Baltimore, Md.: Johns Hopkins University Press, 1984.

Amirsadeghi, Hossein. *The Security of the Persian Gulf*. New York: St. Martin's Press, 1981.

Badeau, John S. *The American Approach to the Arab World*. New York: Harper & Row, 1968.

Badri, H., Magdoub, T., and M. D. Zohdy. *The Ramadan War, 1973*. Dunn Loring, Va.: Dupuy Press, 1978.

Bidwell, Robin. *The Two Yemens*. Boulder, Colo.: Westview Press, 1983.

Bradley, C. Paul. *The Camp David Peace Process: A Study of Carter Administration Policies, 1977-1980*. Grantham, N.H.: Tompson & Rutter, 1981.

Campbell, John C. *Defense of the Middle East*. New York: Praeger, 1960.

Cooley, John K. *Libyan Sandstorm: The Complete Account of Qaddafi's Revolution*. New York: Holt, Reinhart and Winston, 1982.

Elazar, Daniel J. *The Camp David Framework for Peace: A Shift Toward Shared Rule.* Washington, D.C.: American Enterprise Institute, 1979.

Finer, Herman. *Dulles over Suez.* Chicago: Quadrangle, 1964.

Fischer, Michael M. J. *Iran: From Religious Dispute to Revolution.* Cambridge, Mass.: Harvard University Press, 1980.

Forbis, William H. *Fall of the Peacock Throne.* New York: Harper & Row, 1980.

Freedman, Robert O., Ed. *World Politics and the Arab-Israeli Conflict.* Elmsford, N.Y.: Pergamon Press, 1979.

Heikal, Mohamed. *The Sphinx and the Commissar: The Rise and Fall of Soviet Influence in the Arab World.* New York: Harper & Row, 1979.

Jansen, Godfrey. *Militant Islam.* New York: Harper & Row, 1980.

Khourie, Fred J. *The Arab-Israeli Dilemma,* 2nd ed. Syracuse, N.Y.: Syracuse University Press, 1976.

Kuniholm, Bruce R. *The Origins of the Cold War in the Near East: The Great Power Conflict and Diplomacy in Iran, Turkey, and Greece.* Princeton, N.J.: Princeton University Press, 1981.

Laqueur, Walter Z. *The Struggle for the Middle East: The Soviet Union in the Mediterranean, 1958-1968.* New York: Macmillan, 1969.

Ledeen, Michael, and William Lewis. *Debacle: The American Failure in Iran.* New York: Knopf, 1981.

Lenczowski, George. *The Middle East in World Affairs,* 4th ed. Ithaca, N.Y.: Cornell University Press, 1980.

Mortimer, Edward. *Faith and Power: The Politics of Islam.* New York: Random House, 1982.

Novik, Nimrod, and Joyce Starr, Eds. *Challenges in the Middle East: Regional Dynamics and Western Security.* New York: Praeger, 1981.

Polk, William. *The Arab World.* Cambridge, Mass.: Harvard University Press, 1980.

Pollock, David. *The Politics of Pressure: American Arms and Israeli Policy since the Six-Day War.* Westport, Conn.: Greenwood Press, 1982.

Quabin, Fahim I. *Crisis in Lebanon.* Washington, D.C.: Middle East Institute, 1961.

Quandt, William B. *Decade of Decisions: American Policy Toward the Arab-Israeli Conflict, 1967-1976.* Berkeley, Calif.: University of California Press, 1977.

Ramazani, R. K. *The Persian Gulf and the Strait of Hormuz.* Alphen aan den Rijn, The Netherlands: Sijthoff, 1979.

_____. *The United States and Iran: The Patterns of Influence.* New York: Praeger, 1982.

Reich, Berhard. *The United States and Israel: Influence in the Special Relationship.* New York: Praeger, 1984.

Rubin, Barry. *Paved with Good Intentions: The American Experience and Iran.* New York: Oxford University Press, 1980.

Rustow, Dankwert A. *Oil and Turmoil: America Faces OPEC and the Middle East.* New York: Norton, 1982.

Safran, Nadav. *The United States and Israel.* Cambridge, Mass.: Harvard University Press, 1973.

Shaked, Haim, and Itamar Rabinovich, Eds. *The Middle East and the United States.* New Brunswick, N.J.: Transaction Books, 1980.

Vernon, Raymond. *The Oil Crisis.* New York: Norton, 1976.

## ASIA-PACIFIC

Barnds, William J., Ed. *China and America: The Search for a New Relationship.* New York: New York University Press, 1977.

_____ . *Japan and the United States.* New York: New York University Press, 1979.

Booker, Malcolm. *Last Quarter: The Next Twenty-Five Years in Asia and the Pacific.* Melbourne, Australia: Melbourne University Press, 1978.

Bradsher, Henry S. *Afghanistan and the Soviet Union.* Durham, N.C.: Duke University Press, 1983.

Broinowski, Alison, Ed. *Understanding ASEAN.* New York: St. Martin's Press, 1982.

Brown, W. Norman. *The United States and India and Pakistan.* Cambridge, Mass.: Harvard University Press, 1953.

Buss, Claude A. *The United States and the Republic of Korea: Background for Policy.* Stanford, Calif.: Hoover, 1982.

Crouch, Harold. *The Army and Politics in Indonesia.* Ithaca, N.Y.: Cornell University Press, 1978.

Dorrance, John C. *Oceania and the United States.* Washington, D.C.: National Defense University, 1980.

Fairbank, John K. *The United States and China,* rev. ed. New York: Viking Press, 1981.

Fifield, Russell H. *Southeast Asia in United States Policy.* New York: Praeger, 1963.

Gregor, James A., and Maria H. Chang. *The Iron Triangle: A U.S. Security Policy for Northeast Asia.* Stanford, Calif.: Hoover, 1984.

_____ . *Crisis in the Philippines: A Threat to U.S. Interests.* Washington, D.C.: Ethics and Public Policy Center, 1984.

Jacobsen, C. G. *Sino-Soviet Relations since Mao: The Chairman's Legacy.* New York: Praeger, 1981.

Kim, Samuel S. *China, the United Nations, and World Order.* Princeton, N.J.: Princeton University Press, 1979.

_____ . *China and the World: Chinese Foreign Policy in the Post-Mao Era.* Boulder, Colo.: Westview Press, 1984.

Lall, Arthur. *The Emergence of Modern India.* New York: Columbia University Press, 1981.

Manchester, William. *American Caesar: Douglas MacArthur, 1880–1964.* Boston: Little, Brown, 1978.

Marwah, Onkar, and Jonathan D. Pollock, Eds. *Military Power and Policy in Asian States: China, India, Japan.* Boulder, Colo.: Westview Press, 1980.

Newell, Nancy P., and Richard S. Newell. *The Struggle for Afghanistan.* Ithaca, N.Y.: Cornell University Press, 1981.

Pike, Douglas. *History of Vietnamese Communism, 1925–1976.* Stanford, Calif.: Hoover, 1978.

Pringle, Robert. *Beyond Vietnam: The United States and Asia.* New York: Random House, 1978.

_____ . *Indonesia and the Philippines: American Interests in Island Southeast Asia.* New York: Columbia University Press, 1980.

Reischauer, Edwin O. *The United States and Japan,* rev. ed. New York: Viking Press, 1977.

Rothstein, Robert L. *The Third World and U.S. Foreign Policy.* Boulder, Colo.: Westview Press, 1981.

Schaller, Michael. *The United States and China in the Twentieth Century.* New York: Oxford University Press, 1979.

Sherwain Latif, Ahmed. *Pakistan, China, and America.* Karachi, Pakistan: Council for Pakistan Studies, 1980.

Sigmund, Paul E., Jr., Ed. *The Ideologies of the Developing Nations.* New York: Praeger, 1963.

Stueck, William W., Jr. *The Road to Confrontation: American Policy Toward China and Korea, 1947–1950.* Chapel Hill, N.C.: University of North Carolina Press, 1981.

Tahir-Kheli, Shirin, Ed. *U.S. Strategic Interests in Southwest Asia.* New York: Praeger, 1982.

Tucker, Nancy B. *Patterns in the Dust: Chinese-American Relations and the Recognition Controversy, 1949–1950.* New York: Columbia University Press, 1983.

Watts, William, Packard, George R., Clough, Ralph N., and Robert B. Oxnam. *Japan, Korea and China: American Perceptions and Policies.* Lexington, Mass.: D. C. Heath, 1979.

_____ . *The United States and Japan.* Cambridge, Mass.: Ballinger, 1984.

Weinstein, Franklin B., and Fuji Kamiya, Eds. *The Security of Korea: U.S. and Japanese Perspectives in the 1980s.* Boulder, Colo.: Westview Press.

Zagoria, Donald S., Ed. *Soviet Policy in East Asia.* New Haven, Conn.: Yale University Press, 1982.

## THE VIETNAM WAR

Ashmore, Harry S. *Mission to Hanoi.* New York: Putnam, 1968.

Baskir, Lawrence, and William Strauss. *Chance and Circumstance: The Draft, the War, and the Vietnam Generation.* New York: Random House, 1978.

Braestrap, Peter. *Big Story: How the American Press Reported and Intepreted the Crisis of Tet in 1968 in Vietnam and Washington.* Boulder, Colo.: Westview Press, 1977.

Brandon, Henry. *Anatomy of Error: The Inside Story of the Asian War on the Potomac, 1954–1969.* Boston: Gambit, 1969.

Cantrill, Albert. *The American People, Vietnam, and the Presidency.* Princeton, N.J.: Princeton University Press, 1976.

Goodman, Allen E. *The Lost Peace: America's Search for a Negotiated Settlement of the Vietnam War.* Stanford, Calif.: Hoover, 1978.

Halberstam, David. *The Best and the Brightest.* New York: Random House, 1972.

Haley, P. Edward. *Congress and the Fall of South Vietnam and Cambodia.* East Brunswick, N.J.: Fairleigh Dickinson University Press, 1982.

Hoopes, Townsend. *The Limits of Intervention: An Inside Account of How the Johnson Policy on Vietnam Was Reversed.* New York: McKay, 1969.

Karnow, Stanley. *Vietnam: A History.* New York: Viking, 1983.

Kattenberg, Paul M. *The Vietnam Trauma in American Foreign Policy, 1945–1975.* New Brunswick, N.J.: Transaction Books, 1980.

Lake, Anthony, Ed. *The Vietnam Legacy: The War, American Society, and the Future of American Foreign Policy.* New York: New York University Press, 1976.

Lewy, Guenther. *America in Vietnam.* New York: Oxford University Press, 1978.

Oberdorfer, Donald. *Tet.* Garden City, N.Y.: Doubleday, 1971.

Palmer, Bruce, Jr. *The 25-Year War: America's Military Role in Vietnam.* Lexington, Ky.: University Press of Kentucky, 1984.

Schandler, Herbert Y. *The Unmaking of a President.* Princeton, N.J.: Princeton University Press, 1972.

Sheehan, Neil, Smith, Hedrick, Kenworthy, E. W., and Fox Butterfield. *The Pentagon Papers.* New York: Bantam, 1971.

Windchy, Eugene. *Tonkin Gulf.* Garden City, N.Y.: Doubleday, 1971.

## AFRICA

Adelman, Kenneth L. *African Realities.* New York: Crane, Russak, 1980.

Arkhurst, Frederick S., Ed. *U.S. Policy Toward Africa.* New York: Praeger, 1975.

Chaliand, Gerard. *The Struggle for Africa: Conflict of the Great Powers*. New York: St. Martin's Press, 1982.

Charles, Milène. *The Soviet Union and Africa*. Lanham, Md.: University Press of America, 1980.

Gann, L. H., and Peter Duignan. *Africa South of the Sahara: The Challenge to Western Security*. Stanford, Calif.: Hoover, 1981.

Goldschmidt, Walter, Ed. *The United States and Africa*. New York: Praeger, 1963.

Gorman, Robert F. *Political Conflict in the Horn of Africa*. New York: Praeger, 1981.

Hanf, Theodor, Weiland, Heribert, and Gerda Vierdag. *South Africa: The Prospects of Peaceful Change*. Bloomington, Ind.: Indiana University Press, 1981.

Jackson, Henry F. *From the Congo to Soweto: U.S. Foreign Policy Toward Africa Since 1960*. New York: Morrow, 1982.

LeGrande, William M. *Cuba's Policy in Africa: 1959–1980*. Berkeley, Calif.: Institute of International Studies, University of California, 1980.

Legum, Colin, and Bill Lee. *The Horn of Africa in Continuing Crisis*. New York: Holmes & Meier, 1979.

Legum, Colin, Lee, Bill, and I. William Zartman. *Africa in the 1980s*. New York: McGraw-Hill, 1979.

Ogene, Chidozie F. *Interest Groups and the Shaping of Foreign Policy: Four Case Studies of United States African Policy*. New York: St. Martin's Press, 1983.

Ottaway, David, and Marina Ottaway. *Afro Communism*. New York: Africana, 1981.

Rothenberg, Morris. *The USSR and Africa: New Dimensions of Soviet Global Power*. Washington, D.C.: Advanced International Studies Institute, 1980.

Shaw, Timothy M., and 'Sola Ojo, Eds. *Africa and the International Political System*. Washington, D.C.: University Press of America, 1982.

Wai, Dunstan M. *The African-Arab Conflict in the Sudan*. New York: Holmes & Meier, 1981.

Whitaker, Jennifer, S., Ed. *Africa and the United States: Vital Interests*. New York: New York University Press, 1978.

## FOREIGN-POLICY DECISION MAKING

Abel, Elie. *The Missile Crisis*. New York: Harper & Row, 1966.

Acheson, Dean. *Power and Diplomacy*. Cambridge, Mass.: Harvard University Press, 1958.

Allison, Graham T. *Essence of Decision: Explaining the Missile Crisis*. Boston: Little, Brown, 1971.

Allison, Graham T., and Peter Szanton. *Remaking Foreign Policy: The Organizational Connection*. New York: Basic Books, 1976.

Bloomfield, Lincoln. *The Foreign Policy Process: A Modern Primer*. Englewood Cliffs, N.J.: Prentice-Hall, 1982.

Campbell, John C. *The Foreign Affairs Fudge Factory*. New York: Basic Books, 1971.

*Commission of the Organization of the Government for the Conduct of Foreign Policy*. Report June 1975. Washington, D.C.: U.S. Government Printing Office, 1975.

Dallek, Robert. *The American Style of Foreign Policy*. New York: Knopf, 1983.

Destler, I. M. *Presidents, Bureaucrats, and Foreign Policy*. Princeton, N.J.: Princeton University Press, 1974.

Estes, Thomas S., and E. Allen Lightner, Jr. *The Department of State*. New York: Praeger, 1976.

Foster, Schuyler H. *Activism Replaces Isolationism: U.S, Public Attitudes*. Washington, D.C.: Foxhall Press, 1983.

Franck, Thomas M., and Edward Weisband. *Foreign Policy by Congress*. New York: Oxford University Press, 1979.

Gardner, Lloyd C. *A Covenant with Power: America and World Order from Wilson to Reagan*. New York: Oxford University Press, 1984.

Hoxie, R. Gordon. *Command Decision and the Presidency: A Study in National Security Policy and Organization*. New York: Readers Digest Press, 1977.

Johnson, U. Alexis. *The Right Hand of Power*. Englewood Cliffs, N.J.: Prentice-Hall, 1984.

Kennedy, Robert F. *Thirteen Days*. New York: Norton, 1968.

Kirkpatrick, Lyman B., Jr. *The U.S. Intelligence Community*. New York: Hill & Wang, 1973.

Murphy, Robert. *Diplomat among Warriors*. Garden City, N.Y.: Doubleday, 1964.

Neuchterlein, Donald E. *National Interests and Presidential Leadership: The Setting of Priorities*. Boulder, Colo.: Westview Press, 1978.

Neustadt, Richard E. *Presidential Power: The Politics of Leadership, with Reflections from FDR to Carter*. New York: Wiley, 1980.

Quester, George H. *American Foreign Policy: The Last Consensus*. New York: Praeger, 1982.

Sapin, Burton M. *The Making of United States Foreign Policy*. Washington, D.C.: Brookings Institution, 1966.

Sorensen, Theodore C. *Decision-Making in the White House*. New York: Columbia University Press, 1963.

Steinbruner, John D. *The Cybernetic Theory of Decision*. Princeton, N.J.: Princeton University Press, 1974.

Stoessinger, John G. *Crusaders and Pragmatists: Movers of Modern American Foreign Policy*. New York: Norton, 1979.

Thompson, Kenneth W. *Interpreters and Critics of the Cold War*. Washington, D.C.: University Press of America, 1978.

# INDEXES

# Name Index

# Subject Index